List of the Elements with their Symbols and Atomic Masses*

Element	Symbol	Atomic Number	Atomic Mass†	Element	Symbol	Atomic Number	Atomic Mass†
Actinium	Ac	89	(227)	Mendelevium	Md	101	(256)
Aluminum	Al	13	26.98	Mercury	Hg	80	200.6
Americium	Am	95	(243)	Molybdenum	Mo	42	95.94
Antimony	Sb	51	121.8	Neodymium	Nd	60	144.2
Argon	Ar	18	39.95	Neon	Ne	10	20.18
Arsenic	As	33	74.92	Neptunian	Np	93	(237)
Astatine	At	85	(210)	Nickel	Ni	28	58.69
Barium	Ba	56	137.3	Niobium	Nb	41	92.91
Berkelium	Bk	97	(247)	Nitrogen	N	7	14.01
Beryllium	Be	4	9.012	Nobelium	No	102	(253)
Bismuth	Bi	83	209.0	Osmium	Os	76	190.2
Bohrium	Bh	107	(262)	Oxygen	O	8	16.00
Boron	B	5	10.81	Palladium	Pd	46	106.4
Bromine	Br	35	79.90	Phosphorus	P	15	30.97
Cadmium	Cd	48	112.4	Platinum	Pt	78	195.1
Calcium	Ca	20	40.08	Plutonium	Pu	94	(242)
Californium	Cf	98	(249)	Polonium	Po	84	(210)
Carbon	C	6	12.01	Potassium	K	19	39.10
Cerium	Ce	58	140.1	Praseodymium	Pr	59	140.9
Cesium	Cs	55	132.9	Promethium	Pm	61	(147)
Chlorine	Cl	17	35.45	Protactinium	Pa	91	(231)
Chromium	Cr	24	52.00	Radium	Ra	88	(226)
Cobalt	Co	27	58.93	Radon	Rn	86	(222)
Copper	Cu	29	63.55	Rhenium	Re	75	186.2
Curium	Cm	96	(247)	Rhodium	Rh	45	102.9
Darmstadtium	Ds	110	(281)	Roentgenium	Rg	111	(272)
Dubnium	Db	105	(262)	Rubidium	Rb	37	85.47
Dysprosium	Dy	66	162.5	Ruthenium	Ru	44	101.1
Einsteinium	Es	99	(254)	Rutherfordium	Rf	104	(257)
Erbium	Er	68	167.3	Samarium	Sm	62	150.4
Europium	Eu	63	152.0	Scandium	Sc	21	44.96
Fermium	Fm	100	(253)	Seaborgium	Sg	106	(263)
Fluorine	F	9	19.00	Selenium	Se	34	78.96
Francium	Fr	87	(223)	Silicon	Si	14	28.09
Gadolinium	Gd	64	157.3	Silver	Ag	47	107.9
Gallium	Ga	31	69.72	Sodium	Na	11	22.99
Germanium	Ge	32	72.59	Strontium	Sr	38	87.62
Gold	Au	79	197.0	Sulfur	S	16	32.07
Hafnium	Hf	72	178.5	Tantalum	Ta	73	180.9
Hassium	Hs	108	(265)	Technetium	Tc	43	(99)
Helium	He	2	4.003	Tellurium	Te	52	127.6
Holmium	Ho	67	164.9	Terbium	Tb	65	158.9
Hydrogen	H	1	1.008	Thallium	Tl	81	204.4
Indium	In	49	114.8	Thorium	Th	90	232.0
Iodine	I	53	126.9	Thulium	Tm	69	168.9
Iridium	Ir	77	192.2	Tin	Sn	50	118.7
Iron	Fe	26	55.85	Titanium	Ti	22	47.88
Krypton	Kr	36	83.80	Tungsten	W	74	183.9
Lanthanum	La	57	138.9	Uranium	U	92	238.0
Lawrencium	Lr	103	(257)	Vanadium	V	23	50.94
Lead	Pb	82	207.2	Xenon	Xe	54	131.3
Lithium	Li	3	6.941	Ytterbium	Yb	70	173.0
Lutetium	Lu	71	175.0	Yttrium	Y	39	88.91
Magnesium	Mg	12	24.31	Zinc	Zn	30	65.39
Manganese	Mn	25	54.94	Zirconium	Zr	40	91.22
Meitnerium	Mt	109	(266)				

*All atomic masses have four significant figures. These values are recommended by the Committee on Teaching of Chemistry, International Union of Pure and Applied Chemistry.

†Masses of the longest-lived isotope for radioactive elements are given in parentheses.

General, Organic, *and* Biochemistry

GENERAL CHEMISTRY
Chapters 1-9

General, Organic, *and* Biochemistry

SEVENTH EDITION

Katherine J. Denniston
Towson University

Joseph J. Topping
Towson University

Robert L. Caret
Towson University

Boston   Burr Ridge, IL   Dubuque, IA   New York   San Francisco   St. Louis
Bangkok   Bogotá   Caracas   Lisbon   London   Madrid
Mexico City   Milan   New Delhi   Seoul   Singapore   Sydney   Taipei   Toronto

The **McGraw·Hill** Companies

General Chemistry
Chapters 1-9
GENERAL, ORGANIC, AND BIOCHEMISTRY, Seventh Edition

1 2 3 4 5 6 7 8 9 0   DOW DOW 12 11 10

ISBN-13: 978-0-07-739764-7
ISBN-10: 0-07-739764-9

Learning Solutions Representative: Shirley Grall
Production Editor: Tina Hermsen
Printer/Binder: RR Donnelley

Brief Contents

GENERAL CHEMISTRY

Contents

iv

Perspectives

A Human Perspective

A Medical Perspective

Green Chemistry

Kitchen Chemistry

Chemistry at the Crime Scene

Preface

The seventh edition of *General, Organic, and Biochemistry*, like our earlier editions, has been designed to help undergraduate majors in health-related fields understand key concepts and appreciate the significant connections among chemistry, health, and the treatment of disease. We have tried to strike a balance between theoretical and practical chemistry, while emphasizing material that is unique to health-related studies. We have written at a level intended for students whose professional goals do not include a mastery of chemistry, but for whom an understanding of the principles and practice of chemistry is a necessity.

Although we have stressed the importance of chemistry to the health-related professions, this book was written for all students who need a one- or two-semester introduction to chemistry. Our focus on the relationships between chemistry and the environment, medicine, and the function of the human body is an approach that can engage students in a variety of majors. We have integrated the individual disciplines of inorganic, organic, and biochemistry to emphasize their interrelatedness rather than their differences. This approach provides a sound foundation in chemistry and teaches students that life is not a magical property, but rather depends on a complex sequence of chemical reactions that obey the scientific laws.

Students are introduced to the textbook by the cover photograph. Some may wonder, "Why are there flowers on the cover of a chemistry book? That's biology." When they read the story that accompanies the cover, they discover that each flower, indeed each living thing, is a tiny chemical factory, manufacturing a myriad of chemical compounds. These compounds are certainly useful to the plant, but can be useful to other species, especially humans, that are creative enough to recognize their utility and isolate them from the plant.

The cover sets the theme for the textbook: chemistry is not an abstract study. It is valuable because it is integral to our very lives and all of our interactions with our environment. We try to spark student interest with an art program that uses relevant photography, clear and focused figures, animations that are available on our website, and boxed topics that bring life to abstract ideas. We introduce ideas, explain them in a clear and concise way, and encourage the student to apply the concept to solve a problem. We provide guidance in the form of a large number of in-chapter examples, each solved in a stepwise fashion. Each worked example is immediately followed by a problem that is similar in structure to the solved problem and this, in turn, is supported by one or two similar problems from the end of the chapter. These in-chapter problems enable students to achieve some level of proficiency before attempting the end-of-chapter problems. In short, students are engaged, understand the concepts, and build confidence through problem solving.

We have rewritten sections of several chapters to improve organization and focus, reevaluated the use, size, and appropriateness of all photos and figures, and deleted or reduced coverage of topics not critical to a fundamental understanding of chemistry. By judicious use of margin space and the textbook-related website, coupled with efficient writing, we have succeeded in reducing the length of the book by 32 pages.

Key Features of the Seventh Edition

In the preparation of the seventh edition, we have been guided by the collective wisdom of reviewers who are experts in one or more of the three sub-disciplines covered in the book, and who represent a diversity of teaching experience, including community colleges and four-year colleges and universities. We have retained the core approach of our successful earlier editions, updated material where necessary, and expanded or removed material consistent with retention of the original focus and mission of the book. Throughout the project, we have been careful to ensure that the final product is as student-oriented and readable as its predecessors.

We designed the seventh edition to promote student learning and facilitate teaching. It is important to engage students, to appeal to visual learners, and to provide a variety of pedagogical tools to help them organize and summarize information. We have used a variety of strategies to accomplish our goals.

Engaging Students

Students learn when they can see a clear relationship between the subject material they are studying and real life. We wrote the text to help students make connections between the principles of chemistry and their previous life experiences and/or their future professional experiences. Our strategy to accomplish this integration includes boxed applications and clear learning tools.

Boxed Applications

Each chapter contains boxed applications that present short stories about real-world situations involving one or more topics students will encounter within the chapter. There are 100 boxed applications throughout the text, so students are sure to find many topics that spark their interest. Self-tanning lotions, the ozone problem, fingerprinting, the benefits of garlic, disease and third-world countries, and the most recent strategies for the treatment of HIV/AIDS, are just a few examples of boxed application topics.

- **Medical Perspective** boxes relate chemistry to a health concern or a diagnostic application.
- **Green Chemistry** boxes explore environmental topics, including the impact of chemistry on the ecosystem and how these environmental changes affect human health.
- **Human Perspective** boxes delve into chemistry and society and include such topics as gender issues in science and historical viewpoints.
- **Chemistry at the Crime Scene** boxes are new to this edition. They focus on forensic chemistry, applying the principles of chemistry to help solve crimes.
- **Kitchen Chemistry** boxes discuss the chemistry associated with everyday kitchen products.

Chemistry at the Crime Scene

Adipocere and Mummies of Soap

One November evening in 1911, widower Patrick Higgins stepped into his local pub in Abercorn, Scotland. To the surprise of his drinking companions, he did not have his two young boys with him. Neighbors knew that the boys had been a great burden on Patrick since the death of his wife; so they believed Patrick's story that he left William, age 6, and John, age 4, with two women in Edinburgh who had offered to adopt the boys.

More than 18 months had passed when an object was seen floating in the Hopetoun Quarry, an unused, flooded quarry near town. When the object was fished out, it was obvious that it was the body of a young boy; the rescuers were stunned to find another small body tied to the first by a rope. How were these bodies preserved after such a long time and why did they float? The answer is that their bodies had almost completely turned into adipocere, or more simply, soap.

Forensic scientists are trying to understand the nature of the reaction that creates *adipocere*, the technical term for the yellowish-white, greasy, wax-like substance that results from the saponification of fatty tissue. Some researchers hope that this information may allow determination of the postmortem interval (length of time since death). Others simply value the process because it keeps the body so well that even after long periods, it can be easily recognized and any wounds or injuries can be observed.

It is known that adipocere is produced when body fat is hydrolyzed (water is needed) to release fatty acids. Because the fatty acids lower the pH in the tissues, they inhibit many of the bacteria that would begin the process of decay. Certain other bacteria, particularly *Clostridium welchii*, an organism that cannot grow in the presence of oxygen, is known to speed up the formation of adipocere in moist, warm, anaerobic (oxygenless) environments. Adipocere forms first in subcutaneous tissues, including the cheeks, breasts, and buttocks. Given appropriate warmth and damp conditions, it may be seen as early as 3 to 4 weeks after death; but more commonly it is not observed until 5 to 6 months after death.

Adipocere formation in John and William Higgins was so extensive that their former neighbors had no trouble recognizing them. At the postmortem, another advantage of adipocere formation became obvious—it had preserved the stomach contents of the boys! From this, the coroner learned that the boys had eaten Scotch broth about an hour before they died. Investigators were able to find the woman who had given

the broth to the boys and, from her testimony, learned that she had fed them on the last day they were seen in the village. Clearly their father had lied about the adoption by two Edinburgh women! In under one and one-half hours, a jury convicted the father of murdering his sons and he was hanged in October 1913.

For Further Understanding

▶ Adipocere is the technical term for "soap mummification." It comes from the Latin words *adipis* or fat, as in adipose tissue, and *cera*, which means wax. Draw a triglyceride composed of the fatty acids myristic acid, stearic acid, and oleic acid. Write a balanced equation showing a possible reaction that would lead to the formation of adipocere.

▶ Forensic scientists are studying adipocere formation as a possible source of information to determine postmortem interval (length of time since death) of bodies of murder or accident victims. Among the factors being studied are the type of soil, including pH, moisture, temperature, and presence or absence of lime. How might each of these factors influence the rate of adipocere formation and hence the determination of the postmortem interval?

Learning Tools

In designing the original learning system we asked ourselves: "If we were students, what would help us organize and understand the material covered in this chapter?" Based on the feedback of reviewers and users of our text, we include a variety of learning tools:

- **Chapter Overview** pages begin each chapter, listing learning goals and the chapter outline. Both students and professor can see, all in one place, the plan for the chapter.
- **Learning Goal Icons** mark the sections and examples in the chapter that focus on each learning goal.
- **Chapter Cross-References** help students locate pertinent background material. These references to previous chapters, sections, and perspectives are noted in the margins of the text. Marginal cross references also alert students to upcoming topics related to the information currently being studied.
- **End-of-Chapter Problems** are arranged according to the major headings in the chapter outline, with further subdivision into Foundations (basic concepts) and Applications.

Note: Refer to A Human Perspective: Food Calories, Section 1.5.

LEARNING GOAL

3 ▶ Describe experiments that yield thermochemical information and calculate fuel values based on experimental data.

Question 7.7 Using the conversion factor in Chapter 1, convert the energy released in Example 7.3 to joules (J).

Question 7.8 Using the conversion factor in Chapter 1, convert the energy absorbed in Example 7.4 to J.

Many chemical reactions that produce heat are combustion reactions. In our bodies many food substances (carbohydrates, proteins, and fats; Chapters 21 and 22) are oxidized to release energy. **Fuel value** is the amount of energy per g of food.

The fuel value of food is an important concept in nutrition science. The fuel value is generally reported in units of *nutritional Calories*. One **nutritional Calorie (Cal)** is equivalent to one kilocalorie (1000 cal). It is also known as the *large Calorie* (uppercase C).

Energy necessary for our daily activity and bodily function comes largely from the "combustion" of carbohydrates. Chemical energy from foods that is not used to maintain normal body temperature or in muscular activity is stored in the bonds of chemical compounds known collectively as fat. Thus "high-calorie" foods are implicated in obesity.

A special type of calorimeter, a *bomb calorimeter*, is useful for the measurement of the fuel value (Cal) of foods. Such a device is illustrated in Figure 7.6. Its design is similar, in principle, to that of the "coffee cup" calorimeter discussed earlier. It incorporates the insulation from the surroundings, solution pool, reaction chamber, and thermometer. Oxygen gas is added as one of the reactants, and

- **Chapter Summaries** are detailed and similarly organized by major sections. These summaries serve as mini–study guides, covering the major concepts in the chapter.

- **Key Terms** are italicized in the summaries and listed at the end of each chapter, accompanied by the appropriate section number. Each key term is defined and listed alphabetically in the **Glossary Terms** at the end of the book.

- **Summary of Reactions** in the organic chemistry chapters highlight each major reaction type on a green background. Major chemical reactions are summarized by equations at the end of the chapter, facilitating review.

Detailed List of Changes

- **New Problems:** There are 2300 problems included in this edition, 240 of them completely new. In the same spirit, older problems have been replaced and many problems have been reorganized to better follow the flow of the text.

- **New Boxed Applications:** Boxes that focus on forensic chemistry, green chemistry, and kitchen chemistry have been added to this edition to give students a better feel for how chemistry principles apply to the world around them.

- **Chapter 2:** The discussion of the Bohr theory has been rewritten to emphasize its historical value and its importance in explaining atomic spectroscopy. We removed the Bohr orbit diagrams, fearful that students would misinterpret this as a currently correct atomic model. A greater emphasis has been given to electron configurations, including, for the first time, orbital diagrams. We carefully, in a low-key way, introduce Hund's rule and the Pauli exclusion principle, allowing the student to begin to understand magnetic properties of the elements. We have made a special effort to gather together the related concepts of periodic table arrangement, electron configurations, the octet rule, valence electrons, and ion formation. Previously, we felt that the ion concept

was introduced too early; we now have a solid foundation for the concept.

- **Chapter 3:** The guidelines for writing Lewis structures have been rewritten to improve the clarity of a difficult topic. The relationship of atoms in the skeletal structure is now shown with red "connectors" to avoid confusion with bonds. Many of the examples have been rewritten to conform to the new guidelines. Eight worked examples guide students as they write Lewis structures for covalent compounds, cations and anions, resonance forms, and exceptions to the octet rule.

- **Chapter 4:** The coverage of solubility and precipitation has been enhanced by an improved table of solubility rules and the introduction of rules to write net ionic equations for precipitation reactions. The website contains even more information dealing with net ionic equations, particularly representing acid-base reactions with net ionic equations. The topic of limiting reactants is one that many do not cover in introductory non-major courses. However, the concept is important, and we have included a short explanation; a detailed discussion of problem solving using limiting reactants is available on our website, for those who want a more detailed coverage of stoichiometry.

- **Chapter 6:** The desire for consistent use of SI units motivated us to replace older (but still often-used) terms such as formula weight, weight/weight percent, and weight/volume percent with formula mass, mass/mass percent, and mass/volume percent. Explanation of colligative properties has been enhanced. The coverage of equivalents in aqueous solutions has been rewritten for clarity, and molality is now used to calculate freezing-point depression and boiling-point elevation.
- **Chapter 7:** The sections dealing with thermodynamics and kinetics have been rewritten. Enthalpy, entropy, and free energy are now more closely tied to the first two laws of thermodynamics. The importance of free energy as a predictor of spontaneity has been emphasized. The discussion of kinetics has been enhanced with problem-solving examples, and the boxed topic *Too Fast or Too Slow?* examines a variety of real-life situations in which kinetics is relevant, such as food storage, dentistry, art conservation, the environment, and the automobile.
- **Chapter 10:** New to this chapter is the boxed application *Chemistry at the Crime Scene: Arson and Alkanes,* which discusses gas chromatography and the role it plays when examining fire scenes. This chapter also includes a new explanation of halogenation of branched alkanes.
- **Chapter 11:** This chapter includes expanded information on physical properties of alkenes and alkynes and provides a clearer description of the difference between addition and substitution reactions.

- **Chapter 12:** Three new boxed applications have been added to this chapter to help connect the student's real-world interests and experiences with the chemistry concepts presented in the text. They include:
  - *Chemistry at the Crime Scene: Fingerprinting*
  - *Kitchen Chemistry: The Magic of Garlic*
  - *Chemistry at the Crime Scene: Drinking and Driving,* which has been rewritten to focus on forensic chemistry
- **Chapter 13:** Identifying criminals through the use of "odor prints" is the topic of the new introduction to this chapter centered on aldehydes and ketones.
- **Chapter 14:** The new boxed application *Chemistry at the Crime Scene: Carboxylic Acids and the Body Farm* explains how the University of Tennessee Anthropological Research Facility measures the air and soil around decomposing bodies to predict accurate "time since death."
- **Chapter 16:** In response to reviewers, the coverage of stereoisomers has been extended to include racemic mixtures, meso compounds, and diastereomers. This provides a much more complete view of the world of stereoisomers.
- **Chapter 17:** This chapter includes a new boxed application, *Chemistry at the Crime Scene: Adipocere and Mummies of Soap.* This application tells the tale of two young boys whose bodies were turned to adipocere, or soap, and demonstrates how this reaction can help determine time since death.
- **Chapter 19:** This chapter includes the new boxed application *Chemistry at the Crime Scene: Enzymes, Nerve Agents, and Poisoning.*

Problem Solving and Critical Thinking

Perhaps the best preparation for a successful and productive career is the development of problem-solving and critical thinking skills. To this end, we created a variety of problems that require recall, fundamental calculations, and complex reasoning. In this edition we have used suggestions from our reviewers, as well as from our own experience, to enhance our 2300 problems. This edition includes 240 new problems and hundreds of example problems with step-by-step solutions.

- **In-Chapter Examples, Solutions, and Problems:** Each chapter includes examples that show the student, step-by-step, how to properly reach the correct solution to model problems. Each example contains a practice problem, as well as a referral to further practice questions. These questions allow students to test their mastery of information and to build self-confidence.

EXAMPLE 6.4   Calculating ppt and ppm

A 1.00-g sample of stream water was found to contain 1.0×10^{-6} g lead. Calculate the concentration of lead in the stream water in units of % (m/m), ppt, and ppm. Which is the most suitable unit?

Solution

mass percent:

$$\% \left(\frac{m}{m} \right) = \frac{\text{g solute}}{\text{g solution}} \times 100\%$$

$$\% \left(\frac{m}{m} \right) = \frac{1.0 \times 10^{-6} \text{ g Pb}}{1.0 \text{ g solution}} \times 100\%$$

$$\% \left(\frac{m}{m} \right) = 1.0 \times 10^{-4}\%$$

parts per thousand:

$$\text{ppt} = \frac{\text{g solute}}{\text{g solution}} \times 10^3 \text{ ppt}$$

$$\text{ppt} = \frac{1.0 \times 10^{-6} \text{ g Pb}}{1.0 \text{ g solution}} \times 10^3 \text{ ppt}$$

$$\text{ppt} = 1.0 \times 10^{-3} \text{ ppt}$$

parts per million:

$$\text{ppm} = \frac{\text{g solute}}{\text{g solution}} \times 10^6 \text{ ppm}$$

$$\text{ppm} = \frac{1.0 \times 10^{-6} \text{ g Pb}}{1.0 \text{ g solution}} \times 10^6 \text{ ppm}$$

$$\text{ppm} = 1.0 \text{ ppm}$$

Parts per million is the most reasonable unit.

Practice Problem 6.4

Calculate the ppt and ppm of oxygen gas in a mixture containing

a. 20.0 g of oxygen gas and 80.0 g of nitrogen gas
b. 50.0 g of argon gas and 80.0 g of helium gas

▶ **For Further Practice: Questions 6.33 and 6.34.**

- **In-Chapter and End-of-Chapter Problems:**
  We have created a wide variety of paired
  concept problems. The answers to the
  odd-numbered questions are found in
  the back of the book as reinforcement for
  students as they develop problem-solving
  skills. However, students must then be able
  to apply the same principles to the related
  even-numbered problems.

- **Critical Thinking Problems:** Each chapter
  includes a set of critical thinking problems.
  These problems are intended to challenge
  students to integrate concepts to solve more
  complex problems. They make a perfect complement
  to the classroom lecture because they provide an
  opportunity for in-class discussion of complex
  problems dealing with daily life and the health care
  sciences.

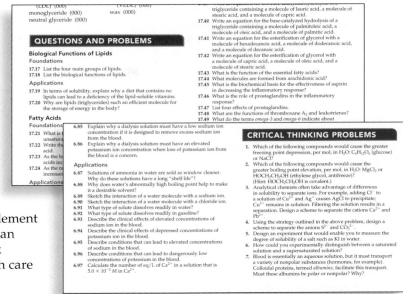

Over the course of the last six editions, hundreds of reviewers have shared
their knowledge and wisdom with us, as well as the reactions of their students
to elements of this book. Their contributions, as well as our own continuing
experience in the area of teaching and learning science, have resulted in a text
that we are confident will provide a strong foundation in chemistry, while
enhancing the learning experience of students.

The Art Program

Today's students are much more visually oriented than previous generations. Television and the computer
represent alternate modes of learning. We have built upon this observation through the use of color, figures,
and three-dimensional computer-generated models. This art program enhances the readability of the text
and provides alternative pathways to learning.

- **Dynamic Illustrations:** Each chapter is amply illustrated using figures, tables, and chemical formulas.
  All of these illustrations are carefully annotated for clarity. To help students better understand difficult
  concepts, there are approximately 350 illustrations and 250 photos in the seventh edition.
- **Color-Coding Scheme:** We have color-coded equations so that chemical groups being added or removed
  in a reaction can be quickly recognized.

1. **Red print** is used in
   chemical equations or
   formulas to draw the
   reader's eye to key
   elements or properties
   in a reaction or
   structure.

2. **Blue print** is used when
   additional features
   must be highlighted.

acids glycine and alanine, is a dehydration reaction, because a water molecule is
lost as the amide bond is formed.

Glycine   Alanine   Peptide bond
                                  (amide bond)

Glycyl-alanine

The molecule formed by condensing two amino acids is called a *dipeptide*. The
amino acid with a free α-N^+H_3 group is known as the amino terminal, or sim-

To understa
acid is place

3. **Green background** screens denote generalized chemical and mathematical equations. In the organic chemistry chapters, the Summary of Reactions at the end of the chapter is also highlighted with a green background screen for ease of recognition.

> Because amines are bases, they react with acids to form alkylammonium salts.
>
> R—N: + HCl ⟶ R—N⁺—HCl⁻
>
> Amine   Acid   Alkylammonium salt
>
> The reaction of methylamine with hydrochloric acid shown is typical of these reactions.

4. Yellow backgrounds illustrate energy, stored either in electrons or groups of atoms, in the general and biochemistry sections of the text. In the organic chemistry section of the text, yellow background screens also reveal the parent chain of an organic compound.

Fructose-6-phosphate   Fructose-1,6-bisphosphate

5. There are situations in which it is necessary to adopt a unique color convention tailored to the material in a particular chapter. For example, in Chapter 18, the structures of amino acids require three colors to draw attention to key features of these molecules. For consistency, red is used to denote the acid portion of an amino acid and blue is used to denote the basic portion of an amino acid. Green print is used to denote the R groups, and a yellow background screen directs the eye to the α-carbon.

- **Computer-Generated Models:** The ability of students to understand the geometry and three-dimensional structure of molecules is essential to the understanding of organic and biochemical reactions. Computer-generated models are used throughout the text because they are both accurate and easily visualized.

Figure 18.1 General structure of an α-amino acid. All amino acids isolated from proteins, with the exception of proline, have this general structure.

Supplementary Materials

This text is supported by a complete package for instructors and students. Several print and media supplements have been prepared to accompany the text and make learning as meaningful and up-to-date as possible.

For the Instructor and Student:

- **McGraw-Hill Connect™ Chemistry**

McGraw-Hill Connect Chemistry is a web-based assignment and assessment platform that gives students the means to better connect with their coursework, with their instructors, and with the important concepts that they need to know for success now and in the future.

With Connect Chemistry, instructors can deliver assignments, quizzes, and tests online. Nearly all the questions from the text are presented in an auto-gradable format and tied to the text's learning objectives. Instructors can edit existing questions and write entirely new problems. They can track individual student performance—by question, assignment, or in relation to the class overall—with detailed grade reports. Instructors can also integrate grade reports easily with Learning Management Systems (LMS) such as WebCT and Blackboard, and much more.

By choosing Connect Chemistry, instructors provide their students with a powerful tool for improving academic performance and truly mastering course material. Connect Chemistry allows students to practice important skills at their own pace and on their own schedule. Importantly, students' assessment results and instructors' feedback are all saved online—so students can continually review their progress and plot their course to success.

- **McGraw-Hill Connect ChemistryPlus™**
  Like Connect Chemistry, Connect ChemistryPlus provides students with online assignments and assessments, plus 24/7 online access to an eBook—an online edition of the text—to aid them in successfully completing their work, wherever and whenever they choose.

For the Instructor

- **Instructor's Manual:** Written by the authors and developed by Danáe Quirk Dorr, this ancillary contains suggestions for organizing lectures, instructional objectives, perspectives on boxed readings from the text, answers to the even-numbered problems from the text, a list of each chapter's key problems and concepts, and more. The Instructor's Manual is available through the Connect website for this text.
- **Test Bank:** The electronic test bank offers questions that can be used for homework assignments or the preparation of exams. The test bank can be utilized to quickly create customized exams. It allows instructors to sort questions by format or level of difficulty, edit existing questions or add new ones, and scramble questions and answer keys for multiple versions of the same test.
- **Laboratory Manual for General, Organic, and Biochemistry:** The seventh edition, by Charles H. Henrickson, Larry C. Byrd, and Norman W. Hunter of Western Kentucky University, offers clear and concise laboratory experiments to reinforce students' understanding of concepts. Pre-laboratory exercises, questions, and report sheets are coordinated with each experiment to ensure active student involvement and comprehension. An updated student tutorial on graphing with Excel has been added to this edition.
- **Laboratory Instructor's Manual:** Written by Charles H. Henrickson, Larry C. Byrd, and Norman W. Hunter of Western Kentucky University, this helpful guide contains hints that the authors have learned over the years to ensure students' success in the laboratory. This Resource Guide is available through the Connect Chemistry website for this text.
- **McGraw-Hill Presentation Center:** Build instructional material wherever, whenever, and however you want! McGraw-Hill Presentation Center is an online digital library containing assets such as photos, artwork, and other media that can be used to create customized lectures, visually enhanced tests and quizzes, compelling course websites, or attractive printed support materials. The McGraw-Hill Presentation Center Library includes thousands of assets from many McGraw-Hill titles. This ever-growing resource gives instructors the power to use assets specific to an adopted textbook as well as content from all other books in the library. The Presentation Center can be accessed from the instructor side of your textbook's Connect website, and the Presentation Center's dynamic search engine allows you to explore by discipline, course, textbook chapter, asset type, or key word. Simply browse, select, and download the files you need to build engaging course materials. All assets are copyrighted by McGraw-Hill Higher Education but can be used by instructors for classroom purposes.
- **More than 300 animations available through the Connect website:** Many animations are linked to appropriate sections of the textbook using the ●. They supplement the textbook material in much the same way as instructor demonstrations. However, for students, they are only a few mouse-clicks away, any time, day or night. Because many students are visual learners and quite computer-literate, the animations add another dimension of learning; they bring a greater degree of reality to the written word.

For the Student

- **Student Study Guide/Solutions Manual:** A separate Student Study Guide/Solutions Manual, prepared by Kim Woodrum and Danáe Quirk Dorr, is available. It contains the answers and complete solutions for the odd-numbered problems. It also offers students a variety of exercises and keys for testing their comprehension of basic, as well as difficult, concepts.
- **Schaum's Outline of General, Organic, and Biological Chemistry:** Written by George Odian and Ira Blei, this supplement provides students with more than 1400 solved problems with complete solutions. It also teaches effective problem-solving techniques.

Acknowledgments

We are thankful to our families, whose patience and support made it possible for us to undertake this project. We are also grateful to our many colleagues at McGraw-Hill for their support, guidance, and assistance. In particular, we would like to thank Gloria Schiesl, Senior Project Manager, Jodi Rhomberg, Developmental Editor II, Tami Hodge, Senior Sponsoring Editor, Ryan Blankenship, Publisher, and Thomas Timp, Marketing Director. We also wish to acknowledge the assistance of Danáe Quirk Dorr, who, in conjunction with the authors, carefully prepared the Instructor's Manual and Student Solutions Manual to accompany this text. We would also like to thank Kim Woodrum, who updated the Student Study Guide, prepared the PowerPoint® Lecture Outlines, and revised the test bank for the seventh edition.

A revision cannot move forward without the feedback of professors teaching the course. The following reviewers have our gratitude and assurance that their comments received serious consideration. The following professors provided reviews, participated in a focus group, or gave valuable advice for the preparation of the seventh edition:

Jennifer Adamski *Old Dominion University*
Jamie Adcock *The University of Tennessee–Knoxville*
Stanley A. Bajue *Medgar Evers College, CUNY*
Roderick S. Black *University of Kansas*
James Braun *Clayton State University*
Eric Elisabeth *Johnson County Community College*
Karen L. Ericson *Indiana University–Purdue University Fort Wayne*
Fatima Fakhreddine *University of Texas at Austin*
David J. Gelormo *Northampton Community College*
Kevin A. Gratton *Johnson County Community College*

Bobbie Grey *Riverside Community College*
Michael Hailu *Columbus State Community College*
James Harman *South Plains College*
Martina Kaledin *Kennesaw State University*
Mushtaq Khan *Union County College*
Myung-Hoon Kim *Georgia Perimeter College*
Edith Preciosa Kippenhan *University of Toledo, Department of Chemistry*
Julie Lowe *Bakersfield College*
Ying Mao *Camden County College*
Craig McClure *University of Alabama at Birmingham*
Charlene McMahon *Milwaukee Area Technical College–Milwaukee*
Jonathan McMurry *Kennesaw State University*
Mary Bethe Neely *University of Colorado–Colorado Springs*
Glenn Nomura *Georgia Perimeter College*
Beng Guat Ooi *Middle Tennessee State University*
Richard Petersen *The University of Memphis*
Lesley Putnam *Northern Michigan University*
Douglas Raynie *South Dakota State*
Emily S. Resar *North Hennepin Community College*
Gillian E. A. Rudd *Northwestern State University*
Raymond Sadeghi *University of Texas at San Antonio*
John Salinas *Rogue Community College*
Colleen Scott *Southern Illinois University Carbondale*
John W. Singer *Jackson Community College*
Heather Sklenicka *Rochester Community and Technical College*
John Tansey *Otterbein College*
Susan T. Thomas *University of Texas at San Antonio*
David A. Tramontozzi *Macomb Community College*
Zhiqiang Yang *Macomb Community College*

Chemistry
Methods and Measurement

1

LEARNING GOALS

1 ▶ Describe the interrelationship of chemistry with other fields of science and medicine.

2 ▶ Discuss the approach to science, the scientific method, and distinguish among the terms *hypothesis, theory,* and *scientific law*.

3 ▶ Distinguish between data and results.

4 ▶ Describe the properties of the solid, liquid, and gaseous states.

5 ▶ Provide specific examples of physical and chemical properties and physical and chemical change.

6 ▶ Distinguish between intensive and extensive properties.

7 ▶ Classify matter as element, compound, or mixture.

8 ▶ Report data and results using scientific notation and the proper number of significant figures.

9 ▶ Learn the major units of measure in the English and metric systems, and be able to convert from one system to another.

10 ▶ Know the three common temperature scales and be able to convert from one to another.

11 ▶ Use density, mass, and volume in problem solving, and calculate the specific gravity of a substance from its density.

OUTLINE

Name the types of measurement associated with this activity.

INTRODUCTION

Louis Pasteur, a chemist and microbiologist, said, "Chance favors the prepared mind." In the history of science and medicine there are many examples in which individuals made important discoveries because they recognized the value of an unexpected observation.

One such example is the use of ultraviolet (UV) light to treat infant jaundice. Infant jaundice is a condition in which the skin and the whites of the eyes appear yellow because of high levels of the bile pigment bilirubin in the blood. Bilirubin is a breakdown product of the oxygen-carrying blood protein hemoglobin. If bilirubin accumulates in the body, it can cause brain damage and death. The immature liver of the baby cannot remove the bilirubin.

An observant nurse in England noticed that when jaundiced babies were exposed to sunlight, the jaundice faded. Research based on her observation showed that the UV light changes the bilirubin into another substance, which can be excreted. To this day, jaundiced newborns are treated with UV light.

In this first chapter of your study of chemistry, you will learn about the scientific method: the process of developing hypotheses to explain observations and the design of experiments to test those hypotheses.

You will also see that measurement of properties of matter, and careful observation and recording of data, are essential to scientific inquiry. So too is assessment of the precision and accuracy of measurements. Measurements (data) must be reported to allow others to determine their significance. So an understanding of significant figures, and the ability to represent data in the most meaningful units, enables other scientists to interpret data and results.

Helping you develop the skills needed to represent and communicate data and results from scientific inquiry is the goal of this introductory chapter.

1.1 The Discovery Process

Chemistry

Chemistry is the study of matter, its chemical and physical properties, the chemical and physical changes it undergoes, and the energy changes that accompany those processes. **Matter** is anything that has mass and occupies space. The changes that matter undergoes always involve either gain or loss of energy. **Energy** is the ability to do work to accomplish some change. The study of chemistry involves matter, energy, and their interrelationship. Matter and energy are at the heart of chemistry.

Major Areas of Chemistry

Chemistry is a broad area of study covering everything from the basic parts of an atom to interactions between huge biological molecules. Because of this, chemistry encompasses the following specialties.

Biochemistry is the study of life at the molecular level and the processes associated with life, such as reproduction, growth, and respiration. *Organic chemistry* is the study of matter that is composed principally of carbon and hydrogen. Organic chemists study methods of preparing such diverse substances as plastics, drugs, solvents, and a host of industrial chemicals. *Inorganic chemistry* is the study of matter that consists of all of the elements other than carbon and hydrogen and their combinations. Inorganic chemists have been responsible for the development of unique substances such as semiconductors and high-temperature

LEARNING GOAL

1 ▶ Describe the interrelationship of chemistry with other fields of science and medicine.

A Medical Perspective

Curiosity, Science, and Medicine

Curiosity is one of the most important human traits. Small children constantly ask "why?". As we get older, our questions become more complex, but the curiosity remains.

Curiosity is also the basis of the scientific method. A scientist observes an event, wonders why it happens, and sets out to answer the question. Dr. Michael Zasloff's curiosity may lead to the development of an entirely new class of antibiotics. When he was a geneticist at the National Institutes of Health, Zasloff's experiments involved the surgical removal of the ovaries of African clawed frogs. After surgery he sutured (sewed up) the incision and put the frogs back in their tanks. These water-filled tanks were teeming with bacteria, but the frogs healed quickly, and the incisions did not become infected!

Of all the scientists to observe this remarkable healing, only Zasloff was curious enough to ask whether there were chemicals in the frogs' skin that defended the frogs against bacterial infections—a new type of antibiotic. All currently used antibiotics are produced by fungi or are synthesized in the laboratory. One big problem in medicine today is more and more pathogenic (disease-causing) bacteria are becoming resistant to these antibiotics. Zasloff hoped to find an antibiotic that worked in an entirely new way so the current problems with antibiotic resistance might be overcome.

Dr. Zasloff found two molecules in frog skin that can kill bacteria. Both are small proteins. Zasloff named them *magainins,* from the Hebrew word for shield. Most of the antibiotics that we now use enter bacteria and kill them by stopping some biochemical process inside the cell. Magainins are more direct; they simply punch holes in the bacterial membrane, and the bacteria explode.

One of the magainins, now chemically synthesized in the laboratory so that no frogs are harmed, may be available to the public in the near future. This magainin can kill a wide variety

Dr. Zasloff's uninfected patient.

of bacteria (broad-spectrum antibiotic), and it has passed the Phase I human trials. If this compound passes all the remaining tests, it will be used in treating deep infected wounds and ulcers, providing an alternative to traditional therapy.

The curiosity that enabled Zasloff to advance the field of medicine also catalyzed the development of chemistry. We will see the product of this fundamental human characteristic as we study the work of many extraordinary chemists throughout this textbook.

For Further Understanding

▶ Why is it important for researchers to continually design and develop new antibacterial substances?

▶ What common characteristics do you find in this work and the discovery discussed in the introduction to this chapter?

ceramics for industrial use. *Analytical chemistry* involves the analysis of matter to determine its composition and the quantity of each kind of matter that is present. Analytical chemists detect traces of toxic chemicals in water and air. They also develop methods to analyze human body fluids for drugs, poisons, and levels of medication. *Physical chemistry* is a discipline that attempts to explain the way in which matter behaves. Physical chemists develop theoretical concepts and try to prove them experimentally. This helps us understand how chemical systems behave.

Over the last 30 years, the boundaries between the traditional sciences of chemistry, physics, and biology, as well as mathematics and computer science, have gradually faded. Medical practitioners, physicians, nurses, and medical technologists use therapies that contain elements of all these disciplines. The rapid expansion of the pharmaceutical industry is based on recognition of the relationship between the function of an organism and its basic chemical makeup. Function is a consequence of changes that chemical substances undergo.

For these reasons, an understanding of basic chemical principles is essential for anyone considering a medically related career; indeed, a worker in any

The study of the causes of rapid melting of glaciers is a global application of chemistry. How does this illustrate the interaction of matter and energy?

science-related field will benefit from an understanding of the principles and applications of chemistry.

The Scientific Method

The **scientific method** is a systematic approach to the discovery of new information. How do we learn about the properties of matter, the way it behaves in nature, and how it can be modified to make useful products? Chemists do this by using the scientific method to study the way in which matter changes under carefully controlled conditions.

The scientific method is not a "cookbook recipe" that, if followed faithfully, will yield new discoveries; rather, it is an organized approach to solving scientific problems. Every scientist brings his or her own curiosity, creativity, and imagination to scientific study. But scientific inquiry does involve some of the "cookbook approach."

Characteristics of the scientific process include the following:

- *Observation.* The description of, for example, the color, taste, or odor of a substance is a result of observation. The measurement of the temperature of a liquid or the size or mass of a solid results from observation.
- *Formulation of a question.* Humankind's fundamental curiosity motivates questions of why and how things work.
- *Pattern recognition.* If a scientist finds a cause-and-effect relationship, it may be the basis of a generalized explanation of substances and their behavior.
- *Theory development.* When scientists observe a phenomenon, they want to explain it. The process of explaining observed behavior begins with a hypothesis. A **hypothesis** is simply an attempt to explain an observation, or series of observations, in a commonsense way. If many experiments support a hypothesis, it may attain the status of a theory. A **theory** is a hypothesis supported by extensive testing (experimentation) that explains scientific facts and can predict new facts.
- *Experimentation.* Demonstrating the correctness of hypotheses and theories is at the heart of the scientific method. This is done by carrying out carefully designed experiments that will either support or disprove the theory or hypothesis.
- *Information summarization.* A scientific **law** is nothing more than the summary of a large quantity of information. For example, the law of conservation of matter states that matter cannot be created or destroyed, only converted from one form to another. This statement represents a massive body of chemical information gathered from experiments.

The scientific method involves the interactive use of hypotheses, development of theories, and thorough testing of theories using well-designed experiments. It is summarized in Figure 1.1.

Models in Chemistry

Hypotheses, theories, and laws are frequently expressed using mathematical equations. These equations may confuse all but the best of mathematicians. For this reason, a *model* of a chemical unit or system is often used to make ideas more clear. A good model based on everyday experience, although imperfect, gives a great deal of information in a simple fashion. Consider the fundamental unit of methane, the major component of natural gas, which is composed of one carbon atom (symbolized by C) and four hydrogen atoms (symbolized by H).

A geometrically correct model of methane can be constructed from balls and sticks. The balls represent the individual units (atoms) of hydrogen and carbon,

LEARNING GOAL

2 ▸ Discuss the approach to science, the scientific method, and distinguish among the terms *hypothesis*, *theory*, and *scientific law*.

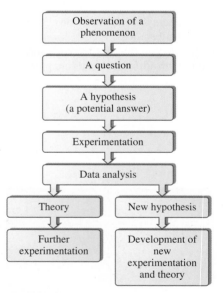

Figure 1.1 The scientific method, an organized way of doing science. A degree of trial and error is apparent here. If experimentation does not support the hypothesis, the cycle must begin again.

A Human Perspective

The Scientific Method

The discovery of penicillin by Alexander Fleming is an example of the scientific method at work. Fleming was studying the growth of bacteria. One day, his experiment was ruined because colonies of mold were growing on his plates. From this failed experiment, Fleming made an observation that would change the practice of medicine: Bacterial colonies could not grow in the area around the mold colonies. Fleming hypothesized that the mold was making a chemical compound that inhibited the growth of the bacteria. He performed a series of experiments designed to test this hypothesis.

The key to the scientific method is the design of carefully controlled experiments that will either support or disprove the hypothesis. This is exactly what Fleming did.

In one experiment, he used two sets of tubes containing sterile nutrient broth. To one set he added mold cells. The second set (the control tubes) remained sterile. The mold was allowed to grow for several days. Then the broth from each of the tubes (experimental and control) was passed through a filter to remove any mold cells. Next, bacteria were placed in each tube. If Fleming's hypothesis was correct, the tubes in which the mold had grown would contain the chemical that inhibits growth, and the bacteria would not grow. On the other hand, the control tubes (which were never used to grow mold) would allow bacterial growth. This is exactly what Fleming observed.

Within a few years this *antibiotic*, penicillin, was being used to treat bacterial infections in patients.

A nurse administers an injection of penicillin to a young patient.

For Further Understanding

▶ What is the purpose of the control tubes used in this experiment?

▶ What common characteristics do you find in this story and the Medical Perspective on page 3?

and the sticks correspond to the attractive forces that hold the hydrogen and carbon together. The model consists of four balls representing hydrogen symmetrically arranged around a center ball representing carbon. The "carbon" ball is attached to each "hydrogen" ball by sticks, as shown:

Color-coding the balls distinguishes one type of matter from another; the geometrical form of the model, all of the angles and dimensions of a tetrahedron, are the same for each methane unit found in nature. Methane is certainly not a collection of balls and sticks; but such models are valuable because they help us understand the chemical behavior of methane and other, more complex substances.

Figure 1.2 Examples of technology originating from scientific inquiry: (a) synthesis of a new drug, (b) solar energy cells, (c) preparation of solid-state electronics, (d) use of a gypsy moth sex attractant for insect control.

(a)　(b)　(c)　(d)

Molecules that maximize therapeutic properties and minimize undesirable side effects can be designed on the computer and synthesized and purified in the laboratory.

Chemists and physicists have used the observed properties of matter to develop models of the individual units of matter. These models collectively make up what we now know as the atomic theory of matter.

These models have been developed from experimental observations over the past 200 years. Theory and experiment are mutually reinforcing. We must gain some insight into atomic structure to appreciate the behavior of atoms themselves, as well as larger aggregates of atoms: compounds.

The structure-properties concept has advanced so far that compounds are designed and synthesized in the laboratory with the hope that they will perform very specific functions, such as curing diseases that have been resistant to other forms of treatment. Figure 1.2 shows some of the variety of modern technology that has its roots in the understanding of the atom.

1.2 Matter and Properties

Properties are characteristics of matter and are classified as either physical or chemical. In this section we will learn the meaning of physical and chemical properties and how they are used to characterize matter.

Data and Results

LEARNING GOAL

3 ▸ Distinguish between data and results.

A scientific experiment produces **data.** Each piece of data is the individual result of a single measurement or observation. Examples include the *mass* of a sample and the *time* required for a chemical reaction to occur. Mass, length, volume, time, temperature, and energy are common types of data obtained from chemical experiments.

A **result** is the outcome of an experiment. Data and results may be identical, but more often several related pieces of data are combined, and logic is used to produce a result.

EXAMPLE 1.1   Distinguishing Between Data and Results

In many cases, a drug is less stable in the presence of moisture, and excess moisture can hasten the breakdown of the active ingredient, leading to loss of potency. Therefore we may wish to know how much water a certain quantity of a drug gains when exposed to air. To do this experiment, we must first weigh the drug sample, then expose it to the air for a period of time and reweigh it. The change in weight,

$$[\text{weight}_{final} - \text{weight}_{initial}] = \text{weight difference}$$

indicates the weight of water taken up by the drug formulation. The initial and final weights are individual bits of *data;* by themselves they do not answer the question, but they do provide the information necessary to calculate the answer: the results. The difference in weight and the conclusions based on the observed change in weight are the *results* of the experiment.

Practice Problem 1.1

Describe an experiment that demonstrates that the boiling point of water changes when salt (sodium chloride) is added to the water.

▶ **For Further Practice: Questions 1.33 and 1.34.**

(a)

(b)

(c)

Figure 1.3 The three states of matter exhibited by water: (a) solid, as ice; (b) liquid, as ocean water; (c) gas, as humidity in the air.

The experiment described in Example 1.1 was not a very good experiment because many conditions were not measured. Measurement of the temperature and humidity of the atmosphere and the length of time that the drug was exposed to the air (the creation of a more complete set of data) would make the results less ambiguous.

States of Matter

There are three *states of matter:* the **gaseous state,** the **liquid state,** and the **solid state.** A gas is made up of particles that are widely separated. In fact, a gas will expand to fill any container; it has no definite shape or volume. In contrast, particles of a liquid are closer together; a liquid has a definite volume but no definite shape; it takes on the shape of its container. A solid consists of particles that are close together and that often have a regular and predictable pattern of particle arrangement (crystalline). A solid has both fixed volume and fixed shape. Attractive forces, which exist between all particles, are very pronounced in solids and much less so in gases.

Matter and Physical Properties

Water is the most common example of a substance that can exist in all three states over a reasonable temperature range (Figure 1.3). Conversion of water from one state to another constitutes a *physical change.* A **physical change** produces a recognizable difference in the appearance of a substance without causing any change in its composition or identity. For example, we can warm an ice cube and it will melt, forming liquid water. Clearly its appearance has changed; it has been transformed from the solid to the liquid state. It is, however, still water; its composition and identity remain unchanged. A physical change has occurred. We could in fact demonstrate the constancy of composition and identity by refreezing the liquid water, re-forming the ice cube. This melting and freezing cycle could be repeated over and over. This very process is a hallmark of our global weather changes. The continual interconversion of the three states of water in the environment (snow, rain, and humidity) clearly demonstrates the retention of the identity of water particles or *molecules.*

Animation
• The Three States of Matter

LEARNING GOAL
4 ▶ Describe the properties of the solid, liquid, and gaseous states.

LEARNING GOAL
5 ▶ Provide specific examples of physical and chemical properties and physical and chemical change.

A **physical property** can be observed or measured without changing the composition or identity of a substance. As we have seen, melting ice is a physical change. We can measure the temperature when melting occurs; this is the *melting point* of water. We can also measure the *boiling point* of water, when liquid water becomes a gas. Both the melting and boiling points of water, and of any other substance, are physical properties.

A practical application of separation of materials based upon their differences in physical properties is shown in Figure 1.4.

Matter and Chemical Properties

We have noted that physical properties can be exhibited, measured, or observed without any change in identity or composition. In contrast, **chemical properties** do result in a change in composition and can be observed only through chemical reactions. A **chemical reaction** is a process of rearranging, removing, replacing, or adding atoms to produce new substances. For example, the process of photosynthesis can be shown as

$$\text{carbon dioxide + water} \xrightarrow[\text{Chlorophyll}]{\text{Light}} \text{sugar + oxygen}$$

This chemical reaction involves the conversion of carbon dioxide and water (the *reactants*) to a sugar and oxygen (the *products*). The products and reactants are clearly different. We know that carbon dioxide and oxygen are gases at room temperature and water is a liquid at this temperature; the sugar is a solid white powder. A chemical property of carbon dioxide is its ability to form sugar under certain conditions. The process of formation of this sugar is the *chemical change*.

Light is the energy needed to make the reaction happen. Chlorophyll is the energy absorber, converting light energy to chemical energy.

EXAMPLE 1.2   Identifying Properties

Can the process that takes place when an egg is fried be described as a physical or chemical change?

Solution

Examine the characteristics of the egg before and after frying. Clearly, some significant change has occurred. Furthermore, the change appears irreversible. More than a simple physical change has taken place. A chemical reaction (actually, several) must be responsible; hence chemical change.

Practice Problem 1.2

Classify each of the following as either a chemical change or a physical change:

a. water boiling to become steam
b. butter becoming rancid
c. combustion of wood
d. melting of ice in spring
e. decay of leaves in winter

▶ **For Further Practice: Questions 1.47 and 1.48.**

Figure 1.4 An example of separation based on differences in physical properties. Magnetic iron is separated from nonmagnetic substances. A large-scale version of this process is important in the recycling industry.

Question 1.1 Classify each of the following as either a chemical property or a physical property:

a. color
b. flammability
c. hardness

Question 1.2 Classify each of the following as either a chemical property or a physical property:

    a. odor

    b. taste

    c. temperature

Intensive and Extensive Properties

It is important to recognize that properties can also be classified according to whether they depend on the size of the sample. Consequently, there is a fundamental difference between properties such as density and specific gravity and properties such as mass and volume.

    An **intensive property** is a property of matter that is *independent* of the *quantity* of the substance. Density, boiling and melting points, and specific gravity are intensive properties. For example, the boiling point of one single drop of water is exactly the same as the boiling point of a liter (L) of water.

    An **extensive property** *depends* on the *quantity* of a substance. Mass and volume are extensive properties. There is an obvious difference between 1 gram (g) of silver and 1 kilogram (kg) of silver; the quantities and, incidentally, the monetary values, differ substantially.

See page 29 for a discussion of density and specific gravity.

LEARNING GOAL

6 ▶ Distinguish between intensive and extensive properties.

EXAMPLE 1.3 **Differentiating Between Intensive and Extensive Properties**

Is temperature an extensive or intensive property?

Solution

Imagine two glasses, each containing 100 g of water, and each at 25°C. Now pour the contents of the two glasses into a larger glass. You would predict that the mass of the water in the larger glass would be 200 g (100 g + 100 g) because mass is an *extensive property,* dependent on quantity. However, we would expect the temperature of the water to remain the same (not 25°C + 25°C); hence temperature is an *intensive property* . . . independent of quantity.

Practice Problem 1.3

Pure water freezes at 0° Celsius. Is this an intensive or extensive property? Why?

▶ **For Further Practice: Questions 1.53 and 1.54.**

Question 1.3 Label each property as intensive or extensive:

    a. the length of my pencil

    b. the color of my pencil

Question 1.4 Label each property as intensive or extensive:

    a. the shape of leaves on a tree

    b. the number of leaves on a tree

Classification of Matter

Chemists look for similarities in properties among various types of materials. Recognizing these likenesses simplifies learning the subject and allows us to predict the behavior of new substances on the basis of their relationship to substances already known and characterized.

    Many classification systems exist. The most useful system, based on composition, is described in the following paragraphs (see also Figure 1.5).

LEARNING GOAL

7 ▶ Classify matter as element, compound, or mixture.

Matter
├── Pure substance
│   ├── Element
│   │   └── Example: sodium; hydrogen
│   └── Compound
│   └── Example: salt; water
└── Mixture
     ├── Homogeneous
     │   └── Example: air; salt in water
     └── Heterogeneous
          └── Example: oil and water; salt and pepper

Figure 1.5 Classification of matter. All matter is either a pure substance or a mixture of pure substances. Pure substances are either elements or compounds, and mixtures may be either homogeneous (uniform composition) or heterogeneous (nonuniform composition).

All matter is either a *pure substance* or a *mixture*. A **pure substance** has only one component. Pure water is a pure substance. It is made up only of particles containing two hydrogen atoms and one oxygen atom, that is, water molecules (H_2O).

There are different types of pure substances. Elements and compounds are both pure substances. An **element** is a pure substance that cannot be changed into a simpler form of matter by any chemical reaction. Hydrogen and oxygen, for example, are elements. Alternatively, a **compound** is a substance resulting from the combination of two or more elements in a definite, reproducible way. The elements hydrogen and oxygen, as noted earlier, may combine to form the compound water, H_2O.

A **mixture** is a combination of two or more pure substances in which each substance retains its own identity. Alcohol and water can be combined in a mixture. They coexist as pure substances because they do not undergo a chemical reaction; they exist as thoroughly mixed discrete molecules. This collection of dissimilar particles is the mixture. A mixture has variable composition; there are an infinite number of combinations of quantities of alcohol and water that can be mixed. For example, the mixture may contain a small amount of alcohol and a large amount of water or vice versa. Each is, however, an alcohol-water mixture.

A mixture may be either *homogeneous* or *heterogeneous* (Figure 1.6). A **homogeneous mixture** has uniform composition. Its particles are well mixed, or thoroughly intermingled. A homogeneous mixture, such as alcohol and water, is described as a *solution*. Air, a mixture of gases, is an example of a gaseous solution. A **heterogeneous mixture** has a nonuniform composition. A mixture of salt and pepper is a good example of a heterogeneous mixture. Concrete is also composed of a heterogeneous mixture of materials (various types and sizes of stone and sand with cement in a nonuniform mixture).

At present, more than 100 elements have been characterized. A complete listing of the elements and their symbols is found on the inside front cover of this textbook.

A detailed discussion of solutions (homogeneous mixtures) and their properties is presented in Chapter 6.

(a)   (b)   (c)

Figure 1.6 Schematic representation of some classes of matter. (a) A pure substance, water, consists of a single component. (b) A homogeneous mixture, ethanol and water, has a uniform distribution of components. (c) A heterogeneous mixture, marble, has a nonuniform distribution of components. The lack of homogeneity is readily apparent.

EXAMPLE 1.4 Categorizing Matter

Is seawater a pure substance, a homogeneous mixture, or a heterogeneous mixture?

Solution

Imagine yourself at the beach, filling a container with a sample of water from the ocean. Examine it. You would see a variety of solid particles suspended in the water: sand, green vegetation, perhaps even a small fish! Clearly, it is a mixture, and one in which the particles are not uniformly distributed throughout the water; hence a heterogeneous mixture.

Practice Problem 1.4

Is each of the following materials a pure substance, a homogeneous mixture, or a heterogeneous mixture?

a. ethyl alcohol
b. blood
c. Alka-Seltzer dissolved in water
d. oxygen in a hospital oxygen tank

▶ **For Further Practice: Questions 1.55 and 1.56.**

Question 1.5 Provide two examples of homogeneous mixtures that you encounter in everyday life.

Question 1.6 Provide two examples of heterogeneous mixtures that you encounter in everyday life.

1.3 Significant Figures and Scientific Notation

Information-bearing figures in a number are termed *significant figures*. Data and results arising from a scientific experiment convey information about the way in which the experiment was conducted. The degree of uncertainty or doubt associated with a measurement or series of measurements is indicated by the number of figures used to represent the information.

Significant Figures

Consider the following situation: A student was asked to obtain the length of a section of wire. In the chemistry laboratory, several different types of measuring devices are usually available. Not knowing which was most appropriate, the student decided to measure the object using each device that was available in the laboratory. The following data were obtained:

5.4 cm
(a)

5.36 cm
(b)

Two questions should immediately come to mind:

Are the two answers equivalent?

If not, which answer is correct?

In fact, the two answers are *not* equivalent, but *both* are correct. How do we explain this apparent contradiction?

The data are not equivalent because each is known to a different degree of certainty. The answer 5.36 centimeters (cm), containing three significant figures, specifies the length of the object more exactly than 5.4 cm, which contains only two significant figures. The term **significant figures** is defined to be all digits in a number representing data or results that are known with certainty *plus one uncertain digit*.

In case (a), we are certain that the object is at least 5 cm long and equally certain that it is *not* 6 cm long because the end of the object falls between the calibration lines 5 and 6. We can only estimate between 5 and 6, because there are no calibration indicators between 5 and 6. The end of the wire appears to be approximately four-tenths of the way between 5 and 6, hence 5.4 cm. The 5 is known with certainty, and 4 is estimated; there are two significant figures.

In case (b), the ruler is calibrated in tenths of m. The end of the wire is at least 5.3 cm and not 5.4 cm. Estimation of the second decimal place between the two closest calibration marks leads to 5.36 cm. In this case, 5.3 is certain, and the 6 is estimated (or uncertain), leading to three significant digits.

Both answers are correct because each is consistent with the measuring device used to generate the data. An answer of 5.36 cm obtained from a measurement using ruler (a) would be *incorrect* because the measuring device is not capable of that exact specification. On the other hand, a value of 5.4 cm obtained from ruler (b) would be erroneous as well; in that case the measuring device is capable of generating a higher level of certainty (more significant digits) than is actually reported.

In summary, the number of significant figures associated with a measurement is determined by the measuring device. Conversely, the number of significant figures reported is an indication of the sophistication of the measurement itself.

Recognition of Significant Figures

Only *significant* digits should be reported as data or results. However, are all digits, as written, significant digits? Let's look at a few examples illustrating the rules that are used to represent data and results with the proper number of significant digits.

- All nonzero digits are significant.
  7.314 has *four* significant digits.
- The number of significant digits is independent of the position of the decimal point.
  73.14 has *four* significant digits, as does 7.314.
- Zeros located between nonzero digits are significant.
  60.052 has *five* significant figures.
- Zeros at the end of a number (often referred to as trailing zeros) are significant if the number contains a decimal point.
  4.70 has *three* significant figures.
  Helpful Hint: Trailing zeros are ambiguous; the next section offers a solution for this ambiguity.
- Trailing zeros are insignificant if the number does not contain a decimal point and are significant if a decimal point is indicated.
  100 has *one* significant figure; 100. has *three* significant figures.
- Zeros to the left of the first nonzero integer are not significant; they serve only to locate the position of the decimal point.
  0.0032 has *two* significant figures.

The uncertain digit represents the degree of doubt in a single measurement.

The uncertain digit results from an estimation.

Question 1.7 How many significant figures are contained in each of the following numbers?

a. 7.26 ⟶ 3

b. 726 — 3

c. 700.2 — 4

d. 7.0 2

e. 0.0720 3

Question 1.8 How many significant figures are contained in each of the following numbers?

a. 0.042

b. 4.20

c. 24.0

d. 240

e. 204

Scientific Notation

It is often difficult to express very large numbers to the proper number of significant figures using conventional notation. The solution to this problem lies in the use of **scientific notation,** also referred to as *exponential notation,* which involves the representation of a number as a power of ten.

The speed of light is 299,792,458 meters per second (m/s). For many calculations, two or three significant figures are sufficient. Using scientific notation, two significant figures, and rounding (p. 17), the speed of light is 3.0×10^8 m/s. The conversion is illustrated using simpler numbers:

$$6200 = 6.2 \times 1000 = 6.2 \times 10^3$$

or

$$5340 = 5.34 \times 1000 = 5.34 \times 10^3$$

Rule: To convert a number greater than one to scientific notation, the original decimal point is moved x places to the left, and the resulting number is multiplied by 10^x. The exponent (x) is a *positive* number equal to the number of places the original decimal point was moved.

Scientific notation is also useful in representing numbers less than one. For example, the mass of a single helium atom is

$$0.000000000000000000000006692 \text{ g}$$

a rather cumbersome number as written. Scientific notation would represent the mass of a single helium atom as 6.692×10^{-24} g. The conversion is illustrated by using simpler numbers:

$$0.0062 = 6.2 \times \frac{1}{1000} = 6.2 \times \frac{1}{10^3} = 6.2 \times 10^{-3}$$

or

$$0.0534 = 5.34 \times \frac{1}{100} = 5.34 \times \frac{1}{10^2} = 5.34 \times 10^{-2}$$

Rule: To convert a number less than one to scientific notation, the original decimal point is moved x places to the right, and the resulting number is multiplied by 10^{-x}. The exponent ($-x$) is a *negative* number equal to the number of places the original decimal point was moved.

LEARNING GOAL

8 ▶ Report data and results using scientific notation and the proper number of significant figures.

 A Review of Mathematics

Question 1.9 Represent each of the following numbers in scientific notation, showing only significant digits:

    a. 0.0024

    b. 0.0180

    c. 224

Question 1.10 Represent each of the following numbers in scientific notation, showing only significant digits:

    a. 48.20

    b. 480.0

    c. 0.126

Error, Accuracy, Precision, and Uncertainty

Error is the difference between the true value and our estimation, or measurement, of the value. Some degree of error is associated with any measurement. Two types of error exist: random error and systematic error. *Random error* causes data from multiple measurements of the same quantity to be scattered in a more or less uniform way around some average value. *Systematic error* causes data to be either smaller or larger than the accepted value. Random error is inherent in the experimental approach to the study of matter and its behavior; systematic error can be found and, in many cases, removed or corrected.

Examples of systematic error include such situations as:

- Dust on the balance pan, which causes all objects weighed to appear heavier than they really are.
- Impurities in chemicals used for the analysis of materials, which may interfere with (or block) the desired process.

Accuracy is the degree of agreement between the true value and the measured value. **Uncertainty** is the degree of doubt in a single measurement.

When measuring quantities that show continuous variation, for example, the weight of this page or the volume of one of your quarters, some doubt or uncertainty is present because the answer cannot be expressed with an infinite number of meaningful digits. The number of meaningful digits is determined by the measuring device. The presence of some error is a natural consequence of any measurement.

The simple process of converting the fraction two-thirds to its decimal equivalent can produce a variety of answers that depend on the device used to perform the calculation: pencil and paper, calculator, computer. The answer might be

0.67

0.667

0.6667

and so forth. All are correct, but each value has a different level of uncertainty. The first number listed, 0.67, has the greatest uncertainty.

It is always best to measure a quantity several times. Modern scientific instruments are designed to perform measurements rapidly; this allows many more measurements to be completed in a reasonable period. Replicate measurements of the same quantity minimize the uncertainty of the result. **Precision** is a measure of the agreement of replicate measurements.

It is important to recognize that accuracy and precision are not the same thing. It is possible to have one without the other. However, when scientific measurements are carefully made, the two most often go hand in hand; high-quality data are characterized by high levels of precision and accuracy.

In Figure 1.7, bull's-eye (a) shows the goal of all experimentation: accuracy *and* precision. Bull's-eye (b) shows the results to be repeatable (good precision); however, some error in the experimental procedure has caused the results to center on an incorrect value. This error is systematic, occurring in each replicate measurement. Occasionally, an experiment may show "accidental" accuracy. The precision is poor, but the average of replicate measurements leads to a correct value. We don't want to rely on accidental success; the experiment should be repeated until the precision inspires faith in the accuracy of the method. Modern measuring devices in chemistry, equipped with powerful computers with immense storage capacity, are capable of making literally thousands of individual replicate measurements to enhance the quality of the result. Bull's-eye (c) illustrates the most common situation. A low level of precision is all too often associated with poor accuracy.

Significant Figures in Calculation of Results

Addition and Subtraction

If we combine the following numbers:

$$37.68$$
$$108.428$$
$$6.71862$$

our calculator will show a final result of

$$152.82662$$

Clearly the answer, with eight digits, defines the total much more accurately than *any* of the individual quantities being combined. This cannot be correct; *the answer cannot have greater significance than any of the quantities that produced the answer.* We rewrite the problem:

$$
\begin{array}{r}
37.68|xxx \\
108.428|xx \\
+ \quad 6.71|862 \\
\hline
152.82|662 \quad \text{(should be 152.83)}
\end{array}
$$

where x = no information; x may be any integer from 0 to 9. Adding 2 to two unknown numbers (in the rightmost column) produces no information. Similar logic prevails for the previous two columns. Thus, five digits remain, all of which are significant. Conventional rules for rounding off would dictate a final answer of 152.83.

Question 1.11 Report the result of each of the following to the proper number of significant figures:

   a. 4.26 + 3.831 = = 8.09
   b. 8.321 − 2.4 = = 5.9
   c. 16.262 + 4.33 − 0.40 = 20.19

Question 1.12 Report the result of each of the following to the proper number of significant figures:

   a. 7.939 + 6.26 =
   b. 2.4 − 8.321 =
   c. 2.333 + 1.56 − 0.29 =

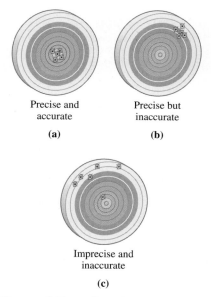

Precise and accurate
(a)

Precise but inaccurate
(b)

Imprecise and inaccurate
(c)

Figure 1.7 An illustration of precision and accuracy in replicate experiments.

LEARNING GOAL

8 ▶ Report data and results using scientific notation and the proper number of significant figures.

Remember the distinction between the words *zero* and *nothing*. Zero is one of the ten digits and conveys as much information as 1, 2, and so forth. *Nothing* implies no information; the digits in the positions indicated by *x* could be 0, 1, 2, or any other.

See rules for rounding off discussed on page 17.

Multiplication and Division

In the preceding discussion of addition and subtraction, the position of the decimal point in the quantities being combined has a bearing on the number of significant figures in the answer. In multiplication and division, this is not the case. The decimal point position is irrelevant when determining the number of significant figures in the answer. It is the number of significant figures in the data that is important. Consider

$$\frac{4.237 \times 1.21 \times 10^{-3} \times 0.00273}{11.125} = 1.26 \times 10^{-6}$$

The answer is limited to three significant figures; the answer can have *only* three significant figures because two numbers in the calculation, 1.21×10^{-3} and 0.00273, have three significant figures and "limit" the answer. Remember, *the answer can be no more precise than the least precise number from which the answer is derived.* The *least precise number* is the number with the fewest significant figures.

Question 1.13 Report the result of each of the following operations using the proper number of significant figures:

a. $63.8 \times 0.80 =$

b. $\dfrac{63.8}{0.80} =$

c. $\dfrac{53.8 \times 0.90}{0.3025} =$

Question 1.14 Report the result of each of the following operations using the proper number of significant figures:

a. $\dfrac{27.2 \times 15.63}{1.84} =$

b. $\dfrac{13.6}{18.02 \times 1.6} =$

c. $\dfrac{12.24 \times 6.2}{18.02 \times 1.6} =$

 A Review of Mathematics

Exponents

Now consider the determination of the proper number of significant digits in the result when a value is multiplied by any power of ten. In each case the number of significant figures in the answer is identical to the number contained in the original term. Therefore

$$(8.314 \times 10^2)^3 = 574.7 \times 10^6 = 5.747 \times 10^8$$

and

$$(8.314 \times 10^2)^{1/2} = 2.883 \times 10^1$$

Each answer contains four significant figures.

Logarithms

Proper use of logarithmic relationships will be particularly important in pH calculations in Chapter 8.

The proper use of the logarithm (or antilogarithm) function often appears to contradict our understanding of significant figures. This is because the logarithm is an exponent that contains two kinds of information: the information in the measurement and the position of the decimal point.

The operative rule is that the number of decimal places in the logarithm is equal to the number of significant figures in the original number.

For example, the pressure P exerted by a gas in a container

$$P = 4.0 \times 10^5 \, \text{atm}$$
$$\text{Log } P = 5.60$$

At first glance the number 5.60 appears incorrect (three significant figures rather than two), but not if we recognize that each part of the number is conveying a different type of information.

Conversely, the antilog operation yields:

$$\text{Antilog } 5.60 = 4.0 \times 10^5 \, \text{atm}$$

Exact (Counted) and Inexact Numbers

Inexact numbers, by definition, have uncertainty (the degree of doubt in the final significant digit). *Exact numbers,* on the other hand, have no uncertainty. Exact numbers may arise from a definition; there are *exactly* 60 minutes (min) in 1 hour (h) or there are exactly 1000 milliliters (mL) in 1 L.

Exact numbers are a consequence of counting. Counting the number of dimes in your pocket or the number of letters in the alphabet are common examples. The fact that exact numbers have no uncertainty means that they do not limit the number of significant figures in the result of a calculation.

Conversion factors are discussed in Section 1.4.

For example, we may want to convert a quantity in ounces (oz) to its corresponding value in pounds (lb).

$$4.00 \, \text{oz} \times 1 \, \text{lb}/16 \, \text{oz} = 0.250 \, \text{lb (three significant figures)}$$

or

$$2568 \, \text{oz} \times 1 \, \text{lb}/16 \, \text{oz} = 160.5 \, \text{lb (four significant figures)}$$

In both examples, the number of significant figures in the result is governed by the data (the number of oz) not the conversion factor, which is *exact,* because it is defined.

A good rule of thumb to follow is: In the metric system, the quantity being converted, not the conversion factor, generally determines the number of significant figures.

Rounding Off Numbers

The use of an electronic calculator generally produces more digits for a result than are justified by the rules of significant figures on the basis of the data input. For example, on your calculator,

$$3.84 \times 6.72 = 25.8048$$

The most correct answer would be 25.8, dropping 048. A convenient way to show this is:

$$3.84 \times 6.72 = 25.8048 \approx 25.8$$

A number of acceptable conventions for rounding exist. Throughout this book we will use the following:

Rule: When the number to be dropped is less than five, the preceding number is not changed. When the number to be dropped is five or larger, the preceding number is increased by one unit.

EXAMPLE 1.5   Rounding Numbers

Round off each of the following to three significant figures.

Solution

a. 63.669 becomes 63.7. *Rationale:* 6 > 5.
b. 8.7715 becomes 8.77. *Rationale:* 1 < 5.
c. 2.2245 becomes 2.22. *Rationale:* 4 < 5.
d. 0.0004109 becomes 0.000411. *Rationale:* 9 > 5.

Helpful Hint: Symbol $x > y$ implies "x greater than y." Symbol $x < y$ implies "x less than y."

Practice Problem 1.5

Round off each of the following numbers to three significant figures.

a. 61.40
b. 6.171
c. 0.066494
d. 6.2262
e. 3895
f. 6.885

▶ **For Further Practice: Questions 1.61 and 1.62.**

1.4 Units and Unit Conversion

Proper use of units is central to all aspects of science. The following sections are designed to develop a fundamental understanding of this vital topic.

Any measurement made in an experiment must specify the units of that measurement. A weight of 3 *oz* is clearly quite different than 3 *lb*. A **unit** defines the basic quantity of mass, volume, time, or whatever quantity is being measured. A number that is not followed by the correct unit usually conveys no useful information.

English and Metric Units

The *English system* is a collection of functionally unrelated units. In the *English system of measurement,* the standard *pound* (lb) is the basic unit of *weight*. The fundamental unit of *length* is the standard *yard* (yd), and the basic unit of *volume* is the standard *gallon* (gal). The English system is used in the United States in business and industry. However, it is not used in scientific work, primarily because it is difficult to convert from one unit to another. For example,

LEARNING GOAL

9 ▶ Learn the major units of measure in the English and metric systems, and be able to convert from one system to another.

$$1 \text{ foot (ft)} = 12 \text{ inches (in)} = 0.33 \text{ yard (yd)} = \frac{1}{5280} \text{ mile (mi)} = \frac{1}{6} \text{ fathom (fath)}$$

Clearly, operations such as the conversion of 1.62 yd to units of mi are not straightforward. In fact, the English "system" is not really a system at all. It is simply a collection of measures accumulated throughout English history. Because they have no common origin, it is not surprising that conversion from one unit to another is not straightforward.

   The United States, the last major industrial country to retain the English system, has begun efforts to convert to the metric system. The *metric system* is truly "systematic." It is composed of a set of units that are related to each other decimally, in other words, as powers of ten. Because the *metric system* is a decimal-based system, it is inherently simpler to use and less ambiguous. For example, the length of an object may be represented as

1 meter (m) = 10 decimeters (dm) = 100 centimeters (cm) = 1000 millimeters (mm)

The metric system was originally developed in France just before the French Revolution in 1789. The more extensive version of this system is the *Système International*, or *S.I. system*. Although the S.I. system has been in existence for over 40 years, it has yet to gain widespread acceptance. To make the S.I. system truly systematic, it utilizes certain units, especially those for pressure, that many find unwieldy.

In this text we will use the metric system, not the S.I. system, and we will use the English system only to the extent of converting *from* it to the more scientifically useful metric system.

In the metric system, there are three basic units. Mass is represented as the *gram*, length as the *meter*, and volume as the *liter*. Any subunit or multiple unit contains one of these units preceded by a prefix indicating the power of ten by which the base unit is to be multiplied to form the subunit or multiple unit. The most common metric prefixes are shown in Table 1.1.

The same prefix may be used for volume, mass, length, time, and so forth. Consider the following examples:

Other metric units, for time, temperature, and energy, will be treated in Section 1.5.

$$1 \text{ mL} = \frac{1}{1000} \text{ L} = 0.001 \text{ L} = 10^{-3} \text{ L}$$

A volume unit is indicated by the base unit, L, and the prefix *milli-*, which indicates that the unit is one thousandth of the base unit. In the same way,

 A Review of Mathematics

$$1 \text{ milligram (mg)} = \frac{1}{1000} \text{ g} = 0.001 \text{ g} = 10^{-3} \text{ g}$$

and

The representation of numbers as powers of ten was discussed in Section 1.3.

$$1 \text{ mm} = \frac{1}{1000} \text{ m} = 0.001 \text{ m} = 10^{-3} \text{ m}$$

Unit Conversion: English and Metric Systems

To convert from one unit to another, we must have a *conversion factor* or series of conversion factors that relate two units. The proper use of these conversion factors is called the *factor-label method*. This method is also termed *dimensional analysis*.

This method is used for two kinds of conversions: to convert from one unit to another within the *same system* or to convert units from *one system to another*.

Conversion of Units Within the Same System

We know, for example, that in the English system,

$$1 \text{ gal} = 4 \text{ quarts (qt)}$$

Table 1.1 Some Common Prefixes Used in the Metric System

Prefix	Multiple	Decimal Equivalent
mega (M)	10^6	1,000,000.
kilo (k)	10^3	1,000.
deka (da)	10^1	10.
deci (d)	10^{-1}	0.1
centi (c)	10^{-2}	0.01
milli (m)	10^{-3}	0.001
micro (μ)	10^{-6}	0.000001
nano (n)	10^{-9}	0.000000001

The speed of an automobile is indicated in both English (mi/h) and metric (km/h) units.

Because dividing both sides of the equation by the same term does not change its identity,

$$\frac{1 \text{ gal}}{1 \text{ gal}} = \frac{4 \text{ qt}}{1 \text{ gal}}$$

The expression on the left is equal to unity (1); therefore

$$1 = \frac{4 \text{ qt}}{1 \text{ gal}} \quad \text{or} \quad 1 = \frac{1 \text{ gal}}{4 \text{ qt}}$$

Now, multiplying any other expression by the ratio 4 qt/1 gal or 1 gal/4 qt will not change the value of the term, because multiplication of any number by 1 produces the original value. However, there is one important difference: The units will have changed.

EXAMPLE 1.6   Using Conversion Factors

Convert 12 gal to units of qt.

Solution

$$12 \text{ gal} \times \frac{4 \text{ qt}}{1 \text{ gal}} = 48 \text{ qt}$$

The conversion factor, 4 qt/1 gal, serves as a bridge, or linkage, between the unit that was given (gal) and the unit that was sought (qt).

The conversion factor may be written as 4 qt/1 gal or 1 gal/4 qt, because both are equal to 1. However, only the first factor, 4 qt/1 gal, will give us the units we need to solve the problem. If we had set up the problem incorrectly, we would obtain

$$12 \text{ gal} \times \frac{1 \text{ gal}}{4 \text{ qt}} = 3 \frac{\text{gal}^2}{\text{qt}}$$

Incorrect units

Clearly, units of gal²/qt are not those asked for in the problem, nor are they reasonable units. The factor-label method is therefore a self-indicating system; the correct units (those required by the problem) will result only if the factor is set up properly.

Practice Problem 1.6

Convert 360 ft to mi.

▶ **For Further Practice: Questions 1.69a, b and 1.70a, b.**

Table 1.2 lists a variety of commonly used English system relationships that may serve as the basis for useful conversion factors.

Table 1.2   Some Common Relationships Used in the English System

A. Weight	1 pound = 16 ounces
	1 ton = 2000 pounds
B. Length	1 foot = 12 inches
	1 yard = 3 feet
	1 mile = 5280 feet
C. Volume	1 gallon = 4 quarts
	1 quart = 2 pints
	1 quart = 32 fluid ounces

Conversion of units within the metric system may be accomplished by using the factor-label method as well. Unit prefixes that dictate the conversion factor facilitate unit conversion (refer to Table 1.1).

EXAMPLE 1.7   Using Conversion Factors

Convert 10.0 cm to m.

Solution

First, recognize that the prefix *centi-* means $\frac{1}{100}$ of the base unit, the meter, just as one cent is $\frac{1}{100}$ of a dollar. There are 100 cents in a dollar and there are 100 cm in 1 m. Thus, our conversion factor is either

$$\frac{1\ m}{100\ cm} \quad \text{or} \quad \frac{100\ cm}{1\ m}$$

each being equal to 1. Only one, however, will result in proper cancellation of units, producing the correct answer to the problem. If we proceed as follows:

$$10.0\ \cancel{cm} \times \frac{1\ m}{100\ \cancel{cm}} = 0.100\ m$$

Data given	Conversion factor	Desired result

we obtain the desired units, m. If we had used the conversion factor 100 cm/1 m, the resulting units would be meaningless and the answer would have been incorrect:

$$10.0\ cm \times \frac{100\ cm}{1\ m} = 1000\frac{cm^2}{m}$$

Incorrect units

Practice Problem 1.7

a. Convert 1.0 L to each of the following units, using the factor-label method:
   _____ milliliters
   _____ microliters
   _____ kiloliters
   _____ centiliters
   _____ dekaliters
b. Convert 1.0 g to each of the following units:
   _____ micrograms
   _____ milligrams
   _____ kilograms
   _____ centigrams
   _____ decigrams

▶ **For Further Practice: Questions 1.71c, d, e and 1.72d, e.**

LEARNING GOAL
9 ▶ Learn the major units of measure in the English and metric systems, and be able to convert from one system to another.

Conversion of Units from One System to Another

The conversion of a quantity expressed in units of one system to an equivalent quantity in the other system (English to metric or metric to English) requires a *bridging* conversion unit. Examples are shown in Table 1.3.

English and metric equivalents are shown in Tables 1.1 and 1.2.

Table 1.3 Commonly Used "Bridging" Units for Intersystem Conversions

Quantity	English		Metric
Mass	1 pound	=	454 grams
	2.2 pounds	=	1 kilogram
Length	1 inch	=	2.54 centimeters
	1 yard	=	0.91 meter
Volume	1 quart	=	0.946 liter
	1 gallon	=	3.78 liters

The conversion may be represented as a three-step process:

Step 1. Conversion from the units given in the problem to a bridging unit.

Step 2. Conversion to the other system using the bridge.

Step 3. Conversion within the desired system to units required by the problem.

EXAMPLE 1.8   Using Conversion Factors Between Systems

Convert 4.00 oz to kg.

Solution

Step 1. A convenient bridging unit for mass is 1 lb = 454 g. To use this conversion factor, we relate oz (given in the problem) to lb:

$$4.00 \text{ oz} \times \frac{1 \text{ lb}}{16 \text{ oz}} = 0.250 \text{ lb}$$

Step 2. Using the bridging unit conversion, we get

$$0.250 \text{ lb} \times \frac{454 \text{ g}}{1 \text{ lb}} = 114 \text{ g}$$

Step 3. Grams may then be directly converted to kg, the desired unit:

$$114 \text{ g} \times \frac{1 \text{ kg}}{1000 \text{ g}} = 0.114 \text{ kg}$$

The calculation may also be done in a single step by arranging the factors in a chain:

$$4.00 \text{ oz} \times \frac{1 \text{ lb}}{16 \text{ oz}} \times \frac{454 \text{ g}}{1 \text{ lb}} \times \frac{1 \text{ kg}}{1000 \text{ g}} = 0.114 \text{ kg}$$

Helpful Hint: Refer to the discussion of rounding off numbers on page 17.

Practice Problem 1.8

Convert:

a. 0.50 in to m
b. 0.75 qt to L
c. 56.8 g to oz
d. 0.50 in to cm
e. 0.75 qt to mL
f. 56.8 mg to oz

▶ **For Further Practice: Questions 1.69c, d, e and 1.70c, d, e.**

LEARNING GOAL

9 ▶ Learn the major units of measure in the English and metric systems, and be able to convert from one system to another.

EXAMPLE 1.9 Using Conversion Factors Involving Exponents

Convert 1.5 m^2 to cm^2.

Solution

The problem is similar to the conversion performed in previous examples. However, we must remember to include the exponent in the units. Thus

$$1.5 \text{ m}^2 \times \left(\frac{10^2 \text{ cm}}{1 \text{ m}}\right)^2 = 1.5 \text{ m}^2 \times \frac{10^4 \text{ cm}^2}{1 \text{ m}^2} = 1.5 \times 10^4 \text{ cm}^2$$

Helpful Hint: The exponent affects both the number *and* unit within the parentheses.

Practice Problem 1.9

Convert:

a. 1.5 cm^2 to m^2
b. 3.6 m^2 to cm^2

▶ **For Further Practice: Questions 1.77 and 1.78.**

LEARNING GOAL

9 ▶ Learn the major units of measure in the English and metric systems, and be able to convert from one system to another.

It is difficult to overstate the importance of paying careful attention to units and unit conversions. Just one example of the tremendous cost that can result from a "small error," is the loss of a 125 million-dollar Mars-orbiting satellite because of failure to convert from English to metric units during one phase of its construction. As a consequence of this error, the satellite established an orbit too close to Mars and burned up in the Martian atmosphere along with 125 million-dollars of the National Aeronautics and Space Administration (NASA) budget.

1.5 Experimental Quantities

Thus far we have discussed the scientific method and its role in acquiring data and converting the data to obtain the results of the experiment. We have seen that such data must be reported in the proper units with the appropriate number of significant figures. The quantities that are most often determined include mass, length, volume, time, temperature, and energy. Now let's look at each of these quantities in more detail.

Mass

Mass describes the quantity of matter in an object. The terms *weight* and *mass,* in common usage, are often considered synonymous. They are not, in fact. **Weight** is the force of gravity on an object:

> Weight = mass × acceleration due to gravity

When gravity is constant, mass and weight are directly proportional. But gravity is not constant; it varies as a function of the distance from the center of the earth. Therefore weight cannot be used for scientific measurement because the weight of an object may vary from one place on the earth to the next.

Mass, on the other hand, is independent of gravity; it is a result of a comparison of an unknown mass with a known mass called a *standard mass.* Balances are instruments used to measure the mass of materials.

Examples of common balances used for the determination of mass are shown in Figure 1.8.

The common conversion units for mass are as follows:

$$1 \text{ g} = 10^{-3} \text{ kg} = \frac{1}{454} \text{ lb}$$

Figure 1.8 Three common balances that are useful for the measurement of mass. (a) A two-pan comparison balance for approximate mass measurement suitable for routine work requiring accuracy to 0.1 g (or perhaps 0.01 g). (b) A top-loading single-pan electronic balance that is similar in accuracy to (a) but has the advantages of speed and ease of operation. The revolution in electronics over the past 20 years has resulted in electronic balances largely supplanting the two-pan comparison balance in routine laboratory usage. (c) An analytical balance that is capable of precise mass measurement (three to five significant figures beyond the decimal point). A balance of this type is used when the highest level of precision and accuracy is required.

(a)

(b)

(c)

In chemistry, when we talk about incredibly small bits of matter such as individual atoms or molecules, units such as g and even micrograms (μg) are much too large. We don't say that a 100-lb individual weighs 0.0500 ton (t); the unit does not fit the quantity being described. Similarly, an atom of a substance such as hydrogen is very tiny. Its mass is only 1.661×10^{-24} g.

One *atomic mass unit* (amu) is a more convenient way to represent the mass of one hydrogen atom, rather than 1.661×10^{-24} g:

$$1 \text{ amu} = 1.661 \times 10^{-24} \text{ g}$$

Units should be chosen to suit the quantity being described. This can easily be done by choosing a unit that gives an exponential term closest to 10^0.

Question 1.15 Convert 325 mg aspirin (the amount of active ingredient in a standard aspirin tablet) to oz of aspirin.

Question 1.16 A tablet prescribed for the treatment of hypertension has a mass of 5.0×10^{-2} oz. What is the mass of the tablet in units of mg?

Length

The standard metric unit of *length,* the distance between two points, is the m. Large distances are measured in km; smaller distances are measured in mm or cm. Very small distances such as the distances between atoms on a surface are measured in *nanometers* (nm):

$$1 \text{ nm} = 10^{-7} \text{ cm} = 10^{-9} \text{ m}$$

Common conversions for length are as follows:

$$1 \text{ m} = 10^2 \text{ cm} = 3.94 \times 10^1 \text{ in}$$

Volume

The standard metric unit of *volume,* the space occupied by an object, is the L. A L is the volume occupied by 1000 g of water at 4 degrees Celsius (°C). The volume, 1 L, also corresponds to:

$$1 \text{ L} = 10^3 \text{ mL} = 1.06 \text{ qt}$$

The relationship between the L and the mL is shown in Figure 1.9.

Volume: 1000 cm³; 1000 mL 1 dm³; 1 L

1 cm
10 cm = 1 dm

Volume: 1 cm³; 1 mL

1 cm

Figure 1.9 The relationships among various volume units.

(a)

(b)

(c)

(d)

Figure 1.10 Common laboratory equipment used for the measurement of volume. Graduated (a) cylinders, (b) pipets, and (c) burets are used for the delivery of liquids. (d) Volumetric flasks are used to contain a specific volume. A graduated cylinder is usually used for measurement of approximate volume; it is less accurate and precise than either pipets or burets.

Typical laboratory devices used for volume measurement are shown in Figure 1.10. These devices are calibrated in units of mL or microliters (μL); 1 mL is, by definition, equal to 1 cm³. The volumetric flask is designed to *contain* a specified volume, and the graduated cylinder, pipet, and buret *dispense* a desired volume of liquid.

LEARNING GOAL

10 ▶ Know the three common temperature scales and be able to convert from one to another.

Time

The standard metric unit of time is the second (s). The need for accurate measurement of time by chemists may not be as apparent as that associated with mass, length, and volume. It is necessary, however, in many applications. In fact, matter may be characterized by measuring the time required for a certain process to occur. The rate of a chemical reaction is a measure of change as a function of time.

Temperature

Temperature is the degree of "hotness" of an object. This may not sound like a very "scientific" definition, and, in a sense, it is not. We know intuitively the difference between a "hot" and a "cold" object, but developing a precise definition to explain this is not easy. We may think of the temperature of an object as a measure of the amount of heat in the object. However, this is not strictly true. An object increases in temperature because its heat content has increased and vice versa; however, the relationship between heat content and temperature depends on the quantity and composition of the material.

Many substances, such as mercury, expand as their temperature increases, and this expansion provides us with a way to measure temperature and temperature changes. If the mercury is contained within a sealed tube, as it is in a thermometer, the height of the mercury is proportional to the temperature. A mercury thermometer may be calibrated, or scaled, in different units, just as a ruler can be. Three common temperature scales are *Fahrenheit* (°F), *Celsius* (°C), and *Kelvin* (K). Two convenient reference temperatures that are used to calibrate a thermometer are the freezing and boiling temperatures of water. Figure 1.11 shows the relationship between the scales and these reference temperatures.

Figure 1.11 The freezing point and boiling point of water, body temperature, and room temperature expressed in the three common units of temperature.

The Kelvin scale is of particular importance because it is directly related to molecular motion. As molecular speed increases, the Kelvin temperature proportionately increases.

The Kelvin symbol does not have a degree sign. The degree sign implies a value that is *relative* to some standard. Kelvin is an *absolute* scale.

LEARNING GOAL

10 ▶ Know the three common temperature scales and be able to convert from one to another.

Although Fahrenheit temperature is most familiar to us, Celsius and Kelvin temperatures are used exclusively in scientific measurements. It is often necessary to convert a temperature reading from one scale to another. To convert from Fahrenheit to Celsius, we use the following formula:

$$°C = \frac{°F - 32}{1.8}$$

To convert from Celsius to Fahrenheit, we solve this formula for °F, resulting in

$$°F = 1.8°C + 32$$

To convert from Celsius to Kelvin, we use the formula

$$K = °C + 273.15$$

EXAMPLE 1.10   Converting from Fahrenheit to Celsius and Kelvin

Normal body temperature is 98.6°F. Calculate the corresponding temperature in degrees Celsius.

Solution

Using the expression relating °C and °F,

$$°C = \frac{°F - 32}{1.8}$$

substituting the information provided,

$$= \frac{98.6 - 32}{1.8} = \frac{66.6}{1.8}$$

results in:

$$= 37.0°C$$

Calculate the corresponding temperature in Kelvin units.

Solution

Using the expression relating K and °C,

$$K = °C + 273.15$$

substituting the value obtained in the first part,

$$= 37.0 + 273.15$$

results in:

$$= 310.2 \text{ K}$$

Practice Problem 1.10

a. The freezing temperature of water is 32°F. Calculate the freezing temperature of water in Celsius units and Kelvin units.

b. When a patient is ill, his or her temperature may increase to 104°F. Calculate the temperature of this patient in Celsius units and Kelvin units.

▶ **For Further Practice: Questions 1.73 and 1.74.**

Energy

Energy, the ability to do work, may be categorized as either **kinetic energy,** the energy of motion, or **potential energy,** the energy of position. Kinetic energy may be considered as energy in process; potential energy is stored energy. All energy is either kinetic or potential.

Another useful way of classifying energy is by form. The principal forms of energy include light, heat, electrical, mechanical, and chemical energy. All of these forms of energy share the following set of characteristics:

- In chemical reactions, energy cannot be created or destroyed.
- Energy may be converted from one form to another.
- Conversion of energy from one form to another always occurs with less than 100% efficiency. Energy is not lost (remember, energy cannot be destroyed) but rather, is not useful. We buy gasoline to move our cars from place to place; however, much of the energy stored in the gasoline is released as heat.
- All chemical reactions involve either a "gain" or a "loss" of energy.

Energy absorbed or liberated in chemical reactions is usually in the form of heat energy. Heat energy may be represented in units of *calories* (cal) or *joules* (J), their relationship being

$$1 \text{ cal} = 4.18 \text{ J}$$

One calorie is defined as the amount of heat energy required to increase the temperature of 1 g of water 1°C.

Heat energy measurement is a quantitative measure of heat content. It is an extensive property, dependent upon the quantity of material. Temperature, as we have mentioned, is an intensive property, independent of quantity.

Not all substances have the same capacity for holding heat; 1 g of iron and 1 g of water, even if they are at the same temperature, do *not* contain the same amount of heat energy. One gram of iron will absorb and store 0.108 cal of heat energy when the temperature is raised 1°C. In contrast, 1 g of water will absorb almost ten times as much energy, 1.00 cal, when the temperature is increased an equivalent amount.

Units for other forms of energy will be introduced in later chapters.

Question 1.17 Convert 595 cal to units of J.

Question 1.18 Convert 2.00×10^2 J to units of cal.

Concentration

Concentration is a measure of the number of particles of a substance, or the mass of those particles, that are contained in a specified volume. Concentration is a widely used way of representing mixtures of different substances. Examples include:

- The concentration of oxygen in the air
- Pollen counts, given during the hay fever seasons, which are simply the number of grains of pollen contained in a measured volume of air
- The amount of an illegal drug in a certain volume of blood, indicating the extent of drug abuse
- The proper dose of an antibiotic, based on a patient's weight

We will describe many situations in which concentration is used to predict useful information about chemical reactions (Sections 6.4 and 8.2, for example). In Chapter 6 we calculate a numerical value for concentration from experimental data.

The *kilocalorie* (kcal) is the familiar nutritional calorie. It is also known as the large Calorie (C); note that in this term the C is uppercase to distinguish it from the normal calorie. The large Calorie is 1000 small calories. Refer to Section 7.2 and A Human Perspective: Food Calories for more information.

Water in the environment (lakes, oceans, and streams) has a powerful effect on the climate because of its ability to store large quantities of energy. In summer, water stores heat energy, moderating temperatures of the surrounding area. In winter, some of this stored energy is released to the air as the water temperature falls; this prevents the surroundings from experiencing extreme changes in temperature.

A Human Perspective

Food Calories

The body gets its energy through the processes known collectively as metabolism, which will be discussed in detail in the chapters on biochemistry and nutrition. The primary energy sources for the body are carbohydrates, fats, and proteins, which we obtain from the foods we eat. The amount of energy available from a given foodstuff is related to the Calories (C) available in the food. Calories are a measure of the energy and heat content that can be derived from the food. One (food) Calorie (symbolized by C) equals 1000 (metric) calories (symbolized by cal):

$$1 \text{ C} = 1000 \text{ cal} = 1 \text{ kcal}$$

The energy available in food can be measured by totally burning the food; in other words, using the food as fuel. The energy given off in the form of heat is directly related to the amount of chemical energy, energy stored in chemical bonds, that is available in the food. Food provides energy to the body through the various metabolic pathways.

The classes of food molecules are not equally energy rich. When oxidized via metabolic pathways, carbohydrates and proteins provide the cell with 4 C/g, whereas fats generate approximately 9 C/g.

In addition, as with all processes, not all the available energy can be efficiently extracted from the food; a certain percentage is always lost. The average person requires between 2000 and 3000 C/day to maintain normal body functions such as the regulation of body temperature, muscle movement, and so on. If a person takes in more C than the body uses, the C-containing substances will be stored as fat, and the person will gain weight. Conversely, if a person uses more C than are ingested, the individual will lose weight.

Excess C are stored in the form of fat, the form that provides the greatest amount of energy per g. Too many C leads to too much fat. Similarly, a lack of C (in the form of food) forces the body to raid its storehouse, the fat. Weight is lost in this process as the fat is consumed. Unfortunately, it always seems easier to add fat to the storehouse than to remove it.

The "rule of thumb" is that 3500 C are equivalent to approximately 1 lb of body weight. You have to take in 3500 C more than you use to gain 1 lb, and you have to expend 3500 C more than you normally use to lose 1 lb. If you eat as few as 100 C/day beyond your body's needs, you could gain about 10–11 lb per year (yr):

$$\frac{100 \text{ C}}{\text{day}} \times \frac{365 \text{ day}}{1 \text{ yr}} \times \frac{1 \text{ lb}}{3500 \text{ C}} = \frac{10.4 \text{ lb}}{\text{yr}}$$

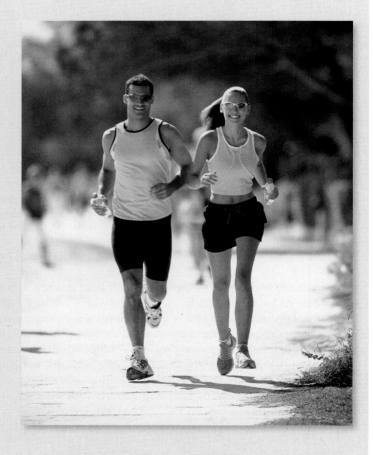

A frequently recommended procedure for increasing the rate of weight loss involves a combination of dieting (taking in fewer C) and exercise. Running, swimming, jogging, and cycling are particularly efficient forms of exercise. Running burns 0.11 C/min/lb of body weight; swimming burns approximately 0.05 C/min/lb of body weight.

For Further Understanding

▶ Sarah runs 1 h each day, and Nancy swims 2 h each day. Assuming that Sarah and Nancy are the same weight, which girl burns more calories in 1 week?

▶ Would you expect a runner to burn more calories in summer or winter? Why?

Table 1.4 Densities of Some Common Materials

Substance	Density (g/mL)	Substance	Density (g/mL)
Air	0.00129 (at 0°C)	Methyl alcohol	0.792
Ammonia	0.000771 (at 0°C)	Milk	1.028–1.035
Benzene	0.879	Oxygen	0.00143 (at 0°C)
Bone	1.7–2.0	Rubber	0.9–1.1
Carbon dioxide	0.001963 (at 0°C)	Turpentine	0.87
Ethyl alcohol	0.789	Urine	1.010–1.030
Gasoline	0.66–0.69	Water	1.000 (at 4°C)
Gold	19.3	Water	0.998 (at 20°C)
Hydrogen	0.000090 (at 0°C)	Wood	0.3–0.98
Kerosene	0.82	(balsa, least dense; ebony and teak, most dense)	
Lead	11.3		
Mercury	13.6		

Figure 1.12 Density (mass/volume) is a unique property of a material. A mixture of wood, water, brass, and mercury is shown, with the cork—the least dense—floating on water. Additionally, brass, with a density greater than water but less than liquid mercury, floats on the interface between these two liquids.

Density and Specific Gravity

Both mass and volume are functions of the *amount* of material present (extensive properties). **Density,** the ratio of mass to volume,

$$\text{Density } (d) = \frac{\text{mass}}{\text{volume}} = \frac{m}{V}$$

is *independent* of the amount of material (intensive property). Density is a useful way to characterize or identify a substance because each substance has a unique density (Figure 1.12).

In density calculations, mass is usually represented in g, and volume is given in either mL or cubic centimeters (cm^3 or cc):

$$1 \text{ mL} = 1 \text{ cm}^3 = 1 \text{ cc}$$

The unit of density would therefore be g/mL, g/cm^3, or g/cc.

A 1 mL sample of air and 1 mL sample of iron do not weigh the same amount. There is much more mass in 1 mL of iron; its density is greater. Density measurements were used to discriminate between real gold and "fool's gold" during the gold rush era. Today the measurement of the density of a substance is still a valuable analytical technique. The densities of a number of common substances are shown in Table 1.4.

LEARNING GOAL

11 ▶ Use density, mass, and volume in problem solving, and calculate the specific gravity of a substance from its density.

Animation
Solid-Liquid Density

EXAMPLE 1.11   Calculating the Density of a Solid

A 2.00 cm^3 sample of aluminum is found to weigh 5.40 g. Calculate the density of aluminum in units of g/cm^3 and g/mL.

Continued—

Solution

The density expression is:

$$d = \frac{m}{V} = \frac{g}{cm^3}$$

Substituting the information given in the problem,

$$= \frac{5.40 \text{ g}}{2.00 \text{ cm}^3}$$

results in:

$$= 2.70 \text{ g/cm}^3$$

Since $1 \text{ mL} = 1 \text{ cm}^3$ (p. 29), we can use this identity as a conversion factor

$$2.70 \frac{g}{cm^3} \times \frac{1 \text{ cm}^3}{1 \text{ mL}} = 2.70 \text{ g/mL}$$

Practice Problem 1.11

A 0.500-mL sample of mercury has a mass of 6.80 g. Calculate the density of mercury in units of g/mL and g/cm^3.

▶ **For Further Practice: Questions 1.87 and 1.88.**

LEARNING GOAL

11 ▶ Use density, mass, and volume in problem solving, and calculate the specific gravity of a substance from its density.

EXAMPLE 1.12   Calculating the Mass of a Gas from Its Density

Air has a density of 0.0013 g/mL. What is the mass of a 6.0-L sample of air?

Solution

$$0.0013 \text{ g/mL} = 1.3 \times 10^{-3} \text{ g/mL}$$

(The decimal point is moved three positions to the right.) This problem can be solved by using conversion factors:

$$6.0 \text{ L air} \times \frac{10^3 \text{ mL air}}{1 \text{ L air}} \times \frac{1.3 \times 10^{-3} \text{ g air}}{\text{mL air}} = 7.8 \text{ g air}$$

Practice Problem 1.12

What mass of air in (g) would be found in a 2.0-L party balloon?

▶ **For Further Practice: Questions 1.89 and 1.90.**

A Medical Perspective

Assessing Obesity: The Body-Mass Index

Density, the ratio of two extensive properties, mass and volume, is an intensive property that can provide useful information about the identity and properties of a substance. The Body-Mass Index (BMI) is also a ratio of two extensive properties, the weight and height (actually the square of the height) of an individual. As a result, the BMI is also an intensive property. It is widely used by physical trainers, medical professionals, and life insurance companies to quantify obesity, which is a predictor of a variety of potential medical problems.

In metric units, the Body-Mass Index is expressed:

$$BMI = \frac{Weight\ (kg)}{Height\ (m^2)}$$

This can be converted to the English system:

$$BMI = \frac{Weight\ (lb)}{Height\ (in^2)} \times 703$$

The number 703 is the commonly used conversion factor to convert from English units (in and lb) to metric units (m and kg) that are the units in the definition of BMI.

The conversion is accomplished in the following way:

$$BMI = \frac{kg}{m^2} = \frac{lb}{in^2} \times \frac{1\ kg}{2.205\ lb} \times \left(\frac{39.37\ in}{1\ m}\right)^2$$

$$\underset{\substack{Weight \\ and \\ height \\ (metric)}}{\uparrow} \quad \underset{\substack{Weight \\ and \\ height \\ (English)}}{\uparrow}$$

$$= \frac{lb}{in^2} \times 703\ \frac{kg \cdot in^2}{lb \cdot m^2}$$

The units of the conversion factor are generally not shown, and the BMI in English units is reduced to:

$$BMI = \frac{Weight\ in\ lb}{(Height\ in\ in)^2} \times 703$$

Computer website BMI calculators generally use this form of the equation.

An individual with a BMI of 25 or greater is considered overweight; if the BMI is 30 or greater, the individual is described as obese. The BMI, once known, can be used as a guideline in the design of suitable diet and exercise programs.

BMI values for a variety of weights and heights are shown as a function of individuals' height and weight:

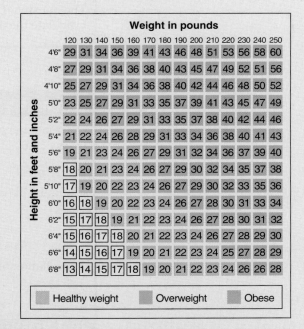

								Weight in pounds							
	120	130	140	150	160	170	180	190	200	210	220	230	240	250
4'6"	29	31	34	36	39	41	43	46	48	51	53	56	58	60
4'8"	27	29	31	34	36	38	40	43	45	47	49	52	51	56
4'10"	25	27	29	31	34	36	38	40	42	44	46	48	50	52
5'0"	23	25	27	29	31	33	35	37	39	41	43	45	47	49
5'2"	22	24	26	27	29	31	33	35	37	38	40	42	44	46
5'4"	21	22	24	26	28	29	31	33	34	36	38	40	41	43
5'6"	19	21	23	24	26	27	29	31	32	34	36	37	39	40
5'8"	18	20	21	23	24	26	27	29	30	32	34	35	37	38
5'10"	17	19	20	22	23	24	26	27	29	30	32	33	35	36
6'0"	16	18	19	20	22	23	24	26	27	28	30	31	33	34
6'2"	15	17	18	19	21	22	23	24	26	27	28	30	31	32
6'4"	15	16	17	18	20	21	22	23	24	26	27	28	29	30
6'6"	14	15	16	17	19	20	21	22	23	24	25	27	28	29
6'8"	13	14	15	17	18	19	20	21	22	23	24	26	26	28

Height in feet and inches

■ Healthy weight ■ Overweight ■ Obese

Developed by the National Center for Health Statistics in collaboration with the National Center for Chronic Disease Prevention and Health Promotion

For Further Understanding

▶ Refer to A Human Perspective: Food Calories (p. 28) and describe connections between these two perspectives.

▶ Calculate your BMI in both metric and English units. Should they agree? Do they?

EXAMPLE 1.13 Using the Density to Calculate the Mass of a Liquid

Calculate the mass, in g, of 10.0 mL of mercury (symbolized Hg) if the density of mercury is 13.6 g/mL.

Continued—

Solution

Using the density as a conversion factor from volume to mass, we have

$$m = (10.0 \text{ mL Hg}) \left(13.6 \, \frac{\text{g Hg}}{\text{mL Hg}} \right)$$

Cancellation of units results in:

$$= 136 \text{ g Hg}$$

Practice Problem 1.13

The density of ethyl alcohol (200 proof, or pure alcohol) is 0.789 g/mL at 20°C. Calculate the mass of a 30.0-mL sample.

▶ **For Further Practice: Questions 1.91 and 1.92.**

EXAMPLE 1.14   Using the Density to Calculate the Volume of a Liquid

Calculate the volume, in mL, of a liquid that has a density of 1.20 g/mL and a mass of 5.00 g.

Solution

Using the density as a conversion factor from mass to volume, we have

$$V = (5.00 \text{ g liquid}) \left(\frac{1 \text{ mL liquid}}{1.20 \text{ g liquid}} \right)$$

Cancellation of units results in:

$$= 4.17 \text{ mL liquid}$$

Practice Problem 1.14

Calculate the volume, in mL, of 10.0 g of a saline solution that has a density of 1.05 g/mL.

▶ **For Further Practice: Questions 1.96 and 1.99.**

Specific gravity is frequently referenced to water at 4°C, its temperature of maximum density (1.000 g/mL). Other reference temperatures may be used. However, the temperature must be specified.

For convenience, values of density are often related to a standard, well-known reference, the density of pure water at 4°C. This "referenced" density is called the **specific gravity,** the ratio of the density of the object in question to the density of pure water at 4°C.

$$\text{specific gravity} = \frac{\text{density of object (g/mL)}}{\text{density of water (g/mL)}}$$

Specific gravity is a *unitless* term. Because the density of water at 4.0°C is 1.00 g/mL, the numerical values for the density and specific gravity of a substance are equal. That is, an object with a density of 2.00 g/mL has a specific gravity of 2.00 at 4°C.

Routine hospital tests involving the measurement of the specific gravity of urine and blood samples are frequently used as diagnostic tools. For example, diseases such as kidney disorders and diabetes change the composition of urine. This compositional change results in a corresponding change in the specific gravity. This change is easily measured and provides the basis for a quick preliminary diagnosis. This topic is discussed in greater detail in A Human Perspective: Quick and Useful Analysis.

A Human Perspective

Quick and Useful Analysis

Measurement of the specific gravity of a liquid is fast, easy, and nondestructive of the sample. Changes in specific gravity over time can provide a wealth of information. Two examples follow:

Urine, a waste product consisting of a wide variety of metabolites, may be analyzed to indicate abnormalities in various metabolic processes or even unacceptable behavior (recall the steroid tests in Olympic competition).

Many of these tests must be performed by using sophisticated and sensitive instrumentation. However, a very simple test, the measurement of the specific gravity of urine, can be an indicator of diabetes mellitus or Bright's disease. The normal range for human urine specific gravity is 1.010–1.030.

A hydrometer, a weighted glass bulb inserted in a liquid, may be used to determine specific gravity. The higher it floats in the liquid, the more dense the liquid. A hydrometer that is calibrated to indicate the specific gravity of urine is called a urinometer.

Winemaking is a fermentation process (Chapter 12). The flavor, aroma, and composition of wine depend upon the extent of fermentation. As fermentation proceeds, the specific gravity of the wine gradually changes. Periodic measurement of the specific gravity during fermentation enables the winemaker to determine when the wine has reached its optimal composition.

For Further Understanding

▶ Give reasons that may account for such a broad range of "normal" values for urine specific gravity.

▶ Could results for a diabetes test depend on food or medicine consumed prior to the test?

Monitoring the winemaking process.

A hydrometer, used in the measurement of the specific gravity of urine.

SUMMARY

1.1 The Discovery Process

Chemistry is the study of matter and the changes that matter undergoes. *Matter* is anything that has mass and occupies space. The changes that matter undergoes always involve either gain or loss of energy. *Energy* is the ability to do work (to accomplish some change). Thus a study of chemistry involves matter, energy, and their interrelationship.

The major areas of chemistry include biochemistry, organic chemistry, inorganic chemistry, analytical chemistry, and physical chemistry.

The *scientific method* consists of six interrelated processes: observation, questioning, pattern recognition, development of *theories* from *hypotheses*, experimentation, and summarizing information. A *law* summarizes a large quantity of information.

The development of the scientific method has played a major role in civilization's rapid growth during the past two centuries.

1.2 Matter and Properties

A scientific experiment produces *data*. Each piece of data arises from a single measurement. Mass, length, volume, time, temperature, and energy are the most common types of data obtained from chemical experiments.

Results are the outcome of an experiment. Usually, several pieces of data are combined, often using a mathematical equation, to produce a result.

Properties (characteristics) of matter may be classified as either physical or chemical. *Physical properties* can be observed without changing the chemical composition of the sample. *Chemical properties* result in a change in composition and can be observed only through *chemical reactions. Intensive properties* are independent of the quantity of the substance. *Extensive properties* depend on the quantity of a substance.

Three states of matter exist (*solid, liquid,* and *gas*); these states of matter are distinguishable by differences in physical properties.

All matter is classified as either a *pure substance* or a *mixture*. A pure substance is a substance that has only one component. A mixture is a combination of two or more pure substances in which the combined substances retain their identity.

A *homogeneous mixture* has uniform composition. Its particles are well mixed. A *heterogeneous mixture* has a non-uniform composition.

An *element* is a pure substance that cannot be converted into a simpler form of matter by any chemical reaction. A *compound* is a substance produced from the combination of two or more elements in a definite, reproducible fashion.

1.3 Significant Figures and Scientific Notation

Significant figures are all digits in a number representing data or results that are known with certainty plus the first uncertain digit. The number of significant figures associated with a measurement is determined by the measuring device. Results should be rounded off to the proper number of significant figures.

Error is defined as the difference between the true value and our estimation, or measurement, of the value. *Accuracy* is the degree of agreement between the true and measured values. *Uncertainty* is the degree of doubt in a single measurement. The number of meaningful digits in a measurement is determined by the measuring device. *Precision* is a measure of the agreement of replicate measurements.

Very large and very small numbers may be represented with the proper number of significant figures by using *scientific notation.*

1.4 Units and Unit Conversion

A *unit* defines the basic quantity of mass, volume, time, and so on. A number that is not followed by the correct unit usually conveys no useful information.

The metric system is a decimal-based system, in contrast to the English system. In the metric system, mass is represented as the gram (g), length as the meter (m), and volume as the liter (L). Any subunit or multiple unit contains one of these units preceded by a prefix indicating the power of ten by which the base unit is to be multiplied to form the subunit or multiple unit. Scientists favor this system over the not-so-systematic English units of measurement.

To convert one unit to another, we must set up a *conversion factor* or series of conversion factors that relate two units. The proper use of these conversion factors is referred to as the factor-label method. This method is used either to convert from one unit to another within the same system or to convert units from one system to another. It is a very useful problem-solving tool.

1.5 Experimental Quantities

Mass describes the quantity of matter in an object. The terms weight and mass are often used interchangeably, but they are not equivalent. *Weight* is the force of gravity on an object. The fundamental unit of mass in the metric system is the gram (g). One atomic mass unit (amu) is equal to 1.661×10^{-24} g.

The standard metric unit of length is the meter (m). Large distances are measured in kilometers (km); smaller distances are measured in millimeters (mm) or centimeters (cm). Very small distances (on the atomic scale) are measured in nanometers (nm). The standard metric unit of volume is the liter (L). A liter is the volume occupied by 1000 g of water at 4 degrees Celsius (°C). The standard metric unit of time is the second (s), a unit that is used in the English system as well.

Temperature is the degree of "hotness" of an object. Many substances, such as liquid mercury, expand as their temperature increases, and this expansion provides us with a way to measure temperature and temperature changes. Three common temperature scales are Fahrenheit (°F), Celsius (°C), and Kelvin (K).

Energy, the ability to do work, may be categorized as either *kinetic energy,* the energy of motion, or *potential energy,* the energy of position. The principal forms of energy are light, heat, mechanical, electrical, nuclear, and chemical energy.

Energy absorbed or liberated in chemical reactions is most often in the form of heat energy. Heat energy may be represented in units of calories or joules: 1 calorie (cal) = 4.18 joules (J). One calorie is defined as the amount of heat energy required to change the temperature of 1 g of water 1°C.

Concentration is a measure of the number of particles of a substance, or the mass of those particles, that are contained in a specified volume. Concentration is a widely used way of representing relative quantities of different substances in a mixture of those substances.

Density is the ratio of mass to volume and is a useful way of characterizing a substance. Values of density are often related to a standard reference, the density of pure water at 4°C. This "referenced" density is the *specific gravity*, the ratio of the density of the object in question to the density of pure water at 4°C.

KEY TERMS

accuracy (1.3)	error (1.3)
chemical property (1.2)	extensive property (1.2)
chemical reaction (1.2)	gaseous state (1.2)
chemistry (1.1)	heterogeneous mixture (1.2)
compound (1.2)	homogeneous mixture (1.2)
concentration (1.5)	hypothesis (1.1)
data (1.2)	intensive property (1.2)
density (1.5)	kinetic energy (1.5)
element (1.2)	law (1.1)
energy (1.1)	liquid state (1.2)

mass (1.5)
matter (1.1)
mixture (1.2)
physical change (1.2)
physical property (1.2)
potential energy (1.5)
precision (1.3)
properties (1.2)
pure substance (1.2)
result (1.2)

scientific method (1.1)
scientific notation (1.3)
significant figures (1.3)
solid state (1.2)
specific gravity (1.5)
temperature (1.5)
theory (1.1)
uncertainty (1.3)
unit (1.4)
weight (1.5)

QUESTIONS AND PROBLEMS

The Discovery Process

Foundations

1.19 Define chemistry and list the major subdivisions of chemistry.
1.20 Define energy and suggest reasons why it is so important.
1.21 How do matter and energy differ?
1.22 Why is observation a critical starting point for any scientific study?
1.23 The model of methane in Section 1.1 is designed to emphasize certain characteristics of that substance. What are these characteristics?
1.24 The model of methane in Section 1.1 has limitations, as do all models. What are these limitations?

Applications

1.25 Discuss the difference between *hypothesis* and *theory*.
1.26 Discuss the difference between *theory* and *law*.
1.27 We use aspects of the scientific method in our everyday lives. Provide one example of formulating a hypothesis as an aid in solving a practical problem.
1.28 Provide one example of the utility of pattern recognition in your day-to-day activities.
1.29 Discuss the meaning of the term *scientific method*.
1.30 Describe an application of reasoning involving the scientific method that has occurred in your day-to-day life.
1.31 Stem-cell research has the potential to provide replacement "parts" for the human body. Is this statement a hypothesis, theory, or law? Explain your reasoning.
1.32 Observed increases in global temperatures are caused by elevated levels of carbon dioxide. Is this statement a hypothesis, theory, or law? Explain your reasoning.
1.33 Describe an experiment demonstrating that the freezing point of water changes when salt (sodium chloride) is added to water.
1.34 Describe an experiment that would enable you to determine the amount (g) of solids suspended in a 1-L sample of seawater.

Matter and Properties

Foundations

1.35 Describe what is meant by a physical property.
1.36 Describe what is meant by a physical change.
1.37 Describe several chemical properties of matter.
1.38 Describe what is meant by a chemical reaction.
1.39 Distinguish between a pure substance and a mixture.
1.40 Give examples of pure substances and mixtures.

1.41 Distinguish between a homogeneous mixture and a heterogeneous mixture.
1.42 Distinguish between an intensive property and an extensive property.

Applications

1.43 Construct a model to represent a heterogeneous mixture of two different compounds.
1.44 Construct a model to represent a homogeneous mixture of two different compounds.
1.45 What data would be required to estimate the total cost of gasoline needed to drive from New York City to Washington, D.C.?
1.46 What data would be required to estimate the mass of planet earth?
1.47 Label each of the following as either a physical change or a chemical reaction:
   a. An iron nail rusts.
   b. An ice cube melts.
   c. A limb falls from a tree.
1.48 Label each of the following as either a physical change or a chemical reaction:
   a. A puddle of water evaporates.
   b. Food is digested.
   c. Wood is burned.
1.49 Label each of the following properties of sodium as either a physical property or a chemical property:
   a. Sodium is a soft metal (can be cut with a knife).
   b. Sodium reacts violently with water to produce hydrogen gas and sodium hydroxide.
1.50 Label each of the following properties of sodium as either a physical property or a chemical property:
   a. When exposed to air, sodium forms a white oxide.
   b. Sodium melts at 98°C.
   c. The density of sodium metal at 25°C is 0.97 g/cm^3.
1.51 Label each of the following as either a pure substance or a mixture:
   a. water
   b. table salt (sodium chloride)
   c. blood
1.52 Label each of the following as either a pure substance or a mixture:
   a. sucrose (table sugar)
   b. orange juice
   c. urine
1.53 Label each of the following as either an intensive property or an extensive property:
   a. mass
   b. volume
   c. density
1.54 Label each of the following as either an intensive property or an extensive property:
   a. specific gravity
   b. temperature
   c. heat content
1.55 Label each of the following as either a homogeneous mixture or a heterogeneous mixture:
   a. a soft drink
   b. a saline solution
   c. gelatin
1.56 Label each of the following as either a homogeneous mixture or a heterogeneous mixture:
   a. gasoline
   b. vegetable soup
   c. concrete

1.57 Plant varieties may be distinguished, one from another, by observing properties of their leaves.
  a. Suggest two extensive properties of leaves that would be useful in the process.
  b. Suggest two intensive properties of leaves that would be useful in the process.

1.58 Would you expect that intensive properties or extensive properties would be more useful in distinguishing among plant varieties by inspecting their leaves?

Significant Figures and Scientific Notation
Foundations

1.59 How many significant figures are contained in each of the following numbers?
  a. 10.0
  b. 0.214
  c. 0.120
  d. 2.062
  e. 10.50
  f. 1050

1.60 How many significant figures are contained in each of the following numbers?
  a. 3.8×10^{-3}
  b. 5.20×10^{2}
  c. 0.00261
  d. 24
  e. 240
  f. 2.40

1.61 Round the following numbers to three significant figures:
  a. 3.873×10^{-3}
  b. 5.202×10^{-2}
  c. 0.002616
  d. 24.3387
  e. 240.1
  f. 2.407

1.62 Round the following numbers to three significant figures:
  a. 123700
  b. 0.00285792
  c. 1.421×10^{-3}
  d. 53.2995
  e. 16.96
  f. 507.5

1.63 Define each of the following terms:
  a. precision
  b. accuracy

1.64 Define each of the following terms:
  a. error
  b. uncertainty

Applications

1.65 Perform each of the following arithmetic operations, reporting the answer with the proper number of significant figures:
  a. (23)(657)
  b. 0.00521 + 0.236
  c. $\dfrac{18.3}{3.0576}$
  d. 1157.23 − 17.812
  e. $\dfrac{(1.987)(298)}{0.0821}$

1.66 Perform each of the following arithmetic operations, reporting the answer with the proper number of significant figures:
  a. $\dfrac{(16.0)(0.1879)}{45.3}$
  b. $\dfrac{(76.32)(1.53)}{0.052}$

  c. (0.0063)(57.8)
  d. 18 + 52.1
  e. 58.17 − 57.79

1.67 Express the following numbers in scientific notation (use the proper number of significant figures):
  a. 12.3
  b. 0.0569
  c. −1527
  d. 0.000000789
  e. 92,000,000
  f. 0.005280
  g. 1.279
  h. −531.77

1.68 Express each of the following numbers in decimal notation:
  a. 3.24×10^{3}
  b. 1.50×10^{4}
  c. 4.579×10^{-1}
  d. -6.83×10^{5}
  e. -8.21×10^{-2}
  f. 2.9979×10^{8}
  g. 1.50×10^{0}
  h. 6.02×10^{23}

Units and Unit Conversion
Foundations

1.69 Convert 2.0 lb to:
  a. oz
  b. tons (t)
  c. g
  d. mg
  e. dekagrams (dag)

1.70 Convert 5.0 qt to:
  a. gal
  b. pints (pt)
  c. L
  d. mL
  e. μL

1.71 Convert 3.0 g to:
  a. lb
  b. oz
  c. kg
  d. centigrams (cg)
  e. mg

1.72 Convert 3.0 m to:
  a. yd
  b. in
  c. ft
  d. cm
  e. mm

1.73 Convert 50.0°F to:
  a. °C
  b. K

1.74 Convert −10.0°F to:
  a. °C
  b. K

1.75 Convert 20.0°C to:
  a. K
  b. °F

1.76 Convert 300.0 K to:
  a. °C
  b. °F

1.77 A typical office has 144 ft^2 of floor space. Calculate the floor space in m^2.

1.78 Tire pressure is measured in units of lb/in^2. Convert 32 lb/in^2 to g/cm^2.

Applications

1.79 A 150-lb adult has approximately 9 pt of blood. How many L of blood does the individual have?

1.80 If a drop of blood has a volume of 0.05 mL, how many drops of blood are in the adult described in Problem 1.79?

1.81 A patient's temperature is found to be 38.5°C. To what Fahrenheit temperature does this correspond?

1.82 A newborn is 21 in in length and weighs 6 lb 9 oz. Describe the baby in metric units.

1.83 Which distance is shorter: 5.0 cm or 5.0 in?

1.84 Which volume is smaller: 50.0 mL or 0.500 L?

1.85 Which mass is smaller: 5.0 mg or 5.0 μg?

1.86 Which volume is smaller: 1.0 L or 1.0 qt?

Experimental Quantities

Foundations

1.87 Calculate the density of a 3.00×10^2-g object that has a volume of 50.0 mL.

1.88 Calculate the density of 50.0 g of an isopropyl alcohol–water mixture (commercial rubbing alcohol) that has a volume of 63.6 mL.

1.89 What volume, in L, will 8.00×10^2 g of air occupy if the density of air is 1.29 g/L?

1.90 In Question 1.89, you calculated the volume of 8.00×10^2 g of air with a density of 1.29 g/L. The temperature of the air sample was lowered and the density increased to 1.50 g/L. Calculate the new volume of the air sample.

1.91 What is the mass, in g, of a piece of iron that has a volume of 1.50×10^2 mL and a density of 7.20 g/mL?

1.92 What is the mass of a femur (leg bone) having a volume of 118 cm^3? The density of bone is 1.8 g/cm^3.

Applications

1.93 You are given a piece of wood that is maple, teak, or oak. The piece of wood has a volume of 1.00×10^2 cm^3 and a mass of 98 g. The densities of maple, teak, and oak are as follows:

Wood	Density (g/cm^3)
Maple	0.70
Teak	0.98
Oak	0.85

What is the identity of the piece of wood?

1.94 The specific gravity of a patient's urine sample was measured to be 1.008. Given that the density of water is 1.000 g/mL at 4°C, what is the density of the urine sample?

1.95 The density of grain alcohol is 0.789 g/mL. Given that the density of water at 4°C is 1.00 g/mL, what is the specific gravity of grain alcohol?

1.96 The density of mercury is 13.6 g/mL. If a sample of mercury weighs 272 g, what is the volume of the sample in mL?

1.97 You are given three bars of metal. Each is labeled with its identity (lead, uranium, platinum). The lead bar has a mass of 5.0×10^1 g and a volume of 6.36 cm^3. The uranium bar has a mass of 75 g and a volume of 3.97 cm^3. The platinum bar has a mass of 2140 g and a volume of 1.00×10^2 cm^3. Which of these metals has the lowest density? Which has the greatest density?

1.98 Refer to Problem 1.97. Suppose that each of the bars had the same mass. How could you determine which bar had the lowest density or highest density?

1.99 The density of methanol at 20°C is 0.791 g/mL. What is the volume of a 10.0-g sample of methanol?

1.100 The density of methanol at 20°C is 0.791 g/mL. What is the mass of a 50.0-mL sample of methanol?

CRITICAL THINKING PROBLEMS

1. An instrument used to detect metals in drinking water can detect as little as 1 μg of mercury in 1 L of water. Mercury is a toxic metal; it accumulates in the body and is responsible for the deterioration of brain cells. Calculate the number of mercury atoms you would consume if you drank 1 L of water that contained only 1 μg of mercury. (The mass of one mercury atom is 3.3×10^{-22} g.)

2. Yesterday's temperature was 40°F. Today it is 80°F. Bill tells Sue that it is twice as hot today. Sue disagrees. Do you think Sue is correct or incorrect? Why or why not?

3. Aspirin has been recommended to minimize the chance of heart attacks in persons who have already had one or more occurrences. If a patient takes one aspirin tablet per day for 10 years, how many pounds of aspirin will the patient consume? (Assume that each tablet is approximately 325 mg.)

4. Design an experiment that will allow you to measure the density of your favorite piece of jewelry.

5. The diameter of an aluminum atom is 250 picometers (pm) (1 pm = 10^{-12} m). How many aluminum atoms must be placed end to end to make a "chain" of aluminum atoms 1 ft long?

The Structure of the Atom and the Periodic Table

2

LEARNING GOALS

1 ▷ Describe the important properties of protons, neutrons, and electrons.

2 ▷ Calculate the number of protons, neutrons, and electrons in any atom.

3 ▷ Distinguish between the terms *atom* and *isotope* and calculate atomic masses from isotopic abundance.

4 ▷ Trace the history of the development of atomic theory, beginning with Dalton.

5 ▷ Explain the critical role of spectroscopy in the development of atomic theory and in our everyday lives.

6 ▷ State the basic postulates of Bohr's theory, its utility, and its limitations.

7 ▷ Recognize the important subdivisions of the periodic table: periods, groups (families), metals, and nonmetals.

8 ▷ Use the periodic table to obtain information about an element.

9 ▷ Describe the relationship between the electronic structure of an element and its position in the periodic table.

10 ▷ Write electron configurations and orbital diagrams for atoms of the most commonly occurring elements.

11 ▷ Use the octet rule to predict the charges of common cations and anions.

12 ▷ Utilize the periodic table and its predictive power to estimate the relative sizes of atoms and ions, as well as relative magnitudes of ionization energy and electron affinity.

OUTLINE

The learning process depends on organizing information efficiently. How does the organization of the periodic table help us to predict properties of the elements?

INTRODUCTION

Why does ice float on water? Why don't oil and water mix? Why does blood transport oxygen to our cells, and why does carbon monoxide inhibit this process? Questions such as these are best answered by understanding the behavior of substances at the atomic level.

In this chapter, we will learn some of the properties of the major particles that make up the atom, and look at early experiments that enabled the development of theories of atomic structure. These theories, in turn, help us to explain the behavior of atoms themselves, as well as the compounds that result from their combination, such as water and carbon dioxide.

The structure of atoms of each element is unique, so it is useful to consider relationships and differences among the elements themselves. The unifying concept is called the periodic law, and it gives rise to an organized "map" of the elements that relates their structure to their chemical and physical properties. This "map" is the periodic table.

As we study the periodic law and periodic table, we shall see that the chemical and physical properties of elements follow directly from the electronic structure of the atoms that make up these elements. A thorough familiarity with the arrangement of the periodic table is vital to the study of chemistry. It not only allows us to predict the structure and properties of the various elements, but it also serves as the basis for developing an understanding of chemical bonding, or the process of forming molecules. Additionally, the properties and behavior of these larger units (bulk properties) are fundamentally related to the properties of the atoms that comprise them.

2.1 Composition of the Atom

The basic structural unit of an element is the **atom,** which is the smallest unit of an element that retains the chemical properties of that element. A tiny sample of the element copper, too small to be seen by the naked eye, is composed of billions of copper atoms arranged in some orderly fashion. Each atom is incredibly small. Only recently have we been able to "see" atoms using modern instruments such as the scanning tunneling electron microscope (Figure 2.1).

Electrons, Protons, and Neutrons

We know from experience that certain kinds of atoms can "split" into smaller particles and release large amounts of energy; this process is *radioactive decay.* We also know that the atom is composed of three primary particles: the *electron,* the *proton,* and the *neutron.* Although other subatomic fragments with unusual names (neutrinos, gluons, quarks, and so forth) have also been discovered, we shall concern ourselves only with the primary particles: the protons, neutrons, and electrons.

We can consider the atom to be composed of two distinct regions:

1. The **nucleus** is a small, dense, positively charged region in the center of the atom. The nucleus is composed of positively charged **protons** and uncharged **neutrons.**
2. Surrounding the nucleus is a diffuse region of negative charge populated by **electrons,** the source of the negative charge. Electrons are very low in mass in contrast to the protons and neutrons.

The properties of these particles are summarized in Table 2.1.

Figure 2.1 Sophisticated techniques, such as scanning tunneling electron microscopy, provide visual evidence for the structure of atoms and molecules. Each dot represents the image of a single iron atom. Even more amazing, the iron atoms have been arranged on a copper surface in the form of the Chinese characters representing the word *atom.*

Table 2.1 Selected Properties of the Three Basic Subatomic Particles

Name	Charge	Mass (amu)	Mass (g)
Electron (e)	-1	5.4×10^{-4}	9.1095×10^{-28}
Proton (p)	$+1$	1.00	1.6725×10^{-24}
Neutron (n)	0	1.00	1.6750×10^{-24}

LEARNING GOAL

1 ▶ Describe the important properties of protons, neutrons, and electrons.

Atoms of various types differ in their number of protons, neutrons, and electrons. The number of protons determines the identity of the atom. As such, the number of protons is *characteristic* of the element. When the number of protons is equal to the number of electrons, the atom is neutral because the charges are balanced and effectively cancel one another.

We may represent an element symbolically as follows:

Mass number

Charge of particle

$$^{A}_{Z}X^{C}$$

Atomic number

Symbol of the element

The **atomic number** (Z) is equal to the number of protons in the atom, and the **mass number** (A) is equal to the *sum* of the number of protons and neutrons (the mass of the electrons is so small as to be insignificant in comparison to that of the nucleus).

If

$$\text{number of protons} + \text{number of neutrons} = \text{mass number}$$

then, if the number of protons is subtracted from each side,

$$\text{number of neutrons} = \text{mass number} - \text{number of protons}$$

or, because the number of protons equals the atomic number,

$$\text{number of neutrons} = \text{mass number} - \text{atomic number}$$

For an atom, in which positive and negative charges cancel, the number of protons and electrons must be equal and identical to the atomic number.

LEARNING GOAL

2 ▶ Calculate the number of protons, neutrons, and electrons in any atom.

Recall from Chapter 1 that one atomic mass unit (amu) is equivalent to 1.661×10^{-24} grams (g).

EXAMPLE 2.1   Determining the Composition of an Atom

Calculate the numbers of protons, neutrons, and electrons in an atom of fluorine. The atomic symbol for the fluorine atom is $^{19}_{9}\text{F}$.

Solution

Step 1. The mass number 19 tells us that the total number of protons + neutrons is 19.

Step 2. The atomic number 9 represents the number of protons.

Step 3. The difference, $19 - 9$, or 10, is the number of neutrons.

Step 4. The number of electrons must be the same as the number of protons, hence 9, for a neutral fluorine atom.

Continued—

Practice Problem 2.1

Calculate the numbers of protons, neutrons, and electrons in each of the following atoms:

a. $^{32}_{16}S$

b. $^{23}_{11}Na$

c. $^{1}_{1}H$

d. $^{244}_{94}Pu$

▶ **For Further Practice: Questions 2.25 and 2.26.**

Isotopes

LEARNING GOAL

3 ▶ Distinguish between the terms *atom* and *isotope* and calculate atomic masses from isotopic abundance.

Isotopes are atoms of the same element having different masses *because they contain different numbers of neutrons.* In other words, isotopes have different mass numbers. For example, all of the following are isotopes of hydrogen:

$^{1}_{1}H$
Hydrogen
(Hydrogen-1)

$^{2}_{1}H$
Deuterium
(Hydrogen-2)

$^{3}_{1}H$
Tritium
(Hydrogen-3)

Isotopes are often written with the name of the element followed by the mass number. For example, the isotopes $^{12}_{6}C$ and $^{14}_{6}C$ may be written as carbon-12 (or C-12) and carbon-14 (or C-14), respectively.

Question 2.1 How many protons, neutrons, and electrons are present in a single atom of:

a. bromine-79

b. bromine-81

c. iron-56

Question 2.2 How many protons, neutrons, and electrons are present in a single atom of:

a. phosphorus-30

b. sulfur-32

c. chlorine-35

A detailed discussion of the use of radioactive isotopes in the diagnosis and treatment of diseases is found in Chapter 9.

Certain isotopes (radioactive isotopes) of elements emit particles and energy that can be used to trace the behavior of biochemical systems. These isotopes otherwise behave identically to any other isotope of the same element. Their chemical behavior is identical; it is their nuclear behavior that is unique. As a result, a radioactive isotope can be substituted for the "nonradioactive" isotope, and its biochemical activity can be followed by monitoring the particles or energy emitted by the isotope as it passes through the body.

Amu are convenient for representing the masses of very small particles, such as individual atoms. Refer to the discussion of units in Chapter 1.

The existence of isotopes explains why the average masses, measured in amu, of the various elements are not whole numbers. This is contrary to what we would expect from proton and neutron masses, which are very close to unity.

Consider, for example, the mass of one chlorine atom, containing seventeen protons (atomic number) and eighteen neutrons:

$$17 \text{ protons} \times \frac{1.00 \text{ amu}}{\text{proton}} = 17.00 \text{ amu}$$

$$18 \text{ neutrons} \times \frac{1.00 \text{ amu}}{\text{neutron}} = 18.00 \text{ amu}$$

$$17.00 \text{ amu} + 18.00 \text{ amu} = 35.00 \text{ amu (mass of chlorine atom)}$$

Inspection of the periodic table reveals that the mass of chlorine is actually 35.45 amu, *not* 35.00 amu. The existence of isotopes accounts for this difference. A natural sample of chlorine is composed principally of two isotopes, chlorine-35 and chlorine-37, in approximately a 3:1 ratio, and the tabulated mass is the *weighted average* of the two isotopes. In our calculation, the chlorine atom referred to was the isotope that has a mass number of 35 amu.

The weighted average of the masses of all of the isotopes of an element is the **atomic mass** and should be distinguished from the mass number, which is the sum of the number of protons and neutrons in a single isotope of the element.

Example 2.2 demonstrates the calculation of the atomic mass of chlorine.

The weighted average is not a true average but is corrected by the relative amounts (the weighting factor) of each isotope present in nature.

EXAMPLE 2.2 Determining Atomic Mass

Calculate the atomic mass of naturally occurring chlorine if 75.77% of chlorine atoms are $^{35}_{17}Cl$ (chlorine-35) and 24.23% of chlorine atoms are $^{37}_{17}Cl$ (chlorine-37).

LEARNING GOAL

3 ▶ Distinguish between the terms *atom* and *isotope* and calculate atomic masses from isotopic abundance.

Solution

Step 1. Convert each percentage to a decimal fraction.

$$75.77\% \text{ chlorine-35} \times \frac{1}{100\%} = 0.7577 \text{ chlorine-35}$$

$$24.23\% \text{ chlorine-37} \times \frac{1}{100\%} = 0.2423 \text{ chlorine-37}$$

Step 2. Multiply the decimal fraction of each isotope by the mass of that isotope to determine the isotopic contribution to the average atomic mass.

$$
\begin{array}{llll}
\text{contribution to} & \text{(fraction of all} & & \text{(mass of a} \\
\text{atomic mass} & = \text{Cl atoms that} & \times & \text{chlorine-35} \\
\text{by chlorine-35} & \text{are chlorine-35)} & & \text{atom)} \\
& = 0.7577 & & \times\ 35.00 \text{ amu} \\
& = 26.52 \text{ amu} & &
\end{array}
$$

$$
\begin{array}{llll}
\text{contribution to} & \text{(fraction of all} & & \text{(mass of a} \\
\text{atomic mass} & = \text{Cl atoms that} & \times & \text{chlorine-37} \\
\text{by chlorine-37} & \text{are chlorine-37)} & & \text{atom)} \\
& = 0.2423 & & \times\ 37.00 \text{ amu} \\
& = 8.965 \text{ amu} & &
\end{array}
$$

Step 3. The weighted average is the sum of the isotopic contributions:

$$
\begin{array}{lll}
\text{atomic mass} & \text{(contribution} & \text{(contribution} \\
\text{of naturally} & = \text{of} & + \text{of} \\
\text{occurring Cl} & \text{chlorine-35)} & \text{chlorine-37)} \\
& = 26.52 \text{ amu} & + 8.965 \text{ amu} \\
& = 35.49 \text{ amu} &
\end{array}
$$

which is very close to the tabulated value of 35.45 amu. An even more exact value would be obtained by using a more exact value of the mass of the proton and neutron (experimentally known to a greater number of significant figures).

Practice Problem 2.2

The element nitrogen has two naturally occurring isotopes. One of these has a mass of 14.003 amu and a natural abundance of 99.63%; the other isotope has a mass of 15.000 amu and a natural abundance of 0.37%. Calculate the atomic mass of nitrogen.

▶ **For Further Practice: Question 2.33.**

A hint for numerical problem solving: Estimate (at least to an order of magnitude) your answer before beginning the calculation using your calculator.

Whenever you do calculations such as those in Example 2.2, before even beginning the calculation you should look for an approximation of the value sought. Then do the calculation and see whether you obtain a reasonable number (similar to your anticipated value). In the preceding problem, if the two isotopes have masses of 35 and 37, the atomic mass must lie somewhere between the two extremes. Furthermore, because the majority of a naturally occurring sample is chlorine-35 (about 75%), the value should be closer to 35 than to 37. An analysis of the results often avoids problems stemming from untimely events such as pushing the wrong button on a calculator.

Chemistry at the Crime Scene

Microbial Forensics

We have learned that atoms of the same element are not identical; common elements are really a mixture of two or more isotopes, differing in mass because they contain different numbers of neutrons. Furthermore, the atomic mass is the weighted average of the masses of these various isotopes.

It seems to follow from this that the relative amounts of these isotopes would be the same, no matter where in the world we obtain a sample of the element. In reality, this is not true. There exist small, but measurable, differences between elemental isotopic ratios; these differences correlate with their locations.

Water, of course, contains oxygen atoms, and a small fraction of these atoms are oxygen-18. We know that lakes and rivers across the United States contain oxygen-18 in different concentrations. Ocean water is richer in oxygen-18. Consequently, freshwater supplies closest to oceans are similarly enriched, perhaps because water containing oxygen-18 is a bit heavier and falls to earth more rapidly, before the clouds are carried inland, far from the coast. Scientists have been able to map the oxygen-18 distribution throughout the United States, creating contour maps, similar to weather maps, showing regions of varying concentrations of the isotope.

How can we use these facts to our advantage? The Federal Bureau of Investigation (FBI) certainly has an interest in ascertaining the origin of microbes that may be used by terrorists. Anthrax, distributed to several sites shortly after September 11, 2001 through the United States Postal Service (USPS), is but one familiar example. If we could carefully measure the ratio of oxygen-18 to oxygen-16 in weaponized biological materials, it might be possible to match this ratio to that found in water supplies in a specific location. We would then have an indication of the region of the country where the material was cultured, perhaps leading to the arrest and prosecution of the perpetrators of the terrorist activity.

This is certainly not an easy task. However, the FBI has assembled an advisory board of science and forensic experts to study this and other approaches to tracking the origin of biological weapons of mass destruction. Just like the "smoking gun," these strategies, termed *microbial forensics*, could lead to more effective prosecution and a safer society for all of us.

For Further Understanding

▶ Search the Web for more information on the properties of anthrax.

▶ How might the approach, described above, be applied to determining the origin of an oil spill at sea?

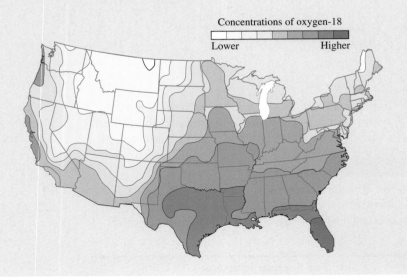

Concentrations of oxygen-18

Lower   Higher

EXAMPLE 2.3   Determining Atomic Mass

Calculate the atomic mass of naturally occurring carbon if 98.90% of carbon atoms are $^{12}_{6}C$ (carbon-12) with a mass of 12.00 amu and 1.11% are $^{13}_{6}C$ (carbon-13) with a mass of 13.00 amu. (Note that a small amount of $^{14}_{6}C$ is also present but is small enough to ignore in a calculation involving three or four significant figures.)

LEARNING GOAL

3 ▶ Distinguish between the terms *atom* and *isotope* and calculate atomic masses from isotopic abundance.

Solution

Step 1. Convert each percentage to a decimal fraction.

$$98.90\% \text{ carbon-12} \times \frac{1}{100\%} = 0.9890 \text{ carbon-12}$$

$$1.11\% \text{ carbon-13} \times \frac{1}{100\%} = 0.0111 \text{ carbon-13}$$

Step 2.

$$\begin{array}{l} \text{contribution to} \\ \text{atomic mass} \\ \text{by carbon-12} \end{array} = \begin{array}{l} \text{(fraction of all} \\ \text{C atoms that} \\ \text{are carbon-12)} \end{array} \times \begin{array}{l} \text{(mass of a} \\ \text{carbon-12} \\ \text{atom)} \end{array}$$

$$= 0.9890 \times 12.00 \text{ amu}$$

$$= 11.87 \text{ amu}$$

$$\begin{array}{l} \text{contribution to} \\ \text{atomic mass} \\ \text{by carbon-13} \end{array} = \begin{array}{l} \text{(fraction of all} \\ \text{C atoms that} \\ \text{are carbon-13)} \end{array} \times \begin{array}{l} \text{(mass of a} \\ \text{carbon-13} \\ \text{atom)} \end{array}$$

$$= 0.0111 \times 13.00 \text{ amu}$$

$$= 0.144 \text{ amu}$$

Step 3. The weighted average is:

$$\begin{array}{l} \text{atomic mass} \\ \text{of naturally} \\ \text{occurring carbon} \end{array} = \begin{array}{l} \text{(contribution} \\ \text{of} \\ \text{carbon-12)} \end{array} + \begin{array}{l} \text{(contribution} \\ \text{of} \\ \text{carbon-13)} \end{array}$$

$$= 11.87 \text{ amu} + 0.144 \text{ amu}$$

$$= 12.01 \text{ amu}$$

Helpful Hint: Because most of the carbon is carbon-12, with very little carbon-13 present, the atomic mass should be very close to that of carbon-12. Approximations, before performing the calculation, provide another check on the accuracy of the final result.

Practice Problem 2.3

The element neon has three naturally occurring isotopes. One of these has a mass of 19.99 amu and a natural abundance of 90.48%. A second isotope has a mass of 20.99 amu and a natural abundance of 0.27%. A third has a mass of 21.99 amu and a natural abundance of 9.25%. Calculate the atomic mass of neon.

▶ **For Further Practice: Question 2.34.**

2.2 Development of Atomic Theory

LEARNING GOAL

4 ▶ Trace the history of the development of atomic theory, beginning with Dalton.

With this overview of our current understanding of the structure of the atom, we now look at a few of the most important scientific discoveries that led to modern atomic theory.

Atoms of element X   Atoms of element Y

(a)

Compound formed from
elements X and Y

(b)

Figure 2.2 An illustration of John Dalton's atomic theory. (a) Atoms of the same element are identical but different from atoms of any other element. (b) Atoms combine in whole-number ratios to form compounds.

Animations
- Thomson's Cathode Ray Tube
- The Rutherford Experiment

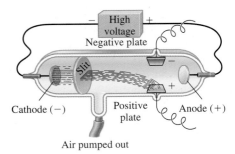

Figure 2.3 Illustration of an experiment demonstrating the charge of cathode rays. The application of an external electric field causes the electron beam to deflect toward a positive charge, implying that the cathode ray is negative.

Dalton's Theory

The first experimentally based theory of atomic structure was proposed by John Dalton, an English schoolteacher, in the early 1800s. Dalton proposed the following description of atoms:

1. All matter consists of tiny particles called atoms.
2. An atom cannot be created, divided, destroyed, or converted to any other type of atom.
3. Atoms of a particular element have identical properties.
4. Atoms of different elements have different properties.
5. Atoms of different elements combine in simple whole-number ratios to produce compounds (stable aggregates of atoms).
6. Chemical change involves joining, separating, or rearranging atoms.

Although Dalton's theory was founded on meager and primitive experimental information, we regard much of it as correct today. Postulates 1, 4, 5, and 6 are currently regarded as true. The discovery of the processes of nuclear fusion, fission ("splitting" of atoms), and radioactivity has disproved the postulate that atoms cannot be created or destroyed. Postulate 3, that all the atoms of a particular element are identical, was disproved by the discovery of isotopes.

Fusion, fission, radioactivity, and isotopes are discussed in some detail in Chapter 9. Figure 2.2 uses a simple model to illustrate Dalton's theory.

Evidence for Subatomic Particles: Electrons, Protons, and Neutrons

The next major discoveries occurred almost a century later (1879–1897). Although Dalton pictured atoms as indivisible, various experiments, particularly those of William Crookes and Eugene Goldstein, indicated that the atom is composed of charged (+ and −) particles.

Crookes connected two metal electrodes (metal disks connected to a source of electricity) at opposite ends of a sealed glass vacuum tube. When the electricity was turned on, rays of light were observed to travel between the two electrodes. They were called **cathode rays** because they traveled from the *cathode* (the negative electrode) to the *anode* (the positive electrode).

Later experiments by J. J. Thomson, an English scientist, demonstrated the electrical and magnetic properties of cathode rays (Figure 2.3). The rays were deflected toward the positive electrode of an external electric field. Because opposite charges attract, this indicates the negative character of the rays. Similar experiments with an external magnetic field showed a deflection as well; hence these cathode rays also have magnetic properties.

A change in the material used to fabricate the electrode disks brought about no change in the experimental results. This suggested that the ability to produce cathode rays is a characteristic of all materials.

In 1897, Thomson announced that cathode rays are streams of negative particles of energy. These particles are *electrons.* Similar experiments, conducted by Goldstein, led to the discovery of particles that are equal in charge to the electron but opposite in sign. These particles, much heavier than electrons (actually 1837 times as heavy), are called *protons.*

As we have seen, the third fundamental atomic particle is the *neutron.* It has a mass virtually identical (it is less than 1% heavier) to that of the proton and has zero charge. The neutron was first postulated in the early 1920s, but it was not until 1932 that James Chadwick demonstrated its existence with a series of experiments involving the use of small-particle bombardment of nuclei.

Evidence for the Nucleus

In the early 1900s it was believed that protons and electrons were uniformly distributed throughout the atom. However, an experiment by Hans Geiger led Ernest Rutherford (in 1911) to propose that the majority of the mass and positive charge of

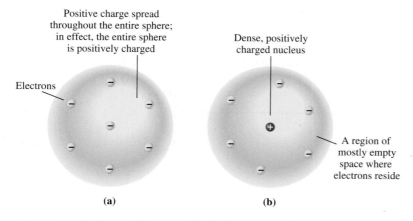

Figure 2.4 The alpha-particle scattering experiment. Most alpha particles passed through the foil without being deflected; a few were deflected from their path by nuclei in the gold atoms.

Figure 2.5 (a) A model of the atom (credited to Thomson) prior to the work of Geiger and Rutherford. (b) A model of the atom supported by the alpha-particle scattering experiments of Geiger and Rutherford.

the atom was actually located in a small, dense region, the *nucleus*, with small, negatively charged electrons occupying a much larger volume outside of the nucleus.

To understand how Rutherford's theory resulted from the experimental observations of Geiger, let us examine this experiment in greater detail. Rutherford and others had earlier demonstrated that some atoms spontaneously "decay" to produce three types of radiation: alpha (α), beta (β), and gamma (γ) radiation. This process is known as *natural radioactivity*. Geiger used radioactive materials, such as *radium*, as projectile sources, "firing" alpha particles at a thin metal foil target (gold leaf). He then observed the interaction of the metal and alpha particles with a detection screen (Figure 2.4) and found that:

a. Most alpha particles passed through the foil without being deflected.
b. A small fraction of the particles were deflected, some even *directly back to the source*.

Rutherford interpreted this to mean that most of the atom is empty space, because most alpha particles were not deflected. Further, most of the mass and positive charge must be located in a small, dense region; collision of the heavy and positively charged alpha particle with this small dense and positive region (the nucleus) caused the great deflections. Rutherford summarized his astonishment at observing the deflected particles: "It was almost as incredible as if you fired a 15-inch shell at a piece of tissue and it came back and hit you."

The significance of Rutherford's contribution cannot be overstated. It caused a revolutionary change in the way that scientists pictured the atom (Figure 2.5). His discovery of the nucleus is fundamental to our understanding of chemistry. Chapter 9 will provide much more information about the nucleus and its unique properties.

2.3 Light, Atomic Structure, and the Bohr Atom

Light and Atomic Structure

The Rutherford atom leaves us with a picture of a tiny, dense, positively charged nucleus containing protons and surrounded by electrons. The electron arrangement, or configuration, is not clearly detailed. More information is needed regarding

LEARNING GOAL

4 ▶ Trace the history of the development of atomic theory, beginning with Dalton.

Animation
• Rutherford's Experiment and a New Atomic Model

LEARNING GOAL

5 ▶ Explain the critical role of spectroscopy in the development of atomic theory and in our everyday lives.

Figure 2.6 The visible spectrum of light. Light passes through a prism, producing a continuous spectrum. Color results from the way in which our eyes interpret the various wavelengths.

the relationship of the electrons to each other and to the nucleus. In dealing with dimensions on the order of 10^{-9} meters (m) (the atomic level), conventional methods for measurement of location and distance of separation become impossible. An alternative approach involves the measurement of *energy* rather than the *position* of the atomic particles to determine structure. For example, information obtained from the absorption or emission of *light* by atoms (energy changes) can yield valuable insight into structure. Such studies are referred to as **spectroscopy.**

In a general sense we refer to light as **electromagnetic radiation.** Electromagnetic radiation travels in *waves* from a source. The most recognizable source of this radiation is the sun. We are aware of a rainbow, in which visible white light from the sun is broken up into several characteristic bands of different colors. Similarly, visible white light, when passed through a glass prism, is separated into its various component colors (Figure 2.6). These various colors are simply light (electromagnetic radiation) of differing *wavelengths.* Light is propagated as a collection of sine waves, and the wavelength is the distance between identical points on successive waves:

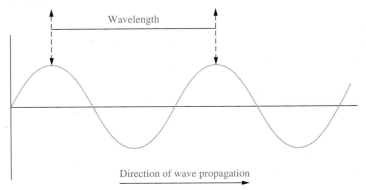

All electromagnetic radiation travels at a speed of 3.0×10^8 m/second (s), the **speed of light.** However, each wavelength of light, although traveling with identical velocity, has its own characteristic energy. A collection of all electromagnetic radiation, including each of these wavelengths, is referred to as the **electromagnetic spectrum.** For convenience in discussing this type of radiation, we subdivide electromagnetic radiation into various spectral regions, which are characterized by physical properties of the radiation, such as its *wavelength* or its *energy* (Figure 2.7). Some of these regions are quite familiar to us from our everyday experiences; the visible and microwave regions are two common examples.

Figure 2.7 The electromagnetic spectrum. Note that the visible spectrum is only a small part of the total electromagnetic spectrum.

Green Chemistry

Electromagnetic Radiation and Its Effects on Our Everyday Lives

From the preceding discussion of the interaction of electromagnetic radiation with matter—spectroscopy—you might be left with the impression that the utility of such radiation is limited to theoretical studies of atomic structure. Although this is a useful application that has enabled us to learn a great deal about the structure and properties of matter, it is by no means the only application. Useful, everyday applications of the theories of light energy and transmission are all around us. Let's look at just a few examples.

Transmission of sound and pictures is conducted at radio frequencies or radio wavelengths. We are immersed in radio waves from the day we are born. A radio or television is our "detector" of these waves. Radio waves are believed to cause no physical harm because of their very low energy, although some concern for people who live very close to transmission towers has resulted from recent research.

X-rays are electromagnetic radiation, and they travel at the speed of light just like radio waves. However, because of their higher energy, they can pass through the human body and leave an image of the body's interior on a photographic film. X-ray photographs are invaluable for medical diagnosis. However, caution is advised in exposing oneself to X-rays, because the high energy can remove electrons from biological molecules, causing subtle and potentially harmful changes in their chemistry.

The sunlight that passes through our atmosphere provides the basis for a potentially useful technology for providing heat and electricity: *solar energy*. Light is captured by absorbers, referred to as *solar collectors*, which convert the light energy into heat energy. This heat can be transferred to water circulating beneath the collectors to provide heat and hot water for homes or industry. Wafers of a silicon-based material can convert light energy to electrical energy; many believe that if the efficiency of these processes can be improved, such approaches may provide

An image of a tumor detected by a CT scanner.

at least a partial solution to the problems of rising energy costs and pollution associated with our fossil fuel–based energy economy.

Microwave radiation for cooking, *infrared* (IR) lamps for heating and remote sensing, *ultraviolet* (UV) lamps used to kill microorganisms on environmental surfaces, *gamma radiation* from nuclear waste, the *visible* light from the lamp you are using to read this chapter—all are forms of the same type of energy that, for better or worse, plays such a large part in our twenty-first century technological society.

Electromagnetic radiation and spectroscopy also play a vital role in the field of diagnostic medicine. They are routinely used as diagnostic and therapeutic tools in the detection and treatment of disease.

The radiation therapy used in the treatment of many types of cancer has been responsible for saving many lives and extending the span of many others. When radiation is used as a treatment, it destroys cancer cells. This topic will be discussed in detail in Chapter 9.

As a diagnostic tool, spectroscopy has the benefit of providing data quickly and reliably; it can also provide information that might not be available through any other means. Additionally, spectroscopic procedures are often nonsurgical, outpatient procedures. Such procedures involve less risk, can be more routinely performed, and are more acceptable to the general public than surgical procedures. The potential cost savings because of the elimination of many unnecessary surgical procedures is an added benefit.

The most commonly practiced technique uses the CT scanner, an acronym for *computer-accentuated tomography*. In this technique, X-rays are directed at the tissue of interest. As the X-rays pass through the tissue, detectors surrounding the tissue gather the signal, compare it to the original X-ray beam, and, using the computer, produce a three-dimensional image of the tissue.

The intensity of IR radiation from a solid or liquid is an indicator of relative temperature. This has been used to advantage in the design of IR cameras, which can obtain images without the benefit of the visible light that is necessary for conventional cameras. The IR photograph shows the coastline surrounding the city of San Francisco.

For Further Understanding

▶ Diane says that a medical X-ray is risky, but a CT scan is risk free. Is Diane correct? Explain your answer.

▶ Why would the sensor (detector) for a conventional camera and an IR camera have to be designed differently?

A spectrophotometer, an instrument that utilizes a prism (or similar device) and a light-sensitive detector, is capable of very accurate and precise wavelength measurement.

Animation
Atom Structure

LEARNING GOAL

6 ▶ State the basic postulates of Bohr's theory, its utility, and its limitations.

Figure 2.8 (a) The emission spectrum of hydrogen. Certain wavelengths of light, characteristic of the atom, are emitted upon electrical excitation. (b) The line spectrum of hydrogen is compared with (c and d) the line spectra of helium and sodium and the spectrum of visible light (e).

Light of shorter wavelength has higher energy; this means that the magnitude of the energy and wavelength are inversely proportional. The wavelength of a particular type of light can be measured, and from this the energy may be calculated.

If we take a sample of some element, such as hydrogen, in the gas phase, place it in an evacuated glass tube containing a pair of electrodes, and pass an electrical charge (cathode ray) through the hydrogen gas, light is emitted. Not all wavelengths (or energies) of light are emitted—only certain wavelengths that are characteristic of the gas under study. This is referred to as an *emission spectrum* (Figure 2.8). If a different gas, such as helium, is used, a different spectrum (different wavelengths of light) is observed. The reason for this behavior was explained by Niels Bohr.

The Bohr Atom

Niels Bohr hypothesized that surrounding each atomic nucleus were certain fixed **energy levels** that could be occupied by electrons. He also believed that each level was defined by a spherical *orbit* around the nucleus, located at a specific distance from the nucleus. The concept of certain fixed energy levels is referred to as the **quantization** of energy. The implication is that only these orbits, or *quantum levels*, are allowed locations for electrons. If an atom *absorbs* energy, an electron undergoes *promotion* from an orbit closer to the nucleus (lower energy) to one farther from the nucleus (higher energy), creating an *excited state*. Similarly, the release of energy by an atom, or *relaxation*, results from an electron falling into an orbit closer to the nucleus (lower energy level).

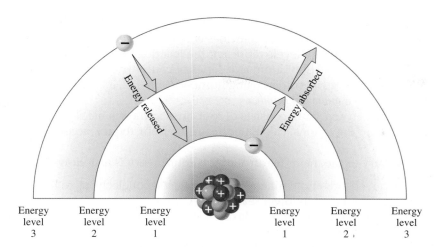

Figure 2.9 The Bohr representation of atoms. Excitation involves promotion of an electron to a higher energy level when energy is absorbed. Relaxation is the reverse process; atoms return to the ground state when the electron relaxes to a lower energy level, releasing energy.

| Energy level 3 | Energy level 2 | Energy level 1 | | Energy level 1 | Energy level 2 | Energy level 3 |

Promotion and relaxation processes are referred to as *electronic transitions*. The amount of energy absorbed in jumping from one energy level to a higher energy level is a precise quantity (hence, quantum), and that energy corresponds exactly to the energy difference between the orbits involved. Electron promotion resulting from absorption of energy results in an *excited state atom;* the process of relaxation allows the atom to return to the ground state (Figure 2.9) with the simultaneous release of light energy. The *ground state* is the lowest possible energy state. This emission process, such as the release of energy after excitation of hydrogen atoms

The line spectrum of each known element is unique. Consequently, spectroscopy is a very useful tool for identifying elements.

A Human Perspective

Atomic Spectra and the Fourth of July

At one time or another we have all marveled at the bright, multicolored display of light and sound that is a fireworks display. These sights and sounds are produced by a chemical reaction that generates the energy necessary to excite a variety of elements to their higher energy electronic states. Light emission results from relaxation of the excited atoms to the ground state. Each atom releases light of specific wavelengths. The visible wavelengths are seen as colored light.

Fireworks need a chemical reaction to produce energy. We know from common experience that oxygen and a fuel will release energy. The fuel in most fireworks preparations is sulfur or aluminum. Each reacts slowly with oxygen; a more potent solid-state source of oxygen is potassium perchlorate ($KClO_4$). The potassium perchlorate reacts with the fuel (an oxidation-reduction reaction, Chapter 8), producing a bright white flash of light. The heat produced excites the various elements packaged with the fuel and oxidant.

Sodium salts, such as sodium chloride, furnish sodium ions, which, when excited, produce yellow light. Red colors arise from salts of strontium, which emit several shades of red corresponding to wavelengths in the 600- to 700-nm region of the visible spectrum. Copper salts produce blue radiation, because copper emits in the 400- to 500-nm spectral region.

The beauty of fireworks is a direct result of the skill of the manufacturer. Selection of the proper oxidant, fuel, and color-producing elements is critical to the production of a spectacular display. Packaging these chemicals in proper quantities so

that they can be stored and used safely is an equally important consideration.

For Further Understanding

▶ Explain why excited sodium emits a yellow color. (Refer to Figure 2.8.)

▶ How does this story illustrate the interconversion of potential and kinetic energy?

A fireworks display is a dramatic illustration of light emission by excited atoms.

Each electronic transition produces "bundles," or quanta, of energy. These quanta are termed "photons." Photons resulting from a certain electronic transition have their own unique wavelength, frequency, and energy.

Animation
- Emission Spectrum of Hydrogen and Electron Energy Transitions

by an electric arc, produces the series of emission lines (emission spectrum). Measurement of the wavelengths of these lines enables the calculation of energy levels in the atom. These energy levels represent the location of the atom's electrons.

We may picture the Bohr atom as a series of concentric orbits surrounding the nucleus. The orbits are identified using numbers ($n = 1, 2, 3, \ldots$, etc.). The number n is referred to as a *quantum number*.

The hydrogen spectrum consists of four lines in the visible region of the spectrum. Electronic transitions, calculated from the Bohr theory, account for each of these lines.

A summary of the major features of the Bohr theory is as follows:

- Atoms can absorb and emit energy via *promotion* of electrons to higher energy levels and *relaxation* to lower levels.
- Energy that is emitted upon relaxation is observed as a single wavelength of light, a collection of photons.
- These *spectral lines* are a result of electron transitions between *allowed levels* in the atom.
- The allowed levels are quantized energy levels, or orbits.
- Electrons are found only in these energy levels.
- The highest energy orbits are located farthest from the nucleus.
- Atoms absorb energy by excitation of electrons to higher energy levels.
- Atoms release energy by relaxation of electrons to lower energy levels.
- Energy differences may be calculated from the wavelengths of light emitted.

Modern Atomic Theory

The Bohr model was an immensely important contribution to the understanding of atomic structure. The idea that electrons exist in specific energy states and that transitions between states involve quanta of energy provided the linkage between atomic structure and atomic spectra. However, some limitations of this model quickly became apparent. Although it explained the hydrogen spectrum, it provided only a crude approximation of the spectra for more complex atoms. Subsequent development of more sophisticated experimental techniques demonstrated that there are problems with the Bohr theory even in the case of hydrogen.

Although Bohr's concept of principal energy levels is still valid, restriction of electrons to fixed orbits is too rigorous. All current evidence shows that electrons do *not*, in fact, orbit the nucleus. We now speak of the *probability* of finding an electron in a *region* of space within the principal energy level, referred to as an **atomic orbital.** The rapid movement of the electron spreads the charge into a *cloud* of charge. This cloud is more dense in certain regions, the **electron density** being proportional to the probability of finding the electron at any point in time. Insofar as these atomic orbitals are part of the principal energy levels, they are referred to as sublevels. In Chapter 3 we will see that the orbital model of the atom can be used to predict how atoms can bond together to form compounds. Furthermore, electron arrangement in orbitals enables us to predict various chemical and physical properties of these compounds.

Question 2.3 What is meant by the term *electron density*?

Question 2.4 How do *orbits* and *orbitals* differ?

The theory of atomic structure has progressed rapidly, from a very primitive level to its present point of sophistication, in a relatively short time. Before we proceed, let us insert a note of caution. We must not think of the present picture of the atom as final. Scientific inquiry continues, and we should view the present theory as a step in an evolutionary process. *Theories are subject to constant refinement*, as was noted in our discussion of the scientific method.

2.4 The Periodic Law and the Periodic Table

In 1869, Dmitri Mendeleev, a Russian, and Lothar Meyer, a German, working independently, found ways of arranging elements in order of increasing atomic mass such that elements with similar properties were grouped together in a *table of elements.* The **periodic law** is embodied by Mendeleev's statement, "the elements if arranged according to their atomic weights (masses), show a distinct *periodicity* (regular variation) of their properties." The *periodic table* (Figure 2.10) is a visual representation of the periodic law.

Chemical and physical properties of elements correlate with the electronic structure of the atoms that make up these elements. In turn, the electronic structure correlates with position on the periodic table.

A thorough familiarity with the arrangement of the periodic table allows us to predict electronic structure and physical and chemical properties of the various elements. It also serves as the basis for understanding chemical bonding.

The concept of "periodicity" may be illustrated by examining a portion of the modern periodic table. The elements in the second row (beginning with lithium, Li, and proceeding to the right) show a marked difference in properties. However, sodium (Na) has properties similar to those of lithium, and sodium

LEARNING GOAL

7 ▶ Recognize the important subdivisions of the periodic table: periods, groups (families), metals, and nonmetals.

Figure 2.10 Classification of the elements: the periodic table.

is therefore placed below lithium; once sodium is fixed in this position, the elements Mg through Ar have properties remarkably similar (though not identical) to those of the elements just above them. The same is true throughout the complete periodic table.

Mendeleev arranged the elements in his original periodic table in order of increasing atomic mass. However, as our knowledge of atomic structure increased, atomic numbers became the basis for the organization of the table. Remarkably, his table was able to predict the existence of elements not known at the time.

The modern periodic law states that *the physical and chemical properties of the elements are periodic functions of their atomic numbers.* If we arrange the elements in order of increasing number of protons, the properties of the elements repeat at regular intervals.

Not all of the elements are of equal importance to an introductory study of chemistry. Table 2.2 lists twenty of the elements that are most important to biological systems, along with their symbols and a brief description of their functions.

We will use the periodic table as our "map," just as a traveler would use a road map. A short time spent learning how to read the map (and remembering to carry it along on your trip!) is much easier than memorizing every highway and intersection. The information learned about one element relates to an entire family of elements grouped as a recognizable unit within the table.

Numbering Groups in the Periodic Table

Mendeleev's original periodic table included only the elements known at the time, fewer than half of the current total.

The periodic table created by Mendeleev has undergone numerous changes over the years. These modifications occurred as more was learned about the chemical and physical properties of the elements. The labeling of groups with Roman

Table 2.2 Summary of the Most Important Elements in Biological Systems

Element	Symbol	Significance
Hydrogen	H	
Carbon	C	
Oxygen	O	Components of major biological molecules
Nitrogen	N	
Phosphorus	P	
Sulfur	S	
Potassium	K	Produce electrolytes responsible for fluid balance and nerve transmission
Sodium	Na	
Chlorine	Cl	
Calcium	Ca	Bones, nerve function
Magnesium	Mg	
Zinc	Zn	
Strontium	Sr	
Iron	Fe	Essential trace metals in human metabolism
Copper	Cu	
Cobalt	Co	
Manganese	Mn	
Cadmium	Cd	"Heavy metals" toxic to living systems
Mercury	Hg	
Lead	Pb	

numerals followed by the letter *A* (representative elements) or *B* (transition elements) was standard, until 1983, in North America and Russia. However, in other parts of the world, the letters *A* and *B* were used in a different way. Consequently, two different periodic tables were in widespread use. This certainly created some confusion.

The International Union of Pure and Applied Chemistry (I.U.P.A.C.), in 1983, recommended that a third system, using numbers 1–18 to label the groups, replace both of the older systems. Unfortunately, multiple systems now exist, and this can cause confusion for both students and experienced chemists.

The periodic tables in this textbook are "double labeled." Both the old (Roman numeral) and new (1–18) systems are used to label the groups. The label that you use is simply a guide to reading the table; the real source of information is in the structure of the table itself. The following sections will show you how to extract useful information from this structure.

Copper is a metal that has many uses. Can you provide other uses of copper?

Periods and Groups

A **period** is a horizontal row of elements in the periodic table. The periodic table consists of six periods containing two, eight, eight, eighteen, eighteen, and thirty-two elements. The seventh period is still incomplete but potentially holds thirty-two elements. Note that the *lanthanide series,* a collection of fourteen elements that are chemically and physically similar to the element lanthanum, is a part of period six. It is written separately for convenience of presentation and is inserted between lanthanum (La), atomic number 57, and hafnium (Hf), atomic number 72. Similarly, the *actinide series,* consisting of fourteen elements similar to the element actinium, is inserted between actinium, atomic number 89, and rutherfordium, atomic number 104.

Groups or *families* are columns of elements in the periodic table. The elements of a particular group or family share many similarities, as in a human family. The similarities extend to physical and chemical properties that are related to similarities in electronic structure (that is, the way in which electrons are arranged in an atom).

Group A elements are called **representative elements,** and Group B elements are **transition elements.** Certain families also have common names. For example, Group IA (or 1) elements are also known as the **alkali metals;** Group IIA (or 2), the **alkaline earth metals;** Group VIIA (or 17), the **halogens;** and Group VIIIA (or 18), the **noble gases.**

LEARNING GOAL
7 ▶ Recognize the important subdivisions of the periodic table: periods, groups (families), metals, and nonmetals.

Representative elements are also known as *main-group elements.* These terms are synonymous.

Metals and Nonmetals

A **metal** is a substance whose atoms tend to lose electrons during chemical change. A **nonmetal,** on the other hand, is a substance whose atoms may gain electrons.

A closer inspection of the periodic table reveals a bold zigzag line running from top to bottom, beginning to the left of boron (B) and ending between polonium (Po) and astatine (At). This line acts as the boundary between *metals,* to the left, and *nonmetals,* to the right. Elements straddling the boundary have properties intermediate between those of metals and nonmetals. These elements are referred to as **metalloids.** The metalloids include boron (B), silicon (Si), germanium (Ge), arsenic (As), antimony (Sb), and tellurium (Te).

Metals and nonmetals may be distinguished by differences in their physical properties in addition to their chemical tendency to lose or gain electrons. Metals have a characteristic luster and generally conduct heat and electricity well. Most (except mercury) are solids at room temperature. Nonmetals, on the other hand, are poor conductors, and several are gases at room temperature.

Note that aluminum (Al) is classified as a metal, not a metalloid.

A Medical Perspective

Copper Deficiency and Wilson's Disease

An old adage tells us that we should consume all things in moderation. This is very true of many of the trace minerals, such as copper. Too much copper in the diet causes toxicity and too little copper results in a serious deficiency disease.

Copper is extremely important for the proper functioning of the body. It aids in the absorption of iron from the intestine and facilitates iron metabolism. It is critical for the formation of hemoglobin and red blood cells in the bone marrow. Copper is also necessary for the synthesis of collagen, a protein that is a major component of the connective tissue. It is essential to the central nervous system in two important ways. First, copper is needed for the synthesis of norepinephrine and dopamine, two chemicals that are necessary for the transmission of nerve signals. Second, it is required for the deposition of the myelin sheath (a layer of insulation) around nerve cells. Release of cholesterol from the liver depends on copper, as does bone development and proper function of the immune and blood clotting systems.

The estimated safe and adequate daily dietary intake (ESADDI) for adults is 1.5–3.0 milligrams (mg). Meats, cocoa, nuts, legumes, and whole grains provide significant amounts of copper.

Although getting enough copper in the diet would appear to be relatively simple, it is estimated that Americans often ingest only marginal levels of copper, and we absorb only 25–40% of that dietary copper. Despite these facts, it appears that copper deficiency is not a serious problem in the United States.

Individuals who are at risk for copper deficiency include people who are recovering from abdominal surgery, which causes decreased absorption of copper from the intestine. Others at risk are premature babies and people who are sustained solely by intravenous feedings that are deficient in copper. In addition, people who ingest high doses of antacids or take excessive supplements of zinc, iron, or vitamin C can develop copper deficiency because of reduced copper absorption. Because copper is involved in so many processes in the body, it is not surprising that the symptoms of copper deficiency are many and diverse. They include anemia; decreased red and white blood cell counts; heart disease; increased levels of serum cholesterol; loss of bone; defects in the nervous system, immune system, and connective tissue; and abnormal hair.

Just as too little copper causes serious problems, so does an excess of copper. At doses greater than about 15 mg, copper causes toxicity that results in vomiting. The effects of extended exposure to excess copper are apparent when we look at Wilson's disease. This is a genetic disorder in which excess copper cannot be removed from the body and accumulates in the cornea of the eye, liver, kidneys, and brain. The symptoms include a greenish ring around the cornea, cirrhosis of the liver, copper in the urine, dementia and paranoia, drooling, and progressive tremors. As a result of the condition, the victim generally dies in early adolescence. Wilson's disease can be treated with medication and diet modification, with moderate success, if it is recognized early, before permanent damage has occurred to any tissues.

For Further Understanding

▶ Why is there an upper limit on the recommended daily amount of copper?

▶ Iron is another essential trace metal in our diet. Go to the Web and find out if upper limits exist for daily iron consumption.

Question 2.5 Using the periodic table on the inside front cover, write the symbol for each of the following metals:

    a. sodium

    b. radium

    c. manganese

    d. magnesium

Question 2.6 Using the periodic table on the inside front cover, write the symbol for each of the following nonmetals:

    a. sulfur

    b. oxygen

    c. phosphorus

    d. nitrogen

LEARNING GOAL

8 ▶ Use the periodic table to obtain information about an element.

Atomic Number and Atomic Mass

The atomic number is the number of protons in the nucleus of an atom of an element. It also corresponds to the nuclear charge, the positive charge from the nucleus. Both the atomic number and the average atomic mass of each element are readily available from the periodic table. For example,

More detailed periodic tables may also include such information as the electron arrangement, relative sizes of atoms and ions, and most probable ion charges.

Question 2.7 Refer to the periodic table (Figure 2.10) and find the following information:

a. the symbol of the element with an atomic number of 40

b. the mass of the element sodium (Na)

c. the element whose atoms contain 24 protons

d. the known element that should most resemble the as-yet undiscovered element with an atomic number of 117

Question 2.8 Refer to the periodic table (Figure 2.10) and find the following information:

a. the symbol of the noble gas in period 3

b. the element in Group IVA with the smallest mass

c. the only metalloid in Group IIIA

d. the element whose atoms contain 18 protons

Question 2.9 For each of the following element symbols, give the name of the element, its atomic number, and its atomic mass.

a. He

b. F

c. Mn

Question 2.10 For each of the following element symbols, give the name of the element, its atomic number, and its atomic mass:

a. Mg

b. Ne

c. Se

2.5 Electron Arrangement and the Periodic Table

A primary objective of studying chemistry is to understand the way in which atoms join together to form chemical compounds. This *bonding process* is a direct consequence of the arrangement of the electrons in the atoms that combine. The **electron configuration** describes the arrangement of electrons in atoms. The organization of the periodic table, originally developed from careful measurement of properties of the elements, also correlates well with similarities in electron configuration. This reveals a very important fact: the properties of collections of atoms are a direct consequence of their electron arrangement.

LEARNING GOAL

9 ▶ Describe the relationship between the electronic structure of an element and its position in the periodic table.

The Quantum Mechanical Atom

As we noted in Section 2.3, the success of Bohr's theory was short-lived. Emission spectra of multi-electron atoms (recall that the hydrogen atom has only one electron) could not be explained by Bohr's theory. Evidence that electrons have wave properties was problematic. Bohr stated that electrons in atoms had very specific locations, now termed *principal energy levels.* The very nature of waves, spread out in space, defies such an exact model of electrons in atoms. Furthermore, the exact model is contradictory to theory and subsequent experiments.

The basic concept of the Bohr theory, that the energy of an electron in an atom is quantized, was refined and expanded by an Austrian physicist, Erwin Schröedinger. He described electrons in atoms in probability terms, developing equations that emphasize the wavelike character of electrons. Although Schröedinger's approach was founded on complex mathematics, we can readily use models of electron probability regions to enable us to gain an insight into atomic structure without the need to understand the underlying mathematics.

Schröedinger's theory, often described as quantum mechanics, incorporates Bohr's principal energy levels ($n = 1, 2$, and so forth); however, it is proposed that each of these levels is made up of one or more sublevels. Each sublevel, in turn, contains one or more atomic orbitals. In the following section, we shall look at each of these regions in more detail and learn how to predict the way that electrons are arranged in stable atoms.

Principal Energy Levels, Sublevels, and Orbitals

Principal Energy Levels

Bohr concluded that electrons in atoms do not roam freely in space; rather they are confined to certain specific regions of space outside of the nucleus of an atom. **Principal energy levels** (analogous to Bohr's orbits) are regions where electrons may be found, and have integral values designated $n = 1, n = 2, n = 3$, and so forth. The principal energy level is related to the average distance from the nucleus. An $n = 1$ level is closest to the nucleus; the larger the value of n, the greater the average distance of an electron in that level from the nucleus.

The maximum number of electrons that a principal energy level can hold is equal to $2(n)^2$. For example:

$n = 1$	$2(1)^2$	Capacity $= 2e^-$
$n = 2$	$2(2)^2$	Capacity $= 8e^-$
$n = 3$	$2(3)^2$	Capacity $= 18e^-$

Sublevels

A **sublevel** is a set of equal-energy orbitals within a principal energy level. The sublevels, or subshells, are symbolized as *s, p, d,* and so forth; they increase in energy in the following order:

$$s < p < d$$

We specify both the principal energy level and type of sublevel when describing the location of an electron—for example, 1*s*, 2*s*, 2*p*. Energy level designations for the first three principal energy levels follow:

- The first principal energy level ($n = 1$) has one possible sublevel: 1*s*.
- The second principal energy level ($n = 2$) has two possible sublevels: 2*s* and 2*p*.
- The third principal energy level ($n = 3$) has three possible sublevels: 3*s*, 3*p*, and 3*d*.

Orbitals

An **atomic orbital** is a specific region of a sublevel containing a maximum of two electrons.

Figure 2.11 depicts a model of an *s* orbital. It is spherically symmetrical, much like a Ping-Pong ball. Its volume represents a region where there is a high probability of finding electrons of similar energy. This probability decreases as we approach the outer region of the atom. The nucleus is at the center of the *s* orbital. At that point the probability of finding the electron is zero; electrons cannot reside in the nucleus. Only one *s* orbital can be found in any *n* level. Atoms with many electrons, occupying a number of *n* levels, have an *s* orbital in each *n* level. Consequently 1*s*, 2*s*, 3*s*, and so forth are possible orbitals.

Figure 2.12 illustrates the shapes of the three possible *p* orbitals within a given level. Each has the same shape, and that shape appears much like a dumbbell; these three orbitals differ only in the direction they extend into space. Imaginary coordinates *x*, *y*, and *z* are superimposed on these models to emphasize this fact. These three orbitals, termed p_x, p_y, and p_z, may coexist in a single atom.

Figure 2.13 depicts the shapes of the five possible *d* orbitals within a given *n* level. These *d* orbitals are important in determining the properties of the transition metals.

Higher energy orbitals (*f*, *g*, and so forth) also exist, but they are important only in the description of the electron arrangements of the heaviest elements.

It is important to remember that *shape* of the orbital represents regions in the atom (but outside of the nucleus) where electrons *may* be found. Not all orbitals are occupied by electrons; the shaded regions really represent the probability of finding the electrons in specific regions of the atom.

Electrons in Sublevels

We can deduce the maximum electron capacity of each sublevel based on the information just given.

For the *s* sublevel:

$$1 \text{ orbital} \times \frac{2e^- \text{ capacity}}{\text{orbital}} = 2e^- \text{ capacity}$$

For the *p* sublevel:

$$3 \text{ orbitals} \times \frac{2e^- \text{ capacity}}{\text{orbital}} = 6e^- \text{ capacity}$$

For the *d* sublevel:

$$5 \text{ orbitals} \times \frac{2e^- \text{ capacity}}{\text{orbital}} = 10e^- \text{ capacity}$$

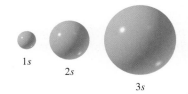

Figure 2.11 Representation of *s* orbitals.

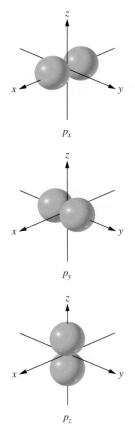

Figure 2.12 Representation of the three *p* orbitals, p_x, p_y, and p_z.

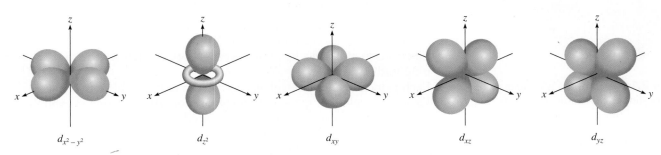

Figure 2.13 Representation of the five *d* orbitals.

Section 2.2 discusses the properties of electrons demonstrated by Thomson.

Animation
• Electron Configurations

Electron Spin

As we have noted, each atomic orbital has a maximum capacity of two electrons. The electrons are perceived to *spin* on an imaginary axis, and the two electrons in the same orbital must have opposite spins: clockwise and counterclockwise. Their behavior is analogous to two ends of a magnet. Remember, electrons have magnetic properties. The electrons exhibit sufficient magnetic attraction to hold themselves together despite the natural repulsion that they "feel" for each other, owing to their similar charge (remember, like charges repel). Electrons must have opposite spins to coexist in an orbital. Two electrons in one orbital that possess opposite spins are referred to as *paired* electrons. The number and arrangement of unpaired electrons in an atom are responsible for the magnetic properties of elements (Figure 2.14.)

Electron Configurations

We can write the electron arrangement (electron configuration) for an atom of any element if we know a few simple facts. We need to know the number of electrons in the atom, which is readily available from the periodic table. (Remember, the number of electrons in a neutral atom is equal to the atomic number.) We know that each principal energy level has a maximum capacity of $2(n)^2$ electrons. No more than two electrons can be placed in any orbital, and each principal energy level, n, can contain only n subshells. Additionally, the aufbau principle, the Pauli exclusion principle, and Hund's rule will complete our strategy.

Aufbau Principle

The *aufbau*, or building up, *principle* helps us to represent the electron configuration of atoms of various elements. According to this principle, electrons fill the lowest energy orbital that is available. Figure 2.15 is a useful way of depicting the theoretical order in which orbitals fill with electrons. It is easily memorized and will prove to be a useful guide to constructing electron configurations for the elements.

Pauli Exclusion Principle

Wolfgang Pauli was a renowned quantum physicist who is credited with providing the most complete explanation of the relationship between electrons in orbitals. Although the theory behind the *Pauli exclusion principle* is rooted in the mathematics of quantum theory, the practical application is straightforward: Each orbital can hold up to two electrons with spins paired.

Hund's Rule

All electrons in atoms are typically in their lowest energy state, termed the *ground state,* at room temperature. *Hund's rule* is a consequence of this: When there is a set of orbitals of equal energy (for example, three p orbitals in the $n = 2$ level) each orbital becomes half-filled (one electron per orbital) before any become completely filled (two electrons).

Guidelines for Writing Electron Configurations

• Obtain the total number of electrons in the atoms from the atomic number found on the periodic table.
• Electrons in atoms occupy the lowest energy orbitals that are available, beginning with 1s.
• Each principal energy level, n, can contain only n sublevels.
• Each sublevel is composed of one (s) or more (three p, five d) orbitals.
• No more than two electrons can be placed in any orbital, and two electrons in a single orbital must be paired.
• The maximum number of electrons in any principal energy level is $2(n)^2$.
• The theoretical order of orbital filling is depicted in Figure 2.15.

Figure 2.14 A compass is a familiar direction-finder that aligns the magnetic field of the compass needle with the earth's natural magnetic field. Unpaired electrons in iron atoms (in the needle and in the earth) are responsible for the magnetic fields.

Now let us look at several examples:

Hydrogen

Hydrogen is the simplest atom; it has only one electron. That electron must be in the lowest principal energy level ($n = 1$) and the lowest orbital (s). We indicate the number of electrons in a region with a *superscript,* so we write $1s^1$. The electron configuration for hydrogen is $1s^1$.

An alternate way of depicting electron arrangement in atoms is the *orbital diagram*. Each orbital is represented as a box, and each electron as an arrow, indicating the relative direction of its spin. The orbital diagram for hydrogen is:

$1s^1$

Helium

Helium has two electrons, which will fill the lowest energy level. The ground state (lowest energy) electron configuration for helium is $1s^2$, and the corresponding orbital diagram is:

$1s^2$

The arrows show paired (opposite) spins, in accordance with the Pauli exclusion principle.

Lithium

Lithium has three electrons. The first two are configured the same as helium. The third must go into the orbital of the lowest energy in the second principal energy level; therefore the configuration is $1s^2\,2s^1$.
The orbital diagram is:

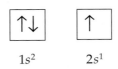

$1s^2$ $2s^1$

Beryllium

Beryllium has four electrons. The first three are configured the same as lithium. The fourth electron fills the $2s$ orbital; therefore the configuration is $1s^2\,2s^2$, and the orbital diagram is:

$1s^2$ $2s^2$

Boron

Boron has five electrons. The first four are configured the same as beryllium. The fifth electron must go into the $2p$ level; therefore the configuration is $1s^2\,2s^2\,2p^1$.
The orbital diagram is:

$1s^2$ $2s^2$ $2p_x^1$

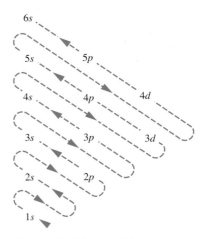

Figure 2.15 A useful way to remember the filling order for electrons in atoms. Begin adding electrons at the bottom (lowest energy) and follow the arrows. Remember: no more than two electrons in each orbital.

The subscripts x, y, and z are often used to distinguish among equivalent orbitals according to their orientation in three-dimensional space (see Figure 2.12).

Carbon

Carbon has six electrons. The first five are configured the same as boron. The sixth electron, according to Hund's rule, enters a second $2p$ orbital, with the same spin as the fifth electron. The electron configuration for carbon is $1s^2\,2s^2\,2p^2$, and the orbital diagram is:

$$
\begin{array}{ccc}
\boxed{\uparrow\downarrow} & \boxed{\uparrow\downarrow} & \boxed{\uparrow}\,\boxed{\uparrow}\,\boxed{} \\
1s^2 & 2s^2 & 2p_x^1 \quad 2p_y^1
\end{array}
$$

Note that Hund's rule requires the two p electrons to occupy different $2p$ orbitals.

Nitrogen

Nitrogen, following the same logic, is $1s^2, 2s^2, 2p^3$, and the orbital diagram is:

$$
\begin{array}{ccc}
\boxed{\uparrow\downarrow} & \boxed{\uparrow\downarrow} & \boxed{\uparrow}\,\boxed{\uparrow}\,\boxed{\uparrow} \\
1s^2 & 2s^2 & 2p_x^1 \quad 2p_y^1 \quad 2p_z^1
\end{array}
$$

Oxygen, Fluorine, and Neon

Each of these elements adds one more electron, pairing one of the three unpaired electrons, resulting in:

for oxygen, $1s^2\,2s^2\,2p^4$ and

$$
\begin{array}{ccc}
\boxed{\uparrow\downarrow} & \boxed{\uparrow\downarrow} & \boxed{\uparrow\downarrow}\,\boxed{\uparrow}\,\boxed{\uparrow} \\
1s^2 & 2s^2 & 2p_x^2 \quad 2p_y^1 \quad 2p_z^1
\end{array}
$$

for fluorine, $1s^2\,2s^2\,2p^5$ and

$$
\begin{array}{ccc}
\boxed{\uparrow\downarrow} & \boxed{\uparrow\downarrow} & \boxed{\uparrow\downarrow}\,\boxed{\uparrow\downarrow}\,\boxed{\uparrow} \\
1s^2 & 2s^2 & 2p_x^2 \quad 2p_y^2 \quad 2p_z^2
\end{array}
$$

for neon, $1s^2\,2s^2\,2p^6$ and

$$
\begin{array}{ccc}
\boxed{\uparrow\downarrow} & \boxed{\uparrow\downarrow} & \boxed{\uparrow\downarrow}\,\boxed{\uparrow\downarrow}\,\boxed{\uparrow\downarrow} \\
1s^2 & 2s^2 & 2p_x^2 \quad 2p_y^2 \quad 2p_z^2
\end{array}
$$

Sodium Through Argon

Electrons in these elements retain the basic $1s^2\,2s^2\,2p^6$ arrangement of the preceding element, neon; new electrons enter the third principal energy level:

Na	$1s^2\,2s^2\,2p^6\,3s^1$	
Mg	$1s^2\,2s^2\,2p^6\,3s^2$	
Al	$1s^2\,2s^2\,2p^6\,3s^2\,3p^1$	Three $3p$ orbitals can
Si	$1s^2\,2s^2\,2p^6\,3s^2\,3p^2$	hold a maximum of six e⁻.
P	$1s^2\,2s^2\,2p^6\,3s^2\,3p^3$	Argon has a complete
S	$1s^2\,2s^2\,2p^6\,3s^2\,3p^4$	$n = 3$ level; that
Cl	$1s^2\,2s^2\,2p^6\,3s^2\,3p^5$	explains its unusual
Ar	$1s^2\,2s^2\,2p^6\,3s^2\,3p^6$	stability.

By knowing the order of filling of atomic orbitals, lowest to highest energy, you may write the electron configuration for any element. The order of orbital filling can be represented by the diagram in Figure 2.15. Such a diagram provides an easy way of predicting the electron configuration of the elements. Remember that the diagram is based on an energy scale, with the lowest energy orbital at the beginning of the "path" and the highest energy orbital at the end of the "path." An alternative way of representing orbital energies is through the use of an energy level diagram, such as the one in Figure 2.16.

We have seen that elements in the periodic table are classified as either representative or transition. Representative elements consist of all Group 1, 2, and 13–18 elements (IA–VIIIA). All others are transition elements. The guidelines that we have developed for writing electron configurations work well for representative elements. Electron configurations for transition elements include several exceptions to the rules, due to more complex interactions among electrons that occur in atoms with large numbers of electrons.

Let us now look at the electron configuration for tin, a representative element with a large number of electrons, hence, a more complex electronic structure.

Figure 2.16 An orbital energy level diagram. Electrons fill orbitals in the order of increasing energy.

EXAMPLE 2.4 Writing the Electron Configuration of Tin

Write the electron configuration for tin.

Solution

Step 1. Tin (Sn) has an atomic number of fifty; thus we must place fifty electrons in atomic orbitals.

Step 2. Recall the total electron capacities of orbital types: s, two; p, six; and d, ten. The first principal energy level has one sublevel, the second has two sublevels, and so on. The order of filling (Figure 2.15) is $1s$, $2s$, $2p$, $3s$, $3p$, $4s$, $3d$, $4p$.

Step 3. The electron configuration is as follows:

$$1s^2\ 2s^2\ 2p^6\ 3s^2\ 3p^6\ 4s^2\ 3d^{10}\ 4p^6\ 5s^2\ 4d^{10}\ 5p^2$$

Helpful Hint: As a check, count electrons in the electron configuration (add all of the superscript numbers) to ensure that we have accounted for all fifty electrons of the Sn atom.

Practice Problem 2.4

Write the electron configuration for an atom of:

a. sulfur
b. calcium
c. potassium
d. phosphorus

▶ **For Further Practice: Questions 2.75 and 2.76.**

EXAMPLE 2.5 Writing the Electron Configuration and Orbital Diagram for Silicon

Write the electron configuration and orbital diagram for silicon.

Solution

Step 1. Silicon (Si) has an atomic number of fourteen; thus we must place fourteen electrons in atomic orbitals.

Continued—

LEARNING GOAL

10 ▶ Write electron configurations and orbital diagrams for atoms of the most commonly occurring elements.

Step 2. Recall the total electron capacities of orbital types (*s*, two electrons and *p*, six electrons) and that the first principal energy level has one sublevel, the second two, and so on. The order of filling is 1*s*, 2*s*, 2*p*, 3*s*, 3*p*.

Step 3. The electron configuration is as follows:

$$1s^2 \ 2s^2 \ 2p^6 \ 3s^2 \ 3p^2$$

Step 4. Be sure to count the superscript numbers in the electron configuration to ensure that all fourteen electrons are accounted for.

Step 5. Writing the orbital box diagram follows from the electron configuration. Remember that Hund's rule tells us to enter *p* electrons unpaired until each orbital contains one electron.

$$\quad\ 1s^2 \qquad\quad 2s^2 \qquad\quad 2p_x^2 \quad 2p_y^2 \quad 2p_z^2 \qquad\quad 3s^2 \qquad\quad 3p_x^1 \quad 3p_y^1 \quad 3p_z$$

Practice Problem 2.5

Write the orbital diagram for each element in Practice Problem 2.4.

▶ **For Further Practice: Questions 2.77 and 2.78.**

Electron Configurations and the Periodic Table

Mendeleev's periodic table was based on extensive observation of physical and chemical properties. Its unusual shape is nicely explained by electron configurations resulting from atomic orbital theory. Elements in the same group (column) have the same outer shell electron configuration. Group IA(1) is ns^1, Group IIA(2), is ns^2, and so forth. The prefix n corresponds to the period (row) containing the element whose principal energy level (also n) is filling. The link between electron configuration and physical properties is, in fact, the periodic table and its unusual shape!

This relationship is shown in Figure 2.17.

Figure 2.17 The shape of the periodic table shows four distinct regions, corresponding to the type of subshell that is filling with electrons.

2.6 Valence Electrons and the Octet Rule

Valence Electrons

If we picture two spherical objects that we wish to join together, perhaps with glue, the glue can be applied to the surface and the two objects can then be brought into contact. We can extend this analogy to two atoms that are modeled as spherical objects. Although this is not a perfect analogy, it is apparent that the surface interaction is of primary importance. Although the positively charged nucleus and "interior" electrons certainly play a role in bonding, we can most easily understand the process by considering only the outermost electrons. We refer to these as *valence electrons*. **Valence electrons** are the outermost electrons in an atom, which are involved, or have the potential to become involved, in the bonding process.

Metals tend to have fewer valence electrons, and nonmetals tend to have more valence electrons.

For representative elements the number of valence electrons in an atom corresponds to the number of the *group* or *family* in which the atom is found. For example, elements such as hydrogen and sodium (in fact, all alkali metals, Group IA or 1) have one valence electron. From left to right in period 2, beryllium, Be (Group IIA or 2), has two valence electrons; boron, B (Group IIIA or 3), has three; carbon, C (Group IVA or 4), has four; and so forth.

EXAMPLE 2.6   Determining Electron Arrangement

Provide the total number of electrons, total number of valence electrons, and energy level in which the valence electrons are found for the silicon (Si) atom.

Solution

Step 1. Determine the position of silicon in the periodic table. Silicon is found in Group IVA and period 3 of the table. Silicon has an atomic number of fourteen.

Step 2. The atomic number provides the number of electrons in an atom. Silicon therefore has fourteen electrons.

Step 3. Because silicon is in Group IV, only 4 of the 14 electrons are valence electrons.

Step 4. Silicon has two electrons in $n = 1$, eight electrons in $n = 2$, and four electrons in the $n = 3$ level.

Practice Problem 2.6

For each of the following elements, provide the *total* number of electrons and *valence* electrons in its atoms as well as the number of the energy level in which the valence electrons are found:

  a. Na
  b. Mg
  c. S
  d. Cl
  e. Ar

▶ **For Further Practice: Questions 2.83 and 2.84.**

We may think of stability as a type of
contentment; a noble gas atom does not
need to rearrange its electrons or lose
or gain any electrons to get to a more
stable, lower energy, or more "contented"
configuration.

The Octet Rule

Elements in the last family, the noble gases, have either two valence electrons (helium) or eight valence electrons (neon, argon, krypton, xenon, and radon). These elements are extremely stable and were often termed *inert gases* because they do not readily bond to other elements, although they can be made to do so under extreme experimental conditions. A full $n = 1$ energy level (as in helium) or an outer *octet* of electrons (eight valence electrons, as in all of the other noble gases) is responsible for this unique stability.

Atoms of elements in other groups are more reactive than the noble gases because in the process of chemical reaction they are trying to achieve a more stable "noble gas" configuration by gaining or losing electrons. This is the basis of the **octet rule,** which states that elements usually react in such a way as to attain the electron configuration of the noble gas closest to them in the periodic table (a stable octet of electrons). In chemical reactions they will gain, lose, or share the minimum number of electrons necessary to attain this more stable energy state. The octet rule, although simple in concept, is a remarkably reliable predictor of chemical change, especially for representative elements.

Shorthand Electron Configurations

As we noted earlier the electron configuration for the sodium atom (Na, atomic number eleven) is

$$1s^2 \; 2s^2 \; 2p^6 \; 3s^1$$

The electron configuration for the preceding noble gas, neon (Ne, atomic number ten), is

$$1s^2 \; 2s^2 \; 2p^6$$

The electron configuration for sodium is really the electron configuration of Ne, with $3s^1$ added to represent one additional electron. So it is permissible to write

[Ne] $3s^1$ as equivalent to $1s^2 \; 2s^2 \; 2p^6 \; 3s^1$
[Ne] $3s^1$ is the *shorthand electron configuration* for sodium.

Similarly,

[Ne] $3s^2$ representing Mg
[Ne] $3s^2 \; 3p^5$ representing Cl
[Ar] $4s^1$ representing K

are valid electron configurations.

The use of abbreviated electron configurations, in addition to being faster and easier to write, serves to highlight the valence electrons, those electrons involved in bonding. The symbol of the noble gas represents the *core,* nonvalence electrons and the valence electron configuration follows the noble gas symbol.

Question 2.11 Give the *shorthand* electron configuration for:

  a. sulfur

  b. calcium

Question 2.12 Give the *shorthand* electron configuration for:

  a. potassium

  b. phosphorus

Ions

Ions are electrically charged particles that result from a gain of one or more electrons by the parent atom (forming negative ions, or **anions**) or a loss of one or more electrons from the parent atom (forming positive ions, or **cations**).

Formation of an anion may occur as follows:

9 protons, 9 electrons   9 protons, 10 electrons

$$^{19}_{9}F + 1e^- \longrightarrow {}^{19}_{9}F^-$$

The neutral atom   The fluorine anion
gains an electron   is formed

Alternatively, formation of a cation of sodium may proceed as follows:

Ions are often formed in chemical reactions, when one or more electrons are transferred from one substance to another.

11 protons, 11 electrons   11 protons, 10 electrons

$$^{23}_{11}Na \longrightarrow 1e^- + {}^{23}_{11}Na^+$$

The neutral atom   The sodium cation
loses an electron   is formed

Note that the electrons gained are written to the left of the reaction arrow (they are reactants), whereas the electrons lost are written as products to the right of the reaction arrow. For simplification, the atomic and mass numbers are often omitted, because they do not change during ion formation. For example, the sodium cation would be written as Na^+ and the anion of fluorine as F^-.

Ion Formation and the Octet Rule

Metals and nonmetals differ in the way in which they form ions. Metallic elements (located at the left of the periodic table) tend to form positively charged *cations*. Positive ions are formed when an atom loses one or more electrons, for example,

Na	$\longrightarrow$	Na^+	$+ e^-$
Sodium atom		Sodium ion	
($11e^-$, 1 valence e^-)		($10e^-$)	

Mg	$\longrightarrow$	Mg^{2+}	$+ 2e^-$
Magnesium atom		Magnesium ion	
($12e^-$, 2 valence e^-)		($10e^-$)	

Al	$\longrightarrow$	Al^{3+}	$+ 3e^-$
Aluminum atom		Aluminum ion	
($13e^-$, 3 valence e^-)		($10e^-$)	

In each of these cases the atom has lost *all* of its valence electrons. The resulting ion has the same number of electrons as the nearest noble gas atom:

$Na^+(10e^-)$ and $Mg^{2+}(10e^-)$ and $Al^{3+}(10e^-)$ are all isoelectronic with Ne ($10e^-$).

These ions are particularly stable. Each ion is **isoelectronic** (that is, it has the same number of electrons) with its nearest noble gas neighbor and has an octet of electrons in its outermost energy level.

Recall that the prefix *iso* (Greek *isos*) means equal.

Section 3.2 discusses the naming of ions.

Sodium is typical of each element in its group. Knowing that sodium forms a 1+ ion leads to the prediction that H, Li, K, Rb, Cs, and Fr also will form 1+ ions. Furthermore, magnesium, which forms a 2+ ion, is typical of each element in its group; Be^{2+}, Ca^{2+}, Sr^{2+}, and so forth are the resulting ions.

Nonmetallic elements, located at the right of the periodic table, tend to gain electrons to become isoelectronic with the nearest noble gas element, forming negative *anions*.

Consider:

The ion of fluorine is the *fluoride ion*; the ion of oxygen is the *oxide ion*; and the ion of nitrogen is the *nitride ion*.

F	$+ 1e^-$ $\longrightarrow$	F^-	(isoelectronic with Ne, $10e^-$)
Fluorine atom		Fluoride ion	
($9e^-$, 7 valence e^-)		($10e^-$)	
O	$+ 2e^-$ $\longrightarrow$	O^{2-}	(isoelectronic with Ne, $10e^-$)
Oxygen atom		Oxide ion	
($8e^-$, 6 valence e^-)		($10e^-$)	
N	$+ 3e^-$ $\longrightarrow$	N^{3-}	(isoelectronic with Ne, $10e^-$)
Nitrogen atom		Nitride ion	
($7e^-$, 5 valence e^-)		($10e^-$)	

As in the case of positive ion formation, each of these negative ions has an octet of electrons in its outermost energy level.

The element fluorine, forming F^-, indicates that the other halogens, Cl, Br, and I, behave as a true family and form Cl^-, Br^-, and I^- ions. Also, oxygen and the other nonmetals in its group form 2^- ions; nitrogen and phosphorus form 3^- ions. It is important to recognize that ions are formed by gain or loss of *electrons*. No change occurs in the nucleus; the number of protons remains the same.

Question 2.13 Give the charge of the most probable ion resulting from each of the following elements. With what element is the ion isoelectronic?

a. Ca

b. Sr

c. S

d. Mg

e. P

Question 2.14 Which of the following pairs of atoms and ions are isoelectronic?

a. Cl^-, Ar

b. Na^+, Ne

c. Mg^{2+}, Na^+

d. Li^+, Ne

e. O^{2-}, F^-

The transition metals tend to form positive ions by losing electrons, just like the representative metals. Metals, whether representative or transition, share this characteristic. However, the transition elements are characterized as "variable valence" elements; depending on the type of substance with which they react, they may form more than one stable ion. For example, iron has two stable ionic forms:

$$Fe^{2+} \text{ and } Fe^{3+}$$

A Medical Perspective

Dietary Calcium

"Drink your milk!" "Eat all of your vegetables!" These imperatives are almost universal memories from our childhood. Our parents knew that calcium, present in abundance in these foods, was an essential element for the development of strong bones and healthy teeth.

Recent studies, spanning the fields of biology, chemistry, and nutrition science, indicate that the benefits of calcium go far beyond bones and teeth. This element has been found to play a role in the prevention of disease throughout our bodies.

Calcium is the most abundant mineral (metal) in the body. It is ingested as the calcium ion (Ca^{2+}) either in its "free" state or "combined," as a part of a larger compound; calcium dietary supplements often contain ions in the form of calcium carbonate. The acid naturally present in the stomach produces the calcium ion:

$$CaCO_3 \ + \ 2H^+ \ \longrightarrow \ Ca^{2+} \ + H_2O + \ CO_2$$

| calcium carbonate | stomach acid | calcium ion | water | carbon dioxide |

Calcium is responsible for a variety of body functions including:

- transmission of nerve impulses
- release of "messenger compounds" that enable communication among nerves
- blood clotting
- hormone secretion
- growth of living cells throughout the body

The body's storehouse of calcium is bone tissue. When the supply of calcium from external sources, the diet, is insufficient, the body uses a mechanism to compensate for this shortage. With vitamin D in a critical role, this mechanism removes calcium from bone to enable other functions to continue to take place. It is evident then that prolonged dietary calcium deficiency can weaken the bone structure. Unfortunately, current studies show that as much as 75% of the American population may not be consuming sufficient amounts of calcium. Developing an understanding of the role of calcium in premenstrual syndrome, cancer, and blood pressure regulation is the goal of three current research areas.

Calcium and premenstrual syndrome (PMS). Dr. Susan Thys-Jacobs, a gynecologist at St. Luke's-Roosevelt Hospital Center in New York City, and colleagues at eleven other medical centers are conducting a study of calcium's ability to relieve the discomfort of PMS. They believe that women with chronic PMS have calcium blood levels that are normal only because calcium is continually being removed from the bone to maintain an adequate supply in the blood. To complicate the situation, vitamin D levels in many young women are very low (as much as 80% of a person's vitamin D is made in the skin, upon exposure to sunlight; many of us now minimize our exposure to the sun because of concerns about ultraviolet radiation and skin cancer). Because vitamin D plays an essential role in calcium metabolism, even if sufficient calcium is consumed, it may not be used efficiently in the body.

Colon cancer. The colon is lined with a type of cell (epithelial cell) that is similar to those that form the outer layers of skin. Various studies have indicated that by-products of a high-fat diet are irritants to these epithelial cells and produce abnormal cell growth in the colon. Dr. Martin Lipkin, of Rockefeller University in New York, and his colleagues have shown that calcium ions may bind with these irritants, reducing their undesirable effects. It is believed that a calcium-rich diet, low in fat, and perhaps use of a calcium supplement can prevent or reverse this abnormal colon cell growth, delaying or preventing the onset of colon cancer.

Blood pressure regulation. Dr. David McCarron, a blood pressure specialist at the Oregon Health Sciences University, believes that dietary calcium levels may have a significant influence on hypertension (high blood pressure). Preliminary studies show that a diet rich in low-fat dairy products, fruits, and vegetables, all high in calcium, may produce a significant lowering of blood pressure in adults with mild hypertension.

The take-home lesson appears clear: a high-calcium, low-fat diet promotes good health in many ways. Once again, our parents were right!

For Further Understanding

▶ Distinguish between "free" and "combined" calcium in the diet.
▶ Why might calcium supplements be ineffective in treating all cases of calcium deficiency?

Copper can exist as

$$Cu^+ \text{ and } Cu^{2+}$$

and elements such as vanadium (V) and manganese (Mn) each can form four different stable ions.

Predicting the charge of an ion or the various possible ions for a given transition metal is not an easy task. Energy differences between valence electrons of transition metals are small and not easily predicted from the position of the element in the periodic table. In fact, in contrast to representative metals, the transition metals show great similarities within a *period* as well as within a *group*.

2.7 Trends in the Periodic Table

Atomic Size

Many atomic properties correlate with electronic structure, hence, with their position in the periodic table. Given the fact that interactions among multiple charged particles are very complex, we would not expect the correlation to be perfect. Nonetheless, the periodic table remains an excellent guide to the prediction of properties.

If our model of the atom is a tiny sphere whose radius is determined by the distance between the center of the nucleus and the boundary of the region where the valence electrons have a probability of being located, the size of the atom will be determined principally by two factors.

The radius of an atom is traditionally defined as one-half of the distance between atoms in a covalent bond. The covalent bond is discussed in Section 3.1.

Animation
• Atomic Radius

1. The energy level (*n* level) in which the outermost electron(s) is (are) found increases as we go *down* a group. (Recall that the outermost *n* level correlates with period number.) Thus the size of atoms should increase from top to bottom of the periodic table as we fill successive energy levels of the atoms with electrons (Figure 2.18).
2. As the magnitude of the positive charge of the nucleus increases, its "pull" on all of the electrons increases, and the electrons are drawn closer to the nucleus. This results in a contraction of the atomic radius and therefore a decrease in atomic size. This effect is apparent as we go *across* the periodic table within a period. Atomic size decreases from left to right in the periodic table. See how many exceptions you can find in Figure 2.18.

Ion Size

Animation
• Atomic and Ionic Radii

Positive ions (cations) are smaller than the parent atom. The cation has more protons than electrons (an increased nuclear charge). The excess nuclear charge pulls the remaining electrons closer to the nucleus. Also, cation formation often results in the loss of all outer-shell electrons, resulting in a significant decrease in radius.

Negative ions (anions) are larger than the parent atom. The anion has more electrons than protons. Owing to the excess negative charge, the nuclear "pull" on

Figure 2.18 Variation in the size of atoms as a function of their position in the periodic table. Note particularly the decrease in size from left to right in the periodic table and the increase in size as we proceed down the table, although some exceptions do exist. (Lanthanide and actinide elements are not included here.)

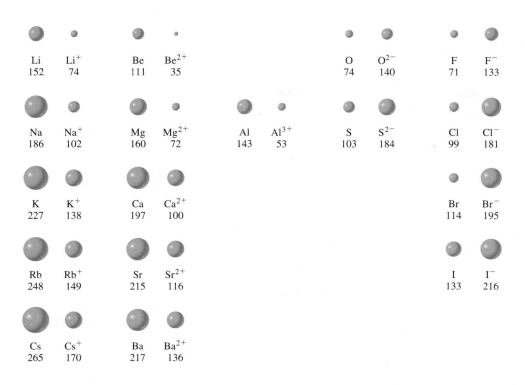

Figure 2.19 Relative size of ions and their parent atoms. Atomic radii are provided in units of picometers (pm).

each individual electron is reduced. The electrons are held less tightly, resulting in a larger anion radius in contrast to the neutral atom.

Ions with multiple positive charge (such as Cu^{2+}) are even *smaller* than their corresponding monopositive ion (Cu^+); ions with multiple negative charge (such as O^{2-}) are *larger* than their corresponding less negative ion.

Figure 2.19 depicts the relative sizes of several atoms and their corresponding ions.

Ionization Energy

The energy required to remove an electron from an isolated atom is the **ionization energy.** The process for sodium is represented as follows:

$$\text{ionization energy} + Na \longrightarrow Na^+ + e^-$$

The magnitude of the ionization energy should correlate with the strength of the attractive force between the nucleus and the outermost electron.

- Reading *down* a group, note that the ionization energy decreases, because the atom's size is increasing. The outermost electron is progressively farther from the nuclear charge, hence easier to remove.
- Reading *across* a period, note that atomic size decreases, because the outermost electrons are closer to the nucleus, more tightly held, and more difficult to remove. Therefore the ionization energy generally increases.

A correlation does indeed exist between trends in atomic size and ionization energy. Atomic size generally *decreases* from the bottom to top of a group and from left to right in a period. Ionization energies generally *increase* in the same periodic way. Note also that ionization energies are highest for the noble gases (Figure 2.20a). A high value for ionization energy means that it is difficult to remove electrons from the atom, and this, in part, accounts for the extreme stability and nonreactivity of the noble gases.

LEARNING GOAL

12 ▶ Utilize the periodic table and its predictive power to estimate the relative sizes of atoms and ions, as well as relative magnitudes of ionization energy and electron affinity.

Remember: ionization energy and electron affinity are predictable from *trends* in the periodic table. As with most trends, exceptions occur.

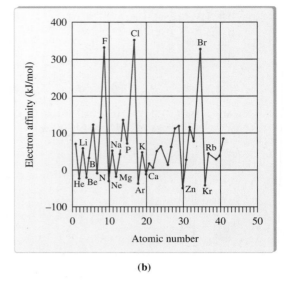

(a)   (b)

Figure 2.20 (a) The ionization energies of the first forty elements versus their atomic numbers. Note the very high values for elements located on the right in the periodic table, and low values for those on the left. Some exceptions to the trends are evident. (b) The periodic variation of electron affinity. Note the very low values for the noble gases and the elements on the far left of the periodic table. These elements do not form negative ions. In contrast, F, Cl, and Br readily form negative ions.

Electron Affinity

The energy released when a single electron is added to an isolated atom is the **electron affinity.** If we consider ionization energy in relation to positive ion formation (remember that the magnitude of the ionization energy tells us the ease of *removal* of an electron, hence the ease of forming positive ions), then electron affinity provides a measure of the ease of forming negative ions. A large electron affinity (energy released) indicates that the atom becomes more stable as it becomes a negative ion (through gaining an electron). Consider the gain of an electron by a bromine atom:

$$\text{Br} + \text{e}^- \longrightarrow \text{Br}^- + \text{energy}$$
Electron affinity

Periodic trends for electron affinity are as follows:

- Electron affinities generally decrease down a group.
- Electron affinities generally increase across a period.

Remember these trends are not absolute. Exceptions exist, as seen in the irregularities in Figure 2.20b.

Question 2.15   Rank Be, N, and F in order of increasing

 a. atomic size

 b. ionization energy

 c. electron affinity

Question 2.16   Rank Cl, Br, I, and F in order of increasing

 a. atomic size

 b. ionization energy

 c. electron affinity

SUMMARY

2.1 Composition of the Atom

The basic structural unit of an element is the *atom,* which is the smallest unit of an element that retains the chemical properties of that element.

The atom has two distinct regions. The *nucleus* is a small, dense, positively charged region in the center of the atom composed of positively charged *protons* and uncharged *neutrons.* Surrounding the nucleus is a diffuse region of negative charge occupied by *electrons,* the source of the negative charge. Electrons are very low in mass in comparison to protons and neutrons.

The *atomic number* is equal to the number of protons in the atom. The *mass number* is equal to the sum of the protons and neutrons (the mass of the electrons is insignificant).

Isotopes are atoms of the same element that have different masses because they have different numbers of neutrons (different mass numbers). Isotopes have chemical behavior identical to that of any other isotope of the same element.

2.2 Development of Atomic Theory

The first experimentally based theory of atomic structure was proposed by John Dalton. Although Dalton pictured atoms as indivisible, the experiments of William Crookes, Eugene Goldstein, and J. J. Thomson indicated that the atom is composed of charged particles: protons and electrons. The third fundamental atomic particle is the neutron. An experiment conducted by Hans Geiger led Ernest Rutherford to propose that the majority of the mass and positive charge of the atom is located in a small, dense region, the *nucleus,* with small, negatively charged electrons occupying a much larger, diffuse space outside of the nucleus.

2.3 Light, Atomic Structure, and the Bohr Atom

The study of the interaction of *light* and *matter* is termed *spectroscopy.* Light, *electromagnetic radiation,* travels at a speed of 3.0×10^8 m/s, the *speed of light.* Light is made up of many wavelengths. Collectively, they make up the *electromagnetic spectrum.* Samples of elements emit certain wavelengths of light when an electrical current is passed through the sample. Different elements emit a different pattern (different wavelengths) of light.

Niels Bohr proposed an atomic model that described the atom as a nucleus surrounded by fixed *energy levels* (or *quantum levels*) that can be occupied by electrons. He believed that each level was defined by a spherical *orbit* located at a specific distance from the nucleus.

Promotion and relaxation processes are referred to as *electronic transitions.* Electron promotion resulting from absorption of energy results in an excited state atom; the process of relaxation allows the atom to return to the ground state by emitting a certain wavelength of light.

The modern view of the atom describes the probability of finding an electron in a region of space within the principal energy level, referred to as an *atomic orbital.* The rapid movement of the electrons spreads them into a cloud of charge. This cloud is more dense in certain regions, the density being proportional to the probability of finding the electron at any point in time. The orbital is strikingly different from Bohr's orbit. The electron does not orbit the nucleus; rather, its behavior is best described as that of a wave.

2.4 The Periodic Law and the Periodic Table

The *periodic law* is an organized "map" of the elements that relates their structure to their chemical and physical properties. It states that the elements, when arranged according to their atomic numbers, show a distinct periodicity (regular variation) of their properties. The periodic table is the result of the periodic law.

The modern periodic table exists in several forms. The most important variation is in group numbering. The tables in this text use the two most commonly accepted numbering systems.

A horizontal row of elements in the periodic table is referred to as a *period.* The periodic table consists of seven periods. The lanthanide series is a part of period 6; the actinide series is a part of period 7.

The columns of elements in the periodic table are called *groups* or *families.* The elements of a particular family share many similarities in physical and chemical properties because of the similarities in electronic structure. Some of the most important groups are named; for example, the *alkali metals* (IA or 1), *alkaline earth metals* (IIA or 2), the *halogens* (VIIA or 17), and the *noble gases* (VIIIA or 18).

Group A elements are called *representative elements;* Group B elements are *transition elements.* A bold zigzag line runs from top to bottom of the table, beginning to the left of boron (B) and ending between polonium (Po) and astatine (At). This line acts as the boundary between *metals* to the left and *nonmetals* to the right. Elements straddling the boundary, *metalloids,* have properties intermediate between those of metals and nonmetals.

2.5 Electron Arrangement and the Periodic Table

Electron configuration of the elements is predictable, using the aufbau principle, the Pauli exclusion principle, and Hund's rule. Knowing the electron configuration, we can identify electrons potentially involved in bonding and begin to predict the kinds of reactions that the elements will undergo.

2.6 Valence Electrons and the Octet Rule

The outermost electrons in an atom are *valence electrons.* For representative elements, the number of valence electrons in an atom corresponds to the group or family number (old numbering system using Roman numerals). Metals tend to have fewer valence electrons than nonmetals.

The *octet rule* tells us that in chemical reactions, elements will gain, lose, or share the minimum number of electrons necessary to achieve the electron configuration of the nearest noble gas.

Ions are electrically charged particles that result from a gain or loss of one or more electrons by the parent atom. *Anions,* negative ions, are formed by a gain of one or more electrons by the parent atom. *Cations,* positive ions, are formed by a loss of one or more electrons from the parent atom.

Metallic elements tend to form cations. The ion is *isoelectronic* with its nearest noble gas neighbor and has a stable octet of electrons in its outermost energy level. Nonmetallic elements tend to gain electrons to become isoelectronic with the nearest noble gas element, forming anions.

Elements in the last family, the noble gases, have either two valence electrons (helium) or eight valence electrons (neon, argon, krypton, xenon, and radon). Their most important properties are their extreme stability and lack of reactivity. A full valence level is responsible for this unique stability.

2.7 Trends in the Periodic Table

Atomic size decreases from left to right and from bottom to top in the periodic table. Remember, this is a trend, and exceptions exist. *Cations* are smaller than the parent atom. *Anions* are larger than the parent atom. Ions with multiple positive charge are even smaller than their corresponding monopositive ion; ions with multiple negative charge are larger than their corresponding less negative ion.

The energy required to remove an electron from the atom is the *ionization energy.* Down a group, the ionization energy generally decreases. Across a period, the ionization energy generally increases.

The energy released when a single electron is added to a neutral atom in the gaseous state is known as the *electron affinity.* Electron affinities generally decrease proceeding down a group and increase proceeding across a period.

KEY TERMS

alkali metal (2.4)
alkaline earth metal (2.4)
anion (2.6)
atom (2.1)
atomic mass (2.1)
atomic number (2.1)
atomic orbital (2.3 and 2.5)
cathode rays (2.2)
cation (2.6)
electromagnetic
　radiation (2.3)
electromagnetic
　spectrum (2.3)
electron (2.1)
electron affinity (2.7)
electron configuration (2.5)
electron density (2.3)
energy level (2.3)
group (2.4)

halogen (2.4)
ion (2.6)
ionization energy (2.7)
isoelectronic (2.6)
isotope (2.1)
mass number (2.1)
metal (2.4)
metalloid (2.4)
neutron (2.1)
noble gas (2.4)
nonmetal (2.4)
nucleus (2.1)
octet rule (2.6)
period (2.4)
periodic law (2.4)
principal energy level (2.5)
proton (2.1)
quantization (2.3)
representative element (2.4)

spectroscopy (2.3)
speed of light (2.3)
sublevel (2.5)

transition element (2.4)
valence electron (2.6)

QUESTIONS AND PROBLEMS

Composition of the Atom

Foundations

2.17 Calculate the number of protons, neutrons, and electrons in:
　　a. $^{16}_{8}O$
　　b. $^{31}_{15}P$

2.18 Calculate the number of protons, neutrons, and electrons in:
　　a. $^{136}_{56}Ba$
　　b. $^{209}_{84}Po$

2.19 State the mass and charge of the:
　　a. electron
　　b. proton
　　c. neutron

2.20 Calculate the number of protons, neutrons, and electrons in:
　　a. $^{37}_{17}Cl$
　　b. $^{23}_{11}Na$
　　c. $^{84}_{36}Kr$

2.21 An atom has nine protons, ten neutrons, and nine electrons. Write the symbol of the atom.

2.22 An atom has nineteen protons, twenty neutrons, and nineteen electrons. Write the symbol of the atom.

Applications

2.23 How many protons are in the nucleus of the isotope Rn-220?

2.24 How many neutrons are in the nucleus of the isotope Rn-220?

2.25 Selenium-80 is a naturally occurring isotope. It is found in over-the-counter supplements.
　　a. How many protons are found in one atom of selenium-80?
　　b. How many neutrons are found in one atom of selenium-80?

2.26 Iodine-131 is an isotope used in thyroid therapy.
　　a. How many protons are found in one atom of iodine-131?
　　b. How many neutrons are found in one atom of iodine-131?

2.27 Write symbols for each isotope:
　　a. Each atom contains one proton and zero neutrons.
　　b. Each atom contains six protons and eight neutrons.

2.28 Write symbols for each isotope:
　　a. Each atom contains one proton and two neutrons.
　　b. Each atom contains 92 protons and 146 neutrons.

2.29 What is the major difference among isotopes of an element?

2.30 What is the major similarity among isotopes of an element?

2.31 Fill in the blanks:
　　a. An isotope of an element differs in mass because the atom has a different number of _____.
　　b. The atomic number gives the number of _____ in the nucleus.
　　c. The mass number of an atom is due to the number of _____ and _____ in the nucleus.
　　d. Electrons surround the _____ and have a _____ charge.

2.32 Label each of the following statements as true or false:
　　a. An atom with an atomic number of 7 and a mass of 14 is identical to an atom with an atomic number of 6 and a mass of 14.
　　b. Neutral atoms have the same number of electrons as protons.
　　c. The mass of an atom is due to the sum of the number of protons, neutrons, and electrons.

2.33 The element copper has two naturally occurring isotopes. One of these has a mass of 62.93 amu and a natural abundance of 69.09%. A second isotope has a mass of 64.9278 amu and a natural abundance of 30.91%. Calculate the atomic mass of copper.

2.34 The element lithium has two naturally occurring isotopes. One of these has a mass of 6.0151 amu and a natural abundance of 7.49%. A second isotope has a mass of 7.0160 amu and a natural abundance of 92.51%. Calculate the atomic mass of lithium.

Development of Atomic Theory

Foundations

2.35 What are the major postulates of Dalton's atomic theory?

2.36 What points of Dalton's theory are no longer current?

2.37 Note the major accomplishment of each of the following:
  a. Chadwick
  b. Goldstein

2.38 Note the major accomplishment of each of the following:
  a. Geiger
  b. Bohr

2.39 Note the major accomplishment of each of the following:
  a. Dalton
  b. Crookes

2.40 Note the major accomplishment of each of the following:
  a. Thomson
  b. Rutherford

Applications

2.41 Describe the experiment that provided the basis for our understanding of the nucleus.

2.42 Describe the series of experiments that characterized the electron.

2.43 List at least three properties of the electron.

2.44 Describe the process that occurs when electrical energy is applied to a sample of hydrogen gas.

2.45 What is a cathode ray? Which subatomic particle is detected?

2.46 Explain how Rutherford concluded that the atom is principally empty space.

Light, Atomic Structure, and the Bohr Atom

Foundations

2.47 Rank the various regions of the electromagnetic spectrum in order of increasing wavelength.

2.48 Rank the various regions of the electromagnetic spectrum in order of increasing energy.

2.49 Which form of radiation has greater energy, microwave or infrared?

2.50 Which form of radiation has the longer wavelength, ultraviolet or infrared?

2.51 What is meant by the term *spectroscopy*?

2.52 What is meant by the term *electromagnetic spectrum*?

Applications

2.53 Critique this statement: Electrons can exist in any position outside of the nucleus.

2.54 Critique this statement: Promotion of electrons is accompanied by a release of energy.

2.55 What are the most important points of the Bohr theory?

2.56 Give two reasons why the Bohr theory did not stand the test of time.

2.57 What was the major contribution of Bohr's atomic model?

2.58 What was the major deficiency of Bohr's atomic model?

The Periodic Law and the Periodic Table

Foundations

2.59 Provide the name of the element represented by each of the following symbols:
  a. Na   **c.** Mg
  b. K   **d.** B

2.60 Provide the name of the element represented by each of the following symbols:
  a. Ca   **c.** Co
  b. Cu   **d.** Si

2.61 Which group of the periodic table is known as the alkali metals? List them.

2.62 Which group of the periodic table is known as the alkaline earth metals? List them.

2.63 Which group of the periodic table is known as the halogens? List them.

2.64 Which group of the periodic table is known as the noble gases? List them.

Applications

2.65 For each of the elements Na, Ni, Al, P, Cl, and Ar, provide the following information:
  a. Which are metals?
  b. Which are representative metals?
  c. Which are inert or noble gases?

2.66 For each of the elements Ca, K, Cu, Zn, Br, and Kr, provide the following information:
  a. Which are metals?
  b. Which are representative metals?
  c. Which are inert or noble gases?

2.67 Using the information below, for Group I elements:

Element	Atomic Number	Melting Point (°C)
Li	3	180.5
Na	11	97.8
K	19	63.3
Rb	37	38.9
Cs	55	28.4

Prepare a graph relating melting point and atomic number. How does this demonstrate the periodic law?

2.68 Use the graph prepared in Question 2.67 to predict the melting point of francium (Fr).

Electron Arrangement and the Periodic Table

Foundations

2.69 Distinguish between a principal energy level and a sublevel.

2.70 Distinguish between a sublevel and an orbital.

2.71 Sketch a diagram and describe our current model of an *s* orbital.

2.72 How is a 2*s* orbital different from a 1*s* orbital?

Applications

2.73 What is the maximum number of electrons in each of the following energy levels?
  a. $n = 1$
  b. $n = 2$
  c. $n = 3$

2.74 **a.** What is the maximum number of *s* electrons that can exist in any one principal energy level?
  b. How many *p* electrons?
  c. How many *d* electrons?

2.75 Using the periodic table, write the electron configuration of each of the following atoms:
  a. Al
  b. Na
  c. Sc

2.76 Using the periodic table, write the electron configuration of each of the following atoms:
  a. Ca
  b. Fe
  c. Cl

2.77 Using the periodic table, write the electron configuration and orbital diagram of each of the following atoms:
  a. B
  b. S
  c. Ar

2.78 Using the periodic table, write the electron configuration and orbital diagram for each of the following atoms:
  a. V
  b. Cd
  c. Te

2.79 Which of the following electron configurations are not possible? Why?
  a. $1s^2 \, 1p^2$
  b. $1s^2 \, 2s^2 \, 2p^2$
  c. $2s^2, \, 2s^2, \, 2p^6, \, 2d^1$
  d. $1s^2, \, 2s^3$

2.80 For each incorrect electron configuration in Question 2.79, assume that the number of electrons is correct, identify the element, and write the correct electron configuration.

Valence Electrons and the Octet Rule

Foundations

2.81 Fill in the blanks:

Symbol	No. of Protons	No. of Neutrons	No. of Electrons	Charge
Example:				
$^{40}_{20}\text{Ca}$	20	20	20	0
$^{23}_{11}\text{Na}$	11	——	11	0
$^{32}_{16}\text{S}^{2-}$	16	16	——	2^-
———	8	8	8	0
$^{24}_{12}\text{Mg}^{2+}$	——	12	——	2^+
———	19	20	18	——

2.82 Fill in the blanks:

Atomic Symbol	No. of Protons	No. of Neutrons	No. of Electrons	Charge
Example:				
$^{27}_{13}\text{Al}$	13	14	13	0
$^{39}_{19}\text{K}$	19	——	19	0
$^{31}_{15}\text{P}^{3-}$	15	16	——	——
———	29	34	27	$2+$
$^{55}_{26}\text{Fe}^{2+}$	——	29	——	$2+$
———	8	8	10	——

2.83 How many total electrons and valence electrons are found in an atom of each of the following elements? What is the number of the principal energy level in which the valence electrons are found?
  a. H   **d.** F
  b. Na   **e.** Ne
  c. B   **f.** He

2.84 How many total electrons and valence electrons are found in an atom of each of the following elements? What is the number of the principal energy level in which the valence electrons are found?
  a. Mg   **d.** Br
  b. K   **e.** Ar
  c. C   **f.** Xe

2.85 What process results in the formation of a cation?

2.86 What process results in the formation of an anion?

2.87 Predict the number of valence electrons in an atom of:
  a. calcium   **c.** cesium
  b. potassium   **d.** barium

2.88 Predict the number of valence electrons in an atom of:
  a. carbon   **c.** sulfur
  b. phosphorus   **d.** chlorine

2.89 Give the most probable ion formed from each of the following elements:
  a. Li   **d.** Br
  b. O   **e.** S
  c. Ca   **f.** Al

2.90 Using only the periodic table or list of elements, write the electron configuration of each of the following ions:
  a. I^- **c.** Se^{2-}
  b. Ba^{2+} **d.** Al^{3+}

2.91 Which of the following pairs of atoms and/or ions are isoelectronic with one another?
  a. O^{2-}, Ne
  b. S^{2-}, Cl^-

2.92 Which of the following pairs of atoms and/or ions are isoelectronic with one another?
  a. F^-, Cl^-
  b. K^+, Ar

Applications

2.93 Write the electron configuration of each of the following biologically important ions:
  a. Ca^{2+}
  b. Mg^{2+}

2.94 Write the electron configuration of each of the following biologically important ions:
  a. K^+
  b. Cl^-

Trends in the Periodic Table

Foundations

2.95 Arrange each of the following lists of elements in order of increasing atomic size:
  a. N, O, F
  b. Li, K, Cs
  c. Cl, Br, I

2.96 Arrange each of the following lists of elements in order of increasing atomic size:
  a. Al, Si, P, Cl, S
  b. In, Ga, Al, B, Tl
  c. Sr, Ca, Ba, Mg, Be
  d. P, N, Sb, Bi, As

2.97 Arrange each of the following lists of elements in order of increasing ionization energy:
  a. N, O, F
  b. Li, K, Cs
  c. Cl, Br, I

2.98 Arrange each of the following lists of elements in order of decreasing electron affinity:
  a. Na, Li, K
  b. Br, F, Cl
  c. S, O, Se

Applications

2.99 **a.** Explain why a positive ion is always smaller than its parent atom.

b. Explain why a negative ion is always larger than its parent atom.

2.100 **a.** Explain why a fluoride ion is commonly found in nature but a fluorine atom is not.

b. Explain why a sodium ion is commonly found in nature but a sodium atom is not.

2.101 Cl^- and Ar are isoelectronic. Which is larger? Why?

2.102 K^+ and Ar are isoelectronic. Which is larger? Why?

CRITICAL THINKING PROBLEMS

1. A natural sample of chromium, taken from the ground, will contain four isotopes: Cr-50, Cr-52, Cr-53, and Cr-54. Predict which isotope is in greatest abundance. Explain your reasoning.

2. Crookes's cathode ray tube experiment inadvertently supplied the basic science for a number of modern high-tech devices. List a few of these devices and describe how they involve one or more aspects of this historic experiment.

3. Name five elements that you came in contact with today. Were they in combined form or did they exist in the form of atoms? Were they present in pure form or in mixtures? If mixtures, were they heterogeneous or homogeneous? Locate each in the periodic table by providing the group and period designation, for example: Group IIA (2), period 3.

4. The periodic table is incomplete. It is possible that new elements will be discovered from experiments using high-energy particle accelerators. Predict as many properties as you can that might characterize the element that would have an atomic number of 118. Can you suggest an appropriate name for this element?

5. The element titanium is now being used as a structural material for bone and socket replacement (shoulders, knees). Predict properties that you would expect for such applications; go to the library or Internet and look up the properties of titanium and evaluate your answer.

6. Imagine that you have undertaken a voyage to an alternate universe. Using your chemical skills, you find a collection of elements quite different than those found here on earth. After measuring their properties and assigning symbols for each, you wish to organize them as Mendeleev did for our elements. Design a periodic table using the information you have gathered:

Symbol	Mass (amu)	Reactivity	Electrical Conductivity
A	2.0	High	High
B	4.0	High	High
C	6.0	Moderate	Trace
D	8.0	Low	0
E	10.0	Low	0
F	12.0	High	High
G	14.0	High	High
H	16.0	Moderate	Trace
I	18.0	Low	0
J	20.0	None	0
K	22.0	High	High
L	24.0	High	High

Predict the reactivity and conductivity of an element with a mass of 30.0 amu. What element in our universe does this element most closely resemble?

Structure and Properties of Ionic and Covalent Compounds

3

LEARNING GOALS

1 ▷ Classify compounds as having ionic, covalent, or polar covalent bonds.

2 ▷ Write the formula of a compound when provided with the name of the compound.

3 ▷ Name common inorganic compounds using standard naming conventions and recognize the common names of frequently used substances.

4 ▷ Predict differences in physical state, melting and boiling points, solid-state structure, and solution chemistry that result from differences in bonding.

5 ▷ Draw Lewis structures for covalent compounds and polyatomic ions.

6 ▷ Describe the relationship between stability and bond energy.

7 ▷ Predict the geometry of molecules and ions using the octet rule and Lewis structures.

8 ▷ Understand the role that molecular geometry plays in determining the polarity of compounds.

9 ▷ Understand the role of polarity in determining solubility as well as melting and boiling points of compounds.

OUTLINE

Structure determines properties. Provide other examples of objects that illustrate the structure-property relationship.

INTRODUCTION

A chemical compound is formed when two or more atoms of different elements are joined by attractive forces called chemical bonds. These bonds result from either a transfer of electrons from one atom to another (the ionic bond) or a sharing of electrons between two atoms (the covalent bond). The elements, once converted to a compound, cannot be recovered by any physical process. A chemical reaction must take place to regenerate the individual elements. The chemical and physical properties of a compound are related to the structure of the compound, and this structure is, in turn, determined by the arrangement of electrons in the atoms that produced the compound. Properties such as solubility, boiling point, and melting point correlate well with the shape and charge distribution, hence, polarity, in the individual units of the compound.

You need to learn how to properly name and write formulas for ionic and covalent compounds. You should also become familiar with some of their properties and be able to relate these properties to the structure and bonding of the compounds.

3.1 Chemical Bonding

When two or more atoms form a chemical compound, the atoms are held together in a characteristic arrangement by attractive forces. The **chemical bond** is the force of attraction between any two atoms in a compound. The attraction is the force that overcomes the repulsion of the positively charged nuclei of the two atoms.

Interactions involving valence electrons are responsible for the chemical bond. We shall focus our attention on these electrons and the electron arrangement of atoms both before and after bond formation.

Lewis Symbols

Recall that the number of valence electrons for a representative element can be determined from the Roman numeral above the group in the periodic table (see Figure 2.10).

The **Lewis symbol,** developed by G. N. Lewis early in the twentieth century, uses the atomic symbol to represent the nucleus and core electrons and dots to represent valence electrons. Its principal advantage is that *only* valence electrons (those that may participate in bonding) are shown. Lewis symbolism is based on the octet rule that was described in Chapter 2.

To draw Lewis symbols, we first write the chemical symbol of the atom; this symbol represents the nucleus and all of the lower energy nonvalence electrons. The valence electrons are indicated by dots arranged around the atomic symbol. Figure 3.1 depicts the Lewis symbols for the representative elements.

Note particularly that the number of dots corresponds to the number of electrons in the outermost shell of the atoms of the element (valence electrons). The four "sides" of the chemical symbol each represent an atomic orbital (one s orbital and three p orbitals) capable of holding one or two valence electrons. Because each atomic orbital can hold no more than two electrons, we can show a maximum of two dots on each side of the element's symbol. Using the same logic employed in writing electron configurations in Chapter 2, we place one dot on each side then sequentially add a second dot, filling each side in turn. This process is limited by the total number of available valence electrons. Each unpaired dot (representing an unpaired electron) is available to form a chemical bond with another atom.

Principal Types of Chemical Bonds: Ionic and Covalent

Two principal classes of chemical bonds exist: ionic and covalent. Both involve valence electrons.

Ionic bonding involves a transfer of one or more electrons from one atom to another, leading to the formation of an ionic bond. **Covalent bonding** involves a sharing of electrons, resulting in the covalent bond.

Animation
• Ionic, Covalent, and Polar Covalent Bonds

A Medical Perspective

Unwanted Crystal Formation

Conventional wisdom says that the painful symptoms associated with the presence of stones in the bladder and kidneys are just one more problem associated with aging. Unfortunately, recent observations by many clinicians and physicians across the country seem to indicate that these problems are not limited to the elderly. Children as young as 5 years old are developing kidney stones while doctors search for reasons to explain this phenomenon.

Kidney stones most often result from the combination of calcium cations (Ca^{2+}) with anions such as oxalate ($C_2O_4^{2-}$) and phosphate (PO_4^{3-}). Calcium oxalate and calcium phosphate are ionic compounds that are only sparingly soluble in water. They grow in a three-dimensional crystal lattice. When the crystals become large enough to inhibit the flow of urine

in the kidney or bladder, painful symptoms necessitate some strategy to remove the stones.

Conditions that favor stone formation are the same as those that favor the formation of the same material in a beaker: high concentrations of the ions and insufficient water to dissolve the stones.

Many physicians believe that children who tend to form stones share several behavioral characteristics. They do not drink enough water and they consume too much salt. Salt in the diet appears to favor the transport of calcium ions to the kidney. Potato chips, French fries, and other snack foods, as well as processed foods such as frozen dinners, sandwich meats, canned soups, and sport drinks are very high in salt content. Obesity appears associated with stone formation, but this may be linked through the unhealthy diet of many children.

Although limiting calcium ion intake would appear to inhibit stone formation (remember, the stones are calcium compounds), reduction of calcium in the diet is not the answer! Dietary calcium is actually beneficial because it binds with oxalate ions before they reach the kidneys. Dietary calcium is important in preventing osteoporosis and dental caries as well. The take-home lesson? A balanced diet, in moderation, with minimal salt intake, especially in the formative years, is recommended.

For Further Understanding

Consult reliable references to answer the following questions:

▶ Describe another disease that is associated with a diet rich in salt.

▶ Describe one useful function of phosphate ion in the diet.

Covalent Bonding

The octet rule is not just for ionic compounds. In covalent bonding, atoms share electrons to complete the octet of electrons for each of the atoms participating in the bond. Consider the bond formed between two hydrogen atoms, producing the diatomic form of hydrogen: H_2. Individual hydrogen atoms are not stable, and two hydrogen atoms readily combine to produce diatomic hydrogen:

$$H + H \longrightarrow H_2$$

If a hydrogen atom were to gain a second electron, it would be isoelectronic with the stable electron configuration of helium. However, because two identical hydrogen atoms have an equal tendency to gain or lose electrons, an electron transfer from one atom to the other is unlikely to occur under normal conditions. Each atom may attain a noble gas structure only by *sharing* its electron with the other, as shown with Lewis symbols and a Lewis structure:

$$\dot{H} + .H \longrightarrow H : H$$

When electrons are shared rather than transferred, the *shared electron pair* is referred to as a *covalent bond* (Figure 3.3). Compounds characterized by covalent bonding are called *covalent compounds*. Covalent compounds are collections

A diatomic molecule is one that is composed of two atoms joined by a covalent bond.

Fourteen valence electrons are arranged in such a way that each fluorine atom is surrounded by eight electrons. The octet rule is satisfied for each fluorine atom.

of *molecules.* **Molecules** are neutral (uncharged) species made up of two or more atoms joined by covalent bonds. Molecules are represented by *Lewis structures.* **Lewis structures** depict valence electrons of all atoms in the molecule, arranged to satisfy the octet rule. Covalent bonds tend to form between atoms with similar tendencies to gain or lose electrons. The most obvious examples are the diatomic molecules H_2, N_2, O_2, F_2, Cl_2, Br_2, and I_2. Bonding in these molecules is *totally covalent* because there can be no net tendency for electron transfer between identical atoms. The formation of F_2, for example, may be represented as

$$:\ddot{F}\cdot \ + \ \cdot\ddot{F}: \ \longrightarrow \ :\ddot{F}:\ddot{F}:$$

As in H_2, a single covalent bond is formed. The bonding electron pair is said to be *localized,* or largely confined to the region between the two fluorine nuclei. Paired electrons around an atom that are not shared are termed **lone pairs.** The lone pairs in F_2 are shown in red.

Two atoms do not have to be identical to form a covalent bond. Consider compounds such as the following:

$$H:\ddot{F}: \qquad H:\ddot{O}:H \qquad H:\overset{\displaystyle H}{\underset{\displaystyle H}{C}}:H \qquad H:\ddot{N}:H$$
$$\overset{}{} \qquad\qquad\qquad\qquad\qquad\qquad \overset{}{H}$$

As you examine each of these structures, notice the numbered of electrons associated with each atom. The octet rule is satisfied for each atom. The hydrogen atoms have two electrons (shared electrons with the atom to which they are attached), and the other (non-hydrogen) atoms have eight valence electrons, which are counted as follows:

- Fluorine (in HF) has two electrons shared with hydrogen and six lone-pair electrons.
- Oxygen (in H_2O) has four electrons shared with the two hydrogen atoms and four lone-pair electrons.
- Carbon (in CH_4) has eight electrons shared with the four hydrogen atoms.
- Nitrogen (in NH_3) has six electrons shared with the three hydrogen atoms and two lone-pair electrons.

In each of these cases, bond formation satisfies the octet rule. A total of eight electrons surrounds each atom other than hydrogen. Hydrogen has only two electrons (corresponding to the electronic structure of helium).

Polar Covalent Bonding and Electronegativity

The Polar Covalent Bond

Covalent bonding is the sharing of an electron pair by two atoms. However, just as we may observe in our day-to-day activities, sharing is not always equal. In a molecule like H_2 (or N_2, or any other diatomic molecule composed of only one element), the electrons, on average, spend the same amount of time in the vicinity of each atom; the electrons have no preference because both atoms are identical.

Now consider a diatomic molecule composed of two different elements; HF is a common example. It has been experimentally shown that the electrons in the H—F bond between hydrogen and fluorine atoms are not equally shared; the electrons spend more time in the vicinity of the fluorine atom. This unequal sharing can be described in various ways:

Partial electron transfer: This describes the bond as having both covalent and ionic properties.

Unequal electron density: The density of electrons around F is greater than the density of electrons around H.

Hydrogen atoms approach at high velocity.

Hydrogen nuclei begin to attract each other's electrons.

Hydrogen atoms form the hydrogen molecule; atoms are held together by the shared electrons, the covalent bond.

Figure 3.3 Covalent bonding in hydrogen.

Polar covalent bond is the preferred term for a bond made up of unequally shared electron pairs. One end of the bond (in this case, the F atom) is more electron rich (higher electron density), hence, more negative. The other end of the bond (in this case, the H atom) is less electron rich (lower electron density), hence, more positive. These two ends, one somewhat positive (δ^+) and the other somewhat negative (δ^-) may be described as electronic poles, hence the term polar covalent bond (Figure 3.4).

Figure 3.4 Polar covalent bonding in HF. Fluorine is electron rich (δ^-) and hydrogen is electron deficient (δ^+) due to unequal electron sharing.

Once again, we can use the predictive power of the periodic table to help us determine whether a particular bond is polar or nonpolar covalent. We already know that elements that tend to form negative ions (by gaining electrons) are found to the right of the table, whereas positive ion formers (that may lose electrons) are located on the left side of the table. Elements whose atoms strongly attract electrons are described as electronegative elements. Linus Pauling, a chemist noted for his theories on chemical bonding, developed a scale of relative electronegativities that correlates reasonably well with the positions of the elements in the periodic table.

Electronegativity

Electronegativity (E_n) is a measure of the ability of an atom to attract electrons in a chemical bond. Elements with high electronegativity have a greater ability to attract electrons than do elements with low electronegativity. Pauling developed a method to assign values of electronegativity to many of the elements in the periodic table. These values range from a low of 0.7 to a high of 4.0, 4.0 being the most electronegative element.

Figure 3.5 shows that the most electronegative elements (excluding the nonreactive noble gas elements) are located in the upper right corner of the periodic table, whereas the least electronegative elements are found in the lower left corner of the table. In general, electronegativity values increase as we proceed left to right and bottom to top of the table. Like other periodic trends, numerous exceptions occur.

If we picture the covalent bond as a competition for electrons between two positive centers, it is the difference in electronegativity, ΔE_n, that determines the extent of polarity. Consider: H_2 or H—H

$$\Delta E_n = \left[\begin{array}{c}\text{Electronegativity}\\\text{of hydrogen}\end{array}\right] - \left[\begin{array}{c}\text{Electronegativity}\\\text{of hydrogen}\end{array}\right]$$

$$\Delta E_n = 2.1 - 2.1 = 0$$

The bond in H_2 is nonpolar covalent. Bonds between *identical* atoms are *always* nonpolar covalent. Also, Cl_2 or Cl—Cl

$$\Delta E_n = \left[\begin{array}{c}\text{Electronegativity}\\\text{of chlorine}\end{array}\right] - \left[\begin{array}{c}\text{Electronegativity}\\\text{of chlorine}\end{array}\right]$$

$$\Delta E_n = 3.0 - 3.0 = 0$$

The bond in Cl_2 is nonpolar covalent. Now consider HCl or H—Cl

$$\Delta E_n = \left[\begin{array}{c}\text{Electronegativity}\\\text{of chlorine}\end{array}\right] - \left[\begin{array}{c}\text{Electronegativity}\\\text{of hydrogen}\end{array}\right]$$

$$\Delta E_n = 3.0 - 2.1 = 0.9$$

The bond in HCl is polar covalent.

Recall that metals and nonmetals usually react to produce ionic compounds resulting from the transfer of one or more electrons from the metal to the nonmetal.

An electronegativity difference of 1.9 is generally accepted as the boundary between polar covalent and ionic bonds. Although, strictly speaking, any electronegativity difference, no matter how small, produces a polar bond, the degree

Animation
• Electronegativity

Linus Pauling is the only person to receive two Nobel Prizes in very unrelated fields; the chemistry award in 1954 and 8 years later, the Nobel Peace Prize. His career is a model of interdisciplinary science, with important contributions ranging from chemical physics to molecular biology.

By convention, the electronegativity difference is calculated by subtracting the less electronegative element's value from the value for the more electronegative element. In this way, negative numbers are avoided.

Figure 3.5 Electronegativities of the elements.

of polarity for bonds with electronegativity differences less than 0.5 is minimal. Consequently, we shall classify these bonds as nonpolar.

3.2 Naming Compounds and Writing Formulas of Compounds

Nomenclature is the assignment of a correct and unambiguous name to each and every chemical compound. Assigning a name to a structure or deducing the structure from a name is a necessary first step in any discussion of these compounds.

Ionic Compounds

The **formula** is the representation of the fundamental compound using chemical symbols and numerical subscripts. It is the "shorthand" symbol for a compound—for example,

$$NaCl \quad \text{and} \quad MgBr_2$$

The formula identifies the number and type of the various atoms that make up the compound unit. The number of like atoms in the unit is shown by the use of a subscript. The presence of only one atom is understood when no subscript is present.

The formula NaCl indicates that each ion pair consists of one sodium cation (Na^+) and one chloride anion (Cl^-). Similarly, the formula $MgBr_2$ indicates that one magnesium ion and two bromide ions combine to form the compound.

The *formula* of an ionic compound is the smallest whole-number ratio of ions in the substance.

Writing Formulas of Ionic Compounds from the Identities of the Component Ions

It is important to be able to write the formula of an ionic compound when provided with the identities of the ions that make up the compound. The charge of each ion can usually be determined from the group (family) of the periodic table in which the parent element is found. The cations and anions must combine in such a way that the resulting formula unit has a net charge of zero.

Consider the following examples.

LEARNING GOAL

2 ▶ Write the formula of a compound when provided with the name of the compound.

EXAMPLE 3.1 **Predicting the Formula of an Ionic Compound**

Predict the formula of the ionic compound formed from the reaction of sodium and oxygen atoms.

Solution

Step 1. Sodium is in Group IA (or 1); it has *one* valence electron. Loss of this electron produces Na^+.

Step 2. Oxygen is in Group VIA (or 16); it has *six* valence electrons. A gain of two electrons (to create a stable octet) produces O^{2-}.

Step 3. Two positive charges are necessary to counterbalance two negative charges on the oxygen anion. Because each sodium ion carries a 1+ charge, two sodium ions are needed for each O^{2-}.

Step 4. The subscript 2 is used to indicate that the formula unit contains two sodium ions. Thus the formula of the compound is Na_2O.

Practice Problem 3.1

Predict the formulas of the compounds formed from the combination of ions of the following elements:

a. lithium and bromine

b. calcium and bromine

c. potassium and chlorine

▶ **For Further Practice: Questions 3.17 and 3.18.**

EXAMPLE 3.2 **Predicting the Formula of an Ionic Compound**

Predict the formula of the compound formed by the reaction of aluminum and oxygen atoms.

Solution

Step 1. Aluminum is in Group IIIA (or 13) of the periodic table; we predict that it has three valence electrons. Loss of these electrons produces Al^{3+}.

Step 2. Oxygen is in Group VIA (or 16) of the periodic table and has six valence electrons. A gain of two electrons (to create a stable octet) produces O^{2-}.

Step 3. How can we combine Al^{3+} and O^{2-} to yield a unit of zero charge? It is necessary that *both* the cation and anion be multiplied by factors that will result in a zero net charge:

Step 4.
$$2 \times (+3) = +6 \quad \text{and} \quad 3 \times (-2) = -6$$
$$2 \times Al^{3+} = +6 \quad \text{and} \quad 3 \times O^{2-} = -6$$

Hence the formula is Al_2O_3.

Practice Problem 3.2

Predict the formulas of the compounds formed from the combination of ions of the following elements:

a. calcium and nitrogen — Ca_3N_2 Ca^{2+} N^{3-}

b. magnesium and bromine — $MgBr_2$ Mg^{2+} Br^{1}

c. magnesium and nitrogen — Mg_3N_2 N^{3-}

▶ **For Further Practice: Questions 3.19 and 3.20.**

Writing Names of Ionic Compounds from the Formulas of the Compounds

Nomenclature, the way in which compounds are named, is based on their formulas. The name of the cation appears first, followed by the name of the anion. The positive ion has the name of the element; the negative ion is named by using the *stem* of the name of the element joined to the suffix *-ide*. Some examples follow.

Formula	cation	and	anion stem	+ ide	=	Compound name
NaCl	sodium		chlor	+ ide		sodium chloride
Na_2O	sodium		ox	+ ide		sodium oxide
Li_2S	lithium		sulf	+ ide		lithium sulfide
$AlBr_3$	aluminum		brom	+ ide		aluminum bromide
CaO	calcium		ox	+ ide		calcium oxide

If the cation and anion exist in only one common charged form, there is no ambiguity between formula and name. Sodium chloride *must be* NaCl, and lithium sulfide *must be* Li_2S, so that the sum of positive and negative charges is zero. With many elements, such as the transition metals, several ions of different charge may exist. Fe^{2+}, Fe^{3+} and Cu^+, Cu^{2+} are two common examples. Clearly, an ambiguity exists if we use the name iron for both Fe^{2+} and Fe^{3+} or copper for both Cu^+ and Cu^{2+}. Two systems have been developed to avoid this problem: the *Stock system* and the *common nomenclature system.*

In the Stock system (systematic name), a Roman numeral placed immediately after the name of the ion indicates the magnitude of the cation's charge. In the older common nomenclature system, the suffix *-ous* indicates the lower ionic charge, and the suffix *-ic* indicates the higher ionic charge. Consider the examples in Table 3.1.

Systematic names are easier and less ambiguous than common names. Whenever possible, we will use this system of nomenclature. The older, common names (-ous, -ic) are less specific; furthermore, they often use the Latin names of the elements (for example, iron compounds use *ferr-*, from *ferrum,* the Latin word for iron).

Monatomic ions are ions consisting of a single atom. Common monatomic ions are listed in Table 3.2. The ions that are particularly important in biological systems are highlighted in red.

Table 3.1 Systematic (Stock) and Common Names for Iron and Copper Ions

For systematic name:			
Formula	**+ Ion Charge**	**Cation Name**	**Compound Name**
$FeCl_2$	2+	Iron(II)	Iron(II) chloride
$FeCl_3$	3+	Iron(III)	Iron(III) chloride
Cu_2O	1+	Copper(I)	Copper(I) oxide
CuO	2+	Copper(II)	Copper(II) oxide
For common nomenclature:			
Formula	**+ Ion Charge**	**Cation Name**	**Common -ous/ic Name**
$FeCl_2$	2+	Ferr*ous*	Ferrous chloride
$FeCl_3$	3+	Ferr*ic*	Ferric chloride
Cu_2O	1+	Cupr*ous*	Cuprous oxide
CuO	2+	Cupr*ic*	Cupric oxide

Table 3.2 Common Monatomic Cations and Anions

Cation	Name	Anion	Name
H^+	Hydrogen ion	H^-	Hydride ion
Li^+	Lithium ion	F^-	Fluoride ion
Na^+	Sodium ion	Cl^-	Chloride ion
K^+	Potassium ion	Br^-	Bromide ion
Cs^+	Cesium ion	I^-	Iodide ion
Be^{2+}	Beryllium ion	O^{2-}	Oxide ion
Mg^{2+}	Magnesium ion	S^{2-}	Sulfide ion
Ca^{2+}	Calcium ion	N^{3-}	Nitride ion
Ba^{2+}	Barium ion	P^{3-}	Phosphide ion
Al^{3+}	Aluminum ion		
Ag^+	Silver ion		

Note: The ions of principal importance are highlighted in red.

Polyatomic ions, such as the hydroxide ion, OH^-, are composed of two or more atoms bonded together. These ions, although bonded to other ions with ionic bonds, are themselves held together by covalent bonds.

The polyatomic ion has an *overall* positive or negative charge. Some common polyatomic ions are listed in Table 3.3. You should memorize the formulas,

Table 3.3 Common Polyatomic Cations and Anions

Ion	Name
H_3O^+	Hydronium
NH_4^+	Ammonium
NO_2^-	Nitrite
NO_3^-	Nitrate
SO_3^{2-}	Sulfite
SO_4^{2-}	Sulfate
HSO_4^-	Hydrogen sulfate
OH^-	Hydroxide
CN^-	Cyanide
PO_4^{3-}	Phosphate
HPO_4^{2-}	Hydrogen phosphate
$H_2PO_4^-$	Dihydrogen phosphate
CO_3^{2-}	Carbonate
HCO_3^-	Bicarbonate
ClO^-	Hypochlorite
ClO_2^-	Chlorite
ClO_3^-	Chlorate
ClO_4^-	Perchlorate
CH_3COO^- (or $C_2H_3O_2^-$)	Acetate
MnO_4^-	Permanganate
$Cr_2O_7^{2-}$	Dichromate
CrO_4^{2-}	Chromate
O_2^{2-}	Peroxide

Note: The most commonly encountered ions are highlighted in red.

charges, and names of these polyatomic ions, especially those highlighted in red.

The following examples are formulas of several compounds containing polyatomic ions.

Formula	Cation	Anion	Name
NH_4Cl	NH_4^+	Cl^-	ammonium chloride
$Ca(OH)_2$	Ca^{2+}	OH^-	calcium hydroxide
Na_2SO_4	Na^+	SO_4^{2-}	sodium sulfate
$NaHCO_3$	Na^+	HCO_3^-	sodium bicarbonate

Sodium bicarbonate may also be named sodium hydrogen carbonate, a preferred and less ambiguous name. Likewise, Na_2HPO_4 is named sodium hydrogen phosphate, and other ionic compounds are named similarly.

Question 3.1 Name each of the following compounds:

a. KCN

b. MgS

c. $Mg(CH_3COO)_2$

Question 3.2 Name each of the following compounds:

a. Li_2CO_3

b. $FeBr_2$

c. $CuSO_4$

Writing Formulas of Ionic Compounds from the Names of the Compounds

LEARNING GOAL

2 ▸ Write the formula of a compound when provided with the name of the compound.

It is also important to be able to write the correct formula when given the compound name. To do this, we must be able to predict the charge of monatomic ions and remember the charge and formula of polyatomic ions. Equally important, the relative number of positive and negative ions in the unit must result in a net (compound) charge of zero. The compounds are electrically neutral. Two examples follow.

EXAMPLE 3.3   Writing a Formula When Given the Name of the Compound

Write the formula of sodium sulfate.

Solution

Step 1. The sodium ion is Na^+, a Group IA (or 1) element. The sulfate ion is SO_4^{2-} (from Table 3.3).

Step 2. Two positive charges, two sodium ions, are needed to cancel the charge on one sulfate ion (two negative charges).

Hence the formula is Na_2SO_4.

Practice Problem 3.3

Write the formula for each of the following compounds:

a. calcium carbonate

b. copper(I) sulfate

▸ **For Further Practice: Questions 3.37 and 3.38.**

EXAMPLE 3.4 **Writing a Formula When Given the Name of the Compound**

Write the formula of magnesium phosphate.

Solution

Step 1. The magnesium ion is Mg^{2+}, a Group IIA (2) element. The phosphate ion is PO_4^{3-} (from Table 3.3).

Step 2. Adding a subscript to one ion will not result in a neutral compound. Strive to balance the charges by obtaining the lowest common multiple of 2 and 3; that is, 6. Three Mg^{2+} ions will yield a $+6$ charge and two PO_4^{3-} ions will yield a -6 charge.

Hence the formula is $Mg_3(PO_4)_2$.

Note that parentheses must be used whenever a subscript accompanies a polyatomic ion.

Practice Problem 3.4

Write the formula for each of the following compounds:

a. iron(III) sulfide
b. calcium sulfate
c. aluminum oxide

▶ **For Further Practice: Questions 3.39 and 3.40.**

Covalent Compounds

Naming Covalent Compounds

Most covalent compounds are formed by the reaction of nonmetals. We saw earlier that ionic compounds are not composed of single units but are a part of a massive three-dimensional crystal structure in the solid state. Covalent compounds typically exist as discrete molecules in the solid, liquid, and gas states. This is a distinctive feature of covalently bonded substances.

The conventions for naming covalent compounds follow:

1. The names of the elements are written in the order in which they appear in the formula.
2. A prefix (Table 3.4) indicating the number of each kind of atom found in the unit is placed before the name of the element.

LEARNING GOAL

3 ▶ Name common inorganic compounds using standard naming conventions and recognize the common names of frequently used substances.

By convention the prefix *mono-* is often omitted from the second element as well (dinitrogen oxide, not dinitrogen monoxide). In other cases, common usage retains the prefix (carbon monoxide, not carbon oxide).

Table 3.4 Prefixes Used to Denote Numbers of Atoms in a Compound

Prefix	Number of Atoms
Mono-	1
Di-	2
Tri-	3
Tetra-	4
Penta-	5
Hexa-	6
Hepta-	7
Octa-	8
Nona-	9
Deca-	10

3. If only one atom of a particular kind is the first element present in the molecule, the prefix *mono-* is usually omitted from that first element.
4. The stem of the name of the last element is used with the suffix *-ide.*
5. The final vowel in a prefix is often dropped before a vowel in the stem name.

LEARNING GOAL

3 ▶ Name common inorganic compounds using standard naming conventions and recognize the common names of frequently used substances.

EXAMPLE 3.5   Naming a Covalent Compound

Name the covalent compound N_2O_4.

Solution

Step 1. two nitrogen atoms   four oxygen atoms

Step 2. di-   tetra-

Step 3. dinitrogen   tetr(a)oxide

The name is dinitrogen tetroxide.

Practice Problem 3.5

Name each of the following compounds:

  a. B_2O_3 c. ICl e. PCl_5

  b. NO d. PCl_3 f. P_2O_5

▶ **For Further Practice: Questions 3.31 and 3.32.**

The following are examples of other covalent compounds.

Formula	Name
N_2O	dinitrogen monoxide
NO_2	nitrogen dioxide
SiO_2	silicon dioxide
CO_2	carbon dioxide
CO	carbon monoxide

Writing Formulas of Covalent Compounds

LEARNING GOAL

2 ▶ Write the formula of a compound when provided with the name of the compound.

Many compounds are so familiar to us that their *common names* are generally used. For example, H_2O is water, NH_3 is ammonia, C_2H_5OH (ethanol) is ethyl alcohol, and $C_6H_{12}O_6$ is glucose. It is useful to be able to correlate both systematic and common names with the corresponding molecular formula and vice versa.

When common names are used, formulas of covalent compounds can be written *only* from memory. You *must* remember that water is H_2O, ammonia is NH_3, and so forth. This is the major disadvantage of common names. Because of their widespread use, however, they cannot be avoided and must be memorized.

Compounds named by using Greek prefixes are easily converted to formulas. Consider the following examples.

EXAMPLE 3.6   Writing the Formula of a Covalent Compound

Write the formula of nitrogen monoxide.

Solution

Step 1. Nitrogen has no prefix; *one* is understood.

Step 2. Oxide has the prefix *mono*—one oxygen.

Step 3. Hence the formula is NO.

Practice Problem 3.6

Write the formula of each of the following compounds:

a. nitrogen trifluoride
b. carbon monoxide

▶ **For Further Practice: Question 3.45.**

EXAMPLE 3.7   Writing the Formula of a Covalent Compound

Write the formula of dinitrogen tetroxide.

Solution

Step 1. Nitrogen has the prefix *di*—two nitrogen atoms.

Step 2. Oxygen has the prefix *tetr(a)*—four oxygen atoms.

Step 3. Hence the formula is N_2O_4.

Practice Problem 3.7

Write the formula of each of the following compounds:

a. diphosphorus pentoxide
b. silicon dioxide

▶ **For Further Practice: Question 3.46.**

3.3 Properties of Ionic and Covalent Compounds

The differences in ionic and covalent bonding result in markedly different properties for ionic and covalent compounds. Because covalent compounds are made up of molecules, distinct units, they have less tendency to form an extended structure in the solid state. Ionic compounds, with ions joined by electrostatic attraction, do not have definable units but form a crystal lattice composed of enormous numbers of positive and negative ions in an extended three-dimensional network. The effects of this basic structural difference are summarized in this section.

LEARNING GOAL

4 ▶ Predict differences in physical state, melting and boiling points, solid-state structure, and solution chemistry that result from differences in bonding.

Physical State

All ionic compounds (for example, NaCl, KCl, and $NaNO_3$) are solids at room temperature; covalent compounds may be solids (sugar), liquids (H_2O, ethanol), or gases (carbon monoxide, carbon dioxide). The three-dimensional crystal structure that is characteristic of ionic compounds holds them in a rigid, solid arrangement, whereas molecules of covalent compounds may be fixed, as in a solid, or more mobile, a characteristic of liquids and gases.

Melting and Boiling Points

The **melting point** is the temperature at which a solid is converted to a liquid, and the **boiling point** is the temperature at which a liquid is converted to a gas at a specified pressure. Considerable energy is required to break apart an ionic crystal lattice with uncountable numbers of ionic interactions and convert the ionic substance to a liquid or a gas. As a result, the melting and boiling temperatures for ionic compounds are generally higher than those of covalent compounds, whose

A Medical Perspective

Rebuilding our Teeth

Tooth decay (dental caries) is an unpleasant fact of life. Aging, diet, and improper dental hygiene lead to the breakdown of a critical building block of teeth, hydroxyapatite, $Ca_5(PO_4)_3OH$. The hydroxyapatite forms a three-dimensional crystalline structure, and this structural unit is the principal component in the exterior, the enamel part of the tooth. Hydroxyapatite is also a major component in the dentin, which is directly underneath the enamel.

Hydroxyapatite breakdown causes the super-strong enamel to become porous and weak. The pores created are ideal hiding places for bacteria that form acids from foods (especially

sugars) that hasten the decay of the tooth. The traditional remedy is the familiar whine of the drill, removing the decayed material, and unfortunately, some of the unaffected tooth. This step is followed by filling with a carbon-based polymer material or metal amalgam. In extreme cases, removal of the entire tooth is the only suitable remedy.

Researchers at a variety of institutions, such as the University of California, San Francisco, are studying other alternatives, collectively termed *remineralization.* What if teeth, in the early stages of enamel decay, were exposed to solutions containing calcium, phosphate, and fluoride ions? Could the hydroxyapatite be rebuilt through the uptake of its critical components, calcium and phosphate ions? Can the hydroxide ion in the hydroxyapatite be replaced by fluoride ion, producing a more decay-resistant $Ca_5(PO_4)_3F$?

Although conventional drill and fill procedures will be with us for the foreseeable future, early remineralization research is encouraging. Already toothpastes and mouthwashes containing calcium, phosphate, and/or fluoride ions are commercially available. Regular use of these products may at least extend the life of our valuable and irreplaceable natural teeth.

For Further Understanding

▶ Examine the labels of a variety of toothpastes and mouthwashes on your drugstore shelves. Do these products contain any of the ions discussed above? Describe their potential benefit.

▶ Many mouthwashes claim to kill bacteria. How can this reduce the incidence of tooth decay?

molecules interact less strongly in the solid state. A typical ionic compound, sodium chloride, has a melting point of 801°C; methane, a covalent compound, melts at −182°C. Exceptions to this general rule do exist; quartz, a covalent compound of silicon dioxide with an extremely high melting point, is a familiar example.

Structure of Compounds in the Solid State

Ionic solids are *crystalline,* characterized by a regular structure, whereas covalent solids may either be crystalline or have no regular structure. In the latter case they are said to be *amorphous.*

Solutions of Ionic and Covalent Compounds

The role of the solvent in the dissolution of solids is discussed in Section 3.5.

In Chapter 1 we saw that mixtures are either heterogeneous or homogeneous. A homogeneous mixture is a solution. Many ionic solids dissolve in solvents, such as water. An ionic solid, if soluble, will form positive and negative ions in solution by **dissociation.**

Because ions in water are capable of carrying (conducting) a current of electricity, we refer to these compounds as **electrolytes,** and the solution is termed an **electrolytic solution.** Covalent solids dissolved in solution usually retain their neutral (molecular) character and are **nonelectrolytes.** The solution is not an electrical conductor.

3.4 Drawing Lewis Structures of Molecules and Polyatomic Ions

Lewis Structures of Molecules

In Section 3.1, we used Lewis symbols of individual atoms to help us understand the bonding process. Lewis symbols for atoms are building blocks that enable construction of *Lewis structures* for compounds and polyatomic ions that depict the role of valence electrons in bonding and structure. To begin to explain the relationship between molecular structure and molecular properties, we will first need a set of guidelines to help us write Lewis structures for molecules and polyatomic ions:

- *Use chemical symbols for the various elements to write the skeletal structure of the compound.* To accomplish this, place the bonded atoms next to one another. This is relatively easy for simple compounds; however, as the number of atoms in the compound increases, the possible number of arrangements increases dramatically. We may be told the pattern of arrangement of the atoms in advance; if not, we can make an intelligent guess and see if a reasonable Lewis structure can be constructed. Three considerations are very important here:

    the least electronegative atom will be placed in the central position (the central atom),

    hydrogen and fluorine must occupy terminal positions, and

    carbon often forms chains of carbon-carbon covalent bonds.

- *Determine the number of valence electrons associated with each atom; combine them to determine the total number of valence electrons in the compound.* However, if we are representing polyatomic cations or anions, we must account for the charge on the ion. Specifically:

    for polyatomic cations, subtract one electron for each unit of positive charge. This accounts for the fact that the positive charge arises from electron loss.

    for polyatomic anions, add one electron for each unit of negative charge. This accounts for excess negative charge resulting from electron gain.

- *Connect the central atom to each of the surrounding atoms with single bonds.* Connection of the atoms uses two electrons per bond. Keep a count of how many valence electrons you placed in the Lewis structure so as not to exceed the previously determined number.

- *Place electrons as lone pairs around the terminal atoms to complete the octet for each.* Remember that hydrogen only needs two electrons. Hydrogen's octet is satisfied simply by a single bond between it and the central atom. Remember to keep a count of electrons used and do not exceed the number of available electrons. Once the terminal atoms have their octet rule satisfied, do the same for the central atom (if you have enough electrons to do so).

- *If the octet rule is not satisfied for all the atoms, move one or more lone pairs on a terminal atom in to make a bond with the central atom.* Double and triple bonds may be formed to ensure that all atoms have an octet.

- *After you are satisfied with the Lewis structure that you have constructed, perform a final electron count.* Count each electron used in the structure; the total must match the number of electrons available.

LEARNING GOAL

5 ▶ Draw Lewis structures for covalent compounds and polyatomic ions.

In each of the following examples, we emphasize the connectivity of the bonded atoms using dashed red lines. These lines represent the probable location of bonds.

The central atom is often the element farthest to the left and/or lowest in the periodic table.

The central atom is often the element in the compound for which there is only one atom.

Hydrogen is *never* the central atom.

Sometimes the octet rule is satisfied for all atoms but electrons are left over from the valence electron count. This problem is addressed under Exceptions to the Octet Rule on page 105.

A Medical Perspective

Blood Pressure and the Sodium Ion/Potassium Ion Ratio

When you have a physical exam, the physician measures your blood pressure. This indicates the pressure of blood against the walls of the blood vessels each time the heart pumps. A blood pressure reading is always characterized by two numbers. With every heartbeat there is an increase in pressure; this is the systolic blood pressure. When the heart relaxes between contractions, the pressure drops; this is the diastolic pressure. Thus the blood pressure is expressed as two values—for instance, 117/72—measured in millimeters (mm) of mercury. Hypertension is simply defined as high blood pressure. To the body it means that the heart must work too hard to pump blood, and this can lead to heart failure or heart disease.

Heart disease accounts for 50% of all deaths in the United States. Epidemiological studies correlate the following major risk factors with heart disease: heredity, sex, race, age, diabetes, cigarette smoking, high blood cholesterol, and hypertension. Obviously, we can do little about our age, sex, and genetic heritage, but we can stop smoking, limit dietary cholesterol, and maintain a normal blood pressure.

The number of Americans with hypertension is alarmingly high: sixty million adults and children. More than ten million of these individuals take medication to control blood pressure, at a cost of nearly 2.5 billion dollars each year. In many cases, blood pressure can be controlled without medication by increasing physical activity, losing weight, decreasing consumption of alcohol, and limiting intake of sodium.

It has been estimated that the average American ingests 7.5–10 grams (g) of salt (NaCl) each day. Because NaCl is about 40% (by mass) sodium ions, this amounts to 3–4 g of sodium daily. Until 1989 the Food and Nutrition Board of the National Academy of Sciences National Research Council's defined estimated safe and adequate daily dietary intake (ESADDI)

of sodium ion was 1.1–3.3 g. Clearly, Americans exceed this recommendation.

Recently, studies have shown that excess sodium is not the sole consideration in the control of blood pressure. More important is the sodium ion/potassium ion (Na^+/K^+) ratio. That ratio should be about 0.6; in other words, our diet should contain about 67% more potassium than sodium. Does the typical American diet fall within this limit? Definitely not! Young American males (25–30 years old) consume a diet with a $Na^+/K^+ = 1.07$, and the diet of females of the same age range has a $Na^+/K^+ = 1.04$. It is little wonder that so many Americans suffer from hypertension.

How can we restrict sodium in the diet, while increasing potassium? A variety of foods are low in sodium and high in potassium. These include fresh fruits and vegetables and fruit juices, a variety of cereals, unsalted nuts, and cooked dried beans (legumes). Unfortunately, some high-sodium, low-potassium foods are very popular. Most of these are processed or prepared foods. This points out how difficult it can be to control sodium in the diet. The majority of the sodium that we ingest comes from commercially prepared foods. The consumer must read the nutritional information printed on cans and packages to determine whether the sodium levels are within acceptable limits.

For Further Understanding

▶ Find several processed food products on the shelves of your local grocery store; read the labels and calculate the sodium ion/potassium ion ratio.

▶ Describe each product that you have chosen in terms of its suitability for inclusion in the diet of a person with moderately elevated blood pressure.

Now, let us see how these guidelines are applied in the examples that follow.

LEARNING GOAL

5 ▶ Draw Lewis structures for covalent compounds and polyatomic ions.

The central atom in the skeletal structure is typically written first in the formula.

EXAMPLE 3.8   Drawing Lewis Structures of Covalent Compounds

Draw the Lewis structure of carbon dioxide, CO_2.

Solution

Step 1.   Draw a skeletal structure of the molecule, arranging the atoms in their most probable order and indicating potential locations of bonds.

For CO_2, two possibilities exist:

$$C—O—O \quad \text{and} \quad O—C—O$$

Referring to Figure 3.5, we find that the electronegativity of oxygen is 3.5 whereas that of carbon is 2.5. Our strategy dictates that the least electronegative atom, in this case carbon, is the central atom. Hence the skeletal structure O—C—O may be presumed correct.

Step 2. Next, we want to determine the number of valence electrons on each atom and add them to arrive at the total for the compound.

For CO_2,

$$1 \text{ C atom} \times 4 \text{ valence electrons} = 4 \text{ e}^-$$
$$\underline{2 \text{ O atoms} \times 6 \text{ valence electrons} = 12 \text{ e}^-}$$
$$4 \text{ e}^- \text{ total}$$

Step 3. Now, use electron pairs to connect the central atom, C, to each oxygen with a single bond.

O : C : O

Step 4. Distribute the electrons around the terminal atoms in pairs, in an attempt to satisfy the octet rule.

:Ö : C : Ö :

Step 5. At this point all sixteen electrons have been used. This structure satisfies the octet rule for each oxygen atom, but not the carbon atom (only four electrons surround the carbon). However, when this structure is modified by moving two electrons from each oxygen atom to a position between C and O, each oxygen and carbon atom is surrounded by eight electrons. The octet rule is satisfied, and the structure below is the most probable Lewis structure for CO_2.

Ö :: C :: Ö

In this structure, four electrons (two electron pairs) are located between C and each O, and these electrons are shared in covalent bonds. Because a **single bond** is composed of two electrons (one electron pair) and because four electrons "bond" the carbon atom to each oxygen atom in this structure, there must be two bonds between each oxygen atom and the carbon atom, a **double bond:**

The notation for a single bond : is equivalent to — (one pair of electrons).

The notation for a double bond : : is equivalent to = (two pairs of electrons).

We may write CO_2 as shown above or, replacing dots with dashes to indicate bonding electron pairs,

Ö=C=Ö

Step 6. As a final step, let us do some "electron accounting." There are eight electron pairs, and they correspond to sixteen valence electrons (8 pair × 2 e⁻/pair). Furthermore, there are eight electrons around each atom and the octet rule is satisfied. Therefore

Ö=C=Ö

is a satisfactory way to depict the structure of CO_2.

Practice Problem 3.8

Draw a Lewis structure for each of the following compounds:

a. H_2O (water)
b. CH_4 (methane)

▶ **For Further Practice: Question 3.63.**

EXAMPLE 3.9   Drawing Lewis Structures of Covalent Compounds

Draw the Lewis structure of ammonia, NH_3.

Solution

Step 1. When trying to implement the first step in our strategy, we may be tempted to make H our central atom because it is less electronegative than N. But, remember the margin note in this section:

"Hydrogen is *never* the central atom."

Hence:

$$
\begin{array}{c}
H \\
| \\
H-\underset{\cdot\cdot}{N}-H
\end{array}
$$

is our skeletal structure.

Step 2. Applying our strategy to determine the total valence electrons for the molecule, we find that there are five valence electrons in nitrogen and one in each of the three hydrogens, for a total of eight valence electrons.

Step 3. Applying our strategy for connection of the terminal atoms to the central atom with single bonds results in the following Lewis structure:

$$
\begin{array}{c}
H \\
\cdot\cdot \\
H:N:H
\end{array}
$$

Step 4. The terminal atoms already have the octet rule satisfied since each hydrogen atom requires only two valence electrons. The structure in step 3 only has six valence electrons on the N atom. Place two additional electrons on N, giving the following structure:

$$
\begin{array}{c}
H \\
| \\
H-\underset{\cdot\cdot}{N}-H
\end{array}
$$

This structure uses the eight valence electrons available and satisfies the octet rule for each atom. No further work is necessary.

Practice Problem 3.9

Draw a Lewis structure for each of the following compounds:

a. C_2H_6 (ethane)
b. N_2 (nitrogen gas)

▶ **For Further Practice: Question 3.64.**

Notice the lines used to represent the sharing of electrons or the bond between the atoms. Each line represents two valence electrons.

LEARNING GOAL

5 ▶ Draw Lewis structures for covalent compounds and polyatomic ions.

Lewis Structures of Polyatomic Ions

The strategies for writing the Lewis structures of polyatomic ions are similar to those for neutral compounds. There is, however, one major difference: the charge on the ion must be accounted for when computing the total number of valence electrons.

LEARNING GOAL

5 ▶ Draw Lewis structures for covalent compounds and polyatomic ions.

EXAMPLE 3.10   Drawing Lewis Structures of Polyatomic Cations

Draw the Lewis structure of the ammonium ion, NH_4^+.

Solution

Step 1. Nitrogen in the central atom, surrounded by four hydrogen atoms:

$$\left[\begin{array}{c} H \\ | \\ H-N-H \\ | \\ H \end{array}\right]^+$$

Step 2. The total number of valence electrons is determined by subtracting one electron for each unit of positive charge.

$$\begin{array}{lll} 1\ \text{N atom} & \times 5\ \text{valence electrons} = & 5\ e^- \\ 4\ \text{H atoms} & \times 1\ \text{valence electrons} = & 4\ e^- \\ -1\ \text{electron for} +1\ \text{charge} & = & -1\ e^- \\ \hline & & 4\ e^-\ \text{total} \end{array}$$

Steps 3, 4, and *5.* Distribute the eight electrons around our skeletal structure:

$$\left[\begin{array}{c} H \\ \cdot\cdot \\ H:N:H \\ \cdot\cdot \\ H \end{array}\right]^+ \quad \text{or} \quad \left[\begin{array}{c} H \\ | \\ H-N-H \\ | \\ H \end{array}\right]^+$$

The bonds alone satisfy the octet rule; no lone-pair electrons are needed.

Step 6. A final check shows eight total electrons, eight around the central atom, nitrogen, and two electrons associated with each hydrogen. Hence the structure is satisfactory.

Practice Problem 3.10

Draw the Lewis structure of H_3O^+ (the hydronium ion).

▶ **For Further Practice: Question 3.67.**

EXAMPLE 3.11   Drawing Lewis Structures of Polyatomic Anions

Draw the Lewis structure of the carbonate ion, CO_3^{2-}.

Solution

Step 1. Carbon is less electronegative than oxygen. Therefore carbon is the central atom. The carbonate ion has the following skeletal structure and charge:

$$\left[\begin{array}{c} O \\ | \\ O-C-O \end{array}\right]^{2-}$$

Continued—

Step 2. The total number of valence electrons is determined by adding one electron for each unit of negative charge:

$$
\begin{aligned}
1\ \text{C atom} \times 4\ \text{valence electrons} &= 4\ e^- \\
3\ \text{O atoms} \times 6\ \text{valence electrons} &= 18\ e^- \\
+2\ \text{negative charge} &= 2\ e^- \\
\hline
24\ e^-\ \text{total}
\end{aligned}
$$

Step 3. Connect the O atoms to the central atom using single bonds. This step uses six of the valence electrons.

$$
\left[
\begin{array}{c}
O \\
| \\
O - C - O
\end{array}
\right]^{2-}
$$

Step 4. Start placing lone-pair electrons around the terminal atoms, giving each an octet. Do not exceed the twenty-four available electrons.

$$
\left[
\begin{array}{c}
:\ddot{O}: \\
| \\
:\ddot{O} - C - \ddot{O}:
\end{array}
\right]^{2-}
$$

Step 5. The central atom only has six valence electrons surrounding it. Move a lone pair from one of the O atoms to form another bond with C. In this example, a lone pair from the top O was moved to make a second bond between it and the C.

$$
\left[
\begin{array}{c}
:O: \\
\| \\
:\ddot{O} - C - \ddot{O}:
\end{array}
\right]^{2-}
$$

Step 6. Each atom has eight valence electrons surrounding it, and the total number of electrons used is twenty-four.

Practice Problem 3.11

Draw the Lewis structure of O_2^{2-}.

▶ **For Further Practice: Question 3.68.**

LEARNING GOAL

5 ▶ Draw Lewis structures for covalent compounds and polyatomic ions.

EXAMPLE 3.12   Drawing Lewis Structures of Polyatomic Anions

Draw the Lewis structure of the acetate ion, CH_3COO^-.

Solution

Step 1. A commonly encountered anion, the acetate ion has a skeletal structure that is more complex than any of the examples that we have studied thus far. Which element should we choose as the central atom? We have three choices: H, O, and C. H is eliminated because hydrogen can never be the central atom. Oxygen is more electronegative than carbon, so carbon must be the central atom. There are two carbon atoms; often they are joined. Further clues are obtained from the formula itself; CH_3COO^- implies three hydrogen atoms attached to the first carbon atom and two oxygen atoms joined to the second carbon. A plausible skeletal structure is:

$$
\left[
\begin{array}{c}
\quad H \quad\ O \\
\quad | \quad\ \ | \\
H - C - C - O \\
\quad | \\
\quad H
\end{array}
\right]^{-}
$$

Step 2. The pool of valence electrons for anions is determined by adding one electron for each unit of negative charge:

$$2 \text{ C atoms} \times 4 \text{ valence electrons} = 8 \text{ e}^-$$
$$3 \text{ H atoms} \times 1 \text{ valence electron} = 3 \text{ e}^-$$
$$4 \text{ O atoms} \times 6 \text{ valence electrons} = 12 \text{ e}^-$$
$$+1 \text{ negative charge} = 1 \text{ e}^-$$

$$\overline{\hspace{6cm} 24 \text{ e}^- \text{ total}}$$

Step 3. Connect the terminal atoms to the two central carbon atoms.

$$\left[\begin{array}{c} \text{H} \quad \text{O} \\ | \quad\; | \\ \text{H}-\text{C}-\text{C}-\text{O} \\ | \\ \text{H} \end{array}\right]^-$$

This step used twelve valence electrons.

Step 4. Place lone-pair electrons around the atoms to give an octet, starting with terminal O atoms. (Remember to keep in mind the twenty-four electrons available, and do not put lone-pair electrons around H.)

$$\left[\begin{array}{c} \text{H} \quad :\ddot{\text{O}}: \\ | \quad\; | \\ \text{H}-\text{C}-\text{C}-\ddot{\text{O}}: \\ | \\ \text{H} \end{array}\right]^-$$

This structure uses all twenty-four electrons, but one of the C atoms only has six valence electrons.

Step 5. Move one of the lone pairs on an O to create an additional bond between C and O.

$$\left[\begin{array}{c} \text{H} \quad :\text{O}: \\ | \quad\; \| \\ \text{H}-\text{C}-\text{C}-\ddot{\text{O}}: \\ | \\ \text{H} \end{array}\right]^-$$

Step 6. All twenty-four electrons are used, and the octet rule is satisfied for all atoms in the structure.

Practice Problem 3.12

Write a Lewis structure describing the bonding in each of the following polyatomic ions:

a. the bicarbonate ion, HCO_3^-
b. the phosphate ion, PO_4^{3-}

▶ **For Further Practice: Question 3.69.**

Lewis Structure, Stability, Multiple Bonds, and Bond Energies

Hydrogen, oxygen, and nitrogen are present in the atmosphere as diatomic gases, H_2, O_2, and N_2. All are covalent molecules. Their stability and reactivity, however, are quite different. Hydrogen is an explosive material, sometimes used as a fuel. Oxygen, although more stable than hydrogen, reacts with fuels in combustion.

LEARNING GOAL

6 ▶ Describe the relationship between stability and bond energy.

The explosion of the space shuttle *Challenger* resulted from the reaction of massive amounts of hydrogen and oxygen. Nitrogen, on the other hand, is extremely nonreactive. Because nitrogen makes up about 80% of the atmosphere, it dilutes the oxygen, which accounts for only about 20% of the atmosphere.

Breathing pure oxygen for long periods, although necessary in some medical situations, causes the breakdown of nasal and lung tissue over time. Oxygen diluted with nonreactive nitrogen is an ideal mixture for humans and animals to breathe.

Why is there such a great difference in reactivity among these three gases? We can explain this, in part, in terms of their bonding characteristics. The Lewis structure for H_2 (two valence electrons) is

$$H:H \qquad or \qquad H-H$$

For oxygen (twelve valence electrons, six on each atom), the only Lewis structure that satisfies the octet rule is

$$\ddot{O}:\,:\ddot{O} \qquad or \qquad \ddot{O}=\ddot{O}$$

The Lewis structure of N_2 (ten total valence electrons) must be

$$:N:::N: \qquad or \qquad :N\equiv N:$$

Therefore:

> N_2 has a *triple bond* (six bonding electrons).
> O_2 has a *double bond* (four bonding electrons).
> H_2 has a *single bond* (two bonding electrons).

A **triple bond,** in which three pairs of electrons are shared by two atoms, is very stable. More energy is required to break a triple bond than a double bond, and a double bond is stronger than a single bond. Stability is related to the bond energy. The **bond energy** is the amount of energy, in units of kilocalories (kcal) or kilojoules (kJ), required to break a bond holding two atoms together. Bond energy is therefore a *measure* of stability. The values of bond energies decrease in the order *triple bond > double bond > single bond*. The H—H bond energy is 436 kJ/mol. This amount of energy is necessary to break a H—H bond. In contrast, the O=O bond energy is 499 kJ/mol and the N≡N bond energy is 941 kJ/mol.

The bond length is related to the presence or absence of multiple bonding. The distance of separation of two nuclei is greatest for a single bond, less for a double bond, and still less for a triple bond. The *bond length* decreases in the order *single bond > double bond > triple bond*.

> **Question 3.3** Contrast a single and double bond with regard to:
>
> a. distance of separation of the bonded nuclei
>
> b. strength of the bond
>
> How are these two properties related?

> **Question 3.4** Two nitrogen atoms in a nitrogen molecule are held together more strongly than the two chlorine atoms in a chlorine molecule. Explain this fact by comparing their respective Lewis structures.

Isomers

Isomers are compounds that share the same molecular formula but have different structures. Hydrocarbons (compounds that contain only hydrogen and carbon atoms) frequently exhibit this property. For example, butane, C_4H_{10}, has two isomeric forms. One isomer, termed normal butane, *n*-butane, has a structure characterized by the four carbon atoms being linked in a chain; the other, termed isobutane, has a three-carbon chain, with the fourth carbon attached to the middle carbon.

The term *bond order* is sometimes used to distinguish among single, double, and triple bonds. A bond order of one corresponds to a single bond, two corresponds to a double bond, and three corresponds to a triple bond.

The mole is simply a unit denoting quantity, just as a *dozen* eggs represents twelve eggs. A mole of bonds is 6.022×10^{23} bonds (see Chapter 4).

H H H H
| | | |
H—C—C—C—C—H
| | | |
H H H H

n-Butane (C₄H₁₀)

H
|
H—C—H
H | H
| | |
H—C—C—C—H
| | |
H H H

Isobutane (C₄H₁₀)

n-pentane

2-methylbutane

2,2-dimethylpropane

Notice that both structures, although clearly different, contain four carbon atoms and ten hydrogen atoms. Owing to their structural differences, each has a different melting point and boiling point. In fact, all of their physical properties differ at least slightly. These differences in properties clearly show that, in fact, *n*-butane and isobutane are different compounds.

As the size of the hydrocarbon increases, the number of possible isomers increases dramatically. A five-carbon hydrocarbon has three isomers, but a thirty-carbon hydrocarbon has over 400 million possible isomers. Petroleum is largely a complex mixture of hydrocarbons, and the principal reason for this complexity lies in the tremendous variety of possible isomers present.

The three isomers of pentane (a five-carbon hydrocarbon) are depicted in the figure in the margin.

Lewis Structures and Resonance

In some cases we find that it is possible to write more than one Lewis structure that satisfies the octet rule for a particular compound. Consider sulfur dioxide, SO_2. Its skeletal structure is

$$O—S—O$$

Total valence electrons may be calculated as follows:

$$
\begin{array}{ll}
1 \text{ sulfur atom} \times 6 \text{ valence e}^-/\text{atom} = & 6 \text{ e}^- \\
+2 \text{ oxygen atoms} \times 6 \text{ valence e}^-/\text{atom} = & 12 \text{ e}^- \\
\hline
& 18 \text{ e}^- \text{ total}
\end{array}
$$

The resulting Lewis structures are

$$\ddot{O}{=}\ddot{S}{-}\ddot{O}: \quad \text{and} \quad :\ddot{O}{-}\ddot{S}{=}\ddot{O}$$

Both satisfy the octet rule. However, experimental evidence shows no double bond in SO_2. The two sulfur-oxygen bonds are equivalent. Apparently, neither structure accurately represents the structure of SO_2, and neither actually exists. The actual structure is said to be an average or *hybrid* of these two Lewis structures. When a compound has two or more Lewis structures that contribute to the real structure, we say that the compound displays the property of **resonance.** The contributing Lewis structures are **resonance forms.** The true structure, a hybrid of the resonance forms, is known as a **resonance hybrid** and may be represented as:

$$\ddot{O}{=}\ddot{S}{-}\ddot{O}: \quad \leftrightarrow \quad :\ddot{O}{-}\ddot{S}{=}\ddot{O}$$

A common analogy might help to clarify this concept. A horse and a donkey may be crossbred to produce a hybrid, the mule. The mule doesn't look or behave exactly like either parent, yet it has attributes of both. The resonance hybrid of a molecule has properties of each resonance form but is not identical to any one form. Unlike the mule, resonance hybrids *do not actually exist.* Rather, they comprise a model that results from the failure of any one Lewis structure to agree with experimentally obtained structural information.

It is a misconception to picture the real molecule as oscillating back and forth among the various resonance structures. Resonance is a modeling strategy designed to help us visualize electron arrangements too complex to be adequately explained by the simple Lewis structure.

The presence of resonance enhances molecular stability. The more resonance forms that exist, the greater is the stability of the molecule they represent. This concept is important in understanding the chemical reactions of many complex organic molecules and is used extensively in organic chemistry.

EXAMPLE 3.13　Drawing Resonance Hybrids of Covalently Bonded Compounds

Draw the possible resonance structures of the nitrate ion, NO_3^-, and represent them as a resonance hybrid.

Solution

Step 1.　Nitrogen is less electronegative than oxygen; therefore, nitrogen is the central atom and the skeletal structure is:

$$\left[\begin{array}{c} O \\ | \\ O-N-O \end{array}\right]^-$$

Step 2.　The pool of valence electrons for anions is determined by adding one electron for each unit of negative charge:

$$
\begin{aligned}
1 \text{ N atom} \times 5 \text{ valence electrons} &= 5 \text{ e}^- \\
3 \text{ O atoms} \times 6 \text{ valence electrons} &= 18 \text{ e}^- \\
+1 \text{ negative charge} &= 1 \text{ e}^- \\
\hline
&24 \text{ e}^- \text{ total}
\end{aligned}
$$

Step 3.　First, connect O atoms to the N atom using single bonds.

$$\left[\begin{array}{c} O \\ | \\ O-N-O \end{array}\right]^-$$

Step 4.　Place lone-pair electrons around the terminal O atoms until each atom has an octet. Do not exceed twenty-four electrons.

$$\left[\begin{array}{c} :\ddot{O}: \\ | \\ :\ddot{O}-N-\ddot{O}: \end{array}\right]^-$$

This structure uses twenty-four electrons; however, the central atom only has six valence electrons.

Step 5.　Shift a lone pair on one of the O atoms to become a bond between the O and N. To draw all possible resonance structures, this shift can be drawn for each of the oxygen atoms.

$$\left[\begin{array}{c} :\ddot{O}: \\ | \\ :\ddot{O}=N-\ddot{O}: \end{array}\right]^- \longleftrightarrow \left[\begin{array}{c} :\ddot{O}: \\ \| \\ :\ddot{O}-N-\ddot{O}: \end{array}\right]^- \longleftrightarrow \left[\begin{array}{c} :\ddot{O}: \\ | \\ :\ddot{O}-N=\ddot{O}: \end{array}\right]^-$$

Step 6.　Each resonance structure used twenty-four valence electrons and the octet rule is obeyed for each atom.

Practice Problem 3.13

a.　SeO_2, like SO_2, has two resonance forms. Draw their Lewis structures.

b.　Explain any similarities between the structures for SeO_2 and SO_2 in light of periodic relationships.

▶ **For Further Practice: Questions 3.73 and 3.74.**

Lewis Structures and Exceptions to the Octet Rule

The octet rule is remarkable in its ability to realistically model bonding and structure in covalent compounds. But, like any model, it does not adequately describe all systems. Beryllium, boron, and aluminum, in particular, tend to form compounds in which they are surrounded by fewer than eight electrons. This situation is termed an *incomplete octet*.

Other molecules, such as nitric oxide:

$$\ddot{N}=\ddot{O}$$

are termed *odd-electron* molecules. Note that it is impossible to pair all electrons to achieve an octet simply because the compound contains an odd number of valence electrons.

Elements in the third period and beyond may involve *d* orbitals and form an *expanded octet*, with ten or even twelve electrons surrounding the central atom. Examples 3.14 and 3.15 illustrate common exceptions to the octet rule.

EXAMPLE 3.14   Drawing Lewis Structures of Covalently Bonded Compounds That Are Exceptions to the Octet Rule

Draw the Lewis structure of beryllium hydride, BeH_2.

Solution

Step 1. A reasonable skeletal structure of BeH_2 is:

$$H — Be — H$$

Step 2. The total number of valence electrons in BeH_2 is:

$$1 \text{ beryllium atom } \times 2 \text{ valence } e^-/\text{atom } = 2\ e^-$$
$$2 \text{ hydrogen atoms } \times 1 \text{ valence } e^-/\text{atom } = 2\ e^-$$
$$\overline{ 4\ e^- \text{ total}}$$

Step 3. The resulting Lewis structure must be:

$$H : Be : H \qquad \text{or} \qquad H — Be — H$$

Step 4. It is apparent that there is no way to satisfy the octet rule for Be in this compound. Consequently, BeH_2 is an exception to the octet rule. It contains an incomplete octet.

Practice Problem 3.14

The BCl_3 molecule has an incomplete octet around B. Draw the Lewis structure of BCl_3.

▶ **For Further Practice: Question 3.91.**

EXAMPLE 3.15   Drawing Lewis Structures of Covalently Bonded Compounds That Are Exceptions to the Octet Rule

Draw the Lewis structure of phosphorus pentafluoride.

Solution

Step 1. The formula is PF_5. Phosphorus is the central atom, with five terminal fluorine atoms.

$$\begin{array}{c} \quad F \\ \quad | \quad F \\ F — P \\ \quad | \quad F \\ \quad F \end{array}$$

Continued—

Step 2. Phosphorus is a third-period element; it may have an expanded octet. The total number of valence electrons is:

$$1 \text{ phosphorus atom} \times 5 \text{ valence } e^-/\text{atom} = 5 \text{ } e^-$$
$$5 \text{ fluorine atoms} \times 7 \text{ valence } e^-/\text{atom} = 35 \text{ } e^-$$
$$\overline{ 40 \text{ } e^- \text{ total}}$$

Steps 3 and 4. Connect five fluorine atoms to the phosphorus atom with single bonds. Distribute the electrons around each F in the skeletal structure (completing the fluorine octets), which results in the Lewis structure:

$$:\!\overset{\displaystyle :\!\ddot{F}\!:}{\underset{\displaystyle :\!\ddot{F}\!:}{\overset{|}{\underset{|}{F}}\!-\!P}}\!\!\overset{\ddot{F}\!:}{\underset{\ddot{F}\!:}{\diagdown}}$$

PF_5 is an example of a compound with an expanded octet. The central phosphorus atom is surrounded by ten electrons.

Practice Problem 3.15

The SF_6 molecule has an expanded octet around S. Draw the Lewis structure of SF_6.

▶ **For Further Practice: Question 3.92.**

Lewis Structures and Molecular Geometry; VSEPR Theory

LEARNING GOAL

7 ▶ Predict the geometry of molecules and ions using the octet rule and Lewis structures.

Animations
• Valence-Shell Electron-Pair Repulsion Theory
• VSEPR and Molecular Geometry

The shape of a molecule plays a large part in determining its properties and reactivity. We may predict the shapes of various molecules by inspecting their Lewis structures for the orientation of their electron pairs. The covalent bond, for instance, in which bonding electrons are localized between the nuclear centers of the atoms, is *directional*; the bond has a specific orientation in space between the bonded atoms. Electrostatic forces in ionic bonds, in contrast, are *nondirectional*; they have no specific orientation in space. The specific orientation of electron pairs in covalent molecules imparts a characteristic shape to the molecules. Consider the following series of molecules whose Lewis structures are shown.

$$BeH_2 \qquad H\!-\!Be\!-\!H$$

$$BF_3 \qquad :\!\ddot{F}\!-\!\underset{\displaystyle |}{\overset{\displaystyle :\!\ddot{F}\!:}{B}}\!-\!\ddot{F}\!:$$

$$CH_4 \qquad H\!-\!\underset{\displaystyle |}{\overset{\displaystyle |}{\underset{\displaystyle H}{\overset{\displaystyle H}{C}}}}\!-\!H$$

$$NH_3 \qquad H\!-\!\underset{\displaystyle |}{\overset{\displaystyle \cdot\cdot}{\underset{\displaystyle H}{N}}}\!-\!H$$

$$H_2O \qquad H\!-\!\ddot{O}\!-\!H$$

The electron pairs around the central atom of the molecule arrange themselves to minimize electronic repulsion. This means that the electron pairs arrange themselves so that they can be as far as possible from each other. We may use this fact to

(a)   (b)

predict molecular shape. This approach is termed the *valence-shell electron-pair repulsion* (VSEPR) theory.

Let's see how the VSEPR theory can be used to describe the bonding and structure of each of the preceding molecules.

BeH₂

As we saw in Example 3.14, beryllium hydride has two bonded atoms around the beryllium atom. These electron pairs have minimum repulsion if they are located as far apart as possible while still bonding the hydrogen atoms to the central atom. This condition is met if the electron pairs are located on opposite sides of the molecule, resulting in a **linear structure,** 180° apart:

$$H-Be-H$$

The *bond angle,* the angle between H—Be and Be—H bonds, formed by the two bonding pairs is 180° (Figure 3.6).

BeF_2, CS_2, and HCN are other examples of molecules that exhibit linear geometry. Multiple bonds are treated identically to single bonds in VSEPR theory. For example, the Lewis structure of HCN is H—C≡N:. The bonded atoms on either side of carbon are positioned 180° from each other. Instead of counting bonding electrons to predict molecular shape, it is more appropriate to count bonded atoms. The central atom has two bonded atoms.

BF₃

Boron trifluoride has three bonded atoms around the central atom. Placing the electron pairs in a plane, forming a triangle, minimizes the electron-pair repulsion in this molecule, as depicted in Figure 3.7 and the following sketch:

Such a structure is *trigonal planar,* and each F—B—F bond angle is 120°. We also find that compounds with central atoms in the same group of the periodic table have similar geometry. Aluminum, in the same group as boron, produces compounds such as AlH_3, which is also trigonal planar.

CH₄

Methane has four bonded atoms around carbon. Here, minimum electron repulsion is achieved by arranging the electrons at the corners of a tetrahedron (Figure 3.8). Each H—C—H bond angle is 109.5°. Methane has a three-dimensional **tetrahedral structure.** Silicon, in the same group as carbon, forms compounds such as $SiCl_4$ and SiH_4 that also have tetrahedral structures.

NH₃

Ammonia has three bonded atoms and one lone pair (four groups) about the central atom. In contrast to methane, in which all four electron pairs are bonding, ammonia has three pairs of bonding electrons and one nonbonding lone pair of electrons. We might expect CH_4 and NH_3 to have electron-pair arrangements that are similar but not identical. The lone pair in ammonia is more negative than the

Only four electrons surround the beryllium atom in BeH_2. Consequently, BeH_2 is a stable exception to the octet rule.

Animations
- The Geometry of BeF_2
- The Geometry of BF_3

BF_3 has only six electrons around the central atom, B. It is one of a number of stable compounds that are exceptions to the octet rule.

CH_4, NH_3, and H_2O all have eight electrons around their central atoms; all obey the octet rule.

(a)   (b)

Figure 3.7 Bonding and geometry in boron trifluoride, BF_3. (a) Trigonal planar geometry in BF_3. (b) Computer-generated model of trigonal planar BF_3.

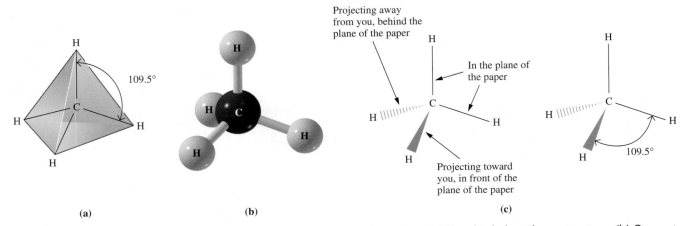

Figure 3.8 Representations of the three-dimensional structure of methane, CH_4. (a) Tetrahedral methane structure. (b) Computer-generated model of tetrahedral methane. (c) Three-dimensional representation of structure (b).

Animations
- The Geometry of CH_4
- The Geometry of NH_3
- The Geometry of H_2O

bonding pairs; some of the negative charge on the bonding pairs is offset by the presence of the hydrogen atoms with their positive nuclei. Thus the arrangement of electron pairs in ammonia is distorted.

The hydrogen atoms in ammonia are pushed closer together than in methane (Figure 3.9). The bond angle is 107° because lone pair–bond pair repulsions are greater than bond pair–bond pair repulsions. The structure or shape is termed *trigonal pyramidal*, and the molecule is termed a **trigonal pyramidal molecule.**

H_2O

Water has two bonded atoms and two lone pairs (four groups) about the central atom. These four electron pairs are approximately tetrahedral to each other; however, because of the difference between bonding and nonbonding electrons, noted earlier, the tetrahedral relationship is only approximate.

The **angular** (or *bent*) **structure** has a bond angle of 104.5° , which is 5° smaller than the tetrahedral angle, because of the repulsive effects of the lone pairs of electrons (Figure 3.10).

The characteristics of linear, trigonal planar, trigonal pyramidal, angular, and tetrahedral structures are summarized in Table 3.5.

Periodic Structural Relationships

The molecules considered previously contain the central atoms Be (Group IIA), B (Group IIIA), C (Group IVA), N (Group VA), and O (Group VIA). We may expect that a number of other compounds containing the same central atom will have

Figure 3.9 The structure of the ammonia molecule. (a) Pyramidal ammonia structure. (b) Computer-generated model of pyramidal ammonia. (c) A three-dimensional sketch showing the H—N—H bond angle.

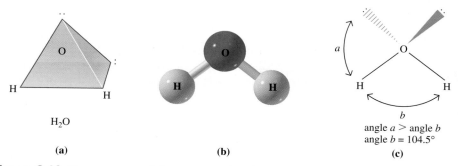

angle a > angle b
angle $b = 104.5°$

(a)   (b)   (c)

Figure 3.10 The structure of the water molecule. (a) Angular water structure. (b) Computer-generated model of angular water. (c) A three-dimensional sketch showing the H—O—H bond angle in water.

structures with similar geometries. This is an approximation, not always true, but still useful in expanding our ability to write reasonable, geometrically accurate structures for a large number of compounds.

The periodic similarity of group members is also useful in predictions involving bonding. Consider Group VIA, oxygen, sulfur, and selenium (Se). Each has six valence electrons. Each needs two more electrons to complete its octet. Each should react with hydrogen, forming H_2O, H_2S, and H_2Se.

If we recall that H_2O is an angular molecule with the following Lewis structure,

$$H—\overset{..}{\underset{|}{O}}:$$
$$H$$

it follows that H_2S and H_2Se would also be angular molecules with similar Lewis structures, or

$$H—\overset{..}{\underset{|}{S}}: \quad \text{and} \quad H—\overset{..}{\underset{|}{Se}}:$$
$$H \qquad\qquad\qquad H$$

This logic applies equally well to the other representative elements.

Table 3.5   Molecular Structure: The Geometry of a Molecule Is Affected by the Number of Nonbonded Electron Pairs Around the Central Atom and the Number of Bonded Atoms

Bonded Atoms	Nonbonding Electron Pairs	Bond Angle	Molecular Structure	Example	Structure
2	0	180°	Linear	CO_2	
3	0	120°	Trigonal planar	SO_3	
2	1	<120°	Angular	SO_2	
4	0	109.5°	Tetrahedral	CH_4	
3	1	~107°	Trigonal pyramidal	NH_3	
2	2	~104.5°	Angular	H_2O	

More Complex Molecules

A molecule such as dimethyl ether, CH_3—O—CH_3, has three distinct central atoms: one oxygen atom and two carbon atoms. We could picture the parts of the molecule containing the CH_3 group (commonly referred to as the *methyl group*) as exhibiting tetrahedral geometry (analogous to methane):

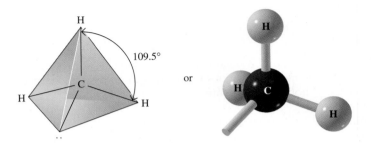

The part of the molecule connecting these two methyl groups (the oxygen) would have a bond angle similar to that of water (in which oxygen is also the central atom), approximately 104°, as seen in Figure 3.11. This is a reasonable way to represent the molecule dimethyl ether.

Trimethylamine, $(CH_3)_3N$, is a member of the amine family. As in the case of dimethyl ether, two different central atoms are present. Carbon and nitrogen determine the geometry of amines. In this case the methyl group should assume the tetrahedral geometry of methane. The nitrogen atom should have the methyl groups in a pyramidal arrangement, similar to the hydrogen atoms in ammonia, as seen in Figure 3.12. This creates a pyramidal geometry around nitrogen. H—N—H bond angles in ammonia are 107°; experimental information shows a very similar C—N—C bond angle in trimethylamine.

Question 3.5 Sketch the geometry of each of the following molecules (basing your sketch on the Lewis structure of the molecule):

    a. PH_3

    b. SiH_4

Question 3.6 Sketch the geometry of each of the following molecules (basing your sketch on the Lewis structure of the molecule):

    a. C_2H_4

    b. C_2H_2

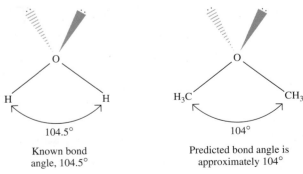

Figure 3.11 A comparison of the bonding in water and dimethyl ether.

Figure 3.12 A comparison of the bonding in ammonia and trimethylamine.

It is essential to represent the molecule in its correct geometric form, using the Lewis and VSEPR theories, to understand its physical and chemical behavior. In the rest of this section we use these models to predict molecular behavior.

Lewis Structures and Polarity

A molecule is *polar* if its centers of positive and negative charge do not coincide. When molecules whose positive and negative charges are separated are placed in an electric field, they align themselves with the field. The molecule behaves as a *dipole* (having two "poles" or ends, one pole is more negative and the other pole is more positive) and is said to be polar.

Nonpolar molecules do not align with an electric field because their positive and negative centers are the same; no dipole exists. These molecules are nonpolar.

The hydrogen molecule is the simplest nonpolar molecule:

$$H : H \quad \text{or} \quad H—H$$

Both electrons, on average, are located at the center of the molecule and positively charged nuclei are on either side. The centers of both positive and negative charge are at the center of the molecule; therefore the bond is nonpolar.

We may arrive at the same conclusion by considering the equality of electron sharing between the atoms being bonded. Electron sharing is related to the concept of electronegativity introduced in Section 3.1.

The atoms that comprise H_2 are identical; their electronegativity (electron attracting power) is the same. Thus the electrons remain at the center of the molecule, and the molecule is nonpolar.

Similarly, O_2, N_2, Cl_2, and F_2 are nonpolar molecules with nonpolar bonds. Arguments analogous to those made for hydrogen explain these observations as well.

Let's next consider hydrogen fluoride, HF. Fluorine is more electronegative than hydrogen. This indicates that the electrons are more strongly attracted to a fluorine atom than they are to a hydrogen atom. This results in a bond and molecule that are polar. The symbol

Less electronegative part of bond ⟋ ⟍ More electronegative part of bond

placed below a bond indicates the direction of polarity. The more negative end of the bond is near the head of the arrow, the less negative end of the bond is next to the tail of the arrow. Symbols using the Greek letter *delta* (δ) may also be used to designate polarity. In this system the more negative end of the bond is designated δ^- (partial negative), and the less negative end is designated δ^+ (partial positive). The symbols are applied to the hydrogen fluoride molecule as follows:

$$\delta^+ H—F \delta^-$$

Less electronegative end of bond ⟋ ⟍ More electronegative end of bond

HF is a **polar covalent molecule** characterized by **polar covalent bonding.** This implies that the electrons are shared unequally.

A molecule containing only nonpolar bonds must be a nonpolar molecule. In contrast, a molecule containing polar bonds may be either polar or nonpolar, depending on the relative arrangement of the bonds and any lone pair(s) of electrons. It is important to be able to determine if a molecule is polar or nonpolar, because this information helps predict properties of solubility as well as melting points and boiling points. These properties will be discussed in Section 3.5.

Think of the polarity of a bond as a rope tied around the central atom pulling in the direction of the more electronegative atom. (Or in the case of lone pairs, the pull will always be in the direction of the lone pair.) Each terminal-atom to

Animation
• Molecular Polarity

LEARNING GOAL

8 ▶ Understand the role that molecular geometry plays in determining the polarity of compounds.

Remember: Electronegativity deals with atoms in molecules, whereas electron affinity and ionization energy deal with isolated atoms.

The word *partial* implies less than a unit charge. Thus δ^+ and δ^- do not imply overall charge on a unit (such as the + or −sign on an ion); they are meant to show only the relative distribution of charge within a unit. The HF molecule shown is *neutral* but has an unequal charge distribution *within* the molecule.

Animations
• The Structure and Dipole Moment of HF
• The Structure and Dipole Moment of CCl_4
• The Structure and Dipole Moment of H_2O

central-atom connection is a separate tug-of-war. If all the pulls are equal, the molecule is nonpolar; otherwise the molecule is polar. To determine if a molecule with polar bonds is polar or nonpolar, draw the Lewis structure and follow these guidelines:

Molecules that have no lone pair on the central atom, and all terminal atoms the same are *nonpolar.* For example, the molecule CO_2 has two bonded O atoms and no lone pairs on the central atom. It is linear and nonpolar. The molecule CCl_4 has no lone pairs on the central atom and four bonded Cl atoms. Its shape is tetrahedral and it is nonpolar.

Molecules with one lone pair on the central atom are *polar.* Ammonia (NH3) is an example. Its nitrogen atom has three bonded H atoms and one lone pair. It is based upon the tetrahedral shape but is a trigonal pyramid. Because the nitrogen atom is more electronegative than the hydrogen atoms, the arrow points toward nitrogen and ammonia is polar. The pull of lone-pair electrons is always away from the atom.

Molecules that have more than one lone pair on the central atom are *usually polar,* **but there are exceptions.** The Lewis structure of water has two lone pairs and two bonded H atoms on the central atom of oxygen. Water is an angular molecule, and it is polar.

The electron density is shifted away from the hydrogens toward oxygen in the water molecule.

EXAMPLE 3.16   Determining if a Molecule Is Polar Covalent or Nonpolar Covalent

Is PCl_3 a polar or nonpolar covalent compound?

Solution

Step 1. Follow all steps to correctly draw the Lewis structure.

Skeletal Structure	Count Valence Electrons	Distribute Valence Electrons
Cl | Cl — P — Cl	$1\,P \times 5\,e^- = 5\,e^-$ $\underline{3\,Cl \times 7\,e^- = 21\,e^-}$ $26\,e^-$ total	:Cl: | :Cl — P — Cl:

Step 2. Examine the central atom to determine if it is polar. The molecule has three chlorine atoms and one lone pair. The one lone pair makes the molecule polar covalent.

Practice Problem 3.16

Determine whether the AsCl₃ molecule is polar.

▶ **For Further Practice: Questions 3.85 and 3.86.**

Question 3.7 Predict which of the following bonds are polar, and, if polar, in which direction the electrons are pulled:

a. O—S
c. Cl—Cl

b. C≡N
d. I—Cl

Question 3.8 Predict which of the following bonds are polar, and, if polar, in which direction the electrons are pulled:

a. Si—Cl
c. H—C

b. S—Cl
d. C—C

Question 3.9 Using Lewis structures and VSEPR, predict whether each of the following molecules is polar:

a. BCl₃
c. HCl

b. NH₃
d. SiCl₄

Question 3.10 Using Lewis structures and VSEPR, predict whether each of the following molecules is polar:

a. CO₂
c. BrCl

b. SCl₂
d. CS₂

3.5 Properties Based on Electronic Structure and Molecular Geometry

Intramolecular forces are attractive forces *within* molecules. They are the chemical bonds that determine the shape and polarity of individual molecules. **Intermolecular forces,** on the other hand, are forces *between* molecules.

It is important to distinguish between these two kinds of forces. It is the *intermolecular* forces that determine such properties as the solubility of one substance in another and the freezing and boiling points of liquids. But, at the same time, we must realize that these forces are a direct consequence of the *intramolecular* forces in the individual units, the molecules.

In the following section we will see some of the consequences of bonding that are directly attributable to differences in intermolecular forces (solubility, boiling and melting points). In Section 5.2 we will investigate, in some detail, the nature of the intermolecular forces themselves.

LEARNING GOAL

9 ▶ Understand the role of polarity in determining solubility as well as melting and boiling points of compounds.

Solubility

Solubility is defined as the maximum amount of solute that dissolves in a given amount of solvent at a specified temperature. Polar molecules are most soluble in polar solvents, whereas nonpolar molecules are most soluble in nonpolar solvents. This is the rule of *"like dissolves like."* Substances of similar polarity are mutually soluble, and large differences in polarity lead to insolubility.

The solute is the substance that is present in lesser quantity, and the solvent is the substance that is present in the greater amount (see Section 6.3).

Figure 3.13 The interaction of polar covalent water molecules (the solvent) with polar covalent solute molecules such as ammonia, resulting in the formation of a solution.

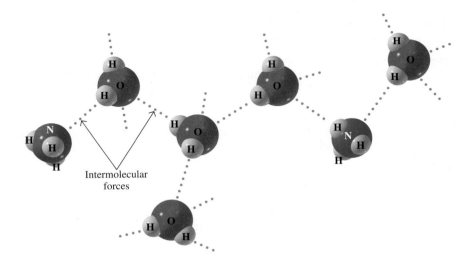

Intermolecular forces

The interaction of water and ammonia is an example of a particularly strong intermolecular force, the hydrogen bond; this phenomenon is discussed in Chapter 5.

Case I: Ammonia and Water

Ammonia is soluble in water because both ammonia and water are polar molecules:

Dissolution of ammonia in water is a consequence of the intermolecular forces present among the ammonia and water molecules. The δ^- end (a nitrogen) of the ammonia molecule is attracted to the δ^+ end (a hydrogen) of the water molecule; at the same time the δ^+ end (a hydrogen) of the ammonia molecule is attracted to the δ^- end (an oxygen) of the water molecule. These attractive forces thus "pull" ammonia into water (and water into ammonia), and the ammonia molecules are randomly distributed throughout the solvent, forming a homogeneous solution (Figure 3.13).

Case II: Oil and Water

Oil and water do not mix; oil is a nonpolar substance composed primarily of molecules containing carbon and hydrogen. Water molecules, on the other hand, are quite polar. The potential solvent, water molecules, have partially charged ends, whereas the molecules of oil do not. As a result, water molecules exert their attractive forces on other water molecules, not on the molecules of oil; the oil remains insoluble, and because it is less dense than water, the oil simply floats on the surface of the water. This is illustrated in Figure 3.14.

Boiling Points of Liquids and Melting Points of Solids

Boiling a liquid requires energy. The energy is used to overcome the intermolecular attractive forces in the liquid, driving the molecules into the less-associated gas phase. The amount of energy required to accomplish this is related to the boiling temperature. This, in turn, depends on the strength of the intermolecular attractive forces in the liquid, which parallels the polarity. This is not the only determinant of boiling point. Molecular mass is also an important consideration. The larger the mass of the molecule, the more difficult it becomes to convert the collection of molecules to the gas phase.

A similar argument can be made for the melting points of solids. The ease of conversion of a solid to a liquid also depends on the magnitude of the attractive forces in the solid. The situation actually becomes very complex for ionic solids because of the complexity of the crystal lattice.

Figure 3.14 The interaction of polar water molecules and nonpolar oil molecules. The familiar salad dressing, oil and vinegar, forms two layers. The oil does not dissolve in vinegar, an aqueous solution of acetic acid.

Table 3.6 Melting and Boiling Points of Selected Compounds in Relation to Their Bonding Type

Formula (Name)	Bonding Type	M.P. (°C)	B.P. (°C)
N_2 (nitrogen)	Nonpolar covalent	−210	−196
O_2 (oxygen)	Nonpolar covalent	−219	−183
NH_3 (ammonia)	Polar covalent	−78	−33
H_2O (water)	Polar covalent	0	100
NaCl (sodium chloride)	Ionic	801	1413
KBr (potassium bromide)	Ionic	730	1435

As a general rule, polar compounds have strong attractive (intermolecular) forces, and their boiling and melting points tend to be higher than those of non-polar substances of similar molecular mass.

Melting and boiling points of a variety of substances are included in Table 3.6.

Question 3.11 Predict which compound in each of the following pairs should have the higher melting and boiling points (Hint: Write the Lewis structure and determine whether the molecule is polar or nonpolar.):

a. H_2O and C_2H_4

b. CO and CH_4

c. NH_3 and N_2

d. Cl_2 and ICl

Question 3.12 Predict which compound in each of the following pairs should have the higher melting and boiling points (Hint: Write the Lewis structure and determine whether the molecule is polar or nonpolar.):

a. C_2H_6 and CH_4

b. CO and NO

c. F_2 and Br_2

d. $CHCl_3$ and CCl_4

SUMMARY

3.1 Chemical Bonding

When two atoms are joined to make a chemical compound, the force of attraction between the two atoms is the *chemical bond*. *Ionic bonding* is characterized by an electron transfer process occurring before bond formation, forming an *ion pair*. In *covalent bonding,* electrons are shared between atoms in the bonding process. *Polar covalent bonding,* like covalent bonding, is based on the concept of electron sharing; however, the sharing is unequal and based on the *electronegativity* difference between joined atoms. The *Lewis symbol,* showing only valence electrons, is a convenient way of representing atoms and *Lewis structures* use Lewis symbols as building blocks to construct combinations of atoms.

3.2 Naming Compounds and Writing Formulas of Compounds

The "shorthand" symbol for a compound is its *formula.* The formula identifies the number and type of atoms in the compound.

An ion that consists of only a single atom is said to be *monatomic. Polyatomic ions,* such as the hydroxide ion, OH^-, are composed of two or more atoms bonded together.

Names of ionic compounds are derived from the names of their ions. The name of the cation appears first, followed by the name of the anion. In the Stock system for naming an ion (the systematic name), a Roman numeral indicates the charge of the cation. In the older common nomenclature system, the suffix *-ous* indicates the lower of the ionic charges, and the suffix *-ic* indicates the higher ionic charge.

Most covalent compounds are formed by the reaction of nonmetals. Covalent compounds exist as *molecules.*

The convention used for naming covalent compounds is as follows:

- The names of the elements are written in the order in which they appear in the formula.
- A prefix indicating the number of each kind of atom found in the unit is placed before the name of the element.
- The stem of the name of the last element is used with the suffix *-ide.*

Many compounds are so familiar to us that their common names are used. It is useful to be able to correlate both systematic and common names with the corresponding molecular formula.

3.3 Properties of Ionic and Covalent Compounds

Covalently bonded molecules are discrete units, and they have less tendency to form an extended structure in the solid state. Ionic compounds, with ions joined by electrostatic attraction, do not have definable units but form a *crystal lattice* composed of positive and negative ions in an extended three-dimensional network.

The *melting point* is the temperature at which a solid is converted to a liquid; the *boiling point* is the temperature at which a liquid is converted to a gas. Melting and boiling temperatures for ionic compounds are generally higher than those of covalent compounds.

Ionic solids are crystalline, whereas covalent solids may be either crystalline or amorphous.

Many ionic solids dissolve in water, *dissociating* into positive and negative ions (an *electrolytic solution*). Because these ions can carry (conduct) a current of electricity, they are called *electrolytes.* Covalent solids in solution usually retain their neutral character and are *nonelectrolytes.*

3.4 Drawing Lewis Structures of Molecules and Polyatomic Ions

The procedure for drawing Lewis structures of molecules involves writing a skeletal structure of the molecule, arranging the atoms in their most probable order, determining the number of valence electrons on each atom, and combining them to get the total for the compound. The electrons are then distributed around the atoms (in pairs if possible) to satisfy the octet rule. At this point electron pairs may be moved, creating double or triple bonds, in an effort to satisfy the octet rule for all atoms and produce the final structure. Lewis structures are useful in representing bonding in polyatomic ions as well.

Stability of a covalent compound is related to the *bond energy.* The magnitude of the bond energy decreases in the order *triple bond > double bond > single bond.* The bond length decreases in the order *single bond > double bond > triple bond.*

The valence-shell electron-pair repulsion theory states that electron pairs around the central atom of the molecule arrange themselves to minimize electronic repulsion; the electrons orient themselves as far as possible from each other. Two electron pairs around the central atom lead to a *linear* arrangement of the attached atoms; three indicate a *trigonal planar* arrangement, and four result in a *tetrahedral geometry.* Both *lone-pair* and *bonding pair* electrons must be taken into account when predicting structure. Molecules with fewer than four and as many as five or six electron pairs around the central atom also exist. They are exceptions to the octet rule.

A molecule is polar if its centers of positive and negative charge do not coincide. A *polar covalent* molecule has at least one *polar covalent bond.* An understanding of the concept of *electronegativity,* the relative electron-attracting power of atoms in molecules, helps us to assess the polarity of a bond.

A molecule containing all nonpolar bonds must be nonpolar. A molecule containing polar bonds may be either polar or nonpolar, depending on the relative position of the bonds.

3.5 Properties Based on Electronic Structure and Molecular Geometry

Attractions between molecules are called *intermolecular forces. Intramolecular forces,* on the other hand, are the attractive forces within molecules. It is the intermolecular forces that determine such properties as the solubility of one substance in another and the freezing and boiling points of liquids.

Solubility is the maximum amount of solute that dissolves in a given amount of solvent at a specified temperature. Polar molecules are most soluble in polar solvents; nonpolar molecules are most soluble in nonpolar solvents. This is the rule of "like dissolves like."

As a general rule, polar compounds have strong intermolecular forces, and their boiling and melting points tend to be higher than nonpolar compounds of similar molecular mass.

KEY TERMS

angular structure (3.4)	melting point (3.3)
boiling point (3.3)	molecule (3.1)
bond energy (3.4)	monatomic ion (3.2)
chemical bond (3.1)	nomenclature (3.2)
covalent bonding (3.1)	nonelectrolyte (3.3)
crystal lattice (3.1)	polar covalent
dissociation (3.3)	bonding (3.4)
double bond (3.4)	polar covalent molecule (3.4)
electrolyte (3.3)	polyatomic ion (3.2)
electrolytic solution (3.3)	resonance (3.4)
electronegativity (3.1)	resonance form (3.4)
formula (3.2)	resonance hybrid (3.4)
intermolecular force (3.5)	single bond (3.4)
intramolecular force (3.5)	solubility (3.5)
ionic bonding (3.1)	tetrahedral structure (3.4)
ion pair (3.1)	trigonal pyramidal
isomers (3.4)	molecule (3.4)
Lewis structure (3.1)	triple bond (3.4)
Lewis symbol (3.1)	*valence-shell electron-pair*
linear structure (3.4)	*repulsion* (VSEPR)
lone pair (3.1)	theory (3.4)

QUESTIONS AND PROBLEMS

Chemical Bonding

Foundations

3.13 Classify each of the following compounds as ionic or covalent:
    a. $MgCl_2$ **c.** H_2S
    b. CO_2 **d.** NO_2

3.14 Classify each of the following compounds as ionic or covalent:
    a. NaCl   **c.** ICl
    b. CO   **d.** H_2

3.15 Classify each of the following compounds as ionic or covalent:
    a. SiO_2 **c.** SO_3
    b. SO_2 **d.** $CaCl_2$

3.16 Classify each of the following compounds as ionic or covalent:
    a. NF_3 **c.** CsF
    b. NaF   **d.** $SiCl_4$

Applications

3.17 Using Lewis symbols and structures, write an equation predicting the product of the reaction of:
    a. Li + Br
    b. Mg + Cl

3.18 Using Lewis symbols and structures, write an equation predicting the product of the reaction of:
    a. Na + O
    b. Na + S

3.19 Using Lewis symbols and structures, write an equation predicting the product of the reaction of:
    a. S + H
    b. P + H

3.20 Using Lewis symbols and structures, write an equation predicting the product of the reaction of:
    a. Si + H
    b. Ca + F

3.21 Explain, using Lewis symbols and the octet rule, why helium is so nonreactive.

3.22 Explain, using Lewis symbols and the octet rule, why neon is so nonreactive.

Naming Compounds and Writing Formulas of Compounds

Foundations

3.23 Name each of the following ions:
    a. Na^+
    b. Cu^+
    c. Mg^{2+}

3.24 Name each of the following ions:
    a. Cu^{2+}
    b. Fe^{2+}
    c. Fe^{3+}

3.25 Name each of the following ions:
    a. S^{2-}
    b. Cl^-
    c. CO_3^{2-}

3.26 Name each of the following ions:
    a. ClO^-
    b. NH_4^+
    c. CH_3COO^-

3.27 Name each of the following compounds:
    a. $MgCl_2$
    b. $AlCl_3$

3.28 Name each of the following compounds:
    a. Na_2O
    b. $Fe(OH)_3$

3.29 Name each of the following covalent compounds:
    a. NO_2 **b.** SeO_3

3.30 Name each of the following covalent compounds:
    a. N_2O_4
    b. CCl_4

3.31 Name each covalent compound:
    a. SO_2
    b. SO_3

3.32 Name each covalent compound:
    a. N_2O_5
    b. CO

3.33 Write the formula for each of the following monatomic ions:
    a. the potassium ion
    b. the bromide ion

3.34 Write the formula for each of the following monatomic ions:
    a. the calcium ion
    b. the chromium(VI) ion

3.35 Write the formula for each of the following complex ions:
    a. the sulfate ion
    b. the nitrate ion

3.36 Write the formula for each of the following complex ions:
    a. the phosphate ion
    b. the bicarbonate ion

3.37 Write the correct formula for each of the following:
    a. sodium chloride
    b. magnesium bromide

3.38 Write the correct formula for each of the following:
    a. potassium oxide
    b. potassium nitride

3.39 Write the correct formula for each of the following:
    a. silver cyanide
    b. ammonium chloride

3.40 Write the correct formula for each of the following:
    a. magnesium carbonate
    b. magnesium bicarbonate

3.41 Write the correct formula for each of the following:
    a. copper(II) oxide
    b. iron(III) oxide

3.42 Write the correct formula for each of the following:
    a. manganese(II) oxide
    b. manganese(III) oxide

Applications

3.43 Predict the formula of a compound formed from:
    a. aluminum and oxygen
    b. lithium and sulfur

3.44 Predict the formula of a compound formed from:
    a. boron and hydrogen
    b. magnesium and phosphorus

3.45 Write a suitable formula for:
    a. silicon dioxide
    b. sulfur dioxide

3.46 Write a suitable formula for:
    a. vanadium pentoxide
    b. vanadium trioxide

3.47 Write a suitable formula for:
    a. sodium nitrate
    b. magnesium nitrate

3.48 Write a suitable formula for:
    a. aluminum nitrate
    b. ammonium nitrate

3.49 Write a suitable formula for:
    a. ammonium iodide
    b. ammonium sulfate

3.50 Write a suitable formula for:
    a. ammonium acetate
    b. ammonium cyanide

Properties of Ionic and Covalent Compounds
Foundations

3.51   Contrast ionic and covalent compounds with respect to their solid-state structure.

3.52   Contrast ionic and covalent compounds with respect to their behavior in solution.

3.53   Contrast ionic and covalent compounds with respect to their relative boiling points.

3.54   Contrast ionic and covalent compounds with respect to their relative melting points.

Applications

3.55   Would KCl be expected to be a solid at room temperature? Why?

3.56   Would CCl_4 be expected to be a solid at room temperature? Why?

3.57   Would H_2O or CCl_4 be expected to have a higher boiling point? Why?

3.58   Would H_2O or CCl_4 be expected to have a higher melting point? Why?

Drawing Lewis Structures of Molecules and Polyatomic Ions
Foundations

3.59   Draw the appropriate Lewis symbol for each of the following atoms:
    a. H   **c.** C
    b. He   **d.** N

3.60   Draw the appropriate Lewis symbol for each of the following atoms:
    a. Be   **c.** F
    b. B   **d.** S

3.61   Draw the appropriate Lewis symbol for each of the following ions:
    a. Li^+ **c.** Cl^-
    b. Mg^{2+} **d.** P^{3-}

3.62   Draw the appropriate Lewis symbol for each of the following ions:
    a. Be^{2+} **c.** O^{2-}
    b. Al^{3+} **d.** S^{2-}

Applications

3.63   Give the Lewis structure for each of the following compounds:
    a. NCl_3
    b. CH_3OH
    c. CS_2

3.64   Give the Lewis structure for each of the following compounds:
    a. HNO_3
    b. CCl_4
    c. PBr_3

3.65   Using the VSEPR theory, predict the geometry, polarity, and water solubility of each compound in Question 3.63.

3.66   Using the VSEPR theory, predict the geometry, polarity, and water solubility of each compound in Question 3.64.

3.67   Draw the Lewis structure of NO^+.

3.68   Draw the Lewis structure of NO_2^-.

3.69   Draw the Lewis structure of OH^-.

3.70   Draw the Lewis structure of HS^-.

3.71   Discuss the concept of resonance, being certain to define the terms *resonance, resonance form,* and *resonance hybrid.*

3.72   Why is resonance an important concept in bonding?

3.73   The acetate ion (Example 3.12) exhibits resonance. Draw two resonance forms of the acetate ion.

3.74   Ozone, O_3, has two resonance forms. Draw each form.

3.75   Ethanol (ethyl alcohol or grain alcohol) has a molecular formula of C_2H_5OH. Draw the Lewis structure of ethanol.

3.76   Formaldehyde, H_2CO, in water solution has been used as a preservative for biological specimens. Draw the Lewis structure of formaldehyde.

3.77   Acetone, C_3H_6O, is a common solvent. It is found in such diverse materials as nail polish remover and industrial solvents. Draw its Lewis structure if its skeletal structure is

$$\overset{\displaystyle O}{\underset{\displaystyle }{\overset{\displaystyle |}{C}}-C-C}$$

3.78   Ethylamine is an example of an important class of organic compounds. The molecular formula of ethylamine is $CH_3CH_2NH_2$. Draw its Lewis structure.

3.79   Predict whether the bond formed between each of the following pairs of atoms would be ionic, nonpolar, or polar covalent:
    a. S and O
    b. Si and P
    c. Na and Cl
    d. Na and O
    e. Ca and Br

3.80   Predict whether the bond formed between each of the following pairs of atoms would be ionic, nonpolar, or polar covalent:
    a. Cl and Cl
    b. H and H
    c. C and H
    d. Li and F
    e. O and O

3.81   Draw an appropriate covalent Lewis structure formed by the simplest combination of atoms in Problem 3.79 for each solution that involves a nonpolar or polar covalent bond.

3.82   Draw an appropriate covalent Lewis structure formed by the simplest combination of atoms in Problem 3.80 for each solution that involves a nonpolar or polar covalent bond.

3.83   Write the Lewis structure of each of the following compounds and predict its geometry using VSEPR.
    a. SO_2
    b. SO_3

3.84   Write the Lewis structure of each of the following compounds and predict its geometry using VSEPR.
    a. SeO_2
    b. SeO_3

3.85   Predict the polarity of each compound in Question 3.83.

3.86   Predict the polarity of each compound in Question 3.84.

3.87   All of the following Lewis structures are incorrect. Find the errors and write the correct structures.

    a. $:\ddot{C}=\ddot{O}:$

    b. $:\ddot{H}-\ddot{O}-\ddot{H}:$

    c. $:\ddot{O}-\ddot{C}-\ddot{O}:$

3.88   All of the following Lewis structures are incorrect. Find the errors and write the correct structures.

    a. $:\ddot{F}-\underset{\displaystyle :\ddot{F}:}{\overset{\displaystyle :\ddot{F}:}{S}}-\ddot{F}:$

b.

$$:O:$$
$$|$$
$$H-C-H$$

c.

$$H$$
$$|$$
$$H-C=O=H$$
$$|$$
$$H$$

3.89 Which of the following compounds have polar bonds but are nonpolar covalent compounds?
a. CO_2
b. NF_3
c. CF_4

3.90 Which of the following compounds have polar bonds but are nonpolar covalent compounds?
a. SO_2
b. CH_4
c. NH_3

3.91 $BeCl_2$ has an incomplete octet around Be. Draw the Lewis structure of $BeCl_2$.

3.92 SeF_6 has an expanded octet around Se. Draw the Lewis structure of SeF_6.

Properties Based on Electronic Structure and Molecular Geometry
Foundations

3.93 What is the relationship between the polarity of a bond and the polarity of the molecule?

3.94 What effect does polarity have on the solubility of a compound in water?

3.95 What effect does polarity have on the melting point of a pure compound?

3.96 What effect does polarity have on the boiling point of a pure compound?

Applications

3.97 Would you expect KCl to dissolve in water?

3.98 Would you expect ethylamine (Question 3.78) to dissolve in water?

3.99 Rank the following in order of increasing boiling point:

$$N_2, CO, O_2, NaCl$$

3.100 Rank the following in order of increasing melting point:

$$NF_3, NCl_3, PCl_3$$

$$KCl, CO_2, H_2O, H_2$$

CRITICAL THINKING PROBLEMS

1. Predict differences in our global environment that may have arisen if the freezing point and boiling point of water were 20°C higher than they are.

2. Would you expect the compound $C_2S_2H_4$ to exist? Why or why not?

3. Draw the resonance forms of the carbonate ion. What conclusions, based on this exercise, can you draw about the stability of the carbonate ion?

4. Which of the following compounds would be predicted to have the higher boiling point? Explain your reasoning.

$$H \quad H$$
$$| \quad |$$
$$H-C-C-O-H$$
$$| \quad |$$
$$H \quad H$$
Ethanol

$$H \quad H$$
$$| \quad |$$
$$H-C-C-H$$
$$| \quad |$$
$$H \quad H$$
Ethane

5. Why does the octet rule not work well for compounds of lanthanide and actinide elements? Suggest a number other than eight that may be more suitable.

Calculations and the Chemical Equation 4

LEARNING GOALS

1 ▶ Know the relationship between the mole and Avogadro's number, and the usefulness of these quantities.

2 ▶ Perform calculations using Avogadro's number and the mole.

3 ▶ Write chemical formulas for common inorganic substances.

4 ▶ Calculate the formula mass and molar mass of a compound.

5 ▶ Know the major function served by the chemical equation, the basis for chemical calculations.

6 ▶ Classify chemical reactions by type: combination, decomposition, or replacement.

7 ▶ Balance chemical equations given the identity of products and reactants.

8 ▶ Recognize the various classes of chemical reactions: precipitation, reactions with oxygen, acid-base, and oxidation-reduction.

9 ▶ Calculate the number of moles or grams of product resulting from a given number of moles or grams of reactants or the number of moles or grams of reactant needed to produce a certain number of moles or grams of product.

10 ▶ Calculate theoretical and percent yield.

OUTLINE

Careful measurements validate chemical equations.

INTRODUCTION

The calculation of chemical quantities based on chemical equations, termed stoichiometry, is the application of logic and arithmetic to chemical systems to answer questions such as the following:

A pharmaceutical company wishes to manufacture 1000 kilograms (kg) of a product next year. How much of each of the starting materials must be ordered? If the starting materials cost 20 dollars per gram (g), how much money must be budgeted for the project?

We often need to predict the quantity of a product produced from the reaction of a given amount of material. This calculation is possible. It is equally possible to calculate how much of a material would be necessary to produce a desired amount of product.

What is required is a recipe: a procedure to follow. The basis for our recipe is the chemical equation. A properly written chemical equation provides all of the necessary information for the chemical calculation. That critical information is the combining ratio of elements or compounds that must occur to produce a certain amount of product or products.

In this chapter we define the mole (mol), the fundamental unit of measure of chemical arithmetic; learn to write and balance chemical equations; and use these tools to perform calculations of chemical quantities.

4.1 The Mole Concept and Atoms

Atoms are exceedingly small, yet their masses have been experimentally determined for each of the elements. The unit of measurement for these determinations is the **atomic mass unit** (amu):

$$1 \text{ amu} = 1.661 \times 10^{-24} \text{ g}$$

The Mole and Avogadro's Number

The exact value of the amu is defined in relation to a standard, just as the units of the metric system represent defined quantities. The carbon-12 isotope has been chosen and is assigned a mass of exactly 12 amu. Hence this standard reference point defines an amu as exactly one-twelfth the mass of a carbon-12 atom.

The periodic table provides atomic weights in amu. These atomic weights are average values, based on the contribution of all naturally occurring isotopes of the particular element. For example, the average mass of a carbon atom is 12.01 amu and

$$\frac{12.01 \text{ amu C}}{\text{C atom}} \times \frac{1.661 \times 10^{-24} \text{ g C}}{1 \text{ amu C}} = 1.995 \times 10^{-23} \frac{\text{g C}}{\text{C atom}}$$

The average mass of a helium atom is 4.003 amu and

$$\frac{4.003 \text{ amu He}}{\text{He atom}} \times \frac{1.661 \times 10^{-24} \text{ g He}}{1 \text{ amu He}} = 6.649 \times 10^{-24} \frac{\text{g He}}{\text{He atom}}$$

In everyday work, chemists use much larger quantities of matter (typically, g or kg). A more practical unit for defining a "collection" of atoms is the *mol*. The **mole** (mol) is the amount of a substance that contains as many atoms, molecules, or ions as are found in exactly 12 g of the carbon-12 isotope. That number, experimentally determined is **Avogadro's number,** named in honor of the nineteenth-century Italian scientist, Amadeo Avogadro.

Avogadro's number is expressed as:

$$1 \text{ mol of atoms} = 6.022 \times 10^{23} \text{ atoms of an element}$$

The practice of defining a unit for a quantity of small objects is common; a *dozen* eggs, a *ream* of paper, and a *gross* of pencils are well-known examples. Similarly, a mol is 6.022×10^{23} individual units of anything. We could, if we desired, speak of a mol of eggs or a mol of pencils. However, in chemistry we use the mol to represent a specific quantity of atoms, ions, or molecules.

The mol and the amu are related. The atomic mass of an element corresponds to the average mass of a single atom in amu *and* the mass of a mol of atoms in g.

The mass of 1 mol of atoms, in g, is defined as the **molar mass**. Consider this relationship for sodium in Example 4.1.

EXAMPLE 4.1 **Relating Avogadro's Number to Molar Mass**

LEARNING GOAL

2 ▶ Perform calculations using Avogadro's number and the mol.

Calculate the mass, in g, of Avogadro's number of sodium atoms.

Solution

Step 1. The periodic table indicates that the average mass of one sodium atom is 22.99 amu. This may be represented as:

$$\frac{22.99 \text{ amu Na}}{1 \text{ atom Na}}$$

Step 2. In order to answer the question, we must calculate the molar mass in units of g/mol. We need two conversion factors; one to convert amu⟶g and another to convert atoms⟶mol.

Step 3. As previously noted, 1 amu is 1.661×10^{-24} g, and 6.022×10^{23} atoms of sodium is Avogadro's number. These relationships may be written as:

$$1.661 \times 10^{-24} \frac{\text{g Na}}{\text{amu}} \quad \text{and} \quad 6.022 \times 10^{23} \frac{\text{atoms Na}}{\text{mol Na}}$$

Step 4. Representing this information as a series of conversion factors, using the factor-label method, we have

$$22.99 \frac{\text{amu Na}}{\text{atom Na}} \times 1.661 \times 10^{-24} \frac{\text{g Na}}{\text{amu Na}} \times 6.022 \times 10^{23} \frac{\text{atoms Na}}{\text{mol Na}} = 22.99 \frac{\text{g Na}}{\text{mol Na}}$$

Step 5. The average mass of one *atom* of sodium, in units of amu, is *numerically identical* to the mass of *Avogadro's number of atoms*, expressed in units of g. Hence the molar mass of sodium is 22.99 g Na/mol.

Helpful Hint: Section 1.4 discusses the use of conversion factors.

Practice Problem 4.1

Calculate the mass, in g, of Avogadro's number of:

a. aluminum atoms
b. mercury atoms

▶ **For Further Practice: Questions 4.15 and 4.16.**

Figure 4.1 The comparison of approximately 1 mol each of silver (as Morgan and Peace dollars), gold (as Canadian Maple Leaf coins), and copper (as pennies) shows the considerable difference in mass (as well as economic value) of equivalent mol of different substances.

The sodium example is not unique. The relationship holds for every element in the periodic table.

Because Avogadro's number of particles (atoms) is 1 mol, it follows that the average mass of one atom of hydrogen is 1.008 amu and the mass of 1 mol of hydrogen atoms is 1.008 g, or the average mass of one atom of carbon is 12.01 amu and the mass of 1 mol of carbon atoms is 12.01 g.

In fact, 1 mol of atoms of *any element* contains the same number, Avogadro's number, of atoms, 6.022×10^{23} atoms.

The difference in mass of a mol of two different elements can be quite striking (Figure 4.1). For example, a mol of hydrogen atoms is 1.008 g, and a mol of lead atoms is 207.19 g.

Calculating Atoms, Moles, and Mass

Performing calculations based on a chemical equation requires a facility for relating the number of atoms of an element to a corresponding number of mol of that element and ultimately to their mass in g. Such calculations involve the use of conversion factors. The use of conversion factors was first described in Chapter 1. Some examples follow.

LEARNING GOAL

2 ▶ Perform calculations using Avogadro's number and the mol.

EXAMPLE 4.2   Converting Moles to Atoms

How many iron atoms are present in 3.0 mol of iron metal?

Solution

Step 1. The calculation is based on the choice of the appropriate conversion factor. The relationship

$$\frac{6.022 \times 10^{23} \text{ atoms Fe}}{1 \text{ mol Fe}}$$

follows directly from

$$1 \text{ mol Fe} = 6.022 \times 10^{23} \text{ atoms Fe}$$

Step 2. Using this conversion factor, we have

$$\text{number of atoms of Fe} = 3.0 \text{ mol Fe} \times \frac{6.022 \times 10^{23} \text{ atoms Fe}}{1 \text{ mol Fe}}$$

$$= 18 \times 10^{23} \text{ atoms of Fe, or}$$

$$= 1.8 \times 10^{24} \text{ atoms of Fe}$$

Practice Problem 4.2

How many oxygen atoms are present in 2.50 mol of:

a. oxygen atoms
b. oxygen molecules

▶ **For Further Practice: Questions 4.17 and 4.18.**

EXAMPLE 4.3   Converting Atoms to Moles

Calculate the number of mol of sulfur represented by 1.81×10^{24} atoms of sulfur.

Solution

Step 1. Just as in the previous example, the calculation is based on the choice of the appropriate conversion factor. The relationship

$$\frac{1 \text{ mol S}}{6.022 \times 10^{23} \text{ atoms S}}$$

follows directly from

$$1 \text{ mol S} = 6.022 \times 10^{23} \text{ atoms S}$$

Step 2. $1.81 \times 10^{24} \text{ atoms S} \times \dfrac{1 \text{ mol S}}{6.022 \times 10^{23} \text{ atoms S}} = 3.01 \text{ mol S}$

Note that this conversion factor is the inverse of that used in Example 4.2. Remember, the conversion factor must cancel units that should not appear in the final answer.

Practice Problem 4.3

How many mol of sodium are represented by 9.03×10^{23} atoms of sodium?

▶ **For Further Practice: Questions 4.19 and 4.20.**

EXAMPLE 4.4 Converting Moles of a Substance to Mass in Grams

What is the mass, in g, of 3.01 mol of sulfur?

LEARNING GOAL

2 ▶ Perform calculations using Avogadro's number and the mol.

Solution

Step 1. We know from the periodic table that 1 mol of sulfur has a mass of 32.06 g. Setting up a suitable conversion factor between g and mol results in

Step 2. $$\frac{32.06 \text{ g S}}{1 \text{ mol S}}$$

which is based on:

$$1 \text{ mol S} = 32.06 \text{ g S}$$

Step 3. Using this conversion factor (ensuring that the units *mol S* cancel):

$$3.01 \text{ mol S} \times \frac{32.06 \text{ g S}}{1 \text{ mol S}} = 96.5 \text{ g S}$$

Practice Problem 4.4

What is the mass, in g, of 3.50 mol of the element helium?

▶ **For Further Practice: Questions 4.21 and 4.22.**

The following examples demonstrate the use of a sequence of conversion factors to proceed from the information *provided* in the problem to the information *requested* by the problem.

EXAMPLE 4.5   Converting Grams to Number of Atoms

Calculate the number of atoms of sulfur in 1.00 g of sulfur.

Solution

It is generally useful to map out a pattern for the required conversion. We are given the number of grams and need the number of atoms that correspond to that mass.

Begin by "tracing a path" to the answer:

$$\text{grams sulfur} \xrightarrow{\text{Step 1}} \text{moles sulfur} \xrightarrow{\text{Step 2}} \text{atoms sulfur}$$

Two transformations, or conversions, are required:

Step 1. Convert g to mol.

Step 2. Convert mol to atoms.

To perform step 1, we could consider either

$$\frac{1 \text{ mol S}}{32.06 \text{ g S}} \quad \text{or} \quad \frac{32.06 \text{ g S}}{1 \text{ mol S}}$$

If we want g to cancel, $\dfrac{1 \text{ mol S}}{32.06 \text{ g S}}$ is the correct choice, resulting in

$$g\,S \times \frac{1 \text{ mol S}}{32.06 \text{ g S}} = \text{value in mol S}$$

To perform step 2, the conversion of mol to atoms, the mol of S must cancel; therefore

$$\text{mol S} \times \frac{6.022 \times 10^{23} \text{ atom S}}{1 \text{ mol S}} = \text{number of atoms S}$$

which are the units necessary for the solution. Combining step 1 and step 2 we have

$$1.00 \text{ g S} \times \frac{1 \text{ mol S}}{32.06 \text{ g S}} \times \frac{6.022 \times 10^{23} \text{ atoms S}}{1 \text{ mol S}} = 1.88 \times 10^{22} \text{ atoms S}$$

Practice Problem 4.5

How many oxygen atoms are present in 40.0 g of oxygen molecules?

▶ **For Further Practice: Questions 4.29 and 4.30.**

EXAMPLE 4.6   Converting Kilograms to Moles

Calculate the number of mol of sulfur in 1.00 kg of sulfur.

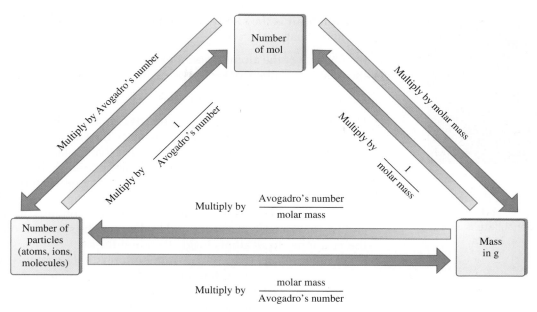

Figure 4.2 Interconversion between numbers of mol, particles, and g. The mol concept is central to chemical calculations involving measured quantities of matter.

Solution

Using the strategy developed in Example 4.5

$$1.00 \ \text{kg S} \times \frac{10^3 \ \text{g S}}{1 \ \text{kg S}} \times \frac{1 \ \text{mol S}}{32.06 \ \text{g S}} = 31.2 \ \text{mol S}$$

Practice Problem 4.6

Calculate the number of mol of silver in a silver ring that has a mass of 3.42 g.

▶ **For Further Practice: Questions 4.25 and 4.26.**

The conversion between the three principal measures of quantity of matter—the number of g (mass), the number of mol, and the number of individual particles (atoms, ions, or molecules)—is essential to the art of problem solving in chemistry. Their interrelationship is depicted in Figure 4.2.

Question 4.1 What is the mass, in g, of 1.00×10^{12} mercury (Hg) atoms?

Question 4.2 How many mol of lead (Pb) atoms are equivalent to six billion lead atoms?

4.2 The Chemical Formula, Formula Mass, and Molar Mass

The Chemical Formula

Compounds are pure substances. They are composed of two or more elements that are chemically combined. A **chemical formula** is a combination of symbols of the various elements that make up the compound. It serves as a convenient way to represent a compound. The chemical formula is based on the formula unit.

LEARNING GOAL

3 ▶ Write chemical formulas for common inorganic substances.

(a)   **(b)**

Figure 4.3 The marked difference in color of (a) hydrated, and (b) anhydrous copper sulfate is clear evidence that they are, in fact, different compounds.

Determination of Composition and Formulas of Compounds

It is possible to determine the correct molecular formula of a compound from experimental data.

LEARNING GOAL

4 ▶ Calculate the formula mass and molar mass of a compound.

The **formula unit** is the smallest collection of atoms that provides two important pieces of information:

- the identity of the atoms present in the compound and
- the relative numbers of each type of atom.

Let's look at the following formulas:

- *Hydrogen gas*, H_2. This indicates that two atoms of hydrogen are chemically bonded forming diatomic hydrogen, hence the subscript two.
- *Water*, H_2O. Water is composed of molecules that contain two atoms of hydrogen (subscript two) and one atom of oxygen (lack of a subscript means *one* atom).
- *Sodium chloride*, NaCl. One atom of sodium and one atom of chlorine combine to make sodium chloride.
- *Calcium hydroxide*, $Ca(OH)_2$. Calcium hydroxide contains one atom of calcium and two atoms each of oxygen and hydrogen. The subscript outside the parentheses applies to *all* atoms inside the parentheses.
- *Ammonium sulfate*, $(NH_4)_2SO_4$. Ammonium sulfate contains two ammonium ions (NH_4^+) and one sulfate ion (SO_4^{2-}). Each ammonium ion contains one nitrogen and four hydrogen atoms. The formula shows that ammonium sulfate contains two nitrogen atoms, eight hydrogen atoms, one sulfur atom, and four oxygen atoms.
- *Copper(II) sulfate pentahydrate*, $CuSO_4 \cdot 5H_2O$. This is an example of a compound that has water in its structure. Compounds containing one or more water molecules as an integral part of their structure are termed **hydrates.** Copper sulfate pentahydrate has five units of water (or ten H atoms and five O atoms) in addition to one copper atom, one sulfur atom, and four oxygen atoms for a total atomic composition of:

> 1 copper atom
> 1 sulfur atom
> 9 oxygen atoms
> 10 hydrogen atoms

Note that the symbol for water is preceded by a dot, indicating that, although the water is a formula unit capable of standing alone, in this case it is a part of a larger structure. Copper sulfate also exists as a structure free of water, $CuSO_4$. This form is described as anhydrous (no water) copper sulfate. The physical and chemical properties of a hydrate often differ markedly from the anhydrous form (Figure 4.3).

Formula Mass and Molar Mass

Just as the atomic mass of an element is the average atomic mass for one atom of the naturally occurring element, expressed in amu, the **formula mass** of a compound is the sum of the atomic masses of all atoms in the compound, as represented by its formula. To calculate the formula mass of a compound we *must* know the correct formula. The formula mass is expressed in amu.

When working in the laboratory, we do not deal with individual molecules; instead, we use units of mol or g. Eighteen grams of water (less than 1 ounce (oz)) contain approximately Avogadro's number of molecules (6.022×10^{23} molecules). Defining our working units as mol and g makes good chemical sense.

We earlier concluded that the atomic mass of an element in amu from the periodic table corresponds to the mass of a mol of atoms of that element in units of g/mol. It follows that *molar mass*, the mass of a mol of compound, is numerically equal to the formula mass in amu.

In Example 4.8, Na_2SO_4 is an ionic compound. As we have seen, it is not technically correct to describe ionic compounds as molecules; similarly, the term *molecular mass* is not appropriate for Na_2SO_4. The term *formula mass* may be used to describe the formula unit of a substance, whether it is made up of ions,

EXAMPLE 4.7 Calculating Formula Mass and Molar Mass

Calculate the formula mass and molar mass of water, H_2O.

LEARNING GOAL

4 ▶ Calculate the formula mass and molar mass of a compound.

Solution

Step 1. Each water molecule contains two hydrogen atoms and one oxygen atom.

Step 2. The formula mass is

$$\begin{array}{ll} \text{2 atoms of hydrogen} \times 1.008 \text{ amu/atom} = & 2.016 \text{ amu} \\ \underline{\text{1 atom of oxygen} \quad\;\; \times 16.00 \text{ amu/atom} = 16.00 \;\; \text{amu}} \\ 18.02 \;\; \text{amu} \end{array}$$

Step 3. The average mass of a single molecule of H_2O is 18.02 amu and is the formula mass. Therefore the mass of a mol of H_2O is 18.02 g or 18.02 g/mol.

Helpful Hint: Adding 2.016 and 16.00 shows a result of 18.016 on your calculator. Proper use of significant figures (Chapter 1) dictates rounding that result to 18.02.

Practice Problem 4.7

Calculate the formula mass and molar mass of NH_3 (ammonia).

▶ **For Further Practice: Questions 4.33 and 4.34.**

EXAMPLE 4.8 Calculating Formula Mass and Molar Mass

Calculate the formula mass and molar mass of sodium sulfate.

Solution

Step 1. The sodium ion is Na^+, and the sulfate ion is SO_4^{2-}. Two sodium ions must be present to neutralize the negative charges on the sulfate ion. The formula is Na_2SO_4. Sodium sulfate contains two sodium atoms, one sulfur atom, and four oxygen atoms.

Step 2. The formula mass is

$$\begin{array}{ll} \text{2 atoms of sodium} \times 22.99 \text{ amu/atom} = & 45.98 \text{ amu} \\ \text{1 atom of sulfur} \quad \times 32.06 \text{ amu/atom} = & 32.06 \text{ amu} \\ \underline{\text{4 atoms of oxygen} \times 16.00 \text{ amu/atom} = 64.00 \text{ amu}} \\ 142.04 \text{ amu} \end{array}$$

Step 3. The average mass of a single unit of Na_2SO_4 is 142.04 amu and is the formula mass. Therefore the mass of a mol of Na_2SO_4 is 142.04 g, or 142.04 g/mol.

Practice Problem 4.8

Calculate the formula mass and molar mass of $C_6H_{12}O_6$ (a sugar, glucose).

▶ **For Further Practice: Questions 4.35 and 4.36.**

ion pairs, or molecules. We shall use the term *formula mass* in a general way to represent each of these species.

Figure 4.4 illustrates the difference between molecules and ion pairs.

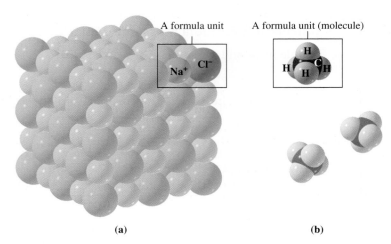

Figure 4.4 Formula units of (a) sodium chloride, an ionic compound, and (b) methane, a covalent compound.

EXAMPLE 4.9 Calculating Formula Mass and Molar Mass

Calculate the formula mass and molar mass of calcium phosphate.

Solution

Step 1. The calcium ion is Ca^{2+}, and the phosphate ion is PO_4^{3-}. To form a neutral unit, three Ca^{2+} must combine with two PO_4^{3-}; $[3 \times (+2)]$ calcium ion charges are balanced by $[2 \times (-3)]$ phosphate ion charges.

Step 2. Thus, for calcium phosphate, $Ca_3(PO_4)_2$, the subscript two for phosphate dictates that there are two phosphorus atoms and eight oxygen atoms (2×4) in the formula unit.

Step 3. Therefore

$$
\begin{array}{lcl}
\text{3 atoms of Ca} \times 40.08 \text{ amu/atom} & = & 120.24 \text{ amu} \\
\text{2 atoms of P } \times 30.97 \text{ amu/atom} & = & 61.94 \text{ amu} \\
\underline{\text{8 atoms of O } \times 16.00 \text{ amu/atom}} & = & \underline{128.00 \text{ amu}} \\
& & 310.18 \text{ amu}
\end{array}
$$

Step 4. The formula mass of calcium phosphate is 310.18 amu, and the molar mass is 310.18 g/mol.

Practice Problem 4.9

Calculate the formula mass and molar mass of $CoCl_2 \cdot 6H_2O$ (cobalt chloride hexahydrate).

▶ **For Further Practice: Questions 4.37 and 4.38.**

Question 4.3 Caffeine occurs naturally in coffee and tea, and is present in many soft drinks. The formula of caffeine is $C_8H_{10}N_4O_2$. Calculate the formula mass and molar mass of caffeine.

Question 4.4 The formula of ascorbic acid, commonly known as vitamin C, is $C_6H_8O_6$. Calculate the formula mass and molar mass of vitamin C.

4.3 The Chemical Equation and the Information It Conveys

A Recipe for Chemical Change

The **chemical equation** is the shorthand notation for a chemical reaction. It describes all of the substances that react and all the products that form. **Reactants,** or starting materials, are all substances that undergo change in a chemical reaction; **products** are substances produced by a chemical reaction.

The chemical equation also describes the physical state of the reactants and products as solid, liquid, or gas. It tells us whether the reaction occurs and identifies the solvent and experimental conditions employed, such as heat, light, or electrical energy added to the system.

Most important, the relative number of mol of reactants and products appears in the equation. According to the **law of conservation of mass,** matter cannot be either gained or lost in the process of a chemical reaction. The total mass of the products must be equal to the total mass of the reactants. In other words, the law of conservation of mass tells us that we must have a balanced chemical equation.

LEARNING GOAL

5 ▶ Know the major function served by the chemical equation, the basis for chemical calculations.

Animation
• Conservation of Mass

Features of a Chemical Equation

Consider the decomposition of calcium carbonate:

$$CaCO_3(s) \xrightarrow{\Delta} CaO(s) + CO_2(g)$$

Calcium carbonate   Calcium oxide   Carbon dioxide

This equation reads: One mole of solid calcium carbonate decomposes upon heating to produce one mole of solid calcium oxide and one mole of gaseous carbon dioxide.

The factors involved in writing equations of this type are described as follows:

1. *The identity of products and reactants must be specified using chemical symbols.* In some cases it is possible to predict the products of a reaction. More often, the reactants and products must be verified by chemical analysis. (Generally, you will be given information regarding the identity of the reactants and products.)
2. *Reactants are written to the left of the reaction arrow (→), and products are written to the right.* The direction in which the arrow points indicates the direction in which the reaction proceeds. In the decomposition of calcium carbonate, the reactant on the left ($CaCO_3$) is converted to products on the right ($CaO + CO_2$) during the course of the reaction.
3. *The physical states of reactants and products may be shown in parentheses.* For example:
   • $Cl_2(g)$ means that chlorine is in the gaseous state.
   • $Mg(s)$ indicates that magnesium is a solid.
   • $Br_2(l)$ indicates that bromine is present as a liquid.
   • $NH_3(aq)$ tells us that ammonia is present as an aqueous solution (dissolved in water).
4. *The symbol Δ over the reaction arrow means that energy is necessary for the reaction to occur.* Often this and other special conditions are noted above or below the reaction arrow. For example, "light" means that a light source provides energy necessary for the reaction. Such reactions are termed photochemical reactions.
5. *The equation must be balanced.* All of the atoms of every reactant must also appear in the products, although in different compounds. We will treat this topic in detail later in this chapter.

According to the factors outlined, the equation for the decomposition of calcium carbonate may now be written as

$$CaCO_3(s) \xrightarrow{\Delta} CaO(s) + CO_2(g)$$

See discussion of acid-base reactions in Chapter 8.

See A Medical Perspective: Hot and Cold Packs in Chapter 7.

The Experimental Basis of a Chemical Equation

The chemical equation must represent a chemical change: One or more substances are changed into new substances, with different chemical and physical properties. Evidence for the reaction may be based on observations such as

- the release of carbon dioxide gas when an acid is added to a carbonate,
- the formation of a solid (or precipitate) when solutions of iron ions and hydroxide ions are mixed,
- the production of heat when using hot packs for treatment of injury, and
- the change in color of a solution upon addition of a second substance.

Many reactions are not so obvious. Sophisticated instruments are now available to the chemist. These instruments allow the detection of subtle changes in chemical systems that would otherwise go unnoticed. Such instruments may measure

- heat or light absorbed or emitted as the result of a reaction,
- changes in the way the sample behaves in an electric or magnetic field before and after a reaction, and
- changes in electrical properties before and after a reaction.

Whether we use our senses or a million-dollar computerized instrument, the "bottom line" is the same: We are measuring a change in one or more chemical or physical properties in an effort to understand the changes taking place in a chemical system.

Disease can be described as a chemical system (actually a biochemical system) gone awry. Here, too, the underlying changes may not be obvious. Just as technology has helped chemists see subtle chemical changes in the laboratory, medical diagnosis has been revolutionized in our lifetimes using very similar technology. Some of these techniques are described in A Medical Perspective: Magnetic Resonance Imaging, in Chapter 9.

Strategies for Writing Chemical Equations

LEARNING GOAL

6 ▸ Classify chemical reactions by type: combination, decomposition, or replacement.

Chemical reactions, whether they involve the formation of precipitate, reaction with oxygen, acids and bases, or oxidation-reduction, generally follow one of a few simple patterns: combination, decomposition, and single- or double-replacement. Recognizing the underlying pattern will improve your ability to write chemical equations and understand chemical reactions.

Combination Reactions

Combination reactions involve the joining of two or more elements or compounds, producing a product of different composition. The general form of a combination reaction is

$$A + B \longrightarrow AB$$

in which A and B represent reactant elements or compounds and AB is the product.

Examples include

1. combination of a metal and a nonmetal to form a salt,

$$Ca(s) + Cl_2(g) \longrightarrow CaCl_2(s)$$

2. combination of hydrogen and chlorine molecules to produce hydrogen chloride,

$$H_2(g) + Cl_2(g) \longrightarrow 2HCl(g)$$

3. formation of water from hydrogen and oxygen molecules,

$$2H_2(g) + O_2(g) \longrightarrow 2H_2O(g)$$

4. reaction of magnesium oxide and carbon dioxide to produce magnesium carbonate,

$$MgO(s) + CO_2(g) \longrightarrow MgCO_3(s)$$

Decomposition Reactions

Decomposition reactions produce two or more products from a single reactant. The general form of these reactions is the reverse of a combination reaction:

$$AB \longrightarrow A + B$$

Some examples are

1. the heating of calcium carbonate to produce calcium oxide and carbon dioxide,

$$CaCO_3(s) \longrightarrow CaO(s) + CO_2(g)$$

2. the removal of water from a hydrated material (a *hydrate* is a substance that has water molecules incorporated in its structure),

$$CuSO_4 \cdot 5H_2O(s) \longrightarrow CuSO_4(s) + 5H_2O(g)$$

Hydrated compounds are described on page 128.

Replacement Reactions

Replacement reactions include both *single-replacement* and *double-replacement*. In a **single-replacement reaction,** one atom replaces another in the compound, producing a new compound:

$$A + BC \longrightarrow AC + B$$

Examples include

1. the replacement of copper by zinc in copper sulfate,

$$Zn(s) + CuSO_4(aq) \longrightarrow ZnSO_4(aq) + Cu(s)$$

2. the replacement of aluminum by sodium in aluminum nitrate,

$$3Na(s) + Al(NO_3)_3(aq) \longrightarrow 3NaNO_3(aq) + Al(s)$$

A **double-replacement reaction,** on the other hand, involves *two compounds* undergoing a "change of partners." Two compounds react by exchanging atoms to produce two new compounds:

$$AB + CD \longrightarrow AD + CB$$

Examples include

1. the reaction of an acid (hydrochloric acid) and a base (sodium hydroxide) to produce water and salt, sodium chloride,

$$HCl(aq) + NaOH(aq) \longrightarrow H_2O(l) + NaCl(aq)$$

2. the formation of solid barium sulfate from barium chloride and potassium sulfate,

$$BaCl_2(aq) + K_2SO_4(aq) \longrightarrow BaSO_4(s) + 2KCl(aq)$$

Question 4.5 Classify each of the following reactions as decomposition (D), combination (C), single-replacement (SR), or double-replacement (DR):

a. $HNO_3(aq) + KOH(aq) \longrightarrow KNO_3(aq) + H_2O(aq)$

b. $Al(s) + 3NiNO_3(aq) \longrightarrow Al(NO_3)_3(aq) + 3Ni(s)$

c. $KCN(aq) + HCl(aq) \longrightarrow HCN(aq) + KCl(aq)$

d. $MgCO_3(s) \longrightarrow MgO(s) + CO_2(g)$

Question 4.6 Classify each of the following reactions as decomposition (D), combination (C), single-replacement (SR), or double-replacement (DR):

a. $2Al(OH)_3(s) \xrightarrow{\Delta} Al_2O_3(s) + 3H_2O(g)$

b. $Fe_2S_3(s) \xrightarrow{\Delta} 2Fe(s) + 3S(s)$

c. $Na_2CO_3(aq) + BaCl_2(aq) \longrightarrow BaCO_3(s) + 2NaCl(aq)$

d. $C(s) + O_2(g) \xrightarrow{\Delta} CO_2(g)$

4.4 Chemical Equations Represent Chemical Change

The chemical equation shows the *molar quantity* of reactants needed to produce a certain *molar quantity* of products.

Balancing Chemical Equations

The relative number of mol of each product and reactant is indicated by placing a whole-number *coefficient* before the formula of each substance in the chemical equation. A coefficient of two (for example, 2NaCl) indicates that 2 mol of sodium chloride are involved in the reaction. Also, $3NH_3$ signifies 3 mol of ammonia; it means that 3 mol of nitrogen atoms and 3×3, or 9, mol of hydrogen atoms are involved in the reaction. The coefficient one is understood, not written. Therefore H_2SO_4 would be interpreted as 1 mol of sulfuric acid, or 2 mol of hydrogen atoms, 1 mol of sulfur atoms, and 4 mol of oxygen atoms.

The equation

$$CaCO_3(s) \xrightarrow{\Delta} CaO(s) + CO_2(g)$$

is balanced as written. On the reactant side we have

    1 mol Ca

    1 mol C

    3 mol O

On the product side there are

    1 mol Ca

    1 mol C

    3 mol O

Animation

• Conservation of Mass

Therefore the law of conservation of mass is obeyed, and the equation is balanced as written.

Now consider the reaction of aqueous hydrogen chloride with solid calcium metal in aqueous solution:

$$HCl(aq) + Ca(s) \longrightarrow CaCl_2(aq) + H_2(g)$$

The equation, as written, is not balanced.

Reactants	Products
1 mol H atoms	2 mol H atoms
1 mol Cl atoms	2 mol Cl atoms
1 mol Ca atoms	1 mol Ca atoms

We need 2 mol of both H and Cl on the left, or reactant, side. An *incorrect* way of balancing the equation is as follows:

$$H_2Cl_2(aq) + Ca(s) \longrightarrow CaCl_2(aq) + H_2(g)$$
NOT a correct equation

The equation satisfies the law of conservation of mass; however, we have altered one of the reacting species. Hydrogen chloride is HCl, not H_2Cl_2. We must remember that *we cannot alter any chemical substance in the process of balancing the equation.* We can *only* introduce coefficients into the equation. Changing subscripts changes the identity of the chemicals involved, and that is not permitted. The equation must represent the reaction accurately. The correct equation is

$$2HCl(aq) + Ca(s) \longrightarrow CaCl_2(aq) + H_2(g)$$
Correct equation

This process is illustrated in Figure 4.5.

Many equations are balanced by trial and error. After the identity of the products and reactants, the physical states, and the reaction conditions are known, the following steps provide a method for correctly balancing a chemical equation:

Step 1. Count the number of mol of atoms of each element on both product and reactant side.

Step 2. Determine which elements are not balanced.

Step 3. Balance one element at a time using coefficients.

Step 4. After you believe that you have successfully balanced the equation, check, as in step 1, to be certain that mass conservation has been achieved.

Coefficients placed in front of the formula indicate the relative numbers of mol of compound (represented by the formula) that are involved in the reaction. Subscripts placed to the lower right of the atomic symbol indicate the relative number of atoms in the compound.

Water (H_2O) and hydrogen peroxide (H_2O_2) illustrate the effect a subscript can have. The two compounds show marked differences in physical and chemical properties.

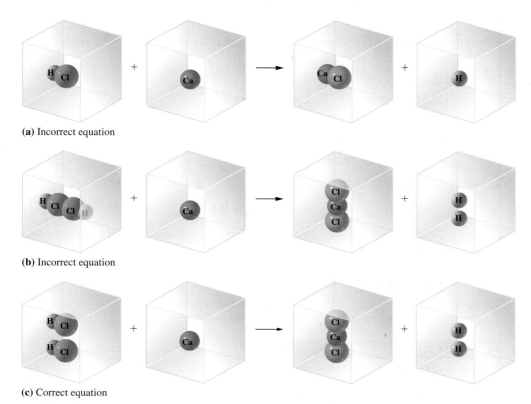

(a) Incorrect equation

(b) Incorrect equation

(c) Correct equation

Figure 4.5 Balancing the equation HCl + Ca $\longrightarrow$ CaCl₂ + H₂. (a) Neither product is the correct chemical species. (b) The reactant, HCl, is incorrectly represented as H_2Cl_2. (c) This equation is correct; all species are correct, and the law of conservation of mass is obeyed.

Let us apply these steps to the reaction of calcium with aqueous hydrogen chloride:

$$HCl(aq) + Ca(s) \longrightarrow CaCl_2(aq) + H_2(g)$$

Step 1.   **Reactants**   **Products**

1 mol H atoms   2 mol H atoms

1 mol Cl atoms   2 mol Cl atoms

1 mol Ca atoms   1 mol Ca atoms

Step 2.   The numbers of mol of H and Cl are not balanced.

Step 3.   Insertion of a 2 before HCl on the reactant side should balance the equation:

$$2HCl(aq) + Ca(s) \longrightarrow CaCl_2(aq) + H_2(g)$$

Step 4.   Check for mass balance:

Reactants   **Products**

2 mol H atoms   2 mol H atoms

2 mol Cl atoms   2 mol Cl atoms

1 mol Ca atoms   1 mol Ca atoms

Hence the equation is balanced.

LEARNING GOAL

7 ▶ Balance chemical equations given the identity of products and reactants.

EXAMPLE 4.10   Balancing Equations

Balance the following equation: Hydrogen gas and oxygen gas react explosively to produce gaseous water.

Solution

Recall that hydrogen and oxygen are diatomic gases; therefore

$$H_2(g) + O_2(g) \longrightarrow H_2O(g)$$

Step 1.   Count the number of mol of atoms of each element on both product and reactant side.

Reactants   **Products**

2 mol H atoms   2 mol H atoms

2 mol O atoms   1 mol O atoms

Step 2.   Note that the mol of hydrogen atoms are balanced but that the mol of oxygen atoms are not.

Step 3.   We must first balance the mol of oxygen atoms. Insert 2 before H_2O.

$$H_2(g) + O_2(g) \longrightarrow 2H_2O(g)$$

Balancing mol of oxygen atoms creates an imbalance in the number of mol of hydrogen atoms, so

$$2H_2(g) + O_2(g) \longrightarrow 2H_2O(g)$$

Step 4.   The equation is balanced, with 4 mol of hydrogen atoms and 2 mol of oxygen atoms on each side of the reaction arrow.

Practice Problem 4.10

Balance the chemical equation: $Fe(s) + O_2(g) \longrightarrow Fe_2O_3(s)$

▶ **For Further Practice: Questions 4.67 and 4.68.**

EXAMPLE 4.11 Balancing Equations

Balance the following equation: Propane gas, C_3H_8, a fuel, reacts with oxygen gas to produce carbon dioxide and water vapor. The reaction is

$$C_3H_8(g) + O_2(g) \longrightarrow CO_2(g) + H_2O(g)$$

Solution

Step 1. Count the number of mol of atoms of each element on both product and reactant side.

Reactants	Products
3 mol C atoms	1 mol C atoms
8 mol H atoms	2 mol H atoms
2 mol O atoms	3 mol O atoms

Step 2. Note that C, H, and O atoms are not balanced.

Step 3. First, balance the carbon atoms; there are 3 mol of carbon atoms on the left and only 1 mol of carbon atoms on the right. We need $3CO_2$ on the right side of the equation:

$$C_3H_8(g) + O_2(g) \longrightarrow 3CO_2(g) + H_2O(g)$$

Next, balance the hydrogen atoms; there are 2 mol of hydrogen atoms on the right and 8 mol of hydrogen atoms on the left. We need $4H_2O$ on the right:

$$C_3H_8(g) + O_2(g) \longrightarrow 3CO_2(g) + 4H_2O(g)$$

There are now 10 mol of oxygen atoms on the right and 2 mol of oxygen atoms on the left. To balance, we must have $5O_2$ on the left side of the equation:

$$C_3H_8(g) + 5O_2(g) \longrightarrow 3CO_2(g) + 4H_2O(g)$$

Step 4. *Remember:* In every case, be sure to check the final equation for mass balance.

Practice Problem 4.11

Balance the chemical equation:

$$C_2H_5OH(l) + O_2(g) \longrightarrow CO_2(g) + H_2O(g)$$

▶ **For Further Practice: Questions 4.69 and 4.70.**

EXAMPLE 4.12 Balancing Equations

Balance the following equation: Butane gas, C_4H_{10}, a fuel used in pocket lighters, reacts with oxygen gas to produce carbon dioxide and water vapor. The reaction is

$$C_4H_{10}(g) + O_2(g) \longrightarrow CO_2(g) + H_2O(g)$$

LEARNING GOAL

7 ▶ Balance chemical equations given the identity of products and reactants.

Continued—

Solution

Step 1. Count the number of mol of atoms of each element on both product and reactant side.

Reactants	Products
4 mol C atoms	1 mol C atoms
10 mol H atoms	2 mol H atoms
2 mol O atoms	3 mol O atoms

Step 2. Note that C, H, and O atoms are not balanced.

Step 3. First, balance the carbon atoms; there are 4 mol of carbon atoms on the left and only 1 mol of carbon atoms on the right:

$$C_4H_{10}(g) + O_2(g) \longrightarrow 4CO_2(g) + H_2O(g)$$

Next, balance hydrogen atoms; there are 10 mol of hydrogen atoms on the left and only 2 mol of hydrogen atoms on the right:

$$C_4H_{10}(g) + O_2(g) \longrightarrow 4CO_2(g) + 5H_2O(g)$$

There are now 13 mol of oxygen atoms on the right and only 2 mol of oxygen atoms on the left. Therefore a coefficient of 6.5 is necessary for O_2.

$$C_4H_{10}(g) + 6.5O_2(g) \longrightarrow 4CO_2(g) + 5H_2O(g)$$

Fractional or decimal coefficients are often needed and used. However, the preferred form requires all integer coefficients. Multiplying each term in the equation by a suitable integer (2, in this case) satisfies this requirement. Hence

$$2C_4H_{10}(g) + 13O_2(g) \longrightarrow 8CO_2(g) + 10H_2O(g)$$

Step 4. The equation is balanced, with 8 mol of carbon atoms, 20 mol of hydrogen atoms, and 26 mol of oxygen atoms on each side of the reaction arrow.

Helpful Hint: When balancing equations, it is often most efficient to begin by balancing the atoms in the most complicated formulas.

Practice Problem 4.12

Balance the chemical equation: $C_6H_6(l) + O_2(g) \longrightarrow CO_2(g) + H_2O(g)$

▶ **For Further Practice: Questions 4.71 and 4.72.**

EXAMPLE 4.13   Balancing Equations

Balance the following equation: Aqueous ammonium sulfate reacts with aqueous lead nitrate to produce aqueous ammonium nitrate and solid lead sulfate. The reaction is

$$(NH_4)_2SO_4(aq) + Pb(NO_3)_2(aq) \longrightarrow NH_4NO_3(aq) + PbSO_4(s)$$

Solution

In this case the polyatomic ions remain as intact units. Therefore we can balance them as we would balance molecules rather than as atoms.

There are two ammonium ions on the left and only one ammonium ion on the right. Hence

$$(NH_4)_2SO_4(aq) + Pb(NO_3)_2(aq) \longrightarrow 2NH_4NO_3(aq) + PbSO_4(s)$$

No further steps are necessary. The equation is now balanced. There are two ammonium ions, two nitrate ions, one lead ion, and one sulfate ion on each side of the reaction arrow.

Practice Problem 4.13

Balance the chemical equation:

$$S_2Cl_2(s) + NH_3(g) \longrightarrow N_4S_4(s) + NH_4Cl(s) + S_8(s)$$

▶ **For Further Practice: Questions 4.73 and 4.74.**

Classifying Chemical Reactions

The most commonly encountered chemical reactions involve:

- the combination of soluble ions to produce an insoluble solid, a *precipitate*
- the reaction of a substance with oxygen, *oxidation,* to produce a new substance
- the reaction of acids and bases involving the transfer of hydrogen ions
- the transfer of one or more electrons from one reactant to another, *oxidation-reduction*

Animations
- Types of Reactions
- Predicting Precipitation Reactions

Precipitation Reactions

Precipitation reactions include any chemical change in solution that results in one or more insoluble product(s). For aqueous solution reactions the product is insoluble in water.

An understanding of precipitation reactions is useful in many ways. They may explain natural phenomena, such as the formation of stalagmites and stalactites in caves; these are simply precipitates in rocklike form. Kidney stones may result from the precipitation of calcium oxalate (CaC_2O_4). The routine act of preparing a solution requires that none of the solutes will react to form a precipitate.

How do you know whether a precipitate will form? Readily available solubility tables, such as Table 4.1, make prediction rather easy.

LEARNING GOAL

8 ▶ Recognize the various classes of chemical reactions: precipitation, reactions with oxygen, acid-base, and oxidation-reduction.

Precipitation reactions may be written as net ionic equations. See page 141.

Table 4.1 Solubilities of Some Common Ionic Compounds

Soluble Compounds	Exceptions
Compounds containing alkali metal ions (Li^+, Na^+, K^+, Rb^+, Cs^+) and the ammonium ion (NH_4^+)	
Nitrates (NO_3^-), bicarbonates (HCO_3^-), and chlorates (ClO_3^-)	
Halides (Cl^-, Br^-, I^-)	Halides of Ag^+, Hg_2^{2+}, and Pb^{2+}
Sulfates (SO_4^{2-})	Sulfates of Ag^+, Ca^{2+}, Sr^{2+}, Ba^{2+}, Hg_2^{2+}, and Pb^{2+}

Insoluble Compounds	Exceptions
Carbonates (CO_3^{2-}), phosphates (PO_4^{3-}), chromates (CrO_4^{2-}), and sulfides (S^{2-})	Compounds containing alkali metal ions and the ammonium ion
Hydroxides (OH^-)	Compounds containing alkali metal ions and the Ba^{2+} ion

The following example illustrates the process.

EXAMPLE 4.14   Predicting Whether Precipitation Will Occur

Will a precipitate form if two solutions of the soluble salts NaCl and $AgNO_3$ are mixed?

Solution

Step 1. Two soluble salts, if they react to form a precipitate, will probably "exchange partners":

$$NaCl(aq) + AgNO_3(aq) \longrightarrow AgCl(?) + NaNO_3(?)$$

Step 2. Refer to Table 4.1 to determine the solubility of AgCl and $NaNO_3$. We predict that $NaNO_3$ is soluble and AgCl is not:

$$NaCl(aq) + AgNO_3(aq) \longrightarrow AgCl(s) + NaNO_3(aq)$$

Step 3. The fact that the solid AgCl is predicted to form classifies this double-replacement reaction as a precipitation reaction.

Helpful Hints: (aq) indicates a soluble species; (s) indicates a solid, an insoluble species.

Practice Problem 4.14

Predict whether the following reactants, when mixed in aqueous solution, undergo a precipitation reaction. Write a balanced equation for each precipitation reaction.

 a. potassium chloride and silver nitrate
 b. potassium acetate and silver nitrate
 c. sodium hydroxide and ammonium chloride
 d. sodium hydroxide and iron(II) chloride

▶ **For Further Practice: Questions 4.77 and 4.78.**

Animations
• Precipitation of Barium Sulfate
• Precipitation of Lead Iodide

Formation of a precipitate, $BaSO_4$.

Some reactions of metals with oxygen are very rapid. A dramatic example is the reaction of magnesium with oxygen.

$$2Mg(s) + O_2(g) \longrightarrow 2MgO(s)$$

Reactions with Oxygen

Many substances react with oxygen. These reactions generally release energy. The combustion of gasoline is used for transportation. Fossil fuel combustion is used to heat homes and provide energy for industry. Reactions involving oxygen provide energy for all sorts of biochemical processes.

When organic (carbon-containing) compounds react with the oxygen in air (burning), carbon dioxide is usually produced. If the compound contains hydrogen, water is the other product.

The reaction between oxygen and methane, CH_4, the major component of natural gas, is

$$CH_4(g) + 2O_2(g) \longrightarrow CO_2(g) + 2H_2O(g)$$

CO_2 and H_2O are waste products, and CO_2 may contribute to the greenhouse effect and global warming. The really important, unseen product is heat energy. That is why we use this reaction in our furnaces!

Inorganic substances also react with oxygen and produce heat, but these reactions usually proceed more slowly. *Corrosion* (rusting iron) is a familiar example:

$$4Fe(s) + 3O_2(g) \longrightarrow 2Fe_2O_3(s)$$
$$\text{Rust}$$

Acid-Base Reactions

Another approach to the classification of chemical reactions is based on the gain or loss of hydrogen ions. **Acid-base reactions** involve the transfer of a *hydrogen ion,* H^+, from one reactant (the acid) to another (the base).

A common example of an acid-base reaction involves hydrochloric acid and sodium hydroxide:

$$\underset{\text{Acid}}{HCl(aq)} + \underset{\text{Base}}{NaOH(aq)} \longrightarrow \underset{\text{Water}}{H_2O(l)} + \underset{\text{Salt}}{Na^+(aq) + Cl^-(aq)}$$

A hydrogen ion is transferred from the acid to the base, producing water and a salt in solution. Acid and base properties and reactions are important in virtually all aspects of chemistry and biochemistry; for this reason, they are considered in much greater detail in Chapter 8.

Oxidation-Reduction Reactions

Another important reaction type, **oxidation-reduction,** takes place because of the transfer of negative charge (one or more *electrons*) from one reactant to another.

The reaction of zinc metal with copper(II) ions is one example of oxidation-reduction:

$$\underset{\substack{\text{Substance} \\ \text{to be oxidized}}}{Zn(s)} + \underset{\substack{\text{Substance to be} \\ \text{reduced}}}{Cu^{2+}(aq)} \longrightarrow \underset{\substack{\text{Oxidized} \\ \text{product}}}{Zn^{2+}(aq)} + \underset{\substack{\text{Reduced} \\ \text{product}}}{Cu(s)}$$

Zinc metal atoms each donate two electrons to copper(II) ions; consequently zinc atoms become zinc(II) ions and copper(II) ions become copper atoms. Zinc is oxidized (increased positive charge) and copper is reduced (decreased positive charge) as a result of electron transfer.

Oxidation-reduction processes will be discussed more fully in Section 8.5.

Writing Precipitation Reactions as Net Ionic Equations

Writing Net Ionic Equations

The equation that we developed in Example 4.14 is written as a *molecular equation.* Although technically correct and properly balanced, it conveys no information about the way the products and reactants exist in solution, other than the precipitate. In reality, all four species are ionic compounds; both reactants and one product are actually *dissociated* in solution, existing as ions. Only the product, AgCl, is associated. Our solubility rules predicted that AgCl is a solid, crystalline precipitate. A more useful representation would show all of the reactants and products in the form in which they are actually present in solution, solid AgCl surrounded by an aqueous collection of ions. This is an *ionic equation.* Even greater clarity can be achieved by removing the ions that do not change during the course of the reaction (spectator ions), to produce a *net ionic equation.* The net ionic equation only shows the chemical species that actually undergo change. This is the approach that is most faithful to our original concept of a chemical equation: a depiction of chemical *change.* The process we use to write a net ionic equation for a precipitation reaction is as follows:

1. Write a balanced molecular equation for the process being considered. Use the solubility rules to identify any precipitates.
2. Write the ionic equation showing all reactants and products as free ions unless they are precipitates.
3. Ions that appear on both sides of the equation are *spectator ions* (they do not undergo change) and are cancelled out. What remains is the net ionic equation.
4. Ensure that charges and numbers of atoms are balanced, just as they must be in a conventional equation.

Passing an electrical current through water causes an oxidation-reduction reaction. The products are H_2 and O_2 in a 2:1 ratio. Is this ratio of products predicted by the equation for the decomposition of water, $2H_2O(l) \longrightarrow 2H_2(g) + O_2(g)$? Explain.

All of the reactions with oxygen (discussed earlier) are oxidation-reduction reactions as well.

 Writing Net Ionic Equations

Example 4.15 shows how this procedure is applied.

EXAMPLE 4.15   Writing Net Ionic Equations

In Example 4.14 we considered the reaction of NaCl and $AgNO_3$. We wrote the chemical equation for this process in the form of a molecular equation. Now, write this process as a net ionic equation.

Solution

Step 1. Write the balanced molecular equation. In Example 4.14 we found:

$$NaCl(aq) + AgNO_3(aq) \longrightarrow AgCl(?) + NaNO_3(?)$$

The solubility rules predicted that AgCl is a precipitate; rewriting our equation to show this information results in:

$$NaCl(aq) + AgNO_3(aq) \longrightarrow AgCl(s) + NaNO_3(aq)$$

Step 2. AgCl is a precipitate and should be written in its associated form; all others are not, and should be written in ionic form:

$$Na^+(aq) + Cl^-(aq) + Ag^+(aq) + NO_3^-(aq) \longrightarrow AgCl(s) + Na^+(aq) + NO_3^-(aq)$$

This is the form of the ionic equation.

Step 3. $Na^+(aq)$ and $NO_3^-(aq)$ appear on both sides of the equation and are *spectator ions* that cancel out because they are unchanged during the course of the reaction:

$$\cancel{Na^+(aq)} + Cl^-(aq) + Ag^+(aq) + \cancel{NO_3^-(aq)} \longrightarrow AgCl(s) + \cancel{Na^+(aq)} + \cancel{NO_3^-(aq)}$$

Step 4. We must now ensure that both net charge and number of atoms of each kind are the same on both sides of the reaction arrow.

Counting charges:

Reactants: one positive charge, $Ag^+(aq)$, and one negative charge, $Cl^-(aq)$, results in a net charge of zero.

Products: the only product, AgCl, has a zero charge

Counting atoms:

Reactants: one Ag and one Cl atom.

Products: one Ag and one Cl atom.

Charges and numbers of atoms are balanced. The final net ionic equation representing the precipitation of silver chloride is:

$$Ag^+(aq) + Cl^-(aq) \longrightarrow AgCl(s)$$

Practice Problem 4.15

Write net ionic equations for the following reactions:

a. $BaCl_2(aq) + ZnSO_4(aq) \longrightarrow$

b. $AgNO_3(aq) + Na_2SO_4(aq) \longrightarrow$

▶ **For Further Practice: Questions 4.79 and 4.80.**

Net ionic equations are useful, not only for precipitation reactions, but for any process involving ionic compounds in aqueous solution. We will see net ionic equations representing acid-base and oxidation-reduction reactions in Chapter 8. Further information about writing these equations may be found on the website under the heading "Writing Net Ionic Equations."

Writing Net Ionic Equations

Question 4.7 Write the net ionic equation representing a solution of Na_2S mixed with a solution of $CuCl_2$.

Question 4.8 Write the net ionic equation representing a solution of Na_2CO_3 mixed with a solution of $CaCl_2$.

4.5 Calculations Using the Chemical Equation

General Principles

The calculation of quantities of products and reactants based on a balanced chemical equation is termed *stoichiometry*, and is important in many fields. The synthesis of drugs and other complex molecules on a large scale is conducted on the basis of a balanced equation. This minimizes the waste of expensive chemical compounds used in these reactions. Similarly, the ratio of fuel and air in a home furnace or automobile must be adjusted carefully, according to their combining ratio, to maximize energy conversion, minimize fuel consumption, and minimize pollution.

In carrying out chemical calculations, we apply the following guidelines:

1. The chemical formulas of all reactants and products must be known.
2. The basis for the calculations is a balanced equation because the conservation of mass must be obeyed. If the equation is not properly balanced, the calculation is meaningless.
3. The calculations are performed in terms of mol. The coefficients in the balanced equation represent the relative number of mol of products and reactants.

We have seen that the number of mol of products and reactants often differs in a balanced equation. For example,

$$C(s) + O_2(g) \longrightarrow CO_2(g)$$

is a balanced equation. Two mol of reactants combine to produce 1 mol of product:

$$1 \text{ mol C} + 1 \text{ mol O}_2 \longrightarrow 1 \text{ mol CO}_2$$

However, 1 mol of C *atoms* and 2 mol of O *atoms* produce 1 mol of C *atoms* and 2 mol of O *atoms*. In other words, the number of mol of reactants and products may differ, but the number of mol of atoms cannot. The formation of CO_2 from C and O_2 may be described as follows:

$$C(s) + O_2(g) \longrightarrow CO_2(g)$$
$$1 \text{ mol C} + 1 \text{ mol O}_2 \longrightarrow 1 \text{ mol CO}_2$$
$$12.0 \text{ g C} + 32.0 \text{ g O}_2 \longrightarrow 44.0 \text{ g CO}_2$$

The mol is the basis of our calculations. However, mol are generally measured in g (or kg). A facility for interconversion of mol and g is fundamental to chemical arithmetic (see Figure 4.2). These calculations, discussed earlier in this chapter, are reviewed in Example 4.16.

LEARNING GOAL

9 ▶ Calculate the number of mol or g of product resulting from a given number of mol or g of reactants or the number of mol or g of reactant needed to produce a certain number of mol or g of product.

Animation
• Stoichiometry

Use of Conversion Factors

Conversion Between Moles and Grams

Conversion from mol to g, and vice versa, requires only the formula mass of the compound of interest. Consider the following examples.

LEARNING GOAL

9 ▶ Calculate the number of mol or g of product resulting from a given number of mol or g of reactants or the number of mol or g of reactant needed to produce a certain number of mol or g of product.

EXAMPLE 4.16   **Converting Between Moles and Grams**

a. Convert 1.00 mol of oxygen gas, O_2, to g.

Solution

Step 1. Use the following path:

$$\text{mol of oxygen} \longrightarrow \text{g of oxygen}$$

Step 2. The molar mass of oxygen (O_2) is 32.0 g O_2, and the conversion factor becomes:

$$\frac{32.0 \text{ g } O_2}{1 \text{ mol } O_2}$$

Step 3. Using the conversion factor (ensure that mol cancel):

$$1.00 \text{ mol } O_2 \times \frac{32.0 \text{ g } O_2}{1 \text{ mol } O_2} = 32.0 \text{ g } O_2$$

b. How many g of carbon dioxide are contained in 10.0 mol of carbon dioxide?

Solution

Step 1. Use the following path:

$$\text{mol of carbon dioxide} \longrightarrow \text{g of carbon dioxide}$$

Step 2. The molar mass of CO_2 is 44.0 g CO_2, and the conversion factor becomes:

$$\frac{44.0 \text{ g } CO_2}{1 \text{ mol } CO_2}$$

Step 3. Using the conversion factor (ensure that mol cancel):

$$10.0 \text{ mol } CO_2 \times \frac{44.0 \text{ g } CO_2}{1 \text{ mol } CO_2} = 44.0 \times 10^2 \text{ g } CO_2$$

c. How many mol of sodium are contained in 1 pound (lb) (454 g) of sodium metal?

Solution

Step 1. Use the following path:

$$\text{g of sodium} \longrightarrow \text{mol of sodium}$$

Step 2. The molar mass of Na is 22.99 g Na, and the conversion factor becomes:

$$\frac{1 \text{ mol Na}}{22.99 \text{ g Na}}$$

Step 3. Using the conversion factor (ensure that g Na cancel):

$$454 \text{ g Na} \times \frac{1 \text{ mol Na}}{22.99 \text{ g Na}} = 19.7 \text{ mol Na}$$

Helpful Hint: Note that each factor can be inverted, producing a second possible factor. Only one will allow the appropriate unit cancellation.

Practice Problem 4.16

Perform each of the following conversions:

a. 5.00 mol of water to g of water
b. 25.0 g of LiCl to mol of LiCl
c. 1.00×10^{-5} mol of $C_6H_{12}O_6$ to micrograms (μg) of $C_6H_{12}O_6$
d. 35.0 g of $MgCl_2$ to mol of $MgCl_2$

▶ **For Further Practice: Questions 4.27 and 4.28.**

Conversion of Moles of Reactants to Moles of Products

In Example 4.11 we balanced the equation for the reaction of propane and oxygen as follows:

$$C_3H_8(g) + 5O_2(g) \longrightarrow 3CO_2(g) + 4H_2O(g)$$

In this reaction, 1 mol of C_3H_8 corresponds to, or results in,

5 mol of O_2 being consumed and
3 mol of CO_2 being formed and
4 mol of H_2O being formed.

This information may be written in the form of a conversion factor or ratio:

$$1 \text{ mol } C_3H_8 / 5 \text{ mol } O_2$$

Translated: 1 mol of C_3H_8 reacts with 5 mol of O_2.

$$1 \text{ mol } C_3H_8 / 3 \text{ mol } CO_2$$

Translated: 1 mol of C_3H_8 produces 3 mol of CO_2.

$$1 \text{ mol } C_3H_8 / 4 \text{ mol } H_2O$$

Translated: 1 mol of C_3H_8 produces 4 mol of H_2O.

Conversion factors based on the chemical equation permit us to perform a variety of calculations.

Let us look at a few examples, based on the combustion of propane and the equation that we balanced in Example 4.11.

LEARNING GOAL

9 ▶ Calculate the number of mol or g of product resulting from a given number of mol or g of reactants or the number of mol or g of reactant needed to produce a certain number of mol or g of product.

EXAMPLE 4.17   Calculating Reacting Quantities

Calculate the number of g of O_2 that will react with 1.00 mol of C_3H_8.

Solution

Step 1. Two conversion factors are necessary to solve this problem:

• conversion from mol of C_3H_8 to mol of O_2 and
• conversion of mol of O_2 to g of O_2.

Continued—

Step 2. Therefore our path is:

$$\boxed{\begin{array}{c}\text{mol}\\ C_3H_8\end{array}} \longrightarrow \boxed{\begin{array}{c}\text{mol}\\ O_2\end{array}} \longrightarrow \boxed{\begin{array}{c}\text{g}\\ O_2\end{array}}$$

Step 3. Set up conversion factors to cancel mol C_3H_8 and mol O_2:

$$1.00 \text{ mol } C_3H_8 \times \frac{5 \text{ mol } O_2}{1 \text{ mol } C_3H_8} \times \frac{32.0 \text{ g } O_2}{1 \text{ mol } O_2} = 1.60 \times 10^2 \text{ g } O_2$$

Practice Problem 4.17

When potassium cyanide (KCN) reacts with acids, hydrogen cyanide (HCN), a poisonous gas, is produced. The equation is

$$KCN(aq) + HCl(aq) \longrightarrow KCl(aq) + HCN(g)$$

Calculate the number of g of KCN that will react with 1.00 mol of HCl.

▶ **For Further Practice: Questions 4.85 and 4.86.**

A Human Perspective

The Chemistry of Automobile Air Bags

Each year, thousands of individuals are killed or seriously injured in automobile accidents. Perhaps most serious is the front-end collision. The car decelerates or stops virtually on impact; the momentum of the passengers, however, does not stop, and the driver and passengers are thrown forward toward the dashboard and the windshield. Suddenly, passive parts of the automobile, such as control knobs, the rearview mirror, the steering wheel, the dashboard, and the windshield, become lethal weapons.

Automobile engineers have been aware of these problems for a long time. They have made a series of design improvements to lessen the potential problems associated with front-end impact. Smooth switches rather than knobs, recessed hardware, and padded dashboards are examples. These changes, coupled with the use of lap and shoulder belts, which help to immobilize occupants of the car, have decreased the frequency and severity of occupant impact and lowered the death rate for this type of accident.

An almost ideal protection would be a soft, fluffy pillow, providing a cushion against impact. Such a device, an air bag inflated only on impact, is now standard equipment for the protection of the driver and front-seat passenger.

How does it work? Ideally, it inflates only when severe front-end impact occurs; it inflates very rapidly (in approximately 40 milliseconds (ms)), then deflates to provide a steady deceleration, cushioning the occupants from impact. A remarkably simple chemical reaction makes this a reality.

When solid sodium azide (NaN_3) is detonated by mechanical energy produced by an electrical current, it decomposes to form solid sodium and nitrogen gas:

$$2NaN_3(s) \longrightarrow 2Na(s) + 3N_2(g)$$

The nitrogen gas inflates the air bag, cushioning the driver and front-seat passenger.

The solid sodium azide has a high density (characteristic of solids) and thus occupies a small volume. It can easily be stored in the center of a steering wheel or in the dashboard. The rate of detonation is very rapid. In ms, the reaction produces 3 mol of N_2 gas for every 2 mol of NaN_3. The N_2 gas occupies a relatively large volume because its density is low. This is a general property of gases.

Figuring out how much sodium azide is needed to produce enough nitrogen to properly inflate the bag is an example of a practical application of the chemical arithmetic that we are learning in this chapter.

For Further Understanding

▶ Why is nitrogen gas preferred for this application?
▶ If this reaction occurs in 5 ms, how many seconds (s) does this represent?

EXAMPLE 4.18 Calculating Grams of Product from Moles of Reactant

Calculate the number of g of CO_2 produced from the combustion of 1.00 mol of C_3H_8.

Solution

Steps 1. and 2. Employ logic similar to that used in Example 4.17 and use the following path:

$$\underset{C_3H_8}{mol} \longrightarrow \underset{CO_2}{mol} \longrightarrow \underset{CO_2}{g}$$

Step 3. Set up conversion factors to cancel mol C_3H_8 and mol CO_2:

$$1.00 \ \text{mol } C_3H_8 \times \frac{3 \ \text{mol } CO_2}{1 \ \text{mol } C_3H_8} \times \frac{44.0 \ \text{g } CO_2}{1 \ \text{mol } CO_2} = 132 \ \text{g } CO_2$$

Practice Problem 4.18

Fermentation is a critical step in the process of winemaking. The reaction is

$$\underset{\text{glucose}}{C_6H_{12}O_6(aq)} \longrightarrow \underset{\text{ethanol}}{2CH_3CH_2OH(aq)} + 2CO_2(g)$$

Calculate the number of g of ethanol produced from the fermentation of 5.00 mol of glucose.

▶ **For Further Practice: Questions 4.87 and 4.88.**

LEARNING GOAL

9 ▶ Calculate the number of mol or g of product resulting from a given number of mol or g of reactants or the number of mol or g of reactant needed to produce a certain number of mol or g of product.

EXAMPLE 4.19 Relating Masses of Reactants and Products

Calculate the number of g of C_3H_8 required to produce 36.0 g of H_2O using the balanced equation from Example 4.11.

Solution

Steps 1. and 2. It is necessary to convert

g of H_2O to mol of H_2O,
mol of H_2O to mol of C_3H_8, and
mol of C_3H_8 to g of C_3H_8.

Use the following path:

$$\underset{H_2O}{g} \longrightarrow \underset{H_2O}{mol} \longrightarrow \underset{C_3H_8}{mol} \longrightarrow \underset{C_3H_8}{g}$$

Step 3. Set up conversion factors to cancel g H_2O, mol H_2O, and mol C_3H_8:

$$36.0 \ \text{g } H_2O \times \frac{1 \ \text{mol } H_2O}{18.0 \ \text{g } H_2O} \times \frac{1 \ \text{mol } C_3H_8}{4 \ \text{mol } H_2O} \times \frac{44.0 \ \text{g } C_3H_8}{1 \ \text{mol } C_3H_8} = 22.0 \ \text{g } C_3H_8$$

Practice Problem 4.19

The balanced equation for the combustion of ethanol (ethyl alcohol) is:

$$C_2H_5OH(l) + 3O_2(g) \longrightarrow 2CO_2(g) + 3H_2O(g)$$

a. How many mol of O_2 will react with 1 mol of ethanol?
b. How many g of O_2 will react with 1 mol of ethanol?
c. How many g of CO_2 will be produced by the combustion of 1 mol of ethanol?

▶ **For Further Practice: Questions 4.89 and 4.90.**

Let's consider an example that requires us to write and balance the chemical equation, use conversion factors, and calculate the amount of a reactant consumed in the chemical reaction.

EXAMPLE 4.20   Calculating a Quantity of Reactant

Calcium hydroxide may be used to neutralize (completely react with) aqueous hydrochloric acid. Calculate the number of g of hydrochloric acid that would be neutralized by 0.500 mol of solid calcium hydroxide.

Solution

Step 1. The formula for calcium hydroxide is $Ca(OH)_2$, and that for hydrochloric acid is HCl. The unbalanced equation produces calcium chloride and water as products:

$$Ca(OH)_2(s) + HCl(aq) \longrightarrow CaCl_2(aq) + H_2O(l)$$

Step 2. Balance the equation:

$$Ca(OH)_2(s) + 2HCl(aq) \longrightarrow CaCl_2(aq) + 2H_2O(l)$$

Step 3. Determine the necessary conversion:

- mol of $Ca(OH)_2$ to mol of HCl and
- mol of HCl to g of HCl

Step 4. Use the following path:

$$\boxed{\text{mol } Ca(OH)_2} \longrightarrow \boxed{\text{mol } HCl} \longrightarrow \boxed{\text{g } HCl}$$

Step 5. $0.500 \text{ mol Ca(OH)}_2 \times \dfrac{2 \text{ mol HCl}}{1 \text{ mol Ca(OH)}_2} \times \dfrac{36.5 \text{ g HCl}}{1 \text{ mol HCl}} = 36.5 \text{ g HCl}$

This reaction is illustrated in Figure 4.6.

Helpful Hints:

1. The reaction between an acid and a base produces a salt and water (Chapter 8).
2. Remember to balance the chemical equation; the proper coefficients are essential parts of the subsequent calculations.

Practice Problem 4.20

Metallic iron reacts with O_2 gas to produce iron(III) oxide.

a. Write and balance the equation.
b. Calculate the number of g of iron needed to produce 5.00 g of product.

▶ **For Further Practice: Questions 4.93 and 4.94.**

Ca(OH)$_2$ +   2HCl   ⟶   CaCl$_2$ +   2H$_2$O

1 mol   2 mol   1 mol   2 mol

74 g/mol   36.5 g/mol   111 g/mol   18 g/mol

74 g   73 g   111 g   36 g

147 g of reactants   147 g of products

Figure 4.6 An illustration of the law of conservation of mass. In this example, 1 mol of calcium hydroxide and 2 mol of hydrogen chloride react to produce 3 mol of product (2 mol of water and 1 mol of calcium chloride). The total mass, in g, of reactant(s) consumed is equal to the total mass, in g, of product(s) formed. *Note:* In reality, HCl does not exist as discrete molecules in water. The HCl separates to form H$^+$ and Cl$^-$. Ionization in water will be discussed with the chemistry of acids and bases in Chapter 8.

A Medical Perspective

Carbon Monoxide Poisoning: A Case of Combining Ratios

A fuel, such as methane, CH$_4$, burned in an excess of oxygen produces carbon dioxide and water:

$$CH_4(g) + 2O_2(g) \longrightarrow CO_2(g) + 2H_2O(g)$$

The same combustion in the presence of insufficient oxygen produces carbon monoxide and water:

$$2CH_4(g) + 3O_2(g) \longrightarrow 2CO(g) + 4H_2O(g)$$

The combustion of methane, repeated over and over in millions of gas furnaces, is responsible for heating many of our homes in the winter. The furnace is designed to operate under conditions that favor the first reaction and minimize the second; excess oxygen is available from the surrounding atmosphere. Furthermore, the vast majority of exhaust gases (containing principally CO, CO$_2$, H$_2$O, and unburned fuel) are removed from the home through the chimney. However, if the chimney becomes obstructed, or the burner malfunctions, carbon monoxide levels within the home can rapidly reach hazardous levels.

Why is exposure to carbon monoxide hazardous? Hemoglobin, an iron-containing compound, binds with O$_2$ and transports it throughout the body. Carbon monoxide also combines with hemoglobin, thereby blocking oxygen transport. The binding affinity of hemoglobin for carbon monoxide is about

200 times as great as for O$_2$. Therefore, to maintain O$_2$ binding and transport capability, our exposure to carbon monoxide must be minimal. Proper ventilation and suitable oxygen-to-fuel ratio are essential for any combustion process in the home, automobile, or workplace. In recent years carbon monoxide sensors have been developed. These sensors sound an alarm when toxic levels of CO are reached. These warning devices have helped to create a safer indoor environment.

The example we have chosen is an illustration of what is termed the *law of multiple proportions*. This law states that identical reactants may produce different products, depending on their combining ratio. The experimental conditions (in this case, the quantity of available oxygen) determine the preferred path of the chemical reaction.

For Further Understanding

▶ Why may new, more strict insulation standards for homes and businesses inadvertently increase the risk of carbon monoxide poisoning?

▶ Explain the link between smoking and carbon monoxide that has motivated many states and municipalities to ban smoking in restaurants, offices, and other indoor spaces.

LEARNING GOAL

9 ▶ Calculate the number of mol or g
of product resulting from a given
number of mol or g of reactants
or the number of mol or g of
reactant needed to produce a
certain number of mol or g of
product.

EXAMPLE 4.21   Calculating Reactant Quantities

What mass of sodium hydroxide, NaOH, would be required to produce 8.00 g of the antacid milk of magnesia, $Mg(OH)_2$, by the reaction of $MgCl_2$ with NaOH?

Solution

Step 1. Write and balance the equation:

$$MgCl_2(aq) + 2NaOH(aq) \longrightarrow Mg(OH)_2(s) + 2NaCl(aq)$$

Step 2. Determine the strategy:

The equation tells us that 2 mol of NaOH form 1 mol of $Mg(OH)_2$. If we calculate the number of mol of $Mg(OH)_2$ in 8.00 g of $Mg(OH)_2$, we can determine the number of mol of NaOH necessary and then the mass of NaOH required:

$$\boxed{\begin{array}{c}\text{mass}\\ Mg(OH)_2\end{array}} \longrightarrow \boxed{\begin{array}{c}\text{mol}\\ Mg(OH)_2\end{array}} \longrightarrow \boxed{\begin{array}{c}\text{mol}\\ NaOH\end{array}} \longrightarrow \boxed{\begin{array}{c}\text{mass}\\ NaOH\end{array}}$$

Step 3. Determine the conversion factor to convert mass to mol $Mg(OH)_2$:

$$\text{Since } 58.3 \text{ g } Mg(OH)_2 = 1 \text{ mol } Mg(OH)_2$$

The conversion factor is:

$$\frac{1 \text{ mol } Mg(OH)_2}{58.3 \text{ g } Mg(OH)_2}$$

Step 4. $8.00 \text{ g } Mg(OH)_2 \times \dfrac{1 \text{ mol } Mg(OH)_2}{58.3 \text{ g } Mg(OH)_2} = 0.137 \text{ mol } Mg(OH)_2$

Step 5. Two moles of NaOH react to give 1 mol of $Mg(OH)_2$. Therefore

$$0.137 \text{ mol } Mg(OH)_2 \times \frac{2 \text{ mol NaOH}}{1 \text{ mol } Mg(OH)_2} = 0.274 \text{ mol NaOH}$$

Step 6. 40.0 g of NaOH = 1 mol of NaOH. Therefore

$$0.274 \text{ mol NaOH} \times \frac{40.0 \text{ g NaOH}}{1 \text{ mol NaOH}} = 11.0 \text{ g NaOH}$$

However, the calculation may be done in a single step:

$$8.00 \text{ g } Mg(OH)_2 \times \frac{1 \text{ mol } Mg(OH)_2}{58.3 \text{ g } Mg(OH)_2} \times \frac{2 \text{ mol NaOH}}{1 \text{ mol } Mg(OH)_2}$$

$$\times \frac{40.0 \text{ g NaOH}}{1 \text{ mol NaOH}} = 11.0 \text{ g NaOH}$$

Note once again that we have followed a logical and predictable path to the solution:

$$\boxed{\begin{array}{c}\text{g}\\ Mg(OH)_2\end{array}} \longrightarrow \boxed{\begin{array}{c}\text{mol}\\ Mg(OH)_2\end{array}} \longrightarrow \boxed{\begin{array}{c}\text{mol}\\ NaOH\end{array}} \longrightarrow \boxed{\begin{array}{c}\text{g}\\ NaOH\end{array}}$$

Helpful Hint: Mass is a laboratory unit, whereas mol is a calculation unit. The laboratory balance is calibrated in units of mass (g). Although mol are essential for calculation, often the starting point and objective are in mass units. As a result, our path is often g⟶mol⟶g.

Practice Problem 4.21

Barium carbonate decomposes upon heating to barium oxide and carbon dioxide.

a. Write and balance the equation.
b. Calculate the number of g of carbon dioxide produced by heating 50.0 g of barium carbonate.

▶ **For Further Practice: Questions 4.95 and 4.96.**

A general problem-solving strategy is summarized in Figure 4.7. By systematically applying this strategy, you will be able to solve virtually any problem requiring calculations based on the chemical equation.

Theoretical and Percent Yield

The **theoretical yield** is the *maximum* amount of product that can be produced (in an ideal world). In the "real" world it is difficult to produce the amount calculated as the theoretical yield. This is true for a variety of reasons. Some experimental error is unavoidable. Moreover, many reactions simply are not complete; some amount of reactant remains at the end of the reaction. We will study these processes, termed *equilibrium reactions* in Chapter 7.

A **percent yield,** the ratio of the actual and theoretical yields multiplied by 100%, is often used to show the relationship between predicted and experimental quantities. Thus

$$\% \text{ yield} = \frac{\text{actual yield}}{\text{theoretical yield}} \times 100\%$$

In Example 4.18, the theoretical yield of CO_2 is 132 g. For this reaction let's assume that a chemist actually obtained 125 g CO_2. This is the actual yield and would normally be provided as a part of the data in the problem.

LEARNING GOAL

10 ▶ Calculate theoretical and percent yield.

For a reaction of the general type:
$$A + B \longrightarrow C$$

(a) Given a specified number of g of A, calculate mol of C.

(b) Given a specified number of g of A, calculate g of C.

(c) Given a volume of A in milliliters (mL), calculate g of C.

Figure 4.7 A general problem-solving strategy, using molar quantities.

A Medical Perspective

Pharmaceutical Chemistry: The Practical Significance of Percent Yield

In recent years, the major pharmaceutical industries have introduced a wide variety of new drugs targeted to cure or alleviate the symptoms of a host of diseases that afflict humanity.

The vast majority of these drugs are synthetic; they are made in a laboratory or by an industrial process. These substances are complex molecules that are patiently designed and constructed from relatively simple molecules in a series of chemical reactions. A series of ten to twenty "steps," or sequential reactions, is not unusual to put together a final product that has the proper structure, geometry, and reactivity for efficacy against a particular disease.

Although a great deal of research occurs to ensure that each of the steps in the overall process is efficient (having a large percent yield), the overall process is still very inefficient (low percent yield). This inefficiency, and the research needed to minimize it, at least in part determines the cost and availability of both prescription and over-the-counter preparations.

Consider a hypothetical five-step sequential synthesis. If each step has a percent yield of 80%, our initial impression might be that this synthesis is quite efficient. However, on closer inspection we find quite the contrary to be true.

The overall yield of the five-step reaction is the product of the decimal fraction of the percent yield of each of the sequential reactions. So, if the decimal fraction corresponding to 80% is 0.80:

$$0.80 \times 0.80 \times 0.80 \times 0.80 \times 0.80 = 0.33$$

Converting the decimal fraction to percentage:

$$0.33 \times 100\% = 33\% \text{ yield}$$

Many reactions are considerably less than 80% efficient, especially those that are used to prepare large molecules with complex arrangements of atoms. Imagine a more realistic scenario in which one step is only 20% efficient (a 20% yield) and the other four steps are 50%, 60%, 70%, and 80% efficient. Repeating the calculation with these numbers (after conversion to a decimal fraction):

$$0.20 \times 0.50 \times 0.60 \times 0.70 \times 0.80 = 0.0336$$

Converting the decimal fraction to a percentage:

$$0.0336 \times 100\% = 3.36\% \text{ yield}$$

a very inefficient process.

If we apply this logic to a fifteen- or twenty-step synthesis we gain some appreciation of the difficulty of producing modern pharmaceutical products. Add to this the challenge of predicting the most appropriate molecular structure that will have the desired biological effect and be relatively free of side effects. All these considerations give new meaning to the term *wonder drug* that has been attached to some of the more successful synthetic products.

We will study some of the elementary steps essential to the synthesis of a wide range of pharmaceutical compounds in later chapters, beginning with Chapter 10.

For Further Understanding

▶ Explain the possible connection of this perspective to escalating costs of pharmaceutical products.

▶ Can you describe other situations, not necessarily in the field of chemistry, where multiple-step processes contribute to inefficiency?

Calculate the percent yield as follows:

$$\% \text{ yield} = \frac{\text{actual yield}}{\text{theoretical yield}} \times 100\%$$

$$= \frac{125 \text{ g } CO_2 \text{ actual}}{132 \text{ g } CO_2 \text{ theoretical}} \times 100\% = 94.7\%$$

EXAMPLE 4.22   Calculation of Percent Yield

Assume that the theoretical yield of iron in the process

$$2Al(s) + Fe_2O_3(s) \longrightarrow Al_2O_3(l) + 2Fe(l)$$

was 30.0 g.

If the actual yield of iron were 25.0 g in the process, calculate the percent yield.

Solution

$$\% \text{ yield} = \frac{\text{actual yield}}{\text{theoretical yield}} \times 100\%$$

$$= \frac{25.0 \text{ g}}{30.0 \text{ g}} \times 100\%$$

$$= 83.3\%$$

Practice Problem 4.22

Given the reaction represented by the balanced equation

$$CH_4(g) + 3Cl_2(g) \longrightarrow 3HCl(g) + CHCl_3(g)$$

a. Calculate the number of g of $CHCl_3$ produced by mixing 105 g Cl_2 with excess CH_4.

b. If 10.0 g $CHCl_3$ were produced, calculate the % yield.

▶ **For Further Practice: Questions 4.101 and 4.102.**

Question 4.9 It is believed that the reaction responsible for the depletion of ozone in the atmosphere is:

$$O_3(g) + NO(g) \longrightarrow O_2(g) + NO_2(g)$$

a. If 50.0 g of O_3 reacts with excess NO, how many g of NO_2 will be produced?

b. If the actual yield of NO_2 is 25.0 g, what is the % yield?

Question 4.10 The reaction:

$$2NO(g) + O_2(g) \longrightarrow 2NO_2(g)$$

is one step in the process of forming atmospheric smog.

a. How many g of NO_2 can be produced by the reaction of excess O_2 with 50.0 g of NO?

b. If the actual yield of NO_2 is 50.0 g, what is the % yield?

A Special Case—The Limiting Reactant

We have learned that reactants combine in molar proportions dictated by the coefficients in the balanced equation. However, we often encounter situations where the reactants are not mixed to match the theoretical proportions. In cases such as this, one reactant will be completely consumed, leaving some of the other reactant unchanged. In effect, the extent of the reaction is *limited* by the amount of the reactant that is completely consumed. This completely consumed reactant is termed the *limiting reactant.* In order to correctly calculate the amount of product formed, the *theoretical yield,* we must base the amount of product formed on the number of mol of the compound "in short supply," the limiting reactant.

Imagine that you are making cheeseburgers. You have twenty buns, eight slices of cheese, and nine hamburger patties. What is the limiting ingredient? How many cheeseburgers can you make? What are the leftover ingredients? If you can answer these questions, you can do limiting reactant problems.

We know that twenty hamburger buns could make twenty cheeseburgers if we had twenty hamburger patties and twenty slices of cheese. But we do not, so it is obvious that we cannot make twenty cheeseburgers, even though we certainly have enough buns. It can be reasoned that only eight burgers are possible. We are limited by the availability of only eight slices of cheese. In our example, cheese is the limiting reactant. Furthermore, nine minus eight, or one hamburger patty and twenty minus eight, or twelve buns, would be left over.

The Limiting Reactant Problem

The strategy outlined above is the same as that used in solving problems involving limiting reactants. You can learn more about this topic on the website, by referring to "The Limiting Reactant Problem."

SUMMARY

4.1 The Mole Concept and Atoms

Atoms are exceedingly small, yet their masses have been experimentally determined for each of the elements. The unit of measurement for these determinations is the *atomic mass unit*, (amu):

$$1\,\text{amu} = 1.661 \times 10^{-24}\ \text{g}$$

The periodic table provides atomic masses in amu.

A more practical unit for defining a "collection" of atoms is the *mole* (mol):

$$1\ \text{mol of atoms} = 6.022 \times 10^{23}\ \text{atoms of an element}$$

This number is referred to as *Avogadro's number*.

The mol and the amu are related. The atomic mass of a given element corresponds to the average mass of a single atom in amu and the mass of a mol of atoms in g. The mass of 1 mol of atoms is termed the *molar mass* of the element. One mole of atoms of any element contains the same number, Avogadro's number, of atoms.

4.2 The Chemical Formula, Formula Mass, and Molar Mass

Compounds are pure substances that are composed of two or more elements that are chemically combined. They are represented by their *chemical formula,* a combination of symbols of the various elements that make up the compounds. The chemical formula is based on the *formula unit.* This is the smallest collection of atoms that provides the identity of the atoms present in the compound and the relative numbers of each type of atom.

Just as a mol of atoms is based on the atomic mass, a mol of a compound is based on the *formula mass.* The formula mass is calculated by addition of the masses of all the atoms or ions of which the unit is composed. To calculate the formula mass, the formula unit must be known. The formula mass of 1 mol of a compound is its *molar mass* in units of g/mol.

4.3 The Chemical Equation and the Information It Conveys

The *chemical equation* is the shorthand notation for a chemical reaction. It describes all of the substances that react to produce the product(s). *Reactants,* or starting materials, are all substances that undergo change in a chemical reaction; *products* are substances produced by a chemical reaction.

According to the *law of conservation of mass,* matter can neither be gained nor lost in the process of a chemical reaction. The law of conservation of mass states that we must have a balanced chemical equation.

Features of a suitable equation include the following:

- The identity of products and reactants must be specified.
- Reactants are written to the left of the reaction arrow ($\rightarrow$) and products to the right.
- The physical states of reactants and products are shown in parentheses.

- The symbol Δ over the reaction arrow means that heat energy is necessary for the reaction to occur.
- The equation must be balanced.

Chemical reactions involve the *combination* of reactants to produce products, the *decomposition* of reactant(s) into products, or the *replacement* of one or more elements in a compound to yield products. Replacement reactions are subclassified as either *single-* or *double-*replacement.

4.4 Chemical Equations Represent Chemical Change

The chemical equation enables us to determine the quantity of reactants needed to produce a certain molar quantity of products. The chemical equation expresses these quantities in terms of mol.

The relative number of mol of each product and reactant is indicated by placing a whole-number coefficient before the formula of each substance in the chemical equation.

Many equations are balanced by trial and error. If the identity of the products and reactants, the physical states, and the reaction conditions are known, the following steps provide a method for correctly balancing a chemical equation:

- Count the number of atoms of each element on both product and reactant sides.
- Determine which atoms are not balanced.
- Balance one element at a time using coefficients.
- After you believe that you have successfully balanced the equation, check to be certain that mass conservation has been achieved.

Reactions that produce products with similar characteristics are often classified as a single group. The formation of an insoluble solid, a *precipitate,* is very common. Such reactions are precipitation reactions, and are represented using net ionic equations.

Chemical reactions that have a common reactant may be grouped together. Reactions involving oxygen, *combustion reactions,* are such a class.

Another approach to the classification of chemical reactions is based on transfer of hydrogen ions (+ charge) or electrons (− charge). *Acid-base reactions* involve the transfer of a hydrogen ion, H^+, from one reactant to another. Another important reaction type, *oxidation-reduction,* takes place because of the transfer of negative charge, one or more electrons, from one reactant to another.

4.5 Calculations Using the Chemical Equation

Calculations involving chemical quantities are based on the following requirements:

- The basis for the calculations is a balanced equation.
- The calculations are performed in terms of mol.
- The conservation of mass must be obeyed.

The mol is the basis for calculations. However, masses are generally measured in g (or kg). Therefore you must be able to interconvert mol and g to perform chemical arithmetic.

KEY TERMS

acid-base reaction (4.4)
atomic mass unit (4.1)
Avogadro's number (4.1)
chemical equation (4.3)
chemical formula (4.2)
combination reaction (4.3)
decomposition reaction (4.3)
double-replacement
    reaction (4.3)
formula mass (4.2)
formula unit (4.2)
hydrate (4.2)

law of conservation of
    mass (4.3)
molar mass (4.1)
mole (4.1)
oxidation-reduction
    reaction (4.4)
percent yield (4.5)
product (4.3)
reactant (4.3)
single-replacement
    reaction (4.3)
theoretical yield (4.5)

QUESTIONS AND PROBLEMS

The Mole Concept and Atoms

Foundations

4.11 We purchase eggs by the dozen. Name several other familiar packaging units.

4.12 One dozen eggs is a convenient consumer unit. Explain why the mol is a convenient chemist's unit.

4.13 What is the average molar mass of:
  a. Si
  b. Ag

4.14 What is the average molar mass of:
  a. S
  b. Na

4.15 What is the mass of Avogadro's number of argon atoms?

4.16 What is the mass of Avogadro's number of iron atoms?

Applications

4.17 How many carbon atoms are present in 1.0×10^{-4} mol of carbon?

4.18 How many mercury atoms are present in 1.0×10^{-10} mol of mercury?

4.19 How many mol of arsenic correspond to 1.0×10^2 atoms of arsenic?

4.20 How many mol of sodium correspond to 1.0×10^{15} atoms of sodium?

4.21 How many g are contained in 2.00 mol of neon atoms?

4.22 How many g are contained in 3.00 mol of carbon atoms?

4.23 What is the mass in g of 1.00 mol of helium atoms?

4.24 What is the mass in g of 1.00 mol of nitrogen atoms?

4.25 Calculate the number of mol corresponding to:
  a. 20.0 g He
  b. 0.040 kg Na
  c. 3.0 g Cl_2

4.26 Calculate the number of mol corresponding to:
  a. 0.10 g Ca
  b. 4.00 g Fe
  c. 2.00 kg N_2

4.27 What is the mass, in g, of 15.0 mol of silver?

4.28 What is the mass, in g, of 15.0 mol of carbon?

4.29 Calculate the number of atoms in 15.0 g of silver.

4.30 Calculate the number of atoms in 15.0 g of carbon.

The Chemical Formula, Formula Mass, and Molar Mass

Foundations

4.31 Distinguish between the terms *molecule* and *ion pair*.

4.32 Distinguish between the terms *formula mass* and *molar mass*.

4.33 Calculate the molar mass, in g/mol, of each of the following formula units:
  a. NaCl
  b. Na_2SO_4
  c. $Fe_3(PO_4)_2$

4.34 Calculate the molar mass, in g/mol, of each of the following formula units:
  a. S_8
  b. $(NH_4)_2SO_4$
  c. CO_2

4.35 Calculate the molar mass, in g/mol, of oxygen gas, O_2.

4.36 Calculate the molar mass, in g/mol, of ozone, O_3.

4.37 Calculate the molar mass of $CuSO_4 \cdot 5H_2O$.

4.38 Calculate the molar mass of $CaCl_2 \cdot 2H_2O$.

Applications

4.39 Calculate the number of mol corresponding to:
  a. 15.0 g NaCl
  b. 15.0 g Na_2SO_4

4.40 Calculate the number of mol corresponding to:
  a. 15.0 g NH_3
  b. 16.0 g O_2

4.41 Calculate the mass in g corresponding to:
  a. 1.000 mol H_2O
  b. 2.000 mol NaCl

4.42 Calculate the mass in g corresponding to:
  a. 0.400 mol NH_3
  b. 0.800 mol $BaCO_3$

4.43 Calculate the mass in g corresponding to:
  a. 10.0 mol He
  b. 1.00×10^2 mol H_2

4.44 Calculate the mass in g corresponding to:
  a. 2.00 mol CH_4
  b. 0.400 mol $Ca(NO_3)_2$

4.45 How many g are required to have 0.100 mol of each of the following?
  a. Mg
  b. $CaCO_3$

4.46 How many g are required to have 0.100 mol of each of the following?
  a. $C_6H_{12}O_6$ (glucose)
  b. NaCl

4.47 How many g are required to have 0.100 mol of each of the following compounds?
  a. NaOH
  b. H_2SO_4

4.48 How many g are required to have 0.100 mol of each of the following compounds?
  a. C_2H_5OH (ethanol)
  b. $Ca_3(PO_4)_2$

4.49 How many mol are in 50.0 g of each of the following substances?
  a. KBr
  b. $MgSO_4$

4.50 How many mol are in 50.0 g of each of the following substances?
  a. Br_2
  b. NH_4Cl

4.51 How many mol are in 50.0 g of each of the following substances?
  a. CS_2
  b. $Al_2(CO_3)_3$

4.52 How many mol are in 50.0 g of each of the following substances?
  a. $Sr(OH)_2$
  b. $LiNO_3$

The Chemical Equation and the Information It Conveys

Foundations

4.53 What law is the ultimate basis for a correct chemical equation?

4.54 List the general types of information that a chemical equation provides.

4.55 What is the meaning of the subscript in a chemical formula?

4.56 What is the meaning of the coefficient in a chemical equation?

4.57 What is the meaning of Δ over the reaction arrow?

4.58 What is the meaning of (s), (l), or (g) immediately following the symbol for a chemical substance?

Applications

4.59 Will a precipitate form if solutions of the soluble salts $Pb(NO_3)_2$ and KI are mixed?

4.60 Will a precipitate form if solutions of the soluble salts $AgNO_3$ and NaOH are mixed?

Chemical Equations Represent Chemical Change

Foundations

4.61 When you are balancing an equation, why must the subscripts in the chemical formula remain unchanged?

4.62 Describe the process of checking to ensure that an equation is properly balanced.

4.63 What is a reactant?

4.64 On which side of the reaction arrow are reactants found?

4.65 What is a product?

4.66 On which side of the reaction arrow are products found?

Applications

4.67 Balance each of the following equations:
a. $C_2H_6(g) + O_2(g) \longrightarrow CO_2(g) + H_2O(g)$
b. $K_2O(s) + P_4O_{10}(s) \longrightarrow K_3PO_4(s)$
c. $MgBr_2(aq) + H_2SO_4(aq) \longrightarrow HBr(g) + MgSO_4(aq)$

4.68 Balance each of the following equations:
a. $C_6H_{12}O_6(s) + O_2(g) \longrightarrow CO_2(g) + H_2O(g)$
b. $H_2O(l) + P_4O_{10}(s) \longrightarrow H_3PO_4(aq)$
c. $PCl_5(g) + H_2O(l) \longrightarrow HCl(aq) + H_3PO_4(aq)$

4.69 Complete, then balance, each of the following equations:
a. $Ca(s) + F_2(g) \longrightarrow$
b. $Mg(s) + O_2(g) \longrightarrow$
c. $H_2(g) + N_2(g) \longrightarrow$

4.70 Complete, then balance, each of the following equations:
a. $Li(s) + O_2(g) \longrightarrow$
b. $Ca(s) + N_2(g) \longrightarrow$
c. $Al(s) + S(s) \longrightarrow$

4.71 Balance each of the following equations:
a. $C_4H_{10}(g) + O_2(g) \longrightarrow H_2O(g) + CO_2(g)$
b. $Au_2S_3(s) + H_2(g) \longrightarrow Au(s) + H_2S(g)$
c. $Al(OH)_3(s) + HCl(aq) \longrightarrow AlCl_3(aq) + H_2O(l)$
d. $(NH_4)_2Cr_2O_7(s) \longrightarrow Cr_2O_3(s) + N_2(g) + H_2O(g)$
e. $C_2H_5OH(l) + O_2(g) \longrightarrow CO_2(g) + H_2O(g)$

4.72 Balance each of the following equations:
a. $Fe_2O_3(s) + CO(g) \longrightarrow Fe_3O_4(s) + CO_2(g)$
b. $C_6H_6(l) + O_2(g) \longrightarrow CO_2(g) + H_2O(g)$
c. $I_4O_9(s) + I_2O_6(s) \longrightarrow I_2(s) + O_2(g)$
d. $KClO_3(s) \longrightarrow KCl(s) + O_2(g)$
e. $C_6H_{12}O_6(s) \longrightarrow C_2H_6O(l) + CO_2(g)$

4.73 Write a balanced equation for each of the following reactions:
a. Ammonia is formed by the reaction of nitrogen and hydrogen.
b. Hydrochloric acid reacts with sodium hydroxide to produce water and sodium chloride.

4.74 Write a balanced equation for each of the following reactions:
a. Nitric acid reacts with calcium hydroxide to produce water and calcium nitrate.
b. Butane (C_4H_{10}) reacts with oxygen to produce water and carbon dioxide.

4.75 Write a balanced equation for each of the following reactions:
a. Glucose, a sugar, $C_6H_{12}O_6$, is oxidized in the body to produce water and carbon dioxide.
b. Sodium carbonate, upon heating, produces sodium oxide and carbon dioxide.

4.76 Write a balanced equation for each of the following reactions:
a. Sulfur, present as an impurity in coal, is burned in oxygen to produce sulfur dioxide.
b. Hydrofluoric acid (HF) reacts with glass (SiO_2) in the process of etching to produce silicon tetrafluoride and water.

4.77 Solutions containing $(NH_4)_2CO_3(aq)$ and $CaCl_2(aq)$ are mixed. Will a precipitate form? If so, write its formula.

4.78 Solutions containing $Mg(NO_3)_2(aq)$ and $NaOH(aq)$ are mixed. Will a precipitate form? If so, write its formula.

4.79 Write the net ionic equation for the reaction of $NaBr(aq)$ with $AgNO_3(aq)$.

4.80 Write the net ionic equation for the reaction of $Pb(NO_3)_2(aq)$ with $K_2S(aq)$.

Calculations Using the Chemical Equation

Foundations

4.81 What is the law that forms the basis of chemical calculations?

4.82 Why is it essential to use balanced equations to solve mol problems?

4.83 Balancing equations involves changing coefficients, not subscripts. Why?

4.84 Describe the steps used in the calculation of g of product resulting from the reaction of a specified number of g of reactant.

Applications

4.85 How many g of B_2H_6 will react with 3.00 mol of O_2?

$$B_2H_6(l) + 3O_2(g) \longrightarrow B_2O_3(s) + 3H_2O(l)$$

4.86 How many g of Al will react with 3.00 mol of O_2?

$$4Al(s) + 3O_2(g) \longrightarrow 2Al_2O_3(s)$$

4.87 Calculate the amount of $CrCl_3$ that could be produced from 50.0 g Cr_2O_3 according to the equation

$$Cr_2O_3(s) + 3CCl_4(l) \longrightarrow 2CrCl_3(s) + 3COCl_2(aq)$$

4.88 A 3.5-g sample of water reacts with PCl_3 according to the following equation:

$$3H_2O(l) + PCl_3(g) \longrightarrow H_3PO_3(aq) + 3HCl(aq)$$

How many g of H_3PO_3 are produced?

4.89 For the reaction

$$N_2(g) + H_2(g) \longrightarrow NH_3(g)$$

a. Balance the equation.
b. How many mol of H_2 would react with 1 mol of N_2?
c. How many mol of product would form from 1 mol of N_2?
d. If 14.0 g of N_2 were initially present, calculate the number of mol of H_2 required to react with all of the N_2.
e. For conditions outlined in part (d), how many g of product would form?

4.90 Aspirin (acetylsalicylic acid) may be formed from salicylic acid and acetic acid as follows:

$$C_7H_6O_3(aq) + CH_3COOH(aq) \longrightarrow C_9H_8O_4(s) + H_2O(l)$$

Salicylic acid   Acetic acid   Aspirin

a. Is this equation balanced? If not, complete the balancing.
b. How many mol of aspirin may be produced from 1.00×10^2 mol salicylic acid?
c. How many g of aspirin may be produced from 1.00×10^2 mol salicylic acid?
d. How many g of acetic acid would be required to react completely with the 1.00×10^2 mol salicylic acid?

4.91 The proteins in our bodies are composed of molecules called amino acids. One amino acid is methionine; its molecular formula is $C_5H_{11}NO_2S$. Calculate:
a. the formula mass of methionine
b. the number of oxygen atoms in a mol of this compound
c. the mass of oxygen in a mol of the compound
d. the mass of oxygen in 50.0 g of the compound

4.92 Triglycerides (Chapters 17 and 23) are used in biochemical systems to store energy; they can be formed from glycerol and fatty acids. The molecular formula of glycerol is $C_3H_8O_3$. Calculate:
a. the formula mass of glycerol
b. the number of oxygen atoms in a mol of this compound
c. the mass of oxygen in a mol of the compound
d. the mass of oxygen in 50.0 g of the compound

4.93 Joseph Priestley discovered oxygen in the eighteenth century by using heat to decompose mercury(II) oxide:

$$2HgO(s) \xrightarrow{\Delta} 2Hg(l) + O_2(g)$$

How much oxygen is produced from 1.00×10^2 g HgO?

4.94 Dinitrogen monoxide (also known as nitrous oxide and used as an anesthetic) can be made by heating ammonium nitrate:

$$NH_4NO_3(s) \longrightarrow N_2O(g) + 2H_2O(g)$$

How much dinitrogen monoxide can be made from 1.00×10^2 g of ammonium nitrate?

4.95 The burning of acetylene (C_2H_2) in oxygen is the reaction in the oxyacetylene torch. How much CO_2 is produced by burning 20.0 kg of acetylene in an excess of O_2? The unbalanced equation is

$$C_2H_2(g) + O_2(g) \longrightarrow CO_2(g) + H_2O(g)$$

4.96 The reaction of calcium hydride with water can be used to prepare hydrogen gas:

$$CaH_2(s) + 2H_2O(l) \longrightarrow Ca(OH)_2(aq) + 2H_2(g)$$

How many g of hydrogen gas are produced in the reaction of 1.00×10^2 g calcium hydride with water?

4.97 Various members of a class of compounds called alkenes (Chapter 11), react with hydrogen to produce a corresponding alkane (Chapter 10). Termed hydrogenation, this type of reaction is used to produce products such as margarine. A typical hydrogenation reaction is

$$C_{10}H_{20}(l) + H_2(g) \longrightarrow C_{10}H_{22}(s)$$

Decene   Decane

How much decane can be produced in a reaction of excess decene with 1.00 g hydrogen?

4.98 A Human Perspective: Alcohol Consumption and the Breathalyzer Test (Chapter 12), describes the reaction between the dichromate ion and ethanol to produce acetic acid. How much acetic acid can be produced from a mixture containing excess of dichromate ion and 1.00×10^{-1} g of ethanol?

4.99 A rocket can be powered by the reaction between dinitrogen tetroxide and hydrazine:

$$N_2O_4(l) + 2N_2H_4(l) \longrightarrow 3N_2(g) + 4H_2O(g)$$

An engineer designed the rocket to hold 1.00 kg N_2O_4 and excess N_2H_4. How much N_2 would be produced according to the engineer's design?

4.100 A 4.00-g sample of Fe_3O_4 reacts with O_2 to produce Fe_2O_3:

$$4Fe_3O_4(s) + O_2(g) \longrightarrow 6Fe_2O_3(s)$$

Determine the number of g of Fe_2O_3 produced.

4.101 If the actual yield of decane in Problem 4.97 is 65.4 g, what is the % yield?

4.102 If the actual yield of acetic acid in Problem 4.98 is 0.110 g, what is the % yield?

4.103 If the % yield of nitrogen gas in Problem 4.99 is 75.0%, what is the actual yield of nitrogen?

4.104 If the % yield of Fe_2O_3 in Problem 4.100 is 90.0%, what is the actual yield of Fe_2O_3?

CRITICAL THINKING PROBLEMS

1. Which of the following has fewer mol of carbon: 100 g of $CaCO_3$ or 0.5 mol of CCl_4?
2. Which of the following has fewer mol of carbon: 6.02×10^{22} molecules of C_2H_6 or 88 g of CO_2?
3. How many molecules are found in each of the following?
   a. 1.0 lb of sucrose, $C_{12}H_{22}O_{11}$ (table sugar)
   b. 1.57 kg of N_2O (anesthetic)
4. How many molecules are found in each of the following?
   a. 4×10^5 tons (t) of SO_2 (produced by the 1980 eruption of the Mount St. Helens volcano)
   b. 25.0 lb of SiO_2 (major constituent of sand)
5. Based on the information in Questions 4.9 and 4.10, it appears that we could solve some of our atmospheric problems by reducing the amount of NO that we put into the air. Do some literature (or Internet) research and determine the sources of atmospheric NO. Can we control atmospheric NO? If so, how?

States of Matter
Gases, Liquids, and Solids

LEARNING GOALS

1 Describe the major points of the kinetic molecular theory of gases.

2 Explain the relationship between the kinetic molecular theory and the physical properties of measurable quantities of gases.

3 Describe the behavior of gases expressed by the gas laws: Boyle's law, Charles's law, combined gas law, Avogadro's law, the ideal gas law, and Dalton's law.

4 Use gas law equations to calculate conditions and changes in conditions of gases.

5 Describe properties of the liquid state in terms of the properties of the individual molecules that comprise the liquid.

6 Describe the processes of melting, boiling, evaporation, and condensation.

7 Describe the dipolar attractions known collectively as van der Waals forces.

8 Describe hydrogen bonding and its relationship to boiling and melting temperatures.

9 Relate the properties of the various classes of solids (ionic, covalent, molecular, and metallic) to the structure of these solids.

OUTLINE

Volcanic activity is a dramatic example of interconversion among the states of matter.

Section 1.2 introduces the properties of the three states of matter.

INTRODUCTION

We have learned that the major differences between solids, liquids, and gases are due to the relationships among particles. These relationships include:

- the average distance of separation of particles in each state,
- the kinds of interactions between the particles, and
- the degree of organization of particles.

We have already discovered that the solid state is the most organized, with particles close together, allowing significant interactions among the particles. This results in high melting and boiling points for solid substances. Large amounts of energy are needed to overcome the attractive forces and disrupt the orderly structure.

Substances that are gases, on the other hand, are disordered, with particles widely separated and weak interactions between particles. Their melting and boiling points are relatively low. Gases at room temperature must be cooled a great deal for them to liquefy or solidify. For example, the melting and boiling points of N_2 are $-210°C$ and $-196°C$, respectively.

Liquids are intermediate in character. The molecules of a liquid are close together, like those of solids. However, the molecules of a liquid are disordered, like those of a gas.

Can a substance such as O_2 gas or N_2 gas also exist as a liquid, or even as a solid? We will see that a reduction in temperature or an increase in pressure can force atoms or molecules closer together, allowing them to behave as liquids or solids. Dry ice, for example, is solid carbon dioxide. Changes in state are described as physical changes. When a substance undergoes a change in state, many of its physical properties change. For example, when ice forms from liquid water, changes occur in density and hardness, but it is still water. Table 5.1 summarizes the important differences in physical properties among gases, liquids, and solids.

5.1 The Gaseous State

Ideal Gas Concept

An **ideal gas** is simply a model of the way that particles (molecules or atoms) behave at the microscopic level. The behavior of the individual particles can be inferred from the measurable behavior of samples of real gases. We can easily measure temperature, volume, pressure, and quantity (mass) of real gases. Similarly,

Table 5.1 A Comparison of Physical Properties of Gases, Liquids, and Solids

	Gas	Liquid	Solid
Volume and Shape	Expands to fill the volume of its container; consequently, it takes the shape of the container	Has a fixed volume at a given mass and temperature; volume principally dependent on its mass and secondarily on temperature; it assumes the shape of its container	Has a fixed volume; volume principally dependent on its mass and secondarily on temperature; it has a definite shape
Density	Low (typically~10^{-3} g/mL)	High (typically~1 g/mL)	High (typically 1–10 g/mL)
Compressibility	High	Very low	Virtually incompressible
Particle Motion	Virtually free	Molecules or atoms "slide" past each other	Vibrate about a fixed position
Intermolecular Distance	Very large	Molecules or atoms are close to each other	Molecules, ions, or atoms are close to each other

when we systematically change one of these properties, we can determine the effect on each of the others. For example, putting more molecules in a balloon (the act of blowing up a balloon) causes its volume to increase in a predictable way. In fact, careful measurements show a direct proportionality between the number of molecules and the volume of the balloon, an observation made by Amadeo Avogadro more than 200 years ago.

We owe a great deal of credit to the efforts of scientists Boyle, Charles, Avogadro, Dalton, and Gay-Lussac, whose careful work elucidated the relationships among the gas properties. Their efforts are summarized in the ideal gas law and are the subject of the first section of this chapter.

Measurement of Gases

The most important gas laws (Boyle's law, Charles's law, Avogadro's law, Dalton's law, and the ideal gas law) involve the relationships between pressure (P), volume (V), temperature (T), and number of moles (mol) (n) of gas. We are already familiar with the measurement of temperature, volume, and mass (allowing the calculation of number of mol) from our laboratory experience. Measurement of pressure is perhaps not as obvious.

Gas pressure is a result of the force exerted by the collision of particles with the walls of the container. **Pressure** is force per unit area. The pressure of a gas may be measured with a **barometer,** invented by Evangelista Torricelli in the mid-1600s. The most common type of barometer is the mercury barometer depicted in Figure 5.1. A tube, sealed at one end, is filled with mercury and inverted in a dish of mercury. The pressure of the atmosphere pushing down on the mercury surface in the dish supports the column of mercury. The height of the column is proportional to the atmospheric pressure. The tube can be calibrated to give a numerical reading in millimeters (mm), centimeters (cm), or inches (in) of mercury. A commonly used unit of measurement is the atmosphere (atm). One standard atmosphere (1 atm) of pressure is equivalent to a height of mercury that is equal to

Figure 5.1 A mercury barometer of the type invented by Torricelli. The height of the column of mercury is a function of the magnitude of the surrounding atmospheric pressure. The mercury in the tube is supported by atmospheric pressure.

760 mm Hg (millimeters of mercury)

76.0 cm Hg (centimeters of mercury)

1 mm of Hg is also = 1 torr, in honor of Torricelli.

The English system equivalent is a pressure of 14.7 lb/in^2 (pounds per square inch) or 29.9 in Hg (inches of mercury). A recommended, yet less frequently used, systematic unit is the pascal (or kilopascal), named in honor of Blaise Pascal, a seventeenth-century French mathematician and scientist:

$$1 \text{ atm} = 1.01 \times 10^5 \text{ Pa (pascal)} = 101 \text{ kPa (kilopascal)}$$

Atmospheric pressure is due to the cumulative force of the air molecules (N_2 and O_2, for the most part) that are attracted to the earth's surface by gravity.

Question 5.1 Express each of the following in units of atm:

a. 725 mm Hg

b. 29.0 cm Hg

c. 555 torr

Question 5.2 Express each of the following in units of atm:

a. 10.0 torr

b. 61.0 cm Hg

c. 275 mm Hg

Kinetic Molecular Theory of Gases

The kinetic molecular theory of gases provides a reasonable explanation of the behavior of gases. The macroscopic properties result from the action of the individual molecules comprising the gas.

The **kinetic molecular theory** can be summarized as follows:

LEARNING GOAL

1 ▶ Describe the major points of the kinetic molecular theory of gases.

1. Gases are made up of tiny atoms or molecules that are in constant, random motion.
2. The distance of separation among these atoms or molecules is very large in comparison to the size of the individual atoms or molecules. In other words, a gas is mostly empty space.
3. All of the atoms and molecules behave independently. No attractive or repulsive forces exist between atoms or molecules in a gas.
4. Atoms and molecules collide with each other and with the walls of the container without *losing* energy. The energy is *transferred* from one atom or molecule to another.
5. The average kinetic energy of the atoms or molecules increases or decreases in proportion to absolute temperature.

Kinetic energy (K.E.) is equal to $1/2\ mv^2$, in which m = mass and v = velocity. Thus increased velocity at higher temperature correlates with an increase in kinetic energy.

LEARNING GOAL

2 ▶ Explain the relationship between the kinetic molecular theory and the physical properties of measurable quantities of gases.

Properties of Gases and the Kinetic Molecular Theory

We know that gases are easily *compressible*. The reason is that a gas is mostly empty space, providing space for the particles to be pushed closer together.

A Human Perspective

The Demise of the Hindenburg

One of the largest and most luxurious airships of the 1930s, the Hindenburg completed thirty-six transatlantic flights within a year after its construction. It was the flagship of a new era of air travel. But, on May 6, 1937, while making a landing approach near Lakehurst, New Jersey, the hydrogen-filled airship exploded and burst into flames. In this tragedy, thirty-seven of the ninety-six passengers were killed and many others were injured.

We may never know the exact cause. Many believe that the massive ship (it was more than 800 feet (ft) long) struck an overhead power line. Others speculate that lightning ignited the hydrogen, and some believe that sabotage may have been involved.

In retrospect, such an accident was inevitable. Hydrogen gas is very reactive, it combines with oxygen readily and rapidly, and this reaction liberates a large amount of energy. An explosion is the result of rapid, energy-releasing reactions.

Why was hydrogen chosen? Hydrogen is the lightest element. One mole of hydrogen has a mass of 2 grams (g). Hydrogen can be easily prepared in pure form, an essential requirement; more than seven million cubic feet (ft^3) of hydrogen were needed for each airship. Hydrogen has a low density; hence it provides great lift. The lifting power of a gas is based on the difference in density of the gas and the surrounding air (air is composed of gases with much greater molar masses; N_2 is 28 g and O_2 is 32 g). Engineers believed that the hydrogen would be safe when enclosed by the hull of the airship.

Today, airships are filled with helium (its molar mass is 4 g) and are used principally for advertising and television.

Hindenburg

A Goodyear blimp can be seen hovering over almost every significant outdoor sporting event.

For Further Understanding

▶ Would a gas such as methane (CH_4) provide lifting power for an airship? Why or why not?

▶ What property would immediately rule out methane as a replacement gas for hydrogen in an airship?

Gases will *expand* to fill any available volume because they move freely with sufficient energy to overcome their attractive forces.

Gases have a *low density.* Density is defined as mass per volume. Because gases are mostly empty space, they have a low mass per volume.

Gases readily *diffuse* through each other simply because they are in continuous motion and paths are readily available because of the large space between adjacent atoms or molecules. Light molecules diffuse rapidly; heavier molecules diffuse more slowly (Figure 5.2).

Gases exert *pressure* on their containers. Pressure is a force per unit area resulting from collisions of gas particles with the walls of their container.

Gases behave most *ideally at low pressures and high temperatures.* At low pressures, the average distance of separation among atoms or molecules is greatest, minimizing interactive forces. At high temperatures, the atoms and molecules are in rapid motion and are able to overcome interactive forces more easily.

Boyle's Law

The Irish scientist Robert Boyle found that the volume of a gas varies *inversely* with the pressure exerted by the gas if the number of mol and temperature of gas are held constant. This relationship is known as **Boyle's law.**

Mathematically, the *product* of pressure (P) and volume (V) is a constant:

$$PV = k_1$$

This relationship is illustrated in Figure 5.3.

Boyle's law is often used to calculate the volume resulting from a pressure change or vice versa. We consider

$$P_iV_i = k_1$$

the *initial* condition and

$$P_fV_f = k_1$$

the *final* condition. Because *PV*, initial or final, is constant and is equal to k_1,

$$P_iV_i = P_fV_f$$

Consider a gas occupying a volume of 10.0 liters (L) at 1.00 atm of pressure. The product, $PV = (10.0 \text{ L})(1.00 \text{ atm})$, is a constant, k_1. Doubling the pressure, to 2.0 atm, decreases the volume to 5.0 L:

$$(2.0 \text{ atm})(V_x) = (10.0 \text{ L})(1.00 \text{ atm})$$
$$V_x = 5.0 \text{ L}$$

Tripling the pressure decreases the volume by a factor of three:

$$(3.0 \text{ atm})(V_x) = (10.0 \text{ L})(1.00 \text{ atm})$$
$$V_x = 3.3 \text{ L}$$

(a)

(b)

Figure 5.2 Gaseous diffusion. (a) Ammonia (17.0 g/mol) and hydrogen chloride (36.5 g/mol) are introduced into the ends of a glass tube containing indicating paper. Red indicates the presence of hydrogen chloride and green indicates ammonia. (b) Note that ammonia has diffused much farther than hydrogen chloride in the same amount of time. This is a verification of the kinetic molecular theory. Light molecules move faster than heavier molecules at a specified temperature.

LEARNING GOAL

3 ▶ Describe the behavior of gases expressed by the gas laws: Boyle's law, Charles's law, combined gas law, Avogadro's law, the ideal gas law, and Dalton's law.

 A Review of Mathematics

EXAMPLE 5.1 Calculating a Final Pressure

A sample of oxygen, at 25°C, occupies a volume of 5.00×10^2 milliliters (mL) at 1.50 atm pressure. What pressure must be applied to compress the gas to a volume of 1.50×10^2 mL, with no temperature change?

Solution

Step 1. Boyle's law applies directly, because there is no change in temperature or number of mol (no gas enters or leaves the container).

LEARNING GOAL

4 ▶ Use gas law equations to calculate conditions and changes in conditions of gases.

Continued—

A Review of Mathematics

Step 2. Begin by identifying each term in the Boyle's law expression:

$$P_i = 1.50 \text{ atm}$$
$$P_f = ?$$
$$V_i = 5.00 \times 10^2 \text{ mL}$$
$$V_f = 1.50 \times 10^2 \text{ mL}$$

Step 3. The Boyle's law expression is:

$$P_iV_i = P_fV_f$$

Step 4. Solving for P_f:

$$P_f = \frac{P_iV_i}{V_f}$$

Step 5. Substituting:

$$P_f = \frac{(1.50 \text{ atm})(5.00 \times 10^2 \text{ mL})}{1.50 \times 10^2 \text{ mL}}$$
$$= 5.00 \text{ atm}$$

Helpful Hint: The calculation can be done with any volume units. It is important only that the units be the *same* on both sides of the equation.

Practice Problem 5.1

Complete the following table:

Sample Number	Initial Pressure (atm)	Final Pressure (atm)	Initial Volume (L)	Final Volume (L)
1	X	5.0	1.0	7.5
2	5.0	X	1.0	0.20
3	1.0	0.50	X	0.30
4	1.0	2.0	0.75	X

▶ **For Further Practice: Questions 5.35 and 5.36.**

Figure 5.3 An illustration of Boyle's law. Note the inverse relationship of pressure and volume.

Charles's Law

Jacques Charles, a French scientist, studied the relationship between gas volume and temperature. This relationship, **Charles's law,** states that the volume of a gas varies *directly* with the absolute temperature (K) if pressure and number of mol of gas are constant.

Mathematically, the *ratio* of volume (V) and temperature (T) is a constant:

$$\frac{V}{T} = k_2$$

In a way analogous to Boyle's law, we may establish a set of initial conditions,

$$\frac{V_i}{T_i} = k_2$$

and final conditions,

$$\frac{V_f}{T_f} = k_2$$

Because k_2 is a constant, we may equate them, resulting in

$$\frac{V_i}{T_i} = \frac{V_f}{T_f}$$

and we may use this expression to solve some practical problems.

Consider a gas occupying a volume of 10.0 L at 273 K. The ratio V/T is a constant, k_2. Doubling the temperature, to 546 K, increases the volume to 20.0 L, as shown here:

$$\frac{10.0 \text{ L}}{273 \text{ K}} = \frac{V_f}{546 \text{ K}}$$
$$V_f = 20.0 \text{ L}$$

Tripling the temperature, to 819 K, increases the volume by a factor of three:

$$\frac{10.0 \text{ L}}{273 \text{ K}} = \frac{V_f}{819 \text{ K}}$$
$$V_f = 30.0 \text{ L}$$

These relationships are illustrated in Figure 5.4.

LEARNING GOAL

3 ▶ Describe the behavior of gases expressed by the gas laws: Boyle's law, Charles's law, combined gas law, Avogadro's law, the ideal gas law, and Dalton's law.

Temperature is a measure of the energy of molecular motion. The Kelvin scale is *absolute*, that is, directly proportional to molecular motion. Celsius and Fahrenheit are simply numerical scales based on the melting and boiling points of water. It is for this reason that Kelvin is used for energy-dependent relationships such as the gas laws.

 A Review of Mathematics

 Animation
• Charles's Law

EXAMPLE 5.2 Calculating a Final Volume

A balloon filled with helium has a volume of 4.0×10^3 L at 25°C. What volume will the balloon occupy at 50°C if the pressure surrounding the balloon remains constant?

LEARNING GOAL

4 ▶ Use gas law equations to calculate conditions and changes in conditions of gases.

Solution
Step 1. Summarize the data, remembering that the temperature must be converted to Kelvin before Charles's law is applied:

$$T_i = 25°C + 273 = 298 \text{ K}$$
$$T_f = 50°C + 273 = 323 \text{ K}$$
$$V_i = 4.0 \times 10^3 \text{ L}$$
$$V_f = ?$$

Continued—

Step 2. Using the Charles's law expression relating initial and final conditions:

$$\frac{V_i}{T_i} = \frac{V_f}{T_f}$$

Step 3. Rearrange and solve for V_f

$$V_f = \frac{(V_i)(T_f)}{T_i}$$

Step 4. Substituting our data, we get

$$V_f = \frac{(V_i)(T_f)}{T_i} = \frac{(4.0 \times 10^3 \text{ L})(323 \text{ K})}{298 \text{ K}} = 4.3 \times 10^3 \text{ L}$$

Practice Problem 5.2

A sample of nitrogen gas has a volume of 3.00 L at 25°C. What volume will it occupy at each of the following temperatures if the pressure and number of mol are constant?

a. 100°C
b. 150°F
c. 273 K
d. 546 K
e. 0°C
f. 373 K

▶ **For Further Practice: Questions 5.43 and 5.44.**

Figure 5.4 An illustration of Charles's law. Note the direct relationship between volume and temperature.

The behavior of a hot-air balloon is a commonplace consequence of Charles's law. The balloon rises because air expands when heated (Figure 5.5). The volume of the balloon is fixed because the balloon is made of an inelastic material; as a result, when the air expands some of it must be forced out. Hence the density of the remaining air is less (less mass contained in the same volume), and the balloon rises. Turning down the heat reverses the process, and the balloon descends.

Combined Gas Law

Boyle's law describes the inverse proportional relationship between volume and pressure; Charles's law shows the direct proportional relationship between volume and temperature. Often, a sample of gas (a fixed number of mol of gas) undergoes change involving volume, pressure, and temperature simultaneously. It would be useful to have one equation that describes such processes.

The **combined gas law** is such an equation. It can be derived from Boyle's law and Charles's law and takes the form:

$$\frac{P_i V_i}{T_i} = \frac{P_f V_f}{T_f}$$

Let's look at two examples that use this expression.

EXAMPLE 5.3   Using the Combined Gas Law

Calculate the volume of N_2 that results when 0.100 L of the gas is heated from 300.0 K to 350.0 K at 1.00 atm.

Solution

Step 1. Summarize the data:

$$P_i = 1.00 \text{ atm} \qquad P_f = 1.00 \text{ atm}$$
$$V_i = 0.100 \text{ L} \qquad V_f = ? \text{ L}$$
$$T_i = 300.0 \text{ K} \qquad T_f = 350.0 \text{ K}$$

Step 2. The combined gas law expression is:

$$\frac{P_i V_i}{T_i} = \frac{P_f V_f}{T_f}$$

Step 3. Rearrange:

$$P_f V_f T_i = P_i V_i T_f$$

and

$$V_f = \frac{P_i V_i T_f}{P_{fi} T}$$

Step 4. Because $P_i = P_f$

$$V_f = \frac{V_i T_f}{T_i}$$

Step 5. Substituting gives

$$V_f = \frac{(0.100 \text{ L})(350.0 \text{ K})}{300.0 \text{ K}}$$
$$= 0.117 \text{ L}$$

Helpful Hint: In this case, because the pressure is constant, the combined gas law reduces to Charles's law.

Practice Problem 5.3

Hydrogen sulfide, H_2S, has the characteristic odor of rotten eggs. If a sample of H_2S gas at 760.0 torr and 25.0°C in a 2.00-L container is allowed to expand into a 10.0-L container at 25.0°C, what is the pressure in the 10.0-L container?

▶ **For Further Practice: Questions 5.49 and 5.50.**

Figure 5.5 Charles's law predicts that the volume of air in the balloon will increase when heated. We assume that the volume of the balloon is fixed; consequently, some air will be pushed out. The air remaining in the balloon is less dense (same volume, less mass) and the balloon will rise. When the heater is turned off the air cools, the density increases, and the balloon returns to earth.

Animation
• Interactive Gas Law

LEARNING GOAL

3 ▶ Describe the behavior of gases expressed by the gas laws: Boyle's law, Charles's law, combined gas law, Avogadro's law, the ideal gas law, and Dalton's law.

LEARNING GOAL

4 ▶ Use gas law equations to calculate conditions and changes in conditions of gases.

A Review of Mathematics

A Review of Mathematics

EXAMPLE 5.4   Using the Combined Gas Law

A sample of helium gas has a volume of 1.27 L at 149 K and 5.00 atm. When the gas is compressed to 0.320 L at 50.0 atm, the temperature increases markedly. What is the final temperature?

Solution

Step 1. Summarize the data:

$$P_i = 5.00 \text{ atm} \quad P_f = 50.0 \text{ atm}$$
$$V_i = 1.27 \text{ L} \quad V_f = 0.320 \text{ L}$$
$$T_i = 149 \text{ K} \quad T_f = ? \text{ K}$$

Step 2. The combined gas law expression is

$$\frac{P_i V_i}{T_i} = \frac{P_f V_f}{T_f}$$

Step 3. Rearrange:

$$P_f V_f T_i = P_i V_i T_f$$

and

$$T_f = \frac{P_f V_f T_i}{P_i V_i}$$

Step 4. Substituting yields

$$T_f = \frac{(50.0 \text{ atm})(0.320 \text{ L})(149 \text{ K})}{(5.00 \text{ atm})(1.27 \text{ L})}$$

$$= 375 \text{ K}$$

Practice Problem 5.4

Cyclopropane, C_3H_6, is used as a general anesthetic. If a sample of cyclopropane stored in a 2.00-L container at 10.0 atm and 25.0°C is transferred to a 5.00-L container at 5.00 atm, what is the resulting temperature?

▶ **For Further Practice: Questions 5.51 and 5.52.**

Avogadro's Law

The relationship between the volume and number of mol of a gas at constant temperature and pressure is known as **Avogadro's law.** It states that equal volumes of any ideal gas contain the same number of mol if measured under the same conditions of temperature and pressure.

Mathematically, the *ratio* of volume (V) to number of mol (n) is a constant:

$$\frac{V}{n} = k_3$$

Consider 1 mol of gas occupying a volume of 10.0 L; using logic similar to the application of Boyle's and Charles's laws, 2 mol of the gas would occupy 20.0 L, 3 mol would occupy 30.0 L, and so forth. As we have done with the previous laws, we can formulate a useful expression relating initial and final conditions:

$$\frac{V_i}{n_i} = \frac{V_f}{n_f}$$

EXAMPLE 5.5 Using Avogadro's Law

If 5.50 mol of CO occupy 20.6 L, how many L will 16.5 mol of CO occupy at the same temperature and pressure?

Solution

Step 1. The quantities and volume are related through Avogadro's law. Summarizing the data:

$$V_i = 20.6 \text{ L} \qquad V_f = ? \text{ L}$$
$$n_i = 5.50 \text{ mol} \qquad n_f = 16.5 \text{ mol}$$

Step 2. Using the mathematical expression for Avogadro's law:

$$\frac{V_i}{n_i} = \frac{V_f}{n_f}$$

Step 3. Rearranging:

$$V_f = \frac{V_i n_f}{n_i}$$

Step 4. Substitution yields:

$$V_f = \frac{(20.6 \text{ L})(16.5 \text{ mol})}{(5.50 \text{ mol})}$$
$$= 61.8 \text{ L of CO}$$

Practice Problem 5.5

a. A 1.00 mol sample of hydrogen gas occupies 22.4 L. How many mol of hydrogen are needed to fill a 100.0 L container at the same pressure and temperature?

b. How many mol of hydrogen are needed to triple the volume occupied by 0.25 mol of hydrogen, assuming no changes in pressure or temperature?

▶ **For Further Practice: Questions 5.55 and 5.56.**

LEARNING GOAL

4 ▶ Use gas law equations to calculate conditions and changes in conditions of gases.

Molar Volume of a Gas

The volume occupied by *1 mol* of any gas is referred to as its **molar volume**. At **standard temperature and pressure (STP)**, the molar volume of any gas is 22.4 L. STP conditions are defined as follows:

$$T = 273 \text{ K (or } 0°\text{C)}$$
$$P = 1 \text{ atm}$$

Thus, 1 mol of N_2, O_2, H_2, or He all occupy the *same volume, 22.4 L*, at STP.

Gas Densities

It is also possible to compute the density of various gases at STP. If we recall that density is the mass/unit volume,

$$d = \frac{m}{V}$$

and that 1 mol of helium weighs 4.00 g,

$$d_{He} = \frac{4.00 \text{ g}}{22.4 \text{ L}} = 0.178 \text{ g/L at STP}$$

Gas densities are most often expressed in units of g/L. Recall that units of g/mL are generally preferred for solids and liquids.

or, because 1 mol of nitrogen weighs 28.0 g, then

$$d_{N_2} = \frac{28.0 \text{ g}}{22.4 \text{ L}} = 1.25 \text{ g/L at STP}$$

The large difference in gas densities of helium and nitrogen (which makes up about 80% of the air) accounts for the lifting power of helium. A balloon filled with helium will rise through a predominantly nitrogen atmosphere because its gas density is less than 15% of the density of the surrounding atmosphere:

$$\frac{d_{He}}{d_{N_2}} \times 100\% = \% \text{ density}$$

$$\frac{0.178 \text{ g/L}}{1.25 \text{ g/L}} \times 100\% = 14.2\%$$

Heating a gas, such as air, will decrease its density and have a lifting effect as well.

The Ideal Gas Law

Boyle's law (relating volume and pressure), Charles's law (relating volume and temperature), and Avogadro's law (relating volume to the number of mol) may be combined into a single expression relating all four terms. This expression is the **ideal gas law:**

$$PV = nRT$$

in which R, based on k_1, k_2, and k_3 (Boyle's, Charles's, and Avogadro's law constants), is a constant and is referred to as the *ideal gas constant:*

$$R = 0.0821 \text{ L} \cdot \text{atm} \cdot \text{K}^{-1} \cdot \text{mol}^{-1}$$

if the units

> atmospheres, for P
> liters, for V
> number of moles, for n
> and
> Kelvin for T

are used.

Consider some examples of the application of the ideal gas equation.

LEARNING GOAL

3 ▶ Describe the behavior of gases expressed by the gas laws: Boyle's law, Charles's law, combined gas law, Avogadro's law, the ideal gas law, and Dalton's law.

Remember that 0.0821 L · atm/K · mol is identical to 0.0821 L · atm·K⁻¹ · mol⁻¹.

Animation
• Ideal Gas Law

LEARNING GOAL

4 ▶ Use gas law equations to calculate conditions and changes in conditions of gases.

EXAMPLE 5.6   Calculating a Molar Volume

Show by calculation that the molar volume of oxygen gas at STP is 22.4 L.

Solution

Step 1. At STP,

$$T = 273 \text{ K}$$
$$P = 1.00 \text{ atm}$$

and the other terms are

$$n = 1.00 \text{ mol}$$
$$R = 0.0821 \text{ L} \cdot \text{atm} \cdot \text{K}^{-1} \cdot \text{mol}^{-1}$$

Step 2. The ideal gas expression is:

$$PV = nRT$$

Step 3. Rearrange and solve for V:

$$V = \frac{nRT}{P}$$

Step 4. Substitute and solve:

$$V = \frac{(1.00 \ \cancel{mol})(0.0821 \ L \cdot \cancel{atm} \cdot \cancel{K^{-1}} \cdot \cancel{mol^{-1}})(273 \ \cancel{K})}{(1.00 \ \cancel{atm})}$$

$$= 22.4 \ L$$

Practice Problem 5.6

Explain why the molar volume of helium (or any other ideal gas) is also 22.4 L.

▶ **For Further Practice: Questions 5.59 and 5.60.**

EXAMPLE 5.7 Calculating the Number of Moles of a Gas

Calculate the number of mol of helium in a 1.00-L balloon at 27°C and 1.00 atm of pressure.

LEARNING GOAL

4 ▶ Use gas law equations to calculate conditions and changes in conditions of gases.

Solution

Step 1. The data are:

$$P = 1.00 \ atm$$
$$V = 1.00 \ L$$
$$T = 27°C + 273 = 3.00 \times 10^2 \ K$$
$$R = 0.0821 \ L \cdot atm \cdot K^{-1} \cdot mol^{-1}$$
$$n = ?$$

Step 2. The ideal gas expression is:

$$PV = nRT$$

Step 3. Rearrange and solve for n:

$$n = \frac{PV}{RT}$$

Step 4. Substitute and solve:

$$n = \frac{(1.00 \ \cancel{atm})(1.00 \ \cancel{L})}{(0.0821 \ \cancel{L} \cdot \cancel{atm} \cdot \cancel{K^{-1}} \cdot mol^{-1})(3.00 \times 10^2 \ \cancel{K})}$$

$$n = 0.0406 \ or \ 4.06 \times 10^{-2} \ mol$$

Practice Problem 5.7

How many mol of N_2 gas will occupy a 5.00-L container at STP?

▶ **For Further Practice: Questions 5.61 and 5.67.**

LEARNING GOAL

4 ▶ Use gas law equations to calculate conditions and changes in conditions of gases.

EXAMPLE 5.8   Converting Mass to Volume

Oxygen used in hospitals and laboratories is often obtained from cylinders containing liquefied oxygen. If a cylinder contains 1.00×10^2 kilograms (kg) of liquid oxygen, how many L of oxygen can be produced at 1.00 atm of pressure at room temperature (20.0°C)?

Solution

Step 1. Data include:

mass of oxygen (O_2) = 1.00×10^2 kg
$T = 20.0°C$
$P = 1.00$ atm
V of O_2 = ?

Step 2. Using conversion factors, we obtain

$$n_{O_2} = 1.00 \times 10^2 \text{ kg } O_2 \times \frac{10^3 \text{ g } O_2}{1 \text{ kg } O_2} \times \frac{1 \text{ mol } O_2}{32.0 \text{ g } O_2}$$

and

$$n_{O_2} = 3.13 \times 10^3 \text{ mol } O_2$$

Step 3. Convert °C to K:

$$T = 20.0°C + 273 = 293 \text{ K}$$

Step 4. The ideal gas expression is:

$$PV = nRT$$

Step 5. Rearrange and solve for V:

$$V = \frac{nRT}{P}$$

Step 6. Substitute and solve:

$$V = \frac{(3.13 \times 10^3 \text{ mol})(0.0821 \text{ L} \cdot \text{atm} \cdot \text{K}^{-1} \cdot \text{mol}^{-1})(293 \text{ K})}{1.00 \text{ atm}}$$

$$= 7.53 \times 10^4 \text{ L}$$

Practice Problem 5.8

What volume is occupied by 10.0 g N_2 at 30.0°C and a pressure of 750 torr?

▶ **For Further Practice: Questions 5.63 and 5.64.**

Question 5.3 A 20.0-L gas cylinder contains 4.80 g H_2 at 25°C. What is the pressure of this gas?

Question 5.4 At what temperature will 2.00 mol of He fill a 2.00-L container at standard pressure?

LEARNING GOAL

3 ▶ Describe the behavior of gases expressed by the gas laws: Boyle's law, Charles's law, combined gas law, Avogadro's law, the ideal gas law, and Dalton's law.

Dalton's Law of Partial Pressures

Our discussion of gases so far has presumed that we are working with a single pure gas. A *mixture* of gases exerts a pressure that is the *sum* of the pressures that each gas would exert if it were present alone under the same conditions. This is known as **Dalton's law** of partial pressures.

Green Chemistry

The Greenhouse Effect and Global Climate Change

A greenhouse is a bright, warm, and humid environment for growing plants, vegetables, and flowers even during the cold winter months. It functions as a closed system in which the concentration of water vapor is elevated and visible light streams through the windows; this creates an ideal climate for plant growth.

Some of the visible light is absorbed by plants and soil in the greenhouse and radiated as infrared radiation. This radiated energy is blocked by the glass or absorbed by water vapor and carbon dioxide (CO_2). This trapped energy warms the greenhouse and is a form of solar heating: light energy is converted to heat energy.

On a global scale, the same process takes place. Although more than half of the sunlight that strikes the earth's surface is reflected back into space, the fraction of light that is absorbed produces sufficient heat to sustain life. How does this happen? Greenhouse gases, such as CO_2, trap energy radiated from the earth's surface and store it in the atmosphere. This moderates our climate. The earth's surface would be much colder and more inhospitable if the atmosphere was not able to capture some reasonable amount of solar energy.

Can we have too much of a good thing? It appears so. Since 1900 the atmospheric concentration of CO_2 has increased from 296 parts per million (ppm) to over 350 ppm (approximately 17% increase). The energy demands of technological and population growth have caused massive increases in the combustion of organic matter and carbon-based fuels (coal, oil, and natural gas), adding over 50 billion tons of CO_2 to that already present in the atmosphere. Photosynthesis naturally removes CO_2 from the atmosphere. However, the removal of forestland to create living space and cropland has decreased the amount of vegetation available to consume atmospheric CO_2 through photosynthesis. The rapid destruction of the Amazon rain forest is just the latest of many examples.

If our greenhouse model is correct, an increase in CO_2 levels should produce global warming, perhaps changing our climate in unforeseen and undesirable ways.

For Further Understanding

▶ What steps might be taken to decrease levels of CO_2 in the atmosphere over time?

▶ In what ways might our climate and our lives change as a consequence of significant global warming?

(a) A greenhouse traps solar radiation as heat. (b) Our atmosphere also acts as a solar collector. Carbon dioxide, like the windows of a greenhouse, allows the visible light to enter and traps the heat.

Stated another way, the total pressure of a mixture of gases is the sum of the **partial pressures.** That is,

$$P_t = p_1 + p_2 + p_3 + \cdots$$

The ideal gas law applies to mixtures of gases as well as pure gases.

in which P_t = total pressure and $p_1, p_2, p_3, \ldots$, are the partial pressures of the component gases. For example, the total pressure of our atmosphere is equal to the sum of the pressures of N_2 and O_2 (the principal components of air):

$$P_{air} = p_{N_2} + p_{O_2}$$

Other gases, such as argon (Ar), carbon dioxide (CO_2), carbon monoxide (CO), and methane (CH_4) are present in the atmosphere at very low partial pressures. However, their presence may result in dramatic consequences; one such gas is carbon dioxide. Classified as a "greenhouse gas," it exerts a significant effect on our climate. Its role is described in Green Chemistry: The Greenhouse Effect and Global Climate Change.

Ideal Gases Versus Real Gases

To this point we have assumed, in both theory and calculations, that all gases behave as ideal gases. However, in reality there is no such thing as an ideal gas. As we noted at the beginning of this section, the ideal gas is a model (a very useful one) that describes the behavior of individual atoms and molecules; this behavior translates to the collective properties of measurable quantities of these atoms and molecules. Limitations of the model arise from the fact that interactive forces, even between the widely spaced particles of gas, are not totally absent in any sample of gas.

Attractive forces are present in gases composed of polar molecules. Nonuniform charge distribution on polar molecules creates positive and negative regions, resulting in electrostatic attraction and deviation from ideality.

Calculations involving polar gases such as HF, NO, and SO_2 based on ideal gas equations (which presume no such interactions) are approximations. However, at low pressures, such approximations certainly provide useful information. Nonpolar molecules, on the other hand, are only weakly attracted to each other and behave much more ideally in the gas phase.

See Sections 3.5 and 5.2 for a discussion of interactions of polar molecules.

5.2 The Liquid State

Molecules in the liquid state are close to one another. Attractive forces are large enough to keep the molecules together, in contrast to gases, whose cohesive forces are so low that a gas expands to fill any volume. However, these attractive forces in a liquid are not large enough to restrict movement, as in solids. Let's look at the various properties of liquids in more detail.

LEARNING GOAL

5 ▶ Describe properties of the liquid state in terms of the properties of the individual molecules that comprise the liquid.

Compressibility

Liquids are practically incompressible. In fact, the molecules are so close to one another that even the application of many atm of pressure does not significantly decrease the volume. This makes liquids ideal for the transmission of force, as in the brake lines of an automobile. The force applied by the driver's foot on the brake pedal does not compress the brake fluid in the lines; rather, it transmits the force directly to the brake pads, and the friction between the brake pads and rotors (that are attached to the wheel) stops the car.

Viscosity

The **viscosity** of a liquid is a measure of its resistance to flow. Viscosity is a function of both the attractive forces between molecules and molecular geometry.

Molecules with complex structures, which do not "slide" smoothly past each other, and polar molecules, tend to have higher viscosity than less structurally complex, less polar liquids. Glycerol, which is used in a variety of skin treatments, has the structural formula:

$$\begin{array}{c} H \\ | \\ H-C-O-H \\ | \\ H-C-O-H \\ | \\ H-C-O-H \\ | \\ H \end{array}$$

It is quite viscous, owing to its polar nature and its significant intermolecular attractive forces. This is certainly desirable in a skin treatment because its viscosity

A Medical Perspective

Blood Gases and Respiration

Respiration must deliver oxygen to cells and carbon dioxide, the waste product, to the lungs to be exhaled. Dalton's law of partial pressures helps to explain the way in which this process occurs.

Gases (such as O_2 and CO_2) move from a region of higher partial pressure to one of lower partial pressure in an effort to establish an equilibrium. At the interface of the lung, the membrane barrier between the blood and the surrounding atmosphere, the following situation exists: Atmospheric O_2 partial pressure is high, and atmospheric CO_2 partial pressure is low. The reverse is true on the other side of the membrane (blood). Thus CO_2 is efficiently removed from the blood, and O_2 is efficiently moved into the bloodstream.

At the other end of the line, capillaries are distributed in close proximity to the cells that need to expel CO_2 and gain O_2. The partial pressure of CO_2 is high in these cells, and the partial pressure of O_2 is low, having been used up by the energy-harvesting reaction, the oxidation of glucose:

$$C_6H_{12}O_6 + 6O_2 \longrightarrow 6CO_2 + 6H_2O + \text{energy}$$

The O_2 diffuses into the cells (from a region of high to low partial pressure), and the CO_2 diffuses from the cells to the blood (again from a region of high to low partial pressure).

The net result is a continuous process proceeding according to Dalton's law. With each breath we take, oxygen is distributed to the cells and used to generate energy, and the waste product, CO_2, is expelled by the lungs.

For Further Understanding

▶ Carbon dioxide and carbon monoxide can be toxic, but for different reasons. Use the Internet to research this topic and:

▶ Explain why carbon dioxide is toxic.

▶ Explain why carbon monoxide is toxic.

---

keeps it on the area being treated. Gasoline, on the other hand, is much less viscous and readily flows through the gas lines of your auto; it is composed of nonpolar molecules.

Viscosity generally decreases with increasing temperature. The increased kinetic energy at higher temperatures overcomes some of the intermolecular attractive forces. The temperature effect is an important consideration in the design of products that must remain fluid at low temperatures, such as motor oils and transmission fluids found in automobiles.

Surface Tension

The **surface tension** of a liquid is a measure of the attractive forces exerted among molecules at the surface of a liquid. It is only the surface molecules that are not totally surrounded by other liquid molecules (the top of the molecule faces the atmosphere). These surface molecules are surrounded and attracted by fewer liquid molecules than those below and to each side. Hence the net attractive forces on surface molecules pull them downward, into the body of the liquid. As a result, the surface molecules behave as a "skin" that covers the interior.

This increased surface force is responsible for the spherical shape of drops of liquid. Drops of water "beading" on a polished surface, such as a waxed automobile, illustrate this effect.

Because surface tension is related to the attractive forces exerted among molecules, surface tension generally decreases with an increase in temperature or a decrease in the polarity of molecules that make up the liquid.

Substances known as **surfactants** can be added to a liquid to decrease surface tension. Common surfactants include soaps and detergents that reduce water's surface tension; this promotes the interaction of water with grease and dirt, making them easier to remove.

 Animation
• Surface Tension of Water

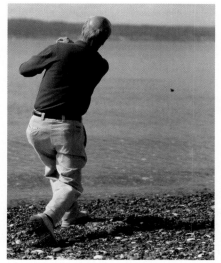

Skimming stones is possible due to the surface tension of water. Explain.

Question 5.5 What molecular properties favor high viscosity?

Question 5.6 What molecular properties favor high surface tension?

Figure 5.6 The temperature dependence of liquid vapor pressure is illustrated. The average molecular kinetic energy increases with temperature. Note that the average values are indicated by dashed lines. The small number of high-energy molecules may evaporate.

Animation
• Vapor Pressure

The process of evaporation of perspiration from the skin produces a cooling effect, because heat is stored in the evaporating molecules.

Vapor Pressure of a Liquid

Evaporation, condensation, and the meaning of the term *boiling point* are all related to the concept of liquid vapor pressure. Consider the following example. A liquid, such as water, is placed in a sealed container. After a time the contents of the container are analyzed. Both liquid water and water vapor are found at room temperature, when we might expect water to be found only as a liquid. In this closed system, some of the liquid water was converted to a gas:

$$\text{energy} + H_2O(l) \longrightarrow H_2O(g)$$

How did this happen? The temperature is too low for conversion of a liquid to a gas by boiling. According to the kinetic theory, liquid molecules are in continuous motion, with their *average* kinetic energy directly proportional to the Kelvin temperature. The word *average* is the key. Although the average kinetic energy is too low to allow "average" molecules to escape from the liquid phase to the gas phase, there exists a range of molecules with different energies, some low and some high, that make up the "average" (Figure 5.6). Thus some of these high-energy molecules possess sufficient energy to escape from the bulk liquid.

At the same time, a fraction of these gaseous molecules lose energy (perhaps by collision with the walls of the container) and return to the liquid state:

$$H_2O(g) \longrightarrow H_2O(l) + \text{energy}$$

The process of conversion of liquid to gas, at a temperature too low to boil, is **evaporation.** The reverse process, conversion of the gas to the liquid state, is **condensation.** After some time the rates of evaporation and condensation become *equal,* and this sets up a dynamic equilibrium between liquid and vapor states. The **vapor pressure of a liquid** is defined as the pressure exerted by the vapor *at equilibrium.*

$$H_2O(g) \rightleftarrows H_2O(l)$$

The equilibrium process of evaporation and condensation of water is depicted in Figure 5.7.

The boiling point of a liquid is defined as the temperature at which the vapor pressure of the liquid becomes equal to the atmospheric pressure. The "normal" atmospheric pressure is 760 torr, or 1 atm, and the **normal boiling point** is the temperature at which the vapor pressure of the liquid is equal to 1 atm.

It follows from the definition that the boiling point of a liquid is not constant. It depends on the atmospheric pressure. At high altitudes, where the atmospheric pressure is low, the boiling point of a liquid, such as water, is lower than the normal boiling point (for water, 100°C). High atmospheric pressure increases the boiling point.

Figure 5.7 Liquid water in equilibrium with water vapor. (a) Initiation: process of evaporation exclusively. (b, c) After a time, both evaporation and condensation occur, but evaporation predominates. (d) Dynamic equilibrium established. Rates of evaporation and condensation are equal.

Symbolizes the rate of evaporation   Symbolizes the rate of condensation

(a)   (b)   (c)   (d)

Apart from its dependence on the surrounding atmospheric pressure, the boiling point depends on the nature of the attractive forces between the liquid molecules. Polar liquids, such as water, with large intermolecular attractive forces have *higher* boiling points than nonpolar liquids, such as gasoline, which exhibit weak attractive forces.

Compounds may be detected and identified because they have a measurable vapor pressure, as you will see in the discussion Chemistry at the Crime Scene: Explosives at the Airport.

Question 5.7 Distinguish between the terms *evaporation* and *condensation*.

Question 5.8 Distinguish between the terms *evaporation* and *boiling*.

van der Waals Forces

Physical properties of liquids, such as those discussed in the previous section, can be explained in terms of their intermolecular forces. We have seen (see Section 3.5) that attractive forces between polar molecules, **dipole-dipole interactions,** significantly decrease vapor pressure and increase the boiling point. However, nonpolar substances can exist as liquids as well; many are liquids and even solids at room temperature. What is the nature of the attractive forces in these nonpolar compounds?

In 1930, Fritz London demonstrated that he could account for a weak attractive force between any two molecules, whether polar or nonpolar. He postulated

> **LEARNING GOAL**
> **7** ▶ Describe the dipolar attractions known collectively as van der Waals forces.

Chemistry at the Crime Scene

Explosives at the Airport

The images flash across our television screens: a "bomb sniffing" dog being led through an airport or train station, pausing to sniff packages or passengers, looking for anything of a suspicious nature. Or, perhaps, we see a long line of people waiting to pass through a scanning device surrounded by what appears to be hundreds of thousands of dollars worth of electronic gadgetry.

At one level, we certainly know what is happening. These steps are taken to increase the likelihood that our trip, as well as everyone else's, will be as safe and worry-free as possible. From a scientific standpoint, we may wonder how these steps actually detect explosive materials. What do the dog and some electronic devices have in common? How can a dog sniff a solid or a liquid? Surely everyone knows that the nose can only sense gases, and explosive devices are solids or liquids, or a combination of the two.

One potential strategy is based on the concept of vapor pressure, which you have just studied. We now know that liquids, such as water, have a measurable vapor pressure at room temperature. In fact, most liquids and many solids have vapor pressures large enough to allow detection of the molecules in the gas phase. The challenge is finding devices that are sufficiently sensitive and selective, enabling them to detect low concentrations of molecules characteristic of explosives, without becoming confused by thousands of other compounds routinely present in the air.

Each explosive device has its own "signature," a unique mix of chemicals used in its manufacture and assembly. If only one, or perhaps a few, of these compounds has a measurable vapor pressure, it may be detected with a sensitive measuring device.

Dogs are renowned for their keen sense of smell, and some breeds are better than others. Dogs can be trained to signal the presence of certain scents by barking or exhibiting unusual agitation. A qualified handler can recognize these cues and alert appropriate authorities.

Scientific instruments are designed to mimic the scenario described here. A device, the mass spectrometer, can detect very low concentrations of molecules in the air. Additionally, it can distinguish certain "target" molecules, because each different compound has its own unique molar mass. Detection of molecules of interest generates an electrical signal, and an alarm is sounded.

Compounds with high vapor pressures are most easily detected. Active areas of forensic research involve designing a new generation of instruments that are even more sensitive and selective than those currently available. Decreased cost and increased portability and reliability will enable many sites not currently being monitored to have the same level of protection as major transit facilities.

For Further Understanding

▶ Would you expect nonpolar or polar molecules of similar mass to be more easily detected? Why?

▶ Why must an explosives detection device be highly selective?

that the electron distribution in molecules is not fixed; electrons are in continuous motion, relative to the nucleus. So, for a short time a nonpolar molecule could experience an *instantaneous dipole,* a short-lived polarity caused by a temporary dislocation of the electron cloud. These temporary dipoles could interact with other temporary dipoles, just as permanent dipoles interact in polar molecules. We now call these intermolecular forces **London forces.**

London forces and dipole-dipole interactions are collectively known as **van der Waals forces.** London forces exist among polar and nonpolar molecules because electrons are in constant motion in all molecules. Dipole-dipole attractions occur only among polar molecules. In addition to van der Waals forces, a special type of dipole-dipole force, the *hydrogen bond,* has a very significant effect on molecular properties, particularly in biological systems.

Hydrogen Bonding

Typical forces in polar liquids, discussed above, are only about 1–2% as strong as ionic and covalent bonds. However, certain liquids have boiling points that are much higher than we would predict from these dipolar interactions alone. This indicates the presence of some strong intermolecular force. This attractive force is due to **hydrogen bonding.** Molecules in which a hydrogen atom is bonded to a small, highly electronegative atom such as nitrogen, oxygen, or fluorine exhibit this effect. The presence of a highly electronegative atom bonded to a hydrogen atom creates a large dipole:

Recall that the most electronegative elements are in the upper right corner of the periodic table, and these elements exert strong electron attraction in molecules, as described in Chapter 3.

This arrangement of atoms produces a very polar bond, often resulting in a polar molecule with strong intermolecular attractive forces. Although the hydrogen bond is weaker than bonds formed *within* molecules (covalent and polar covalent *intra*molecular forces), it is the strongest attractive force *between* molecules (intermolecular force).

Consider the boiling points of four small molecules:

$$CH_4 \quad NH_3 \quad H_2O \quad HF$$
$$-161°C \quad -33°C \quad +100°C \quad +19.5°C$$

Clearly, ammonia, water, and hydrogen fluoride boil at significantly higher temperatures than methane. The N—H, O—H, and F—H bonds are far more polar than the C—H bond, owing to the high electronegativity of N, O, and F.

It is interesting to note that the boiling points increase as the electronegativity of the element bonded to hydrogen increases, with one exception: Fluorine, with the highest electronegativity, should cause HF to have the highest boiling point. This is not the case. The order of boiling points is

water > hydrogen fluoride > ammonia > methane

not

hydrogen fluoride > water > ammonia > methane

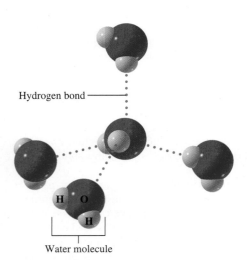

Hydrogen bond ⎯

Water molecule

Figure 5.8 Hydrogen bonding in water. Note that the central water molecule is hydrogen bonded to four other water molecules. The attractive force between the hydrogen (δ^+) part of one water molecule and the oxygen (δ^-) part of another water molecule constitutes the hydrogen bond.

Why? To answer this question we must look at the *number of potential bonding sites* in each molecule. Water has two partial positive sites (located at each hydrogen atom) and two partial negative sites (two lone pairs of electrons on the oxygen atom); it can form hydrogen bonds at each site. This results in a complex network of attractive forces among water molecules in the liquid state, and the strength of the forces holding this network together accounts for water's unusually high boiling point. This network is depicted in Figure 5.8.

Ammonia and hydrogen fluoride can form only one hydrogen bond per molecule. Ammonia has three partial positive sites (three hydrogen atoms bonded to nitrogen) but only one partial negative site (the lone pair); the single lone pair is the limiting factor. One positive site and one negative site are needed for each hydrogen bond. Hydrogen fluoride has only one partial positive site and three partial negative sites (three lone pairs); the single positive site is the limiting factor. Consequently, hydrogen fluoride, like ammonia, can form only one hydrogen bond per molecule. The network of attractive forces in ammonia and hydrogen fluoride is, therefore, much less extensive than that found in water, and their boiling points are considerably lower than that of water.

Hydrogen bonding has an extremely important influence on the behavior of many biological systems. Molecules such as proteins and DNA require extensive hydrogen bonding to maintain their structures and hence functions. DNA (deoxyribonucleic acid, Section 20.2) is a giant among molecules, with intertwined chains of atoms held together by thousands of hydrogen bonds.

Intramolecular hydrogen bonding between polar regions helps keep proteins folded in their proper three-dimensional structure. See Chapter 18.

Question 5.9 Arrange the following compounds in order of increasing boiling point:

$$CO_2 \quad CH_3OH \quad CH_3Cl$$

Explain your logic.

Question 5.10 Explain the large difference in boiling point for the isomers butanol and diethyl ether.

butanol
b.p. = 117°C

diethyl ether
b.p. = 34.5°C

5.3 The Solid State

The close packing of the particles of a solid results from attractive forces that are strong enough to restrict motion. This occurs because the kinetic energy of the particles is insufficient to overcome the attractive forces among particles. The particles are "locked" together in a defined and highly organized fashion. This results in fixed shape and volume, although, at the atomic level, vibrational motion is observed.

Properties of Solids

Solids are virtually incompressible, owing to the small distance between particles. Most will convert to liquids at a higher temperature, when the increased heat energy overcomes some of the attractive forces within the solid. The temperature at which a solid is converted to the liquid phase is its **melting point.** The melting point depends on the strength of the attractive forces in the solid, hence its structure. As we might expect, polar solids have higher melting points than nonpolar solids of the same molecular weight.

A solid may be a **crystalline solid,** having a regular repeating structure, or an **amorphous solid,** having no organized structure. Diamond and sodium chloride (Figure 5.9) are examples of crystalline substances; glass, plastic, and concrete are examples of amorphous solids.

LEARNING GOAL

9 ▶ Relate the properties of the various classes of solids (ionic, covalent, molecular, and metallic) to the structure of these solids.

Figure 5.9 Crystalline solids.

Cl⁻   Na⁺

(a) The crystal structure of diamond

(b) The crystal structure of sodium chloride

(c) The crystal structure of methane, a frozen molecular solid. Only one methane molecule is shown in detail.

(d) The crystal structure of a metallic solid. The gray area represents mobile electrons around fixed metal cations.

Types of Crystalline Solids

Crystalline solids may exist in one of four general groups:

1. *Ionic solids.* The units that comprise an **ionic solid** are positive and negative ions. Electrostatic forces hold the crystal together. Ionic solids generally have high melting points, and are hard and brittle. A common example of an ionic solid is sodium chloride.

2. *Covalent solids.* The units that comprise a **covalent solid** are atoms held together by covalent bonds. Covalent solids have very high melting points (1200°C to 2000°C or more is not unusual) and are extremely hard. They are insoluble in most solvents. Diamond is a covalent solid composed of covalently bonded carbon atoms. Diamonds are used for industrial cutting because they are so hard and as gemstones because of their crystalline beauty.

3. *Molecular solids.* The units that make up a **molecular solid,** molecules, are held together by intermolecular attractive forces (London forces, dipole-dipole interactions, and hydrogen bonding). Molecular solids are usually soft and have low melting points. They are frequently volatile and are poor electrical conductors. A common example is ice (solid water; Figure 5.10).

4. *Metallic solids.* The units that comprise a **metallic solid** are metal atoms held together by metallic bonds. **Metallic bonds** are formed by the overlap of orbitals of metal atoms, resulting in regions of high electron density surrounding the positive metal nuclei. Electrons in these regions are extremely mobile. They are able to move freely from atom to atom through pathways

Intermolecular forces are also discussed in Sections 3.5 and 5.2.

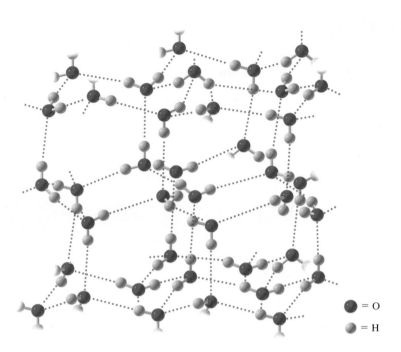

Figure 5.10 The structure of ice, a molecular solid. Hydrogen bonding among water molecules produces a regular open structure that is less dense than liquid water.

● = O

● = H

that are, in reality, overlapping atomic orbitals. This results in the high *conductivity* (ability to carry electrical current) *exhibited by many metallic solids.* Silver and copper are common examples of metallic solids. Metals are easily shaped and are used for a variety of purposes. Most of these are practical applications such as hardware, cookware, and surgical and dental tools. Others are purely for enjoyment and decoration, such as silver and gold jewelry.

Sublimation of Solids

Sublimation is the process in which some molecules in the solid state convert directly to the gaseous state.

As we saw in the Chemistry at the Crime Scene discussion of the development of new devices for airport security (p. 177), some molecular solids possess measurable vapor pressures. Recall that vapor pressure of a liquid is the key concept in explaining the conversion of a liquid to a gas by evaporation or by boiling. Certain molecular solids such as dry ice (frozen carbon dioxide) and naphthalene (moth balls) will, at room temperature, convert to a gas without passing through the liquid state because they have a sufficiently high vapor pressure. This process is termed *sublimation.*

If you live in a very cold climate, you may have observed that, over a period of several days, snow and ice "disappear," even though the temperature is continuously below the melting point of water. Snow and ice, molecular solids, have simply sublimed, converting from solid to water vapor.

Solid-state chemistry is critically important to the semiconductor industry. "Chips," crystalline solids made of silicon and traces of other elements such as arsenic and germanium, are the "brains" behind our computers, cell phones, and a host of other electronic devices.

Question 5.11

  a. What properties are associated with ionic solids?

  b. Provide two examples of ionic solids.

Question 5.12

  a. What properties are associated with molecular solids?

  b. Provide two examples of molecular solids.

SUMMARY

5.1 The Gaseous State

The *kinetic molecular theory* describes an *ideal gas* in which gas particles exhibit no interactive or repulsive forces and the volumes of the individual gas particles are assumed to be negligible.

Boyle's law states that the volume of a gas varies inversely with the pressure exerted by the gas if the number of mol and temperature of gas are held constant ($PV = k_1$).

Charles's law states that the volume of a gas varies directly with the absolute temperature (K) if pressure and number of mol of gas are constant ($V/T = k_2$).

The *combined gas law* provides a convenient expression for performing gas law calculations involving the most common variables: pressure, volume, and temperature.

Avogadro's law states that equal volumes of any gas contain the same number of mol if measured at constant temperature and pressure ($V/n = k_3$).

The volume occupied by 1 mol of any gas is its *molar volume*. At *standard temperature and pressure* (STP), the molar volume of any ideal gas is 22.4 L. STP conditions are defined as 273 K (or 0°C) and 1 atm pressure.

Boyle's law, Charles's law, and Avogadro's law may be combined into a single expression relating all four terms, the *ideal gas law: PV = nRT*. R is the ideal gas constant ($0.0821 \, L \cdot atm \cdot K^{-1} \cdot mol^{-1}$) if the units P (atm), V (L), n (number of mol), and T (Kelvin) are used.

Dalton's law of partial pressures states that a mixture of gases exerts a pressure that is the sum of the pressures that each gas would exert if it were present alone under similar conditions ($P_t = p_1 + p_2 + p_3 + \ldots$).

5.2 The Liquid State

Liquids are practically incompressible because of the closeness of their molecules. The *viscosity* of a liquid is a measure of its resistance to flow. Viscosity generally decreases with increasing temperature. The *surface tension* of a liquid is a measure of the attractive forces at the surface of a liquid. *Surfactants* decrease surface tension.

The conversion of liquid to vapor at a temperature below the boiling point of the liquid is *evaporation*. Conversion of the gas to the liquid state is *condensation*. The *vapor pressure of the liquid* is defined as the pressure exerted by the vapor at equilibrium at a specified temperature. The *normal boiling point* of a liquid is the temperature at which the vapor pressure of the liquid is equal to 1 atm.

Molecules in which a hydrogen atom is bonded to a small, highly electronegative atom such as nitrogen, oxygen, or fluorine exhibit *hydrogen bonding*. Hydrogen bonding in liquids is responsible for lower than expected vapor pressures and higher than expected boiling points. The presence of *van der Waals forces* and hydrogen bonds significantly affects the boiling points of liquids as well as the melting points of solids.

5.3 The Solid State

Solids have fixed shapes and volumes. They are *incompressible*, owing to the closeness of their particles. Solids may be *crystalline*, having a regular, repeating structure, or *amorphous*, having no organized structure.

Crystalline solids may exist as *ionic solids, covalent solids, molecular solids,* or *metallic solids*. Electrons in metallic solids are extremely mobile, resulting in the high *conductivity* (ability to carry electrical current) exhibited by many metallic solids. Sublimation is a process whereby more molecular solids convert directly from solid to gas.

KEY TERMS

amorphous solid (5.3)
Avogadro's law (5.1)
barometer (5.1)
Boyle's law (5.1)
Charles's law (5.1)
combined gas law (5.1)
condensation (5.2)
covalent solid (5.3)
crystalline solid (5.3)
Dalton's law (5.1)
dipole-dipole interactions (5.2)
evaporation (5.2)
hydrogen bonding (5.2)
ideal gas (5.1)
ideal gas law (5.1)
ionic solid (5.3)
kinetic molecular theory (5.1)

London forces (5.2)
melting point (5.3)
metallic bond (5.3)
metallic solid (5.3)
molar volume (5.1)
molecular solid (5.3)
normal boiling point (5.2)
partial pressure (5.1)
pressure (5.1)
standard temperature and pressure (STP) (5.1)
sublimation (5.3)
surface tension (5.2)
surfactant (5.2)
van der Waals forces (5.2)
vapor pressure of a liquid (5.2)
viscosity (5.2)

QUESTIONS AND PROBLEMS

Kinetic Molecular Theory of Gases

Foundations

5.13 Compare and contrast the gas, liquid, and solid states with regard to the average distance of particle separation.

5.14 Compare and contrast the gas, liquid, and solid states with regard to the nature of the interactions among the particles.

5.15 Describe the molecular/atomic basis of gas pressure.

5.16 Describe the measurement of gas pressure.

Applications

5.17 Why are gases easily compressible?

5.18 Why are gas densities much lower than those of liquids or solids?

5.19 Why do gases expand to fill any available volume?

5.20 Why do gases with lower molar masses diffuse more rapidly than gases with higher molar masses?

5.21 Do gases exhibit more ideal behavior at low or high pressures? Why?

5.22 Do gases exhibit more ideal behavior at low or high temperatures? Why?

5.23 Use the kinetic molecular theory to explain why dissimilar gases mix more rapidly at high temperatures than at low temperatures.

5.24 Use the kinetic molecular theory to explain why aerosol cans carry instructions warning against heating or disposing of the container in a fire.

5.25 Predict and explain any observed changes taking place when an inflated balloon is cooled (perhaps refrigerated).

5.26 Predict and explain any observed changes taking place when an inflated balloon is heated (perhaps microwaved).

Boyle's Law

Foundations

5.27 State Boyle's law in words.

5.28 State Boyle's law in equation form.

5.29 The pressure on a fixed mass of a gas is tripled at constant temperature. Will the volume increase, decrease, or remain the same?

5.30 By what factor will the volume of the gas in Question 5.29 change?

Applications

A sample of helium gas was placed in a cylinder and the volume of the gas was measured as the pressure was slowly increased. The results of this experiment are shown graphically.

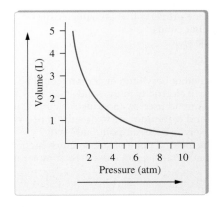

Questions 5.31–5.34 are based on this experiment.

5.31 At what pressure does the gas occupy a volume of 5 L?

5.32 What is the volume of the gas at a pressure of 5 atm?

5.33 Calculate the Boyle's law constant at a volume of 2 L.

5.34 Calculate the Boyle's law constant at a pressure of 2 atm.

5.35 Calculate the pressure, in atm, required to compress a sample of helium gas from 20.9 L (at 1.00 atm) to 4.00 L.

5.36 A balloon filled with helium gas at 1.00 atm occupies 15.6 L. What volume would the balloon occupy in the upper atmosphere, at a pressure of 0.150 atm?

Charles's Law

Foundations

5.37 State Charles's law in words.

5.38 State Charles's law in equation form.

5.39 Explain why the Kelvin scale is used for gas law calculations.

5.40 The temperature on a summer day may be 90°F. Convert this value to Kelvin units.

Applications

5.41 The temperature of a gas is raised from 25°C to 50°C. Will the volume double if mass and pressure do not change? Why or why not?

5.42 Verify your answer to Question 5.41 by calculating the temperature needed to double the volume of the gas.

5.43 Determine the change in volume that takes place when a 2.00-L sample of $N_2(g)$ is heated from 250°C to 500°C.

5.44 Determine the change in volume that takes place when a 2.00-L sample of $N_2(g)$ is heated from 250 K to 500 K.

5.45 A balloon containing a sample of helium gas is warmed in an oven. If the balloon measures 1.25 L at room temperature (20°C), what is its volume at 80°C?

5.46 The balloon described in Problem 5.45 was then placed in a refrigerator at 39°F. Calculate its new volume.

Combined Gas Law

Foundations

5.47 Will the volume of gas increase, decrease, or remain the same if the temperature is increased and the pressure is decreased? Explain.

5.48 Will the volume of gas increase, decrease, or remain the same if the temperature is decreased and the pressure is increased? Explain.

Applications

Use the combined gas law,

$$\frac{P_i V_i}{T_i} = \frac{P_f V_f}{T_f}$$

to answer Questions 5.49 and 5.50.

5.49 Solve the combined gas law expression for the final volume.

5.50 Solve the combined gas law expression for the final temperature.

5.51 If 2.25 L of a gas at 16°C and 1.00 atm is compressed at a pressure of 125 atm at 20°C, calculate the new volume of the gas.

5.52 A balloon filled with helium gas occupies 2.50 L at 25°C and 1.00 atm. When released, it rises to an altitude where the temperature is 20°C and the pressure is only 0.800 atm. Calculate the new volume of the balloon.

Avogadro's Law

Foundations

5.53 State Avogadro's law in words.

5.54 State Avogadro's law in equation form.

Applications

5.55 If 5.00 g helium gas is added to a 1.00-L balloon containing 1.00 g of helium gas, what is the new volume of the balloon? Assume no change in temperature or pressure.

5.56 How many g of helium must be added to a balloon containing 8.00 g helium gas to double its volume? Assume no change in temperature or pressure.

Molar Volume and the Ideal Gas Law

Foundations

5.57 Will 1.00 mol of a gas always occupy 22.4 L?

5.58 H_2O and CH_4 are gases at 150°C. Which exhibits more ideal behavior? Why?

5.59 What are the units and numerical value of standard temperature?

5.60 What are the units and numerical value of standard pressure?

Applications

5.61 A sample of nitrogen gas, stored in a 4.0-L container at 32°C, exerts a pressure of 5.0 atm. Calculate the number of mol of nitrogen gas in the container.

5.62 Seven moles of carbon monoxide are stored in a 30.0-L container at 65°C. What is the pressure of the carbon monoxide in the container?

5.63 Calculate the volume of 44.0 g of carbon monoxide at STP.

5.64 Calculate the volume of 44.0 g of carbon dioxide at STP.

5.65 Calculate the density of carbon monoxide at STP.

5.66 Calculate the density of carbon dioxide at STP.

5.67 Calculate the number of mol of a gas that is present in a 7.55-L container at 45°C, if the gas exerts a pressure of 725 mm Hg.

5.68 Calculate the pressure exerted by 1.00 mol of gas contained in a 7.55-L cylinder at 45°C.

5.69 A sample of argon (Ar) gas occupies 65.0 mL at 22°C and 750 torr. What is the volume of this Ar gas sample at STP?

5.70 A sample of O_2 gas occupies 257 mL at 20°C and 1.20 atm. What is the volume of this O_2 gas sample at STP?

5.71 Calculate the molar volume of Ar gas at STP.

5.72 Calculate the molar volume of O_2 gas at STP.

5.73 Calculate the volume of 4.00 mol Ar gas at 8.25 torr and 27°C.

5.74 Calculate the volume of 6.00 mol O_2 gas at 30 cm Hg and 72°F.

5.75 What is the temperature (°C) of 1.75 g of O_2 gas occupying 2.00 L at 1.00 atm?

5.76 How many g of O_2 gas occupy 10.0 L at STP?

Dalton's Law of Partial Pressures

Foundations

5.77 State Dalton's law in words.

5.78 State Dalton's law in equation form.

Applications

5.79 A gas mixture has three components: N_2, F_2, and He. Their partial pressures are 0.40 atm, 0.16 atm, and 0.18 atm, respectively. What is the pressure of the gas mixture?

5.80 A gas mixture has a total pressure of 0.56 atm and consists of He and Ne. If the partial pressure of the He in the mixture is 0.27 atm, what is the partial pressure of the Ne in the mixture?

The Liquid State

Foundations

5.81 Compare the strength of intermolecular forces in liquids with those in gases.

5.82 Compare the strength of intermolecular forces in liquids with those in solids.

5.83 What is the relationship between the temperature of a liquid and the vapor pressure of that liquid?

5.84 What is the relationship between the strength of the attractive forces in a liquid and its vapor pressure?

5.85 Describe the process occurring at the molecular level that accounts for the property of viscosity.

5.86 Describe the process occurring at the molecular level that accounts for the property of surface tension.

Applications

Questions 5.87–5.90 are based on the following:

methane　　　　chloromethane　　　　methanol

5.87 Which of these molecules exhibit London forces? Why?

5.88 Which of these molecules exhibit dipole-dipole forces? Why?

5.89 Which of these molecules exhibit hydrogen bonding? Why?

5.90 Which of these molecules would you expect to have the highest boiling point? Why?

Questions 5.91 and 5.92 are based on the following:

propane　　　　isopropyl alcohol　　　　propylene glycol

5.91 Predict the compound expected to have the greatest viscosity in the liquid state.

5.92 Predict the compound expected to have the greatest surface tension in the liquid state.

The Solid State

Foundations

5.93 Explain why solids are essentially incompressible.

5.94 Distinguish between amorphous and crystalline solids.

5.95 Describe one property that is characteristic of:
- **a.** ionic solids
- **b.** covalent solids

5.96 Describe one property that is characteristic of:
- **a.** molecular solids
- **b.** metallic solids

Applications

5.97 Predict whether beryllium or carbon would be a better conductor of electricity in the solid state. Why?

5.98 Why is diamond used as an industrial cutting tool?

5.99 Mercury and chromium are toxic substances. Which element is more likely to be an air pollutant? Why?

5.100 Why is the melting point of silicon much higher than that of argon, even though argon has a greater molar mass?

CRITICAL THINKING PROBLEMS

1. An elodea plant, commonly found in tropical fish aquaria, was found to produce 5.0×10^{22} molecules of oxygen per hour (h). What volume of oxygen (at STP) would be produced in an 8-h period?

2. A chemist measures the volume of 1.00 mol of helium gas at STP and obtains a value of 22.4 L. After changing the temperature to 137 K, the experimental value was found to be 11.05 L. Verify the chemist's results using the ideal gas law and explain any apparent discrepancies.

3. A chemist measures the volumes of 1.00 mol of H_2 and 1.00 mol of CO and finds that they differ by 0.10 L. Which gas produced the larger volume? Do the results contradict the ideal gas law? Why or why not?

4. A 100.0-g sample of water was decomposed using an electric current (electrolysis), producing hydrogen gas and oxygen gas. Write the balanced equation for the process and calculate the volume of each gas produced (at STP). Explain any relationship you may observe between the volumes obtained and the balanced equation for the process.

5. An autoclave is used to sterilize surgical equipment. It is far more effective than steam produced from boiling water in the open atmosphere because it generates steam at a pressure of 2 atm. Explain why an autoclave is such an efficient sterilization device.

6. Imagine that you have been asked to design a new solid material to be used in replacement bones and joints. What physical and chemical properties would you deem important?

Solutions 6

LEARNING GOALS

1 ▶ Distinguish among the terms *solution, solute,* and *solvent.*

2 ▶ Describe various kinds of solutions and give examples of each.

3 ▶ Describe the relationship between solubility and equilibrium.

4 ▶ Calculate solution concentration in mass/volume percent, mass/mass percent, parts per thousand, and parts per million.

5 ▶ Calculate solution concentration using molarity.

6 ▶ Perform dilution calculations.

7 ▶ Describe and explain concentration-dependent solution properties.

8 ▶ Describe why the chemical and physical properties of water make it a truly unique solvent.

9 ▶ Interconvert molar concentration of ions and milliequivalents/liter.

10 ▶ Explain the role of electrolytes in blood and their relationship to the process of dialysis.

OUTLINE

Carbonated beverages are a commonplace example of a solution of a gas dissolved in a liquid solvent. Based on your everyday experience, can you predict whether the solubility of carbon dioxide in water (or cola) would increase or decrease as the temperature of the solution increases?

INTRODUCTION

A significant deterrent to achieving optimal athletic performance in strenuous competitive sports, especially in warm weather, is dehydration—the loss of body fluids through perspiration. Perspiration is an aqueous solution and the loss of ions dissolved in water (the solvent) has as great a negative impact on bodily function as the loss of the water itself.

This fact was not lost on researchers at the University of Florida in the 1960s. The University of Florida football team (the Florida 'Gators) plays much of its schedule in a very warm climate. This, coupled with the intense physical effort required and the heavy padding that must be worn to prevent injury, makes dehydration of the athletes a real concern.

The remedy, at that time, was to drink large volumes of water while consuming salt tablets, to replace the lost ions, and high-sugar foods (often oranges) to provide energy. How much of each was pure guesswork. Often the cure was worse than the original problem, and cramping resulted.

The team doctor, along with medical researchers at the university, had an idea. Would it be possible to mix all three components in some proportion to produce a solution that achieved the desired effect without the unwanted side effect? The result of this research was a solution of ionic compounds and sugar dissolved in water, which was similar to the composition of the perspiration being lost, with flavoring added to make it palatable. The identity of the ions: sodium, potassium, and chloride, was certainly important, as were the concentrations of the ions in producing a solution that achieved the desired effect without inducing cramps.

The football team began using the "'Gator-aid" solution and was victorious in the 1966 Orange Bowl, offering some proof that the solution had a positive effect on the team's performance. Now named Gatorade, it was the first "sports drink." Currently, several competing brands are available in the marketplace, differing slightly in composition, concentration, and flavor. They are widely used by college and professional teams, as well as the "weekend athlete." We should not forget that the most important ingredient in all sports drinks is the solvent, water. In fact, some argue that pure water is just as efficient a cell hydrator as sports drinks.

In this chapter, we will learn more about solutions, their composition and their concentration. We will see why some substances are soluble in water and others are not. We will see why the concentration of ions, such as sodium and potassium, is critical to the function and the integrity of the cells in our bodies.

6.1 Properties of Solutions

LEARNING GOAL

1 ▶ Distinguish among the terms *solution, solute,* and *solvent.*

A **solution** is a homogeneous (or uniform) mixture of two or more substances. A solution is composed of one or more *solutes,* dissolved in a *solvent.* The **solute** is a component of a solution that is present in lesser quantity than the solvent. The **solvent** is the solution component present in the largest quantity. For example, when sugar (the solute) is added to water (the solvent), the sugar dissolves in the water to produce a solution. In those instances in which the solvent is water, we refer to the homogeneous mixture as an **aqueous solution,** from the Latin *aqua,* meaning "water."

The dissolution of a solid in a liquid is perhaps the most common example of solution formation. However, it is also possible to form solutions in gases and solids as well as in liquids. For example:

• Air is a gaseous mixture, but it is also a solution; oxygen and a number of trace gases are dissolved in the gaseous solvent, nitrogen.

- Alloys, such as brass and silver and the gold used to make jewelry, are also homogeneous mixtures of two or more kinds of metal atoms in the solid state.

Although solid and gaseous solutions are important in many applications, our emphasis will be on *liquid solutions* because so many important chemical reactions take place in liquid solutions.

General Properties of Liquid Solutions

Liquid solutions are clear and transparent with no visible particles of solute. They may be colored or colorless, depending on the properties of the solute and solvent. Note that the terms *clear* and *colorless* do not mean the same thing; a clear solution has only one state of matter that can be detected; *colorless* simply means the absence of color.

Recall that solutions of **electrolytes** are formed from solutes that are soluble ionic compounds. These compounds dissociate in solution to produce ions that behave as charge carriers. Solutions of electrolytes are good conductors of electricity. For example, sodium chloride dissolving in water:

$$NaCl(s) \xrightarrow{H_2O} Na^+(aq) + Cl^-(aq)$$

Solid sodium   Dissolved sodium
chloride   chloride

In contrast, solutions of **nonelectrolytes** are formed from nondissociating *molecular* solutes (nonelectrolytes), and these solutions are nonconducting. For example, dissolving sugar in water:

$$C_6H_{12}O_6(s) \xrightarrow{H_2O} C_6H_{12}O_6(aq)$$

Solid glucose   Dissolved glucose

A *true solution* is a homogeneous mixture with uniform properties throughout. In a true solution the solute cannot be isolated from the solution by filtration. The particle size of the solute is about the same as that of the solvent, and solvent and solute pass directly through the filter paper. Furthermore, solute particles will not "settle out" after a time. All of the molecules of solute and solvent are intimately mixed. The continuous particle motion in solution maintains the homogeneous, random distribution of solute and solvent particles.

Volumes of solute and solvent are not additive; 1 liter (L) of alcohol mixed with 1 L of water does not result in exactly 2 L of solution. The volume of pure liquid is determined by the way in which the individual molecules "fit together." When two or more kinds of molecules are mixed, the interactions become more complex. Solvent interacts with solvent, solute interacts with solvent, and solute may interact with other solute. This will be important to remember when we solve concentration problems later.

Solutions and Colloids

How can you recognize a solution? A clear liquid in a beaker may be a pure substance, a true solution, or a colloid. Only chemical analysis, determining the identity of all substances in the liquid, can distinguish between a pure substance and a solution. A pure substance has *one* component, pure water being an example. A true solution will contain more than one substance, with the tiny particles homogeneously intermingled.

A **colloidal suspension** also consists of solute particles distributed throughout a solvent. However, the distribution is not completely homogeneous, owing to the size of the colloidal particles. Particles with diameters of 1×10^{-9} meter (m) to 2×10^{-7} m are colloids. (Recall that 1×10^{-9} m = 1 nanometer (nm), therefore 2×10^{-7} m = 200 nm.) Particles smaller than 1 nm are solution particles; those larger than 200 nm are precipitates (solid in contact with solvent).

LEARNING GOAL

2 ▶ Describe various kinds of solutions and give examples of each.

Animations
- Dissolution of Compounds
- Salt Dissolving in Water
- Strong, Weak, and Nonelectrolytes

Particles in electrolyte solutions are ions, making the solution an electrical conductor.

Particles in nonelectrolyte solutions are individual molecules. No ions are formed in the dissolution process.

Section 3.5 relates properties and molecular geometry.

See Section 4.4 for more information on precipitates.

Figure 6.1 The Tyndall effect. The beaker on the left contains a colloidal suspension, which scatters the light. This scattered light is visible as a haze. The beaker on the right contains a true solution; no scattered light is observed.

Section 3.5 describes solute-solvent interactions in detail.

The term *qualitative* implies identity, and the term *quantitative* relates to quantity.

To the naked eye, a colloidal suspension and a true solution appear identical; neither solute nor colloid can be seen. However, a simple experiment, using only a bright light source, can readily make the distinction based upon differences in their interaction with light. Colloid particles are large enough to scatter light; solute particles are not. When a beam of light passes through a colloidal suspension, the large particles scatter light, and the liquid appears hazy. We see this effect in sunlight passing through fog. Fog is a colloidal suspension of tiny particles of liquid water dispersed throughout a gas, air. The haze is light scattered by droplets of water. You may have noticed that your automobile headlights are not very helpful in foggy weather. Visibility becomes worse rather than better because light scattering increases.

The light-scattering ability of colloidal suspensions is termed the *Tyndall effect*. True solutions, with very tiny particles, do not scatter light—no haze is observed—and true solutions are easily distinguished from colloidal suspensions by observing their light-scattering properties (Figure 6.1).

A **suspension** is a heterogeneous mixture that contains particles much larger than a colloidal suspension; over time, these particles may settle, forming a second phase. A suspension is not a true solution, nor is it a precipitate.

Question 6.1 Describe how you would distinguish experimentally between a pure substance and a true solution.

Question 6.2 Describe how you would distinguish experimentally between a true solution and a colloidal suspension.

Degree of Solubility

In our discussion of the relationship of polarity and solubility, the rule *"like dissolves like"* was described as the fundamental condition for solubility. Polar solutes are soluble in polar solvents, and nonpolar solutes are soluble in nonpolar solvents. Thus, knowing a little bit about the structure of the molecule enables us to predict qualitatively the solubility of the compound.

The *degree* of **solubility,** *how much* solute can dissolve in a given volume of solvent, is a quantitative measure of solubility. It is difficult to predict the solubility of each and every compound. However, general solubility trends are based on the following considerations:

- *The magnitude of difference between polarity of solute and solvent.* The greater the difference, the less soluble is the solute.
- *Temperature.* An increase in temperature usually, but not always, increases solubility (Figure 6.2). Often, the effect is dramatic. For example, an increase in temperature from 0°C to 100°C increases the water solubility of KNO_3 from 10 grams per 100 milliliters (10 g/100 mL) to 240 g/100 mL.
- *Pressure.* Pressure has little effect on the solubility of solids and liquids in liquids. However, the solubility of a gas in liquid is directly proportional to the applied pressure. Carbonated beverages, for example, are made by dissolving carbon dioxide in the beverage under high pressure (hence the term *carbonated*).

When a solution contains all the solute that can be dissolved at a particular temperature, it is a **saturated solution.** When solubility values are given—for example, 13.3 g of potassium nitrate in 100 mL of water at 1°C—they refer to the concentration of a saturated solution.

As we have already noted, *increasing* the temperature generally increases the amount of solute a given solution may hold. Conversely, *cooling* a saturated solution often results in a decrease in the amount of solute in solution. The excess

Figure 6.2 The solubility of a variety of ionic compounds in water as a function of temperature. Note that Na_2SO_4 and $Ce_2(SO_4)_3$ become less soluble at higher temperatures.

solute falls to the bottom of the container as a **precipitate** (a solid in contact with the solution). Occasionally, on cooling, the excess solute may remain in solution for a time. Such a solution is described as a **supersaturated solution**. This type of solution is inherently unstable. With time, excess solute will precipitate, and the solution will revert to a saturated solution, which is stable.

Solubility and Equilibrium

When an excess of solute is added to a solvent, it begins to dissolve and continues until it establishes a *dynamic equilibrium* between dissolved and undissolved solute.

Initially, the rate of dissolution is large. After a time the rate of the reverse process, precipitation, increases. The rates of dissolution and precipitation eventually become equal, and there is no further change in the composition of the solution. There is, however, a continual exchange of solute particles between solid and liquid phases because particles are in constant motion. The solution is saturated. The most precise definition of a saturated solution is a solution that is in equilibrium with undissolved solute.

Solubility of Gases: Henry's Law

When a liquid and a gas are allowed to come to equilibrium, the amount of gas dissolved in the liquid reaches some maximum level. This quantity can be predicted from a very simple relationship. **Henry's law** states that the number of moles (mol) of a gas dissolved in a liquid at a given temperature is proportional to the partial pressure of the gas. In other words, the gas solubility is directly proportional to the pressure of that gas in the atmosphere that is in contact with the liquid.

Carbonated beverages are bottled at high pressures of carbon dioxide. When the cap is removed, the fizzing results from the fact that the partial pressure of carbon dioxide in the atmosphere is much less than that used in the bottling process. As a result, the equilibrium quickly shifts to one of lower gas solubility.

LEARNING GOAL

3 ▶ Describe the relationship between solubility and equilibrium.

The concept of equilibrium was introduced in Section 5.2 and will be discussed in detail in Section 7.4.

The concept of partial pressure is a consequence of Dalton's law, discussed in Section 5.1.

Figure 6.3 The water solubility of O_2 gas decreases markedly as the temperature of the water increases; this may have significant environmental implications.

The exchange of O_2 and CO_2 in the lungs and other tissues is a complex series of events described in greater detail in Section 18.9.

See A Medical Perspective: Blood Gases and Respiration, Chapter 5.

Gases are most soluble at low temperatures, and the gas solubility decreases markedly at higher temperatures (Figure 6.3). This explains many common observations. For example, a chilled container of carbonated beverage that is opened quickly goes flat as it warms to room temperature. As the beverage warms up, the solubility of the carbon dioxide decreases.

Henry's law helps to explain the process of respiration. Respiration depends on a rapid and efficient exchange of oxygen and carbon dioxide between the atmosphere and the blood. This transfer occurs through the lungs. The process, oxygen entering the blood and carbon dioxide released to the atmosphere, is accomplished in air sacs called *alveoli,* which are surrounded by an extensive capillary system. Equilibrium is quickly established between alveolar air and the capillary blood. The temperature of the blood is effectively constant. Therefore the equilibrium concentrations of both oxygen and carbon dioxide are determined by the partial pressures of the gases (Henry's law). The oxygen is transported to cells, a variety of reactions take place, and the waste product of respiration, carbon dioxide, is brought back to the lungs to be expelled into the atmosphere.

Question 6.3 Explain why, over time, a bottle of soft drink goes "flat" after it is opened.

Question 6.4 Would the soft drink in Question 6.3 go "flat" faster if the bottle warmed to room temperature? Why?

A Human Perspective

Scuba Diving: Nitrogen and the Bends

A deep-water diver's worst fear is the interruption of the oxygen supply through equipment malfunction, forcing his or her rapid rise to the surface in search of air. If a diver must ascend too rapidly, he or she may suffer a condition known as "the bends."

Key to understanding this problem is recognition of the tremendous increase in pressure that divers withstand as they descend, because of the weight of the water above them. At the surface the pressure is approximately 1 atmosphere (atm). At a depth of 200 feet (ft) the pressure is approximately six times as great; hence, the blood concentration of N_2 increases dramatically. Oxygen solubility increases as well, although its effect is less serious (O_2 is 20% of air, N_2 is 80%). Recall that Henry's law tells us that the number of mol of gas dissolved in blood is directly proportional to the pressure of the gas.

As the diver quickly rises, the pressure decreases rapidly, and the nitrogen "boils" out of the blood, stopping blood flow and impairing nerve transmission. The joints of the body lock in a bent position, hence the name of the condition: the bends.

To minimize the problem, scuba tanks may be filled with mixtures of helium and oxygen rather than nitrogen and oxygen. Helium has a much lower solubility in blood and, like nitrogen, is inert. To avoid the bends, divers are advised to make several decompression stops while ascending to the water's surface. Such "time-outs" allow a more gradual equilibration

Scuba diving.

of nitrogen concentration in the blood; the ideal is to achieve normal (or close to normal) levels upon reaching the surface. Tables and charts relating pressures and decompression times have been developed to aid divers.

For Further Understanding

▶ Why are divers who slowly rise to the surface less likely to be adversely affected?

▶ What design features would be essential in deep-water manned exploration vessels?

6.2 Concentration Based on Percent by Mass

Solution **concentration** is defined as the amount of solute dissolved in a given amount of solution. The concentration of a solution has a profound effect on the properties of a solution, both *physical* (melting and boiling points) and *chemical* (solution reactivity). Solution concentration may be expressed in many different units. Here we consider concentration units based on percent by mass.

Mass/Volume Percent

The concentration of a solution is defined as the amount of solute dissolved in a specified amount of solution,

LEARNING GOAL

4 ▶ Calculate solution concentration in mass/volume percent, mass/mass percent, parts per thousand, and parts per million.

$$\text{concentration} = \frac{\text{amount of solute}}{\text{amount of solution}}$$

If we define the amount of solute as the *mass* of solute (in g) and the amount of solution in *volume* units (mL), concentration is expressed as the ratio

$$\text{concentration} = \frac{\text{g of solute}}{\text{mL of solution}}$$

This concentration can then be expressed as a percentage by multiplying the ratio by the factor 100%. This results in

$$\% \text{ concentration} = \frac{\text{g of solute}}{\text{mL of solution}} \times 100\%$$

The percent concentration expressed in this way is called **mass/volume percent,** or **% (m/V).** Thus

$$\% \left(\frac{m}{V}\right) = \frac{\text{g of solute}}{\text{mL of solution}} \times 100\%$$

Consider the following examples.

EXAMPLE 6.1 Calculating Mass/Volume Percent

Calculate the mass/volume percent composition, or % (m/V), of 3.00×10^2 mL of solution containing 15.0 g of glucose.

Solution

Step 1. The expression for mass/volume percent is:

$$\% \left(\frac{m}{V}\right) = \frac{\text{g of solute}}{\text{mL of solution}} \times 100\%$$

Step 2. There are 15.0 g of glucose, the solute, and 3.00×10^2 mL of total solution. Therefore, substituting in our expression for mass/volume percent:

$$\% \left(\frac{m}{V}\right) = \frac{15.0 \text{ g glucose}}{3.00 \times 10^2 \text{ mL solution}} \times 100\%$$

$$= 5.00\% \left(\frac{m}{V}\right) \text{ glucose}$$

Continued—

Practice Problem 6.1

a. Calculate the % (m/V) of 0.0600 L of solution containing 10.0 g NaCl.
b. Calculate the % (m/V) of 0.200 L of solution containing 15.0 g KCl.
c. 20.0 g of oxygen gas are diluted with 80.0 g of nitrogen gas in a 78.0-L container at standard temperature and pressure. Calculate the % (m/V) of oxygen gas.
d. 50.0 g of argon gas are diluted with 80.0 g of helium gas in a 476-L container at standard temperature and pressure. Calculate the % (m/V) of argon gas.

▶ **For Further Practice: Questions 6.19 and 6.20.**

LEARNING GOAL

4 ▶ Calculate solution concentration in mass/volume percent, mass/mass percent, parts per thousand, and parts per million.

EXAMPLE 6.2   Calculating the Mass or Volume of Solute from a Mass/Volume Percent

Calculate the number of g of NaCl in 5.00×10^2 mL of a 10.0% $\left(\frac{m}{V}\right)$ solution.

Solution

Step 1. The expression for mass/volume percent is:

$$\% \left(\frac{m}{V}\right) = \frac{\text{g of solute}}{\text{mL of solution}} \times 100\%$$

Step 2. Substitute the data from the problem:

$$10.0\% \left(\frac{m}{V}\right) = \frac{X \text{ g NaCl}}{5.00 \times 10^2 \text{ mL solution}} \times 100\%$$

Step 3. Cross-multiplying to simplify:

$$X \text{ g NaCl} \times 100\% = \left(10.0\% \frac{m}{V}\right)(5.00 \times 10^2 \text{ mL solution})$$

Step 4. Dividing both sides by 100% to isolate g NaCl on the left side of the equation:

$$X = 50.0 \text{ g NaCl}$$

Practice Problem 6.2

a. Calculate the mass (in g) of sodium hydroxide required to make 2.00 L of a 1.00% (m/V) solution.
b. Calculate the volume (in mL) of a 25.0% (m/V) solution containing 10.0 g NaCl.

▶ **For Further Practice: Questions 6.29 and 6.30.**

Section 1.4 discusses units and unit conversion.

If the units of mass are other than g, or if the solution volume is in units other than mL, the proper conversion factor must be used to arrive at the units used in the equation.

Mass/Mass Percent

The **mass/mass percent,** or **% (m/m),** is most useful for mixtures of solids, whose masses are easily obtained. The expression used to calculate mass/mass percentage is analogous in form to % (m/V):

$$\% \left(\frac{m}{m}\right) = \frac{\text{g solute}}{\text{g solution}} \times 100\%$$

EXAMPLE 6.3 Calculating Mass/Mass Percent

Calculate the % (m/m) of platinum in a gold ring that contains 14.00 g gold and 4.500 g platinum.

LEARNING GOAL
4 ▶ Calculate solution concentration in mass/volume percent, mass/mass percent, parts per thousand, and parts per million.

Solution

Step 1. Using our definition of mass/mass percent

$$\% \left(\frac{m}{m}\right) = \frac{\text{g solute}}{\text{g solution}} \times 100\%$$

Step 2. Substituting,

$$= \frac{4.500 \text{ g platinum}}{4.500 \text{ g platinum} + 14.00 \text{ g gold}} \times 100\%$$

$$= \frac{4.500 \text{ g}}{18.50 \text{ g}} \times 100\%$$

$$= 24.32\% \text{ platinum}$$

Practice Problem 6.3

a. Calculate the % (m/m) of oxygen gas in a mixture containing 20.0 g of oxygen gas and 80.0 g of nitrogen gas.
b. Calculate the % (m/m) of argon gas in a mixture containing 50.0 g of argon gas and 80.0 g of helium gas.

▶ **For Further Practice: Questions 6.23 and 6.24.**

Parts Per Thousand (ppt) and Parts Per Million (ppm)

The calculation of concentration in parts per thousand (ppt) or parts per million (ppm) is based on the same logic as mass/mass percent. Percentage is actually the number of parts of solute in 100 parts of solution. For example, a 5.00% (m/m) solution is made up of 5.00 g solute in 100 g solution.

$$5.00\% \left(\frac{m}{m}\right) = \frac{5.00 \text{ g solute}}{100 \text{ g solution}} \times 100\%$$

It follows that a 5.00 ppt solution is made up of 5.00 g solute in 1000 g solution.

$$5.00 \text{ ppt} = \frac{5.00 \text{ g solute}}{1000 \text{ g solution}} \times 10^3 \text{ ppt}$$

Using similar logic, a 5.00 ppm solution is made up of 5.00 g solute in 1,000,000 g solution.

$$5.00 \text{ ppm} = \frac{5.00 \text{ g solute}}{1,000,000 \text{ g solution}} \times 10^6 \text{ ppm}$$

The general expressions are:

$$\text{ppt} = \frac{\text{g solute}}{\text{g solution}} \times 10^3 \text{ ppt}$$

and

$$ppm = \frac{g \text{ solute}}{g \text{ solution}} \times 10^6 \text{ ppm}$$

Units of ppt and ppm are most often used for expressing the concentrations of very dilute solutions.

LEARNING GOAL

4 ▶ Calculate solution concentration in mass/volume percent, mass/mass percent, parts per thousand, and parts per million.

EXAMPLE 6.4   Calculating ppt and ppm

A 1.00-g sample of stream water was found to contain 1.0×10^{-6} g lead. Calculate the concentration of lead in the stream water in units of % (m/m), ppt, and ppm. Which is the most suitable unit?

Solution

mass percent:

$$\% \left(\frac{m}{m} \right) = \frac{g \text{ solute}}{g \text{ solution}} \times 100\%$$

$$\% \left(\frac{m}{m} \right) = \frac{1.0 \times 10^{-6} \text{ g Pb}}{1.0 \text{ g solution}} \times 100\%$$

$$\% \left(\frac{m}{m} \right) = 1.0 \times 10^{-4}\%$$

parts per thousand:

$$ppt = \frac{g \text{ solute}}{g \text{ solution}} \times 10^3 \text{ ppt}$$

$$ppt = \frac{1.0 \times 10^{-6} \text{ g Pb}}{1.0 \text{ g solution}} \times 10^3 \text{ ppt}$$

$$ppt = 1.0 \times 10^{-3} \text{ ppt}$$

parts per million:

$$ppm = \frac{g \text{ solute}}{g \text{ solution}} \times 10^6 \text{ ppm}$$

$$ppm = \frac{1.0 \times 10^{-6} \text{ g Pb}}{1.0 \text{ g solution}} \times 10^6 \text{ ppm}$$

$$ppm = 1.0 \text{ ppm}$$

Parts per million is the most reasonable unit.

Practice Problem 6.4

Calculate the ppt and ppm of oxygen gas in a mixture containing

a. 20.0 g of oxygen gas and 80.0 g of nitrogen gas
b. 50.0 g of argon gas and 80.0 g of helium gas

▶ **For Further Practice: Questions 6.33 and 6.34.**

6.3 Concentration Based on Moles

LEARNING GOAL

5 ▶ Calculate solution concentration using molarity.

In our discussion of the chemical arithmetic of reactions in Chapter 4, we saw that the chemical equation represents the relative number of *moles* of reactants producing products. When chemical reactions occur in solution, it is most useful to represent their concentrations on a *molar* basis.

Molarity

The most common mole-based concentration unit is molarity. **Molarity,** symbolized M, is defined as the number of mol of solute per L of solution, or

$$M = \frac{\text{mol solute}}{\text{L solution}}$$

EXAMPLE 6.5   Calculating Molarity from Moles

Calculate the molarity of 2.0 L of solution containing 5.0 mol NaOH.

Solution

Using our expression for molarity

$$M = \frac{\text{mol solute}}{\text{L solution}}$$

Substituting,

$$M_{\text{NaOH}} = \frac{5.0 \text{ mol NaOH}}{2.0 \text{ L solution}}$$
$$= 2.5 \, M$$

Practice Problem 6.5

Calculate the molarity of 2.5 L of solution containing 0.75 mol $MgCl_2$.

▶ **For Further Practice: Questions 6.37 and 6.38.**

LEARNING GOAL

5 ▶ Calculate solution concentration using molarity.

Remember the need for conversion factors to convert from mass to number of mol. Consider the following example:

Section 1.4 discussed units and unit conversion.

EXAMPLE 6.6   Calculating Molarity from Mass

If 5.00 g glucose are dissolved in 1.00×10^2 mL of solution, calculate the molarity, M, of the glucose solution.

Solution

Step 1. To use our expression for molarity it is necessary to convert from units of g of glucose to mol of glucose. The molar mass of glucose is 1.80×10^2 g/mol. Therefore

$$5.00 \, g \times \frac{1 \text{ mol}}{1.80 \times 10^2 \, g} = 2.78 \times 10^{-2} \text{ mol glucose}$$

Step 2. We must convert mL to L:

$$1.00 \times 10^2 \, mL \times \frac{1 \text{ L}}{10^3 \, mL} = 1.00 \times 10^{-1} \text{ L}$$

Step 3. Substituting these quantities:

$$M_{\text{glucose}} = \frac{2.78 \times 10^{-2} \text{ mol}}{1.00 \times 10^{-1} \text{ L}}$$
$$= 2.78 \times 10^{-1} \, M$$

Continued—

Practice Problem 6.6

Calculate the molarity, M, of KCl when 2.33 g KCl are dissolved in 2.50×10^3 mL of solution.

▶ **For Further Practice: Questions 6.39 and 6.40.**

LEARNING GOAL

5 ▶ Calculate solution concentration using molarity.

EXAMPLE 6.7   Calculating Volume from Molarity

Calculate the volume of a 0.750 M sulfuric acid (H_2SO_4) solution containing 0.120 mol of solute.

Solution

Substituting in our basic expression for molarity, we obtain

$$0.750 \; M \; H_2SO_4 = \frac{0.120 \text{ mol } H_2SO_4}{X \text{ L}}$$

$$X \text{ L} = 0.160 \text{ L}$$

Practice Problem 6.7

Calculate the volume of a 0.200 M KCl solution containing 5.00×10^{-2} mol of solute.

▶ **For Further Practice: Questions 6.41 and 6.42.**

Question 6.5 Calculate the number of mol of solute in 5.00×10^2 mL of 0.250 M HCl.

Question 6.6 Calculate the number of g of silver nitrate required to prepare 2.00 L of 0.500 M $AgNO_3$.

Dilution

Laboratory reagents are often purchased as concentrated solutions (for example, 12 M HCl or 6 M NaOH) for reasons of safety, economy, and space limitations. We must often *dilute* such a solution to a larger volume to prepare a less concentrated solution for the experiment at hand. The approach to such a calculation is as follows.

We define

$$M_1 = \text{molarity of solution } before \text{ dilution}$$
$$M_2 = \text{molarity of solution } after \text{ dilution}$$
$$V_1 = \text{volume of solution } after \text{ dilution}$$
$$V_2 = \text{volume of solution } after \text{ dilution}$$

and

$$M = \frac{\text{mol solute}}{\text{L solution}}$$

This equation can be rearranged:

$$\text{mol solute} = (M)(\text{L solution})$$

LEARNING GOAL

6 ▶ Perform dilution calculations.

Animation
• Dilution

The number of mol of solute *before* and *after* dilution is unchanged, because dilution involves only addition of extra solvent:

$$\text{mol}_1 \text{ solute} = \text{mol}_2 \text{ solute}$$

Initial condition   Final condition

or

$$(M_1)(L_1 \text{ solution}) = (M_2)(L_2 \text{ solution})$$

$$(M_1)(V_1) = (M_2)(V_2)$$

Knowing any three of these terms enables us to calculate the fourth.

EXAMPLE 6.8 Calculating Molarity After Dilution

Calculate the molarity of a solution made by diluting 0.050 L of 0.10 M HCl solution to a volume of 1.0 L.

LEARNING GOAL

6 ▶ Perform dilution calculations.

Solution

Step 1. Summarize the information provided in the problem:

$$M_1 = 0.10 \, M$$
$$M_2 = X \, M$$
$$V_1 = 0.050 \text{ L}$$
$$V_2 = 1.0 \text{ L}$$

Step 2. Use the dilution expression:

$$(M_1)(V_1) = (M_2)(V_2)$$

Step 3. Solve for M_2, the final solution concentration:

$$M_2 = \frac{(M_1)(V_1)}{V_2}$$

Step 4. Substituting,

$$X \, M = \frac{(0.10 \, M)(0.050 \, \cancel{L})}{(1.0 \, \cancel{L})}$$

$$= 0.0050 \, M \text{ or } 5.0 \times 10^{-3} \, M \text{ HCl}$$

Practice Problem 6.8

What volume of 0.200 M sugar solution can be prepared from 50.0 mL of 0.400 M solution?

▶ **For Further Practice: Questions 6.44 and 6.45.**

EXAMPLE 6.9 Calculating a Dilution Volume

Calculate the volume, in L, of water that must be added to dilute 20.0 mL of 12.0 M HCl to 0.100 M HCl.

Continued—

Solution

Step 1. Summarize the information provided in the problem:

$$M_1 = 12.0 \, M$$
$$M_2 = 0.100 \, M$$
$$V_1 = 20.0 \text{ mL } (0.0200 \text{ L})$$
$$V_2 = V_{final}$$

Step 2. Then, using the dilution expression:

$$(M_1)(V_1) = (M_2)(V_2)$$

Step 3. Solve for V_2, the final volume:

$$V_2 = \frac{(M_1)(V_1)}{(M_2)}$$

Step 4. Substituting,

$$V_{final} = \frac{(12.0 \, M)(0.0200 \text{ L})}{0.100 \, M}$$
$$= 2.40 \text{ L solution}$$

Note that this is the *total final volume*. The amount of water added equals this volume *minus* the original solution volume, or

$$2.40 \text{ L} - 0.0200 \text{ L} = 2.38 \text{ L water}$$

Practice Problem 6.9

How would you prepare 1.0×10^2 mL of 2.0 M HCl, starting with concentrated (12.0 M) HCl?

▶ **For Further Practice: Questions 6.43 and 6.46.**

The dilution equation is valid with any concentration units, such as % (m/V) *as well as* molarity, which was used in Examples 6.8 and 6.9. However, you must use the same units for both initial *and* final concentration values. Only in this way can you cancel units properly.

6.4 Concentration-Dependent Solution Properties

LEARNING GOAL

7 ▶ Describe and explain concentration-dependent solution properties.

Colligative properties are solution properties that depend on the *concentration of the solute particles,* rather than the *identity of the solute.*

There are four colligative properties of solutions:

- vapor pressure lowering
- freezing point depression
- boiling point elevation
- osmotic pressure

Each of these properties has widespread practical applications. We look at each in some detail in the following sections.

Vapor Pressure Lowering

Raoult's law states that, when a nonvolatile solute is added to a solvent, the vapor pressure of the solvent decreases in proportion to the concentration of the solute.

Perhaps the most important consequence of Raoult's law is the effect of the solute on the freezing and boiling points of a solution.

When a nonvolatile solute is added to a solvent, the freezing point of the resulting solution decreases (a lower temperature is required to convert the liquid to a solid). The boiling point of the solution is found to increase (it requires a higher temperature to form the gaseous state).

Raoult's law may be explained in molecular terms by using the following logic: Vapor pressure of a solution results from the escape of solvent molecules from the liquid to the gas phase, thus increasing the partial pressure of the gas-phase solvent molecules until the equilibrium vapor pressure is reached. Presence of solute molecules hinders the escape of solvent molecules, thus lowering the equilibrium vapor pressure (Figure 6.4).

Figure 6.4 An illustration of Raoult's law: lowering of vapor pressure by addition of solute molecules. White units represent solvent molecules, and red units are solute molecules. Solute molecules present a barrier to escape of solvent molecules, thus decreasing the vapor pressure.

Freezing Point Depression and Boiling Point Elevation

Freezing point depression may be explained by examining the equilibrium between solid and liquid states. At the freezing point, ice is in equilibrium with liquid water:

$$H_2O(l) \underset{(r)}{\overset{(f)}{\rightleftarrows}} H_2O(s)$$

Solute molecules interfere with the rate at which liquid water molecules associate to form the solid state, decreasing the rate of the forward reaction. For a true equilibrium, the rate of the forward (f) and reverse (r) processes must be equal. Lowering the temperature eventually slows the rate of the reverse (r) process sufficiently to match the rate of the forward reaction. At the lower temperature, equilibrium is established, and the solution freezes.

Boiling point elevation can be explained by considering the definition of the boiling point, that is, the temperature at which the vapor pressure of the liquid equals the atmospheric pressure. Raoult's law states that the vapor pressure of a solution is decreased by the presence of a solute. Therefore a higher temperature is necessary to raise the vapor pressure to the atmospheric pressure, hence the boiling point elevation.

The extent of the freezing point depression (ΔT_f) is proportional to the solute concentration over a limited range of concentration:

$$\Delta T_f = k_f \times (\text{solute concentration})$$

The boiling point elevation (ΔT_b) is also proportional to the solute concentration:

$$\Delta T_b = k_b \times (\text{solute concentration})$$

If the value of the proportionality factor (k_f or k_b) is known for the solvent of interest, the magnitude of the freezing point depression or boiling point elevation can be calculated for a solution of known concentration.

Solute concentration must be in *mole*-based units. The number of particles (molecules or ions) is critical here, not the mass of solute. One *heavy* molecule will have exactly the same effect on the freezing or boiling point as one *light* molecule. A mole-based unit, because it is related directly to Avogadro's number, will correctly represent the number of particles in solution.

We have already worked with one mole-based unit, *molarity,* and this concentration unit can be used to calculate either the freezing point depression or the boiling point elevation.

A second mole-based concentration unit, molality, is more commonly used in these types of situations. **Molality** (symbolized m) is defined as the number of mol of solute per kilogram (kg) of solvent in a solution:

$$m = \frac{\text{mol solute}}{\text{kg solvent}}$$

Recall that the concept of liquid vapor pressure was discussed in Section 5.2.

Section 7.4 discusses equilibrium.

Molarity is temperature dependent simply because it is expressed as mol/volume. Volume is temperature dependent—most liquids expand measurably when heated and contract when cooled. Molality is mol/mass; both mol and mass are temperature independent.

Molality does not vary with temperature, whereas molarity is temperature dependent. For this reason, molality is the preferred concentration unit for studies such as freezing point depression and boiling point elevation, in which measurement of *change* in temperature is critical.

Practical applications that take advantage of freezing point depression of solutions by solutes include the following:

- Salt is spread on roads to melt ice in winter. The salt lowers the freezing point of the water, so it exists in the liquid phase below its normal freezing point, 0°C or 32°F.
- Solutes such as ethylene glycol, "antifreeze," are added to car radiators in the winter to prevent freezing by lowering the freezing point of the coolant.

We refer to the concentration of *particles* in our discussion of colligative properties. Why do we stress this term? The reason is that there is a very important difference between electrolytes and nonelectrolytes. That difference is the way that they behave when they dissolve. For example, if we dissolve 1 mol of glucose ($C_6H_{12}O_6$) in 1 kg of water,

$$1\ C_6H_{12}O_6(s) \xrightarrow{\ H_2O\ } 1\ C_6H_{12}O_6(aq)$$

1 mol (Avogadro's number, 6.022×10^{23} particles) of glucose is present in solution. *Glucose is a covalently bonded nonelectrolyte.* Dissolving 1 mol of sodium chloride in 1 kg of water,

$$1\ NaCl(s) \xrightarrow{\ H_2O\ } 1\ Na^+(aq) + 1\ Cl^-(aq)$$

produces 2 mol of particles (1 mol of sodium ions and 1 mol of chloride ions). *Sodium chloride is an ionic electrolyte.*

$$1\ \text{mol glucose} \longrightarrow 1\ \text{mol of particles in solution}$$
$$1\ \text{mol sodium chloride} \longrightarrow 2\ \text{mol of particles in solution}$$

It follows that 1 mol of sodium chloride will decrease the vapor pressure, increase the boiling point, or depress the freezing point of 1 kg of water *twice as much* as 1 mol of glucose in the same quantity of water.

Question 6.7 Comparing pure water and a 0.10 *m* glucose solution, which has the higher freezing point?

Question 6.8 Comparing pure water and a 0.10 *m* glucose solution, which has the higher boiling point?

Calculating Freezing Points and Boiling Points of Aqueous Solutions

The freezing point depression constant for aqueous solutions is:

$$k_f = \frac{1.86°C}{m}$$

The expression for calculating the change (decrease) in freezing point of an aqueous solution is equal to the product of the freezing point depression constant and the molality of the solution:

$$\Delta T_f = \left(\frac{1.86°C}{m}\right)(m)$$

Correspondingly, for boiling point elevation:

$$k_b = \frac{0.52°C}{m}$$

and

$$\Delta T_b = \left(\frac{0.52°C}{m}\right)(m)$$

If we know the solution molality (m),

$$m = \frac{\text{mol solute}}{\text{kg solvent}}$$

we can calculate the decrease (freezing) or increase (boiling) in freezing or boiling temperature. Recalling that pure water freezes at 0°C and boils at 100°C, we can subtract ΔT_f from 0°C to obtain the solution freezing point and add ΔT_b, to 100°C, resulting in the solution boiling point.

Let's review calculations of this type in Example 6.10.

EXAMPLE 6.10   Calculating Freezing and Boiling Points of Aqueous Solutions

Ethylene glycol, H—O—C—C—O—H (with H H above and H H below the two C atoms), is a widely used automobile antifreeze.

a. Calculate the freezing point of an 8.38 m aqueous solution of ethylene glycol.
b. Calculate the boiling point of an 8.38 m aqueous solution of ethylene glycol.

Solution

For part a,

Step 1. Using our expression for freezing point depression:

$$\Delta T_f = \left(\frac{1.86°C}{m}\right)(m)$$

and, substituting solution molality,

$$\Delta T_f = \left(\frac{1.86°C}{m}\right)(8.38\ m) = 15.6°C$$

Step 2. The solution freezing point is 15.6°C *below* 0.0°C, the freezing point of pure water. Therefore

$$\text{Freezing Point} = 0.0°C - 15.6°C = -15.6°C$$

For part b,

Step 1. Substituting our value for molality into the boiling point elevation equation:

$$\Delta T_b = \left(\frac{0.52°C}{m}\right)(m)$$

$$= \left(\frac{0.52°C}{m}\right)(8.38\ m) = 4.4°C$$

Step 2. This means that the solution boiling point is 4.4°C *above* the boiling point of pure water. Therefore

$$\text{Boiling Point} = 100.0°C + 4.4°C = 104.4°C$$

Continued—

Animation
• Osmosis

The terms *selectively permeable* or *differentially permeable* are used to describe biological membranes because such membranes restrict passage of particles based both on size and charge. Even small ions, such as H^+, cannot pass freely across a cell membrane.

Practice Problem 6.10

Calculate the boiling temperature and freezing temperature of a 1.5 *m* solution of KCl. (Remember that **1** mol of KCl produces **2** mol of particles.)

▶ **For Further Practice: Questions 6.63 and 6.64.**

Osmotic Pressure, Osmosis, and Osmolarity

The cell membrane mediates the interaction of the cell with its environment and is responsible for the controlled passage of material into and out of the cell. One of the principal means of transport is termed *diffusion*. **Diffusion** is the net movement of solute or solvent molecules from an area of high concentration to an area of low concentration. This region where the concentration decreases over a distance is termed the **concentration gradient.** Because of the structure of the cell membrane, only small molecules are able to diffuse freely across this barrier. Large molecules and highly charged ions are restricted by the barrier. In other words, the cell membrane is behaving in a selective fashion. Such membranes are termed **selectively permeable membranes.**

Because a cell membrane is selectively permeable, it is not always possible for solutes to pass through it in response to a concentration gradient. In such cases, the solvent diffuses through the membrane. Such membranes, permeable to solvent but not to solute, are specifically called **semipermeable membranes. Osmosis** is the diffusion of a solvent (water in biological systems) through a semipermeable membrane in response to a (water) concentration gradient.

Suppose that we place a 0.5 *M* glucose solution in a dialysis bag that is composed of a membrane with pores that allow the passage of water molecules but not glucose molecules. Consider what will happen when we place this bag into a beaker of pure water. We have created a gradient in which there is a higher concentration of glucose inside the bag than outside, but the glucose cannot diffuse through the bag to achieve equal concentration on both sides of the membrane.

Now let's think about this situation in another way. We have a higher concentration of water molecules outside the bag (where there is only pure water) than inside the bag (where some of the water molecules are occupied in dipole-dipole interactions with solute particles and are consequently unable to move freely in the system). Because water can diffuse through the membrane, a net diffusion of water will occur through the membrane into the bag. This is the process of osmosis (Figure 6.5).

As you have probably already guessed, this system can never reach equilibrium (equal concentrations inside and outside the bag). Regardless of how much water diffuses into the bag, diluting the glucose solution, the concentration of glucose will always be higher inside the bag (and the accompanying free water concentration will always be lower).

Figure 6.5 Osmosis across a membrane. The solvent, water, diffuses from outside the bag (the membrane) to the region of high solute concentration (inside the bag).

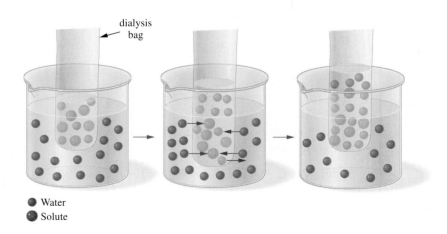

● Water
● Solute

What happens when the bag has taken in as much water as it can, when it has expanded as much as possible? Now the walls of the bag exert a force that will stop the *net* flow of water into the bag. **Osmotic pressure** is the pressure that must be exerted to stop the flow of water across a selectively permeable membrane by osmosis. Stated more precisely, the osmotic pressure of a solution is the net pressure with which water enters it by osmosis from a pure water compartment when the two compartments are separated by a semipermeable membrane.

The osmotic pressure, like the pressure exerted by a gas, may be treated quantitatively. Osmotic pressure, symbolized by π, follows the same form as the ideal gas equation:

Ideal Gas   **Osmotic Pressure**

$$PV = nRT$$ $$\pi V = nRT$$

or   or

$$P = \frac{n}{V}RT$$ $$\pi = \frac{n}{V}RT$$

and since   and since

$$M = \frac{n}{V}$$ $$M = \frac{n}{V}$$

then   then

$$P = MRT$$ $$\pi = MRT$$

The osmotic pressure can be calculated from the solution concentration at any temperature. How do we determine "solution concentration"? Recall that osmosis is a colligative property, dependent on the concentration of solute particles. Again, it becomes necessary to distinguish between solutions of electrolytes and nonelectrolytes. For example, a 1 M glucose solution consists of 1 mol of particles per L; glucose is a nonelectrolyte. A solution of 1 M NaCl produces 2 mol of particles per L (1 mol of Na^+ and 1 mol of Cl^-). A 1 M $CaCl_2$ solution is 3 M in particles (1 mol of Ca^{2+} and 2 mol of Cl^- per L).

Osmolarity, the molarity of particles in solution, and abbreviated osmol, is used for osmotic pressure calculations.

EXAMPLE 6.11   Calculating Osmolarity

Determine the osmolarity of $5.0 \times 10^{-3}\ M$ Na_3PO_4.

Solution

Step 1. Na_3PO_4 is an ionic compound and produces an electrolytic solution:

$$Na_3PO_4 \xrightarrow{H_2O} 3Na^+ + PO_4{}^{3-}$$

Step 2. 1 mol of Na_3PO_4 yields 4 mol of product ions; consequently

$$5.0 \times 10^{-3}\ \frac{\text{mol Na}_3\text{PO}_4}{\text{L}} \times \frac{4\ \text{mol particles}}{1\ \text{mol Na}_3\text{PO}_4} = 2.0 \times 10^{-2}\ \frac{\text{mol particles}}{\text{L}}$$

Step 3. Using our definition of osmolarity,

$$2.0 \times 10^{-2}\ \frac{\text{mol particles}}{\text{L}} = 2.0 \times 10^{-2}\ \text{osmol}$$

Continued—

Practice Problem 6.11

Determine the osmolarity of the following solutions:

   a. $5.0 \times 10^{-3}\,M\ NH_4NO_3$ (electrolyte)
   b. $5.0 \times 10^{-3}\,M\ C_6H_{12}O_6$ (nonelectrolyte)

▶ **For Further Practice: Questions 6.77 and 6.78.**

EXAMPLE 6.12   Calculating Osmotic Pressure

Calculate the osmotic pressure of a $5.0 \times 10^{-2}\,M$ solution of NaCl at 25°C (298 K).

Solution

Step 1. Using our definition of osmotic pressure, π:

$$\pi = MRT$$

Step 2. M should be represented as osmolarity as we have shown in Example 6.11

$$M = 5.0 \times 10^{-2}\,\frac{\text{mol NaCl}}{\text{L}} \times \frac{2\ \text{mol particles}}{1\ \text{mol NaCl}} = 1.0 \times 10^{-1}\,\frac{\text{mol particles}}{\text{L}}$$

Step 3. Substituting in our osmotic pressure expression:

$$\pi = 1.0 \times 10^{-1}\,\frac{\text{mol particles}}{L} \times 0.0821\,\frac{L \cdot \text{atm}}{K \cdot \text{mol}} \times 298\,K$$

$$= 2.4\ \text{atm}$$

Practice Problem 6.12

Calculate the osmotic pressure of each solution described in Practice Problem 6.11. Assume that the solutions are at 298 K.

▶ **For Further Practice: Questions 6.67 and 6.68.**

(a)

(b)

(c)

Figure 6.6 Scanning electron micrographs of red blood cells exposed to (a) hypertonic, (b) isotonic, and (c) hypotonic solutions.

Blood plasma has an osmolarity equivalent to a $0.30\,M$ glucose solution or a $0.15\,M$ NaCl solution. The latter is true because NaCl in solution dissociates into Na^+ and Cl^- and thus contributes twice the number of solute particles as a molecule that does not ionize. If red blood cells, which have an osmolarity equal to blood plasma, are placed in a $0.30\,M$ glucose solution, no net osmosis will occur because the osmolarity and water concentration inside the red blood cells are equal to those of the $0.30\,M$ glucose solution. The solutions inside and outside the red blood cells are said to be **isotonic** (*iso* means "same," and *tonic* means "strength") **solutions.** Because the osmolarity is the same inside and outside, the red blood cells will remain the same size (Figure 6.6b).

What happens if we now place the red blood cells into a **hypotonic solution,** in other words, a solution having a lower osmolarity than the cytoplasm of the cells? In this situation there will be a net movement of water into the cells as water diffuses down its concentration gradient. The membranes of the red blood cells do not have the strength to exert a sufficient pressure to stop this flow of water, and the cells will swell and burst (Figure 6.6c). Alternatively, if we place the red blood cells into a **hypertonic solution** (one with a greater osmolarity than the cells), water will pass out of the cells, and they will shrink dramatically (Figure 6.6a).

A Medical Perspective

Oral Rehydration Therapy

Diarrhea kills millions of children before they reach the age of 5 years. This is particularly true in third world countries where sanitation, water supplies, and medical care are poor. In the case of diarrhea, death results from fluid loss, electrolyte imbalance, and hypovolemic shock (multiple organ failure due to insufficient perfusion). Cholera is one of the best-understood bacterial diarrheas. The organism *Vibrio cholera* survives passage through the stomach and reproduces in the intestine, where it produces a toxin called choleragen. The toxin causes the excessive excretion of Na^+, Cl^-, and HCO_3^- from epithelial cells lining the intestine. The increased ion concentration (hypertonic solution) outside the cell results in movement of massive quantities of water into the intestinal lumen. This causes the severe, abundant, clear vomit and diarrhea that can result in the loss of 10–15 L of fluid per day. Over the 4- to 6-day progress of the disease, a patient may lose from one to two times his or her body mass!

The need for fluid replacement is obvious. Oral rehydration is preferred over intravenous administration of fluids and electrolytes since it is noninvasive. In many third world countries, it is the only therapy available in remote areas. The rehydration formula includes 50–80 g/L rice (or other starch), 3.5 g/L sodium chloride, 2.5 g/L sodium bicarbonate, and 1.5 g/L potassium chloride. Oral rehydration takes advantage of the cotransport of Na^+ and glucose across the cells lining the intestine. Thus, the glucose enters the cells, and Na^+ is carried along. Movement of these materials into the cells helps alleviate the osmotic imbalance, reduces the diarrhea, and corrects the fluid and electrolyte imbalance.

The disease runs its course in less than a week. In fact, antibiotics are not used to combat cholera. The only effective

A woman is shown filtering water through sari cloth.

therapy is oral rehydration, which reduces mortality to less than 1%. A much better option is prevention. In the photo above, a woman is shown filtering water through sari cloth. This simple practice has been shown to reduce the incidence of cholera significantly.

For Further Understanding

▶ Explain dehydration in terms of osmosis.
▶ Explain why even severely dehydrated individuals continue to experience further fluid loss.

These principles have important applications in the delivery of intravenous (IV) solutions into an individual (Figure 6.7). Normally, any fluids infused intravenously must have the correct osmolarity; they must be isotonic with the blood cells and the blood plasma. Such infusions are frequently either 5.5% dextrose (glucose) or "normal saline." The first solution is composed of 5.5 g of glucose per 100 mL of solution (0.30 M), and the latter of 9.0 g of NaCl per 100 mL of solution (0.15 M). In either case, they have the same osmotic pressure and osmolarity as the plasma and blood cells and can therefore be safely administered without upsetting the osmotic balance between the blood and the blood cells.

Practical examples of osmosis abound, including the following:

- A sailor, lost at sea in a lifeboat, dies of dehydration while surrounded by water. Seawater, because of its high salt concentration, dehydrates the cells of the body as a result of the large osmotic pressure difference between it and intracellular fluids.
- A cucumber, soaked in brine, shrivels into a pickle. The water in the cucumber is drawn into the brine (salt) solution because of a difference in osmotic pressure (Figure 6.8).
- A Medical Perspective: Oral Rehydration Therapy describes one of the most lethal and pervasive examples of cellular fluid imbalance.

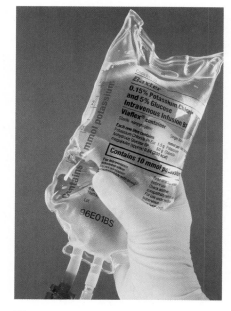

Figure 6.7 Composition and concentration are critically important in medical intervention.

Figure 6.8 A cucumber (a) in an acidic salt solution undergoes considerable shrinkage on its way to becoming a pickle (b) because of osmosis.

(a)   (b)

Question 6.9 Refer to the intravenous solution in Figure 6.7 and calculate the osmolarity of its contents.

Question 6.10 Is the solution osmolarity that you calculated in Question 6.9 isotonic with blood plasma? Why or why not?

6.5 Aqueous Solutions

Water as a Solvent

Water is by far the most abundant substance on earth. It is an excellent solvent for most inorganic substances, and is the principal biological solvent. Approximately 60% of the adult human body is water, and maintenance of this level is essential for survival. These characteristics are a direct consequence of the molecular structure of water.

As we saw in Chapter 3, water is a bent molecule with a 104.5° bond angle. This angular structure, resulting from the effect of the two lone pairs of electrons around the oxygen atom, is responsible for the polar nature of water. The polarity, in turn, gives water its unique properties.

Because water molecules are polar, water is an excellent solvent for other polar substances ("like dissolves like"). Because much of the matter on earth is polar, hence at least somewhat water soluble, water has been described as the universal solvent. The term *universal solvent* is historical; for centuries, water was known to dissolve many commonly used substances. The solvent in blood is water, and it dissolves and transports compounds as diverse as potassium chloride, glucose, and protein throughout our bodies.

Water is readily accessible and easily purified. It is nontoxic and quite nonreactive. The high boiling point of water, 100°C, compared with molecules of similar size such as N_2 (b.p. = −196°C), is also explained by water's polar character. Strong dipole-dipole interactions between a δ^+ hydrogen of one molecule and δ^- oxygen of a second, referred to as hydrogen bonding, create an interactive molecular network in the liquid phase (see Figure 5.8a). The strength of these interactions requires more energy (higher temperature) to cause water to boil. The higher than expected boiling point enhances water's value as a solvent; often, reactions are carried out at higher temperatures to increase their rates. Other solvents, with lower boiling points, would simply boil away, and the reaction would stop.

This idea is easily extended to our own chemistry—because 60% of our bodies is water, we should appreciate the polarity of water on a hot day. As a biological solvent in the human body, water is involved in the transport of ions, nutrients, and waste into and out of cells. Water is also the solvent for biochemical reactions in cells and the digestive tract. Water is a reactant or product in some biochemical processes.

A Human Perspective

An Extraordinary Molecule

Think for a moment. What is the only common molecule that exists in all three physical states of matter (solid, liquid, and gas) under natural conditions on earth? This molecule is absolutely essential for life; in fact, life probably arose in this substance. It is the most abundant molecule in the cells of living organisms (70–95%) and covers 75% of the earth's surface. Without it, cells quickly die, and without it the earth would not be a fit environment in which to live. By now you have guessed that we are talking about the water molecule. It is so abundant on earth that we take this deceptively simple molecule for granted.

What are some of the properties of water that cause it to be essential to life as we know it? Water has the ability to stabilize temperatures on the earth and in the body. This ability is due in part to the energy changes that occur when water changes physical state; but ultimately, this ability is due to the polar nature of the water molecule.

Life can exist only within a fairly narrow range of temperatures. Above or below that range, the chemical reactions necessary for life, and thus life itself, will cease. Water can moderate temperature fluctuation and maintain the range necessary for life, and one property that allows it to do so is its unusually high specific heat, 1 cal/g °C. This means that water can absorb or lose more heat energy than many other substances without a significant temperature change. This is because in the liquid state, every water molecule is hydrogen bonded to other water molecules. Because a temperature increase is really just a measure of increased (more rapid) molecular movement, we must get the water molecules moving more rapidly, independent of one another, to register a temperature increase. Before we can achieve this independent, increased activity, the hydrogen bonds between molecules must be broken. Much of the heat energy that water absorbs is involved in breaking hydrogen bonds and is *not* used to increase molecular movement. Thus a great deal of heat is needed to raise the temperature of water even a little bit.

Water also has a very high heat of vaporization. It takes 540 calories (cal) to change 1 g of liquid water at 100°C to a gas and even more, 603 cal/g, when the water is at 37°C, human body temperature. That is about twice the heat of vaporization of alcohol. As water molecules evaporate, the surface of the liquid cools because only the highest-energy (or "hottest") molecules leave as a gas. Only the "hottest" molecules have enough energy to break the hydrogen bonds that bind them to other water molecules. Indeed, evaporation of water molecules from the surfaces of lakes and oceans helps to maintain stable temperatures in those bodies of water. Similarly, evaporation of perspiration from body surfaces helps to prevent overheating on a hot day or during strenuous exercise.

Beauty is also a property of water.

Even the process of freezing helps stabilize and moderate temperatures. This is especially true in the fall. Water releases heat when hydrogen bonds are formed. This is an example of an exothermic process. Thus, when water freezes, solidifying into ice, additional hydrogen bonds are formed, and heat is released into the environment. As a result, the temperature change between summer and winter is more gradual, allowing organisms to adjust to the change.

One last feature that we take for granted is the fact that when we put ice in our iced tea on a hot summer day, the ice floats. This means that the solid state of water is actually *less* dense than the liquid state! In fact, it is about 10% less dense, having an open lattice structure with each molecule hydrogen bonded to the maximum of four other water molecules. What would happen if ice did sink? All bodies of water, including the mighty oceans would eventually freeze solid, killing all aquatic and marine plant and animal life. Even in the heat of summer, only a few inches of ice at the surface would thaw. Instead, the ice forms at the surface and provides a layer of insulation that prevents the water below from freezing.

As we continue our study of chemistry, we will refer again and again to this amazing molecule. In other Human Perspective features we will examine other properties of water that make it essential to life.

For Further Understanding

▶ Why is the high heat of vaporization of water important to our bodies?

▶ Why is it cooler at the ocean shore than in the desert during summer?

LEARNING GOAL

8 ▶ Describe why the chemical and physical properties of water make it a truly unique solvent.

EXAMPLE 6.13   Predicting Structure from Observable Properties

Sucrose is a common sugar and we know that it is used as a sweetener when dissolved in many beverages. What does this allow us to predict about the structure of sucrose?

Solution

Sucrose is used as a sweetener in teas, coffee, and a host of soft drinks. The solvent in all of these beverages is water, a polar molecule. The rule "like dissolves like" implies that sucrose must also be a polar molecule. Without even knowing the formula or structure of sucrose, we can infer this important information from a simple experiment—dissolving sugar in our morning cup of coffee.

Practice Problem 6.13

Predict whether ammonia or methane would be more soluble in water. Explain your answer. (Hint: Refer to Section 5.2, the discussion of interactions in the liquid state.)

▶ **For Further Practice: Questions 6.89 and 6.90.**

Electrolytes in Solution

LEARNING GOAL

9 ▶ Interconvert molar concentrations of ions and milliequivalents/liter.

Recall (Sections 3.3 and 6.1) that an electrolyte is a material that dissolves in water to produce an *electrolytic solution* that conducts an electrical current. The behavior of many biological systems is critically dependent on the concentration of electrolytic solutions that are a part of these systems.

Molarity (mol/L) is the most commonly used concentration unit; however, another useful concentration unit is based on the *equivalent.* The **equivalent** (eq) is the number of grams of an ion corresponding to Avogadro's number of electrical charges. The resulting concentration unit is eq/L.

When discussing solutions of ionic compounds, molarity emphasizes the number of individual ions. A 1 molar solution of Na^+ contains Avogadro's number, 6.022×10^{23}, of Na^+ per L. In contrast, eq/L emphasize charge; 1 eq of Na^+ contains Avogadro's number of positive charges.

The concentration of any ion in aqueous solution, in units of eq/L, is equal to the product of the equivalents/mol of the ion and the molar concentration of the ion:

$$eq/L = \left(\frac{eq}{mol\ ion}\right)\left(\frac{mol\ ion}{L}\right)$$

Since

$$\frac{mol\ ion}{L} = M$$

$$eq/L = \left(\frac{eq}{mol\ ion}\right)(M)$$

The eq/mol of the ion is simply the number of charges on the ion, regardless of whether that charge is positive or negative. For example:

For Na^+, eq/mol is equal to 1
　　Cl^-, eq/mol is equal to 1
　　Mg^{2+}, eq/mol is equal to 2
　　CO_3^{2-}, eq/mol is equal to 2
and so forth.

The units milliequivalents/liter (meq/L) are often used when describing small amounts or low concentration of ions. These units are routinely used when describing ions in blood, urine, and blood plasma.

We can convert between eq/L and meq/L using conversion factors based on the identity:

$$1 \text{ eq} = 10^3 \text{ meq}$$

EXAMPLE 6.14   Calculating Ion Concentration

For a solution that is 5.0×10^{-3} M in phosphate ion (PO_4^{-3})

a. Calculate the concentration of phosphate ion in units of eq/L
b. Calculate the concentration of phosphate ion in units of meq/L

LEARNING GOAL

9 ▶ Interconvert molar concentration of ions and milliequivalents/liter.

Solution

a. Substituting in the equation:

$$eq/L = \left(\frac{eq}{mol \text{ ion}} \right)(M)$$

$$eq/L = \left(\begin{array}{c} 3 \\ \text{moles of charge} \\ \text{per mol of phosphate ion} \end{array} \right)\left(\begin{array}{c} 5.0 \times 10^{-3} \text{ } M \\ \text{molar concentration} \\ \text{of the phosphate ion} \end{array} \right)$$

$$eq/L = 1.5 \times 10^{-2} \text{ eq/L}$$

Note: The mols of charge in this equation is always positive even if the ion is negative. It represents the number of mol of charge, not the sign of the charge.

b. We need only use the conversion factor

$$\frac{10^3 \text{ meq}}{eq}$$

$$meq/L = 1.5 \times 10^{-2} \frac{\cancel{eq}}{L} \times \frac{10^3 \text{ meq}}{\cancel{eq}} = 15 \text{ meq/L}$$

Practice Problem 6.14

Calculate the number of eq/L of carbonate ion, CO_3^{2-}, in a solution that is 6.4×10^{-4} M carbonate ion.

▶ **For Further Practice: Questions 6.97 and 6.98.**

EXAMPLE 6.15   Calculating Electrolyte Concentrations

A typical concentration of calcium ion in blood plasma is 4 meq/L. Represent this concentration in mol/L.

Solution

Step 1. The calcium ion has a 2+ charge (recall that calcium is in Group IIA of the periodic table; hence, a 2+ charge on the calcium ion).

Continued—

Step 2. We will need two conversion factors:

$$meq \longrightarrow eq$$
$$eq \longrightarrow mol\ of\ calcium\ ion$$

Step 3. Using conversion factors as in Example 6.14,

$$\frac{4\ meq\ Ca^{2+}}{1\ L} \times \frac{1\ eq\ Ca^{2+}}{10^3\ meq\ Ca^{2+}} = 4 \times 10^{-3}\ \frac{eq\ Ca^{2+}}{L}$$

Step 4. Our relationship between meq/L and M is:

$$eq\ Ca^{2+}/L = \left(\frac{eq\ Ca^{2+}}{mol\ Ca^{2+}}\right)(M)$$

Step 5. Rearranging and solving for M,

$$M = \left(\frac{eq\ Ca^{2+}}{L}\right)\left(\frac{mol\ Ca^{2+}}{eq\ Ca^{2+}}\right)$$

Step 6. Substituting,

$$M = \left(\frac{4 \times 10^{-3}\ eq\ Ca^{2+}}{L}\right)\left(\frac{1\ mol\ Ca^{2+}}{2\ eq\ Ca^{2+}}\right)$$

and

$$M = \frac{2 \times 10^{-3}\ mol\ Ca^{2+}}{L}$$

Practice Problem 6.15

Sodium chloride [0.9% (m/V)] is a solution administered intravenously to replace fluid loss. It is frequently used to avoid dehydration. The sodium ion concentration is 15.4 meq/L. Calculate the sodium ion concentration in mol/L.

▶ **For Further Practice: Questions 6.99 and 6.100.**

Biological Effects of Electrolytes in Solution

LEARNING GOAL

10 ▶ Explain the role of electrolytes in blood and their relationship to the process of dialysis.

The concentrations of cations, anions, and other substances in biological fluids are critical to health. Consequently, the osmolarity of body fluids is carefully regulated by the kidney.

The two most important cations in body fluids are Na^+ and K^+. Sodium ion is the most abundant cation in the blood and intercellular fluids, whereas potassium ion is the most abundant intracellular cation. In blood and intercellular fluid, the Na^+ concentration is 135 meq/L and the K^+ concentration is 3.5–5.0 meq/L. Inside the cell, the situation is reversed. The K^+ concentration is 125 meq/L and the Na^+ concentration is 10 meq/L.

If osmosis and simple diffusion were the only mechanisms for transporting water and ions across cell membranes, these concentration differences would not occur. One positive ion would be just as good as any other. However, the situation is more complex than this. Large protein molecules embedded in cell membranes actively pump sodium ions to the outside of the cell and potassium ions into the cell. This is termed *active transport* because cellular energy must be expended to transport those ions. Proper cell function in the regulation of muscles and the nervous system depends on the sodium ion/potassium ion ratio inside and outside of the cell.

If the Na^+ concentration in the blood becomes too low, urine output decreases, the mouth feels dry, the skin becomes flushed, and a fever may develop. The blood level of Na^+ may be elevated when large amounts of water are lost. Diabetes,

A Medical Perspective

Hemodialysis

As we have seen in Section 6.5, blood is the medium for exchange of both nutrients and waste products. The membranes of the kidneys remove waste materials such as urea and uric acid (Chapter 22), excess salts, and large quantities of water. This process of waste removal is termed **dialysis,** a process similar in function to osmosis (Section 6.4). Semipermeable membranes in the kidneys, dialyzing membranes, allow small molecules (principally water and urea) and ions in solution to pass through and ultimately collect in the bladder. From there they can be eliminated from the body.

Unfortunately, a variety of diseases can cause partial or complete kidney failure. Should the kidneys fail to perform their primary function, dialysis of waste products, urea and other waste products rapidly increase in concentration in the blood. This can become a life-threatening situation in a very short time.

The most effective treatment of kidney failure is the use of a machine, an artificial kidney, that mimics the function of the kidney. The artificial kidney removes waste from the blood using the process of hemodialysis (blood dialysis). The blood is pumped through a long semipermeable membrane, the dialysis membrane. The dialysis process is similar to osmosis. However, in addition to water molecules, larger molecules (including the waste products in the blood) and ions can pass across the membrane from the blood into a dialyzing fluid. The dialyzing fluid is isotonic with normal blood; it also is similar in its concentration of all other essential blood components. The waste materials move across the dialysis membrane (from a higher to a lower concentration, as in diffusion). A successful dialysis procedure selectively removes the waste from the body without upsetting the critical electrolyte balance in the blood.

Hemodialysis, although lifesaving, is not by any means a pleasant experience. The patient's water intake must be severely limited to minimize the number of times each week that treatment must be used. Many dialysis patients require two or three treatments per week and each session may require one-half

Dialysis patient.

(or more) day of hospitalization, especially when the patient suffers from complicating conditions such as diabetes.

Improvements in technology, as well as the growth and sophistication of our health care delivery systems over the past several years, have made dialysis treatment much more patient friendly. Dialysis centers, specializing in the treatment of kidney patients, are now found in most major population centers. Smaller, more automated dialysis units are available for home use, under the supervision of a nurse. With the remarkable progress in kidney transplant success, dialysis is becoming, more and more, a temporary solution, sustaining life until a suitable kidney donor match can be found.

For Further Understanding

▶ In what way is dialysis similar to osmosis?

▶ In what way does dialysis differ from osmosis?

certain high-protein diets, and diarrhea may cause elevated blood Na^+ level. In extreme cases, elevated Na^+ levels may cause confusion, stupor, or coma.

Concentrations of K^+ in the blood may rise to dangerously high levels following any injury that causes large numbers of cells to rupture, releasing their intracellular K^+. This may lead to death by heart failure. Similarly, very low levels of K^+ in the blood may also cause death from heart failure. This may occur following prolonged exercise that results in excessive sweating. When this happens, both body fluids and electrolytes must be replaced. Salt tablets containing both NaCl and KCl taken with water, and drinks such as Gatorade effectively provide water and electrolytes and prevent serious symptoms.

The cationic charge in blood is neutralized by two major anions, Cl^- and HCO_3^-. The chloride ion plays a role in acid-base balance, maintenance of osmotic pressure within an acceptable range, and oxygen transport by hemoglobin. The bicarbonate anion is the form in which most waste CO_2 is carried in the blood.

A variety of proteins are also found in the blood. Because of their larger size, they exist in colloidal suspension. These proteins include blood clotting factors, immunoglobulins (antibodies) that help us fight infection, and albumins that act as carriers of nonpolar, hydrophobic substances (fatty acids and steroid hormones) that cannot dissolve in water.

Additionally, blood is the medium for exchange of nutrients and waste products. Nutrients, such as the polar sugar glucose, enter the blood from the intestine or the liver. Because glucose molecules are polar, they dissolve in body fluids and are circulated to tissues throughout the body. As noted above, nonpolar nutrients are transported with the help of carrier proteins. Similarly, nitrogen-containing waste products, such as urea, are passed from cells to the blood. They are continuously and efficiently removed from the blood by the kidneys.

In cases of loss of kidney function, mechanical devices—dialysis machines—mimic the action of the kidney. The process of blood dialysis—hemodialysis—is discussed in A Medical Perspective: Hemodialysis on page 211.

SUMMARY

6.1 Properties of Solutions

A *solution* is a homogeneous (or uniform) mixture of two or more substances. A solution is composed of one or more *solutes,* dissolved in a *solvent.* When the solvent is water, the solution is called an *aqueous solution.*

Liquid solutions are clear and transparent with no visible particles of solute. They may be colored or colorless, depending on the properties of the solute and solvent.

In solutions of *electrolytes* the solutes are ionic compounds that dissociate in solution to produce ions. They are good conductors of electricity. Solutions of *nonelectrolytes* are formed from nondissociating molecular solutes (nonelectrolytes), and their solutions are nonconducting.

The rule "like dissolves like" is the fundamental condition for solubility. Polar solutes are soluble in polar solvents, and nonpolar solutes are soluble in nonpolar solvents.

The degree of solubility depends on the difference between the polarity of solute and solvent, the temperature, and the pressure. Pressure considerations are significant only for solutions of gases.

When a solution contains all the solute that can be dissolved at a particular temperature, it is *saturated.* Excess solute falls to the bottom of the container as a *precipitate.* Occasionally, on cooling, the excess solute may remain in solution for a time before precipitation. Such a solution is a *supersaturated solution.* When excess solute, the precipitate, contacts solvent, the dissolution process reaches a state of dynamic equilibrium. *Colloidal suspensions* have particle sizes between those of true solutions and precipitates. A *suspension* is a heterogeneous mixture that contains particles much larger than a colloidal suspension. Over time, these particles may settle, forming a second phase.

Henry's law describes the solubility of gases in liquids. At a given temperature the solubility of a gas is proportional to the partial pressure of the gas.

6.2 Concentration Based on Percent by Mass

The amount of solute dissolved in a given amount of solution is the solution *concentration.* The more widely used percentage-based concentration units are *mass/volume percent*

and *mass/mass percent. Parts per thousand (ppt)* and *parts per million (ppm)* are used with very dilute solutions.

6.3 Concentration Based on Moles

Molarity, symbolized M, is defined as the number of moles of solute per liter of solution.

Dilution is often used to prepare less concentrated solutions. The expression for this calculation is $(M_1)(V_1) = (M_2)(V_2)$. Knowing any three of these terms enables us to calculate the fourth. The concentration of solute may be represented as mol/L (molarity) or any other suitable concentration units. However, both concentrations must be in the same units when using the dilution equation.

6.4 Concentration-Dependent Solution Properties

Solution properties that depend on the concentration of solute particles, rather than the identity of the solute, are *colligative properties.*

There are four colligative properties of solutions, all of which depend on the concentration of *particles* in solution.

1. *Vapor pressure lowering. Raoult's law* states that when a solute is added to a solvent, the vapor pressure of the solvent decreases in proportion to the concentration of the solute.

2. and 3. *Freezing point depression and boiling point elevation.* When a nonvolatile solid is added to a solvent, the freezing point of the resulting solution decreases, and the boiling point increases. The magnitudes of both the freezing point depression (ΔT_f) and the boiling point elevation (ΔT_b) are proportional to the solute concentration over a limited range of concentrations. The mole-based concentration unit, molality, is more commonly used in calculations involving colligative properties. This is due to the fact that molality is temperature independent. *Molality* (symbolized m) is defined as the number of mol of solute per kg of solvent in a solution.

4. *Osmosis and osmotic pressure. Osmosis* is the movement of solvent from a dilute solution to a more concentrated solution through a *semipermeable membrane.* The pressure that must be applied to the more concentrated solution to stop this flow is the *osmotic pressure.* The osmotic pressure, like the pressure exerted by a gas, may be treated

quantitatively by using an equation similar in form to the ideal gas equation: $\pi = MRT$. By convention the molarity of particles that is used for osmotic pressure calculations is termed *osmolarity (osmol).*

In biological systems, if the concentration of the fluid surrounding red blood cells is higher than that inside the cell (a *hypertonic* solution), water flows from the cell, causing it to collapse. Too low a concentration of this fluid relative to the solution within the cell (a *hypotonic* solution) will cause cell rupture.

Two solutions are *isotonic* if they have identical osmotic pressures. In that way the osmotic pressure differential across the cell is zero, and no cell disruption occurs.

6.5 Aqueous Solutions

The role of water in the solution process deserves special attention. It is often referred to as the "universal solvent" because of the large number of ionic and polar covalent compounds that are at least partially soluble in water. It is the principal biological solvent. These characteristics are a direct consequence of the molecular geometry and structure of water and its ability to undergo hydrogen bonding.

When discussing solutions of ionic compounds, molarity emphasizes the number of individual ions. A 1 M solution of Na^+ contains Avogadro's number of sodium ions. In contrast, equivalents per liter emphasizes charge; a solution containing 1 eq of Na^+ per L contains Avogadro's number of positive charge. One *equivalent* of an ion is the number of grams of the ion corresponding to Avogadro's number of electrical charges. Changing from mol/L to eq/L (or the reverse) is done using conversion factors.

Concentration of charge in these electrolytic solutions is even more important than the molar concentration of the ions that are responsible for the charge. Consequently, we often use concentration units (eq/L and meq/L) that emphasize charge rather than number of ions in solution.

The concentrations of cations, anions, and other substances in biological fluids are critical to health. As a result, the osmolarity of body fluids is carefully regulated by the kidney using the process of *dialysis.*

KEY TERMS

aqueous solution (6.1)	isotonic solution (6.4)
colligative property (6.4)	mass/mass percent
colloidal suspension (6.1)	(% [m/m]) (6.2)
concentration (6.2)	mass/volume percent
concentration gradient (6.4)	(% [m/V]) (6.2)
dialysis (6.5)	molality (6.4)
diffusion (6.4)	molarity (6.3)
electrolyte (6.1)	nonelectrolyte (6.1)
equivalent (6.5)	osmolarity (6.4)
Henry's law (6.1)	osmosis (6.4)
hypertonic solution (6.4)	osmotic pressure (6.4)
hypotonic solution (6.4)	precipitate (6.1)

Raoult's law (6.4)	solute (6.1)
saturated solution (6.1)	solution (6.1)
selectively permeable	solvent (6.1)
membrane (6.4)	supersaturated
semipermeable	solution (6.1)
membrane (6.4)	suspension (6.1)
solubility (6.1)	

QUESTIONS AND PROBLEMS

Properties of Solutions
Foundations

6.11 Classify each of the following solutes as an electrolyte or a nonelectrolyte:
  a. $NaNO_3$
  b. $C_6H_{12}O_6$
  c. $FeCl_3$
6.12 Classify each of the following solutes as an electrolyte or a nonelectrolyte:
  a. HCl
  b. Na_2SO_4
  c. Ethanol (CH_3CH_2OH)
6.13 Distinguish among the terms true solution, colloid, and suspension.
6.14 What is the difference between saturated and supersaturated solutions?

Applications

6.15 Fly fishermen in the Northeast have known for a long time that their chances of catching trout are much greater in early spring than in mid-August. Suggest an explanation based on your reading of this chapter.
6.16 Fish kills (the sudden death of thousands of fish) often occur during periods of prolonged elevated temperatures. Pollution is often, but not always, the cause. Suggest another reason, based on your reading of this chapter.
6.17 Can a solution be both clear and red? Explain.
6.18 Two liters of solvent A are mixed with two liters of solvent B. The resulting volume is only 3.95 L. Explain what happened on the molecular level.

Concentration Based on Percent by Mass
Foundations

6.19 Calculate the composition of each of the following solutions in mass/volume %:
  a. 20.0 g NaCl in 1.00 L solution
  b. 33.0 g sugar, $C_6H_{12}O_6$, in 5.00×10^2 mL solution
6.20 Calculate the composition of each of the following solutions in mass/volume %:
  a. 0.700 g KCl per 1.00 mL
  b. 1.00 mol $MgCl_2$ in 2.50×10^2 mL solution
6.21 Calculate the composition of each of the following solutions in mass/volume %:
  a. 50.0 g ethanol dissolved in 1.00 L solution
  b. 50.0 g ethanol dissolved in 5.00×10^2 mL solution
6.22 Calculate the composition of each of the following solutions in mass/volume %:
  a. 20.0 g acetic acid dissolved in 2.50 L solution
  b. 20.0 g benzene dissolved in 1.00×10^2 mL solution
6.23 Calculate the composition of each of the following solutions in mass/mass %:
  a. 21.0 g NaCl in 1.00×10^2 g solution
  b. 21.0 g NaCl in 5.00×10^2 mL solution ($d = 1.12$ g/mL)

6.24 Calculate the composition of each of the following solutions in mass/mass %:
  a. 1.00 g KCl in 1.00×10^2 g solution
  b. 50.0 g KCl in 5.00×10^2 mL solution ($d = 1.14$ g/mL)

Applications

6.25 How many g of solute are needed to prepare each of the following solutions?
  a. 2.50×10^2 g of 0.900% (m/m) NaCl
  b. 2.50×10^2 g of 1.25% (m/m) $NaC_2H_3O_2$ (sodium acetate)

6.26 How many g of solute are needed to prepare each of the following solutions?
  a. 2.50×10^2 g of 5.00% (m/m) NH_4Cl (ammonium chloride)
  b. 2.50×10^2 g of 3.50% (m/m) Na_2CO_3

6.27 A solution was prepared by dissolving 14.6 g of KNO_3 in sufficient water to produce 75.0 mL of solution. What is the mass/volume % of this solution?

6.28 A solution was prepared by dissolving 12.4 g of $NaNO_3$ in sufficient water to produce 95.0 mL of solution. What is the mass/volume % of this solution?

6.29 How many g of sugar would you use to prepare 100 mL of a 1.00 mass/volume % solution?

6.30 How many mL of 4.0 mass/volume % $Mg(NO_3)_2$ solution would contain 1.2 g of magnesium nitrate?

6.31 Which solution is more concentrated: a 0.04% (m/m) solution or a 50 ppm solution?

6.32 Which solution is more concentrated: a 20 ppt solution or a 200 ppm solution?

6.33 A solution contains 1.0 mg of Cu^{2+} per 0.50 kg solution. Calculate the concentration in ppt.

6.34 A solution contains 1.0 mg of Cu^{2+} per 0.50 kg solution. Calculate the concentration in ppm.

Concentration Based on Moles

Foundations

6.35 Why is it often necessary to dilute solutions in laboratory?

6.36 Write the dilution expression and define each term.

6.37 Calculate the molarity of 5.0 L of solution containing 2.5 mol HNO_3.

6.38 Calculate the molarity of 2.75 L of solution containing 1.35×10^{-2} mol HCl.

Applications

6.39 Calculate the number of g of solute that would be needed to make each of the following solutions:
  a. 2.50×10^2 mL of 0.100 M NaCl
  b. 2.50×10^2 mL of 0.200 M $C_6H_{12}O_6$ (glucose)

6.40 Calculate the number of g of solute that would be needed to make each of the following solutions:
  a. 2.50×10^2 mL of 0.100 M NaBr
  b. 2.50×10^2 mL of 0.200 M KOH

6.41 Calculate the volume of a 0.500 M sucrose solution (table sugar, $C_{12}H_{22}O_{11}$) containing 0.133 mol of solute.

6.42 Calculate the volume of a 1.00×10^{-2} M KOH solution containing 3.00×10^{-1} mol of solute.

6.43 It is desired to prepare 0.500 L of a 0.100 M solution of NaCl from a 1.00 M stock solution. How many mL of the stock solution must be taken for the dilution?

6.44 A 50.0-mL sample of a 0.250 M sucrose solution was diluted to 5.00×10^2 mL. What is the molar concentration of the resulting solution?

6.45 A 50.0-mL portion of a stock solution was diluted to 500.0 mL. If the resulting solution was 2.00 M, what was the molarity of the original stock solution?

6.46 A 6.00-mL portion of an 8.00 M stock solution is to be diluted to 0.400 M. What will be the final volume after dilution?

6.47 Calculate the molarity of a solution that contains 2.25 mol of $NaNO_3$ dissolved in 2.50 L.

6.48 Calculate the molarity of a solution that contains 1.75 mol of KNO_3 dissolved in 3.00 L.

6.49 How many g of glucose ($C_6H_{12}O_6$) are present in 1.75 L of a 0.500 M solution?

6.50 How many g of sodium hydroxide are present in 675 mL of a 0.500 M solution?

6.51 A 50.0-mL sample of 0.500 M NaOH was diluted to 500.0 mL. What is the new molarity?

6.52 A 300.0-mL portion of H_2O is added to 300.0 mL of 0.250 M H_2SO_4. What is the new molarity?

Concentration-Dependent Solution Properties

Foundations

6.53 What is meant by the term *colligative property?*

6.54 Name and describe four colligative solution properties.

6.55 Explain, in terms of solution properties, why salt is used to melt ice in the winter.

6.56 Explain, in terms of solution properties, why a wilted plant regains its "health" when watered.

Applications

6.57 In what way do colligative properties and chemical properties differ?

6.58 Look up the meaning of the term "colligative." Why is it an appropriate title for these properties?

6.59 State Raoult's law.

6.60 What is the major importance of Raoult's law?

6.61 Why does 1 mol of $CaCl_2$ lower the freezing point of water more than 1 mol of NaCl?

6.62 Using salt to try to melt ice on a day when the temperature is $-20°C$ will be unsuccessful. Why?

Answer Questions 6.63–6.68 by comparing two solutions: 0.50 M sodium chloride (an ionic compound) and 0.50 M sucrose (a covalent compound).

6.63 Calculate the freezing temperature of each solution. Assume that the molality of each solution is 0.50 m. (The molar and molal concentrations of dilute aqueous solutions are often identical, to two significant figures.)

6.64 Calculate the boiling temperature of each solution. Assume that the molality of each solution is 0.50 m. (The molar and molal concentrations of dilute aqueous solutions are often identical, to two significant figures.)

6.65 Which solution has the higher vapor pressure?

6.66 Each solution is separated from water by a semipermeable membrane. Which solution has the higher osmotic pressure?

6.67 Calculate the osmotic pressure of 0.50 M sodium chloride.

6.68 Calculate the osmotic pressure of 0.50 M sucrose.

Answer Questions 6.69–6.72 based on the following scenario: Two solutions, A and B, are separated by a semipermeable membrane. For each case, predict whether there will be a net flow of water in one direction and, if so, which direction.

6.69 A is pure water and B is 5% glucose.

6.70 A is 0.10 M glucose and B is 0.10 M KCl.

6.71 A is 0.10 M NaCl and B is 0.10 M KCl.

6.72 A is 0.10 M NaCl and B is 0.20 M glucose.

In Questions 6.73–6.76, label each solution as isotonic, hypotonic, or hypertonic in comparison to 0.9% NaCl (0.15 M NaCl).

6.73 0.15 M $CaCl_2$

6.74 0.35 M glucose

6.75 0.15 M glucose

6.76 3% NaCl

6.77 Determine the osmolarity of 5.0×10^{-4} M KNO_3 (electrolyte).

6.78 Determine the osmolarity of 2.5×10^{-4} M $C_6H_{12}O_6$ (nonelectrolyte).

Aqueous Solutions

Foundations

6.79 What properties make water such a useful solvent?

6.80 Sketch the "interactive network" of water molecules in the liquid state.

6.81 Sketch the interaction of water with an ammonia molecule.

6.82 Sketch the interaction of water with an ethanol molecule.

6.83 Why is it important to distinguish between electrolytes and nonelectrolytes when discussing colligative properties?

6.84 Name the two most important cations in biological fluids.

6.85 Explain why a dialysis solution must have a low sodium ion concentration if it is designed to remove excess sodium ion from the blood.

6.86 Explain why a dialysis solution must have an elevated potassium ion concentration when loss of potassium ion from the blood is a concern.

Applications

6.87 Solutions of ammonia in water are sold as window cleaner. Why do these solutions have a long "shelf life"?

6.88 Why does water's abnormally high boiling point help to make it a desirable solvent?

6.89 Sketch the interaction of a water molecule with a sodium ion.

6.90 Sketch the interaction of a water molecule with a chloride ion.

6.91 What type of solute dissolves readily in water?

6.92 What type of solute dissolves readily in gasoline?

6.93 Describe the clinical effects of elevated concentrations of sodium ion in the blood.

6.94 Describe the clinical effects of depressed concentrations of potassium ion in the blood.

6.95 Describe conditions that can lead to elevated concentrations of sodium in the blood.

6.96 Describe conditions that can lead to dangerously low concentrations of potassium in the blood.

6.97 Calculate the number of eq/L of Ca^{2+} in a solution that is 5.0×10^{-2} M in Ca^{2+}.

6.98 Calculate the number of eq/L of SO_4^{2-} in a solution that is 2.5×10^{-3} M in SO_4^{2-}.

6.99 A potassium chloride solution that also contains 5% (m/V) dextrose is administered intravenously to treat some forms of malnutrition. The potassium ion concentration in this solution is 40 meq/L. Calculate the potassium ion concentration in mol/L.

6.100 If the potassium ion concentration in the solution described in Question 6.99 was only 35 meq/L, calculate the potassium ion concentration in units of mol/L.

CRITICAL THINKING PROBLEMS

1. Which of the following compounds would cause the greater freezing point depression, per mol, in H_2O: $C_6H_{12}O_6$ (glucose) or NaCl?

2. Which of the following compounds would cause the greater boiling point elevation, per mol, in H_2O: $MgCl_2$ or $HOCH_2CH_2OH$ (ethylene glycol, antifreeze)? (Hint: $HOCH_2CH_2OH$ is covalent.)

3. Analytical chemists often take advantage of differences in solubility to separate ions. For example, adding Cl^- to a solution of Cu^{2+} and Ag^+ causes AgCl to precipitate; Cu^{2+} remains in solution. Filtering the solution results in a separation. Design a scheme to separate the cations Ca^{2+} and Pb^{2+}.

4. Using the strategy outlined in the above problem, design a scheme to separate the anions S^{2-} and CO_3^{2-}.

5. Design an experiment that would enable you to measure the degree of solubility of a salt such as KI in water.

6. How could you experimentally distinguish between a saturated solution and a supersaturated solution?

7. Blood is essentially an aqueous solution, but it must transport a variety of nonpolar substances (hormones, for example). Colloidal proteins, termed *albumins,* facilitate this transport. Must these albumins be polar or nonpolar? Why?

Energy, Rate, and Equilibrium

7

LEARNING GOALS

1 ▶ Correlate the terms *endothermic* and *exothermic* with heat flow between a *system* and its *surroundings*.

2 ▶ State the meaning of the terms *enthalpy*, *entropy*, and *free energy* and know their implications.

3 ▶ Describe experiments that yield thermochemical information and calculate fuel values based on experimental data.

4 ▶ Describe the concept of reaction rate and the role of kinetics in chemical and physical change.

5 ▶ Describe the importance of *activation energy* and the *activated complex* in determining reaction rate.

6 ▶ Predict the way reactant structure, concentration, temperature, and catalysis affect the rate of a chemical reaction.

7 ▶ Write rate laws and use these equations to calculate the effect of concentration on rate.

8 ▶ Recognize and describe equilibrium situations.

9 ▶ Write equilibrium constant expressions and use these expressions to calculate equilibrium constants.

10 ▶ Use LeChatelier's principle to predict changes in equilibrium position.

OUTLINE

36

Describe the relationship of the modern automobile engine to the topics discussed in this chapter.

INTRODUCTION

In Chapter 4 we calculated quantities of matter involved in chemical change, assuming that all of the reacting material was consumed and that only products of the reaction remain at the end of the reaction. Often this is not true. Furthermore, not all chemical reactions take place at the same speed; some occur almost instantaneously (explosions), whereas others may proceed for many years (corrosion).

Two concepts play important roles in determining the extent and speed of a chemical reaction: (1) thermodynamics, which deals with energy changes in chemical reactions, and (2) kinetics, which describes the rate or speed of a chemical reaction.

Although both thermodynamics and kinetics involve energy, they are two separate considerations. The laws of thermodynamics may predict that a reaction will occur, but the process will not be observed because the reaction is so slow; conversely, a reaction may be very fast because it is kinetically favorable yet produce very little (or no) product because it is thermodynamically unfavorable.

In this chapter we investigate the fundamentals of thermodynamics and kinetics, with an emphasis on the critical role that energy changes play in chemical reactions. We consider physical change and chemical change, including the conversions that take place among the states of matter (solid, liquid, and gas). We use these concepts to explain the behavior of reactions that do not go to completion. These are termed *equilibrium reactions*. We develop the equilibrium constant expression and demonstrate how equilibrium composition can be altered using LeChatelier's principle.

7.1 Thermodynamics

Thermodynamics is the study of energy, work, and heat. It may be applied to chemical change, such as the calculation of the quantity of heat obtainable from the combustion of 1 gallon (gal) of fuel oil. Similarly, energy released or consumed in physical change, such as the boiling or freezing of water, may be determined.

There are three basic laws of thermodynamics.

1. Energy cannot be created or destroyed, only converted from one form to another.
2. The universe spontaneously tends toward increasing disorder or randomness.
3. The disorder of a pure, perfect crystal at absolute zero (0 Kelvin) is zero.

Only the first two laws of thermodynamics will be of concern here. They help us to predict why some chemical reactions may occur spontaneously and others do not. A spontaneous reaction does occur under a specific set of conditions; a nonspontaneous reaction does not occur under specified conditions. Whether we are synthesizing compounds in the laboratory, manufacturing industrial chemicals, or trying to determine causes of cancer, the ability to predict spontaneity is essential.

Energy, its various forms, and commonly used energy units were introduced in Chapter 1.

The Chemical Reaction and Energy

John Dalton believed that chemical change involved joining, separating, or rearranging atoms. Two centuries later, this statement stands as an accurate description of chemical reactions. However, we now know much more about the nonmaterial energy changes that are an essential part of every reaction.

The kinetic molecular theory of gases was introduced in Section 5.1. The basic ideas of this theory will be useful to remember throughout the discussion of thermodynamics and kinetics. Keep in mind that molecules and atoms are in constant, random motion and frequently collide with each other. Remember that the average kinetic energy of the atoms or molecules increases with increasing temperature. In addition to these statements of the kinetic molecular theory, we will add the following concepts as they pertain to chemical reactions:

- some collisions, those with sufficient energy, will break bonds in molecules, and
- when reactant bonds are broken, new bonds may be formed and products result.

It is worth noting that we cannot measure an absolute value for energy stored in a chemical system. We can only measure the *change* in energy (energy absorbed or released) as a chemical reaction occurs. Also, it is often both convenient and necessary to establish a boundary between the *system* and its *surroundings.*

The **system** contains the process under study. The **surroundings** encompass the rest of the universe. Energy is lost from the system to the surroundings or energy may be gained by the system at the expense of the surroundings. This energy change, most often in the form of heat, may be determined because the temperature of the system or surroundings will change, and this change can be measured. This process is illustrated in Figure 7.1.

Consider the combustion of methane; that is, the reaction of methane and oxygen to form carbon dioxide and water. If we define the reaction as the system, the temperature of the air surrounding the reaction increases, indicating that some of the potential energy (energy stored in the bonds) is converted to kinetic energy, causing the molecules surrounding the reaction to speed up. This type of kinetic energy is called *thermal energy.* The transfer of the thermal energy to the surroundings is known as **heat,** and is sometimes called *heat flow.*

Now, an exact temperature measurement of the air before and after the reaction is difficult. However, if we could insulate a portion of the surroundings, to isolate and trap the heat, we could calculate a useful quantity, the heat of the reaction. Experimental strategies for measuring temperature change and calculating heats of reactions, termed *calorimetry,* are discussed in Section 7.2.

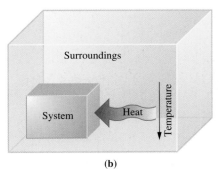

Figure 7.1 Illustration of heat flow in (a) exothermic and (b) endothermic reactions.

The First Law of Thermodynamics

Exothermic and Endothermic Reactions

The first law of thermodynamics states that the energy of the universe is constant. It is the law of conservation of energy. The study of energy changes that occur in chemical reactions is a very practical application of the first law. Consider, for example, the generalized reaction:

$$A\text{—}B + C\text{—}D \longrightarrow A\text{—}D + C\text{—}B$$

An **exothermic reaction** releases energy to the surroundings. The surroundings become warmer.

Each chemical bond is stored chemical energy (potential energy). For the reaction to take place, bond A—B and bond C—D must break; this process *always* requires energy. At the same time, bonds A—D and C—B must form; this process always releases energy.

If the energy required to break the A—B and C—D bonds is *less* than the energy given off when the A—D and C—B bonds form, the reaction will release the excess energy. The energy is a *product,* and the reaction is called an exothermic (*Greek exo,* "out," and *Greek therm,* "heat") reaction.

An example of an exothermic reaction is the combustion of methane, represented by a *thermochemical equation:*

$$CH_4(g) + 2O_2(g) \longrightarrow CO_2(g) + 2H_2O(g) + 211 \text{ kilocalories (kcal)}$$
Exothermic reaction

This thermochemical equation reads: the combustion of 1 mole (mol) of methane releases 211 kcal of heat.

An **endothermic reaction** absorbs energy from the surroundings. The surroundings become colder.

If the energy required to break the *A—B* and *C—D* bonds is *greater* than the energy released when the *A—D* and *C—B* bonds form, the reaction will need an external supply of energy. Insufficient energy is available in the system to initiate the bond-breaking process. Such a reaction is called an endothermic (*Greek endo,* "to take on," and *Greek therm,* "heat") reaction, and energy is a *reactant.*

The decomposition of ammonia into nitrogen and hydrogen is one example of an endothermic reaction:

$$22 \text{ kcal} + 2NH_3(g) \longrightarrow N_2(g) + 3H_2(g)$$
Endothermic reaction

This thermochemical equation reads: the decomposition of 2 mol of ammonia requires 22 kcal of heat.

The examples used here show the energy absorbed or released as heat energy. Depending on the reaction and the conditions under which the reaction is run, the energy may take the form of light energy or electrical energy. A firefly releases energy as a soft glow of light on a summer evening. An electrical current results from a chemical reaction in a battery, enabling your car to start.

> In an exothermic reaction, heat is released *from the system* to the surroundings. In an endothermic reaction, heat is absorbed *by the system* from the surroundings.

LEARNING GOAL

1 ▶ Correlate the terms *endothermic* and *exothermic* with heat flow between a *system* and its *surroundings.*

EXAMPLE 7.1   Determining Whether a Process Is Exothermic or Endothermic

An ice cube is dropped into a glass of water at room temperature. The ice cube melts. Is the melting of the ice exothermic or endothermic?

Solution

Step 1. Consider the ice cube to be the system and the water, the surroundings.

Step 2. Recognize that the water (the surroundings) will decrease in temperature. The surroundings are transferring heat to the system, the ice cube. The ice cube uses the heat to overcome hydrogen bonding among molecules, and the ice melts.

Step 3. The heat flow is from surroundings to system.

Step 4. The system gains energy (+energy); hence, the melting process (physical change) is endothermic.

Practice Problem 7.1

Are the following processes exothermic or endothermic?

a. Fuel oil is burned in a furnace.

b. When solid NaOH is dissolved in water, the solution temperature increases.

▶ **For Further Practice: Questions 7.23 and 7.24.**

Green Chemistry

Twenty-First Century Energy

When we purchase gasoline for our automobiles or oil for the furnace we are certainly buying matter. But that matter is only a storage device; we are really purchasing the energy stored in the chemical bonds. Combustion, burning in oxygen, releases the stored energy (potential energy) in a form suited to its function: mechanical energy to power a vehicle or heat energy to warm a home.

Energy release is a consequence of change. In fuel combustion, this change results in the production of waste products that may be detrimental to our environment. This necessitates the expenditure of time, money, and *more* energy to clean up our surroundings.

If we are paying a considerable price for our energy supply, it would be nice to believe that we are at least getting full value for our expenditure. Even that is not the case. Removal of energy from molecules also extracts a price. For example, a properly tuned automobile engine is perhaps 30% efficient. That means that less than one-third of the available energy actually moves the car. The other two-thirds is released into the atmosphere as wasted energy, mostly heat energy. The law of conservation of energy tells us that the energy is not destroyed, but it is certainly no longer available to us in a useful form.

Can we build a 100%-efficient energy transfer system? Is there such a thing as cost-free energy? The answer to these questions is no, on both counts. It is theoretically impossible, and the laws of thermodynamics tell us why this is so.

Although 100% energy conversion is not possible, there is still room for improvement in our current energy usage. Consuming vast quantities of nonrenewable resources (fossil fuels: coal, oil, and natural gas) and expelling the waste products (carbon dioxide and sulfur oxides) into the atmosphere does not seem to be the best energy generation system that human ingenuity can devise.

The process of generating electricity is simply finding ways to move electrons. Converting water to steam, then using the steam pressure to drive a turbine (a mechanical device to "push" electrons) requires massive quantities of heat to boil the water and produce steam. Nuclear reactions produce heat, which is the basis of a nuclear power plant. Combustion of coal, oil, and natural gas (exothermic reactions) also produces heat. So we see that the essential difference among the various types of power plants lies in the identity and technological complexity of the heat source.

Newer approaches to moving electrons involve wind energy and solar energy. It has been estimated that twenty-first century, high-tech windmills erected in unpopulated areas (the shallow waters of the Atlantic Ocean, and the plains of the western portion of the United States), coupled with a modern electrical transmission grid, could satisfy the electrical demands of virtually the entire country. Solar energy, collected by photovoltaic cells arranged in solar panels, is converted to electrical energy.

Improvement in the design and efficiency of these "alternate energy sources" holds promise of reducing dependence on polluting, nonrenewable resources.

For Further Understanding

▶ Solar and wind power have been mentioned as energy alternatives. Suggest a third alternative.

▶ What do you see as potential advantages (and potential shortcomings) of the alternative that you have suggested?

Enthalpy

Enthalpy is the term used to represent heat. The *change in enthalpy* is the energy difference between the products and reactants of a chemical reaction and is symbolized as ΔH. By convention, energy released is represented with a negative sign (indicating an exothermic reaction), and energy absorbed is shown with a positive sign (indicating an endothermic reaction). This is based on the relationship:

$$\Delta H_{\text{reaction}} = H_{\text{products}} - H_{\text{reactants}}$$

If $H_{\text{reactants}} > H_{\text{products}}$, ΔH must be negative and the reaction is exothermic.

On the other hand,

if $H_{\text{reactants}} < H_{\text{products}}$, ΔH must be positive and the reaction is endothermic.

For the combustion of methane, an exothermic process, energy is a *product* in the thermochemical equation, and

$$\Delta H = -211 \text{ kcal}$$

For the decomposition of ammonia, an endothermic process, energy is a *reactant* in the thermochemical equation, and

$$\Delta H = +22 \text{ kcal}$$

LEARNING GOAL

2 ▶ State the meaning of the terms *enthalpy*, *entropy*, and *free energy* and know their implications.

Animation

• Heat Flow in Endothermic and Exothermic Reactions

In these discussions, we consider the enthalpy change and energy change to be identical. This is true for most common reactions carried out in lab, with minimal volume change.

Figure 7.2 (a) An exothermic reaction. ΔH represents the energy released during the progress of the exothermic reaction:
$A + B \longrightarrow C + D + \Delta H$. (b) An endothermic reaction. ΔH represents the energy absorbed during the progress of the endothermic reaction:
$\Delta H + A + B \longrightarrow C + D$.

LEARNING GOAL

2 ▶ State the meaning of the terms *enthalpy, entropy,* and *free energy* and know their implications.

A *system* is a part of the universe upon which we wish to focus our attention. For example, it may be a beaker containing reactants and products.

Animation
• Entropy and Rubber Bands

Diagrams representing changes in enthalpy for exothermic (a) and endothermic (b) reactions are shown in Figure 7.2.

Question 7.1 Are the following processes exothermic or endothermic?
  a. $C_6H_{12}O_6(s) \longrightarrow 2C_2H_5OH(l) + 2CO_2(g)$, $\Delta H = -16$ kcal
  b. $N_2O_5(g) + H_2O(l) \longrightarrow 2HNO_3(l) + 18.3$ kcal

Question 7.2 Are the following processes exothermic or endothermic?
  a. $S(s) + O_2(g) \longrightarrow SO_2(g)$, $\Delta H = -71$ kcal
  b. $N_2(g) + 2O_2(g) + 16.2$ kcal $\longrightarrow 2NO_2(g)$

Spontaneous and Nonspontaneous Reactions

It seems that all exothermic reactions should be spontaneous. After all, an external supply of energy does not appear to be necessary; in fact, energy is a product of the reaction. It also seems that all endothermic reactions should be nonspontaneous: energy is a reactant that we must provide. However, these hypotheses are not supported by experimentation.

Experimental measurement has shown that most *but not all* exothermic reactions are spontaneous. Likewise, most *but not all*, endothermic reactions are not spontaneous. There must be some factor in addition to enthalpy that will help us to explain the less obvious cases of nonspontaneous exothermic reactions and spontaneous endothermic reactions. This other factor is entropy.

The Second Law of Thermodynamics

Entropy

The first law of thermodynamics considers the enthalpy of chemical reactions. The second law states that the universe spontaneously tends toward increasing disorder or randomness.

A measure of the randomness of a chemical system is its **entropy.** The entropy of a substance is represented by the symbol S. A random, or disordered, system is characterized by *high entropy;* a well-organized system has *low entropy.*

What do we mean by disorder in chemical systems? Disorder is simply the absence of a regular repeating pattern. Disorder or randomness increases as we convert from the solid to the liquid to the gaseous state. As we have seen, solids often have an ordered crystalline structure, liquids have, at best, a loose arrangement, and gas particles are virtually random in their distribution. Therefore gases have high entropy, and crystalline solids have very low entropy. Figures 7.3 and 7.4 illustrate properties of entropy in systems.

The second law describes the entire universe or any isolated system within the universe. On a more personal level, we all fall victim to the law of increasing disorder. Chaos in our room or workplace is certainly not our intent! It happens almost effortlessly. However, reversal of this process requires work and energy. The same is true at the molecular level. The gradual deterioration of our cities' infrastructure (roads, bridges, water mains, and so forth) is an all-too-familiar example. Millions of dollars (translated into energy and work) are needed annually just to try to maintain the status quo.

The entropy of a reaction is measured as a difference, ΔS, between the entropies, S, of products and reactants.

The drive toward increased entropy, along with a tendency to achieve a lower potential energy, is responsible for spontaneous chemical reactions. Reactions that are exothermic and whose products are more disordered (higher in entropy) will occur spontaneously, whereas endothermic reactions producing products of lower entropy will not be spontaneous. If they are to take place at all, they will need some energy input.

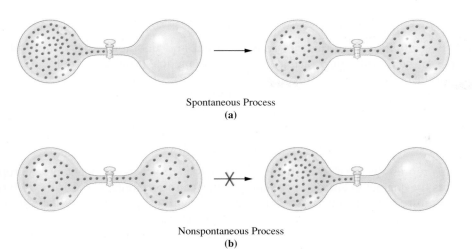

Spontaneous Process
(a)

Nonspontaneous Process
(b)

Figure 7.3 (a) Gas particles, trapped in the left chamber, spontaneously diffuse into the right chamber, initially under vacuum, when the valve is opened. (b) It is unimaginable that the gas particles will rearrange themselves and reverse the process to create a vacuum. This can only be accomplished using a pump, that is, by doing work on the system.

Question 7.3 Which substance has the greatest entropy, He(g) or Na(s)? Explain your reasoning.

Question 7.4 Which substance has the greatest entropy, $H_2O(l)$ or $H_2O(g)$? Explain your reasoning.

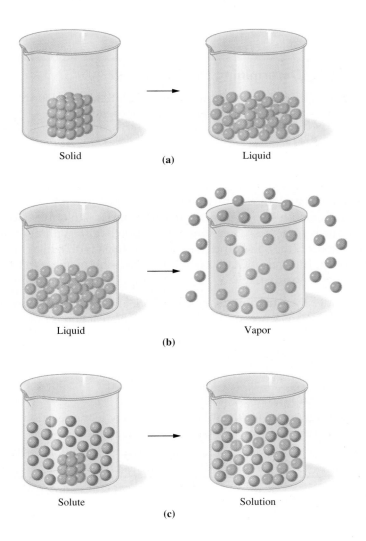

Solid (a) Liquid

Liquid (b) Vapor

Solute (c) Solution

Figure 7.4 Processes such as (a) melting, (b) vaporization, and (c) dissolution increase entropy, or randomness, of the particles.

Free Energy

The two situations just described are clear-cut and unambiguous. In any other situation the reaction may or may not be spontaneous. It depends on the relative size of the enthalpy and entropy values.

Free energy, symbolized by ΔG, represents the combined contribution of the enthalpy *and* entropy values for a chemical reaction. Thus free energy is the ultimate predictor of reaction spontaneity and is expressed as

$$\Delta G = \Delta H - T\Delta S$$

ΔH represents the change in enthalpy between products and reactants, ΔS represents the change in entropy between products and reactants, and T is the Kelvin temperature of the reaction. A reaction with a negative value of ΔG will *always* be spontaneous. Reactions with a positive ΔG will *always* be nonspontaneous.

We need to know both ΔH and ΔS in order to predict the sign of ΔG and make a definitive statement regarding the spontaneity of the reaction. Additionally, the temperature may determine the direction of spontaneity. Consider the four possible situations:

- ΔH positive and ΔS negative: ΔG is always positive, regardless of the temperature. The reaction is always nonspontaneous.
- ΔH negative and ΔS positive: ΔG is always negative, regardless of the temperature. The reaction is always spontaneous.
- Both ΔH and ΔS positive: The sign of ΔG depends on the temperature.
- Both ΔH and ΔS negative: The sign of ΔG depends on the temperature.

EXAMPLE 7.2   Determining the Sign of ΔG

Determine the sign of ΔG for the following reaction. Is the reaction spontaneous, nonspontaneous, or temperature dependent?

$$42.5 \text{ kcal} + CaCO_3(s) \longrightarrow CaO(s) + CO_2(g)$$

Solution

Step 1. Determine the sign of ΔH. Because heat is added as a reactant, the reaction is endothermic. This gives a positive sign for ΔH.

Step 2. Determine the sign of ΔS. This reaction starts with only solid and produces some gas. Therefore the reaction begins with a small amount of disorder (the solid) and produces products with a high amount of disorder (the gas of CO_2). Therefore there is an increase in the disorder and ΔS is positive.

Step 3. Consider the equation $\Delta G = \Delta H - T\Delta S$. Since ΔH and ΔS are both positive, ΔG is temperature dependent. The reaction is only spontaneous if the $T\Delta S$ term becomes so large that when it is subtracted from ΔH the value for ΔG will be negative. Therefore this reaction is spontaneous at high temperature.

Practice Problem 7.2

Determine the sign of ΔG for the following reaction. Is the reaction spontaneous, nonspontaneous, or temperature dependent?

$$2H_2(g) + O_2(g) \longrightarrow 2H_2O(l) + 137 \text{ kcal}$$

▶ **For Further Practice: Questions 7.41 and 7.42.**

A Medical Perspective

Hot and Cold Packs

Hot packs provide "instant warmth" for hikers and skiers and are used in treatment of injuries such as pulled muscles. Cold packs are in common use today for the treatment of injuries and the reduction of swelling. These useful items are an excellent example of basic science producing a technologically useful product.

Both hot and cold packs depend on large energy changes taking place during a chemical reaction. Cold packs rely on an endothermic reaction, and hot packs generate heat energy from an exothermic reaction.

A cold pack is fabricated as two separate compartments within a single package. One compartment contains NH_4NO_3, and the other contains water. When the package is squeezed, the inner boundary between the two compartments ruptures, allowing the components to mix, and the following reaction occurs:

$$6.7 \text{ kcal/mol} + NH_4NO_3(s) \longrightarrow NH_4^+(aq) + NO_3^-(aq)$$

Heating pads.

A cold pack.

This reaction is endothermic; heat taken from the surroundings produces the cooling effect.

The design of a hot pack is similar. Here, finely divided iron powder is mixed with oxygen. Production of iron oxide results in the evolution of heat:

$$4Fe(s) + 3O_2(g) \longrightarrow 2Fe_2O_3(s) + 198 \text{ kcal/mol}$$

This reaction occurs via an oxidation-reduction mechanism (see Chapter 8). The iron atoms are oxidized, O_2 is reduced. Electrons are transferred from the iron atoms to O_2 and Fe_2O_3 forms exothermically. The rate of the reaction is slow; therefore the heat is liberated gradually over a period of several hours.

For Further Understanding

▶ What is the sign of ΔH for each equation in this story?
▶ Predict whether entropy increases or decreases for each equation in this story.

The introduction to this chapter stated that thermodynamics is used to predict whether or not a reaction will occur. The value of ΔG determines if a reaction is thermodynamically favorable or unfavorable.

Question 7.5 Predict whether a reaction with positive ΔH and negative ΔS will be spontaneous, nonspontaneous, or temperature dependent. Explain your reasoning.

Question 7.6 Predict whether a reaction with positive ΔH and positive ΔS will be spontaneous, nonspontaneous, or temperature dependent. Explain your reasoning.

7.2 Experimental Determination of Energy Change in Reactions

The measurement of heat energy changes in a chemical reaction is **calorimetry.** This technique involves the measurement of the change in the temperature of a quantity of water or solution that is in contact with the reaction of interest and isolated from the surroundings. A device used for these measurements is a *calorimeter,* which measures heat changes in calories.

Think of a calorimeter as a self-contained "universe" where heat can exchange between the system and its surroundings but cannot escape the calorimeter. At the same time, external heat is prevented from entering the calorimeter.

A Styrofoam coffee cup is a simple design for a calorimeter, and it produces surprisingly accurate results. It is a good insulator, and, when filled with solution, it can be used to measure temperature changes taking place as the result of a chemical reaction occurring in that solution (Figure 7.5). The change in the temperature of the solution, caused by the reaction, can be used to calculate the gain or loss of heat energy for the reaction.

For an exothermic reaction, heat released by the reaction is absorbed by the surrounding solution. For an endothermic reaction, the reactants absorb heat from the solution.

The **specific heat** of a substance is defined as the number of calories (cal) of heat needed to raise the temperature of 1 gram (g) of the substance 1 degree Celsius (°C). Knowing the specific heat of the water or the aqueous solution along with the total number of g of solution and the temperature increase (measured as the difference between the final and initial temperatures of the solution), enables the experimenter to calculate the heat released during the reaction.

The solution behaves as a "trap" or "sink" for energy released in an exothermic process. The temperature increase indicates a gain in heat energy. Endothermic reactions, on the other hand, take heat energy away from the solution, lowering its temperature.

The quantity of heat absorbed or released by the reaction (Q) is the product of the mass of solution in the calorimeter (m_s), the specific heat of the solution (SH_s), and the change in temperature (ΔT_s) of the solution as the reaction proceeds from the initial to final state.

The heat is calculated by using the following equation:

$$Q = m_s \times \Delta T_s \times SH_s$$

with units

$$cal = g \times °C \times \frac{cal}{g \cdot °C}$$

The details of the experimental approach are illustrated in Example 7.3.

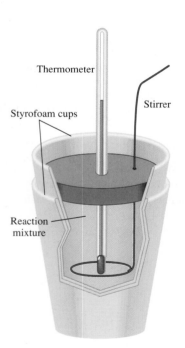

Figure 7.5 A "coffee cup" calorimeter used for the measurement of heat change in chemical reactions. The concentric Styrofoam cups insulate the solution. Heat released by the chemical reaction (the system) enters the solution (the surroundings), raising its temperature, which is measured by using a thermometer.

Thermometer

Stirrer

Styrofoam cups

Reaction mixture

EXAMPLE 7.3   Calculating Energy Involved in Calorimeter Reactions

If 0.050 mol of hydrochloric acid (HCl) is mixed with 0.050 mol of sodium hydroxide (NaOH) in a "coffee cup" calorimeter, the temperature of 1.00×10^2 g of the resulting solution increases from 25.0°C to 31.5°C. If the specific heat of the solution is 1.00 cal/g-°C, calculate the quantity of energy involved in the reaction. Also, is the reaction endothermic or exothermic?

Solution

Step 1. The calorimetry expression is:

$$Q = m_s \times \Delta T_s \times SH_s$$

Step 2. The change in temperature is

$$\Delta T_s = T_{s\,final} - T_{s\,initial}$$
$$= 31.5°C - 25.0°C = 6.5°C$$

Step 3. Substituting:

$$Q = 100 \times 10^2 \text{ g solution} \times 6.5°C \times \frac{1.00 \text{ cal}}{\text{g solution-}°C}$$

$$= 6.5 \times 10^2 \text{ cal}$$

6.5×10^2 cal (or 0.65 kcal) of heat energy were released by this acid-base reaction to the surroundings, the solution; the reaction is exothermic.

Practice Problem 7.3

Calculate the temperature change that would have been observed if 50.0 g solution were in the calorimeter instead of 1.00×10^2 g solution.

▶ **For Further Practice: Question 7.35.**

LEARNING GOAL

3 ▶ Describe experiments that yield thermochemical information and calculate fuel values based on experimental data.

EXAMPLE 7.4   Calculating Energy Involved in Calorimeter Reactions

If 0.10 mol of ammonium chloride (NH_4Cl) is dissolved in water producing 1.00×10^2 g solution, the water temperature decreases from 25.0°C to 18.0°C. If the specific heat of the resulting solution is 1.00 cal/g-°C, calculate the quantity of energy involved in the process. Also, is the dissolution of ammonium chloride endothermic or exothermic?

Solution

Step 1. The calorimetry expression is:

$$Q = m_s \times \Delta T_s \times SH_s$$

Step 2. The change in temperature is

$$\Delta T = T_{s\,final} - T_{s\,initial}$$
$$= 18.0°C - 25.0°C = -7.0°C$$

Step 3. Substituting:

$$Q = 1.00 \times 10^2 \text{ g solution} \times (-7.0°C) \times \frac{1.00 \text{ cal}}{\text{g solution-}°C}$$

$$= -7.0 \times 10^2 \text{ cal}$$

7.0×10^2 cal (or 0.70 kcal) of heat energy were absorbed by the dissolution process because the solution lost ($-$ sign) 7.0×10^2 cal of heat energy to the system. The reaction is endothermic.

Practice Problem 7.4

Calculate the temperature change that would have been observed if 1.00×10^2 g of another liquid, producing a solution with a specific heat capacity of 0.800 cal/g-°C, were substituted for the water in the calorimeter.

▶ **For Further Practice: Question 7.36.**

Question 7.7 Using the conversion factor in Chapter 1, convert the energy released in Example 7.3 to joules (J).

Question 7.8 Using the conversion factor in Chapter 1, convert the energy absorbed in Example 7.4 to J.

Note: Refer to A Human Perspective: Food Calories, Section 1.5.

Many chemical reactions that produce heat are combustion reactions. In our bodies many food substances (carbohydrates, proteins, and fats; Chapters 21 and 22) are oxidized to release energy. **Fuel value** is the amount of energy per g of food.

The fuel value of food is an important concept in nutrition science. The fuel value is generally reported in units of *nutritional Calories*. One **nutritional Calorie (Cal)** is equivalent to one kilocalorie (1000 cal). It is also known as the *large Calorie* (uppercase C).

Energy necessary for our daily activity and bodily function comes largely from the "combustion" of carbohydrates. Chemical energy from foods that is not used to maintain normal body temperature or in muscular activity is stored in the bonds of chemical compounds known collectively as fat. Thus "high-calorie" foods are implicated in obesity.

A special type of calorimeter, a *bomb calorimeter*, is useful for the measurement of the fuel value (Cal) of foods. Such a device is illustrated in Figure 7.6. Its design is similar, in principle, to that of the "coffee cup" calorimeter discussed earlier. It incorporates the insulation from the surroundings, solution pool, reaction chamber, and thermometer. Oxygen gas is added as one of the reactants, and an electrical igniter is inserted to initiate the reaction. However, it is not open to the atmosphere. In the sealed container the reaction continues until the sample is completely oxidized. All of the heat energy released during the reaction is captured in the water.

Figure 7.6 A bomb calorimeter that may be used to measure heat released upon combustion of a sample. This device is commonly used to determine the fuel value of foods. The bomb calorimeter is similar to the "coffee cup" calorimeter. However, note the electrical component necessary to initiate the combustion reaction.

EXAMPLE 7.5 Calculating the Fuel Value of Foods

A 1-g sample of glucose (a common sugar or carbohydrate) was burned in a bomb calorimeter. The temperature of 1.00×10^3 g H_2O was raised from 25.0°C to 28.8°C ($\Delta T_w = 3.8°C$). Calculate the fuel value of glucose.

Solution

Step 1. Recall that the fuel value is the number of nutritional Cal liberated by the combustion of 1 g of material, and 1 g of material was burned in the calorimeter.

Step 2. Then

$$\text{Fuel value} = Q = m_w \times \Delta T_w \times SH_w$$

Step 3. Water is the surroundings in the calorimeter; it has a specific heat capacity equal to 1.00 cal/g H_2O-°C.

Substituting in our expression for fuel value:

$$\text{Fuel value} = Q = \text{g } H_2O \times °C \times \frac{1.00 \text{ cal}}{\text{g } H_2O\text{-°C}}$$

$$= 1.00 \times 10^3 \times \text{g } H_2O \times 3.8°C \times \frac{1.00 \text{ cal}}{\text{g } H_2O\text{-°C}}$$

$$= 3.8 \times 10^3 \text{ cal}$$

Step 4. Converting from cal to nutritional Cal:

$$3.8 \times 10^3 \text{ cal} \times \frac{1 \text{ nutritional Cal}}{10^3 \text{ cal}} = 3.8 \text{ Cal (nutritional Calories, or kcal)}$$

Since the quantity of glucose burned in the calorimeter is 1 g, the fuel value of glucose is 3.8 kcal/g.

Practice Problem 7.5

A 1.0-g sample of a candy bar (which contains lots of sugar and fats!) was burned in a bomb calorimeter. A 3.0°C temperature increase was observed for 1.00×10^3 g of water. The entire candy bar weighed 2.5 ounces (oz). Calculate the fuel value (in Cal) of the sample and the total caloric content of the candy bar.

▶ **For Further Practice: Question 7.38.**

7.3 Kinetics

Chemical Kinetics

Thermodynamics help us to decide whether a chemical reaction is spontaneous. Knowing that a reaction can occur spontaneously tells us nothing about the time that it may take.

Chemical **kinetics** is the study of the **rate** (or speed) of chemical reactions. Kinetics also gives an indication of the *mechanism* of a reaction, a step-by-step description of how reactants become products. Kinetic information may be represented as the *disappearance* of reactants or *appearance* of product over time. A typical graph of number of molecules versus time is shown in Figure 7.7.

LEARNING GOAL

3 ▶ Describe experiments that yield thermochemical information and calculate fuel values based on experimental data.

LEARNING GOAL

4 ▶ Describe the concept of reaction rate and the role of kinetics in chemical and physical change.

Animations
- Kinetics
- Rates of Chemical Reactions

Figure 7.7 For a hypothetical reaction $A \longrightarrow B$ the number of A molecules (reactant molecules) decreases over time and B molecules (product molecules) increase in number over time.

LEARNING GOAL

5 ▶ Describe the importance of *activation energy* and the *activated complex* in determining reaction rate.

Information about the rate at which various chemical processes occur is useful. For example, what is the "shelf life" of processed foods? When will slow changes in composition make food unappealing or even unsafe? Many drugs lose their potency with time because the active ingredient decomposes into other substances. The rate of hardening of dental filling material (via a chemical reaction) influences the dentist's technique. Our very lives depend on the efficient transport of oxygen to each of our cells and the rapid use of the oxygen for energy-harvesting reactions.

The diagram in Figure 7.8 is a useful way of depicting the kinetics of a reaction at the molecular level.

Often a color change, over time, can be measured. Such changes are useful in assessing the rate of a chemical reaction (Figure 7.9).

Let's see what actually happens when two chemical compounds react and what experimental conditions affect the rate of a reaction.

Activation Energy and the Activated Complex

Consider the exothermic reaction that we discussed in Section 7.1:

$$CH_4(g) + 2O_2(g) \longrightarrow CO_2(g) + 2H_2O(g) + 211 \text{ (kcal)}$$

For the reaction to proceed, C—H and O—O bonds must be broken, and C—O and H—O bonds must be formed. Sufficient energy must be available to cause the bonds to break if the reaction is to take place. This energy is provided by the collision of molecules. If sufficient energy is available at the temperature of the reaction, one or more bonds will break, and the atoms will recombine in a lower

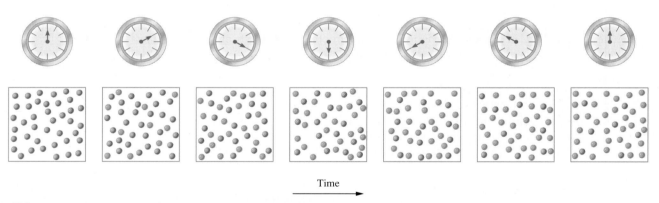

Time

Figure 7.8 An alternate way of representing the information contained in Figure 7.7.

Figure 7.9 The conversion of reddish brown Br_2 in solution to colorless Br^- over time.

Time

energy arrangement, in this case as carbon dioxide and water. A collision producing product molecules is termed an *effective collision.* Only effective collisions lead to chemical reaction.

The minimum amount of energy required to initiate a chemical reaction is called the **activation energy,** E_a, for the reaction.

We can picture the chemical reaction in terms of the changes in potential energy that occur during the reaction. Figure 7.10a graphically shows these changes for an exothermic reaction. Important characteristics of this graph include the following:

- The reaction proceeds from reactants to products through an extremely unstable state that we call the **activated complex.** The activated complex cannot be isolated from the reaction mixture but may be thought of as a short-lived group of atoms structured in such a way that it quickly and easily breaks apart into the products of the reaction.
- Formation of the activated complex requires energy. The difference between the energy of reactants and that of the activated complex is the activation energy. This energy must be provided by the collision of the reacting molecules or atoms at the temperature of the reaction.
- Because this is an exothermic reaction, the overall energy change must be a *net* release of energy. The *net* release of energy is the difference in energy between products and reactants.

For an endothermic reaction, such as the decomposition of water,

$$\text{energy} + 2H_2O(l) \longrightarrow 2H_2(g) + O_2(g)$$

the change of potential energy with reaction time is shown in Figure 7.10b.

The reaction takes place slowly because of the large activation energy required for the conversion of water into the elements hydrogen and oxygen.

Question 7.9 The act of striking a match illustrates the role of activation energy in a chemical reaction. Explain.

Question 7.10 Distinguish between the terms *net energy* and *activation energy.*

Factors That Affect Reaction Rate

The following six factors influence reaction rate:

• Structure of the Reacting Species

Reactions among ions in solution are usually very rapid. Ionic compounds in solution are dissociated; consequently, their bonds are already broken, and the activation energy for their reaction should be very low. On the other hand, reactions involving covalently bonded compounds may proceed more slowly. Covalent bonds must be broken and new bonds formed. The activation energy for this process would be significantly higher than that for the reaction of free ions. Bond strengths certainly play a role in determining reaction rates because the magnitude of the activation energy, or energy barrier, is related to bond strength.

• Molecular Shape and Orientation

The size and shape of reactant molecules influence the rate of the reaction. Large molecules, containing bulky groups of atoms, may block the reactive part of the molecule from interacting with another reactive substance, causing the reaction to proceed slowly. Only molecular collisions that have the correct collision orientation lead to product formation. These collisions are termed *effective collisions.*

(a)

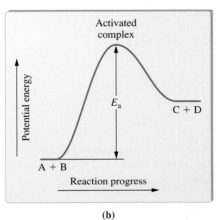

(b)

Figure 7.10 (a) The change in potential energy as a function of reaction time for an exothermic reaction. (b) The change in potential energy as a function of reaction time for an endothermic reaction.

Animation
- Activation Energy
- Importance of Molecular Orientation on a Reaction
- Effect of Molecular Orientation on Collision Effectiveness

LEARNING GOAL

6 ▶ Predict the way reactant structure, concentration, temperature, and catalysis affect the rate of a chemical reaction.

How does a match illustrate the concept of activation energy?

Concentration is introduced in Section 1.5, and units and calculations are discussed in Sections 6.2 and 6.3.

These factors were considered in our discussion of the states of matter (Chapter 5).

Section 11.5 describes the role of catalysis in organic reactions.

Sections 19.1 through 19.6 describe enzyme catalysis.

• The Concentration of Reactants

The rate of a chemical reaction is often a complex function of the concentration of one or more of the reacting substances. The rate will generally *increase* as concentration *increases* simply because a higher concentration means more reactant molecules in a given volume and therefore a greater number of collisions per unit time. If we assume that other variables are held constant, a larger number of collisions leads to a larger number of effective collisions. For example, the rate at which a fire burns depends on the concentration of oxygen in the atmosphere surrounding the fire, as well as the concentration of the fuel (perhaps methane or propane). A common fire-fighting strategy is the use of fire extinguishers filled with carbon dioxide. The carbon dioxide dilutes the oxygen to a level where the combustion process can no longer be sustained.

• The Temperature of Reactants

The rate of a reaction *increases* as the temperature increases, because the average kinetic energy of the reacting particles is directly proportional to the Kelvin temperature. Increasing the speed of particles increases the likelihood of collision, and the higher kinetic energy means that a higher percentage of these collisions will result in product formation (effective collisions). A 10°C rise in temperature has often been found to double the reaction rate.

• The Physical State of Reactants

The rate of a reaction depends on the physical state of the reactants: solid, liquid, or gas. For a reaction to occur the reactants must collide frequently and have sufficient energy to react. In the solid state, the atoms, ions, or molecules are restricted in their motion. In the gaseous and liquid states, the particles have both free motion and proximity to each other. Hence reactions tend to be fastest in the gaseous and liquid states and slowest in the solid state.

• The Presence of a Catalyst

A **catalyst** is a substance that *increases* the reaction rate. If added to a reaction mixture, the catalytic substance undergoes no net change, nor does it alter the outcome of the reaction. However, the catalyst interacts with the reactants to create an alternative pathway for production of products. This alternative path has a lower activation energy. This makes it easier for the reaction to take place and thus increases the rate. This effect is illustrated in Figure 7.11.

Catalysis is important industrially; it may often make the difference between profit and loss in the sale of a product. For example, catalysis is useful in converting double bonds to single bonds. An important application of this principle involves the process of hydrogenation. Hydrogenation converts one or more of

Figure 7.11 The effect of a catalyst on the magnitude of the activation energy of a chemical reaction: (a) uncatalyzed reaction, (b) catalyzed reaction. Note that the presence of a catalyst decreases the activation energy ($E'_a < E_a$), thus increasing the rate of the reaction.

(a) Uncatalyzed reaction

(b) Catalyzed reaction

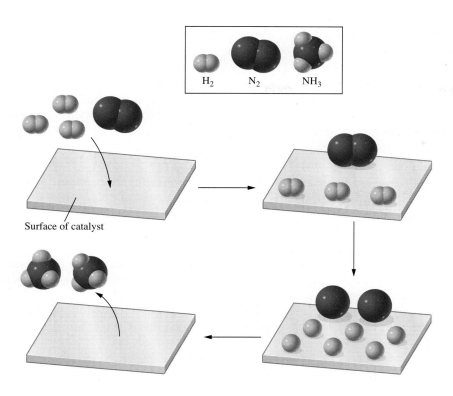

Figure 7.12 The synthesis of ammonia, an important industrial product, is facilitated by a solid-phase catalyst (the Haber process). H_2 and N_2 bind to the surface, their bonds are weakened, dissociation and reformation as ammonia occur, and the newly formed ammonia molecules leave the surface. This process is repeated over and over, with no change in the catalyst.

the carbon-carbon double bonds of unsaturated fats (e.g., corn oil, olive oil) to single bonds characteristic of saturated fats (such as margarine). The use of a metal catalyst, such as nickel, in contact with the reaction mixture dramatically increases the rate of the reaction.

Thousands of essential biochemical reactions in our bodies are controlled and speeded up by biological catalysts called *enzymes.*

A molecular-level view of the action of a solid catalyst widely used in industrial synthesis of ammonia is presented in Figure 7.12.

Question 7.11 Would you imagine that a substance might act as a poison if it interfered with the function of an enzyme? Why?

Question 7.12 Bacterial growth decreases markedly in a refrigerator. Why?

Mathematical Representation of Reaction Rate

Consider the decomposition reaction of N_2O_5 (dinitrogen pentoxide) in the gas phase. When heated, N_2O_5 decomposes and forms two products: NO_2 (nitrogen dioxide) and O_2 (diatomic oxygen). The balanced chemical equation for the reaction is

$$2N_2O_5(g) \xrightarrow{\Delta} 4NO_2(g) + O_2(g)$$

When all of the factors that affect the rate of the reaction (except concentration) are held constant (that is, the nature of the reactant, temperature and physical state of the reactant, and the presence or absence of a catalyst), the rate of the reaction is proportional to the concentration of N_2O_5.

$$\text{rate} \propto \text{concentration } N_2O_5$$

We will represent the concentration of N_2O_5 in units of molarity and represent molar concentration using brackets.

$$\text{concentration } N_2O_5 = [N_2O_5]$$

LEARNING GOAL

7 ▶ Write rate laws and use these equations to calculate the effect of concentration on rate.

Then,

$$\text{rate} \propto [N_2O_5]$$

Laboratory measurement shows that the rate of the reaction depends on the molar concentration raised to an experimentally determined exponent, which we will symbolize as n, the *reaction order*. The **reaction order** represents the number of molecules that are involved in the formation of product.

$$\text{rate} \propto [N_2O_5]^n$$

In expressions such as the one shown, the proportionality symbol, $\propto$, may be replaced by an equality sign and a proportionality constant that we represent as k, the **rate constant.**

$$\text{rate} = k[N_2O_5]^n$$

Equations that follow this format, the rate being equal to the rate constant multiplied by the reactant concentration raised to an exponent that is the reaction order, are termed **rate laws.**

For the reaction described here, n has been experimentally determined and is equal to 1; hence the reaction is first order in N_2O_5 and the rate law for the reaction is:

$$\text{rate} = k[N_2O_5]$$

In general, the rate of reaction for an equation of the general form:

$$A \longrightarrow product$$

is represented by the rate law

$$rate = k[A]^n$$

in which

$$n = \text{the reaction order}$$
$$k = \text{the rate constant of the reaction}$$

An equation of the form

$$A + B \longrightarrow products$$

has a rate law of the form

$$rate = k[A]^n[B]^{n'}$$

Both the value of the rate constant and the reaction order are deduced from a series of experiments. We cannot predict them by simply looking at the chemical equation.

Note that the exponent, n, in the rate law is not the same as the coefficient of N_2O_5 in the balanced equation. However, in some reactions the coefficient in the balanced equation and the exponent n (the order of the reaction) are numerically the same.

LEARNING GOAL

7 ▶ Write rate laws and use these equations to calculate the effect of concentration on rate.

EXAMPLE 7.6   Writing Rate Laws

Write the rate law for the oxidation of ethanol (C_2H_5OH). The reaction has been experimentally determined to be first order in ethanol and third order in oxygen (O_2). The chemical reaction for this process is:

$$C_2H_5OH(l) + 3O_2(g) \longrightarrow 2CO_2(g) + 3H_2O(l)$$

Solution

Step 1. The rate law involves only the reactants, C_2H_5OH and O_2. Depict their concentrations as

$$[C_2H_5OH][O_2]$$

Step 2. Now raise each to an exponent corresponding to its experimentally determined order

$$[C_2H_5OH][O_2]^3$$

Step 3. This is proportional to the rate:

$$\text{rate} \propto [C_2H_5OH][O_2]^3$$

Step 4. Proportionality ($\propto$) is incorporated into an equation using a proportionality constant, k.

$$\text{rate} = k[C_2H_5OH][O_2]^3$$

is the rate law. (Remember that 1 is understood as an exponent; $[C_2H_5OH]$ is correct and $[C_2H_5OH]^1$ is not.)

Practice Problem 7.6

Write the general form of the rate law for each of the following processes. Represent the order as n, n', and so forth.

a. $N_2(g) + O_2(g) \longrightarrow 2NO(g)$
b. $2C_4H_6(g) \longrightarrow C_8H_{12}(g)$
c. $CH_4(g) + 2O_2(g) \longrightarrow CO_2(g) + 2H_2O(g)$
d. $2NO_2(g) \longrightarrow 2NO(g) + O_2(g)$

▶ **For Further Practice: Questions 7.49 and 7.50.**

Knowledge of the form of the rate law, coupled with the experimental determination of the value of the rate constant, k, and the order, n, are valuable in a number of ways. Industrial chemists use this information to establish optimum conditions for preparing a product in the shortest practical time. The design of an entire manufacturing facility may, in part, depend on the rates of the critical reactions.

In Section 7.4 we will see how the rate law forms the basis for describing equilibrium reactions.

EXAMPLE 7.7 Using Rate Laws to Determine the Relationship Between Concentration and Rate

The rate law for the reaction

$$2NO(g) + 2H_2(g) \longrightarrow N_2(g) + 2H_2O(g)$$

is determined to be rate $= k[NO]^2[H_2]$. At 1280°C, the value of k was determined to be $2.5 \times 10^2 \ 1/M^2 \cdot s$. What effect will doubling the concentration of NO have on the rate?

Solution

Step 1. We are not given specific values for the [NO] and [H$_2$], so we will pick easy values to work with. Let's start with [NO] and [H$_2$] equal to $1 \ M$ and determine the rate.

$$\text{Rate} = k[NO]^2[H_2]$$

$$\text{Rate} = 2.5 \times 10^2 \ \frac{1}{M^2 \cdot s}(1 \, M)^2(1 \, M) = 2.5 \times 10^2 \, M/s$$

Continued—

Step 2. Calculate the rate of the reaction by doubling [NO] to 2 M.

$$\text{Rate} = 2.5 \times 10^2 \frac{1}{M^2 \cdot \text{s}} (2\,M)^2(1\,M) = 2.5 \times 10^2 \frac{1}{M^2 \cdot \text{s}} (4\,M^3)$$

$$\text{Rate} = 10 \times 10^2\,M/\text{s} = 1.0 \times 10^3\,M/\text{s}$$

Step 3. Compare the two rates.

$$\frac{\text{Rate (at [NO]} = 2\,M)}{\text{Rate (at [NO]} = 1\,M)} = \frac{1.0 \times 10^3\,M/\text{s}}{2.5 \times 10^2\,M/\text{s}} = 4$$

Doubling the concentration of [NO] caused a four-fold increase in the rate.

Practice Problem 7.7

For the same reaction equation and conditions above, what effect will tripling the concentration of H_2 have on the rate of the reaction?

▶ **For Further Practice: Questions 7.61 and 7.62.**

A Human Perspective

Too Fast or Too Slow?

Kinetics plays a vital role in the development of a wide range of commercial products. We will consider a few of these applications that contribute to our health, our enjoyment, and preservation of our environment.

Refrigeration
Throughout history, few technologies have had a more profound benefit to human health than the development of inexpensive and efficient refrigeration, allowing food to be stored for long periods without spoiling. At room temperature unwanted chemical reactions, with the help of bacteria, rapidly decompose many foods, especially meats and fish, making them unsuitable for human consumption. Storing food at low temperatures slows the rate of decomposition by slowing the rate of bacterial reproduction and the rate of the destructive chemical reactions. Refrigeration is a straightforward application of kinetics: Rates are halved for each 10°C decrease in temperature.

Dentistry
The most widely used strategy for whitening teeth is bleaching with hydrogen peroxide (H_2O_2). Because the reaction is slow, manufacturers of home-use products use devices to trap the H_2O_2 and hold it in contact with the teeth. A better strategy involves higher concentrations of H_2O_2. (Remember, the rate of a reaction is proportional to the reactant concentration.) However, these treatments must be administered by a dentist; used incorrectly, high concentrations of H_2O_2 can damage sensitive tissues, such as the gums and the interior of the mouth.

Artwork and Photography
Old paintings and photographs are very susceptible to the effects of ultraviolet (UV) light. Chemical reactions that produce discoloration are energized by UV light. More molecules achieve the necessary activation energy, and the quality and value of the artwork degrades more rapidly. Glass that absorbs UV radiation (conservation glass) robs these reactions of needed energy, and the lifetime of these valuable materials is extended.

The Environment
An essential requirement for herbicides and pesticides is biodegradability. Ideally, these materials enter soil or vegetation, quickly complete their task of killing weeds or bugs and rapidly decompose, often with the help of bacteria. Most people are aware of the problems caused by earlier, nonbiodegradable pesticides, most famously DDT (dichlorodiphenyltrichloroethane). DDT degrades very slowly in the environment. It is fat-soluble, bioaccumulates in animal tissue, and is blamed for many detrimental effects, most notably its interference with bird reproduction. Even though it has been banned in the United States, DDT can still be found in the environment. It has been replaced with compounds that exhibit more favorable decay kinetics.

Automobiles
The catalytic converter in modern automobiles helps to speed up the rate of conversion of harmful emissions (CO and NO, for example) to less harmful products (CO_2 and N_2 gas). The converter contains the metals platinum and palladium, that serve as solid catalysts, enabling the almost complete conversion of the auto emissions before they leave the tailpipe.

Nuclear Waste
We wish that chemical kinetics applied to radioactive waste. Perhaps we could heat the waste and it would go away. Not so! Radioactive decay (Chapter 9) is a nuclear process and is immune to all of the strategies routinely used to alter the rate of chemical reactions. That leaves us with a serious radioactive waste disposal problem. For more details, refer to Green Chemistry: Nuclear Waste Disposal in Chapter 9.

For Further Understanding
▶ Provide another example of a process that has a less-than-optimal rate. What changes in conditions would improve the rate of this process?
▶ Find the current market values of platinum and palladium in the financial pages of a newspaper. How does this help to explain the high cost of a replacement catalytic converter?

7.4 Equilibrium

Rate and Reversibility of Reactions

We have assumed that most chemical and physical changes considered thus far proceed to completion. A complete reaction is one in which all reactants have been converted to products. However, many important chemical reactions do not go to completion. As a result, after no further obvious change is taking place, measurable quantities of reactants and products remain. Reactions of this type (incomplete reactions) are called **equilibrium reactions.**

Examples of physical and chemical equilibria abound in nature. Many environmental systems depend on fragile equilibria. The amount of oxygen dissolved in a certain volume of lake water (the oxygen concentration) is governed by the principles of equilibrium. The lives of plants and animals within this system are critically related to the levels of dissolved oxygen in the water.

The very form and function of the earth is a consequence of a variety of complex equilibria. Stalactite and stalagmite formations in caves are made up of solid calcium carbonate ($CaCO_3$). They owe their existence to an equilibrium process described by the following equation:

$$Ca^{2+}(aq) + 2HCO_3^-(aq) \rightleftharpoons CaCO_3(s) + CO_2(aq) + H_2O(l)$$

Physical Equilibrium

A physical equilibrium, such as sugar dissolving in water, is a reversible reaction. A **reversible reaction** is a process that can occur in both directions. It is indicated by using a double arrow ($\rightleftharpoons$) symbol.

Dissolution of sugar in water, producing a saturated solution, is a convenient illustration of a state of *dynamic equilibrium.*

A **dynamic equilibrium** is a situation in which the rate of the forward process in a reversible reaction is exactly balanced by the rate of the reverse process.

Let's now look at the sugar and water equilibrium in more detail.

Sugar in Water

Imagine that you mix a small amount of sugar (2 or 3 g) in 100 milliliters (mL) of water. After you stir it for a short time, all of the sugar dissolves; there is no residual solid sugar because the sugar has dissolved *completely.* The reaction clearly has converted all solid sugar to its dissolved state, an aqueous solution of sugar, or

$$sugar(s) \longrightarrow sugar(aq)$$

Now, suppose that you add a very large amount of sugar (100 g), more than can possibly dissolve, to the same volume of water. As you stir the mixture you observe more and more sugar dissolving. After some time the amount of solid sugar remaining in contact with the solution appears constant. Over time, you observe no further decrease in the amount of undissolved sugar. Although nothing further appears to be happening, in reality a great deal of activity is taking place!

An equilibrium situation has been established. Over time the amount of sugar dissolved in the measured volume of water (the concentration of sugar in water) does not change. Hence the amount of undissolved sugar remains the same. However, if you could look at the individual sugar molecules, you would see something quite amazing. Rather than sugar molecules in the solid simply staying in place, you would see them continuing to leave the solid state and go into solution. At the same time, a like number of dissolved sugar molecules would leave the water and form more solid. This active process is described as a *dynamic equilibrium.* The reaction is proceeding in a forward (left to right) and a reverse (right to left) direction at the same time and is a reversible reaction:

$$sugar(s) \rightleftharpoons sugar(aq)$$

LEARNING GOAL

8 ▶ Recognize and describe equilibrium situations.

Animations
- Equilibrium
- Dynamic Equilibrium

An excess of sugar in water produces a saturated solution, discussed in Section 6.1.

The rates of the forward and reverse reactions are identical and the amount of sugar present as solid and in solution is constant. The system is at equilibrium. The double arrow serves as

- an indicator of a reversible process,
- an indicator of an equilibrium process, and
- a reminder of the dynamic nature of the process.

Dynamic equilibrium can be particularly dangerous for living cells because it represents a situation in which nothing is getting done. There is no gain. Let's consider an exothermic reaction designed to produce a net gain of energy for the cell. In a dynamic equilibrium, the rate of the forward (energy-releasing) reaction is equal to the rate of the backward (energy-requiring) reaction. Thus there is no net gain of energy to fuel cellular activity, and the cell will die.

Question 7.13 Construct an example of a dynamic equilibrium using a subway car at rush hour or a busy restaurant at lunchtime.

Question 7.14 A certain change in reaction conditions for an equilibrium process was found to increase the rate of the forward reaction much more than that of the reverse reaction. Did the amount of product increase, decrease, or remain the same? Why?

Chemical Equilibrium

The Reaction of N_2 and H_2

When we mix nitrogen gas (N_2) and hydrogen gas (H_2) at an elevated temperature (perhaps 500°C), some of the molecules will collide with sufficient energy to break N—N and H—H bonds. Rearrangement of the atoms will produce the product (NH_3):

$$N_2(g) + 3H_2O(g) \rightleftharpoons 2NH_3(g)$$

Beginning with a mixture of hydrogen and nitrogen, the rate of the reaction is initially rapid, because the reactant concentration is high; as the reaction proceeds, the concentration of reactants decreases. At the same time the concentration of the product, ammonia, is increasing. At equilibrium the *rate of depletion* of hydrogen and nitrogen *is equal to* the *rate of depletion* of ammonia. In other words, *the rates of the forward and reverse reactions are equal.*

The concentration of the various species is fixed at equilibrium because product is being *consumed and formed at the same rate.* In other words, the reaction continues indefinitely (dynamic), but the concentration of products and reactants is fixed (equilibrium). This is a *dynamic equilibrium.* The rate of this reaction mixture as a function of time is depicted in Figure 7.13.

For systems such as the ammonia/hydrogen/nitrogen equilibrium, an **equilibrium constant** expression can be written; it summarizes the relationship between the concentration of reactants and products in an equilibrium reaction.

The Generalized Equilibrium Constant Expression for a Chemical Reaction

We write the general form of an equilibrium chemical reaction as

$$aA + bB \rightleftharpoons cC + dD$$

in which A and B represent reactants, C and D represent products, and a, b, c, and d are the coefficients of the balanced equation. The equilibrium constant expression for this general case is

$$K_{eq} = \frac{[C]^c[D]^d}{[A]^a[B]^b}$$

For the ammonia system, it follows that the appropriate equilibrium expression is:

$$K_{eq} = \frac{[NH_3]^2}{[N_2][H_2]^3}$$

Figure 7.13 The change of the rate of reaction as a function of time. The rate of reaction, initially rapid, decreases as the concentration of reactant decreases and approaches a limiting value at equilibrium.

It does not matter what initial amounts (concentrations) of reactants or products we choose. When the system reaches equilibrium, the calculated value of K_{eq} will not change. The magnitude of K_{eq} can be altered only by changing the temperature. Thus K_{eq} is temperature dependent. The chemical industry uses this fact to its advantage by choosing a reaction temperature that will maximize the yield of a desired product.

Question 7.15 How could we determine when a reaction has reached equilibrium?

Question 7.16 Does the attainment of equilibrium imply that no further change is taking place in the system?

Writing Equilibrium Constant Expressions

An equilibrium constant expression can be written only after a correct, balanced chemical equation that describes the equilibrium system has been developed. A balanced equation is essential because the *coefficients* in the equation become the *exponents* in the equilibrium constant expression.

Each chemical reaction has a unique equilibrium constant value at a specified temperature. Equilibrium constants listed in the chemical literature are often reported at 25°C, to allow comparison of one system with any other. For any equilibrium reaction, the value of the equilibrium constant changes with temperature.

The brackets represent molar concentration or molarity; recall that molarity has units of moles per liter (mol/L). In our discussion of equilibrium, all equilibrium constants are shown as *unitless*.

A properly written equilibrium constant expression may not include all of the terms in the chemical equation upon which it is based. Only the concentrations of gases and substances in solution are shown, because their concentrations can change. Concentration terms for liquids and solids are *not* shown. The concentration of a liquid is constant. Most often, the liquid is the solvent for the reaction under consideration. A solid also has a fixed concentration and, for solution reactions, is not really a part of the solution. When a solid is formed it exists as a solid phase in contact with a liquid phase (the solution).

LEARNING GOAL

9 ▶ Write equilibrium constant expressions and use these expressions to calculate equilibrium constants.

Products of the overall equilibrium reaction are in the numerator, and *reactants* are in the denominator.

The exponents correspond to the *coefficients* of the balanced equation.

EXAMPLE 7.8 Writing an Equilibrium Constant Expression

Write an equilibrium constant expression for the reversible reaction:

$$H_2(g) + F_2(g) \rightleftharpoons 2NF(g)$$

Solution

Step 1. Inspection of the chemical equation reveals that no solids or liquids are present. Hence all reactants and products appear in the equilibrium constant expression.

Step 2. The numerator term is the product term $[HF]^2$.

Step 3. The denominator terms are the reactants $[H_2]$ and $[F_2]$. Note that each term contains an exponent identical to the corresponding coefficient in the balanced equation.

Step 4. Arranging the numerator and denominator terms as a fraction and setting the fraction equal to K_{eq} yields

$$K_{eq} = \frac{[HF]^2}{[H_2][F_2]}$$

Continued—

Practice Problem 7.8

Write an equilibrium constant expression for each of the following reversible reactions.

   a. $2NO_2(g) \rightleftharpoons N_2(g) + 2O_2(g)$

   b. $2H_2O(l) \rightleftharpoons 2H_2(g) + O_2(g)$

▶ **For Further Practice: Questions 7.77 and 7.78.**

LEARNING GOAL

9 ▶ Write equilibrium constant expressions and use these expressions to calculate equilibrium constants.

EXAMPLE 7.9   Writing an Equilibrium Constant Expression

Write an equilibrium constant expression for the reversible reaction:

$$MnO_2(s) + 4H^+(aq) + 2Cl^-(aq) \rightleftharpoons Mn^{2+}(aq) + Cl_2(g) + 2H_2O(l)$$

Solution

Step 1. MnO_2 is a solid and H_2O, although a product, is negligible compared with the water solvent. Thus they are not written in the equilibrium constant expression.

$$\boxed{MnO_2(s)} + 4H^+(aq) + 2Cl^-(aq) \rightleftharpoons Mn^{2+}(aq) + Cl_2(g) + \boxed{2H_2O(l)}$$
$$\underbrace{\hspace{4cm}}_{\text{Not a part of the } K_{eq} \text{ expression}}$$

Step 2. The numerator term includes the remaining products:

$$[Mn^{2+}] \quad \text{and} \quad [Cl_2]$$

Step 3. The denominator term includes the remaining reactants:

$$[H^+]^4 \quad \text{and} \quad [Cl^-]^2$$

Note that each exponent is identical to the corresponding coefficient in the chemical equation.

Step 4. Arranging the numerator and denominator terms as a fraction and setting the fraction equal to K_{eq} yields

$$K_{eq} = \frac{[Mn^{2+}][Cl_2]}{[H^+]^4[Cl^-]^2}$$

Practice Problem 7.9

Write an equilibrium constant expression for each of the following reversible reactions.

   a. $AgCl(s) \rightleftharpoons Ag^+(aq) + Cl^-(aq)$

   b. $PCl_5(s) \rightleftharpoons PCl_3(g) + Cl_2(g)$

▶ **For Further Practice: Questions 7.81 and 7.83.**

Animation
• NO_2/N_2O_4 Equilibrium

Interpreting Equilibrium Constants

What utility does the equilibrium constant have? The reversible arrow in the chemical equation alerts us to the fact that an equilibrium exists. Some measurable quantity of the product and reactant remain. However, there is no indication whether products predominate, reactants predominate, or significant concentrations of both products and reactants are present at equilibrium.

The numerical value of the equilibrium constant provides this additional information. It tells us the extent to which reactants have converted to products. This is important information for anyone who wants to manufacture and sell the product. It also is important to anyone who studies the effect of equilibrium reactions on environmental systems and living organisms.

Although an absolute interpretation of the numerical value of the equilibrium constant depends on the form of the equilibrium constant expression, the following generalizations are useful:

- K_{eq} greater than 1×10^2. A large numerical value of K_{eq} indicates that the numerator (product term) is much larger than the denominator (reactant term) and that at equilibrium mostly product is present.
- K_{eq} less than 1×10^{-2}. A small numerical value of K_{eq} indicates that the numerator (product term) is much smaller than the denominator (reactant term) and that at equilibrium mostly reactant is present.
- K_{eq} between 1×10^{-2} and 1×10^2. In this case the equilibrium mixture contains significant concentrations of both reactants and products.

Question 7.17 At a given temperature, the equilibrium constant for a certain reaction is 1×10^{20}. Does this equilibrium favor products or reactants? Why?

Question 7.18 At a given temperature, the equilibrium constant for a certain reaction is 1×10^{-18}. Does this equilibrium favor products or reactants? Why?

Calculating Equilibrium Constants

The magnitude of the equilibrium constant for a chemical reaction is determined experimentally. The reaction under study is allowed to proceed until the concentration of products and reactants no longer changes (Figure 7.14). This may be a matter of seconds, minutes, hours, or even months or years, depending on the rate of the reaction. The reaction mixture is then analyzed to determine the molar concentration of each of the products and reactants. These concentrations are substituted in the equilibrium constant expression and the equilibrium constant is calculated. The following example illustrates this process.

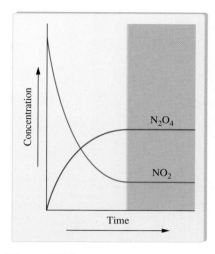

Figure 7.14 For the reaction $2NO_2(g) \rightleftharpoons N_2O_4(g)$, the concentration of reactant (NO_2) diminishes rapidly while the N_2O_4 concentration builds. Eventually, the concentrations of both reactant and product become constant over time (blue area). The equilibrium condition has been attained.

EXAMPLE 7.10 **Calculating an Equilibrium Constant**

Hydrogen iodide is placed in a sealed container and allowed to come to equilibrium. The equilibrium reaction is:

$$2HI(g) \rightleftharpoons H_2(g) + I_2(g)$$

and the equilibrium concentrations are:

$$[HI] = 0.54 \ M$$
$$[H_2] = 1.72 \ M$$
$$[I_2] = 1.72 \ M$$

Calculate the equilibrium constant.

Solution

Step 1. Write the equilibrium constant expression:

$$K_{eq} = \frac{[H_2][I_2]}{[HI]^2}$$

Step 2. Substitute the equilibrium concentrations of products and reactants to obtain

$$K_{eq} = \frac{[1.72][1.72]}{[0.54]^2} = \frac{2.96}{0.29}$$

$$= 10.1 \text{ or } 1.0 \times 10^1 \text{ (two significant figures)}$$

Continued—

LEARNING GOAL

9 ▶ Write equilibrium constant expressions and use these expressions to calculate equilibrium constants.

Practice Problem 7.10

A container holds the following mixture at equilibrium:

$$[NH_3] = 0.25\ M$$
$$[N_2] = 0.11\ M$$
$$[H_2] = 1.91\ M$$

If the reaction is:

$$N_2(g) + 3H_2(g) \rightleftharpoons 2NH_3(g)$$

calculate the equilibrium constant.

▶ **For Further Practice: Questions 7.82 and 7.84.**

Using Equilibrium Constants

We have seen that the equilibrium constant for a reaction can be calculated if we know the equilibrium concentrations of all of the reactants and products. Once known, the equilibrium constant can be used to obtain equilibrium concentrations of one or more reactants or products for a variety of different situations. These calculations can be quite complex. Let's look at one straightforward but useful case, one where the equilibrium concentration of reactants is known and we wish to calculate the product concentration.

LEARNING GOAL

9 ▶ Write equilibrium constant expressions and use these expressions to calculate equilibrium constants.

EXAMPLE 7.11   Using an Equilibrium Constant

Given the equilibrium reaction studied in Example 7.10:

$$2HI(g) \rightleftharpoons H_2(g) + I_2(g)$$

A sample mixture of HI, H_2, and I_2, at equilibrium, was found to have $[H_2] = 1.0 \times 10^{-2}\ M$ and $[HI] = 4.0 \times 10^{-2}\ M$. Calculate the molar concentration of I_2 in the equilibrium mixture.

Solution

Step 1. From Example 7.10, the equilibrium expression and equilibrium constant are:

$$K_{eq} = \frac{[H_2][I_2]}{[HI]^2}; \quad K_{eq} = 1.0 \times 10^1$$

Step 2. To solve the equilibrium expression for $[I_2]$, first multiply both sides of the equation by $[HI]^2$

$$[H_2][I_2] = K_{eq}[HI]^2$$

Then, divide both sides by $[H_2]$

$$[I_2] = \frac{K_{eq}[HI]^2}{[H_2]}$$

Step 3. Substitute the values:

$$K_{eq} = 1.0 \times 10^1$$
$$[H_2] = 1.0 \times 10^{-2}\ M$$
$$[HI] = 4.0 \times 10^{-2}\ M$$

Step 4. Solve:

$$[I_2] = \frac{[1.0 \times 10^1][4.0 \times 10^{-2}]^2}{[1.0 \times 10^{-2}]}$$

$$[I_2] = 1.6 \ M$$

Practice Problem 7.11

Using the reaction (above), calculate the $[I_2]$ if both $[H_2]$ and $[HI]$ were $1.0 \times 10^{-4} \ M$.

▶ **For Further Practice: Questions 7.85 and 7.86.**

LeChatelier's Principle

In the nineteenth century the French chemist LeChatelier discovered that changes in equilibrium depend on the amount of "stress" applied to the system. The stress may take the form of an increase or decrease of the temperature of the system at equilibrium, or perhaps a change in the amount of reactant or product present in a fixed volume (the concentration of reactant or product).

LeChatelier's principle states that if a stress is placed on a system at equilibrium, the system will respond by altering the equilibrium composition in such a way as to minimize the stress.

Consider the equilibrium situation discussed earlier:

$$N_2(g) + 3H_2(g) \rightleftharpoons 2NH_3(g)$$

If the reactants and products are present in a fixed volume, such as 1 liter (L), and more NH_3 (the *product*) is introduced into the container, the system will be stressed—the equilibrium will be disturbed. The system will try to alleviate the stress (as we all do) by *removing* as much of the added material as possible. How can it accomplish this? By converting some NH_3 to H_2 and N_2. The position of the equilibrium shifts to the left, and the dynamic equilibrium is soon reestablished.

Adding extra H_2 or N_2 would apply the stress to the other side of the equilibrium. To minimize the stress, the system would "use up" some of the excess H_2 or N_2 to make product, NH_3. The position of the equilibrium would shift to the right.

In summary,

$$N_2(g) + 3H_2(g) \rightleftharpoons 2NH_3(g)$$

Product introduced: ⟵ position of the equilibrium shifted

Reactant introduced: position of the equilibrium shifted ⟶

What would happen if some of the ammonia molecules were *removed* from the system? The loss of ammonia represents a stress on the system; to relieve that stress, the ammonia would be replenished by the reaction of hydrogen and nitrogen. The position of the equilibrium would shift to the right.

Effect of Concentration

Addition of extra product or reactant to a fixed reaction volume is just another way of saying that we have increased the concentration of product or reactant. Removal of material from a fixed volume decreases the concentration. Therefore, changing the concentration of one or more components of a reaction mixture is a way to alter the equilibrium composition of an equilibrium mixture (Figure 7.15).

LEARNING GOAL

10 ▶ Use LeChatelier's principle to predict changes in equilibrium position.

Animation
• LeChatelier's Principle

Addition of products or reactants may have a profound effect on the composition of a reaction mixture but *does not* affect the value of the equilibrium constant.

(a)   (b)   (c)

Figure 7.15 The effect of concentration on equilibrium position of the reaction:

$$FeSCN^{2+}(aq) \rightleftharpoons Fe^{3+}(aq) + SCN^-(aq)$$
(red)   (yellow)   (colorless)

Solution (a) represents this reaction at equilibrium; addition of SCN^- shifts the position of the equilibrium to the left (b) intensifying the red color. Removal of SCN^- shifts the position of the equilibrium to the right (c) shown by the disappearance of the red color.

Figure 7.16 The effect of heat on equilibrium position. For the reaction:

$$CoCl_4^{2-}(aq) + 6H_2O(l) \rightleftharpoons$$
(blue)
$$Co(H_2O)_6^{2+}(aq) + 4Cl^-(aq)$$
(pink)

Heating the solution favors the blue $CoCl_4^{2-}$ species; cooling favors the pink $Co(H_2O)_6^{2+}$ species.

Expansion and compression of gases and Boyle's law are discussed in Section 5.1.

The industrial process for preparing ammonia, the Haber process, uses pressures of several hundred atmospheres (atm) to increase the yield.

Let's look at some additional experimental variables that may change equilibrium composition.

Effect of Heat

The change in equilibrium composition caused by the addition or removal of heat from an equilibrium mixture can be explained by treating heat as a product or reactant. The reaction of nitrogen and hydrogen is an exothermic reaction:

$$N_2(g) + 3H_2(g) \rightleftharpoons 2NH_3(g) + 22 \text{ kcal}$$

Adding heat by raising the temperature is similar to increasing the amount of product. The position of the equilibrium will shift to the left, increasing the amounts of N_2 and H_2 and decreasing the amount of NH_3. If the reaction takes place in a fixed volume, the concentrations of N_2 and H_2 increase and the NH_3 concentration decreases.

Removal of heat by lowering the temperature produces the reverse effect. More ammonia is produced from N_2 and H_2, and the concentrations of these reactants must decrease.

In the case of an endothermic reaction, such as

$$39 \text{ kcal} + 2N_2(g) + O_2(g) \rightleftharpoons 2N_2O(g)$$

addition of heat is analogous to the addition of reactant, and the position of the equilibrium shifts to the right. Removal of heat would shift the reaction to the left, favoring the formation of reactants.

The dramatic effect of heat on the position of equilibrium is shown in Figure 7.16.

Effect of Pressure

Only gases are affected significantly by changes in pressure because gases are free to expand and compress in accordance with Boyle's law. However, liquids and solids are not compressible, so their volumes are unaffected by pressure.

Therefore pressure changes will alter equilibrium composition only in reactions that involve a gas or variety of gases as products and/or reactants. Again, consider the ammonia example,

$$N_2(g) + 3H_2(g) \rightleftharpoons 2NH_3(g)$$

One mole of N_2 and three moles of H_2 (total of 4 mol of reactants) react to form two moles of NH_3 (2 mol of product). An increase in pressure will cause a stress to the system. To relieve the stress, the system will shift toward the side of the reaction that has fewer mol of gas. As the number of mol decreases, the pressure will decrease. In the example of ammonia, an increase in pressure will shift the position of the equilibrium to the right, producing more NH_3.

A decrease in pressure will be countered by the reaction shifting toward the side that contains more mol of gas. As the number of mol of gas increases, the pressure will increase. Therefore, in the equilibrium reaction of ammonia, a decrease in pressure will cause the position of the equilibrium to shift to the left, and ammonia decomposes to form more nitrogen and hydrogen.

In contrast, the decomposition of hydrogen iodide,

$$2HI(g) \rightleftharpoons H_2(g) + I_2(g)$$

is unaffected by pressure. The number of mol of gaseous product and reactant are identical. No volume advantage is gained by a shift in equilibrium composition. In summary:

- Pressure affects the equilibrium composition only of reactions that involve at least one gaseous substance.

- Additionally, the relative number of mol of gaseous products and reactants must differ.
- The equilibrium composition will shift to increase the number of mol of gas when the pressure decreases; it will shift to decrease the number of mol of gas when the pressure increases.

Effect of a Catalyst

A catalyst has no effect on the equilibrium composition. A catalyst increases the rates of both forward and reverse reactions to the same extent. The equilibrium composition *and* equilibrium concentration do not change when a catalyst is used, but the equilibrium composition is achieved in a shorter time. The role of a solid-phase catalyst in the synthesis of ammonia is shown in Figure 7.12 on page 233.

EXAMPLE 7.12 Predicting Changes in Equilibrium Composition

Earlier in this section we considered the geologically important reaction that occurs in rock and soil:

$$4.67 \text{ kcal} + Ca^{2+}(aq) + 2HCO_3^-(aq) \rightleftharpoons CaCO_3(s) + CO_2(aq) + H_2O(l)$$

Predict the effect on the equilibrium composition for each of the following changes.

  a. The concentration of Ca^{2+} is increased by addition of some $CaCl_2$.
  b. Some solid $CaCO_3$ is removed from the mixture.
  c. The concentration of HCO_3^- is decreased.
  d. The temperature of the system is increased.
  e. A catalyst is added.

Solution

  a. The addition of Ca^{2+} ions will cause the position of the equilibrium to shift to the right, and more products will form.
  b. Because $CaCO_3$ is a solid, addition or removal of the substance will have no effect on the equilibrium composition.
  c. If HCO_3^- (aq) is removed from the system, the position of the equilibrium will shift to the left to produce more HCO_3^- and other reactants.
  d. The reaction is endothermic. The addition of heat by the raising of the temperature will shift the position of the equilibrium to the right, and more products will form.
  e. The addition of a catalyst has no effect on the equilibrium composition.

Practice Problem 7.12

The reaction

$$382 \text{ cal} + Pb(s) + 2H^+(aq) \rightleftharpoons Pb^{2+}(aq) + H_2(g)$$

is carried out at constant pressure. Predict whether the volume of hydrogen gas would increase, decrease, or remain the same for each of the following changes.

  a. Addition of $Pb(s)$.
  b. Addition of Pb^{2+} ions by adding some $Pb(NO_3)_2$ to the solution.
  c. Removal of H^+ ions.
  d. Lowering of the temperature.
  e. Addition of a catalyst.

▶ **For Further Practice: Questions 7.87 and 7.88.**

A Human Perspective

Light-Sensitive Glasses

Most of us are familiar with eyeglasses that darken in bright sunlight, functioning as sunglasses; at lower light levels, they gradually lighten, increasing their transparency. This ability to function both as sunglasses and conventional eyeglasses is an attractive feature for many people. But, how do they work?

Glass is made from the raw material silicon dioxide (SiO_2) mixed with other substances to form a polymeric silicate; silicates are long chains composed of silicon-oxygen groups. The glass is hard, not overly fragile, and can be ground and polished, enabling eyeglass users to compensate for focusing problems in their own eyes.

Adding silver chloride (AgCl) and Cu^+ ions to the mix of raw materials produces photochromic (*photo*, "light" and *chromic*, "color") glass. Literally, glass that changes color in proportion to the intensity of light. Furthermore, this change is reversible and will occur hundreds of thousands of times during the lifetime of the glass.

Although the chemical processes taking place in the glass are complex, we may represent the essential reaction as an equilibrium:

$$Cu^+ + Ag^+ \rightleftharpoons Cu^{2+} + Ag$$

Silver atoms in the glass are responsible for the gray color that forms, and the silver atoms block visible light. When walking into bright light, photons (light energy) shift the equilibrium reaction to the right, forming silver atoms:

$$\text{light energy} + Cu^+ + Ag^+ \rightleftharpoons Cu^{2+} + Ag$$

Removing the light (walking into a darkened room) causes the equilibrium reaction to shift to the left, and silver atoms are converted back to silver ions, which are transparent. The entire process is a practical and useful application of LeChatelier's principle.

The conversion from high to low transparency or vice versa occurs within a few minutes. A critical aspect of the improvement in the design of photochromic glass has been the improvements in the rate of conversion from one form to another. The kinetics of the reaction had to be optimized in order to make a product that people would actually purchase!

Equilibrium and kinetics, as well as thermodynamics (a reaction that will occur), are not abstract concepts but are essential in the development of many commercial products.

For Further Understanding

▶ How can light-sensitive glass improve energy efficiency in homes and offices?

▶ We know that energy cannot be destroyed; rather, it is converted to another form. The sunlight absorbed by sunglasses is no exception. What form of energy results from this absorption process?

SUMMARY

7.1 Thermodynamics

Thermodynamics is the study of energy, work, and heat, and is useful in predicting spontaneity of chemical change. Thermodynamics can be applied to the study of chemical reactions because we can determine the quantity of heat flow (by measuring the temperature change) between the *system* and the *surroundings*. *Exothermic reactions* release energy and produce products that are lower in energy than the reactants. *Endothermic reactions* require energy input. Heat energy is represented as *enthalpy, H*. The energy gain or loss is the change in enthalpy, ΔH, and is one factor that is useful in predicting whether a reaction is spontaneous or nonspontaneous.

Entropy, S, is a measure of the randomness of a system. A random, or disordered system has high entropy; a well-ordered system has low entropy. The change in entropy in a chemical reaction, ΔS, is also a factor in predicting reaction spontaneity.

Free energy, ΔG, incorporates both factors, enthalpy and entropy; as such, it is an absolute predictor of the spontaneity of a chemical reaction.

7.2 Experimental Determination of Energy Change in Reactions

A *calorimeter* measures heat changes (in cal or J) that occur in chemical reactions.

The *specific heat* of a substance is the number of cal of heat needed to raise the temperature of 1 g of the substance 1°C.

The amount of energy per g of food is referred to as its *fuel value*. Fuel values are commonly reported in units of *nutritional Calories* (1 nutritional Cal = 1 kcal). A bomb calorimeter is useful for measurement of the fuel value of foods.

7.3 Kinetics

Chemical *kinetics* is the study of the *rate* or speed of a chemical reaction. Energy for reactions is provided by molecular collisions. If this energy is sufficient, bonds may break, and atoms may recombine in a different arrangement, producing product. A collision producing one or more product molecules is termed an effective collision.

The minimum amount of energy needed for a reaction is the *activation energy*. The reaction proceeds from reactants to products through an intermediate state, the *activated complex*.

Experimental conditions influencing the reaction rate include the structure of the reacting species, the concentration of reactants, the temperature of reactants, the physical state of reactants, and the presence or absence of a catalyst.

A *catalyst* increases the rate of a reaction. The catalytic substance undergoes no net change in the reaction, nor does it alter the outcome of the reaction.

The *rate law* relates the rate of a reaction to the *rate constant* multiplied by the concentration of the reactants raised to a power that is the *reaction order.*

7.4 Equilibrium

Many chemical reactions do not completely convert reactants to products. A mixture of products and reactants exists, and its composition will remain constant until the experimental conditions are changed. This mixture is in a state of *chemical equilibrium.* The reaction continues indefinitely (dynamic), but the concentrations of products and reactants are fixed (equilibrium) because the rates of the forward and reverse reactions are equal. This is a *dynamic equilibrium.*

LeChatelier's principle states that if a stress is placed on an equilibrium system, the system will respond by altering the equilibrium in such a way as to minimize the stress.

KEY TERMS

activated complex (7.3)
activation energy (7.3)
calorimetry (7.2)
catalyst (7.3)
dynamic equilibrium (7.4)
endothermic reaction (7.1)
enthalpy (7.1)
entropy (7.1)
equilibrium constant (7.4)
equilibrium reaction (7.4)
exothermic reaction (7.1)
free energy (7.1)
fuel value (7.2)
heat (7.1)

kinetics (7.3)
LeChatelier's principle (7.4)
nutritional Calorie (7.2)
rate constant (7.3)
rate law (7.3)
rate of chemical
    reaction (7.3)
reaction order (7.3)
reversible reaction (7.4)
specific heat (7.2)
surroundings (7.1)
system (7.1)
thermodynamics (7.1)

QUESTIONS AND PROBLEMS

Thermodynamics

Foundations

7.19 What are the energy units most commonly employed in chemistry?

7.20 What energy unit is commonly employed in nutrition science?

7.21 Describe what is meant by an exothermic reaction.

7.22 Describe what is meant by an endothermic reaction.

7.23 The oxidations of fuels (coal, oil, gasoline) are exothermic reactions. Why?

7.24 Provide an explanation for the fact that most decomposition reactions are endothermic but most combination reactions are exothermic.

7.25 Describe how a calorimeter is used to distinguish between exothermic and endothermic reactions.

7.26 Construct a diagram of a coffee-cup calorimeter.

7.27 Why does a calorimeter have a "double-walled" container?

7.28 Explain why the fuel value of foods is an important factor in nutrition science.

7.29 Explain what is meant by the term *free energy.*

7.30 Explain what is meant by the term *specific heat.*

7.31 State the first law of thermodynamics.

7.32 State the second law of thermodynamics.

7.33 Explain what is meant by the term *enthalpy.*

7.34 Explain what is meant by the term *entropy.*

Applications

7.35 A 5.00-g sample of octane is burned in a bomb calorimeter containing 2.00×10^2 g H_2O. How much energy, in cal, is released if the water temperature increases 6.00°C?

7.36 A 0.0500-mol sample of a nutrient substance is burned in a bomb calorimeter containing 2.00×10^2 g H_2O. If the formula weight of this nutrient substance is 114 g/mol, what is the fuel value (in nutritional Cal) if the temperature of the water increased 5.70°C?

7.37 Calculate the energy released, in J, in Question 7.35 (recall conversion factors, Chapter 1).

7.38 Calculate the fuel value, in kilojoules (kJ), in Question 7.36 (recall conversion factors, Chapter 1).

7.39 Predict whether each of the following processes increases or decreases entropy, and explain your reasoning.
   a. melting of a solid metal
   b. boiling of water

7.40 Predict whether each of the following processes increases or decreases entropy, and explain your reasoning.
   a. burning a log in a fireplace
   b. condensation of water vapor on a cold surface

7.41 Predict whether a reaction with a negative ΔH and a positive ΔS will be spontaneous, nonspontaneous, or temperature dependent. Explain your reasoning.

7.42 Predict whether a reaction with a negative ΔH and a negative ΔS will be spontaneous, nonspontaneous, or temperature dependent. Explain your reasoning.

7.43 Isopropyl alcohol, commonly known as rubbing alcohol, feels cool when applied to the skin. Explain why.

7.44 Energy is required to break chemical bonds during the course of a reaction. When is energy released?

Kinetics

Foundations

7.45 Provide an example of a reaction that is extremely slow, taking days, weeks, or years to complete.

7.46 Provide an example of a reaction that is extremely fast, perhaps quicker than the eye can perceive.

7.47 Define the term *activated complex* and explain its significance in a chemical reaction.

7.48 Define and explain the term *activation energy* as it applies to chemical reactions.

Applications

7.49 Distinguish among the terms *rate, rate constant,* and *reaction order.*

7.50 Write the rate law for:

$$CH_4(g) + 2O_2(g) \longrightarrow 2H_2O(l) + CO_2(g)$$

if the order of all reactants is one.

7.51   Will the rate of the reaction in Question 7.50 increase, decrease, or remain the same if the rate constant doubles?

7.52   Will the rate of the reaction in Question 7.50 increase, decrease, or remain the same if the concentration of methane increases?

7.53   Describe the general characteristics of a catalyst.

7.54   Select one enzyme from a later chapter in this book and describe its biochemical importance.

7.55   Sketch a potential energy diagram for a reaction that shows the effect of a catalyst on an exothermic reaction.

7.56   Sketch a potential energy diagram for a reaction that shows the effect of a catalyst on an endothermic reaction.

7.57   For the equilibrium

$$2I(g) \rightleftharpoons I_2(g)$$

the rate law is:

$$\text{rate} = k[I]^2$$

at 23°C, $k = 7.0 \times 10^9 \ M^{-1} \ s^{-1}$. What effect will doubling the [I] have on the rate?

7.58   For the reaction

$$2H_2O_2(aq) \longrightarrow 2H_2O(l) + O_2(g)$$

the rate law is:

$$\text{rate} = k[H_2O_2]$$

at 25°C, $k = 3.1 \times 10^{-3} \ s^{-1}$. What effect would doubling the [H₂O₂] have on the rate?

7.59   Describe how an increase in the concentration of reactants increases the rate of a reaction.

7.60   Describe how an increase in the temperature of reactants increases the rate of a reaction.

7.61   Write the rate law for the reaction:

$$N_2O_4(g) \rightleftharpoons 2NO_2(g)$$

Represent the order as n, n', and so forth.

7.62   Write the rate law for the reaction:

$$H_2S(aq) + Cl_2(aq) \rightleftharpoons S(s) + 2HCl(aq)$$

Represent the order as n, n', and so forth.

7.63   Describe how a catalyst speeds up a chemical reaction.

7.64   Explain how a catalyst can be involved in a chemical reaction without being consumed in the process.

Equilibrium

Foundations

7.65   Does a large equilibrium constant mean that products or reactants are favored?

7.66   Does a large equilibrium constant mean that the reaction must be rapid?

7.67   The following diagram represents the reversible reaction $A(g) \rightleftharpoons 2B(g)$ at equilibrium with a total pressure of P.

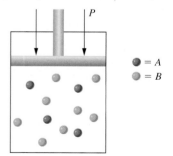

The pressure is increased to P'. Which of the following diagrams would represent the system once equilibrium is reestablished?

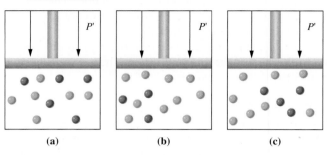

(a)   (b)   (c)

7.68   The following diagram represents the endothermic reaction at equilibrium at 25°C: heat $+ A(g) \rightleftharpoons 2B(g)$

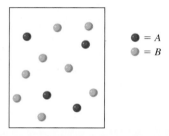

a.   The temperature is increased to 50°C. Which of the following diagrams would represent the system once equilibrium is reestablished?

b.   The temperature is decreased to 15°C. Which of the following diagrams would represent the system once equilibrium is reestablished?

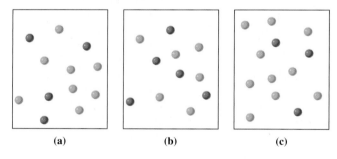

(a)   (b)   (c)

7.69   Explain LeChatelier's principle.

7.70   How can LeChatelier's principle help us to increase yields of chemical reactions?

7.71   Describe the meaning of the term *dynamic equilibrium.*

7.72   What is the relationship between the forward and reverse rates for a reaction at equilibrium?

7.73   Describe the meaning of the term *position of the equilibrium.*

7.74   Can a catalyst alter the position of the equilibrium?

7.75   Name three factors that can shift the position of an equilibrium.

7.76   A change in pressure could have the greatest effect on which type of equilibria: gaseous, liquid, or solid?

Applications

7.77   Write a valid equilibrium constant expression for the reaction shown in Question 7.61.

7.78   Write a valid equilibrium constant expression for the reaction shown in Question 7.62.

7.79 Distinguish between a physical equilibrium and a chemical equilibrium.

7.80 Distinguish between the rate constant and the equilibrium constant for a reaction.

7.81 Write the equilibrium constant expression for the reaction:

$$N_2(g) + 3H_2(g) \rightleftharpoons 2NH_3(g)$$

7.82 Using the equilibrium constant expression in Question 7.81, calculate the equilibrium constant if:

$$[N_2] = 0.071\,M$$
$$[H_2] = 9.2 \times 10^{-3}\,M$$
$$[NH_3] = 1.8 \times 10^{-4}\,M$$

7.83 Write the equilibrium constant expression for the reaction:

$$2H_2(g) + S_2(g) \rightleftharpoons 2H_2S(g)$$

7.84 Using the equilibrium constant expression in Question 7.83, calculate the equilibrium constant if:

$$[H_2] = 2.1 \times 10^{-1}\,M$$
$$[S_2] = 1.1 \times 10^{-6}\,M$$
$$[H_2S] = 7.3 \times 10^{-1}\,M$$

7.85 Use the equilibrium constant expression you wrote in Question 7.81 and the equilibrium constant you calculated in Question 7.82 to determine the equilibrium concentration of NH_3 if:

$$[N_2] = 8.0 \times 10^{-2}\,M$$
$$[H_2] = 5.0 \times 10^{-3}\,M$$

7.86 Use the equilibrium constant expression you wrote in Question 7.83 and the equilibrium constant you calculated in Question 7.84 to determine the equilibrium concentration of H_2S if:

$$[H_2] = 1.0 \times 10^{-1}\,M$$
$$[S_2] = 1.0 \times 10^{-5}\,M$$

7.87 For the reaction

$$CH_4(g) + Cl_2(g) \rightleftharpoons CH_3Cl(g) + HCl(g) + 26.4\text{ kcal}$$

predict the effect on the position of the equilibrium (will it shift to the left or to the right, or will there be no change?) for each of the following changes.
   a. The temperature is increased.
   b. The pressure is increased by decreasing the volume of the container.
   c. A catalyst is added.

7.88 For the reaction

$$47\text{ kcal} + 2SO_3(g) \rightleftharpoons 2SO_2(g) + O_2(g)$$

predict the effect on the position of the equilibrium (will it shift to the left or to the right, or will there be no change?) for each of the following changes.
   a. The temperature is increased.
   b. The pressure is increased by decreasing the volume of the container.
   c. A catalyst is added.

7.89 Label each of the following statements as true or false and explain why.
   a. A slow reaction is an incomplete reaction.
   b. The rates of forward and reverse reactions are never the same.

7.90 Label each of the following statements as true or false and explain why.
   a. A reaction is at equilibrium when no reactants remain.
   b. A reaction at equilibrium is undergoing continual change.

7.91 Use LeChatelier's principle to predict whether the amount of PCl_3 in a 1.00-L container is increased, is decreased, or remains the same for the equilibrium

$$PCl_3(g) + Cl_2(g) \rightleftharpoons PCl_5(g) + \text{heat}$$

when each of the following changes is made.
   a. PCl_5 is added.
   b. Cl_2 is added.
   c. PCl_5 is removed.
   d. The temperature is decreased.
   e. A catalyst is added.

7.92 Use LeChatelier's principle to predict the effects, if any, of each of the following changes on the equilibrium system, described below, in a closed container.

$$C(s) + 2H_2(g) \rightleftharpoons CH_4(g) + 18\text{ kcal}$$

   a. C is added.
   b. H_2 is added.
   c. CH_4 is removed.
   d. The temperature is increased.
   e. A catalyst is added.

7.93 Will an increase in pressure increase, decrease, or have no effect on the concentration of $H_2(g)$ in the reaction:

$$C(s) + H_2O(g) \rightleftharpoons CO(g) + H_2(g)$$

7.94 Will an increase in pressure increase, decrease, or have no effect on the concentration of $NO(g)$ in the reaction:

$$N_2(g) + O_2(g) \rightleftharpoons 2NO(g)$$

7.95 Write the equilibrium constant expression for the reaction described in Question 7.93.

7.96 Write the equilibrium constant expression for the reaction described in Question 7.94.

7.97 True or false: The position of the equilibrium will shift to the right when a catalyst is added to the mixture described in Question 7.93. Explain your reasoning.

7.98 True or false: The position of the equilibrium for an endothermic reaction will shift to the right when the reaction mixture is heated. Explain your reasoning.

7.99 A bottle of carbonated beverage slowly goes "flat" (loses CO_2) after it is opened. Explain, using LeChatelier's principle.

7.100 Carbonated beverages quickly go flat (lose CO_2) when heated. Explain, using LeChatelier's principle.

CRITICAL THINKING PROBLEMS

1. Predict the sign of ΔG for perspiration evaporating. Would you expect the ΔH term or the ΔS term to be more dominant? Explain your reasoning.
2. Can the following statement ever be true? "Heating a reaction mixture increases the rate of a certain reaction but decreases the yield of product from the reaction." Explain why or why not.
3. Molecules must collide for a reaction to take place. Sketch a model of the orientation and interaction of HI and Cl that is most favorable for the reaction:

$$HI(g) + Cl(g) \longrightarrow HCl(g) + I(g)$$

4. Refer to Question 7.88. Choose the statements that are correct.
   a. K_{eq} (at 25°C) $> K_{eq}$ (at 50°C)
   b. K_{eq} (at 25°C) $< K_{eq}$ (at 50°C)
   c. K_{eq} (at 25°C) $= K_{eq}$ (at 50°C)
   d. K_{eq} (at 25°C) $> K_{eq}$ (at 15°C)
   e. K_{eq} (at 25°C) $< K_{eq}$ (at 15°C)
   f. K_{eq} (at 25°C) $= K_{eq}$ (at 15°C)

5. Silver ion reacts with chloride ion to form the precipitate silver chloride:

$$Ag^+(aq) + Cl^-(aq) \rightleftharpoons AgCl(s)$$

After the reaction reached equilibrium, the chemist filtered 99% of the solid silver chloride from the solution, hoping to shift the equilibrium to the right, to form more product. Critique the chemist's experiment.

6. Human behavior often follows LeChatelier's principle. Provide one example and explain in terms of LeChatelier's principle.

7. A clever device found in some homes is a figurine that is blue on dry, sunny days and pink on damp, rainy days. These figurines are coated with substances containing chemical species that undergo the following equilibrium reaction:

$$Co(H_2O)_6{}^{2+}(aq) + 4Cl^-(aq) \rightleftharpoons CoCl_4{}^{2-}(aq) + 6H_2O(l)$$

   a. Which substance is blue?
   b. Which substance is pink?
   c. How is LeChatelier's principle applied here?

8. You have spent the entire morning in a 20°C classroom. As you ride the elevator to the cafeteria, six persons enter the elevator after being outside on a subfreezing day. You suddenly feel chilled. Explain the heat flow situation in the elevator in thermodynamic terms.

Acids and Bases and Oxidation-Reduction

LEARNING GOALS

1 ▶ Identify acids and bases and acid-base reactions.

2 ▶ Describe the role of the solvent in acid-base reactions.

3 ▶ Write equations describing acid-base dissociation and label the conjugate acid-base pairs.

4 ▶ Calculate pH from concentration data.

5 ▶ Calculate hydronium and/or hydroxide ion concentration from pH data.

6 ▶ Provide examples of the importance of pH in chemical and biochemical systems.

7 ▶ Describe the meaning and utility of neutralization reactions.

8 ▶ Describe the applications of buffers to chemical and biochemical systems, particularly blood chemistry.

9 ▶ Explain the meaning of the terms *oxidation* and *reduction,* and describe some practical examples of redox processes.

10 ▶ Diagram a voltaic cell and describe its function.

11 ▶ Compare and contrast voltaic and electrolytic cells.

OUTLINE

Solution properties, including clarity and bacteria levels, are often pH dependent.

LEARNING GOAL

1 ▶ Identify acids and bases and acid-base reactions.

Figure 8.1 The yellow solution on the left, containing CrO_4^{2-} (chromate ion), was made acidic, producing the reddish brown solution on the right. The principal component in solution is now $Cr_2O_7^{2-}$. Addition of base to this solution removes H^+ ions and regenerates the yellow CrO_4^{2-}. This is an example of an acid-base dependent chemical equilibrium.

INTRODUCTION

In this chapter we will learn about two general classes of chemical change: acid-base reactions and oxidation-reduction reactions. Although superficially quite different, their underlying similarity is that both are essentially charge-transfer processes. An acid-base reaction involves the transfer of one or more positively charged units, protons or hydrogen ions; an oxidation-reduction reaction involves the transfer of one or more negatively charged particles, electrons.

Acids and bases include some of the most important compounds in nature. Historically, it was recognized that certain compounds, acids, had a sour taste, were able to dissolve some metals, and caused vegetable dyes to change color. Bases have long been recognized by their bitter taste, slippery feel, and corrosive nature. Bases react strongly with acids and cause many metal ions in solution to form a solid precipitate.

Digestion of proteins is aided by stomach acid (hydrochloric acid), and many biochemical processes such as enzyme catalysis depend on the proper level of acidity. Indeed, a wide variety of chemical reactions critically depend on the acid-base composition of the solution (Figure 8.1). This is especially true of the biochemical reactions occurring in the cells of our bodies. For this reason the level of acidity must be very carefully regulated. This is done with substances called buffers.

Oxidation-reduction processes are also common in living systems. Respiration is driven by oxidation-reduction reactions. Additionally, oxidation-reduction reactions generate heat that warms our homes and workplaces and fuels our industrial civilization. Moreover, oxidation-reduction is the basis for battery design. Batteries are found in automobiles and electronic devices such as cameras and radios, and are even implanted in the human body to regulate heart rhythm.

8.1 Acids and Bases

The properties of acids and bases are related to their chemical structure. All acids have common characteristics that enable them to increase the hydrogen ion concentration in water. All bases lower the hydrogen ion concentration in water.

Two theories, one developed from the other, help us to understand the unique chemistry of acids and bases.

Arrhenius Theory of Acids and Bases

One of the earliest definitions of acids and bases is the **Arrhenius theory.** According to this theory, an **acid,** dissolved in water, dissociates to form *hydrogen ions or protons* (H^+), and a **base,** dissolved in water, dissociates to form *hydroxide ions* (OH^-). For example, hydrochloric acid dissociates in solution according to the reaction

$$HCl(aq) \longrightarrow H^+(aq) + Cl^-(aq)$$

Sodium hydroxide, a base, produces hydroxide ions in solution:

$$NaOH(aq) \longrightarrow Na^+(aq) + OH^-(aq)$$

The Arrhenius theory satisfactorily explains the behavior of many acids and bases. However, a substance such as ammonia, NH_3, has basic properties but cannot be an Arrhenius base, because it contains no OH^-. The *Brønsted-Lowry theory* explains this mystery and gives us a broader view of acid-base theory by considering the central role of the solvent in the dissociation process.

Brønsted-Lowry Theory of Acids and Bases

The **Brønsted-Lowry theory** defines an **acid** as a proton (H^+) donor and a **base** as a proton acceptor.

Hydrochloric acid in solution *donates* a proton to the solvent water, thus behaving as a Brønsted-Lowry acid:

$$HCl(aq) + H_2O(l) \longrightarrow H_3O^+(aq) + Cl^-(aq)$$

H_3O^+ is referred to as the hydrated proton or **hydronium ion.**

The basic properties of ammonia are clearly accounted for by the Brønsted-Lowry theory. Ammonia *accepts* a proton from the solvent water, producing OH^-. An equilibrium mixture of NH_3, H_2O, NH_4^+, and OH^- results.

$$NH_3(aq) + H-OH(l) \rightleftharpoons NH_4^+(aq) + OH^-(aq)$$

Acid-Base Properties of Water

The role that the solvent, water, plays in acid-base reactions is noteworthy. In one example above, the water molecule accepts a proton from the HCl molecule. The water is behaving as a proton acceptor, a base.

However, when water is a solvent for ammonia (NH_3), a base, the water molecule donates a proton to the ammonia molecule. The water, in this situation, is acting as a proton donor, an acid.

Water, owing to the fact that it possesses *both* acid and base properties, is termed **amphiprotic.** Water is the most commonly used solvent for acids and bases. Solute-solvent interactions between water and acids or bases promote both the solubility and the dissociation of acids and bases.

Acid and Base Strength

The terms *acid or base strength* and *acid or base concentration* are easily confused. *Strength* is a measure of the *degree of dissociation* of an acid or base in solution, independent of its concentration. The degree of dissociation is the fraction of acid or base molecules that produce ions in solution. Concentration, as we have learned, refers to the amount of solute (in this case, the amount of acid or base) per quantity of solution.

The strength of acids and bases in water depends on the extent to which they react with the solvent, water. Acids and bases are classified as *strong* when the reaction with water is virtually 100% complete and as *weak* when the reaction with water is much less than 100% complete.

Important strong acids include:

Hydrochloric acid	$HCl(aq) + H_2O(l) \longrightarrow H_3O^+(aq) + Cl^-(aq)$
Nitric acid	$HNO_3(aq) + H_2O(l) \longrightarrow H_3O^+(aq) + NO_3^-(aq)$
Sulfuric acid	$H_2SO_4(aq) + H_2O(l) \longrightarrow H_3O^+(aq) + HSO_4^-(aq)$

Note that the equation for the dissociation of each of these acids is written with a single arrow. This indicates that the reaction has little or no tendency to proceed in the reverse direction to establish equilibrium. Virtually all of the acid molecules are dissociated to form ions.

All common strong bases are *metal hydroxides.* Strong bases completely dissociate in aqueous solution to produce hydroxide ions and metal cations. Of the

LEARNING GOAL

2 ▶ Describe the role of the solvent in acid-base reactions.

Concentration of solutions is discussed in Section 6.3.

The concentration of an acid or base does affect the degree of dissociation. However, the major factor in determining the degree of dissociation is the strength of the acid or base.

Animations
- The Dissociation of Strong and Weak Acids
- Ionization of a Strong Base and a Weak Base
- Dissociation of Acetic Acid

Reversibility of reactions is discussed in Section 7.4.

common metal hydroxides, only NaOH and KOH are soluble in water and are readily usable strong bases:

Sodium hydroxide $NaOH(aq) \longrightarrow Na^+(aq) + OH^-(aq)$
Potassium hydroxide $KOH(aq) \longrightarrow K^+(aq) + OH^-(aq)$

Weak acids and weak bases dissolve in water principally in the molecular form. Only a small percentage of the molecules dissociate to form the hydronium or hydroxide ion.

Two important weak acids are:

Acetic acid $CH_3COOH(aq) + H_2O(l) \rightleftharpoons H_3O^+(aq) + CH_3COO^-(aq)$
Carbonic acid $H_2CO_3(aq) + H_2O(l) \rightleftharpoons H_3O^+(aq) + HCO_3^-(aq)$

We have already mentioned the most common weak base, ammonia. Many organic compounds function as weak bases. Several examples of weak bases follow:

Pyridine $C_5H_5N(aq) + H_2O(l) \rightleftharpoons C_5H_5NH^+(aq) + OH^-(aq)$
Aniline $C_6H_5NH_2(aq) + H_2O(l) \rightleftharpoons C_6H_5NH_3^+(aq) + OH^-(aq)$
Methylamine $CH_3NH_2(aq) + H_2O(l) \rightleftharpoons CH_3NH_3^+(aq) + OH^-(aq)$

The fundamental chemical difference between strong and weak acids or bases is their equilibrium ion concentration. A strong acid, such as HCl, does not, in aqueous solution, exist to any measurable degree in equilibrium with its ions, H_3O^+ and Cl^-. On the other hand, a weak acid, such as acetic acid, establishes a dynamic equilibrium with its ions, H_3O^+ and CH_3COO^-.

Conjugate Acids and Bases

The Brønsted-Lowry theory contributed several fundamental ideas that broadened our understanding of solution chemistry. First of all, an acid-base reaction is a charge-transfer process. Second, the transfer process usually involves the solvent. Water may, in fact, accept or donate a proton. Last, and perhaps most important, the acid-base reaction is seen as a reversible process. This leads to the possibility of a reversible, dynamic equilibrium (see Section 7.4).

Consequently, any acid-base reaction can be represented by the general equation

$$\underset{\text{(acid)}}{HA} + \underset{\text{(base)}}{B} \rightleftharpoons BH^+ + A^-$$

In the forward reaction, the acid (HA) donates a proton (H^+) to the base (B) leading to the formation of BH^+ and A^-. However, in the reverse reaction, it is the BH^+ that behaves as an acid; it donates its "extra" proton to A^-. A^- is therefore a base in its own right because it accepts the proton.

These *product* acids and bases are termed *conjugate acids and bases.*

A **conjugate acid** is the species formed when a base accepts a proton.

A **conjugate base** is the species formed when an acid donates a proton.

The acid and base on the opposite sides of the equation are collectively termed a **conjugate acid-base pair.** In the above equation:

BH^+ is the conjugate acid of the base B.
A^- is the conjugate base of the acid HA.
B and BH^+ constitute a conjugate acid-base pair.
HA and A^- constitute a conjugate acid-base pair.

The double arrow implies an equilibrium between dissociated and undissociated species.

Many organic compounds have acid or base properties. The chemistry of organic acids and bases will be discussed in Chapter 14 (Carboxylic Acids and Carboxylic Acid Derivatives) and 15 (Amines and Amides).

LEARNING GOAL

3 ▶ Write equations describing acid-base dissociation and label the conjugate acid-base pairs.

Rewriting our model equation:

$$\text{HA} + \text{B} \;\rightleftharpoons\; \text{BH}^+ + \text{A}^-$$
(acid) (base)   (acid) (base)

conjugate acid-base pair

— conjugate acid-base pair —

Although we show the forward and reverse arrows to indicate the reversibility of the reaction, seldom are the two processes "equal but opposite." One reaction, either forward or reverse, is usually favored. Consider the reaction of hydrochloric acid in water:

↓ Forward reaction: significant

$$\text{HCl}(aq) + \text{H}_2\text{O}(l) \;\rightleftharpoons\; \text{H}_3\text{O}^+(aq) + \text{Cl}^-(aq)$$
(acid)   (base)   (acid)   (base)

↑ Reverse reaction: not significant

HCl is a much better proton donor than H_3O^+. Consequently the forward reaction predominates, the reverse reaction is inconsequential, and hydrochloric acid is termed a *strong acid*. As we learned in Chapter 7, reactions in which the forward reaction is strongly favored have large equilibrium constants. The dissociation of hydrochloric acid is so favorable that we describe it as 100% dissociated and use only a single forward arrow to represent its behavior in water:

$$\text{HCl}(aq) + \text{H}_2\text{O}(l) \longrightarrow \text{H}_3\text{O}^+(aq) + \text{Cl}^-(aq)$$

The degree of dissociation, or strength, of acids and bases has a profound influence on their aqueous chemistry. For example, vinegar (a 5% mass/volume [m/V] solution of acetic acid in water) is a consumable product; aqueous hydrochloric acid in water is not. Why? Acetic acid is a *weak* acid and, as a result, a dilute solution does no damage to the mouth and esophagus. The following section looks at the strength of acids and bases in solution in more detail.

Animations
• Reaction of a Strong Acid with Water
• Reaction of a Weak Acid with Water

Question 8.1 Write an equation for the reaction of each of the following with water:

a. HF (a weak acid)

b. NH_3 (a weak base)

Question 8.2 Write an equation for the reaction of each of the following with water:

a. H_2S (a weak acid)

b. CH_3NH_2 (a weak base)

Question 8.3 Select the conjugate acid-base pairs for each reaction in Question 8.1.

Question 8.4 Select the conjugate acid-base pairs for each reaction in Question 8.2.

The relative strength of an acid or base is determined by the ease with which it donates or accepts a proton. Acids with the greatest proton-donating capability (strongest acids) have the weakest conjugate bases. Good proton acceptors (strong bases) have weak conjugate acids. This relationship is clearly indicated in Figure 8.2. This figure can be used to help us compare and predict relative acid-base strength.

Figure 8.2 Conjugate acid-base pairs. Strong acids have weak conjugate bases; strong bases have weak conjugate acids. Note that, in every case, the conjugate base has one fewer H^+ than the corresponding conjugate acid.

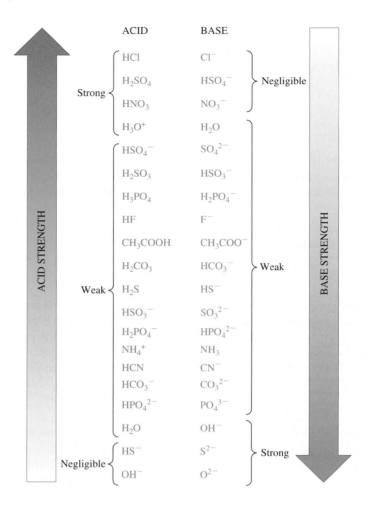

LEARNING GOAL

3 ▶ Write equations describing acid-base dissociation and label the conjugate acid-base pairs.

EXAMPLE 8.1   Predicting Relative Acid-Base Strengths

a. Write the conjugate acid of HS^-.

Solution

The conjugate acid may be constructed by adding a proton (H^+) to the base structure, consequently, H_2S.

b. Using Figure 8.2, identify the stronger base, HS^- or F^-.

Solution

HS^- is the stronger base because it is located farther down the right-hand column.

c. Using Figure 8.2 identify the stronger acid, H_2S or HF.

Solution

HF is the stronger acid because its conjugate base is weaker *and* because it is located farther up the left-hand column.

Practice Problem 8.1

a. In each pair, write the conjugate base of each acid and identify the stronger acid.

H_2O or NH_4^+

H_2SO_4 or H_2SO_3

b. In each pair, write the conjugate acid of each base and identify the stronger base.

CO_3^{2-} or PO_4^{3-}

HCO_3^- or HPO_4^{2-}

▶ **For Further Practice: Questions 8.23 and 8.24.**

Solutions of acids and bases used in the laboratory must be handled with care. Acids burn because of their exothermic reaction with water present on and in the skin. Bases react with proteins, which are principal components of the skin and eyes.

Such solutions are more hazardous if they are strong or concentrated. A strong acid or base produces more H_3O^+ or OH^- than does the corresponding weak acid or base. More-concentrated acids or bases contain more H_3O^+ or OH^- than do less-concentrated solutions of acids or bases of the same strength.

The Dissociation of Water

Aqueous solutions of acids and bases are electrolytes. The dissociation of the acid or base produces ions that can conduct an electrical current. As a result of the differences in the degree of dissociation, *strong acids and bases are strong electrolytes; weak acids and bases are weak electrolytes.* The conductivity of these solutions is principally dependent on the solute and not the solvent (water).

Solutions of electrolytes are discussed in Section 6.5.

Although pure water is virtually 100% molecular, a small number of water molecules do ionize. This process occurs by the transfer of a proton from one water molecule to another, producing a hydronium ion and a hydroxide ion:

$$H_2O(l) + H_2O(l) \rightleftharpoons H_3O^+(aq) + OH^-(aq)$$

This process is the **autoionization,** or self-ionization, of water. Water is therefore a *very* weak electrolyte and a very poor conductor of electricity. Water has *both* acid and base properties; dissociation produces both the hydronium and hydroxide ion.

Pure water at room temperature has a hydronium ion concentration of $1.0 \times 10^{-7}\,M$. One hydroxide ion is produced for each hydronium ion. Therefore, the hydroxide ion concentration is also $1.0 \times 10^{-7}\,M$. Molar equilibrium concentration is conveniently indicated by brackets around the species whose concentration is represented:

$$[H_3O^+] = 1.0 \times 10^{-7}\,M$$
$$[OH^-] = 1.0 \times 10^{-7}\,M$$

The product of hydronium and hydroxide ion concentration in pure water is referred to as the **ion product for water,** symbolized by K_w.

$$K_w = \text{ion product} = [H_3O^+][OH^-]$$
$$= [1.0 \times 10^{-7}][1.0 \times 10^{-7}]$$
$$= 1.0 \times 10^{-14}$$

The ion product is constant because its value does not depend on the nature or concentration of the solute, as long as the temperature does not change. The ion product is a temperature-dependent quantity.

The nature and concentration of the solutes added to water do alter the relative concentrations of H_3O^+ and OH^- present, but the product, $[H_3O^+][OH^-]$, always equals 1.0×10^{-14} at 25°C. This relationship is the basis for a scale that is useful in the measurement of the level of acidity or basicity of solutions. This scale, the pH scale, is discussed next.

LEARNING GOAL

4 ▶ Calculate pH from concentration data.

pH values greater than 14 and less than zero are possible, but largely meaningless, due to ion association characteristics of very concentrated solutions.

8.2 pH: A Measurement Scale for Acids and Bases

A Definition of pH

The **pH scale** gauges the hydronium ion concentration and reflects the degree of acidity or basicity of a solution. The pH scale is somewhat analogous to the temperature scale used for assignment of relative levels of hot or cold. The temperature scale was developed to allow us to indicate how cold or how hot an object is. The pH scale specifies how acidic or how basic a solution is. The pH scale has values that range from 0 (very acidic) to 14 (very basic). A pH of 7, the middle of the scale, is neutral, neither acidic nor basic. Figure 8.3 provides a convenient overview of solution pH.

To help us to develop a concept of pH, let's consider the following:

- Addition of an acid (proton donor) to water *increases* the $[H_3O^+]$ and decreases the $[OH^-]$.
- Addition of a base (proton acceptor) to water *decreases* the $[H_3O^+]$ by increasing the $[OH^-]$.
- $[H_3O^+] = [OH^-]$ when *equal* amounts of acid and base are present.
- In all three cases, $[H_3O^+][OH^-] = 1.0 \times 10^{-14} =$ the ion product for water at 25°C.

Measuring pH

The pH of a solution can be calculated if the concentration of either H_3O^+ or OH^- is known. Alternatively, measurement of pH allows the calculation of H_3O^+ or

Figure 8.3 The pH scale. A pH of 7 is neutral ($[H_3O^+] = [OH^-]$). Values less than 7 are acidic (H_3O^+ predominates) and values greater than 7 are basic (OH^- predominates).

(a)

(b)

Figure 8.4 The measurement of pH. (a) A strip of test paper impregnated with indicator (a material that changes color as the acidity of the surroundings changes) is put in contact with the solution of interest. The resulting color is matched with a standard color chart (colors shown as a function of pH) to obtain the approximate pH. (b) A pH meter uses a sensor (a pH electrode) that develops an electrical potential that is proportional to the pH of the solution.

OH^- concentration. The pH of aqueous solutions may be approximated by using indicating paper (pH paper) that develops a color related to the solution pH. Alternatively, a pH meter can give us a much more exact pH measurement. A sensor measures an electrical property of a solution that is proportional to pH (Figure 8.4).

Calculating pH

One of our objectives in this chapter is to calculate the pH of a solution when the hydronium or hydroxide ion concentration is known, and to calculate $[H_3O^+]$ or $[OH^-]$ from the pH.

The pH of a solution is defined as the negative logarithm of the molar concentration of the hydronium ion:

$$pH = -\log [H_3O^+]$$

LEARNING GOAL

4 ▶ Calculate pH from concentration data.

Refer to the treatment of significant figures using logarithms in Section 1.3.

EXAMPLE 8.2   Calculating pH from Acid Molarity

Calculate the pH of a 1.0×10^{-3} M solution of HCl.

Solution

Step 1. Recognize that HCl is a strong acid.

Step 2. If 1 mole (mol) HCl dissolves and dissociates in 1 liter (L) of aqueous solution, it produces 1 mol H_3O^+ (a 1 M solution of H_3O^+). Therefore a 1.0×10^{-3} M HCl solution has $[H_3O^+] = 1.0 \times 10^{-3}$ M, and

Step 3. Using our expression for pH:

$$pH = -\log [H_3O^+]$$

Step 4. Substituting for $[H_3O^+]$:

$$pH = -\log [1.0 \times 10^{-3}]$$
$$= -[-3.00] = 3.00$$

Practice Problem 8.2

Calculate the pH of a 1.0×10^{-4} M solution of HNO_3.

▶ **For Further Practice: Questions 8.43 and 8.44.**

LEARNING GOAL

5 ▶ Calculate hydronium and/or hydroxide ion concentration from pH data.

EXAMPLE 8.3   Calculating [H₃O⁺] from pH

Calculate the $[H_3O^+]$ of a solution of hydrochloric acid with pH = 4.00.

Solution

Step 1. We use the pH expression:

$$pH = -\log [H_3O^+]$$
$$4.00 = -\log [H_3O^+]$$

Step 2. Multiplying both sides of the equation by −1, we get

$$-4.00 = \log [H_3O^+]$$

Step 3. Taking the antilogarithm of both sides (the reverse of a logarithm), we have

$$\text{antilog} \quad -4.00 = [H_3O^+]$$

Step 4. The antilog is the exponent of 10; therefore

$$1.0 \times 10^{-4} \, M = [H_3O^+]$$

Practice Problem 8.3

Calculate the $[H_3O^+]$ of a solution of HNO_3 that has a pH = 5.00.

▶ **For Further Practice: Questions 8.45 and 8.46.**

EXAMPLE 8.4   Calculating the pH of a Base

Calculate the pH of a $1.0 \times 10^{-5} \, M$ solution of NaOH.

Solution

Step 1. Recognize that NaOH is a strong base.

Step 2. If 1 mol NaOH dissolves and dissociates in 1 L of aqueous solution, it produces 1 mol OH^- (a 1 M solution of OH^-). Therefore a $1.0 \times 10^{-5} \, M$ NaOH solution has $[OH^-] = 1.0 \times 10^{-5} \, M$.

Step 3. To calculate pH, we need $[H_3O^+]$. Recall that

$$[H_3O^+][OH^-] = 1.0 \times 10^{-14}$$

Step 4. Solving this equation for $[H_3O^+]$,

$$[H_3O^+] = \frac{1.0 \times 10^{-14}}{[OH^-]}$$

Step 5. Substituting the information provided in the problem,

$$[H_3O^+] = \frac{1.0 \times 10^{-14}}{1.0 \times 10^{-5}}$$
$$= 1.0 \times 10^{-9} \, M$$

Step 6. The solution is now similar to that in Example 8.2:

$$pH = -\log [H_3O^+]$$
$$= -\log [1.0 \times 10^{-9}]$$
$$= 9.00$$

Practice Problem 8.4

a. Calculate the pH corresponding to a $1.0 \times 10^{-2} \, M$ solution of sodium hydroxide.
b. Calculate the pH corresponding to a $1.0 \times 10^{-6} \, M$ solution of sodium hydroxide.

▶ **For Further Practice: Questions 8.47 and 8.48.**

EXAMPLE 8.5   Calculating Both Hydronium and Hydroxide Ion Concentrations from pH

Calculate the $[H_3O^+]$ and $[OH^-]$ of a sodium hydroxide solution with a pH = 10.00.

LEARNING GOAL

5 ▶ Calculate hydronium and/or hydroxide ion concentration from pH data.

Solution

Step 1. First, calculate $[H_3O^+]$ using our expression for pH:

$$pH = -\log [H_3O^+]$$
$$10.00 = -\log [H_3O^+]$$
$$-10.00 = \log [H_3O^+]$$
$$\text{antilog } -10.00 = [H_3O^+]$$
$$1.0 \times 10^{-10} \, M = [H_3O^+]$$

Step 2. To calculate the $[OH^-]$, we need to solve for $[OH^-]$ by using the following expression:

$$K_w = [H_3O^+][OH^-] = 1.0 \times 10^{-14}$$
$$[OH^-] = \frac{1.0 \times 10^{-14}}{[H_3O^+]}$$

Step 3. Substituting the $[H_3O^+]$ from the first step, we have

$$[OH^-] = \frac{1.0 \times 10^{-14}}{1.0 \times 10^{-10}}$$
$$= 1.0 \times 10^{-4} \, M$$

Practice Problem 8.5

Calculate the $[H_3O^+]$ and $[OH^-]$ of a potassium hydroxide solution with a pH = 8.00.

▶ **For Further Practice: Questions 8.49 and 8.50.**

Often, the pH or $[H_3O^+]$ will not be a whole number (pH = 1.5, pH = 5.3, $[H_3O^+] = 1.5 \times 10^{-3}$ and so forth). With the advent of inexpensive and versatile calculators, calculations with noninteger numbers pose no great problems. Consider Examples 8.6 and 8.7.

LEARNING GOAL

4 ▶ Calculate pH from concentration data.

EXAMPLE 8.6   Calculating pH with Noninteger Numbers

Calculate the pH of a sample of lake water that has a $[H_3O^+] = 6.5 \times 10^{-5}\ M$.

Solution

Step 1. Use the expression for pH:

$$pH = -\log[H_3O^+]$$

Step 2. Substituting

$$pH = -\log[6.5 \times 10^{-5}]$$
$$= 4.19$$

Note: The pH, 4.19, is low enough to suspect acid rain. (See Green Chemistry: Acid Rain in this chapter.)

Practice Problem 8.6

Calculate the pH of a sample of blood that has a $[H_3O^+] = 3.3 \times 10^{-8}\ M$.

▶ **For Further Practice: Questions 8.61 and 8.62.**

LEARNING GOAL

5 ▶ Calculate hydronium and/or hydroxide ion concentration from pH data.

EXAMPLE 8.7   Calculating [H₃O⁺] from pH

The measured pH of a sample of lake water is 6.40. Calculate $[H_3O^+]$.

Solution

Step 1. An alternative mathematical form of

$$pH = -\log[H_3O^+]$$

is the expression

$$[H_3O^+] = 10^{-pH}$$

Step 2. We can use this expression to solve for $[H_3O^+]$.

$$[H_3O^+] = 10^{-6.40}$$

Step 3. Performing the calculation on your calculator results in 3.98×10^{-7} or $4.0 \times 10^{-7}\ M = [H_3O^+]$.

Practice Problem 8.7

a. Calculate the $[H_3O^+]$ corresponding to pH = 8.50.
b. Calculate the $[H_3O^+]$ corresponding to pH = 4.50.

▶ **For Further Practice: Questions 8.57 and 8.58.**

Examples 8.2–8.7 illustrate the most frequently used pH calculations. It is important to remember that in the case of a base you must convert the $[OH^-]$ to $[H_3O^+]$, using the expression for the ion product for the solvent, water. It is also useful to be aware of the following:

- The pH of a 1 *M* solution of any strong acid is 0.
- The pH of a 1 *M* solution of any strong base is 14.
- Each tenfold change in concentration changes the pH by one unit. A tenfold change in concentration is equivalent to moving the decimal point one place.

- A *decrease* in acid concentration *increases* the pH.
- A *decrease* in base concentration *decreases* the pH.

Question 8.5 Calculate the [OH⁻] of the solution in Example 8.2.

Question 8.6 Calculate the [OH⁻] of the solution in Example 8.3.

The Importance of pH and pH Control

Solution pH and pH control play a major role in many facets of our lives. Consider a few examples:

- *Agriculture:* Crops grow best in a soil of proper pH. Proper fertilization involves the maintenance of a suitable pH.
- *Physiology:* If the pH of our blood were to shift by one unit, we would die. Many biochemical reactions in living organisms are extremely pH dependent.
- *Industry:* From manufacture of processed foods to the manufacture of automobiles, industrial processes often require rigorous pH control.
- *Municipal services:* Purification of drinking water and treatment of sewage must be carried out at their optimum pH.
- *Acid rain:* Nitric acid and sulfuric acid, resulting largely from the reaction of components of vehicle emissions and electric power generation (nitrogen and sulfur oxides) with water, are carried down by precipitation and enter aquatic systems (lakes and streams), lowering the pH of the water. A less than optimum pH poses serious problems for native fish populations.

The list could continue on for many pages. However, in summary, any change that takes place in aqueous solution generally has at least some pH dependence.

LEARNING GOAL

6 ▶ Provide examples of the importance of pH in chemical and biochemical systems.

See Green Chemistry: Acid Rain in this chapter.

A Medical Perspective

Drug Delivery

When a doctor prescribes medicine to treat a disease or relieve its symptoms, the medication may be administered in a variety of ways. Drugs may be taken orally, injected into a muscle or a vein, or absorbed through the skin. Specific instructions are often provided to regulate the particular combination of drugs that can or cannot be taken. The diet, both before and during the drug therapy, may be of special importance.

To appreciate why drugs are administered in a specific way, it is necessary to understand a few basic facts about medications and how they interact with the body.

Drugs function by undergoing one or more chemical reactions in the body. Few compounds react in only one way, to produce a limited set of products, even in the simple environment of a beaker or flask. Imagine the number of possible reactions that a drug can undergo in a complex chemical factory like the human body. In many cases a drug can react in a variety of ways other than its intended path. These alternative paths are side reactions, sometimes producing *side effects* such as nausea, vomiting, insomnia, or drowsiness. Side effects may be unpleasant and may actually interfere with the primary function of the drug.

The development of safe, effective medication, with minimal side effects, is a slow and painstaking process, and determining the best drug delivery system is a critical step. For example, a drug that undergoes an unwanted side reaction in an acidic solution would not be very effective if administered orally. The acidic digestive fluids in the stomach could prevent the drug from even reaching the intended organ, let alone retaining its potency. The drug could be administered through a vein into the blood; blood is not acidic, in contrast to digestive fluids. In this way the drug may be delivered intact to the intended site in the body, where it is free to undergo its primary reaction.

Drug delivery has become a science in its own right. Pharmacology, the study of drugs and their uses in the treatment of disease, has a goal of creating drugs that are highly selective. In other words, they will undergo only one reaction, the intended reaction. Encapsulation of drugs, enclosing them within larger molecules or collections of molecules, may protect them from unwanted reactions as they are transported to their intended site.

8.3 Reactions Between Acids and Bases

Neutralization

The reaction of an acid with a base to produce a salt and water is referred to as **neutralization**. In the strictest sense, neutralization requires equal numbers of moles (mol) of H_3O^+ and OH^- to produce a neutral solution (no excess acid or base).

Consider the reaction of a solution of hydrochloric acid and sodium hydroxide:

$$HCl(aq) + NaOH(aq) \longrightarrow NaCl(aq) + H_2O(l)$$

Acid   Base   Salt   Water

Equation balancing is discussed in Chapter 4.

Our objective is to make the balanced equation represent the process actually occurring. We recognize that HCl, NaOH, and NaCl are dissociated in solution:

$$H^+(aq) + Cl^-(aq) + Na^+(aq) + OH^-(aq) \longrightarrow Na^+(aq) + Cl^-(aq) + H_2O(l)$$

We also know that Na^+ and Cl^- are unchanged in the reaction; they are termed *spectator ions*. If we write only those components that actually change, ignoring the spectator ions, we produce a *net, balanced ionic equation:*

$$H^+(aq) + OH^-(aq) \longrightarrow H_2O(l)$$

Writing Net Ionic Equations

If we realize that the H^+ occurs in aqueous solution as the hydronium ion, H_3O^+, the most correct form of the net, balanced ionic equation is

$$H_3O^+(aq) + OH^-(aq) \longrightarrow 2H_2O(l)$$

The equation for any strong acid/strong base neutralization reaction is the same as this equation.

A neutralization reaction may be used to determine the concentration of an unknown acid or base solution. The technique of **titration** involves the addition of measured amounts of a **standard solution** (one whose concentration is known with certainty) to neutralize the second, unknown solution. From the volumes of the two solutions and the concentration of the standard solution, the concentration of the unknown solution may be determined.

Animations
• The Neutralization Reaction of NaOH and HCl
• Titration of HCl with NaOH

A strategy for carrying out an acid-base titration is summarized in Table 8.1. The calculations involved in an acid-base titration are illustrated in Example 8.8.

Table 8.1 Conducting an Acid-Base Titration

1. A known volume, perhaps 25.00 milliliters (mL), of the unknown acid of unknown concentration is measured into a flask using a pipet.

2. An **indicator,** a substance that changes color as the solution reaches a certain pH (Figure 8.5), is added to the unknown solution. We must know, from prior experience, the expected pH at the equivalence point (see step 4). For this titration, phenolphthalein or phenol red would be a logical choice, since the equivalence-point pH is known to be seven.

3. A solution of sodium hydroxide, perhaps 0.1000 *M*, is carefully added to the unknown solution using a **buret** (Figure 8.6), which is a long glass tube calibrated in mL. A stopcock at the bottom of the buret regulates the amount of liquid dispensed. The standard solution is added until the indicator changes color.

4. At this point, the **equivalence point,** the number of mol of hydroxide ion added is equal to the number of mol of hydronium ion present in the unknown acid. The solution is neutral, with a pH equal to seven.

5. The volume dispensed by the buret, perhaps 35.00 mL, is measured.

6. Using the data from the experiment (volume of the unknown, volume of the titrant, and molarity of the titrant), calculate the molar concentration of the unknown substance.

Phenol red is yellow in acid solution and turns red after all acid is neutralized. Phenolphthalein is colorless in acid solution and turns pink after all acid is neutralized (Figure 8.5).

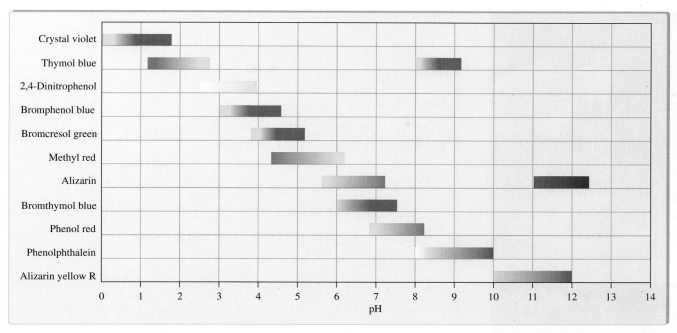

Figure 8.5 The relationship between pH and color of a variety of compounds, some of which are commonly used as acid-base indicators. Many indicators are naturally occurring substances.

EXAMPLE 8.8   **Determining the Concentration of a Solution of Hydrochloric Acid**

A 25.00-mL sample of an acid of unknown concentration was transferred to a flask, a few drops of the indicator phenolphthalein were added, and the resulting solution was titrated with 0.1000 *M* sodium hydroxide solution. After 35.00 mL of sodium hydroxide solution were added, the indicator turned pink, signaling the chemist that the unknown and titrant had reached their equivalence point. Calculate the *M* of the acid.

LEARNING GOAL

7 ▶ Describe the meaning and utility of neutralization reactions.

Solution

Step 1. Pertinent information for this titration includes:

Volume of the unknown acid solution, 25.00 mL

Volume of sodium hydroxide solution added, 35.00 mL

Concentration of the sodium hydroxide solution, 0.1000 *M*

Step 2. From the balanced equation, we know that 1 mol of HCl will react with 1 mol of NaOH:

$$HCl(aq) + NaOH(aq) \longrightarrow NaCl(aq) + H_2O(l)$$

Note: The net, balanced, ionic equation for this reaction provides the same information; 1 mol of H_3O^+ reacts with 1 mol of OH^-.

$$H_3O^+(aq) + OH^-(aq) \longrightarrow 2H_2O(l)$$

Step 3. Using a strategy involving conversion factors

$$35.00 \text{ mL NaOH} \times \frac{1 \text{ L NaOH}}{10^3 \text{ mL NaOH}} \times \frac{0.1000 \text{ mol NaOH}}{1 \text{ L NaOH}} = 3.500 \times 10^{-3} \text{ mol NaOH}$$

Continued—

(a)

(b)

Figure 8.6 An acid-base titration. (a) An exact volume of a standard solution (in this example, a base) is added to a solution of unknown concentration (in this example, an acid). (b) From the volume (read from the buret) and concentration of the standard solution, coupled with the mass or volume of the unknown, the concentration of the unknown may be calculated.

Step 4. Knowing that HCl and NaOH undergo a 1:1 reaction,

$$3.500 \times 10^{-3} \, \text{mol NaOH} \times \frac{1 \, \text{mol HCl}}{1 \, \text{mol NaOH}} = 3.500 \times 10^{-3} \, \text{mol HCl}$$

3.500×10^{-3} mol HCl are contained in 25.00 mL of HCl solution.

Step 5. Thus,

$$\frac{3.500 \times 10^{-3} \, \text{mol HCl}}{25.00 \, \text{mL HCl soln}} \times \frac{10^3 \, \text{mL HCl soln}}{1 \, \text{L HCl soln}} = 1.400 \times 10^{-1} \, \text{mol HCl/L HCl soln}$$

$$= 0.1400 \, M$$

The titration of an acid with a base is depicted in Figure 8.6.

Note: An alternate problem-solving strategy produces the same result:

$$(M_{\text{acid}})(V_{\text{acid}}) = (M_{\text{base}})(V_{\text{base}})$$

and

$$M_{\text{acid}} = M_{\text{base}}\left(\frac{V_{\text{base}}}{V_{\text{acid}}}\right)$$

$$M_{\text{acid}} = (0.1000 \, M)\left(\frac{35.00 \, \text{mL}}{25.00 \, \text{mL}}\right)$$

$$M_{\text{acid}} = 0.1400 \, M$$

Practice Problem 8.8

a. Calculate the molar concentration of a sodium hydroxide solution if 40.00 mL of this solution were required to neutralize 20.00 mL of a 0.2000 M solution of hydrochloric acid.
b. Calculate the molar concentration of a sodium hydroxide solution if 36.00 mL of this solution were required to neutralize 25.00 mL of a 0.2000 M solution of hydrochloric acid.

▶ **For Further Practice: Questions 8.71 and 8.72.**

Polyprotic Substances

Not all acid-base reactions occur in a 1:1 combining ratio (as hydrochloric acid and sodium hydroxide in Example 8.8). Acid-base reactions with other than 1:1 combining ratios occur between what are termed *polyprotic substances*. **Polyprotic substances** donate (as acids) or accept (as bases) more than one proton per formula unit.

Reactions of Polyprotic Substances

HCl dissociates to produce one H^+ ion for each HCl. For this reason, it is termed a *monoprotic acid.* Its reaction with sodium hydroxide is:

$$HCl(aq) + NaOH(aq) \longrightarrow H_2O(l) + Na^+(aq) + Cl^-(aq)$$

Sulfuric acid, in contrast, is a *diprotic acid.* Each unit of H_2SO_4 produces two H^+ ions (the prefix *di-* indicating two). Its reaction with sodium hydroxide is:

$$H_2SO_4(aq) + 2NaOH(aq) \longrightarrow 2H_2O(l) + 2Na^+(aq) + SO_4^{2-}(aq)$$

Phosphoric acid is a *triprotic acid.* Each unit of H_3PO_4 produces three H^+ ions. Its reaction with sodium hydroxide is:

$$H_3PO_4(aq) + 3NaOH(aq) \longrightarrow 3H_2O(l) + 3Na^+(aq) + PO_4^{3-}(aq)$$

Green Chemistry

Acid Rain

Acid rain is a global environmental problem that has raised public awareness of the chemicals polluting the air through the activities of our industrial society. Normal rain has a pH of about 5.6 as a result of the chemical reaction between carbon dioxide gas and water in the atmosphere. The following equation shows this reaction:

$$CO_2(g) \quad + \quad H_2O(l) \rightleftharpoons \quad H_2CO_3(aq)$$
Carbon dioxide   Water   Carbonic acid

Acid rain refers to conditions that are much more acidic than this. In upstate New York, the rain has as much as twenty-five times the acidity of normal rainfall. One rainstorm, recorded in West Virginia, produced rainfall that measured 1.5 on the pH scale. This is approximately the pH of stomach acid or about ten thousand times more acidic than "normal rain" (remember that the pH scale is logarithmic; a 1 pH unit decrease represents a tenfold increase in hydronium ion concentration).

Acid rain is destroying life in streams and lakes. More than half the highland lakes in the western Adirondack Mountains have no native game fish. In addition to these 300 lakes, 140 lakes in Ontario have suffered a similar fate. It is estimated that 48,000 other lakes in Ontario and countless others in the northeastern and central United States are threatened. Our forests are endangered as well. The acid rain decreases soil pH, which in turn alters the solubility of minerals needed by plants. Studies have shown that about 40% of the red spruce and maple trees in New England have died. Increased acidity of rainfall appears to be the major culprit.

What is the cause of this acid rain? The combustion of fossil fuels (gas, oil, and coal) by power plants produces oxides of sulfur and nitrogen. Nitrogen oxides, in excess of normal levels, arise mainly from conversion of atmospheric nitrogen to nitrogen oxides in the engines of gasoline and diesel powered vehicles. Sulfur oxides result from the oxidation of sulfur in fossil fuels. The sulfur atoms were originally a part of the amino acids and proteins of plants and animals that became, over the millenia, our fuel. These react with water, as does the CO_2 in normal rain, but the products are strong acids: sulfuric and nitric acids. Let's look at the equations for these processes.

In the atmosphere, nitric oxide (NO) can react with oxygen to produce nitrogen dioxide as shown:

$$2NO(g) + O_2(g) \longrightarrow 2NO_2(g)$$
Nitric oxide   Oxygen   Nitrogen dioxide

Nitrogen dioxide (which causes the brown color of smog) then reacts with water to form nitric acid:

$$3NO_2(g) + H_2O(l) \longrightarrow 2HNO_3(aq) + NO(g)$$

A similar chemistry is seen with the sulfur oxides. Coal may contain as much as 3% sulfur. When the coal is burned, the sulfur also burns. This produces choking, acrid sulfur dioxide gas:

$$S(s) + O_2(g) \longrightarrow SO_2(g)$$

By itself, sulfur dioxide can cause serious respiratory problems for people with asthma or other lung diseases, but matters are worsened by the reaction of SO_2 with atmospheric oxygen:

$$2SO_2(g) + O_2(g) \longrightarrow 2SO_3(g)$$

Sulfur trioxide will react with water in the atmosphere:

$$SO_3(g) + H_2O(l) \longrightarrow H_2SO_4(aq)$$

The product, sulfuric acid, is even more irritating to the respiratory tract. When the acid rain created by the reactions shown above falls to earth, the impact is significant.

It is easy to balance these chemical equations, but decades could be required to balance the ecological systems that we have disrupted by our massive consumption of fossil fuels. A sudden decrease of even 25% in the use of fossil fuels would lead to worldwide financial chaos. Development of alternative fuel sources, such as solar energy and safe nuclear power, will help to reduce our dependence on fossil fuels and help us to balance the global equation.

For Further Understanding

▶ Criticize this statement: "Passing and enforcing strong legislation against sulfur and nitrogen oxide emission will solve the problem of acid rain in the United States."

▶ Research the literature to determine the percentage of electricity that is produced from coal in your state of residence.

pH Values for a Variety of Substances Compared with the pH of Acid Rain

Indicates the range of pH values ascribed to acid rain

Damage caused by acid rain.

Dissociation of Polyprotic Substances

Sulfuric acid, and other diprotic acids, dissociate in two steps:

Step 1. $H_2SO_4(aq) + H_2O(l) \longrightarrow H_3O^+(aq) + HSO_4^-(aq)$

Step 2. $HSO_4^-(aq) + H_2O(l) \rightleftarrows H_3O^+(aq) + SO_4^{2-}(aq)$

Notice that H_2SO_4 behaves as a strong acid (step 1) and HSO_4^- behaves as a weak acid, indicated by a double arrow (step 2).

Phosphoric acid dissociates in three steps, all forms behaving as weak acids.

Step 1. $H_3PO_4(aq) + H_2O(l) \rightleftarrows H_3O^+(aq) + H_2PO_4^-(aq)$

Step 2. $H_2PO_4^-(aq) + H_2O(l) \rightleftarrows H_3O^+(aq) + HPO_4^{2-}(aq)$

Step 3. $HPO_4^{2-}(aq) + H_2O(l) \rightleftarrows H_3O^+(aq) + PO_4^{3-}(aq)$

Bases exhibit this property as well.

NaOH produces one OH^- ion per formula unit:

$$NaOH(aq) \longrightarrow Na^+(aq) + OH^-(aq)$$

$Ba(OH)_2$, barium hydroxide, produces two OH^- ions per formula unit:

$$Ba(OH)_2(aq) \longrightarrow Ba^{2+}(aq) + 2OH^-(aq)$$

8.4 Acid-Base Buffers

A **buffer solution** contains components that enable the solution to resist large changes in pH when either acids or bases are added. Buffer solutions may be prepared in the laboratory to maintain optimum conditions for a chemical reaction. Buffers are routinely used in commercial products to maintain optimum conditions for product behavior.

Buffer solutions also occur naturally. Blood, for example, is a complex natural buffer solution maintaining a pH of approximately 7.4, optimum for oxygen transport. The major buffering agent in blood is the mixture of carbonic acid (H_2CO_3) and bicarbonate ions (HCO_3^-).

The color of the petals of the hydrangea is formed by molecules that behave as acid-base indicators. The color is influenced by the pH of the soil in which the hydrangea is grown. The plant (a) was grown in soil with lower pH (more acidic) than plant (b).

(a)

(b)

The Buffer Process

The basis of buffer action is the establishment of an equilibrium between either a weak acid and its conjugate base or a weak base and its conjugate acid. Let's consider the case of a weak acid and its salt.

A common buffer solution may be prepared from acetic acid (CH_3COOH) and sodium acetate (CH_3COONa). Sodium acetate is a salt that is the source of the conjugate base CH_3COO^-. An *equilibrium* is established in solution between the weak acid and the conjugate base.

We ignore Na^+ in the description of the buffer. Na^+ does not actively participate in the reaction.

$$CH_3COOH(aq) + H_2O(l) \rightleftharpoons H_3O^+(aq) + CH_3COO^-(aq)$$

Acetic acid   Water   Hydronium ion   Acetate ion
(weak acid)   (conjugate base)

The acetate ion is the conjugate base of acetic acid.

A buffer solution functions in accordance with LeChatelier's principle, which states that an equilibrium system, when stressed, will shift its equilibrium position to relieve that stress. This principle is illustrated by the following examples.

Addition of Base or Acid to a Buffer Solution

Addition of a basic substance to our buffer solution causes the following changes.

- OH^- from the base reacts with H_3O^+, producing water.
- Molecular acetic acid *dissociates* to replace the H_3O^+ consumed by the base, maintaining the pH close to the initial level.

This is an example of LeChatelier's principle, because the loss of H_3O^+ (the *stress*) is compensated for by the dissociation of acetic acid to produce more H_3O^+.

Addition of an acidic solution to a buffer results in the following changes.

- H_3O^+ from the acid increases the overall $[H_3O^+]$.
- The system reacts to this stress, in accordance with LeChatelier's principle, to form more molecular acetic acid; the acetate ion combines with H_3O^+. Thus, the H_3O^+ concentration and therefore, the pH, remain close to the initial level.

These effects may be summarized as follows:

Animation
- Effect of Addition of a Strong Acid and a Strong Base on a Buffer

$$CH_3COOH(aq) + H_2O(l) \rightleftharpoons H_3O^+(aq) + CH_3COO^-(aq)$$

OH^- added, equilibrium position shifts to the right $\longrightarrow$

$\longleftarrow$ H_3O^+ added, equilibrium position shifts to the left

Buffer Capacity

Buffer capacity is a measure of the ability of a solution to resist large changes in pH when a strong acid or strong base is added. More specifically, buffer capacity is described as the amount of strong acid or strong base that a buffer can neutralize without significantly changing its pH. Buffering capacity against base is a function of the concentration of the weak acid (in this case, CH_3COOH). Buffering capacity against acid is dependent on the concentration of the anion of the salt, the conjugate base (CH_3COO^- in this example). Buffer solutions are often designed to have identical buffer capacity for both acids and bases. This is achieved when, in the above example, $[CH_3COO^-]/[CH_3COOH] = 1$. As an added bonus, making the $[CH_3COO^-]$ and $[CH_3COOH]$ as large as is practical ensures a high buffer capacity for both added acid and added base.

Question 8.7 Explain how the molar concentration of H_2CO_3 in the blood would change if the partial pressure of CO_2 in the lungs were to increase. (Refer to A Medical Perspective: Control of Blood pH on page 273.)

Question 8.8 Explain how the molar concentration of H_2CO_3 in the blood would change if the partial pressure of CO_2 in the lungs were to decrease. (Refer to A Medical Perspective: Control of Blood pH on page 273.)

Question 8.9 Explain how the molar concentration of hydronium ion in the blood would change under each of the conditions described in Questions 8.7 and 8.8.

Commercial products that claim improved function owing to their ability to control pH. Can you name other products whose performance is pH dependent?

Question 8.10 Explain how the pH of blood would change under each of the conditions described in Questions 8.7 and 8.8.

Preparation of a Buffer Solution

It is useful to understand how to prepare a buffer solution and how to determine the pH of the resulting solution. Many chemical reactions produce the largest amount of product only when they are run at an optimal, constant pH. The study of biologically important processes in the laboratory often requires conditions that approximate the composition of biological fluids. A constant pH would certainly be essential.

The buffer process is an equilibrium reaction and is described by an equilibrium constant expression. For acids, the equilibrium constant is represented as K_a, the subscript a implying an acid equilibrium. For example, the acetic acid/sodium acetate system is described by

$$CH_3COOH(aq) + H_2O(l) \rightleftharpoons H_3O^+(aq) + CH_3COO^-(aq)$$

and

$$K_a = \frac{[H_3O^+][CH_3COO^-]}{[CH_3COOH]}$$

Using a few mathematical maneuvers we can turn this equilibrium constant expression into one that will allow us to calculate the pH of the buffer if we know how much acid (acetic acid) and salt (sodium acetate) are present in a known volume of the solution.

First, multiply both sides of the equation by the concentration of acetic acid, [CH_3COOH]. This will eliminate the denominator on the right side of the equation.

$$[CH_3COOH]K_a = \frac{[H_3O^+][CH_3COO^-]\cancel{[CH_3COOH]}}{\cancel{[CH_3COOH]}}$$

or

$$[CH_3COOH]K_a = [H_3O^+][CH_3COO^-]$$

Now, dividing both sides of the equation by the acetate ion concentration [CH_3COO^-] will give us an expression for the hydronium ion concentration [H_3O^+]

$$\frac{[CH_3COOH]K_a}{[CH_3COO^-]} = [H_3O^+]$$

The calculation of pH from [H₃O⁺] is discussed in Section 8.2.

Once we know the value for [H_3O^+], we can easily find the pH. To use this equation:

- assume that [CH_3COOH] represents the concentration of the acid component of the buffer.
- assume that [CH_3COO^-] represents the concentration of the conjugate base (principally from the dissociation of the salt, sodium acetate) component of the buffer.

$$\frac{[CH_3COOH]K_a}{[CH_3COO^-]} = [H_3O^+]$$

$$\frac{[acid]K_a}{[conjugate\ base]} = [H_3O^+]$$

Let's look at examples of practical applications of this equation.

EXAMPLE 8.9 Calculating the pH of a Buffer Solution

Calculate the pH of a buffer solution in which both the acetic acid and sodium acetate concentrations are 1.0×10^{-1} M. The equilibrium constant, K_a, for acetic acid is 1.8×10^{-5}.

LEARNING GOAL

8 ▶ Describe the applications of buffers to chemical and biochemical systems, particularly blood chemistry.

Solution

Step 1. Acetic acid is the acid; [acid] $= 1.0 \times 10^{-1}$ M

Sodium acetate is the salt, furnishing the conjugate base; [conjugate base] $= 1.0 \times 10^{-1}$ M

Step 2. The equilibrium is

$$\underset{\text{acid}}{CH_3COOH(aq)} + H_2O(l) \rightleftharpoons H_3O^+(aq) + \underset{\text{conjugate base}}{CH_3COO^-(aq)}$$

Step 3. The hydronium ion concentration is expressed as

$$[H_3O^+] = \frac{[acid]K_a}{[conjugate\ base]}$$

Step 4. Substituting the values given in the problem

$$[H_3O^+] = \frac{[1.0 \times 10^{-1}]1.8 \times 10^{-5}}{[1.0 \times 10^{-1}]}$$

$$[H_3O^+] = 1.8 \times 10^{-5}$$

Step 5. Now we can substitute in our expression for pH:

$$pH = -\log[H_3O^+]$$
$$pH = -\log 1.8 \times 10^{-5}$$
$$= 4.74$$

The pH of the buffer solution is 4.74.

Practice Problem 8.9

A buffer solution is prepared in such a way that the concentrations of propanoic acid and sodium propanoate are each 2.00×10^{-1} M. If the buffer equilibrium is described by

$$\underset{\text{Propanoic acid}}{C_2H_5COOH(aq)} + H_2O(l) \rightleftharpoons H_3O^+(aq) + \underset{\text{Propanoate anion}}{C_2H_5COO^-(aq)}$$

with $K_a = 1.34 \times 10^{-5}$, calculate the pH of the solution.

▶ **For Further Practice: Questions 8.81 and 8.82.**

EXAMPLE 8.10 Calculating the pH of a Buffer Solution

Calculate the pH of a buffer solution similar to that described in Example 8.9 except that the acid concentration is doubled, while the salt concentration remains the same.

LEARNING GOAL

8 ▶ Describe the applications of buffers to chemical and biochemical systems, particularly blood chemistry.

Solution

Step 1. Acetic acid is the acid; [acid] $= 2.0 \times 10^{-1}$ M (remember, the acid concentration is twice that of Example 8.9; $2 \times [1.0 \times 10^{-1}] = 2.0 \times 10^{-1}$ M

Sodium acetate is the salt, furnishing the conjugate base; [conjugate base] $= 1.0 \times 10^{-1}$ M

Continued—

Step 2. The equilibrium is

$$CH_3COOH(aq) + H_2O(l) \rightleftharpoons H_3O^+(aq) + CH_3COO^-(aq)$$

acid   conjugate base

Step 3. The hydronium ion concentration is expressed as,

$$[H_3O^+] = \frac{[acid]K_a}{[conjugate\ base]}$$

Step 4. Substituting the values given in the problem

$$[H_3O^+] = \frac{[2.0 \times 10^{-1}]1.8 \times 10^{-5}}{[1.00 \times 10^{-1}]}$$

$$[H_3O^+] = 3.60 \times 10^{-5}$$

Step 5. Now we can substitute in our expression for pH:

$$pH = -\log[H_3O^+]$$
$$pH = -\log 3.60 \times 10^{-5}$$
$$= 4.44$$

The pH of the buffer solution is 4.44.

Practice Problem 8.10

Calculate the pH of the buffer solution in Practice Problem 8.9 if the concentration of the sodium propanoate were doubled while the acid concentration remained the same.

▶ **For Further Practice: Questions 8.85 and 8.86.**

A comparison of the two solutions described in Examples 8.9 and 8.10 demonstrates a buffer solution's most significant attribute: the ability to stabilize pH. Although the acid concentration of these solutions differs by a factor of two, the difference in their pH is only 0.30 units.

The Henderson-Hasselbalch Equation

The solution of the equilibrium constant expression and the pH are sometimes combined into one operation. The combined expression is termed the **Henderson-Hasselbalch equation.**

For the acetic acid/sodium acetate buffer system,

$$CH_3COOH(aq) + H_2O(l) \rightleftharpoons H_3O^+(aq) + CH_3COO^-(aq)$$

$$K_a = \frac{[H_3O^+][CH_3COO^-]}{[CH_3COOH]}$$

Taking the $-\log$ of both sides of the equation:

$$-\log K_a = -\log[H_3O^+] - \log\frac{[CH_3COO^-]}{[CH_3COOH]}$$

$$pK_a = pH - \log\frac{[CH_3COO^-]}{[CH_3COOH]}$$

$pK_a = -\log K_a$, analogous to $pH = -\log[H_3O^+]$.

the Henderson-Hasselbalch expression is:

$$pH = pK_a + \log\frac{[CH_3COO^-]}{[CH_3COOH]}$$

The form of this equation is especially amenable to buffer problem calculations. In this expression, [CH_3COOH] represents the molar concentration of the

A Medical Perspective

Control of Blood pH

A pH of 7.4 is maintained in blood partly by a carbonic acid–bicarbonate buffer system based on the following equilibrium:

$$H_2CO_3(aq) + H_2O(l) \rightleftharpoons H_3O^+(aq) + HCO_3^-(aq)$$

Carbonic acid   Bicarbonate ion
(weak acid)   (salt)

The regulation process based on LeChatelier's principle is similar to the acetic acid–sodium acetate buffer, which we have already discussed.

Red blood cells transport O_2, bound to hemoglobin, to the cells of body tissue. The metabolic waste product, CO_2, is picked up by the blood and delivered to the lungs.

The CO_2 in the blood also participates in the carbonic acid–bicarbonate buffer equilibrium. Carbon dioxide reacts with water in the blood to form carbonic acid:

$$CO_2(aq) + H_2O(l) \rightleftharpoons H_2CO_3(aq)$$

As a result, the buffer equilibrium becomes more complex:

$$CO_2(aq) + 2H_2O(l) \rightleftharpoons H_2CO_3(aq) + H_2O(l) \rightleftharpoons H_3O^+(aq) + HCO_3^-(l)$$

Through this sequence of relationships the concentration of CO_2 in the blood affects the blood pH.

Higher than normal CO_2 concentrations shift the above equilibrium to the right (LeChatelier's principle), increasing $[H_3O^+]$ and lowering the pH. The blood becomes too acidic, leading to numerous medical problems. A situation of high blood CO_2 levels and low pH is termed *acidosis*. Respiratory acidosis results from various diseases (emphysema, pneumonia) that restrict the breathing process, causing the buildup of waste CO_2 in the blood.

Lower than normal CO_2 levels, on the other hand, shift the equilibrium to the left, decreasing $[H_3O^+]$ and making the pH more basic. This condition is termed *alkalosis* (from "alkali," implying basic). Hyperventilation, or rapid breathing, is a common cause of respiratory alkalosis.

For Further Understanding

▶ Write the Henderson-Hasselbalch expression for the equilibrium between carbonic acid and the bicarbonate ion.
▶ Calculate the $[HCO_3^-]/[H_2CO_3]$ that corresponds to a pH of 7.4. The K_a for carbonic acid is 4.2×10^{-7}.

---

weak acid and $[CH_3COO^-]$ is the molar concentration of the conjugate base of the weak acid. The generalized expression is:

$$pH = pK_a + \log \frac{[\text{conjugate base}]}{[\text{weak acid}]}$$

Substituting concentrations along with the value for the pK_a of the acid allows the calculation of the pH of the buffer solution in problems such as those shown in Examples 8.9 and 8.10.

Question 8.11 Solve the problem illustrated in Example 8.9 using the Henderson-Hasselbalch equation.

Question 8.12 Solve the problem illustrated in Example 8.10 using the Henderson-Hasselbalch equation.

Question 8.13 Solve Practice Problem 8.9 using the Henderson-Hasselbalch equation.

Question 8.14 Solve Practice Problem 8.10 using the Henderson-Hasselbalch equation.

8.5 Oxidation-Reduction Processes

Oxidation-reduction processes are responsible for many types of chemical change. Corrosion, the operation of a battery, and biochemical energy-harvesting reactions are a few examples. In this section we explore the basic concepts underlying this class of chemical reactions.

Oxidation and Reduction

Oxidation is defined as a loss of electrons, loss of hydrogen atoms, or gain of oxygen atoms.

Magnesium metal, is, for example, oxidized to a *Magnesium ion*, losing two electrons when it reacts with a nonmetal such as chlorine:

$$Mg \longrightarrow Mg^{2+} + 2e^-$$

Reduction is defined as a gain of electrons, gain of hydrogen atoms, or loss of oxygen atoms.

Diatomic chlorine is reduced to *chloride ions* by gaining electrons when it reacts with a metal such as magnesium:

$$Cl_2 + 2e^- \longrightarrow 2Cl^-$$

Oxidation and reduction are complementary processes. The *oxidation half-reaction* produces electrons that are the reactants for the *reduction half-reaction*. The combination of two half-reactions, one oxidation and one reduction, produces the complete reaction:

Oxidation half-reaction: $Mg \longrightarrow Mg^{2+} + 2e^-$

Reduction half-reaction: $Cl_2 + 2e^- \longrightarrow 2Cl^-$

Complete reaction: $Mg + Cl_2 \longrightarrow Mg^{2+} + 2Cl^-$

Half-reactions, one oxidation and one reduction, are exactly that: one-half of a complete reaction. The two half-reactions combine to produce the complete reaction. Note that the electrons cancel: in the electron transfer process, no free electrons remain.

In the preceding reaction, magnesium metal is the **reducing agent.** It releases electrons for the reduction of chlorine. Chlorine is the **oxidizing agent.** It accepts electrons from the magnesium, which is oxidized.

The characteristics of oxidizing and reducing agents may be summarized as follows:

Oxidizing Agent	**Reducing Agent**
• Is reduced	• Is oxidized
• Gains electrons	• Loses electrons
• Causes oxidation	• Causes reduction

Question 8.15 Write the oxidation half-reaction, the reduction half-reaction, and the complete reaction for the formation of calcium sulfide from the elements Ca and S.

Question 8.16 Write the oxidation half-reaction, the reduction half-reaction, and the complete reaction for the formation of calcium iodide from calcium metal and I_2. Remember, the electron gain *must* equal the electron loss.

Oxidation-reduction processes are more difficult to identify using half-reactions when covalent compounds are involved. For example, consider the reaction of methane with oxygen, discussed in Chapter 4:

$$CH_4(g) + 2O_2(g) \longrightarrow CO_2(g) + 2H_2O(g)$$

Animation
• Oxidation-Reduction Reactions

Oxidation-reduction reactions are often termed *redox reactions.*

The reducing agent becomes oxidized and the oxidizing agent becomes reduced.

A Medical Perspective

Oxidizing Agents for Chemical Control of Microbes

Before the twentieth century, hospitals were not particularly sanitary establishments. Refuse, including human waste, was disposed of on hospital grounds. Because many hospitals had no running water, physicians often cleaned their hands and instruments by wiping them on their lab coats and then proceeded to treat the next patient! As you can imagine, many patients died of infections in hospitals.

By the late nineteenth century a few physicians and microbiologists had begun to realize that infectious diseases are transmitted by microbes, including bacteria and viruses. To decrease the number of hospital-acquired infections, physicians like Joseph Lister and Ignatz Semmelweis experimented with chemicals and procedures that were designed to eliminate pathogens from environmental surfaces and from wounds.

Many common disinfectants and antiseptics are oxidizing agents. A disinfectant is a chemical that is used to kill or inhibit the growth of pathogens, disease-causing microorganisms, on environmental surfaces. An antiseptic is a milder chemical that is used to destroy pathogens associated with living tissue.

Hydrogen peroxide is an effective antiseptic that is commonly used to cleanse cuts and abrasions. We are all familiar with the furious bubbling that occurs as the enzyme catalase from our body cells catalyzes the breakdown of H_2O_2:

$$2H_2O_2(aq) \longrightarrow 2H_2O(l) + O_2(g)$$

A highly reactive and deadly form of oxygen, the superoxide radical (O_2^-), is produced during this reaction. This superoxide inactivates proteins, especially critical enzyme systems.

At higher concentrations (3–6%), H_2O_2 is used as a disinfectant. It is particularly useful for disinfection of soft contact lenses, utensils, and surgical implants because there is no residual toxicity. Concentrations of 6–25% are even used for complete sterilization of environmental surfaces.

Benzoyl peroxide is another powerful oxidizing agent. Ointments containing 5–10% benzoyl peroxide have been used as antibacterial agents to treat acne. The compound is currently found in over-the-counter facial scrubs because it is also an exfoliant, causing sloughing of old skin and replacement with smoother-looking skin. A word of caution is in order: in sensitive individuals, benzoyl peroxide can cause swelling and blistering of tender facial skin.

Chlorine is a very widely used disinfectant and antiseptic. Calcium hypochlorite [Ca(OCl)$_2$] was first used in hospital maternity wards in 1847 by the pioneering Hungarian physician Ignatz Semmelweis. Semmelweis insisted that hospital workers cleanse their hands in a Ca(OCl)$_2$ solution and dramatically reduced the incidence of infection. Today, calcium hypochlorite is more commonly used to disinfect bedding, clothing, restaurant eating utensils, slaughterhouses, barns, and dairies.

Sodium hypochlorite (NaOCl), sold as Clorox, is used as a household disinfectant and deodorant but is also used to disinfect swimming pools, dairies, food-processing equipment, and kidney dialysis units. It can be used to treat drinking water of questionable quality. Addition of 1/2 teaspoon (tsp) of household bleach (5.25% NaOCl) to 2 gallons (gal) of clear water

renders it drinkable after 1/2 hour (h). The Centers for Disease Control even recommend a 1:10 dilution of bleach as an effective disinfectant against human immunodeficiency virus, the virus that causes acquired immune deficiency syndrome (AIDS).

Chlorine gas (Cl$_2$) is used to disinfect swimming pool water, sewage, and municipal water supplies. This treatment has successfully eliminated epidemics of waterborne diseases. However, chlorine is inactivated in the presence of some organic materials and, in some cases, may form toxic chlorinated organic compounds. For these reasons, many cities are considering the use of ozone (O$_3$) rather than chlorine.

Ozone is produced from O$_2$ by high-voltage electrical discharges. (That fresh smell in the air after an electrical storm is ozone.) Several European cities use ozone to disinfect drinking water. It is a more effective killing agent than chlorine, especially with some viruses: less ozone is required for disinfection; there is no unpleasant residual odor or flavor; and there appear to be fewer toxic by-products. However, ozone is more expensive than chlorine, and maintaining the required concentration in the water is more difficult. Nonetheless, the benefits seem to outweigh the drawbacks, and many U.S. cities may soon follow the example of European cities and convert to the use of ozone for water treatment.

For Further Understanding

▶ Describe the difference between the terms *disinfectant* and *antiseptic*.

▶ Explain why hydrogen peroxide, at higher concentration, is used as a disinfectant, whereas lower concentrations are used as antiseptics.

Our alternate definitions of oxidation and reduction (p. 274) make it clear that this is an oxidation-reduction reaction. Carbon has lost hydrogen and gained oxygen, becoming CO_2 (our alternate definition of oxidation). Oxygen has gained hydrogen, becoming water (the gain of hydrogen indicates reduction).

Consider the reaction of aluminum with atmospheric oxygen:

$$4Al(s) + 3O_2(g) \longrightarrow 2Al_2O_3(s)$$

It is evident that aluminum has been oxidized because it gains oxygen atoms.

Applications of Oxidation and Reduction

Oxidation-reduction processes are important in many areas as diverse as industrial manufacturing and biochemical processes.

Corrosion

The deterioration of metals caused by an oxidation-reduction process is termed **corrosion.** Metal atoms are converted to metal ions; the structure, hence the properties, changes dramatically, and usually for the worse.

Millions of dollars are spent annually in an attempt to correct damage resulting from corrosion. A current area of chemical research is concerned with the development of corrosion-inhibiting processes. In one type of corrosion, elemental iron is oxidized to iron(III) oxide (rust):

$$4Fe(s) + 3O_2(g) \longrightarrow 2Fe_2O_3(s)$$

Aluminum is strong and its low density make it ideal for the wings and cabin exterior of airplanes. Aluminum oxide forms on the metal surface and this oxide coating protects the metal from further reaction.

LEARNING GOAL

9 ▶ Explain the meaning of the terms *oxidation* and *reduction*, and describe some practical examples of redox processes.

At the same time that iron is oxidized, O_2 is being reduced to O^{2-} and is incorporated into the structure of iron(III) oxide. Electrons lost by iron reduce oxygen. This again shows that oxidation and reduction processes go hand in hand.

<table>
<tr><td>(a)</td><td>(b)</td><td>(c)</td></tr>
</table>

The rust (an oxide of iron) that diminishes structural strength and ruins the appearance of (a) automobiles, (b) bridges, and (c) other iron-based objects is a product of a common oxidation-reduction reaction. Can you provide examples of other electron-transfer processes that produce changes in properties?

Combustion of Fossil Fuels

Burning fossil fuel is an extremely exothermic process. Energy is released to heat our homes, offices, and classrooms. The simplest fossil fuel is methane, CH_4, and its oxidation reaction is written:

$$CH_4(g) + 2O_2(g) \longrightarrow CO_2(g) + 2H_2O(g)$$

Methane is a hydrocarbon. The complete oxidation of any hydrocarbon (including those in gasoline, heating oil, liquid propane, and so forth) produces carbon dioxide and water. The energy released by these reactions is of paramount importance. The water and carbon dioxide are viewed as waste products, and the carbon dioxide contributes to the greenhouse effect (see Green Chemistry: The Greenhouse Effect and Global Climate Change on page 174).

Bleaching

Bleaching agents are most often oxidizing agents. Sodium hypochlorite (NaOCl) is the active ingredient in a variety of laundry products. It is an effective oxidizing agent. Products containing NaOCl are advertised for their stain-removing capabilities.

Stains are a result of colored compounds adhering to surfaces. Oxidation of these compounds produces products that are not colored or compounds that are subsequently easily removed from the surface, thus removing the stain.

Biological Processes

Respiration

There are many examples of biological oxidation-reduction reactions. For example, the electron-transport chain of aerobic respiration involves the reversible oxidation and reduction of iron atoms in cytochrome c,

See Chapters 21 and 22 for the details of these energy-harvesting cellular oxidation-reduction reactions.

$$\text{cytochrome } c \ (Fe^{3+}) + e^- \longrightarrow \text{cytochrome } c \ (Fe^{2+})$$

The reduced iron ion transfers an electron to an iron ion in another protein, called cytochrome c oxidase, according to the following reaction:

$$\text{cytochrome } c \ (Fe^{2+}) + \text{cytochrome } c \text{ oxidase } (Fe^{3+}) \longrightarrow \text{cytochrome } c \ (Fe^{3+}) + \text{cytochrome } c \text{ oxidase } (Fe^{2+})$$

Cytochrome c oxidase eventually passes four electrons to O_2, the final electron acceptor of the chain:

$$O_2 + 4e^- + 4H^+ \longrightarrow 2H_2O$$

Metabolism

When ethanol is metabolized in the liver, it is oxidized to acetaldehyde (the molecule partially responsible for hangovers). Continued oxidation of acetaldehyde produces acetic acid, which is eventually oxidized to CO_2 and H_2O. These reactions, summarized as follows, are catalyzed by liver enzymes.

$$CH_3CH_2-OH \longrightarrow \underset{\text{Acetaldehyde}}{CH_3\overset{\overset{\textstyle O}{\|}}{C}-H} \longrightarrow \underset{\text{Acetic acid}}{CH_3\overset{\overset{\textstyle O}{\|}}{C}-OH} \longrightarrow CO_2 + H_2O$$

Ethanol

It is more difficult to recognize these reactions as oxidations because neither the product nor the reactant carries a charge. In previous examples we looked for an increase in positive charge as an indication that an oxidation had occurred. A decrease in positive charge (or increased negative charge) would signify reduction.

Once again our alternative descriptions of oxidation and reduction are useful in identifying these reactions. Recall that:

Oxidation is the *gain* of oxygen or *loss* of hydrogen.
Reduction is the *loss* of oxygen or *gain* of hydrogen.

In the conversion of ethanol to acetaldehyde, ethanol has six hydrogen atoms per molecule; the product acetaldehyde has four hydrogen atoms per molecule. This represents a loss of two hydrogen atoms per molecule. Therefore, ethanol has been oxidized to acetaldehyde, based on the interpretation of the above-mentioned rules.

This strategy is most useful for recognizing oxidation and reduction of *organic compounds* and organic compounds of biological interest, *biochemical compounds.*

Organic compounds and their structures and reactivity are the focus of Chapters 10 through 15 and biochemical compounds are described in Chapters 16 through 23.

Voltaic Cells

LEARNING GOAL

10 ▶ Diagram a voltaic cell and describe its function.

Animations
• The Cu/Zn Voltaic Cell
• Operation of a Voltaic Cell

Recall that solutions of ionic salts are good conductors of electricity (Chapter 6).

When zinc metal is dipped into a copper(II) sulfate solution, zinc atoms are oxidized to zinc ions and copper(II) ions are reduced to copper metal, which deposits on the surface of the zinc metal (Figure 8.7). This reaction is summarized as follows:

$$\overbrace{Zn(s) + Cu^{2+}(aq) \longrightarrow Zn^{2+}(aq) + Cu(s)}$$

Oxidation/e^- loss (top curved arrow)

Reduction/e^- gain (bottom curved arrow)

In the reduction of aqueous copper(II) ions by zinc metal, electrons flow from the zinc rod directly to copper(II) ions in the solution. If electron transfer from the zinc rod to the copper ions in solution could be directed through an external electrical circuit, this spontaneous oxidation-reduction reaction could be used to produce an electrical current that could perform some useful function.

However, when zinc metal in one container is connected by a copper wire with a copper(II) sulfate solution in a separate container, no current flows through the wire. A complete, or continuous circuit is necessary for current to flow. To complete the circuit, we connect the two containers with a tube filled with a solution of an electrolyte such as potassium chloride. This tube is described as a *salt bridge*.

Current now flows through the external circuit (Figure 8.8). The device shown in Figure 8.8 is an example of a *voltaic cell*. A **voltaic cell** is an *electrochemical* cell that converts stored *chemical* energy into *electrical* energy.

This cell consists of two *half-cells*. The oxidation half-reaction occurs in one half-cell and the reduction half-reaction occurs in the other half-cell. The sum of the two half-cell reactions is the overall oxidation-reduction reaction that describes the cell. The electrode at which oxidation occurs is called the **anode,** and the electrode at which reduction occurs is the **cathode.** In the device shown in Figure 8.8, the zinc metal is the anode. At this electrode the zinc atoms are oxidized to zinc ions:

$$\text{Anode half-reaction: } Zn(s) \longrightarrow Zn^{2+}(aq) + 2e^-$$

Figure 8.7 The spontaneous reaction of zinc metal and Cu^{2+} ions is the basis of the cell depicted in Figure 8.8.

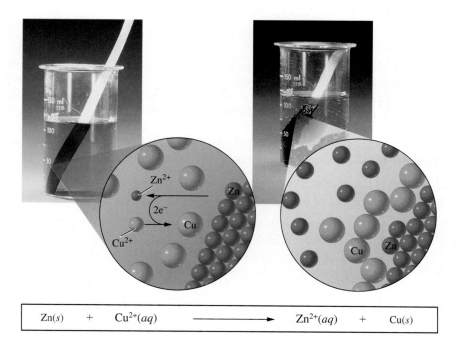

$$Zn(s) + Cu^{2+}(aq) \longrightarrow Zn^{2+}(aq) + Cu(s)$$

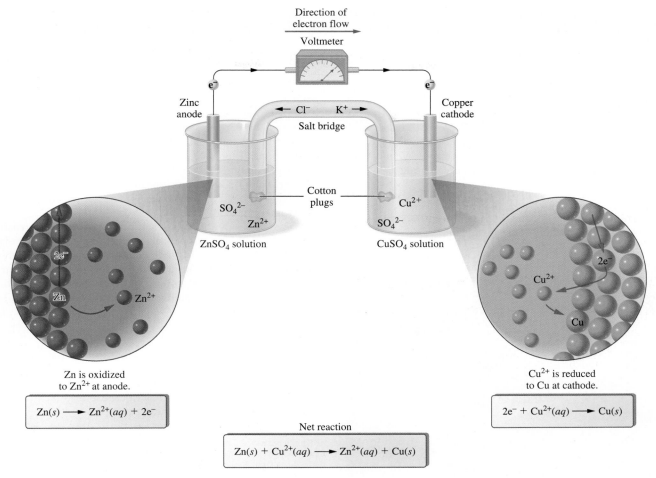

Figure 8.8 A voltaic cell generating electrical current by the reaction:

$$Zn(s) + Cu^{2+}(aq) \longrightarrow Zn^{2+}(aq) + Cu(s)$$

Each electrode consists of the pure metal, zinc or copper. Zinc is oxidized, releasing electrons that flow to the copper, reducing Cu^{2+} to Cu. The salt bridge completes the circuit and the voltmeter displays the voltage (or chemical potential) associated with the reaction.

Electrons released at the anode travel through the external circuit to the cathode (the copper rod) where they are transferred to copper(II) ions in the solution. Copper(II) ions are reduced to copper atoms that deposit on the copper metal surface, the cathode:

Cathode half-reaction: $Cu^{2+}(aq) + 2e^- \longrightarrow Cu(s)$

The sum of these half-cell reactions is the cell reaction:

$$Zn(s) + Cu^{2+}(aq) \longrightarrow Zn^{2+}(aq) + Cu(s)$$

Voltaic cells are found in many aspects of our lives, as those convenient and reliable sources of electrical energy, the battery. Batteries convert stored chemical energy to an electrical current to power a wide array of different commercial appliances: radios, portable televisions and computers, flashlights, and a host of other useful devices.

Technology has made modern batteries smaller, safer, and more dependable than our crudely constructed copper-zinc voltaic cell. In fact, the silver cell (Figure 8.9) is sufficiently safe and nontoxic that it can be implanted in the human body as a part of a pacemaker circuit that is used to improve heart rhythm.

Figure 8.9 A silver battery used in cameras, heart pacemakers, and hearing aids. This battery is small, stable, and nontoxic (hence implantable in the human body).

A Medical Perspective

Electrochemical Reactions in the Statue of Liberty and in Dental Fillings

Throughout history, we have suffered from our ignorance of basic electrochemical principles. For example, during the Middle Ages, our chemistry ancestors (alchemists) placed an iron rod into a blue solution of copper sulfate. They noticed that bright shiny copper plated out onto the iron rod and they thought that they had changed a base metal, iron, into copper. What actually happened was the redox reaction shown in Equation 1.

$$2Fe(s) + 3Cu^{2+}(aq) \longrightarrow 2Fe^{3+}(aq) + 3Cu(s) \qquad (1)$$

This misunderstanding encouraged them to embark on a futile, 1000-year attempt to change base metals into gold.

Statue of Liberty redox reaction.

Over 100 years ago, France presented the United States with the Statue of Liberty. Unfortunately, the French did not anticipate the redox reaction shown in Equation 1 when they mounted the copper skin of the statue on iron support rods. Oxygen in the atmosphere oxidized the copper skin to produce copper ions. Then, because iron is more reactive than copper, the displacement shown in Equation 1 aided the corrosion of the support bars. As a result of this and other reactions, the statue needed refurbishing before we celebrated its one-hundredth anniversary in 1986.

Sometimes dentists also overlook possible redox reactions when placing gold caps over teeth next to teeth with amalgam fillings. The amalgam in tooth fillings is an alloy of mercury, silver, tin, and copper. Because the metals in the amalgam are more reactive than gold, contact between the amalgam fillings and minute numbers of gold ions results in redox reactions such as the following.*

$$3Sn(s) + 2Au^{3+}(aq) \longrightarrow 3Sn^{2+}(aq) + 2Au(s) \qquad (2)$$

As a result, the dental fillings dissolve and the patients are left with a constant metallic taste in their mouths.

These examples show that like our ancestors, we continue to experience unfortunate results because of a lack of understanding of basic electrochemical principles.

Source: Ronald DeLorenzo, *Journal of Chemical Education*, May 1985, pp. 424–425.

*Equation 2 is oversimplified to illustrate more clearly the basic displacement of gold ions by metallic tin atoms. Actually, only complex ions of gold and tin can exist in aqueous solutions, not the simple cations that are shown.

For Further Understanding

▶ Label the oxidizing agent, reducing agent, substance oxidized, and substance reduced in each equation in this perspective.

▶ For each equation, state the substance that gains electrons and the substance that loses electrons.

Electrolysis

Electrolytic cells are the reverse of voltaic cells.

Electrolysis reactions use electrical energy to cause nonspontaneous oxidation-reduction reactions to occur. One common application of electrolysis is the rechargeable battery. When it is being used to power a device, such as a laptop computer, it behaves as a voltaic cell. After some time, the chemical reaction approaches completion and the voltaic cell "runs down." The cell reaction is reversible, and the battery is plugged into a battery charger. The charger is really an external source of electrical energy that reverses the chemical reaction in the battery, bringing it back to its original state. The cell has been operated as an electrolytic cell. Removal of the charging device turns the cell back into a voltaic device, ready to spontaneously react to produce electrical current once again.

The relationship between a voltaic cell and an electrolytic cell is illustrated in Figure 8.10.

Figure 8.10 (a) A voltaic cell is converted to (b) an electrolytic cell by attaching a battery with a voltage sufficiently large to reverse the reaction. This process underlies commercially available rechargeable batteries.

(a) Voltaic cell   **(b)** Electrolytic cell

SUMMARY

8.1 Acids and Bases

One of the earliest definitions of acids and bases is the *Arrhenius theory*. According to this theory, an *acid* dissociates to form hydrogen ions, H^+, and a *base* dissociates to form hydroxide ions, OH^-. The *Brønsted-Lowry theory* defines an acid as a proton (H^+) donor and a base as a proton acceptor.

Water, the solvent in many acid-base reactions, is *amphiprotic*. It has both acid and base properties.

The strength of acids and bases in water depends on their degree of dissociation, the extent to which they react with the solvent, water. Acids and bases are strong when their reaction with water is virtually 100% complete and weak when their reaction with water is much less than 100% complete.

Weak acids and weak bases dissolve in water principally in the molecular form. Only a small percentage of the molecules dissociate to form the *hydronium* ion or *hydroxide* ion.

Aqueous solutions of acids and bases are electrolytes. The dissociation of the acid or base produces ions, which conduct an electrical current. Strong acids and bases are strong electrolytes. Weak acids and bases are weak electrolytes.

Although pure water is virtually 100% molecular, a small number of water molecules do ionize. This process occurs by the transfer of a proton from one water molecule to another, producing a hydronium ion and a hydroxide ion. This process is the *autoionization*, or self-ionization, of water.

Pure water at room temperature has a hydronium ion concentration of $1.0 \times 10^{-7}\ M$. One hydroxide ion is produced for each hydronium ion. Therefore, the hydroxide ion concentration is also $1.0 \times 10^{-7}\ M$. The product of hydronium and hydroxide ion concentration (1.0×10^{-14}) is the *ion product for water*.

8.2 pH: A Measurement Scale for Acids and Bases

The *pH scale* correlates the hydronium ion concentration with a number, the pH, that serves as a useful indicator of the degree of acidity or basicity of a solution. The pH of a solution is defined as the negative logarithm of the molar concentration of the hydronium ion ($pH = -\log[H_3O^+]$).

8.3 Reactions Between Acids and Bases

The reaction of an acid with a base to produce a salt and water is referred to as *neutralization*. Neutralization requires equal numbers of mol of H_3O^+ and OH^- to produce a neutral solution (no excess acid or base). A neutralization reaction may be used to determine the concentration of an unknown acid or base solution. The technique of *titration* involves the addition of measured amounts of a *standard solution* (one whose concentration is known) from a *buret* to neutralize the second, unknown solution. The *equivalence point* is signaled by an *indicator*.

8.4 Acid-Base Buffers

A *buffer solution* contains components that enable the solution to resist large changes in pH when acids or bases are added. The basis of buffer action is an equilibrium between either a weak acid and its conjugate base or a weak base and its conjugate acid.

A buffer solution follows LeChatelier's principle, which states that an equilibrium system, when stressed, will shift its equilibrium position to alleviate that stress.

Buffering against base is a function of the concentration of the weak acid for an acidic buffer. Buffering against acid is dependent on the concentration of the anion of the salt.

A buffer solution can be described by an equilibrium constant expression. The equilibrium constant expression for an acidic system can be rearranged and solved for $[H_3O^+]$. In that way, the pH of a buffer solution can be obtained, if the composition of the solution is known. Alternatively, the *Henderson-Hasselbalch equation,* derived from the equilibrium constant expression, may be used to calculate the pH of a buffer solution.

8.5 Oxidation-Reduction Processes

Oxidation is defined as a loss of electrons, loss of hydrogen atoms, or gain of oxygen atoms. *Reduction* is defined as a gain of electrons, gain of hydrogen atoms, or loss of oxygen atoms.

Oxidation and reduction are complementary processes. The oxidation half-reaction produces an electron that is the reactant for the reduction half-reaction. The combination of two half-reactions, one oxidation and one reduction, produces the complete reaction.

The *reducing agent* releases electrons for the reduction of a second substance to occur. The *oxidizing agent* accepts electrons, causing the oxidation of a second substance to take place.

A *voltaic cell* is an electrochemical cell that converts chemical energy into electrical energy. *Electrolysis* is the opposite of a battery. It converts electrical energy into chemical potential energy.

KEY TERMS

acid (8.1)
amphiprotic (8.1)
anode (8.5)
Arrhenius theory (8.1)
autoionization (8.1)
base (8.1)
Brønsted-Lowry theory (8.1)
buffer capacity (8.4)
buffer solution (8.4)
buret (8.3)
cathode (8.5)

conjugate acid (8.1)
conjugate acid-base pair (8.1)
conjugate base (8.1)
corrosion (8.5)
electrolysis (8.5)
equivalence point (8.3)
Henderson-Hasselbalch
    equation (8.4)
hydronium ion (8.1)
indicator (8.3)
ion product for water (8.1)

neutralization (8.3)
oxidation (8.5)
oxidizing agent (8.5)
pH scale (8.2)
polyprotic substance (8.3)

reducing agent (8.5)
reduction (8.5)
standard solution (8.3)
titration (8.3)
voltaic cell (8.5)

QUESTIONS AND PROBLEMS

Acids and Bases
Foundations

8.17   **a.** Define an acid according to the Arrhenius theory.
       b. Define an acid according to the Brønsted-Lowry theory.
8.18   **a.** Define a base according to the Arrhenius theory.
       b. Define a base according to the Brønsted-Lowry theory.
8.19   What are the essential differences between the Arrhenius and Brønsted-Lowry theories?
8.20   Why is ammonia described as a Brønsted-Lowry base and not an Arrhenius base?

Applications

8.21   Write an equation for the reaction of each of the following with water:
       a. HNO_2
       b. HCN
8.22   Write an equation for the reaction of each of the following with water:
       a. HNO_3
       b. $HCOOH$
8.23   **a.** Write the conjugate acid of NO_3^-.
       b. Which is the stronger base, NO_3^- or CN^-?
       c. Which is the stronger acid, HNO_3 or HCN?
8.24   **a.** Write the conjugate acid of F^-.
       b. Which is the stronger base, F^- or CH_3COO^-?
       c. Which is the stronger acid, HF or CH_3COOH?
8.25   Label each of the following as a strong or weak acid (consult Figure 8.2, if necessary):
       a. H_2SO_3
       b. H_2CO_3
       c. H_3PO_4
8.26   Label each of the following as a strong or weak base (consult Figure 8.2, if necessary):
       a. KOH
       b. CN^-
       c. SO_4^{2-}
8.27   Identify the conjugate acid-base pairs in each of the following chemical equations:
       a. $NH_4^+(aq) + CN^-(aq) \rightleftharpoons NH_3(aq) + HCN(aq)$
       b. $CO_3^{2-}(aq) + HCl(aq) \rightleftharpoons HCO_3^-(aq) + Cl^-(aq)$
8.28   Identify the conjugate acid-base pairs in each of the following chemical equations:
       a. $HCOOH(aq) + NH_3(aq) \rightleftharpoons HCOO^-(aq) + NH_4^+(aq)$
       b. $HCl(aq) + OH^-(aq) \rightleftharpoons H_2O(l) + Cl^-(aq)$
8.29   Distinguish between the terms acid-base *strength* and acid-base *concentration*.
8.30   Of the following diagrams, which one represents:
       a. a concentrated strong acid
       b. a dilute strong acid
       c. a concentrated weak acid
       d. a dilute weak acid

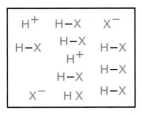

I   II

III   IV

8.31 Classify each of the following as a Brønsted acid, Brønsted base, or both:
  a. H_3O^+
  b. OH^-
  c. H_2O
8.32 Classify each of the following as a Brønsted acid, Brønsted base, or both:
  a. NH_4^+
  b. NH_3
8.33 Classify each of the following as a Brønsted acid, Brønsted base, or both:
  a. H_2CO_3
  b. HCO_3^-
  c. CO_3^{2-}
8.34 Classify each of the following as a Brønsted acid, Brønsted base, or both:
  a. H_2SO_4
  b. HSO_4^-
  c. SO_4^{2-}
8.35 Write the formula of the conjugate acid of CN^-.
8.36 Write the formula of the conjugate acid of Br^-.
8.37 Write the formula of the conjugate base of HI.
8.38 Write the formula of the conjugate base of HCOOH.

pH: A Measurement Scale for Acids and Bases

Foundations

8.39 Calculate the $[H_3O^+]$ of an aqueous solution that is:
  a. 1.0×10^{-7} M in OH^-
  b. 1.0×10^{-3} M in OH^-
8.40 Calculate the $[H_3O^+]$ of an aqueous solution that is:
  a. 1.0×10^{-9} M in OH^-
  b. 1.0×10^{-5} M in OH^-
8.41 Consider two beakers, one containing 0.10 M HCl and the other, 0.10 M CH_3COOH. Which solution has the greater pH? Why?
8.42 Consider two beakers, one containing 0.10 M NaOH and the other, 0.10 M NH_3. Which solution has the greater pH? Why?
8.43 Calculate the pH of a solution that is:
  a. 1.0×10^{-2} M in HCl
  b. 1.0×10^{-4} M in HNO_3
8.44 Calculate the pH of a solution that is:
  a. 1.0×10^{-1} M in HCl
  b. 1.0×10^{-5} M in HNO_3

8.45 Calculate $[H_3O^+]$ for a solution of nitric acid for which:
  a. pH = 1.00
  b. pH = 5.00
8.46 Calculate $[H_3O^+]$ for a solution of hydrochloric acid for which:
  a. pH = 2.00
  b. pH = 3.00
8.47 Calculate the pH of a 1.0×10^{-3} M solution of KOH.
8.48 Calculate the pH of a 1.0×10^{-5} M solution of NaOH.
8.49 Calculate both $[H_3O^+]$ and $[OH^-]$ for a solution for which:
  a. pH = 1.30
  b. pH = 9.70
8.50 Calculate both $[H_3O^+]$ and $[OH^-]$ for a solution for which:
  a. pH = 5.50
  b. pH = 7.00
8.51 What is a neutralization reaction?
8.52 Describe the purpose of a titration.

Applications

8.53 The pH of urine may vary between 4.5 and 8.2. Determine the H_3O^+ concentration and OH^- concentration if the measured pH is:
  a. 6.00
  b. 5.20
  c. 7.80
8.54 The hydronium ion concentration in blood of three different patients was:

Patient	$[H_3O^+]$
A	5.0×10^{-8}
B	3.1×10^{-8}
C	3.2×10^{-8}

What is the pH of each patient's blood? If the normal range is 7.30–7.50, which, if any, of these patients has an abnormal blood pH?
8.55 Criticize the following statement: A lakewater sample of pH = 3.0 is twice as acidic as a lakewater sample of pH = 6.0.
8.56 Can a dilute solution of a strong acid ever have a higher pH than a more concentrated solution of a weak acid? Why or why not?
8.57 What is the H_3O^+ concentration of a solution with a pH of:
  a. 5.00
  b. 12.00
  c. 5.50
8.58 What is the H_3O^+ concentration of a solution with a pH of:
  a. 6.80
  b. 4.60
  c. 2.70
8.59 Calculate the pH of a solution with a H_3O^+ concentration of:
  a. 1.0×10^{-6} M
  b. 1.0×10^{-8} M
  c. 5.6×10^{-4} M
8.60 What is the OH^- concentration of each solution in Problem 8.59?
8.61 Calculate the pH of a solution that has $[H_3O^+] = 7.5 \times 10^{-4}$ M.
8.62 Calculate the pH of a solution that has $[H_3O^+] = 6.6 \times 10^{-5}$ M.
8.63 Calculate the pH of a solution that has $[OH^-] = 5.5 \times 10^{-4}$ M.
8.64 Calculate the pH of a solution that has $[OH^-] = 6.7 \times 10^{-9}$ M.

Reactions Between Acids and Bases

Foundations

8.65 Write an equation to represent the neutralization of an aqueous solution of HNO_3 with an aqueous solution of NaOH.
8.66 Write an equation to represent the neutralization of an aqueous solution of HCl with an aqueous solution of KOH.
8.67 Rewrite the equation in Problem 8.65 as a net, balanced ionic equation.

8.68   Rewrite the equation in Problem 8.66 as a net, balanced ionic equation.

8.69   What function does an indicator perform?

8.70   Choose an indicator from Figure 8.5 that would appear yellow in acid solution and blue in basic solution.

Applications

8.71   Titration of 15.00 mL of HCl solution requires 22.50 mL of 0.1200 M NaOH solution. What is the molarity of the HCl solution?

8.72   Titration of 17.85 mL of HNO_3 solution requires 16.00 mL of 0.1600 M KOH solution. What is the molarity of the HNO_3 solution?

8.73   What volume of 0.1500 M NaOH is required to titrate 20.00 mL of 0.1000 M HCl?

8.74   What volume of 0.2000 M KOH is required to titrate 25.00 mL of 0.1500 M HNO_3?

Acid-Base Buffers

Foundations

8.75   Which of the following are capable of forming a buffer solution?
   a. NH_3 and NH_4Cl
   b. HNO_3 and KNO_3

8.76   Which of the following are capable of forming a buffer solution?
   a. HBr and $MgCl_2$
   b. H_2CO_3 and $NaHCO_3$

8.77   Consider two beakers, one containing a mixture of HCl and NaCl (each solute is 0.10 M) and the other containing a mixture of CH_3COOH and CH_3COONa (each solute is also 0.10 M). If we add 0.10 M NaOH (10.0 mL) to each beaker, which solution will have the greater change in pH? Why?

8.78   Consider two beakers, one containing a mixture of NaOH and NaCl (each solute is 0.10 M) and the other containing a mixture of NH_3 and NH_4Cl (each solute is also 0.10 M). If we add 0.10 M HNO_3 (10.0 mL) to each beaker, which solution will have the greater change in pH? Why?

Applications

8.79   For the equilibrium situation involving acetic acid,

$$CH_3COOH(aq) + H_2O(l) \rightleftharpoons CH_3COO^-(aq) + H_3O^+(aq)$$

explain the equilibrium shift occurring for the following changes:
   a. A strong acid is added to the solution.
   b. The solution is diluted with water.

8.80   For the equilibrium situation involving acetic acid,

$$CH_3COOH(aq) + H_2O(l) \rightleftharpoons CH_3COO^-(aq) + H_3O^+(aq)$$

explain the equilibrium shift occurring for the following changes:
   a. A strong base is added to the solution.
   b. More acetic acid is added to the solution.

8.81   What is $[H_3O^+]$ for a buffer solution that is 0.200 M in acid and 0.500 M in the corresponding salt if the weak acid $K_a = 5.80 \times 10^{-7}$?

8.82   What is the pH of the solution described in Problem 8.81?

8.83   For the buffer system described in Problem 8.79, which substance is responsible for buffering capacity against added hydrochloric acid? Explain.

8.84   For the buffer system described in Problem 8.79, which substance is responsible for buffering capacity against added sodium hydroxide? Explain.

8.85   Calculate the pH of a buffer system containing 1.0 M CH_3COOH and 1.0 M CH_3COONa. (K_a of acetic acid, CH_3COOH, is 1.8×10^{-5}.)

8.86   Calculate the pH of a buffer system containing 1.0 M NH_3 and 1.0 M NH_4Cl. (K_a of NH_4^+, the acid in this system, is 5.6×10^{-10}.)

8.87   The pH of blood plasma is 7.40. The principal buffer system is HCO_3^-/H_2CO_3. Calculate the ratio $[HCO_3^-]/[H_2CO_3]$ in blood plasma. (K_a of H_2CO_3, carbonic acid, is 4.5×10^{-7}.)

8.88   The pH of blood plasma from a patient was found to be 7.6, a life-threatening situation. Calculate the ratio $[HCO_3^-]/[H_2CO_3]$ in this sample of blood plasma. (K_a of H_2CO_3, carbonic acid, is 4.5×10^{-7}.)

Oxidation-Reduction Processes

Foundations

8.89   During an oxidation process in an oxidation-reduction reaction, does the species oxidized gain or lose electrons?

8.90   During an oxidation-reduction reaction, is the oxidizing agent oxidized or reduced?

8.91   During an oxidation-reduction reaction, is the reducing agent oxidized or reduced?

8.92   Do metals tend to be good oxidizing agents or good reducing agents?

Applications

8.93   In the following reaction, identify the oxidized species, reduced species, oxidizing agent, and reducing agent:

$$Cl_2(aq) + 2KI(aq) \longrightarrow 2KCl(aq) + I_2(aq)$$

8.94   In the following reaction, identify the oxidized species, reduced species, oxidizing agent, and reducing agent:

$$Zn(s) + Cu^{2+}(aq) \longrightarrow Zn^{2+}(aq) + Cu(s)$$

8.95   Write the oxidation and reduction half-reactions for the equation in Problem 8.93.

8.96   Write the oxidation and reduction half-reactions for the equation in Problem 8.94.

8.97   Explain the relationship between oxidation-reduction and voltaic cells.

8.98   Compare and contrast a battery and electrolysis.

8.99   Describe one application of voltaic cells.

8.100 Describe one application of electrolytic cells.

CRITICAL THINKING PROBLEMS

1. Acid rain is a threat to our environment because it can increase the concentration of toxic metal ions, such as Cd^{2+} and Cr^{3+}, in rivers and streams. If cadmium and chromium are present in sediment as $Cd(OH)_2$ and $Cr(OH)_3$, write reactions that demonstrate the effect of acid rain. Use the library or Internet to find the properties of cadmium and chromium responsible for their environmental impact.

2. Aluminum carbonate is soluble in acidic solution, forming aluminum cations. Write a reaction (or series of reactions) that explains this observation.

3. Carbon dioxide reacts with the hydroxide ion to produce the bicarbonate anion. Write the Lewis structure for each reactant and product. Label each as a Brønsted acid or base. Explain the reaction using the Brønsted theory. Why would the Arrhenius theory provide an inadequate description of this reaction?

4. Maalox is an antacid composed of $Mg(OH)_2$ and $Al(OH)_3$. Explain the origin of the trade name Maalox. Write chemical reactions that demonstrate the antacid activity of Maalox.

5. Acid rain has been described as a regional problem, whereas the greenhouse effect is a global problem. Do you agree with this statement? Why or why not?

The Nucleus, Radioactivity, and Nuclear Medicine

9

LEARNING GOALS

1 ▷ Enumerate characteristics of alpha, beta, positron, and gamma radiation.

2 ▷ Write balanced equations for nuclear processes.

3 ▷ Calculate the amount of radioactive substance remaining after a specified time has elapsed.

4 ▷ Explain the process of radiocarbon dating.

5 ▷ Describe how nuclear energy can generate electricity: fission, fusion, and the breeder reactor.

6 ▷ Cite examples of the use of radioactive isotopes in medicine.

7 ▷ Describe the use of ionizing radiation in cancer therapy.

8 ▷ Discuss the preparation and use of radioisotopes in diagnostic imaging studies.

9 ▷ Explain the difference between natural and artificial radioactivity.

10 ▷ Describe characteristics of radioactive materials that relate to radiation exposure and safety.

11 ▷ Be familiar with common techniques for the detection of radioactivity.

12 ▷ Know the common units of radiation intensity: the curie, roentgen, rad, and rem.

OUTLINE

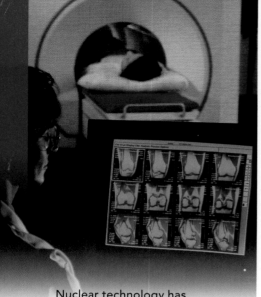

Nuclear technology has revolutionized the practice of medicine.

Animation
• Radioactive Decay

Be careful not to confuse the mass number (a simple count of the neutrons and protons) with the atomic mass, which includes the contribution of electrons and is a true *mass* figure.

Isotopes are introduced in Section 2.1.

INTRODUCTION

Our discussion of the atom and atomic structure in Chapter 2 revealed a nucleus containing protons and neutrons surrounded by electrons. Until now, we have treated the nucleus as simply a region of positive charge in the center of the atom. The focus of our interest has been the electrons and their arrangement around the nucleus. Electron arrangement is an essential part of a discussion of bonding or chemical change.

In this chapter we consider the nucleus and nuclear properties. The behavior of nuclei may have as great an effect on our everyday lives as any of the thousands of synthetic compounds developed over the past several decades. Examples of nuclear technology range from everyday items (smoke detectors) to sophisticated instruments for medical diagnosis and treatment and electrical power generation (nuclear power plants).

Beginning in 1896 with Becquerel's discovery of radiation emitted from uranium ore, the technology arising from this and related findings has produced both risks and benefits. Although early discoveries of radioactivity and its properties expanded our fundamental knowledge and brought fame to the investigators, it was not accomplished without a price. Several early investigators died prematurely of cancer and other diseases caused by the radiation they studied.

Even today, the existence of nuclear energy and its associated technology is a mixed blessing. On one side, the horrors of Nagasaki and Hiroshima, the fear of nuclear war, and potential contamination of populated areas resulting from the peaceful application of nuclear energy are critical problems facing society. Conversely, hundreds of thousands of lives have been saved because of the early detection of disease such as cancer by diagnosis based on the interaction of radiation and the body. The use of techniques such as cobalt-60 treatment are considered a routine part of comprehensive treatment of a variety of tumors. Furthermore, nuclear energy is an alternative energy source, providing an opportunity for us to compensate for the depletion of nonrenewable oil reserves.

9.1 Natural Radioactivity

Radioactivity is the process by which some atoms emit energy and particles. The energy and particles are termed *radiation*. Nuclear radiation occurs as a result of an alteration in nuclear composition or structure. This process occurs in a nucleus that is unstable and hence radioactive. Radioactivity is a nuclear event: *matter and energy released during this process come from the nucleus.*

We shall designate the nucleus using *nuclear symbols,* analogous to the *atomic symbols* that were discussed in Chapter 2. The nuclear symbols consist of the *symbol* of the element, the *atomic number* (the number of protons in the nucleus), and the *mass number,* which is defined as the sum of neutrons and protons in the nucleus.

With the use of nuclear symbols, the fluorine nucleus is represented as

$$\text{Mass number} \longrightarrow {}^{19}_{9}\text{F} \longleftarrow \text{Symbol of the element}$$
$$\text{Atomic number} \longrightarrow$$
$$\text{(or nuclear charge)}$$

This symbol is equivalent to writing *fluorine-19.* This alternative representation is frequently used to denote specific isotopes of elements.

Not all nuclei are unstable. Only unstable nuclei undergo change and produce radioactivity, the process of radioactive decay. Recall that different atoms of the same element having different masses exist as *isotopes.* One isotope of an element may be radioactive, whereas others of the same element may be quite stable. It is important to distinguish between the terms *isotope* and *nuclide.* The term *isotope*

Carbon-12 has
six protons and
six neutrons

Carbon-13 has
six protons and
seven neutrons

Carbon-14 has
six protons and
eight neutrons

Figure 9.1 Three isotopes of carbon. Each nucleus contains the same number of protons. Only the number of neutrons is different; hence, each isotope has a different mass.

refers to any atoms that have the same atomic number but different mass numbers. The term **nuclide** refers to any atom characterized by an atomic number and a mass number.

Many elements in the periodic table occur in nature as mixtures of isotopes. Two common examples include carbon (Figure 9.1),

$$\begin{array}{ccc} {}^{12}_{6}\text{C} & {}^{13}_{6}\text{C} & {}^{14}_{6}\text{C} \\ \text{Carbon-12} & \text{Carbon-13} & \text{Carbon-14} \end{array}$$

and hydrogen,

$$\begin{array}{ccc} {}^{1}_{1}\text{H} & {}^{2}_{1}\text{H} & {}^{3}_{1}\text{H} \\ \text{Hydrogen-1} & \text{Hydrogen-2} & \text{Hydrogen-3} \\ \text{Protium} & \text{Deuterium} & \text{Tritium} \\ & \text{(symbol D)} & \text{(symbol T)} \end{array}$$

Protium is a stable isotope and makes up more than 99.9% of naturally occurring hydrogen. Deuterium (D) can be isolated from hydrogen; it can form compounds such as "heavy water," D_2O. Heavy water is a potential source of deuterium for fusion processes. Tritium (T) is rare and unstable, hence radioactive.

In writing the symbols for a nuclear process, it is essential to indicate the particular isotope involved. This is why the mass number and atomic number are used. These values tell us the number of neutrons in the species, hence the isotope's identity.

Natural radiation emitted by unstable nuclei includes *alpha particles, beta particles, positrons,* and *gamma rays.*

Alpha Particles

An **alpha particle** (α) contains two protons and two neutrons. An alpha particle is identical to the nucleus of the helium atom (He) or a *helium ion* (He^{2+}), which also contains two protons (atomic number = 2) and two neutrons (mass number − atomic number = 2). Having no electrons to counterbalance the nuclear charge, the alpha particle may be symbolized as

$${}^{4}_{2}\text{He}^{2+} \quad \text{or} \quad {}^{4}_{2}\text{He} \quad \text{or} \quad \alpha$$

Alpha particles have a relatively large mass compared to other nuclear particles. Consequently, alpha particles emitted by radioisotopes are relatively slow-moving particles (approximately 10% of the speed of light), and they are stopped by barriers as thin as a few pages of this book.

Beta Particles and Positrons

The **beta particle** (β), in contrast, is a fast-moving electron traveling at approximately 90% of the speed of light as it leaves the nucleus. It is formed in the nucleus by the conversion of a neutron into a proton. The beta particle is represented as

Alpha, beta, positron, and gamma radiation have widespread use in the field of medicine.

 Animation
• The Types of Radioactive Decay

LEARNING GOAL

1 ▶ Enumerate characteristics of alpha, beta, positron, and gamma radiation.

Other radiation particles, such as neutrinos and deuterons, will not be discussed here.

Table 9.1 A Summary of the Major Properties of Alpha, Beta, Positron, and Gamma Radiation

Name and Symbol	Identity	Charge	Mass (amu)	Velocity	Penetration
Alpha (α)	Helium nucleus	+2	4.0026	5–10% of the speed of light	Low
Beta $_{-1}^{0}\beta$	Electron	−1	0.000549	Up to 90% of the speed of light	Medium
Positron $_{+1}^{0}\beta$	Electron	+1	0.000549	Up to 90% of the speed of light	Medium
Gamma (γ)	Radiant energy	0	0	Speed of light	High

$$_{-1}^{0}e \quad \text{or} \quad _{-1}^{0}\beta \quad \text{or} \quad \beta$$

The subscript −1 is written in the same position as the atomic number and, like the atomic number (number of protons), indicates the charge of the particle.

Beta particles are smaller and faster than alpha particles. They are more penetrating and are stopped only by more dense materials such as wood, metal, or several layers of clothing.

A *positron* has the same mass as a beta particle but carries a positive charge and is symbolized as $_{+1}^{0}e$ or $_{+1}^{0}\beta$. Positrons are produced by the conversion of a proton to a neutron in the nucleus of the isotope. The proton, in effect, loses its positive charge as well as a tiny bit of mass. This positively charged mass that is released is the positron.

Gamma Rays

Gamma rays (γ) are the most energetic part of the electromagnetic spectrum (see Section 2.2), and result from nuclear processes; in contrast, alpha radiation and beta radiation are matter. Because electromagnetic radiation has no protons, neutrons, or electrons, the symbol for a gamma ray is simply

$$\gamma$$

Gamma radiation is highly energetic and is the most penetrating form of nuclear radiation. Barriers of lead, concrete, or, more often, a combination of the two are required for protection from this type of radiation.

Properties of Alpha, Beta, Positron, and Gamma Radiation

Important properties of alpha, beta, positron, and gamma radiation are summarized in Table 9.1.

Alpha, beta, positron, and gamma radiation are collectively termed *ionizing radiation*. **Ionizing radiation** produces a trail of ions throughout the material that it penetrates. The ionization process changes the chemical composition of the material. When the material is living tissue, radiation-induced illness may result (Section 9.6).

The penetrating power of alpha radiation is very low. Damage to internal organs from this form of radiation is negligible except when an alpha particle emitter is actually ingested. Beta particles and positrons have much higher velocities than alpha particles; still, they have limited penetrating power. They cause skin and eye damage and, to a lesser extent, damage to internal organs. Shielding is required when working with beta emitters. Pregnant women must take special precautions. The great penetrating power and high energy of gamma radiation make it particularly difficult to shield. Hence, it can damage internal organs.

Anyone working with any type of radiation must take precautions. Radiation safety is required, monitored, and enforced in the United States under provisions of the Occupational Safety and Health Act (OSHA).

Animations
- Alpha, Beta, and Gamma Radiation
- Alpha, Beta, and Gamma Rays

LEARNING GOAL

1 ▶ Enumerate characteristics of alpha, beta, positron, and gamma radiation.

A Human Perspective

Origin of the Elements

The current, most widely held theory of the origin of the universe is the "big bang" theory. An explosion of very dense matter was followed by expansion into space of the fragments resulting from this explosion. This is one of the scenarios that have been created by scientists fascinated by the origins of matter, the stars and planets, and life as we know it today.

The first fragments, or particles, were protons and neutrons moving with tremendous velocity and possessing large amounts of energy. Collisions involving these high-energy protons and neutrons formed deuterium atoms (^{2}H), which are isotopes of hydrogen. As the universe expanded and cooled, tritium (^{3}H), another hydrogen isotope, formed as a result of collisions of neutrons with deuterium atoms. Subsequent capture of a proton produced helium (He). Scientists theorize that a universe that was principally composed of hydrogen atoms and helium atoms persisted for perhaps 100,000 years until the temperature decreased sufficiently to allow the formation of a simple molecule, hydrogen, two atoms of hydrogen bonded together (H_2).

Many millions of years later, the effect of gravity caused these small units to coalesce, first into clouds and eventually into stars, with temperatures of millions of degrees. In this setting, these small collections of protons and neutrons combined to form larger atoms such as carbon (C) and oxygen (O), then sodium (Na), neon (Ne), magnesium (Mg), silicon (Si), and so forth. Subsequent explosions of stars provided the conditions that formed many larger atoms. These fragments, gathered together by the force of gravity, are the most probable origin of the planets in our own solar system.

The reactions that formed the elements as we know them today were a result of a series of *fusion reactions*, the joining of nuclei to produce larger atoms at very high temperatures (millions of degrees Celsius). These fusion reactions are similar to processes that are currently being studied as a possible alternative source of nuclear power.

Nuclear reactions of this type do not naturally occur on the earth today. The temperature is simply too low. As a result we have, for the most part, a collection of stable elements existing as chemical compounds, atoms joined together by chemical bonds while retaining their identity even in the combined state. Silicon exists all around us as sand and soil in a combined form, silicon dioxide; most metals exist as a part of a chemical compound, such as iron ore.

The wonder and complexity of our universe is a legacy of events that happened a long time ago. As our understanding of bonding, molecular structure, and structure-property relationships has developed, our ability to design and synthesize useful new compounds has dramatically increased.

For Further Understanding

▶ How does tritium differ from "normal" hydrogen?
▶ Would you expect to find similar atoms on other planets?

Question 9.1 Gamma radiation is a form of *electromagnetic radiation*. Provide examples of other forms of electromagnetic radiation.

Question 9.2 How does the energy of gamma radiation compare with that of other regions of the electromagnetic spectrum?

9.2 Writing a Balanced Nuclear Equation

Nuclear equations represent nuclear change in much the same way as chemical equations represent chemical change.

A **nuclear equation** can be used to represent the process of radioactive decay. In radioactive decay a *nuclide* breaks down, producing a *new nuclide, smaller particles, and/or energy.* The concept of mass balance, required when writing chemical equations, is also essential for nuclear equations. When writing a balanced equation, remember that:

- the total mass on each side of the reaction arrow must be identical, and
- the sum of the atomic numbers on each side of the reaction arrow must be identical.

Alpha Decay

Consider the decay of one isotope of uranium, $^{238}_{92}$U, into thorium and an alpha particle. Because an alpha particle is lost in this process, this decay is called *alpha decay.*

LEARNING GOAL
2 ▶ Write balanced equations for nuclear processes.

Examine the balanced equation for this nuclear reaction:

$$^{238}_{92}U \longrightarrow ^{234}_{90}Th + ^{4}_{2}He$$

Uranium-238   Thorium-234   Helium-4

The sum of the mass numbers on the right (234 + 4 = 238) is equal to the mass number on the left. The sum of atomic numbers on the right (90 + 2 = 92) is equal to the atomic number on the left.

Beta Decay

Beta decay is illustrated by the decay of one of the less-abundant nitrogen isotopes, $^{16}_{7}N$. Upon decomposition, nitrogen-16 produces oxygen-16 and a beta particle. Conceptually, a neutron = proton + electron. In beta decay, one neutron in nitrogen-16 is converted to a proton and the electron, the beta particle, is released. The reaction is represented as

$$^{16}_{7}N \longrightarrow ^{16}_{8}O + ^{0}_{-1}e$$

or

$$^{16}_{7}N \longrightarrow ^{16}_{8}O + \beta$$

Note that the mass number of the beta particle is zero, because the electron has no protons or neutrons. Sixteen nuclear particles are accounted for on both sides of the reaction arrow. Note also that the product nuclide has the same mass number as the parent nuclide but the atomic number has *increased* by one unit.

The atomic number on the left (+7) is counterbalanced by [8 + (−1)] or (+7) on the right. Therefore the equation is correctly balanced.

Positron Emission

The decay of carbon-11 to a stable isotope, boron-11, is one example of positron emission.

$$^{11}_{6}C \longrightarrow ^{11}_{8}B + ^{0}_{1}e$$

or

$$^{11}_{6}C \longrightarrow ^{11}_{5}B + ^{0}_{+1}\beta$$

A **positron** has the same mass as an electron, or beta particle, but opposite (+) charge. In contrast to beta emission, the product nuclide has the same mass number as the parent nuclide, but the atomic number has *decreased* by one unit.

The atomic number on the left (+6) is counterbalanced by [5 + (+1)] or (+6) on the right. Therefore, the equation is correctly balanced.

Gamma Production

If *gamma radiation* were the only product of nuclear decay, there would be no measurable change in the mass or identity of the radioactive nuclei. This is so because the gamma emitter has simply gone to a lower energy state. An example of an isotope that decays in this way is technetium-99m. It is described as a **metastable isotope,** meaning that it is unstable and increases its stability through gamma decay without change in the mass or charge of the isotope. The letter *m* is used to denote a metastable isotope. The decay equation for $^{99m}_{43}Tc$ is

$$^{99m}_{43}Tc \longrightarrow ^{99}_{43}Tc + \gamma$$

More often, gamma radiation is produced along with other products. For example, iodine-131 decays as follows:

$$^{131}_{53}\text{I} \longrightarrow {}^{131}_{54}\text{Xe} + {}^{0}_{-1}\beta + \gamma$$

Iodine-131   Xenon-131   Beta   Gamma
                                    particle   ray

This reaction may also be represented as

$$^{131}_{53}\text{I} \longrightarrow {}^{131}_{54}\text{Xe} + {}^{0}_{-1}\text{e} + \gamma$$

An isotope of xenon, a beta particle, and gamma radiation are produced.

Predicting Products of Nuclear Decay

It is possible to use a nuclear equation to predict one of the products of a nuclear reaction if the others are known. Consider the following example, in which we represent the unknown product as ?:

$$^{40}_{19}\text{K} \longrightarrow ? + {}^{0}_{-1}\text{e}$$

Step 1. The mass number of this isotope of potassium is 40. Therefore the sum of the mass number of the products must also be 40, and ? must have a mass number of 40.

Step 2. Likewise, the atomic number on the left is 19, and the sum of the unknown atomic number plus the charge of the beta particle (-1) must equal 19.

Step 3. The unknown atomic number must be 20, because $[20 + (-1) = 19]$. The unknown is

$$^{40}_{20}?$$

Step 4. If we consult the periodic table, the element that has atomic number 20 is calcium; therefore $? = {}^{40}_{20}\text{Ca}$.

EXAMPLE 9.1 Predicting the Products of Radioactive Decay

Determine the identity of the unknown product of the alpha decay of curium-245:

$$^{245}_{96}\text{Cm} \longrightarrow {}^{4}_{2}\text{He} + ?$$

LEARNING GOAL

2 ▶ Write balanced equations for nuclear processes.

Solution

Step 1. The mass number of the curium isotope is 245. Therefore the sum of the mass numbers of the products must also be 245, and ? must have a mass number of 241.

Step 2. Likewise, the atomic number on the left is 96, and the sum of the unknown atomic number plus the atomic number of the alpha particle (2) must equal 96.

Step 3. The unknown atomic number must be 94, because $[94 + 2 = 96]$. The unknown is

$$^{241}_{94}?$$

Step 4. Referring to the periodic table, we find that the element that has atomic number 94 is plutonium; therefore $? = {}^{241}_{94}\text{Pu}$.

Continued—

> **Practice Problem 9.1**
>
> Complete each of the following nuclear equations:
>
> a. $^{85}_{36}Kr \longrightarrow ? + ^{0}_{-1}e$
>
> b. $? \longrightarrow ^{4}_{2}He + ^{222}_{86}Rn$
>
> c. $^{239}_{92}U \longrightarrow ? + ^{0}_{-1}e$
>
> d. $^{11}_{5}B \longrightarrow ^{7}_{3}Li + ?$

▶ **For Further Practice: Questions 9.37 and 9.38.**

Question 9.3 Iodine-131, useful in the treatment of certain kinds of thyroid disease, decays by beta emission. Write a balanced nuclear equation for this process.

Question 9.4 Phosphorus-31, known to bioaccumulate in the liver, decays by beta emission. Write a balanced nuclear equation for this process.

9.3 Properties of Radioisotopes

Why are some isotopes radioactive but others are not? Do all radioactive isotopes decay at the same rate? Are all radioactive materials equally hazardous? We address these and other questions in this section.

Nuclear Structure and Stability

A measure of nuclear stability is the **binding energy** of the nucleus. The binding energy of the nucleus is the energy required to break up a nucleus into its component protons and neutrons. This must be very large, because identically charged protons in the nucleus exert extreme repulsive forces on one another. These forces must be overcome if the nucleus is to be stable. When a nuclide decays, some energy is released because the products are more stable than the parent nuclide. This released energy is the source of the high-energy radiation emitted and the basis for all nuclear technology.

Why are some isotopes more stable than others? The answer to this question is not completely clear. Evidence obtained so far points to several important factors that describe stable nuclei:

- Nuclear stability correlates with the ratio of neutrons to protons in the isotope. For example, for light atoms a neutron:proton ratio of 1 characterizes a stable atom.
- Nuclei with large numbers of protons (84 or more) tend to be unstable.
- Naturally occurring isotopes containing 2, 8, 20, 50, 82, or 126 protons or neutrons are stable. These *magic numbers* seem to indicate the presence of energy levels in the nucleus, analogous to electronic energy levels in the atom.
- Isotopes with even numbers of protons or neutrons are generally more stable than those with odd numbers of protons or neutrons.
- All isotopes (except hydrogen-1) with more protons than neutrons are unstable. However, the reverse is not true.

Half-Life

LEARNING GOAL

3 ▶ Calculate the amount of radioactive substance remaining after a specified time has elapsed.

The **half-life** ($t_{1/2}$) is the time required for one-half of a given quantity of a substance to undergo change. Not all radioactive isotopes decay at the same rate. The rate of nuclear decay is generally represented in terms of the half-life of the isotope. Each isotope has its own characteristic half-life that may be as short as a

Table 9.2 Half-Lives of Selected Radioisotopes

Name	Symbol	Half-Life
Carbon-14	$^{14}_{6}C$	5730 years
Cobalt-60	$^{60}_{27}Co$	5.3 years
Hydrogen-3	$^{3}_{1}H$	12.3 years
Iodine-131	$^{131}_{53}I$	8.1 days
Iron-59	$^{59}_{26}Fe$	45 days
Molybdenum-99	$^{99}_{42}Mo$	67 hours
Sodium-24	$^{24}_{11}Na$	15 hours
Strontium-90	$^{90}_{38}Sr$	28 years
Technetium-99m	$^{99m}_{43}Tc$	6 hours
Uranium-235	$^{235}_{92}U$	710 million years

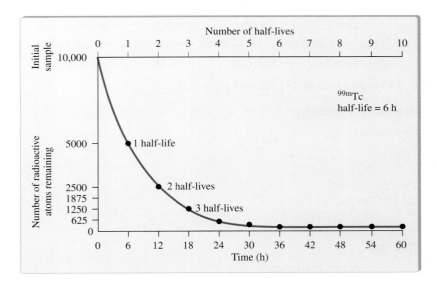

Figure 9.2 The decay curve for the medically useful radioisotope technetium-99m. Note that the number of radioactive atoms remaining—hence the radioactivity—approaches zero.

few millionths of a second or as long as billions of years. Half-lives of some naturally occurring and synthetic isotopes are given in Table 9.2.

The stability of an isotope is indicated by the isotope's half-life. Isotopes with short half-lives decay rapidly; they are very unstable. This is not meant to imply that substances with long half-lives are less hazardous. Often, just the reverse is true.

Imagine that we begin with 100 milligrams (mg) of a radioactive isotope that has a half-life of 24 hours (h). After one half-life, or 24 h, 1/2 of 100 mg will have decayed to other products, and 50 mg remain. After two half-lives (48 h), 1/2 of the remaining material has decayed, leaving 25 mg, and so forth:

$$100 \text{ mg} \xrightarrow[\text{Half-life} \atop \text{(24 h)}]{\text{One}} 50 \text{ mg} \xrightarrow[\text{Half-life} \atop \text{(48 h total)}]{\text{A Second}} 25 \text{ mg} \longrightarrow \text{etc.}$$

Decay of a radioisotope that has a reasonably short $t_{1/2}$ is experimentally determined by following its activity as a function of time. Graphing the results produces a radioactive decay curve, as shown in Figure 9.2.

The mass of any radioactive substance remaining after a period may be calculated with a knowledge of the initial mass and the half-life of the isotope, following the scheme just outlined. The general equation for this process is:

$$m_f = m_i (.5)^n$$

Animation
- Radioactive Half-Life

Refer to the discussion of radiation exposure and safety in Sections 9.6 and 9.7.

where m_f = final or remaining mass
$\qquad m_i$ = initial mass
$\qquad\quad n$ = number of half-lives

EXAMPLE 9.2   Predicting the Extent of Radioactive Decay

A 50.0-mg supply of iodine-131, used in hospitals in the treatment of hyperthyroidism, was stored for 32.4 days (d). If the half-life of iodine-131 is 8.1 d, how many mg remain?

Solution

First calculate n, the number of half-lives elapsed using the half-life as a conversion factor:

$$n = 32.4 \text{ d} \times \frac{1 \text{ half-life}}{8.1 \text{ d}} = 4.0 \text{ half-lives}$$

Then calculate the amount remaining:

$$
\begin{array}{ccccc}
\text{first} & \text{second} & \text{third} & \text{fourth} \\
50.0 \text{ mg} \longrightarrow 25.0 \text{ mg} \longrightarrow 12.5 \text{ mg} \longrightarrow 6.25 \text{ mg} \longrightarrow 3.13 \text{ mg} \\
\text{half-life} & \text{half-life} & \text{half-life} & \text{half-life}
\end{array}
$$

Hence, 3.13 mg of iodine-131 remain after 32.4 d.

An Alternate Strategy

Use the equation:

$$m_f = m_i \,(.5)^n$$

Where
m_i is the initial mass
m_f is the final mass
and
n is the half-life
Substituting:

$$m_f = 50.0 \text{ mg}(.5)^4$$
$$m_f = 3.13 \text{ mg of iodine-131 remain after 32.4 d.}$$

Note that both strategies produce the same answer.

Practice Problem 9.2

a. A 100.0 nanogram (ng) sample of sodium-24 was stored in a lead-lined cabinet for 2.5 d. How much sodium-24 remained? See Table 9.2 for the half-life of sodium-24.

b. If a patient is administered 10 ng of technetium-99m, how much will remain 1 d later, assuming that no technetium has been eliminated by any other process? See Table 9.2 for the half-life of technetium-99m.

▶ **For Further Practice: Questions 9.61 and 9.62.**

Question 9.5 The half-life of molybdenum-99 is 67 h. A 200 (microgram) (μg) quantity decays, over time, to 25 μg. How much time has elapsed?

Question 9.6 The half-life of strontium-87 is 2.8 h. What percentage of this isotope will remain after 8 h and 24 minutes (min)?

A Human Perspective

An Extraordinary Woman in Science

The path to a successful career in science, or any other field for that matter, is seldom smooth or straight. That was certainly true for Madame Marie Sklodowska Curie. Her lifelong ambition was to raise a family and do something interesting for a career. This was a lofty goal for a nineteenth-century woman.

The political climate in Poland, coupled with the prevailing attitudes toward women and careers, especially careers in science, certainly did not make it any easier for Mme. Curie. To support herself and her sister, she toiled at menial jobs until moving to Paris to resume her studies.

It was in Paris that she met her future husband and fellow researcher, Pierre Curie. Working with crude equipment in a laboratory that was primitive, even by the standards of the time, she and Pierre made a most revolutionary discovery only 2 years after Henri Becquerel discovered radioactivity. Radioactivity, the emission of energy from certain substances, was released from *inside* the atom and was independent of the molecular form of the substance. The absolute proof of this assertion came only after the Curies processed over 1 *ton* (t) of a material (pitchblende) to isolate less than a gram (g) of pure radium. The difficult conditions under which this feat was accomplished are perhaps best stated by Sharon Bertsch McGrayne in her book *Nobel Prize Women in Science* (Birch Lane Press, New York, p. 23):

The only space large enough at the school was an abandoned dissection shed. The shack was stifling hot in summer and freezing cold in winter. It had no ventilation system for removing poisonous fumes, and its roof leaked. A chemist accustomed to Germany's modern laboratories called it "a cross between a stable and a potato cellar and, if I had not seen the work table with the chemical apparatus, I would have thought it a practical joke." This ramshackle shed became the symbol of the Marie Curie legend.

The pale green glow emanating from the radium was beautiful to behold. Mme. Curie would go to the shed in the middle of the night to bask in the light of her accomplishment. She did not realize that this wonderful accomplishment would, in time, be responsible for her death.

Mme. Curie received not one, but two Nobel Prizes, one in physics and one in chemistry. She was the first woman in France to earn the rank of professor.

For Further Understanding

▶ Paradoxically, radiation can both cause and cure cancer. Do some Internet research and explain the paradox.

▶ What is the message that you, personally, can take away from this story?

Radiocarbon Dating

Natural radioactivity is useful in establishing the approximate age of objects of archaeological, anthropological, or historical interest. **Radiocarbon dating** is the estimation of the age of objects through measurement of isotopic ratios of carbon.

Radiocarbon dating is based on the measurement of the relative amounts (or ratio) of $^{14}_{6}C$ and $^{12}_{6}C$ present in an object. The $^{14}_{6}C$ is formed in the upper atmosphere by the bombardment of $^{14}_{7}N$ by high-speed neutrons (cosmic radiation):

$$^{14}_{7}N + ^{0}_{1}n \longrightarrow ^{14}_{6}C + ^{1}_{1}H$$

The carbon-14, along with the more abundant carbon-12, is converted into living plant material by the process of photosynthesis. Carbon proceeds up the food chain as the plants are consumed by animals, including humans. When a plant or animal dies, the uptake of both carbon-14 and carbon-12 ceases. However, the amount of carbon-14 slowly decreases because carbon-14 is radioactive ($t_{1/2} = 5730$ years). Carbon-14 decay produces nitrogen:

$$^{14}_{6}C \longrightarrow ^{14}_{7}N + ^{0}_{-1}e$$

When an artifact is found and studied, the relative amounts of carbon-14 and carbon-12 are determined. By using suitable equations involving the $t_{1/2}$ of carbon-14, it is possible to approximate the age of the artifact.

This technique has been widely used to increase our knowledge about the history of the earth, to establish the age of objects (Figure 9.3), and even to detect art forgeries. Early paintings were made with inks fabricated from vegetable dyes (plant material that, while alive, metabolized carbon).

The carbon-14 dating technique is limited to objects that are less than fifty thousand years old, or approximately nine half-lives, which is a practical upper limit. Older objects that have geological or archaeological significance may be dated using naturally occurring isotopes having much longer half-lives.

LEARNING GOAL

4 ▶ Explain the process of radiocarbon dating.

Figure 9.3 Radiocarbon dating was used in the authentication study of the Shroud of Turin. It is a minimally destructive technique and is valuable in estimating the age of historical artifacts. It was found that the Shroud is approximately 700 years old, negating the claim that it was used to wrap the body of Jesus.

Table 9.3 Isotopes Useful in Radioactive Dating

Isotope	Half-Life (years)	Upper Limit (years)	Dating Applications
Carbon-14	5730	5×10^4	Charcoal, organic material, artwork
Tritium ^3_1H	12.3	1×10^2	Aged wines, artwork
Potassium-40	1.3×10^9	Age of earth (4×10^9)	Rocks, planetary material
Rhenium-187	4.3×10^{10}	Age of earth (4×10^9)	Meteorites
Uranium-238	4.5×10^9	Age of earth (4×10^9)	Rocks, earth's crust

Examples of useful dating isotopes are listed in Table 9.3.

9.4 Nuclear Power

Energy Production

Einstein predicted that a small amount of nuclear mass corresponds to a very large amount of energy that is released when the nucleus breaks apart. Einstein's equation is

$$E = mc^2$$

in which

$$E = \text{energy}$$
$$m = \text{mass}$$
$$c = \text{speed of light}$$

This kinetic energy, when rapidly released, is the basis for the greatest instruments of destruction developed by humankind, nuclear bombs. However, when heat energy is released in a controlled fashion, as in a nuclear power plant, the heat energy converts liquid water into steam. The steam, in turn, drives an electrical generator, producing electricity. The entire process takes place in a **nuclear reactor.**

Nuclear Fission

Fission (splitting) occurs when a heavy nuclear particle is split into smaller nuclei by a smaller nuclear particle (such as a neutron). This splitting process is accompanied by the release of large amounts of energy.

A nuclear power plant uses a fissionable material (capable of undergoing fission), such as uranium-235, as fuel. The energy released by the fission process in the nuclear core heats water in an adjoining chamber, producing steam. The high pressure of the steam drives a turbine, which converts this heat energy into electricity using an electric power generator. The energy transformation may be summarized as follows:

nuclear energy	$\longrightarrow$	heat energy	$\longrightarrow$	mechanical energy	$\longrightarrow$	electrical energy
Nuclear reactor		Steam		Turbine		Electricity

The fission reaction, once initiated, is self-perpetuating. For example, neutrons are used to initiate the reaction:

$$^1_0\text{n} + ^{235}_{92}\text{U} \longrightarrow ^{235}_{92}\text{U} \longrightarrow ^{92}_{36}\text{Kr} + ^{141}_{56}\text{Ba} + 3\,^1_0\text{n} + \text{energy}$$

$$\underbrace{\quad\quad}_{\text{Fuel}} \quad \underbrace{\quad\quad}_{\text{Unstable}} \quad \underbrace{\quad\quad\quad\quad}_{\text{Products of reaction}}$$

Note that three neutrons are released as product for each single reacting neutron. Each of the three neutrons produced is available to initiate another fission process.

LEARNING GOAL

5 ▶ Describe how nuclear energy can generate electricity: fission, fusion, and the breeder reactor.

Animations
- Nuclear Fission
- Nuclear Chain Reaction

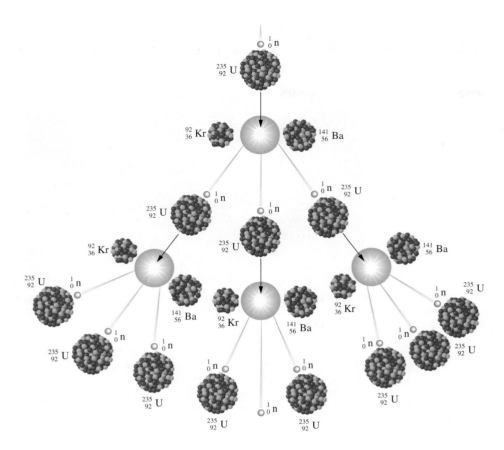

Figure 9.4 The fission of uranium-235 producing a chain reaction. Note that the number of available neutrons, which "trigger" the decomposition of the fissionable nuclei to release energy, increases at each step in the "chain." In this way the reaction builds in intensity. Control rods stabilize (or limit) the extent of the chain reaction to a safe level.

Figure 9.5 A representation of the "energy zones" of a nuclear reactor. Heat produced by the reactor core is carried by water in a second zone to a boiler. Water in the boiler (third zone) is converted to steam, which drives a turbine to convert heat energy to electrical energy. The isolation of these zones from each other allows heat energy transfer without actual physical mixing. This minimizes the transport of radioactive material into the environment.

Nine neutrons are released from this process. These, in turn, react with other nuclei. The fission process continues and intensifies, producing very large amounts of energy (Figure 9.4). This process of intensification is referred to as a **chain reaction.**

To maintain control over the process and to prevent dangerous overheating, rods fabricated from cadmium or boron are inserted into the core. These rods, which are controlled by the reactor's main operating system, absorb free neutrons as needed, thereby moderating the reaction.

A nuclear fission reactor may be represented as a series of energy transfer zones, as depicted in Figure 9.5. A view of the core of a fission reactor is shown in Figure 9.6.

Green Chemistry

Nuclear Waste Disposal

Nuclear waste arises from a variety of sources. A major source is the spent fuel from nuclear power plants. Medical laboratories generate significant amounts of low-level waste from tracers and therapy. Even household items with limited lifetimes, such as certain types of smoke detectors, use a tiny amount of radioactive material.

Virtually everyone is aware, through television and newspapers, of the problems of solid waste (nonnuclear) disposal that our society faces. For the most part, this material will degrade in some reasonable amount of time. Still, we are disposing of trash and garbage at a rate that far exceeds nature's ability to recycle it.

Now imagine the problem with nuclear waste. We cannot alter the rate at which it decays. This is defined by the half-life. We can't heat it, stir it, or add a catalyst to speed up the process as we can with chemical reactions. Furthermore, the half-lives of many nuclear waste products are very long: plutonium, for example, has a half-life in excess of 24,000 years. Ten half-lives represents the approximate time required for the radioactivity of a substance to reach background levels. So we are talking about a *very* long storage time, on the order of 250,000 years!

Where on earth can something so very hazardous be contained and stored with reasonable assurance that it will lie undisturbed for a quarter of a million years? Perhaps this is a rhetorical question. Scientists, engineers, and politicians have debated this question for almost 50 years. As yet, no permanent disposal site has been agreed upon. Most agree that the best solution is burial in a stable rock formation, but there is no firm agreement on the location. Fear of earthquakes, which may release large quantities of radioactive materials into the underground water system, is the most serious consideration. Such a disaster could render large sections of the country unfit for habitation.

A photograph of the earth, taken from the moon, clearly illustrates the limits of resources and the limits to waste disposal.

Many argue for the continuation of temporary storage sites with the hope that the progress of science and technology will, in the years ahead, provide a safer and more satisfactory long-term solution.

The nuclear waste problem, important for its own sake, also affects the development of future societal uses of nuclear chemistry. Before we can fully enjoy its benefits, we must learn to use and dispose of its waste products safely.

For Further Understanding

▶ Summarize the major arguments supporting expanded use of nuclear power for electrical energy.

▶ Enumerate the characteristics of an "ideal" solution to the nuclear waste problem.

Figure 9.6 The core of a nuclear reactor located at Oak Ridge National Laboratories in Tennessee.

Nuclear Fusion

Fusion (meaning *to join together*) results from the combination of two small nuclei to form a larger nucleus with the concurrent release of large amounts of energy. The best example of a fusion reactor is the sun. Continuous fusion processes furnish our solar system with light and heat.

An example of a fusion reaction is the combination of two isotopes of hydrogen, deuterium (^2_1H) and tritium (^3_1H), to produce helium, a neutron, and energy:

$$^2_1H + ^3_1H \longrightarrow ^4_2He + ^1_0n + \text{energy}$$

Although fusion is capable of producing tremendous amounts of energy, no commercially successful fusion plant exists in the United States. Safety concerns relating to problems of containment of the reaction, resulting directly from the technological problems associated with containing high temperatures (millions of degrees) and pressures required to sustain a fusion process, have slowed the development of fusion reactors.

Breeder Reactors

A **breeder reactor** is a variation of a fission reactor that literally manufactures its own fuel. A perceived shortage of fissionable isotopes makes the breeder an attractive alternative to conventional fission reactors. A breeder reactor uses $^{238}_{92}U$, which is abundant but nonfissionable. In a series of steps, the uranium-238 is converted to plutonium-239, which *is* fissionable and undergoes a fission chain reaction, producing energy. The attractiveness of a reactor that makes its own fuel from abundant starting materials is offset by the high cost of the system, potential environmental damage, and fear of plutonium proliferation. Plutonium can be readily used to manufacture nuclear bombs. Currently only France and Japan operate breeder reactors for electrical power generation.

9.5 Medical Applications of Radioactivity

The use of radiation in the treatment of various forms of cancer, as well as the newer area of **nuclear medicine,** the use of radioisotopes in diagnosis, has become widespread in the past quarter century. Let's look at the properties of radiation that make it an indispensable tool in modern medical care.

Cancer Therapy Using Radiation

When high-energy radiation, such as gamma radiation, passes through a cell, it may collide with one of the molecules in the cell and cause it to lose one or more electrons, causing a series of events that result in the production of ion pairs. For this reason, such radiation is termed *ionizing radiation* (Section 9.1).

Ions produced in this way are highly energetic. Consequently they may damage biological molecules and cause changes in cellular biochemical processes. Interaction of ionizing radiation with intracellular water produces free electrons and other particles that can damage DNA. This may result in diminished or altered cell function or, in extreme cases, the death of the cell.

An organ that is cancerous is composed of both healthy cells and malignant cells. Tumor cells are more susceptible to the effects of gamma radiation than normal cells because they are undergoing cell division more frequently. Therefore exposure of the tumor area to carefully targeted and controlled dosages of high-energy gamma radiation from cobalt-60 (a high-energy gamma ray source) will kill a higher percentage of abnormal cells than normal cells. If the dosage is administered correctly, a sufficient number of malignant cells will die, destroying the tumor, and enough normal cells will survive to maintain the function of the affected organ.

Gamma radiation can cure cancer. Paradoxically, the exposure of healthy cells to gamma radiation can actually cause cancer. For this reason, radiation therapy for cancer is a treatment that requires unusual care and sophistication.

Nuclear Medicine

The diagnosis of a host of biochemical irregularities or diseases of the human body has been made routine through the use of radioactive tracers. Medical **tracers** are small amounts of radioactive substances used as probes to study internal organs. Medical techniques involving tracers are **nuclear imaging** procedures.

A small amount of the tracer, an isotope of an element that is known to be attracted to the organ of interest, is administered to the patient. For a variety of reasons, such as ease of administration of the isotope to the patient and targeting the organ of interest, the isotope is often a part of a larger molecule or ion. Because the isotope is radioactive, its path may be followed by using suitable detection devices. A "picture" of the organ is obtained, often far more detailed than is possible with conventional X-rays. Such techniques are noninvasive; that is, surgery is not required to investigate the condition of the internal organ, eliminating the risk associated with an operation.

The radioactive isotope of an element chosen for tracer studies has chemical behavior similar to any other isotope of the same element. For example, iodine-127, the most abundant nonradioactive isotope of iodine, is used by the body in the

Animation
• Operation of a Nuclear Power Plant

LEARNING GOAL
6 ▶ Cite examples of the use of radioactive isotopes in medicine.

LEARNING GOAL
7 ▶ Describe the use of ionizing radiation in cancer therapy.

LEARNING GOAL
8 ▶ Discuss the preparation and use of radioisotopes in diagnostic imaging studies.

Animation
• Nuclear Medical Techniques

A close up of a scanned image of human intestines.

synthesis of thyroid hormones and tends to concentrate in the thyroid gland. Both iodine-127 and radioactive iodine-131 behave in the same way, making it possible to use iodine-131 to study the thyroid. The rate of uptake of the radioactive isotope gives valuable information regarding underactivity or overactivity (hypoactive or hyperactive thyroid).

Isotopes with short half-lives are preferred for tracer studies. These isotopes emit their radiation in a more concentrated burst (short half-life materials have greater activity), facilitating their detection. If the radioactive decay is easily detected, the method is more sensitive and thus capable of providing more information. Furthermore, an isotope with a short half-life decays to background more rapidly. This is a mechanism for removal of the radioactivity from the body. If the radioactive element is also rapidly metabolized and excreted, this is obviously beneficial as well.

The following examples illustrate the use of imaging procedures for diagnosis of disease.

- *Bone disease and injury.* The most widely used isotope for bone studies is technetium-99m, which is incorporated into a variety of ions and molecules that direct the isotope to the tissue being investigated. Technetium compounds containing phosphate are preferentially adsorbed on the surface of bone. New bone formation (common to virtually all bone injuries) increases the incorporation of the technetium compound. As a result, an enhanced image appears at the site of the injury. Bone tumors behave in a similar fashion.
- *Cardiovascular diseases.* Thallium-201 is used in the diagnosis of coronary artery disease. The isotope is administered intravenously and delivered to the heart muscle in proportion to the blood flow. Areas of restricted flow are observed as having lower levels of radioactivity, indicating some type of blockage.
- *Pulmonary disease.* Xenon is one of the noble gases. Radioactive xenon-133 may be inhaled by the patient. The radioactive isotope will be transported from the lungs and distributed through the circulatory system. Monitoring the distribution, as well as the reverse process, the removal of the isotope from the body (exhalation), can provide evidence of obstructive pulmonary disease, such as cancer or emphysema.

Examples of useful isotopes and the organ(s) in which they tend to concentrate are summarized in Table 9.4.

For many years, imaging with radioactive tracers was used exclusively for diagnosis. Recent applications have expanded to other areas of medicine. Imaging is now used extensively to guide surgery, assist in planning radiation therapy, and support the technique of angioplasty.

Question 9.7 Technetium-99m is used in diagnostic imaging studies involving the brain. What fraction of the radioisotope remains after 12 h have elapsed? See Table 9.2 for the half-life of technetium-99m.

Question 9.8 Barium-131 is a radioisotope used to study bone formation. A patient ingested barium-131. How much time will elapse until only one-fourth of the barium-131 remains, assuming that none of the isotope is eliminated from the body through normal processes? The half-life of barium-131 is 11.6 min.

Making Isotopes for Medical Applications

In early experiments with radioactivity, the radioactive isotopes were naturally occurring. For this reason the radioactivity produced by these unstable isotopes is described as **natural radioactivity.** If, on the other hand, a normally stable, nonradioactive nucleus is made radioactive, the resulting radioactivity is termed **artificial radioactivity.** The stable nucleus is made unstable by the introduction of "extra" protons, neutrons, or both.

LEARNING GOAL

8 ▸ Discuss the preparation and use of radioisotopes in diagnostic imaging studies.

LEARNING GOAL

9 ▸ Explain the difference between natural and artificial radioactivity.

Table 9.4 Isotopes Commonly Used in Nuclear Medicine

Area of Body	Isotope	Use
Blood	Red blood cells tagged with chromium-51	Determine blood volume in body
Bone	*Technetium-99m, barium-131, strontium-87	Allow early detection of the extent of bone tumors and active sites of rheumatoid arthritis
Brain	*Technetium-99m	Detect and locate brain tumors and stroke
Coronary artery	Thallium-201	Determine the presence and location of obstructions in coronary arteries
Heart	*Technetium-99m	Determine cardiac output, size, and shape
Kidney	*Technetium-99m	Determine renal function and location of cysts; a common follow-up procedure for kidney transplant patients
Liver-spleen	*Technetium-99m	Determine size and shape of liver and spleen; location of tumors
Lung	Xenon-133	Determine whether lung fills properly; locate region of reduced ventilation and tumors
Thyroid	Iodine-131	Determine rate of iodine uptake by thyroid

*The destination of this isotope is determined by the identity of the compound in which it is incorporated.

Figure 9.7 A portion of a linear accelerator located at Brookhaven National Laboratory in New York. Particles can be accelerated at velocities close to the speed of light and accurately strike small "target" nuclei. At such facilities, rare isotopes can be synthesized and their properties studied.

The process of forming radioactive substances is often accomplished in the core of a *nuclear reactor,* in which an abundance of small nuclear particles, particularly neutrons, is available. Alternatively, extremely high velocity charged particles (such as alpha and beta particles) may be produced in *particle accelerators,* such as a cyclotron. Accelerators are extremely large and use magnetic and electric fields to "push and pull" charged particles toward their target at very high speeds. A portion of the accelerator at the Brookhaven National Laboratory is shown in Figure 9.7.

Many isotopes that are useful in medicine are produced by particle bombardment. A few examples include the following:

• Gold-198, used as a tracer in the liver, is prepared by neutron bombardment.

$$^{197}_{79}\text{Au} + ^{1}_{0}\text{n} \longrightarrow ^{198}_{79}\text{Au}$$

A Medical Perspective

Magnetic Resonance Imaging

The Nobel Prize in physics was awarded to Otto Stern in 1943 and to Isidor Rabi in 1944. They discovered that certain atomic nuclei have a property known as spin, analogous to the spin associated with electrons, which we discussed in Chapter 2. The spin of electrons is responsible for the magnetic properties of atoms. Spinning nuclei behave as tiny magnets, producing magnetic fields as well.

One very important aspect of this phenomenon is the fact that the atoms in close proximity to the spinning nucleus (its chemical environment) exert an effect on the nuclear spin. In effect, measurable differences in spin are indicators of their surroundings. This relationship has been exhaustively studied for one atom in particular, hydrogen, and magnetic resonance techniques have become useful tools for the study of molecules containing hydrogen.

Human organs and tissue are made up of compounds containing hydrogen atoms. In the 1970s and 1980s the experimental technique was extended beyond tiny laboratory samples of pure compounds to the most complex sample possible—the human body. The result of these experiments is termed *magnetic resonance imaging (MRI)*.

MRI is noninvasive to the body, requires no use of radioactive substances, and is quick, safe, and painless. A person

Dr. Paul Barnett of the Greater Baltimore Medical Center studies images obtained using MRI.

is placed in a cavity surrounded by a magnetic field, and an image (based on the extent of radio frequency energy absorption) is generated, stored, and sorted in a computer. Differences between normal and malignant tissue, atherosclerotic thickening of an aortal wall, and a host of other problems may be seen clearly in the final image.

Advances in MRI technology have provided medical practitioners with a powerful tool in diagnostic medicine. This is but one more example of basic science leading to technological advancement.

For Further Understanding

▶ Why is hydrogen a useful atom to study in biological systems?

▶ Why would MRI provide minimal information about bone tissue?

A patient entering an MRI scanner.

- Gallium-67, used in the diagnosis of Hodgkin's disease, is prepared by proton bombardment.

$$^{66}_{20}\text{Zn} + ^{1}_{1}\text{p} \longrightarrow ^{67}_{31}\text{Ga}$$

Some medically useful isotopes with short half-lives must be prepared near the site of the clinical test. Preparation and shipment from a reactor site would waste time and result in an isotopic solution that had already undergone significant decay, resulting in diminished activity.

A common example is technetium-99m. It has a half-life of only 6 h. It is prepared in a small generator, often housed in a hospital's radiology laboratory (Figure 9.8). The generator contains radioactive molybdate ion (MoO_4^{2-}). Molybdenum-99 is more stable than technetium-99m; it has a half-life of 67 h.

(a)   **(b)**

Figure 9.8 Preparation of technetium-99m. (a) A diagram depicting the conversion of $^{99}MoO_4^{2-}$ to $^{99m}TcO_4^-$ through radioactive decay. The radioactive pertechnetate ion is periodically removed from the generator in saline solution and used in tracer studies.
(b) A photograph of a commercially available technetium-99m generator suitable for use in a hospital laboratory.

The molybdenum in molybdate ion decays according to the following nuclear equation:

$$^{99}_{42}Mo \longrightarrow {}^{99m}_{43}Tc + {}^{0}_{-1}e$$

Chemically, radioactive molybdate MoO_4^{2-} converts to radioactive pertechnetate ion (TcO_4^-). The radioactive TcO_4^- is removed from the generator when needed. It is administered to the patient as an aqueous salt solution that has an osmotic pressure identical to that of human blood.

9.6 Biological Effects of Radiation

It is necessary to use suitable precautions in working with radioactive substances. The chosen protocol is based on an understanding of the effects of radiation, dosage levels and "tolerable levels," the way in which radiation is detected and measured, and the basic precepts of radiation safety.

Radiation Exposure and Safety

In working with radioactive materials, the following factors must be considered.

The Magnitude of the Half-Life

Short-half-life radioisotopes produce a larger amount of radioactivity per unit time than a long-half-life substance. For example, consider equal amounts of hypothetical isotopes that produce alpha particles. One has a half-life of 10 days; the other has a half-life of 100 days. In one half-life, each substance will produce exactly the same number of alpha particles. However, the first substance generates the alpha particles in only one-tenth of the time, hence emits ten times as much radiation per unit time. Equal exposure times will result in a higher level of radiation exposure for substances with short half-lives, and lower levels for substances with long half-lives.

On the other hand, materials with short half-lives (weeks, days, or less) may be safer to work with, especially if an accident occurs. Over time (depending on the magnitude of the half-life) radioactive isotopes will decay to **background radiation** levels. This is the level of radiation attributable to our surroundings on a day-to-day basis.

Virtually all matter is composed of both radioactive and nonradioactive isotopes. Small amounts of radioactive material in the air, water, soil, and so forth make up a part of the background levels. Cosmic rays from outer space continually bombard us with radiation, contributing to the total background. Owing to the inevitability of background radiation, there can be no situation on earth where we observe zero radiation levels.

An isotope with a short half-life, for example 5.0 min, may decay to background in less than 1 h:

See Green Chemistry: Nuclear Waste Disposal on page 298.

$$10 \text{ half-lives} \times \frac{5.0 \text{ min}}{1 \text{ half-life}} = 50 \text{ min}$$

A spill of such material could be treated by waiting ten half-lives, perhaps by going to lunch. When you return to the laboratory, the material that was spilled will be no more radioactive than the floor itself. An accident with plutonium-239, which has a half-life of 24,000 years, would be quite a different matter! After 50 min, virtually all of the plutonium-239 would still remain. Long-half-life isotopes, by-products of nuclear technology, pose the greatest problems for safe disposal. Finding a site that will remain undisturbed "forever" is quite a formidable task.

Question 9.9 Describe the advantage of using isotopes with short half-lives for tracer applications in a medical laboratory.

Question 9.10 Can you think of any disadvantage associated with the use of isotopes described in Question 9.9? Explain.

Shielding

Alpha and beta particles, being relatively low in penetrating power, require low-level **shielding.** A lab coat and gloves are generally sufficient protection from this low-penetration radiation. On the other hand, shielding made of lead, concrete, or both is required for gamma rays (and X-rays, which are also high-energy radiation). Extensive manipulation of gamma emitters is often accomplished in laboratory and industrial settings by using robotic control: computer-controlled mechanical devices that can be programmed to perform virtually all manipulations normally carried out by humans.

Distance from the Radioactive Source

Radiation intensity varies *inversely* with the *square* of the distance from the source. Doubling the distance from the source *decreases* the intensity by a factor of four (2^2). Again, the use of robot manipulators is advantageous, allowing a greater distance between the operator and the radioactive source.

Time of Exposure

The effects of radiation are cumulative. Generally, potential damage is directly proportional to the time of exposure. Workers exposed to moderately high levels of radiation on the job may be limited in the time that they can perform that task. For example, workers involved in the cleanup of the Three Mile Island nuclear plant, incapacitated in 1979, observed strict limits on the amount of time that they could be involved in the cleanup activities.

Types of Radiation Emitted

Alpha and beta emitters are generally less hazardous than gamma emitters, owing to differences in energy and penetrating power that require less shielding. However, ingestion or inhalation of an alpha emitter or beta emitter can, over time, cause serious tissue damage; the radioactive substance is in direct contact with sensitive tissue. Green Chemistry: Radon and Indoor Air Pollution (p. 307) expands on this problem.

Waste Disposal

Virtually all applications of nuclear chemistry create radioactive waste and, along with it, the problems of safe handling and disposal. Most disposal sites, at present, are considered temporary, until a long-term safe solution can be found. Figure 9.9 conveys a sense of the enormity of the problem. Also, Green Chemistry: Nuclear Waste Disposal on page 298, examines this problem in more detail.

9.7 Measurement of Radiation

The changes that take place when radiation interacts with matter (such as photographic film) provide the basis of operation for various radiation detection devices.

The principal detection methods involve the use of either photographic film to create an image of the location of the radioactive substance or a counter that allows the measurement of intensity of radiation emitted from some source by converting the radiation energy to an electrical signal.

Nuclear Imaging

This approach is often used in nuclear medicine. An isotope, perhaps iodine-131, is administered to a patient to study the thyroid gland, and the isotope begins to concentrate in the organ of interest. Nuclear images (photographs) of that region of the body are taken at periodic intervals using a special type of film. The emission of radiation from the radioactive substance creates the image, in much the same way as light causes the formation of images on conventional film in a camera. Upon development of the series of photographs, a record of the organ's uptake of the isotope over time enables the radiologist to assess the condition of the organ.

Computer Imaging

The coupling of rapid developments in the technology of television and computers, resulting in the marriage of these two devices, has brought about a versatile alternative to photographic imaging.

A specialized television camera, sensitive to emitted radiation from a radioactive substance administered to a patient, develops a continuous and instantaneous record of the voyage of the isotope throughout the body. The signal, transmitted to the computer, is stored, sorted, and portrayed on a monitor. Advantages include increased sensitivity, allowing a lower dose of the isotope, speed through elimination of the developing step, and versatility of application, limited perhaps only by the creativity of the medical practitioners.

A particular type of computer imaging, useful in diagnostic medicine, is the CT scanner. The CT scanner measures the interaction of X-rays with biological tissue, gathering huge amounts of data and processing the data to produce detailed information, all in a relatively short time. Such a device may be less hazardous than conventional X-ray techniques because it generates more useful information per unit of radiation. It often produces a superior image. A photograph of a CT scanner is shown in Figure 9.10, and an image of a damaged spinal bone, taken by a CT scanner, is shown in Figure 9.11.

The Geiger Counter

A Geiger counter is an instrument that detects ionizing radiation. Ions, produced by radiation passing through a tube filled with an ionizable gas, can conduct an electrical current between two electrodes. This current flow can be measured and is proportional to the level of radiation (Figure 9.12). Such devices, which were routinely used in laboratory and industrial monitoring, have been largely replaced by more sophisticated devices, often used in conjunction with a computer.

Figure 9.9 Photograph of the construction of one-million-gallon (gal) capacity storage tanks for radioactive waste. Located in Hanford, Washington, they are now covered with 6–8 feet (ft) of earth.

LEARNING GOAL

11 ▶ Be familiar with common techniques for the detection of radioactivity.

CT represents *Computerized Tomography*: the computer reconstructs a series of measured images of tissue density (tomography). Small differences in tissue density may indicate the presence of a tumor.

Figure 9.10 An imaging laboratory at the Greater Baltimore Medical Center.

Figure 9.11 Damage observed in a spinal bone on a CT scan image.

Figure 9.12 The design of a Geiger counter used for the measurement of radioactivity.

Film Badges

A common sight in any hospital or medical laboratory or any laboratory that routinely uses radioisotopes is the film badge worn by all staff members exposed in any way to low-level radioactivity.

A film badge is merely a piece of photographic film that is sensitive to energies corresponding to radioactive emissions. It is shielded from light, which would interfere, and mounted in a clip-on plastic holder that can be worn throughout the workday. The badges are periodically collected and developed. The degree of darkening is proportional to the amount of radiation to which the worker has been exposed, just as a conventional camera produces images on film in proportion to the amount of light that it "sees."

Proper record keeping thus allows the laboratory using radioactive substances to maintain an ongoing history of each individual's exposure and, at the same time, promptly pinpoint any hazards that might otherwise go unnoticed.

Units of Radiation Measurement

The amount of radiation emitted by a source or received by an individual is reported in a variety of ways, using units that describe different aspects of radiation. The *curie* and the *roentgen* describe the intensity of the emitted radiation, whereas the *rad* and the *rem* describe the biological effects of radiation.

The Curie

The **curie** is a measure of the amount of radioactivity in a radioactive source. The curie is independent of the nature of the radiation (alpha, beta, or gamma) and its effect on biological tissue. A curie is defined as the amount of radioactive material that produces 3.7×10^{10} atomic disintegrations per second (s).

The Roentgen

The **roentgen** is a measure of very high energy ionizing radiation (X-ray and gamma ray) only. The roentgen is defined as the amount of radiation needed to produce 2×10^9 ion pairs when passing through 1 cubic centimeter (cm^3) of air at 0°C. The roentgen is a measure of radiation's interaction with air and gives no information about the effect on biological tissue.

The Rad

The **rad,** or *radiation absorbed dosage,* provides more meaningful information than either of the previous units of measure. It takes into account the nature of the absorbing material. It is defined as the dosage of radiation able to transfer 2.4×10^{-3} calories (cal) of energy to 1 kilogram (kg) of matter.

The Rem

The **rem,** or *roentgen equivalent for man,* describes the biological damage caused by the absorption of different kinds of radiation by the human body. The *rem* is

Green Chemistry

Radon and Indoor Air Pollution

Marie and Pierre Curie first discovered that air in contact with radium compounds became radioactive. Later experiments by Ernest Rutherford and others isolated the radioactive substance from the air. This substance was an isotope of the noble gas radon (Rn).

We now know that radium (Ra) produces radon by spontaneous decay:

$$^{226}_{88}\text{Ra} \longrightarrow {}^{4}_{2}\text{He} + {}^{222}_{86}\text{Rn}$$

Radium in trace quantities is found in soil and rock, and is unequally distributed in the soil. The decay product, radon, is emitted from the soil to the surrounding atmosphere. Radon is also found in higher concentrations where uranium is found in the soil. This is not surprising, because radium is formed as a part of the stepwise decay of uranium.

If someone constructs a building over soil or rock that has a high radium content (or uses stone with a high radium content to build the foundation!), the radon gas can percolate through the basement and accumulate in the house. Couple this with the need to build more energy-efficient, well-insulated dwellings, and the radon levels in buildings in some regions of the country can become quite high.

Radon itself is radioactive; however, its radiation is not the major problem. Because it is a gas and chemically inert, it is rapidly exhaled after breathing. However, radon decays to polonium:

$$^{222}_{86}\text{Rn} \longrightarrow {}^{4}_{2}\text{He} + {}^{218}_{84}\text{Po}$$

This polonium isotope is radioactive and is a nonvolatile heavy metal that can attach itself to bronchial or lung tissue, emitting hazardous radiation and producing other isotopes that are also radioactive.

In the United States, homes are now being tested and monitored for radon. In many states, proof of acceptable levels of radon is a condition of sale of the property. Studies continue to attempt to find reasonable solutions to the radon problem. Current recommendations include sealing cracks and openings in basements, increasing ventilation, and evaluating sites before construction of buildings. Debate continues within the scientific community regarding a safe and attainable indoor air quality standard for radon.

For Further Understanding

▶ Why is indoor radon more hazardous than outdoor radon?

▶ Polonium-218 has a very long half-life. Explain why this constitutes a potential health problem.

---

obtained by multiplication of the *rad* by a factor called the *relative biological effect (RBE)*. The RBE is a function of the type of radiation (alpha, beta, or gamma). Although a beta particle is more penetrating than an alpha particle, an alpha particle is approximately ten times more damaging to biological tissue. As a result, the RBE is ten for alpha particles and one for beta particles.

The **lethal dose (LD$_{50}$)** of radiation is defined as the acute dosage of radiation that would be fatal for 50% of the exposed population within 30 days. An estimated lethal dose is 500 rems. Some biological effects, however, may be detectable at a level as low as 25 rems. Relative yearly radiation dosages received by Americans are shown in Figure 9.13.

Question 9.11 From a clinical standpoint, what advantages does expressing radiation in rems have over the use of other radiation units?

Question 9.12 Is the roentgen unit used in the measurement of alpha particle radiation? Why or why not?

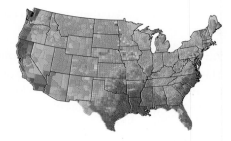

Figure 9.13 Relative yearly radiation dosages for individuals in the continental United States. Red, yellow, and green shading indicates higher levels of background radiation. Blue shading indicates regions of lower background exposure.

SUMMARY

9.1 Natural Radioactivity

Radioactivity is the process by which atoms emit energetic, ionizing particles or rays. These particles or rays are termed radiation. Nuclear radiation occurs because the nucleus is unstable, hence radioactive. Nuclear symbols consist of the elemental symbol, the atomic number, and the mass number.

Not all *nuclides* are unstable. Only unstable nuclides undergo change and produce radioactivity in the process of radioactive decay. Natural radiation emitted by unstable nuclei includes *alpha particles, beta particles, positrons,* and *gamma rays*. This radiation is collectively termed *ionizing radiation*.

9.2 Writing a Balanced Nuclear Equation

A *nuclear equation* represents a nuclear process such as radioactive decay. The total of the mass numbers on each side of the reaction arrow must be identical, and the sum of the atomic numbers of the reactants must equal the sum of the atomic numbers of the products. Nuclear equations can be used to predict products of nuclear reactions.

9.3 Properties of Radioisotopes

The *binding energy* of the nucleus is a measure of nuclear stability. When an isotope decays, energy is released. Nuclear stability correlates with the ratio of neutrons to protons in the isotope. Nuclei with large numbers of protons tend to be unstable, and isotopes containing 2, 8, 20, 50, 82, or 126 protons or neutrons (magic numbers) are stable. Also, isotopes with even numbers of protons or neutrons are generally more stable than those with odd numbers of protons or neutrons.

The *half-life*, $t_{1/2}$, is the time required for one-half of a given quantity of a substance to undergo change. Each isotope has its own characteristic half-life. The degree of stability of an isotope is indicated by the isotope's half-life. Isotopes with short half-lives decay rapidly; they are very unstable.

Radiocarbon dating is based on the measurement of the relative amounts of carbon-12 and carbon-14 present in an object. The ratio of the masses of these isotopes changes slowly over time, making it useful in determining the age of objects containing carbon.

9.4 Nuclear Power

Einstein predicted that a small amount of nuclear mass would convert to a very large amount of energy when the nucleus breaks apart. *Fission* reactors are used to generate electrical power. Technological problems with *fusion* and *breeder* reactors have prevented their commercialization in the United States.

9.5 Medical Applications of Radioactivity

The use of radiation in the treatment of various forms of cancer, and in the newer area of *nuclear medicine*, has become widespread in the past quarter century.

Ionizing radiation causes changes in cellular biochemical processes that may damage or kill the cell. A cancerous organ is composed of both healthy and malignant cells. Exposure of the tumor area to controlled dosages of high-energy gamma radiation from cobalt-60 will kill a higher percentage of abnormal cells than normal cells and is a valuable cancer therapy.

The diagnosis of a host of biochemical irregularities or diseases of the human body has been made routine through the use of radioactive tracers. *Tracers* are small amounts of radioactive substances used as probes to study internal organs. Because the isotope is radioactive, its path may be followed by using suitable detection devices. A "picture" of the organ is obtained, far more detailed than is possible with conventional X-rays.

The radioactivity produced by unstable isotopes is described as *natural radioactivity*. A normally stable, nonradioactive nucleus can be made radioactive, and this is termed *artificial radioactivity* (the process produces synthetic isotopes). Synthetic isotopes are often used in clinical situations. Isotopic synthesis may be carried out in the core of a *nuclear reactor* or in a *particle accelerator*. Short-lived isotopes, such as technetium-99m, are often produced directly at the site of the clinical testing.

9.6 Biological Effects of Radiation

Safety considerations are based on the magnitude of the *half-life, shielding,* distance from the radioactive source, time of exposure, and type of radiation emitted. We are never entirely free of the effects of radioactivity. *Background radiation* is normal radiation attributable to our surroundings.

Virtually all applications of nuclear chemistry create radioactive waste and, along with it, the problems of safe handling and disposal. Most disposal sites are considered temporary, until a long-term safe solution can be found.

9.7 Measurement of Radiation

The changes that take place when radiation interacts with matter provide the basis for various radiation detection devices. Photographic imaging, computer imaging, the Geiger counter, and film badges represent the most frequently used devices for detecting and measuring radiation.

Commonly used radiation units include the *curie,* a measure of the amount of radioactivity in a radioactive source; the *roentgen,* a measure of high-energy radiation (X-ray and gamma ray); the *rad* (radiation absorbed dosage), which takes into account the nature of the absorbing material; and the *rem* (roentgen equivalent for man), which describes the biological damage caused by the absorption of different kinds of radiation by the human body. The *lethal dose* of radiation, LD_{50}, is defined as the dose that would be fatal for 50% of the exposed population within 30 days.

KEY TERMS

alpha particle (9.1)	natural radioactivity (9.5)
artificial radioactivity (9.5)	nuclear equation (9.2)
background radiation (9.6)	nuclear imaging (9.5)
beta particle (9.1)	nuclear medicine (9.5)
binding energy (9.3)	nuclear reactor (9.4)
breeder reactor (9.4)	nuclide (9.1)
chain reaction (9.4)	positron (9.2)
curie (9.7)	rad (9.7)
fission (9.4)	radioactivity (9.1)
fusion (9.4)	radiocarbon dating (9.3)
gamma ray (9.1)	rem (9.7)
half-life ($t_{1/2}$) (9.3)	roentgen (9.7)
ionizing radiation (9.1)	shielding (9.6)
lethal dose (LD_{50}) (9.7)	tracer (9.5)
metastable isotope (9.2)	

QUESTIONS AND PROBLEMS

Natural Radioactivity

Foundations

9.13 Describe the meaning of the term *natural radioactivity*.
9.14 What is background radiation?
9.15 What is the composition of an alpha particle?
9.16 What is alpha decay?
9.17 What is the composition of a beta particle?
9.18 What is the composition of a positron?
9.19 In what way do beta particles and positrons differ?
9.20 In what way are beta particles and positrons similar?
9.21 What are the major differences between alpha and beta particles?
9.22 What are the major differences between alpha particles and gamma radiation?
9.23 How do nuclear reactions and chemical reactions differ?
9.24 We can control the rate of chemical reactions. Can we control the rate of natural radiation?

Applications

9.25 Write the nuclear symbol for an alpha particle.
9.26 Write the nuclear symbol for a beta particle.
9.27 Write the nuclear symbol for uranium-235.
9.28 How many protons and neutrons are contained in the nucleus of uranium-235?
9.29 How many protons and neutrons are contained in each of the three isotopes of hydrogen?
9.30 How many protons and neutrons are contained in each of the three isotopes of carbon?
9.31 Write the nuclear symbol for nitrogen-15.
9.32 Write the nuclear symbol for carbon-14.
9.33 Compare and contrast the three major types of radiation produced by nuclear decay.
9.34 Rank the three major types of radiation in order of size, speed, and penetrating power.
9.35 How does an alpha particle differ from a helium atom?
9.36 What is the major difference between beta and gamma radiation?

Writing a Balanced Nuclear Equation

Foundations

9.37 Write a nuclear equation to represent cobalt-60 decaying to nickel-60 plus a beta particle plus a gamma ray.
9.38 Write a nuclear equation to represent radium-226 decaying to radon-222 plus an alpha particle.
9.39 Complete the following nuclear equation:

$$^{23}_{11}\text{Na} + {}^{2}_{1}\text{H} \longrightarrow ? + {}^{1}_{1}\text{H}$$

9.40 Complete the following nuclear equation:

$$^{238}_{92}\text{U} + {}^{14}_{7}\text{N} \longrightarrow ? + 6{}^{1}_{0}\text{n}$$

9.41 Complete the following nuclear equation:

$$^{24}_{10}\text{Ne} \longrightarrow \beta + ?$$

9.42 Complete the following nuclear equation:

$$^{190}_{78}\text{Pt} \longrightarrow \alpha + ?$$

9.43 Complete the following nuclear equation:

$$? \longrightarrow {}^{140}_{56}\text{Ba} + {}^{0}_{-1}\text{e}$$

9.44 Complete the following nuclear equation:

$$? \longrightarrow {}^{214}_{90}\text{Th} + {}^{4}_{2}\text{He}$$

Applications

9.45 Element 107 was synthesized by bombarding bismuth-209 with chromium-54. Write the equation for this process if one product is a neutron.
9.46 Element 109 was synthesized by bombarding bismuth-209 with iron-58. Write the equation for this process if one product is a neutron.
9.47 Write a balanced nuclear equation for beta emission by magnesium-27.
9.48 Write a balanced nuclear equation for alpha decay of bismuth-212.
9.49 Write a balanced nuclear equation for position emission by nitrogen-12.
9.50 Write a balanced nuclear equation for the formation of polonium-206 through alpha decay.
9.51 Americium-241, found in many home smoke detectors, decays by alpha emission. The alpha particle ionizes surrounding air molecules, and ions produced conduct an electric current. Smoke particles block this process and the change in current triggers an alarm. Write the balanced nuclear equation for the decay of americium-241.
9.52 Element 106 was recently named seaborgium (Sg) in honor of Glenn T. Seaborg, a pioneer in the discovery of lanthanide and actinide elements. Seaborgium-263 decays by alpha emission. Write a balanced nuclear equation for this process.

Properties of Radioisotopes

Foundations

9.53 What is the difference between natural radioactivity and artificial radioactivity?
9.54 Is the fission of uranium-235 an example of natural or artificial radioactivity?
9.55 Summarize the major characteristics of nuclei for which we predict a high degree of stability.
9.56 Explain why the binding energy of a nucleus is expected to be large.

Applications

9.57 Would you predict oxygen-20 to be stable? Explain your reasoning.
9.58 Would you predict cobalt-59 to be stable? Explain your reasoning.
9.59 Would you predict chromium-48 to be stable? Explain your reasoning.
9.60 Would you predict lithium-9 to be stable? Explain your reasoning.
9.61 If 3.2 mg of the radioisotope iodine-131 is administered to a patient, how much will remain in the body after 24 days, assuming that no iodine has been eliminated from the body by any other process? (See Table 9.2 for the half-life of iodine-131.)
9.62 A patient receives 9.0 ng of a radioisotope with a half-life of 12 h. How much will remain in the body after 2.0 days, assuming that radioactive decay is the only path for removal of the isotope from the body?
9.63 A sample containing 1.00×10^2 mg of iron-59 is stored for 135 days. What mass of iron-59 will remain at the end of the storage period? (See Table 9.2 for the half-life of iron-59.)
9.64 An instrument for cancer treatment containing a cobalt-60 source was manufactured in 1978. In 1995 it was removed from service and, in error, was buried in a landfill with the source still in place. What percentage of its initial radioactivity will remain in the year 2010? (See Table 9.2 for the half-life of cobalt-60.)

9.65 Describe the process used to determine the age of the wooden coffin of King Tut.

9.66 What property of carbon enables us to assess the age of a painting?

Nuclear Power

Foundations

9.67 Which type of nuclear process splits nuclei to release energy?

9.68 Which type of nuclear process combines small nuclei to release energy?

9.69 **a.** Describe the process of fission.
  b. How is this reaction useful as the basis for the production of electrical energy?

9.70 **a.** Describe the process of fusion.
  b. How could this process be used for the production of electrical energy?

Applications

9.71 Write a balanced nuclear equation for a fusion reaction.

9.72 What are the major disadvantages of a fission reactor for electrical energy production?

9.73 What is meant by the term *breeder reactor?*

9.74 What are the potential advantages and disadvantages of breeder reactors?

9.75 Describe what is meant by the term *chain reaction*.

9.76 Why are cadmium rods used in a fission reaction?

9.77 What is the greatest barrier to development of fusion reactors?

9.78 What type of nuclear reaction fuels our solar system?

Medical Applications of Radioactivity

Foundations

9.79 Why is radiation therapy an effective treatment for certain types of cancer?

9.80 Describe how medically useful isotopes may be prepared.

9.81 What is the source of background radiation?

9.82 Why do high-altitude jet flights increase a person's exposure to background radiation?

Applications

9.83 The isotope indium-111 is used in medical laboratories as a label for blood platelets. To prepare indium-111, silver-108 is bombarded with an alpha particle, forming an intermediate isotope of indium. Write a nuclear equation for the process, and identify the intermediate isotope of indium.

9.84 Radioactive molybdenum-99 is used to produce the tracer isotope, technetium-99m. Write a nuclear equation for the formation of molybdenum-99 from stable molybdenum-98 bombarded with neutrons.

9.85 Describe an application of each of the following isotopes:
  a. technetium-99m
  b. xenon-133

9.86 Describe an application of each of the following isotopes:
  a. iodine-131
  b. thallium-201

Answer Questions 9.87 through 9.94 based on the assumption that you are employed by a clinical laboratory that prepares radioactive isotopes for medical diagnostic tests. Consider alpha, beta, positron, and gamma emission.

9.87 What would be the effect on your level of radiation exposure if you increase your average distance from a radioactive source?

9.88 Would wearing gloves have any significant effect? Why?

9.89 Would limiting your time of exposure have a positive effect? Why?

9.90 Would wearing a lab apron lined with thin sheets of lead have a positive effect? Why?

9.91 Would the use of robotic manipulation of samples have an effect? Why?

9.92 Would the use of concrete rather than wood paneling help to protect workers in other parts of the clinic? Why?

9.93 Would the thickness of the concrete in Question 9.92 be an important consideration? Why?

9.94 Suggest a protocol for radioactive waste disposal.

Measurement of Radiation

Foundations

9.95 What is meant by the term *relative biological effect?*

9.96 What is meant by the term *lethal dose* of radiation?

9.97 Define each of the following units:
  a. curie
  b. roentgen

9.98 Define each of the following radiation units:
  a. rad
  b. rem

Applications

9.99 X-ray technicians often wear badges containing photographic film. How is this film used to indicate exposure to X-rays?

9.100 Why would a Geiger counter be preferred to film for assessing the immediate danger resulting from a spill of some solution containing a radioisotope?

CRITICAL THINKING PROBLEMS

1. Isotopes used as radioactive tracers have chemical properties that are similar to those of a nonradioactive isotope of the same element. Explain why this is a critical consideration in their use.

2. A chemist proposes a research project to discover a catalyst that will speed up the decay of radioactive isotopes that are waste products of a medical laboratory. Such a discovery would be a potential solution to the problem of nuclear waste disposal. Critique this proposal.

3. A controversial solution to the disposal of nuclear waste involves burial in sealed chambers far below the earth's surface. Describe potential pros and cons of this approach.

4. What type of radioactive decay is favored if the number of protons in the nucleus is much greater than the number of neutrons? Explain.

5. If the proton-to-neutron ratio in Problem 4 (above) were reversed, what radioactive decay process would be favored? Explain.

6. Radioactive isotopes are often used as "tracers" to follow an atom through a chemical reaction, and the following is an example. Acetic acid reacts with methyl alcohol by eliminating a molecule of water to form methyl acetate. Explain how you would use the radioactive isotope oxygen-18 to show whether the oxygen atom in the water product comes from the —OH of the acid or the —OH of the alcohol.

$$\underset{\text{Acetic acid}}{H_3C-\overset{\overset{\displaystyle O}{\|}}{C}-OH} + \underset{\text{Methyl alcohol}}{HOCH_3} \longrightarrow \underset{\text{Methyl acetate}}{H_3C-\overset{\overset{\displaystyle O}{\|}}{C}-O-CH_3} + H_2O$$

7. Chromium-51, used as a tracer to study red blood cells, decays by electron capture. In this process a proton in the chromium nucleus is, in effect, converted to a neutron by combining with (capturing) an electron. Write a balanced equation for this process. What is the identity of the product?

Glossary

A

absolute specificity (19.5) the property of an enzyme that allows it to bind and catalyze the reaction of only one substrate

accuracy (1.3) the nearness of an experimental value to the true value

acetal (13.4) the family of organic compounds formed via the reaction of two molecules of alcohol with an aldehyde in the presence of an acid catalyst; acetals have the following general structure:

$$R^1\!-\!\underset{\underset{H}{|}}{\overset{\overset{OR^2}{|}}{C}}\!-\!OR^3$$

acetyl coenzyme A (acetyl CoA) (14.4, 22.2) a molecule composed of coenzyme A and an acetyl group; the intermediate that provides acetyl groups for complete oxidation by aerobic respiration

acid (8.1) a substance that behaves as a proton donor

acid anhydride (14.3) the product formed by the combination of an acid chloride and a carboxylate ion; structurally they are two carboxylic acids with a water molecule removed:

$$(Ar)R\!-\!\overset{\overset{O}{\|}}{C}\!-\!O\!-\!\overset{\overset{O}{\|}}{C}\!-\!R(Ar)$$

acid-base reaction (4.4) reaction that involves the transfer of a hydrogen ion (H^+) from one reactant to another

acid chloride (14.3) member of the family of organic compounds with the general formula

$$(Ar)R\!-\!\overset{\overset{O}{\|}}{C}\!-\!Cl$$

activated complex (7.3) the arrangement of atoms at the top of the potential energy barrier as a reaction proceeds

activation energy (7.3) the threshold energy that must be overcome to produce a chemical reaction

active site (19.4) the cleft in the surface of an enzyme that is the site of substrate binding

acyl carrier protein (ACP) (23.4) the protein that forms a thioester linkage with fatty acids during fatty acid synthesis

acyl group (14: Intro, 15.3) the functional group found in carboxylic acid derivatives that contains the carbonyl group attached to one alkyl or aryl group:

$$(Ar)R\!-\!\overset{\overset{O}{\|}}{C}\!-$$

addition polymer (11.5) polymers prepared by the sequential addition of a monomer

addition reaction (11.5, 13.4) a reaction in which two molecules add together to form a new molecule; often involves the addition of one molecule to a double or triple bond in an unsaturated molecule; e.g., the addition of alcohol to an aldehyde or ketone to form a hemiacetal or hemiketal

adenosine triphosphate (ATP) (14.4, 21.1) a nucleotide composed of the purine adenine, the sugar ribose, and three phosphoryl groups; the primary energy storage and transport molecule used by the cells in cellular metabolism

adipocyte (23.1) a fat cell

adipose tissue (23.1) fatty tissue that stores most of the body lipids

aerobic respiration (22.3) the oxygen-requiring degradation of food molecules and production of ATP

alcohol (12.1) an organic compound that contains a hydroxyl group (—OH) attached to an alkyl group

aldehyde (13.1) a class of organic molecules characterized by a carbonyl group; the carbonyl carbon is bonded to a hydrogen atom and to another hydrogen or an alkyl or aryl group. Aldehydes have the following general structure:

$$(Ar)\!-\!\overset{\overset{O}{\|}}{C}\!-\!H \qquad R\!-\!\overset{\overset{O}{\|}}{C}\!-\!H$$

aldol condensation (13.4) a reaction in which aldehydes or ketones react to form a larger molecule

aldose (16.2) a sugar that contains an aldehyde (carbonyl) group

aliphatic hydrocarbon (10.1) any member of the alkanes, alkenes, and alkynes or the substituted alkanes, alkenes, and alkynes

alkali metal (2.4) an element within Group IA (1) of the periodic table

alkaline earth metal (2.4) an element within Group IIA (2) of the periodic table

alkaloid (15.2) a class of naturally occurring compounds that contain one or more nitrogen heterocyclic rings; many of the alkaloids have medicinal and other physiological effects

alkane (10.2) a hydrocarbon that contains only carbon and hydrogen and is bonded together through carbon-hydrogen and carbon-carbon single bonds; a saturated hydrocarbon with the general molecular formula C_nH_{2n+2}

alkene (11.1) a hydrocarbon that contains one or more carbon-carbon double bonds; an unsaturated hydrocarbon with the general formula C_nH_{2n}

alkyl group (10.2) a hydrocarbon group that results from the removal of one hydrogen from the original hydrocarbon (e.g., methyl, —CH_3; ethyl, —CH_2CH_3)

alkyl halide (10.5) a substituted hydrocarbon with the general structure R—X, in which R— represents any alkyl group and X = a halogen (F—, Cl—, Br—, or I—)

alkylammonium ion (15.1) the ion formed when the lone pair of electrons of the nitrogen atom of an amine is shared with a proton (H^+) from a water molecule

alkyne (11.1) a hydrocarbon that contains one or more carbon-carbon triple bonds; an unsaturated hydrocarbon with the general formula C_nH_{2n-2}

allosteric enzyme (19.9) an enzyme that has an effector binding site and an active site; effector binding changes the shape of the active site, rendering it either active or inactive

alpha particle (9.1) a particle consisting of two protons and two neutrons; the alpha particle is identical to a helium nucleus

amide bond (15.3) the bond between the carbonyl carbon of a carboxylic acid and the amino nitrogen of an amine

amides (15.3) the family of organic compounds formed by the reaction between a carboxylic acid derivative and an amine and characterized by the amide group

amines (15.1) the family of organic molecules with the general formula RNH_2, R_2NH, or R_3N (R— can represent either an alkyl or aryl group); they may be viewed as substituted ammonia molecules in which one or more of the ammonia hydrogens has been substituted by a more complex organic group

α-amino acid (18.1) the subunits of proteins composed of an α-carbon bonded to a carboxylate group, a protonated amino group, a hydrogen atom, and a variable R group

aminoacyl group (15.4) the functional group that is characteristic of an amino acid; the aminoacyl group has the following general structure:

$$H_3\overset{+}{N}\!-\!\underset{\underset{R}{|}}{\overset{\overset{H}{|}}{C}}\!-\!\overset{\overset{O}{\|}}{C}\!-$$

aminoacyl tRNA (20.6) the transfer RNA covalently linked to the correct amino acid

aminoacyl tRNA binding site of ribosome (A-site) (20.6) a pocket on the surface of a ribosome that holds the aminoacyl tRNA during translation

aminoacyl tRNA synthetase (20.6) an enzyme that recognizes one tRNA and covalently links the appropriate amino acid to it

amorphous solid (5.3) a solid with no organized, regular structure

amphibolic pathway (22.9) a metabolic pathway that functions in both anabolism and catabolism

amphiprotic (8.1) a substance that can behave either as a Brønsted acid or a Brønsted base

amylopectin (16.6) a highly branched form of amylose; the branches are attached to the C-6 hydroxyl by $\alpha(1 \rightarrow 6)$ glycosidic linkage; a component of starch

amylose (16.6) a linear polymer of α-D-glucose molecules bonded in $\alpha(1 \rightarrow 4)$ glycosidic linkage that is a component of starch; a polysaccharide storage form

anabolism (21.1, 22.9) all of the cellular energy-requiring biosynthetic pathways

anaerobic threshold (21.4) the point at which the level of lactate in the exercising muscle inhibits glycolysis and the muscle, deprived of energy, ceases to function

analgesic (15.2) any drug that acts as a painkiller, e.g., aspirin, acetaminophen

anaplerotic reaction (22.9) a reaction that replenishes a substrate needed for a biochemical pathway

anesthetic (15.2) a drug that causes a lack of sensation in part of the body (local anesthetic) or causes unconsciousness (general anesthetic)

angular structure (3.4) a planar molecule with bond angles other than 180°

anion (2.6) a negatively charged atom or group of atoms

anode (8.5) the positively charged electrode in an electrical cell

anomers (16.4) isomers of cyclic monosaccharides that differ from one another in the arrangement of bonds around the hemiacetal carbon

antibodies (18: Intro) immunoglobulins; specific glycoproteins produced by cells of the immune system in response to invasion by infectious agents

anticodon (20.4) a sequence of three ribonucleotides on a tRNA that are complementary to a codon on the mRNA; codon-anticodon binding results in delivery of the correct amino acid to the site of protein synthesis

antigen (18: Intro) any substance that is able to stimulate the immune system; generally a protein or large carbohydrate

antiparallel strands (20.2) a term describing the polarities of the two strands of the DNA double helix; on one strand the sugar-phosphate backbone advances in the $5' \rightarrow 3'$ direction; on the opposite, complementary strand the sugar-phosphate backbone advances in the $3' \rightarrow 5'$ direction

apoenzyme (19.7) the protein portion of an enzyme that requires a cofactor to function in catalysis

aqueous solution (6.1) any solution in which the solvent is water

arachidonic acid (17.2) a fatty acid derived from linoleic acid; the precursor of the prostaglandins

aromatic hydrocarbon (10.1, 11.6) an organic compound that contains the benzene ring or a derivative of the benzene ring

Arrhenius theory (8.1) a theory that describes an acid as a substance that dissociates to produce H^+ and a base as a substance that dissociates to produce OH^-

artificial radioactivity (9.5) radiation that results from the conversion of a stable nucleus to another, unstable nucleus

atherosclerosis (17.4) deposition of excess plasma cholesterol and other lipids and proteins on the walls of arteries, resulting in decreased artery diameter and increased blood pressure

atom (2.1) the smallest unit of an element that retains the properties of that element

atomic mass (2.1) the mass of an atom expressed in atomic mass units

atomic mass unit (4.1) 1/12 of the mass of a ^{12}C atom, equivalent to 1.661×10^{-24} g

atomic number (2.1) the number of protons in the nucleus of an atom; it is a characteristic identifier of an element

atomic orbital (2.3, 2.5) a specific region of space where an electron may be found

ATP synthase (22.6) a multiprotein complex within the inner mitochondrial membrane that uses the energy of the proton (H^+) gradient to produce ATP

autoionization (8.1) also known as *self-ionization*, the reaction of a substance, such as water, with itself to produce a positive and a negative ion

Avogadro's law (5.1) a law that states that the volume is directly proportional to the number of moles of gas particles, assuming that the pressure and temperature are constant

Avogadro's number (4.1) 6.022×10^{23} particles of matter contained in 1 mol of a substance

axial atom (10.4) an atom that lies above or below a cycloalkane ring

B

background radiation (9.6) the radiation that emanates from natural sources

barometer (5.1) a device for measuring pressure

base (8.1) a substance that behaves as a proton acceptor

base pair (20.2) a hydrogen-bonded pair of bases within the DNA double helix; the standard base pairs always involve a purine and a pyrimidine; in particular, adenine always base pairs with thymine and cytosine with guanine

Benedict's reagent (16.4) a buffered solution of Cu^{2+} ions that can be used to test for reducing sugars or to distinguish between aldehydes and ketones

Benedict's test (13.4) a test used to determine the presence of reducing sugars or to distinguish between aldehydes and ketones; it requires a buffered solution of Cu^{2+} ions

that are reduced to Cu^+, which precipitates as brick-red Cu_2O

beta particle (9.1) an electron formed in the nucleus by the conversion of a neutron into a proton

bile (23.1) micelles of lecithin, cholesterol, bile salts, protein, inorganic ions, and bile pigments that aid in lipid digestion by emulsifying fat droplets

binding energy (9.3) the energy required to break down the nucleus into its component parts

bioinformatics (20.10) an interdisciplinary field that uses computer information sciences and DNA technology to devise methods for understanding, analyzing, and applying DNA sequence information

boat conformation (10.4) a form of a six-member cycloalkane that resembles a rowboat. It is less stable than the chair conformation because the hydrogen atoms are not perfectly staggered

boiling point (3.3) the temperature at which the vapor pressure of a liquid is equal to the atmospheric pressure

bond energy (3.4) the amount of energy necessary to break a chemical bond

Boyle's law (5.1) a law stating that the volume of a gas varies inversely with the pressure exerted if the temperature and number of moles of gas are constant

breeder reactor (9.4) a nuclear reactor that produces its own fuel in the process of providing electrical energy

Brønsted-Lowry theory (8.1) a theory that describes an acid as a proton donor and a base as a proton acceptor

buffer capacity (8.4) a measure of the ability of a solution to resist large changes in pH when a strong acid or strong base is added

buffer solution (8.4) a solution containing a weak acid or base and its salt (the conjugate base or acid) that is resistant to large changes in pH upon addition of strong acids or bases

buret (8.3) a device calibrated to deliver accurately known volumes of liquid, as in a titration

C

C-terminal amino acid (18.2) the amino acid in a peptide that has a free α-CO_2^- group; the last amino acid in a peptide

calorimetry (7.2) the measurement of heat energy changes during a chemical reaction

cap structure (20.4) a 7-methylguanosine unit covalently bonded to the 5' end of a mRNA by a 5'-5' triphosphate bridge

carbinol carbon (12.4) that carbon in an alcohol to which the hydroxyl group is attached

carbohydrate (16.1) generally sugars and polymers of sugars; the primary source of energy for the cell

carbonyl group (13: Intro) the functional group that contains a carbon-oxygen double

bond: —C=O; the functional group found in aldehydes and ketones

carboxyl group (14.1) the —COOH functional group; the functional group found in carboxylic acids

carboxylic acid (14.1) a member of the family of organic compounds that contain the —COOH functional group

carboxylic acid derivative (14.2) any of several families of organic compounds, including the esters and amides, that are derived from carboxylic acids and have the general formula

$$(Ar)\overset{\overset{\displaystyle O}{\|}}{-}C-Z \qquad R\overset{\overset{\displaystyle O}{\|}}{-}C-Z$$

Z = —OR or OAr for the esters, and
Z = —NH$_2$ for the amides

carcinogen (20.7) any chemical or physical agent that causes mutations in the DNA that lead to uncontrolled cell growth or cancer

catabolism (21.1, 22.9) the degradation of fuel molecules and production of ATP for cellular functions

catalyst (7.3) any substance that increases the rate of a chemical reaction (by lowering the activation energy of the reaction) and that is not destroyed in the course of the reaction

cathode (8.5) the negatively charged electrode in an electrical cell

cathode rays (2.2) a stream of electrons that is given off by the cathode (negative electrode) in a cathode ray tube

cation (2.6) a positively charged atom or group of atoms

cellulose (16.6) a polymer of β-D-glucose linked by β(1 → 4) glycosidic bonds

central dogma (20.4) a statement of the directional transfer of the genetic information in cells: DNA → RNA → Protein

chain reaction (9.4) the process in a fission reactor that involves neutron production and causes subsequent reactions accompanied by the production of more neutrons in a continuing process

chair conformation (10.4) the most energetically favorable conformation for a six-member cycloalkane; so-called for its resemblance to a lawn chair

Charles's law (5.1) a law stating that the volume of a gas is directly proportional to the temperature of the gas, assuming that the pressure and number of moles of the gas are constant

chemical bond (3.1) the attractive force holding two atomic nuclei together in a chemical compound

chemical equation (4.3) a record of chemical change, showing the conversion of reactants to products

chemical formula (4.2) the representation of a compound or ion in which elemental symbols represent types of atoms and subscripts show the relative numbers of atoms

chemical property (1.2) characteristics of a substance that relate to the substance's participation in a chemical reaction

chemical reaction (1.2) a process in which atoms are rearranged to produce new combinations

chemistry (1.1) the study of matter and the changes that matter undergoes

chiral carbon (16.3) a carbon atom bonded to four different atoms or groups of atoms

chiral molecule (16.3) molecule capable of existing in mirror-image forms

cholesterol (17.4) a twenty-seven-carbon steroid ring structure that serves as the precursor of the steroid hormones

chromosome (20.2) a piece of DNA that carries the genetic instructions, or genes, of an organism

chylomicron (17.5, 23.1) a plasma lipoprotein (aggregate of protein and triglycerides) that carries triglycerides from the intestine to all body tissues via the bloodstream

cis-trans **isomers** (10.3) isomers that differ from one another in the placement of substituents on a double bond or ring

citric acid cycle (22.4) a cyclic biochemical pathway that is the final stage of degradation of carbohydrates, fats, and amino acids. It results in the complete oxidation of acetyl groups derived from these dietary fuels

cloning vector (20.8) a DNA molecule that can carry a cloned DNA fragment into a cell and that has a replication origin that allows the DNA to be replicated abundantly within the host cell

coagulation (18.9) the process by which proteins in solution are denatured and aggregate with one another to produce a solid

codon (20.4) a group of three ribonucleotides on the mRNA that specifies the addition of a specific amino acid onto the growing peptide chain

coenzyme (19.7) an organic group required by some enzymes; it generally serves as a donor or acceptor of electrons or a functional group in a reaction

coenzyme A (22.2) a molecule derived from ATP and the vitamin pantothenic acid; coenzyme A functions in the transfer of acetyl groups in lipid and carbohydrate metabolism

cofactor (19.7) an inorganic group, usually a metal ion, that must be bound to an apoenzyme to maintain the correct configuration of the active site

colipase (23.1) a protein that aids in lipid digestion by binding to the surface of lipid droplets and facilitating binding of pancreatic lipase

colligative property (6.4) property of a solution that is dependent only on the concentration of solute particles

colloidal suspension (6.1) a heterogeneous mixture of solute particles in a solvent; distribution of solute particles is not uniform because of the size of the particles

combination reaction (4.3) a reaction in which two substances join to form another substance

combined gas law (5.1) an equation that describes the behavior of a gas when volume, pressure, and temperature may change simultaneously

combustion (10.5) the oxidation of hydrocarbons by burning in the presence of air to produce carbon dioxide and water

competitive inhibitor (19.10) a structural analog; a molecule that has a structure very similar to the natural substrate of an enzyme, competes with the natural substrate for binding to the enzyme active site, and inhibits the reaction

complementary strands (20.2) the opposite strands of the double helix are hydrogen-bonded to one another such that adenine and thymine or guanine and cytosine are always paired

complete protein (18.10) a protein source that contains all the essential and nonessential amino acids

complex lipid (17.5) a lipid bonded to other types of molecules

compound (1.2) a substance that is characterized by constant composition and that can be chemically broken down into elements

concentration (1.5, 6.2) a measure of the quantity of a substance contained in a specified volume of solution

concentration gradient (6.4) region where concentration decreases over distance

condensation (5.2) the conversion of a gas to a liquid

condensation polymer (14.2) a polymer, which is a large molecule formed by combination of many small molecules (monomers) that results from joining of monomers in a reaction that forms a small molecule, such as water or an alcohol

condensed formula (10.2) a structural formula showing all of the atoms in a molecule and placing them in a sequential arrangement that details which atoms are bonded to each other; the bonds themselves are not shown

conformations, conformers (10.4) discrete, distinct isomeric structures that may be converted, one to the other, by rotation about the bonds in the molecule

conjugate acid (8.1) substance that has one more proton than the base from which it is derived

conjugate acid-base pair (8.1) two species related to each other through the gain or loss of a proton

conjugate base (8.1) substance that has one fewer proton than the acid from which it is derived

constitutional isomers (10.2) two molecules having the same molecular formulas, but different chemical structures

Cori Cycle (21.6) a metabolic pathway in which the lactate produced by working muscle is taken up by cells in the liver and converted back to glucose by gluconeogenesis

corrosion (8.5) the unwanted oxidation of a metal

covalent bonding (3.1) a pair of electrons shared between two atoms

covalent solid (5.3) a collection of atoms held together by covalent bonds

cristae (22.1) the folds of the inner membrane of the mitochondria

crystal lattice (3.1) a unit of a solid characterized by a regular arrangement of components

crystalline solid (5.3) a solid having a regular repeating atomic structure

curie (9.7) the quantity of radioactive material that produces 3.7×10^{10} nuclear disintegrations per second

cycloalkane (10.3) a cyclic alkane; a saturated hydrocarbon that has the general formula C_nH_{2n}

D

Dalton's law (5.1) also called the law of partial pressures; states that the total pressure exerted by a gas mixture is the sum of the partial pressures of the component gases

data (1.2) facts resulting from an experiment

decomposition reaction (4.3) the breakdown of a substance into two or more substances

defense proteins (18: Intro) proteins that defend the body against infectious diseases; antibodies are defense proteins

degenerate code (20.5) a term used to describe the fact that several triplet codons may be used to specify a single amino acid in the genetic code

dehydration (of alcohols) (12.5) a reaction that involves the loss of a water molecule, in this case the loss of water from an alcohol and the simultaneous formation of an alkene

deletion mutation (20.7) a mutation that results in the loss of one or more nucleotides from a DNA sequence

denaturation (18.9) the process by which the organized structure of a protein is disrupted, resulting in a completely disorganized, nonfunctional form of the protein

density (1.5) mass per unit volume of a substance

deoxyribonucleic acid (DNA) (20.1) the nucleic acid molecule that carries all of the genetic information of an organism; the DNA molecule is a double helix composed of two strands, each of which is composed of phosphate groups, deoxyribose, and the nitrogenous bases thymine, cytosine, adenine, and guanine

deoxyribonucleotide (20.1) a nucleoside phosphate or nucleotide composed of a nitrogenous base in β-N-glycosidic linkage to the 1′ carbon of the sugar 2′-deoxyribose and with one, two, or three phosphoryl groups esterified at the hydroxyl of the 5′ carbon

diabetes mellitus (23.3) a disease caused by the production of insufficient levels of insulin and characterized by the appearance of very high levels of glucose in the blood and urine

dialysis (6.5) the removal of waste material via transport across a membrane

diastereomers (16.3) stereoisomers that are not mirror images of one another; these typically occur when the molecule has more than one chiral carbon

diffusion (6.4) net movement of solute or solvent molecules from a region of high concentration to a region of low concentration

diglyceride (17.3) the product of esterification of glycerol at two positions

dipole-dipole interactions (5.2) attractive forces between polar molecules

disaccharide (16.1) a sugar composed of two monosaccharides joined through an oxygen atom bridge

dissociation (3.3) production of positive and negative ions when an ionic compound dissolves in water

disulfide (12.9) an organic compound that contains a disulfide group (—S—S—)

DNA polymerase III (20.3) the enzyme that catalyzes the polymerization of daughter DNA strands using the parental strand as a template

double bond (3.4) a bond in which two pairs of electrons are shared by two atoms

double helix (20.2) the spiral staircase–like structure of the DNA molecule characterized by two sugar-phosphate backbones wound around the outside and nitrogenous bases extending into the center

double-replacement reaction (4.3) a chemical change in which cations and anions "exchange partners"

dynamic equilibrium (7.4) the state that exists when the rate of change in the concentration of products and reactants is equal, resulting in no net concentration change

E

eicosanoid (17.2) any of the derivatives of twenty-carbon fatty acids, including the prostaglandins, leukotrienes, and thromboxanes

electrolysis (8.5) an electrochemical process that uses electrical energy to cause nonspontaneous oxidation-reduction reactions to occur

electrolyte (3.3, 6.1) a material that dissolves in water to produce a solution that conducts an electrical current

electrolytic solution (3.3) a solution composed of an electrolytic solute dissolved in water

electromagnetic radiation (2.3) energy that is propagated as waves at the speed of light

electromagnetic spectrum (2.3) the complete range of electromagnetic waves

electron (2.1) a negatively charged particle outside of the nucleus of an atom

electron affinity (2.7) the energy released when an electron is added to an isolated atom

electron configuration (2.5) the arrangement of electrons around the nucleus of an atom, an ion, or a collection of nuclei of a molecule

electron density (2.3) the probability of finding the electron in a particular location

electron transport system (22.6) the series of electron transport proteins embedded in the inner mitochondrial membrane that accept high-energy electrons from NADH and FADH$_2$ and transfer them in stepwise fashion to molecular oxygen (O_2)

electronegativity (3.1) a measure of the tendency of an atom in a molecule to attract shared electrons

element (1.2) a substance that cannot be decomposed into simpler substances by chemical or physical means

elimination reaction (12.5) a reaction in which a molecule loses atoms or ions from its structure

elongation factor (20.6) proteins that facilitate the elongation phase of translation

emulsifying agent (17.3) a bipolar molecule that aids in the suspension of fats in water

enantiomers (16.3) stereoisomers that are nonsuperimposable mirror images of one another

endothermic reaction (7.1) a chemical or physical change in which energy is absorbed

energy (1.1) the capacity to do work

energy level (2.3) one of numerous atomic regions where electrons may be found

enthalpy (7.1) a term that represents heat energy

entropy (7.1) a measure of randomness or disorder

enzyme (18: Intro, 19: Intro) a protein that serves as a biological catalyst

enzyme specificity (19.5) the ability of an enzyme to bind to only one, or a very few, substrates and thus catalyze only a single reaction

enzyme-substrate complex (19.4) a molecular aggregate formed when the substrate binds to the active site of the enzyme

equatorial atom (10.4) an atom that lies in the plane of a cycloalkane ring

equilibrium constant (7.4) number equal to the ratio of the equilibrium concentrations of products to the equilibrium concentrations of reactants, each raised to the power corresponding to its coefficient in the balanced equation

equilibrium reaction (7.4) a reaction that is reversible and the rates of the forward and reverse reactions are equal

equivalence point (8.3) the situation in which reactants have been mixed in the molar ratio corresponding to the balanced equation

equivalent (6.5) the number of grams of an ion corresponding to Avogadro's number of electrical charges

error (1.3) the difference between the true value and the experimental value for data or results

essential amino acid (18.10) an amino acid that cannot be synthesized by the body and must therefore be supplied by the diet

essential fatty acids (17.2) the fatty acids linolenic and linoleic acids that must be supplied in the diet because they cannot be synthesized by the body

ester (14.2) a carboxylic acid derivative formed by the reaction of a carboxylic acid and an alcohol. Esters have the following general formula:

$$\underset{R-C-OR}{\overset{O}{\|}} \quad \underset{R-C-O(Ar)}{\overset{O}{\|}} \quad \underset{(Ar)-C-O(Ar)}{\overset{O}{\|}}$$

esterification (17.2) the formation of an ester in the reaction of a carboxylic acid and an alcohol

ether (12.8) an organic compound that contains two alkyl and/or aryl groups attached to an oxygen atom; R—O—R, Ar—O—R, and Ar—O—Ar

eukaryote (20.2) an organism having cells containing a true nucleus enclosed by a nuclear membrane and having a variety of membrane-bound organelles that segregate different cellular functions into different compartments

evaporation (5.2) the conversion of a liquid to a gas below the boiling point of the liquid

exon (20.4) protein-coding sequences of a gene found on the final mature mRNA

exothermic reaction (7.1) a chemical or physical change that releases energy

extensive property (1.2) a property of a substance that depends on the quantity of the substance

F

F₀F₁ complex (22.6) an alternative term for the ATP synthase, the multiprotein complex in the inner mitochondrial membrane that uses the energy of the proton gradient to produce ATP

fatty acid (14.1, 17.2) any member of the family of continuous-chain carboxylic acids that generally contain four to twenty carbon atoms; the most concentrated source of energy used by the cell

feedback inhibition (19.9) the process whereby excess product of a biosynthetic pathway turns off the entire pathway for its own synthesis

fermentation (12.3, 21.4) anaerobic (in the absence of oxygen) catabolic reactions that occur with no net oxidation. Pyruvate or an organic compound produced from pyruvate is reduced as NADH is oxidized

fibrous protein (18.4) a protein composed of peptides arranged in long sheets or fibers

Fischer Projection (16.3) a two-dimensional drawing of a molecule, which shows a chiral carbon at the intersection of two lines and horizontal lines representing bonds projecting out of the page and vertical lines representing bonds that project into the page

fission (9.4) the splitting of heavy nuclei into lighter nuclei accompanied by the release of large quantities of energy

fluid mosaic model (17.6) the model of membrane structure that describes the fluid nature of the lipid bilayer and the presence of numerous proteins embedded within the membrane

formula (3.2) the representation of the fundamental compound unit using chemical symbols and numerical subscripts

formula mass (4.2) the mass of a formula unit of a compound relative to a standard (carbon-12)

formula unit (4.2) the smallest collection of atoms from which the formula of a compound can be established

free energy (7.1) the combined contribution of entropy and enthalpy for a chemical reaction

fructose (16.4) a ketohexose that is also called levulose and fruit sugar; the sweetest of all sugars, abundant in honey and fruits

fuel value (7.2) the amount of energy derived from a given mass of material

functional group (10.1) an atom (or group of atoms and their bonds) that imparts specific chemical and physical properties to a molecule

fusion (9.4) the joining of light nuclei to form heavier nuclei, accompanied by the release of large amounts of energy

G

galactose (16.4) an aldohexose that is a component of lactose (milk sugar)

galactosemia (16.5) a human genetic disease caused by the inability to convert galactose to a phosphorylated form of glucose (glucose-1-phosphate) that can be used in cellular metabolic reactions

gamma ray (9.1) a high-energy emission from nuclear processes, traveling at the speed of light; the high-energy region of the electromagnetic spectrum

gaseous state (1.2) a physical state of matter characterized by a lack of fixed shape or volume and ease of compressibility

genome (20.2) the complete set of genetic information in all the chromosomes of an organism

geometric isomer (10.3, 11.3) an isomer that differs from another isomer in the placement of substituents on a double bond or a ring

globular protein (18.5) a protein composed of polypeptide chains that are tightly folded into a compact spherical shape

glucagon (21.7, 23.6) a peptide hormone synthesized by the α-cells of the islets of Langerhans in the pancreas and secreted in response to low blood glucose levels; glucagon promotes glycogenolysis and gluconeogenesis and thereby increases the concentration of blood glucose

gluconeogenesis (21.6) the synthesis of glucose from noncarbohydrate precursors

glucose (16.4) an aldohexose, the most abundant monosaccharide; it is a component of many disaccharides, such as lactose and sucrose, and of polysaccharides, such as cellulose, starch, and glycogen

glyceraldehyde (16.3) an aldotriose that is the simplest carbohydrate; phosphorylated forms of glyceraldehyde are important intermediates in cellular metabolic reactions

glyceride (17.3) a lipid that contains glycerol

glycogen (16.6, 21.7) a long, branched polymer of glucose stored in liver and muscles of animals; it consists of a linear backbone of α-D-glucose in $\alpha(1 \rightarrow 4)$ linkage, with numerous short branches attached to the C-6 hydroxyl group by $\alpha(1 \rightarrow 6)$ linkage

glycogenesis (21.7) the metabolic pathway that results in the addition of glucose to growing glycogen polymers when blood glucose levels are high

glycogen granule (21.7) a core of glycogen surrounded by enzymes responsible for glycogen synthesis and degradation

glycogenolysis (21.7) the biochemical pathway that results in the removal of glucose molecules from glycogen polymers when blood glucose levels are low

glycolysis (21.3) the enzymatic pathway that converts a glucose molecule into two molecules of pyruvate; this anaerobic process generates a net energy yield of two molecules of ATP and two molecules of NADH

glycoprotein (18.6) a protein bonded to sugar groups

glycosidic bond (16.1) the bond between the hydroxyl group of the C-1 carbon of one sugar and a hydroxyl group of another sugar

group (2.4) any one of eighteen vertical columns of elements; often referred to as a family

group specificity (19.5) an enzyme that catalyzes reactions involving similar substrate molecules having the same functional groups

guanosine triphosphate (GTP) (21.6) a nucleotide composed of the purine guanosine, the sugar ribose, and three phosphoryl groups

H

half-life ($t_{1/2}$) (9.3) the length of time required for one-half of the initial mass of an isotope to decay to products

halogen (2.4) an element found in Group VIIA (17) of the periodic table

halogenation (10.5, 11.5) a reaction in which one of the C—H bonds of a hydrocarbon is replaced with a C—X bond (X = Br or Cl generally)

Haworth projection (16.4) a means of representing the orientation of substituent groups around a cyclic sugar molecule

heat (7.1) energy transferred between a system and its surroundings due to a temperature difference between system and surroundings

α-helix (18.4) a right-handed coiled secondary structure maintained by hydrogen bonds between the amide hydrogen of one amino acid and the carbonyl oxygen of an amino acid four residues away

heme group (18.8) the chemical group found in hemoglobin and myoglobin that is responsible for the ability to carry oxygen

hemiacetal (13.4, 16.4) the family of organic compounds formed via the reaction of one molecule of alcohol with an aldehyde in the presence of an acid catalyst; hemiacetals have the following general structure:

$$\begin{array}{c} OH \\ | \\ R^1{-}C{-}OR^2 \\ | \\ H \end{array}$$

hemiketal (13.4, 16.4) the family of organic compounds formed via the reaction of one molecule of alcohol with a ketone in the presence of an acid catalyst; hemiketals have the following general structure:

$$\begin{array}{c} OH \\ | \\ R^1{-}C{-}OR^3 \\ | \\ R^2 \end{array}$$

hemoglobin (18.8) the major protein component of red blood cells; the function of this red, iron-containing protein is transport of oxygen

Henderson-Hasselbalch equation (8.4) an equation for calculating the pH of a buffer system:

$$pH = pK_a + \log \frac{[\text{conjugate base}]}{[\text{weak acid}]}$$

Henry's law (6.1) a law stating that the number of moles of a gas dissolved in a liquid at a given temperature is proportional to the partial pressure of the gas

heterocyclic amine (15.2) a heterocyclic compound that contains nitrogen in at least one position in the ring skeleton

heterocyclic aromatic compound (11.7) cyclic aromatic compound having at least one atom other than carbon in the structure of the aromatic ring

heterogeneous mixture (1.2) a mixture of two or more substances characterized by nonuniform composition

heteropolysaccharide (16.6) a polysaccharide composed of two or more different monosaccharides

hexose (16.2) a six-carbon monosaccharide

high-density lipoprotein (HDL) (17.5) a plasma lipoprotein that transports cholesterol from peripheral tissue to the liver

holoenzyme (19.7) an active enzyme consisting of an apoenzyme bound to a cofactor

homogeneous mixture (1.2) a mixture of two or more substances characterized by uniform composition

homopolysaccharide (16.6) a polysaccharide composed of identical monosaccharides

hybridization (20.8) a technique for identifying DNA or RNA sequences that is based on specific hydrogen bonding between a radioactive probe and complementary DNA or RNA sequences

hydrate (4.2) any substance that has water molecules incorporated in its structure

hydration (11.5, 12.5) a reaction in which water is added to a molecule, e.g., the addition of water to an alkene to form an alcohol

hydrocarbon (10.1) a compound composed solely of the elements carbon and hydrogen

hydrogen bonding (5.2) the attractive force between a hydrogen atom covalently bonded to a small, highly electronegative atom and another atom containing an unshared pair of electrons

hydrogenation (11.5, 13.4, 17.2) a reaction in which hydrogen (H_2) is added to a double or a triple bond

hydrohalogenation (11.5) the addition of a hydrohalogen (HCl, HBr, or HI) to an unsaturated bond

hydrolase (19.1) an enzyme that catalyzes hydrolysis reactions

hydrolysis (14.2) a chemical change that involves the reaction of a molecule with water; the process by which molecules are broken into their constituents by addition of water

hydronium ion (8.1) a protonated water molecule, H_3O^+

hydrophilic amino acid (18.1) "water loving"; a polar or ionic amino acid that has a high affinity for water

hydrophobic amino acid (18.1) "water fearing"; a nonpolar amino acid that prefers contact with other nonpolar molecules over contact with water

hydroxyl group (12.1) the —OH functional group that is characteristic of alcohols

hyperammonemia (22.8) a genetic defect in one of the enzymes of the urea cycle that results in toxic or even fatal elevation of the concentration of ammonium ions in the body

hyperglycemia (21.7) blood glucose levels that are higher than normal

hypertonic solution (6.4) the more concentrated solution of two separated by a semipermeable membrane

hypoglycemia (21.7) blood glucose levels that are lower than normal

hypothesis (1.1) an attempt to explain observations in a commonsense way

hypotonic solution (6.4) the more dilute solution of two separated by a semipermeable membrane

I

ideal gas (5.1) a gas in which the particles do not interact and the volume of the individual gas particles is assumed to be negligible

ideal gas law (5.1) a law stating that for an ideal gas the product of pressure and volume is proportional to the product of the number of moles of the gas and its temperature; the proportionality constant for an ideal gas is symbolized R

incomplete protein (18.10) a protein source that does not contain all the essential and nonessential amino acids

indicator (8.3) a solute that shows some condition of a solution (such as acidity or basicity) by its color

induced fit model (19.4) the theory of enzyme-substrate binding that assumes that the enzyme is a flexible molecule and that both the substrate and the enzyme change their shapes to accommodate one another as the enzyme-substrate complex forms

initiation factors (20.6) proteins that are required for formation of the translation initiation complex, which is composed of the large and small ribosomal subunits, the mRNA, and the initiator tRNA, methionyl tRNA

inner mitochondrial membrane (22.1) the highly folded, impermeable membrane within the mitochondrion that is the location of the electron transport system and ATP synthase

insertion mutation (20.7) a mutation that results in the addition of one or more nucleotides to a DNA sequence

insulin (21.7, 23.6) a hormone released from the pancreas in response to high blood glucose levels; insulin stimulates glycogenesis, fat storage, and cellular uptake and storage of glucose from the blood

intensive property (1.2) a property of a substance that is independent of the quantity of the substance

intermembrane space (22.1) the region between the outer and inner mitochondrial membranes, which is the location of the proton (H^+) reservoir that drives ATP synthesis

intermolecular force (3.5) any attractive force that occurs between molecules

intramolecular force (3.5) any attractive force that occurs within molecules

intron (20.4) a noncoding sequence within a eukaryotic gene that must be removed from the primary transcript to produce a functional mRNA

ion (2.6) an electrically charged particle formed by the gain or loss of electrons

ionic bonding (3.1) an electrostatic attractive force between ions resulting from electron transfer

ionic solid (5.3) a solid composed of positive and negative ions in a regular three-dimensional crystalline arrangement

ionization energy (2.7) the energy needed to remove an electron from an atom in the gas phase

ionizing radiation (9.1) radiation that is sufficiently high in energy to cause ion formation upon impact with an atom

ion pair (3.1) the simplest formula unit for an ionic compound

ion product for water (8.1) the product of the hydronium and hydroxide ion concentrations in pure water at a specified temperature; at 25°C, it has a value of 1.0×10^{-14}

irreversible enzyme inhibitor (19.10) a chemical that binds strongly to the R groups of an amino acid in the active site and eliminates enzyme activity

isoelectric point (18.9) a situation in which a protein has an equal number of positive and negative charges and therefore has an overall net charge of zero

isoelectronic (2.6) atoms, ions, and molecules containing the same number of electrons

isomerase (19.1) an enzyme that catalyzes the conversion of one isomer to another

isomers (3.4) molecules having the same molecular formula but different chemical structures

isotonic solution (6.4) a solution that has the same solute concentration as another solution with which it is being compared; a solution that has the same osmotic pressure as a solution existing within a cell

isotope (2.1) atom of the same element that differs in mass because it contains different numbers of neutrons

I.U.P.A.C. Nomenclature System (10.2) the International Union of Pure and Applied Chemistry (I.U.P.A.C.) standard, universal system for the nomenclature of organic compounds

K

α-keratin (18.4) a member of the family of fibrous proteins that form the covering of most land animals; major components of fur, skin, beaks, and nails

ketal (13.4) the family of organic compounds formed via the reaction of two molecules of alcohol with a ketone in the presence of an acid catalyst; ketals have the following general structure:

$$R^1 - \overset{\overset{\displaystyle OR^3}{|}}{\underset{\underset{\displaystyle R^2}{|}}{C}} - OR^4$$

ketoacidosis (23.3) a drop in the pH of the blood caused by elevated levels of ketone bodies

ketone (13.1) a family of organic molecules characterized by a carbonyl group; the carbonyl carbon is bonded to two alkyl groups, two aryl groups, or one alkyl and one aryl group; ketones have the following general structures:

$$R - \overset{\overset{\displaystyle O}{\|}}{C} - R \qquad R - \overset{\overset{\displaystyle O}{\|}}{C} - (Ar) \qquad (Ar) - \overset{\overset{\displaystyle O}{\|}}{C} - (Ar)$$

ketone bodies (23.3) acetone, acetoacetone, and β-hydroxybutyrate produced from fatty acids in the liver via acetyl CoA

ketose (16.2) a sugar that contains a ketone (carbonyl) group

ketosis (23.3) an abnormal rise in the level of ketone bodies in the blood

kinetic energy (1.5) the energy resulting from motion of an object [kinetic energy = $1/2(\text{mass})(\text{velocity})^2$]

kinetic molecular theory (5.1) the fundamental model of particle behavior in the gas phase

kinetics (7.3) the study of rates of chemical reactions

L

lactose (16.5) a disaccharide composed of β-D-galactose and either α- or β-D-glucose in β(1 → 4) glycosidic linkage; milk sugar

lactose intolerance (16.5) the inability to produce the digestive enzyme lactase, which degrades lactose to galactose and glucose

lagging strand (20.3) in DNA replication, the strand that is synthesized discontinuously from numerous RNA primers

law (1.1) a summary of a large quantity of information

law of conservation of mass (4.3) a law stating that, in chemical change, matter cannot be created or destroyed

leading strand (20.3) in DNA replication, the strand that is synthesized continuously from a single RNA primer

LeChatelier's principle (7.4) a law stating that when a system at equilibrium is disturbed, the equilibrium shifts in the direction that minimizes the disturbance

lethal dose (LD$_{50}$) (9.7) the quantity of toxic material (such as radiation) that causes the death of 50% of a population of an organism

Lewis structure (3.1) representation of a molecule (or polyatomic ion) that shows valence electron arrangement among the atoms in a molecule (or polyatomic ion)

Lewis symbol (3.1) representation of an atom (or ion) using the atomic symbol (for the nucleus and core electrons) and dots to represent valence electrons

ligase (19.1) an enzyme that catalyzes the joining of two molecules

linear structure (3.4) the structure of a molecule in which the bond angle(s) about the central atom(s) is (are) 180°

line formula (10.2) the simplest representation of a molecule, in which it is assumed that there is a carbon atom at any location where two or more lines intersect, there is a carbon at the end of any line, and each carbon is bonded to the correct number of hydrogen atoms

linkage specificity (19.5) the property of an enzyme that allows it to catalyze reactions involving only one kind of bond in the substrate molecule

lipase (23.1) an enzyme that hydrolyzes the ester linkage between glycerol and the fatty acids of triglycerides

lipid (17.1) a member of the group of biological molecules of varying composition that are classified together on the basis of their solubility in nonpolar solvents

liquid state (1.2) a physical state of matter characterized by a fixed volume and the absence of a fixed shape

lock-and-key model (19.4) the theory of enzyme-substrate binding that depicts enzymes as inflexible molecules; the substrate fits into the rigid active site in the same way a key fits into a lock

London forces (5.2) weak attractive forces between molecules that result from short-lived dipoles that occur because of the continuous movement of electrons in the molecules

lone pair (3.1) an electron pair that is not involved in bonding

low-density lipoprotein (LDL) (17.5) a plasma lipoprotein that carries cholesterol to peripheral tissues and helps to regulate cholesterol levels in those tissues

lyase (19.1) an enzyme that catalyzes a reaction involving double bonds

M

maltose (16.5) a disaccharide composed of α-D-glucose and a second glucose molecule in α(1 → 4) glycosidic linkage

Markovnikov's rule (11.5) the rule stating that a hydrogen atom, adding to a carbon-carbon double bond, will add to the carbon having the larger number of hydrogens attached to it

mass (1.5) a quantity of matter

mass/mass percent [% (m/m)] (6.2) the concentration of a solution expressed as a ratio of mass of solute to mass of solution multiplied by 100%

mass number (2.1) the sum of the number of protons and neutrons in an atom

mass/volume percent [% (m/V)] (6.2) the concentration of a solution expressed as a ratio of grams of solute to milliliters of solution multiplied by 100%

matrix space (22.1) the region of the mitochondrion within the inner membrane; the location of the enzymes that carry out the reactions of the citric acid cycle and β-oxidation of fatty acids

matter (1.1) the material component of the universe

melting point (3.3, 5.3) the temperature at which a solid converts to a liquid

meso compound (16.3) a special case of stereoisomers that occurs when a molecule has two chiral carbons and each chiral carbon has identical substituents; these molecules are achiral because they have a plane of symmetry within the molecule

messenger RNA (20.4) an RNA species produced by transcription and that specifies the amino acid sequence for a protein

metal (2.4) an element located on the left side of the periodic table (left of the "staircase" boundary)

metallic bond (5.3) a bond that results from the orbital overlap of metal atoms

metallic solid (5.3) a solid composed of metal atoms held together by metallic bonds

metalloid (2.4)   an element along the "staircase" boundary between metals and nonmetals; metalloids exhibit both metallic and nonmetallic properties

metastable isotope (9.2)   an isotope that will give up some energy to produce a more stable form of the same isotope

micelle (23.1)   an aggregation of molecules having nonpolar and polar regions; the nonpolar regions of the molecules aggregate, leaving the polar regions facing the surrounding water

mitochondria (22.1)   the cellular "power plants" in which the reactions of the citric acid cycle, the electron transport system, and ATP synthase function to produce ATP

mixture (1.2)   a material composed of two or more substances

molality (6.4)   the number of moles of solute per kilogram of solvent

molar mass (4.1)   the mass in grams of 1 mol of a substance

molar volume (5.1)   the volume occupied by 1 mol of a substance

molarity (6.3)   the number of moles of solute per liter of solution

mole (4.1)   the amount of substance containing Avogadro's number of particles

molecular formula (10.2)   a formula that provides the atoms and number of each type of atom in a molecule but gives no information regarding the bonding pattern involved in the structure of the molecule

molecular solid (5.3)   a solid in which the molecules are held together by dipole-dipole and London forces (van der Waals forces)

molecule (3.1)   a unit in which the atoms of two or more elements are held together by chemical bonds

monatomic ion (3.2)   an ion formed by electron gain or loss from a single atom

monoglyceride (17.3)   the product of the esterification of glycerol at one position

monomer (11.5)   the individual molecules from which a polymer is formed

monosaccharide (16.1)   the simplest type of carbohydrate consisting of a single saccharide unit

movement protein (18: Intro)   a protein involved in any aspect of movement in an organism, for instance, actin and myosin in muscle tissue and flagellin that composes bacterial flagella

mutagen (20.7)   any chemical or physical agent that causes changes in the nucleotide sequence of a gene

mutation (20.7)   any change in the nucleotide sequence of a gene

myoglobin (18.8)   the oxygen storage protein found in muscle

N

N-terminal amino acid (18.2)   the amino acid in a peptide that has a free α-N$^+$H$_3$ group; the first amino acid of a peptide

natural radioactivity (9.5)   the spontaneous decay of a nucleus to produce high-energy particles or rays

negative allosterism (19.9)   effector binding inactivates the active site of an allosteric enzyme

neurotransmitter (15.5)   a chemical that carries a message, or signal, from a nerve cell to a target cell

neutral glyceride (17.3)   the product of the esterification of glycerol at one, two, or three positions

neutralization (8.3)   the reaction between an acid and a base

neutron (2.1)   an uncharged particle, with the same mass as the proton, in the nucleus of an atom

nicotinamide adenine dinucleotide (NAD$^+$) (21.3)   a molecule synthesized from the vitamin niacin and the nucleotide ATP and that serves as a carrier of hydride anions; a coenzyme that is an oxidizing agent used in a variety of metabolic processes

noble gas (2.4)   elements in Group VIIIA (18) of the periodic table

nomenclature (3.2)   a system for naming chemical compounds

nonelectrolyte (3.3, 6.1)   a substance that, when dissolved in water, produces a solution that does not conduct an electrical current

nonessential amino acid (18.10)   any amino acid that can be synthesized by the body

nonmetal (2.4)   an element located on the right side of the periodic table (right of the "staircase" boundary)

nonreducing sugar (16.5)   a sugar that cannot be oxidized by Benedict's or Tollens' reagent

normal boiling point (5.2)   the temperature at which a substance will boil at 1 atm of pressure

nuclear equation (9.2)   a balanced equation accounting for the products and reactants in a nuclear reaction

nuclear imaging (9.5)   the generation of images of components of the body (organs, tissues) using techniques based on the measurement of radiation

nuclear medicine (9.5)   a field of medicine that uses radioisotopes for diagnostic and therapeutic purposes

nuclear reactor (9.4)   a device for conversion of nuclear energy into electrical energy

nucleosome (20.2)   the first level of chromosome structure consisting of a strand of DNA wrapped around a small disk of histone proteins

nucleotide (20.1, 21.1)   a molecule composed of a nitrogenous base, a five-carbon sugar, and one, two, or three phosphoryl groups

nucleus (2.1)   the small, dense center of positive charge in the atom

nuclide (9.1)   any atom characterized by an atomic number and a mass number

nutrient protein (18: Intro)   a protein that serves as a source of amino acids for embryos or infants

nutritional Calorie (7.2)   equivalent to 1 kilocalorie (1000 calories); also known as a large Calorie

O

octet rule (2.6)   a rule predicting that atoms form the most stable molecules or ions when they are surrounded by eight electrons in their highest occupied energy level

oligosaccharide (16.1)   an intermediate-sized carbohydrate composed of from three to ten monosaccharides

osmolarity (6.4)   molarity of particles in solution; this value is used for osmotic pressure calculations

osmosis (6.4)   net flow of a solvent across a semipermeable membrane in response to a concentration gradient

osmotic pressure (6.4)   the net force with which water enters a solution through a semipermeable membrane; alternatively, the pressure required to stop net transfer of solvent across a semipermeable membrane

outer mitochondrial membrane (22.1)   the membrane that surrounds the mitochondrion and separates it from the contents of the cytoplasm; it is highly permeable to small "food" molecules

β-oxidation (23.2)   the biochemical pathway that results in the oxidation of fatty acids and the production of acetyl CoA

oxidation (8.5, 12.6, 13.4, 14.1)   a loss of electrons; in organic compounds it may be recognized as a loss of hydrogen atoms or the gain of oxygen

oxidation-reduction reaction (4.4)   also called redox reaction, a reaction involving the transfer of one or more electrons from one reactant to another

oxidative deamination (22.7)   an oxidation-reduction reaction in which NAD$^+$ is reduced and the amino acid is deaminated

oxidative phosphorylation (21.3, 22.6)   production of ATP using the energy of electrons harvested during biological oxidation-reduction reactions

oxidizing agent (8.5)   a substance that oxidizes, or removes electrons from, another substance; the oxidizing agent is reduced in the process

oxidoreductase (19.1)   an enzyme that catalyzes an oxidation-reduction reaction

P

pancreatic serine proteases (19.11)   a family of proteolytic enzymes, including trypsin, chymotrypsin, and elastase, that arose by divergent evolution

parent compound or parent chain (10.2)   in the I.U.P.A.C. Nomenclature System the parent compound is the longest carbon-carbon chain containing the principal functional group in the molecule that is being named

partial pressure (5.1)   the pressure exerted by one component of a gas mixture

pentose (16.2)   a five-carbon monosaccharide

pentose phosphate pathway (21.5)   an alternative pathway for glucose degradation that provides the cell with reducing power in the form of NADPH

peptide bond (15.4, 18.2)   the amide bond between two amino acids in a peptide chain

peptidyl tRNA binding site of ribosome (P-site) (20.6)   a pocket on the surface of the ribosome that holds the tRNA bound to the growing peptide chain

percent yield (4.5)   the ratio of the actual and theoretical yields of a chemical reaction multiplied by 100%

period (2.4)   any one of seven horizontal rows of elements in the periodic table

periodic law (2.4)   a law stating that properties of elements are periodic functions of their atomic numbers (Note that Mendeleev's original statement was based on atomic masses.)

peripheral membrane protein (17.6)   a protein bound to either the inner or the outer surface of a membrane

phenol (12.7)   an organic compound that contains a hydroxyl group (—OH) attached to a benzene ring

phenyl group (11.6)   a benzene ring that has had a hydrogen atom removed, C_6H_5—

pH optimum (19.8)   the pH at which an enzyme catalyzes the reaction at maximum efficiency

phosphatidate (17.3)   a molecule of glycerol with fatty acids esterified to C-1 and C-2 of glycerol and a free phosphoryl group esterified at C-3

phosphoanhydride (14.4)   the bond formed when two phosphate groups react with one another and a water molecule is lost

phosphoester (14.4)   the product of the reaction between phosphoric acid and an alcohol

phosphoglyceride (17.3)   a molecule with fatty acids esterified at the C-1 and C-2 positions of glycerol and a phosphoryl group esterified at the C-3 position

phospholipid (17.3)   a lipid containing a phosphoryl group

phosphopantetheine (23.4)   the portion of coenzyme A and the acyl carrier protein that is derived from the vitamin pantothenic acid

pH scale (8.2)   a numerical representation of acidity or basicity of a solution; $pH = -\log[H_3O^+]$

physical change (1.2)   a change in the form of a substance but not in its chemical composition; no chemical bonds are broken in a physical change

physical property (1.2)   a characteristic of a substance that can be observed without the substance undergoing change (examples include color, density, melting and boiling points)

plasma lipoprotein (17.5)   a complex composed of lipid and protein that is responsible for the transport of lipids throughout the body

β-pleated sheet (18.4)   a common secondary structure of a peptide chain that resembles the pleats of an Oriental fan

point mutation (20.7)   the substitution of one nucleotide pair for another within a gene

polar covalent bonding (3.4)   a covalent bond in which the electrons are not equally shared

polar covalent molecule (3.4)   a molecule that has a permanent electric dipole moment resulting from an unsymmetrical electron distribution; a dipolar molecule

poly(A) tail (20.4)   a tract of 100–200 adenosine monophosphate units covalently attached to the 3′ end of eukaryotic messenger RNA molecules

polyatomic ion (3.2)   an ion containing a number of atoms

polymer (11.5)   a very large molecule formed by the combination of many small molecules (called monomers) (e.g., polyamides, nylons)

polyprotic substance (8.3)   a substance that can accept or donate more than one proton per molecule

polysaccharide (16.1)   a large, complex carbohydrate composed of long chains of monosaccharides

polysome (20.6)   complexes of many ribosomes all simultaneously translating a single mRNA

positive allosterism (19.9)   effector binding activates the active site of an allosteric enzyme

positron (9.2)   particle that has the same mass as an electron but opposite (+) charge

post-transcriptional modification (20.4)   alterations of the primary transcripts produced in eukaryotic cells; these include addition of a poly(A) tail to the 3′ end of the mRNA, addition of the cap structure to the 5′ end of the mRNA, and RNA splicing

potential energy (1.5)   stored energy or energy caused by position or composition

precipitate (6.1)   an insoluble substance formed and separated from a solution

precision (1.3)   the degree of agreement among replicate measurements of the same quantity

pressure (5.1)   a force per unit area

primary (1°) alcohol (12.4)   an alcohol with the general formula RCH_2OH

primary (1°) amine (15.1)   an amine with the general formula RNH_2

primary (1°) carbon (10.2)   a carbon atom that is bonded to only one other carbon atom

primary structure (of a protein) (18.3)   the linear sequence of amino acids in a protein chain determined by the genetic information of the gene for each protein

primary transcript (20.4)   the RNA product of transcription in eukaryotic cells, before post-transcriptional modifications are carried out

principal energy level (2.5)   a region where electrons may be found; has integral values $n = 1$, $n = 2$, and so forth

product (4.3, 19.2)   the chemical species that results from a chemical reaction and that appears on the right side of a chemical equation

proenzyme (19.9)   the inactive form of a proteolytic enzyme

prokaryote (20.2)   an organism with simple cellular structure in which there is no true

nucleus enclosed by a nuclear membrane and there are no true membrane-bound organelles in the cytoplasm

promoter (20.4)   the sequence of nucleotides immediately before a gene that is recognized by the RNA polymerase and signals the start point and direction of transcription

properties (1.2)   characteristics of matter

prostaglandins (17.2)   a family of hormonelike substances derived from the twenty-carbon fatty acid, arachidonic acid; produced by many cells of the body, they regulate many body functions

prosthetic group (18.6)   the nonprotein portion of a protein that is essential to the biological activity of the protein; often a complex organic compound

protein (18: Intro)   a macromolecule whose primary structure is a linear sequence of α-amino acids and whose final structure results from folding of the chain into a specific three-dimensional structure; proteins serve as catalysts, structural components, and nutritional elements for the cell

protein modification (19.9)   a means of enzyme regulation in which a chemical group is covalently added to or removed from a protein. The chemical modification either turns the enzyme on or turns it off

proteolytic enzyme (19.11)   an enzyme that hydrolyzes the peptide bonds between amino acids in a protein chain

proton (2.1)   a positively charged particle in the nucleus of an atom

pure substance (1.2)   a substance with constant composition

purine (20.1)   a family of nitrogenous bases (heterocyclic amines) that are components of DNA and RNA and consist of a six-sided ring fused to a five-sided ring; the common purines in nucleic acids are adenine and guanine

pyridoxal phosphate (22.7)   a coenzyme derived from vitamin B_6 that is required for all transamination reactions

pyrimidine (20.1)   a family of nitrogenous bases (heterocyclic amines) that are components of nucleic acids and consist of a single six-sided ring; the common pyrimidines of DNA are cytosine and thymine; the common pyrimidines of RNA are cytosine and uracil

pyrimidine dimer (20.7)   UV light–induced covalent bonding of two adjacent pyrimidine bases in a strand of DNA

pyruvate dehydrogenase complex (22.2)   a complex of all the enzymes and coenzymes required for the synthesis of CO_2 and acetyl CoA from pyruvate

Q

quantization (2.3)   a characteristic that energy can occur only in discrete units called quanta

quaternary ammonium salt (15.1)   an amine salt with the general formula $R_4N^+A^-$ (in which R— can be an alkyl or aryl group or a hydrogen atom and A^- can be any anion)

quaternary (4°) carbon (10.2) a carbon atom that is bonded to four other carbon atoms

quaternary structure (of a protein) (18.6) aggregation of more than one folded peptide chain to yield a functional protein

R

rad (9.7) abbreviation for *radiation absorbed dose,* the absorption of 2.4×10^{-3} calories of energy per kilogram of absorbing tissue

radioactivity (9.1) the process by which atoms emit high-energy particles or rays; the spontaneous decomposition of a nucleus to produce a different nucleus

radiocarbon dating (9.3) the estimation of the age of objects through measurement of isotopic ratios of carbon

Raoult's law (6.4) a law stating that the vapor pressure of a component is equal to its mole fraction times the vapor pressure of the pure component

rate constant (7.3) the proportionality constant that relates the rate of a reaction and the concentration of reactants

rate law (7.3) expresses the rate of a reaction in terms of reactant concentration and a rate constant

rate of chemical reaction (7.3) the change in concentration of a reactant or product per unit time

reactant (4.3) starting material for a chemical reaction, appearing on the left side of a chemical equation

reaction order (7.3) the exponent of each concentration term in the rate equation

reducing agent (8.5) a substance that reduces, or donates electrons to, another substance; the reducing agent is itself oxidized in the process

reducing sugar (16.4) a sugar that can be oxidized by Benedict's or Tollens' reagents; includes all monosaccharides and most disaccharides

reduction (8.5, 12.6) the gain of electrons; in organic compounds it may be recognized by a gain of hydrogen or loss of oxygen

regulatory proteins (18: Intro) proteins that control cell functions such as metabolism and reproduction

release factor (20.6) a protein that binds to the termination codon in the empty A-site of the ribosome and causes the peptidyl transferase to hydrolyze the bond between the peptide and the peptidyl tRNA

rem (9.7) abbreviation for *roentgen equivalent for man,* the product of rad and RBE

replication fork (20.3) the point at which new nucleotides are added to the growing daughter DNA strand

replication origin (20.3) the region of a DNA molecule where DNA replication always begins

representative element (2.4) member of the groups of the periodic table designated as A

resonance (3.4) a condition that occurs when more than one valid Lewis structure can be written for a particular molecule

resonance form (3.4) one of a number of valid Lewis structures for a particular molecule

resonance hybrid (3.4) a description of the bonding in a molecule resulting from a superimposition of all valid Lewis structures (resonance forms)

restriction enzyme (20.8) a bacterial enzyme that recognizes specific nucleotide sequences on a DNA molecule and cuts the sugar-phosphate backbone of the DNA at or near that site

result (1.2) the outcome of a designed experiment, often determined from individual bits of data

reversible, competitive enzyme inhibitor (19.10) a chemical that resembles the structure and charge distribution of the natural substrate and competes with it for the active site of an enzyme

reversible, noncompetitive enzyme inhibitor (19.10) a chemical that binds weakly to an amino acid R group of an enzyme and inhibits activity; when the inhibitor dissociates, the enzyme is restored to its active form

reversible reaction (7.4) a reaction that will proceed in either direction, reactants to products or products to reactants

ribonucleic acid (RNA) (20.1) single-stranded nucleic acid molecules that are composed of phosphoryl groups, ribose, and the nitrogenous bases uracil, cytosine, adenine, and guanine

ribonucleotide (20.1) a ribonucleoside phosphate or nucleotide composed of a nitrogenous base in β-*N*-glycosidic linkage to the 1′ carbon of the sugar ribose and with one, two, or three phosphoryl groups esterified at the hydroxyl of the 5′ carbon of the ribose

ribose (16.4) a five-carbon monosaccharide that is a component of RNA and many coenzymes

ribosomal RNA (rRNA) (20.4) the RNA species that are structural and functional components of the small and large ribosomal subunits

ribosome (20.6) an organelle composed of a large and a small subunit, each of which is made up of ribosomal RNA and proteins; the platform on which translation occurs and that carries the enzymatic activity that forms peptide bonds

RNA polymerase (20.4) the enzyme that catalyzes the synthesis of RNA molecules using DNA as the template

RNA splicing (20.4) removal of portions of the primary transcript that do not encode protein sequences

roentgen (9.7) the dose of radiation producing 2.1×10^{9} ions in 1 cm^3 of air at 0°C and 1 atm of pressure

S

saccharide (16.1) a sugar molecule

saponification (14.2, 17.2) a reaction in which a soap is produced; more generally, the hydrolysis of an ester by an aqueous base

saturated fatty acid (17.2) a long-chain monocarboxylic acid in which each carbon of the chain is bonded to the maximum number of hydrogen atoms

saturated hydrocarbon (10.1) an alkane; a hydrocarbon that contains only carbon and hydrogen bonded together through carbon-hydrogen and carbon-carbon single bonds

saturated solution (6.1) one in which undissolved solute is in equilibrium with the solution

scientific method (1.1) the process of studying our surroundings that is based on experimentation

scientific notation (1.3) a system used to represent numbers as powers of ten

secondary (2°) alcohol (12.4) an alcohol with the general formula R_2CHOH

secondary (2°) amine (15.1) an amine with the general formula R_2NH

secondary (2°) carbon (10.2) a carbon atom that is bonded to two other carbon atoms

secondary structure (of a protein) (18.4) folding of the primary structure of a protein into an α-helix or a β-pleated sheet; folding is maintained by hydrogen bonds between the amide hydrogen and the carbonyl oxygen of the peptide bond

selectively permeable membrane (6.4) a membrane that restricts diffusion of some ions and molecules (based on size and charge) across the membrane

semiconservative DNA replication (20.3) DNA polymerase "reads" each parental strand of DNA and produces a complementary daughter strand; thus, all newly synthesized DNA molecules consist of one parental and one daughter strand

semipermeable membrane (6.4) a membrane permeable to the solvent but not the solute; a material that allows the transport of certain substances from one side of the membrane to the other

shielding (9.6) material used to provide protection from radiation

sickle cell anemia (18.8) a human genetic disease resulting from inheriting mutant hemoglobin genes from both parents

significant figures (1.3) all digits in a number known with certainty and the first uncertain digit

silent mutation (20.7) a mutation that changes the sequence of the DNA but does not alter the amino acid sequence of the protein encoded by the DNA

single bond (3.4) a bond in which one pair of electrons is shared by two atoms

single-replacement reaction (4.3)   also called substitution reaction, one in which one atom in a molecule is displaced by another

soap (14.2)   any of a variety of the alkali metal salts of fatty acids

solid state (1.2)   a physical state of matter characterized by its rigidity and fixed volume and shape

solubility (3.5, 6.1)   the amount of a substance that will dissolve in a given volume of solvent at a specified temperature

solute (6.1)   a component of a solution that is present in lesser quantity than the solvent

solution (6.1)   a homogeneous (uniform) mixture of two or more substances

solvent (6.1)   the solution component that is present in the largest quantity

specific gravity (1.5)   the ratio of the density of a substance to the density of water at 4°C or any specified temperature

specific heat (7.2)   the quantity of heat (calories) required to raise the temperature of 1 g of a substance 1 degree Celsius

spectroscopy (2.3)   the measurement of intensity and energy of electromagnetic radiation

speed of light (2.3) 2.99×10^8 m/s in a vacuum

sphingolipid (17.4)   a phospholipid that is derived from the amino alcohol sphingosine rather than from glycerol

sphingomyelin (17.4)   a sphingolipid found in abundance in the myelin sheath that surrounds and insulates cells of the central nervous system

standard solution (8.3)   a solution whose concentration is accurately known

standard temperature and pressure (STP) (5.1)   defined as 273 K and 1 atm

stereochemical specificity (19.5)   the property of an enzyme that allows it to catalyze reactions involving only one enantiomer of the substrate

stereochemistry (16.3)   the study of the spatial arrangement of atoms in a molecule

stereoisomers (10.3, 16.3)   a pair of molecules having the same structural formula and bonding pattern but differing in the arrangement of the atoms in space

steroid (17.4)   a lipid derived from cholesterol and composed of one five-sided ring and three six-sided rings; the steroids include sex hormones and anti-inflammatory compounds

structural analog (19.10)   a chemical having a structure and charge distribution very similar to those of a natural enzyme substrate

structural formula (10.2)   a formula showing all of the atoms in a molecule and exhibiting all bonds as lines

structural isomers (10.2)   molecules having the same molecular formula but different chemical structures

structural protein (18: Intro)   a protein that provides mechanical support for large plants and animals

sublevel (2.5)   a set of equal-energy orbitals within a principal energy level

sublimation (5.3)   a process whereby some molecules in the solid state convert directly to the gaseous state

substituted hydrocarbon (10.1)   a hydrocarbon in which one or more hydrogen atoms is replaced by another atom or group of atoms

substitution reaction (10.5, 11.6)   a reaction that results in the replacement of one group for another

substrate (19.1)   the reactant in a chemical reaction that binds to an enzyme active site and is converted to product

substrate-level phosphorylation (21.3)   the production of ATP by the transfer of a phosphoryl group from the substrate of a reaction to ADP

sucrose (16.5)   a disaccharide composed of α-D-glucose and β-D-fructose in (α1 → β2) glycosidic linkage; table sugar

supersaturated solution (6.1)   a solution that is more concentrated than a saturated solution (Note that such a solution is not at equilibrium.)

surface tension (5.2)   a measure of the strength of the attractive forces at the surface of a liquid

surfactant (5.2)   a substance that decreases the surface tension of a liquid

surroundings (7.1)   the universe outside of the system

suspension (6.1)   a heterogeneous mixture of particles; the suspended particles are larger than those found in a colloidal suspension

system (7.1)   the process under study

T

temperature (1.5)   a measure of the relative "hotness" or "coldness" of an object

temperature optimum (19.8)   the temperature at which an enzyme functions optimally and the rate of reaction is maximal

terminal electron acceptor (22.6)   the final electron acceptor in an electron transport system that removes the low-energy electrons from the system; in aerobic organisms the terminal electron acceptor is molecular oxygen

termination codon (20.6)   a triplet of ribonucleotides with no corresponding anticodon on a tRNA; as a result, translation will end, because there is no amino acid to transfer to the peptide chain

terpene (17.4)   the general term for lipids that are synthesized from isoprene units; the terpenes include steroids, bile salts, lipid-soluble vitamins, and chlorophyll

tertiary (3°) alcohol (12.4)   an alcohol with the general formula R_3COH

tertiary (3°) amine (15.1)   an amine with the general formula R_3N

tertiary (3°) carbon (10.2)   a carbon atom that is bonded to three other carbon atoms

tertiary structure (of a protein) (18.5)   the globular, three-dimensional structure of a protein that results from folding the regions of secondary structure; this folding occurs spontaneously as a result of interactions of the side chains or R groups of the amino acids

tetrahedral structure (3.4)   a molecule consisting of four groups attached to a central atom that occupy the four corners of an imagined regular tetrahedron

tetrose (16.2)   a four-carbon monosaccharide

theoretical yield (4.5)   the maximum amount of product that can be produced from a given amount of reactant

theory (1.1)   a hypothesis supported by extensive testing that explains and predicts facts

thermodynamics (7.1)   the branch of science that deals with the relationship between energies of systems, work, and heat

thioester (14.4)   the product of a reaction between a thiol and a carboxylic acid

thiol (12.9)   an organic compound that contains a thiol group (—SH)

titration (8.3)   the process of adding a solution from a buret to a sample until a reaction is complete, at which time the volume is accurately measured and the concentration of the sample is calculated

Tollens' test (13.4)   a test reagent (silver nitrate in ammonium hydroxide) used to distinguish aldehydes and ketones; also called the Tollens' silver mirror test

tracer (9.5)   a radioisotope that is rapidly and selectively transmitted to the part of the body for which diagnosis is desired

transaminase (22.7)   an enzyme that catalyzes the transfer of an amino group from one molecule to another

transamination (22.7)   a reaction in which an amino group is transferred from one molecule to another

transcription (20.4)   the synthesis of RNA from a DNA template

transferase (19.1)   an enzyme that catalyzes the transfer of a functional group from one molecule to another

transfer RNA (tRNA) (15.4, 20.4)   small RNAs that bind to a specific amino acid at the 3' end and mediate its addition at the appropriate site in a growing peptide chain; accomplished by recognition of the correct codon on the mRNA by the complementary anticodon on the tRNA

transition element (2.4)   any element located between Groups IIA (2) and IIIA (13) in the long periods of the periodic table

transition state (19.6)   the unstable intermediate in catalysis in which the enzyme has altered the form of the substrate so that it now shares properties of both the substrate and the product

translation (20.4)   the synthesis of a protein from the genetic code carried on the mRNA

translocation (20.6)   movement of the ribosome along the mRNA during translation

transmembrane protein (17.6)   a protein that is embedded within a membrane and crosses the lipid bilayer, protruding from the membrane both inside and outside the cell

transport protein (18: Intro)   a protein that transports materials across the cell membrane or throughout the body

triglyceride (17.3, 23.1)   triacylglycerol; a molecule composed of glycerol esterified to three fatty acids

trigonal pyramidal molecule (3.4)   a nonplanar structure involving three groups bonded to a central atom in which each group is equidistant from the central atom

triose (16.2)   a three-carbon monosaccharide

triple bond (3.4)   a bond in which three pairs of electrons are shared by two atoms

U

uncertainty (1.3)   the degree of doubt in a single measurement

unit (1.4)   a determinate quantity (of length, time, etc.) that has been adopted as a standard of measurement

unsaturated fatty acid (17.2)   a long-chain monocarboxylic acid having at least one carbon-to-carbon double bond

unsaturated hydrocarbon (10.1, 11: Intro)   a hydrocarbon containing at least one multiple (double or triple) bond

urea cycle (22.8)   a cyclic series of reactions that detoxifies ammonium ions by incorporating them into urea, which is excreted from the body

uridine triphosphate (UTP) (21.7)   a nucleotide composed of the pyrimidine uracil, the sugar ribose, and three phosphoryl groups and that serves as a carrier of glucose-1-phosphate in glycogenesis

V

valence electron (2.6)   electron in the outermost shell (principal quantum level) of an atom

valence-shell electron-pair repulsion (VSEPR) theory (3.4)   a model that predicts molecular geometry using the premise that electron pairs will arrange themselves as far apart as possible, to minimize electron repulsion

van der Waals forces (5.2)   a general term for intermolecular forces that include dipole-dipole and London forces

vapor pressure of a liquid (5.2)   the pressure exerted by the vapor at the surface of a liquid at equilibrium

very low density lipoprotein (VLDL) (17.5)   a plasma lipoprotein that binds triglycerides synthesized by the liver and carries them to adipose tissue for storage

viscosity (5.2)   a measure of the resistance to flow of a substance at constant temperature

vitamin (19.7)   an organic substance that is required in the diet in small amounts; water-soluble vitamins are used in the synthesis of coenzymes required for the function of cellular enzymes; lipid-soluble vitamins are involved in calcium metabolism, vision, and blood clotting

voltaic cell (8.5)   an electrochemical cell that converts chemical energy into electrical energy

W

wax (17.4)   a collection of lipids that are generally considered to be esters of long-chain alcohols

weight (1.5)   the force exerted on an object by gravity

Z

Zaitsev's rule (12.5)   states that in an elimination reaction, the alkene with the greatest number of alkyl groups on the double-bonded carbon (the more highly substituted alkene) is the major product of the reaction

Answers to Odd-Numbered Problems

Chapter 1

1.1 a. Physical property
 b. Chemical property
 c. Physical property

1.3 a. Extensive property
 b. Intensive property

1.5 Many examples exist; two are rubbing alcohol and bottled drinking water.

1.7 a. Three
 b. Three
 c. Four
 d. Two
 e. Three

1.9 a. 2.4×10^{-3}
 b. 1.80×10^{-2}
 c. 2.24×10^{2}

1.11 a. 8.09
 b. 5.9
 c. 20.19

1.13 a. 51
 b. 8.0×10^{1}
 c. 1.6×10^{2}

1.15 1.15×10^{-2} oz

1.17 2.49×10^{3} J

1.19 Chemistry is the study of matter, its chemical and physical properties, the chemical and physical changes it undergoes, and the energy changes that accompany those processes.
 Major subdivisions include biochemistry, organic chemistry, inorganic chemistry, analytical chemistry and physical chemistry.

1.21 Matter has mass and occupies space. Energy is intangible and is manifested by changes that result in matter due to the gain or loss of energy.

1.23 Shape, number of atoms in a unit, the special relationship of the atoms, and the location and number of bonds that hold the unit together.

1.25 A hypothesis is essentially an "educated guess." A theory is a hypothesis supported by extensive experimentation; it can explain and predict new facts.

1.27 Many examples exist; one could involve the time it takes to get to work: hypothesis—taking the "back roads" is faster than choosing the crowded interstate highway. The experiment would involve driving each path several times, starting at the same time, timing each trip and calculating an average time for each path.

1.29 The scientific method is an organized way of doing science.

1.31 A theory.

1.33 Freeze the contents of two beakers, one containing pure water, and the other containing salt dissolved in water. Slowly warm each container and measure the temperature of each as they convert from the solid to the liquid state. This temperature is the melting point, hence, the freezing point. Note that the melting and freezing point of a solution are the same temperature.

1.35 A physical property is a characteristic of a substance that can be observed without the substance undergoing a change in chemical composition.

1.37 Chemical properties of matter include flammability and toxicity.

1.39 A pure substance has constant composition with only a single substance whereas a mixture is composed of two or more substances.

1.41 Mixtures are composed of two or more substances. A homogeneous mixture has uniform composition while a heterogeneous mixture has non-uniform composition.

1.43

1.45 You need the cost per gallon, the average miles per gallon, and the distance between New York City and Washington, D.C.

1.47 a. Chemical reaction
 b. Physical change
 c. Physical change

1.49 a. Physical property
 b. Chemical property

1.51 a. Pure substance
 b. Pure substance
 c. Mixture

1.53 a. Extensive property
 b. Extensive property
 c. Intensive property

1.55 a. Homogeneous
 b. Homogeneous
 c. Homogeneous

1.57 a. Surface area and mass
 b. Color and shape

1.59 a. 3
 b. 3
 c. 3
 d. 4
 e. 4
 f. 3

1.61 a. 3.87×10^{-3}
 b. 5.20×10^{-2}
 c. 2.62×10^{-3}
 d. 2.43×10^{1}
 e. 2.40×10^{2}
 f. 2.41×10^{0}

1.63 a. Precision is a measure of the agreement of replicate results.
 b. Accuracy is the degree of agreement between the true value and measured value.

1.65 a. 1.5×10^{4}
 b. 2.41×10^{-1}
 c. 5.99
 d. 1139.42
 e. 7.21×10^{3}

1.67 **a.** 1.23×10^1
    b. 5.69×10^{-2}
    c. -1.527×10^3
    d. 7.89×10^{-7}
    e. 9.2×10^7
    f. 5.280×10^{-3}
    g. 1.279×10^0
    h. -5.3177×10^2

1.69 **a.** 32 oz
    b. 1.0×10^{-3} t
    c. 9.1×10^2 g
    d. 9.1×10^5 mg
    e. 9.1×10^1 da

1.71 **a.** 6.6×10^{-3} lb
    b. 1.1×10^{-1} oz
    c. 3.0×10^{-3} kg
    d. 3.0×10^2 cg
    e. 3.0×10^3 mg

1.73 **a.** 10.0°C
    b. 283.2 K

1.75 **a.** 293.2 K
    b. 68.0°F

1.77 13.4 m²

1.79 4 L

1.81 101°F

1.83 5 cm is shorter than 5 in.

1.85 5.0 μg is smaller that 5.0 mg.

1.87 6.00 g/mL

1.89 6.20×10^2 L

1.91 1.08×10^3 g

1.93 teak

1.95 0.789

1.97 Lead has the lowest density and platinum has the greatest density.

1.99 12.6 mL

Chapter 2

2.1 **a.** 35 protons, 35 electrons, 44 neutrons
    b. 35 protons, 35 electrons, 46 neutrons
    c. 26 protons, 26 electrons, 30 neutrons

2.3 Electron density is the probability that an electron will be found in a particular region of an atomic orbital.

2.5 **a.** Na
    b. Ra
    c. Mn
    d. Mg

2.7 **a.** Zr (zirconium)
    b. 22.99
    c. Cr (chromium)
    d. At (astatine)

2.9 **a.** Helium, atomic number = 2, mass = 4.00 amu
    b. Fluorine, atomic number = 9, mass = 19.00 amu
    c. Manganese, atomic number = 25, mass = 54.94 amu

2.11 **a.** $[Ne]\ 3s^2, 3p^4$
    b. $[Ar]\ 4s^2$

2.13 **a.** Ca^{2+} and Ar are isoelectronic
    b. Sr^{2+} and Kr are isoelectronic
    c. S^{2-} and Ar are isoelectronic
    d. Mg^{2+} and Ne are isoelectronic
    e. P^{3-} and Ar are isoelectronic

2.15 **a.** (Smallest) F, N, Be (largest)
    b. (Lowest) Be, N, F (highest)
    c. (Lowest) Be, N, F, (highest)

2.17 **a.** 8 protons, 8 electrons, 8 neutrons
    b. 15 protons, 15 electrons, 16 neutrons

2.19

Particle	Mass	Charge
a. electron	5.4×10^{-4} amu	-1
b. proton	1.00 amu	$+1$
c. neutron	1.00 amu	0

2.21 $^{19}_{9}\text{F}$

2.23 From the periodic table, all isotopes of Rn have 86 protons. Isotopes differ in the number of neutrons.

2.25 **a.** 34
    b. 46

2.27 **a.** $^{1}_{1}\text{H}$
    b. $^{14}_{6}\text{C}$

2.29 Isotopes of an element have different numbers of neutrons.

2.31 **a.** Neutrons
    b. Protons
    c. Protons, neutrons
    d. Ion
    e. Nucleus, negative

2.33 63.55 amu

2.35 • All matter consists of tiny particles called atoms.
    • Atoms cannot be created, divided, destroyed, or converted to any other type of atom.
    • All atoms of a particular element have identical properties.
    • Atoms of different elements have different properties.
    • Atoms combine in simple whole-number ratios.
    • Chemical change involves joining, separating, or rearranging atoms.

2.37 **a.** Chadwick—demonstrated the existence of the neutron in 1932.
    b. Goldstein—identified positive charge in the atom.

2.39 **a.** Dalton—developed the Law of Multiple Proportions; determined the relative atomic weights of the elements known at that time; developed the first scientific atomic theory.
    b. Crookes—developed the cathode ray tube and discovered "cathode rays"; characterized electron properties.

2.41 Our understanding of the nucleus is based on the gold foil experiment performed by Geiger and interpreted by Rutherford. In this experiment, Geiger bombarded a piece of gold foil with alpha particles, and observed that some alpha particles passed straight through the foil, others were deflected and some simply bounced back. This led Rutherford to propose that the atom consisted of a small, dense nucleus (alpha particles bounced back), surrounded by a cloud of electrons (some alpha particles were deflected). The size of the nucleus is small when compared to the volume of the atom (alpha particles were able to pass through the foil).

2.43 Crookes used the cathode ray tube. He observed particles emitted by the cathode and traveling toward the anode. This ray was deflected by an electric field. Thomson measured the curvature of the ray influenced by the electric and magnetic fields. This measurement provided the mass to charge ratio of the negative particle. Thomson also gave the particle the name, electron.

2.45 A cathode ray is the negatively charged particle formed in a cathode ray tube.

2.47 Radiowave
    Microwave
    Infrared   Increasing
    Visible   Wavelength
    Ultraviolet
    X-ray
    Gamma ray

2.49 Infrared radiation has greater energy than microwave radiation.

2.51 Spectroscopy is the measurement of intensity and energy of electromagnetic radiation.

2.53 According to Bohr, Planck, and others, electrons exist only in certain allowed regions, quantum levels, outside of the nucleus.

2.55
- Electrons are found in orbits at discrete distances from the nucleus.
- The orbits are quantized—they are of discrete energies.
- Electrons can only be found in these orbits, never in between (they are able to jump instantaneously from orbit to orbit).
- Electrons can undergo transitions—if an electron absorbs energy, it will jump to a higher orbit; when the electron falls back to a lower orbit, it will release energy.

2.57 Bohr's atomic model was the first to successfully account for electronic properties of atoms, specifically, the interaction of atoms and light (spectroscopy).

2.59
a. Sodium
b. Potassium
c. Magnesium
d. Boron

2.61 Group IA (or 1) is known collectively as the alkali metals and consists of lithium, sodium, potassium, rubidium, cesium, and francium.

2.63 Group VIIA (or 17) is known collectively as the halogens and consists of fluorine, chlorine, bromine, iodine, and astatine.

2.65
a. Na, Ni, Al
b. Na, Al
c. Ar

2.67

2.69 A principal energy level is designated $n = 1, 2, 3$, and so forth. It is similar to Bohr's orbit in concept. A sublevel is a part of a principal energy level and is designated $s, p, d,$ and f.

2.71 The s orbital represents the probability of finding an electron in a region of space surrounding the nucleus.

2.73 $2\,e^-$ for $n = 1$
$8\,e^-$ for $n = 2$
$18\,e^-$ for $n = 3$

2.75
a. $1s^2, 2s^2, 2p^6, 3s^2, 3p^1$
b. $1s^2, 2s^2, 2p^6, 3s^1$
c. $1s^2, 2s^2, 2p^6, 3s^2, 3p^6, 4s^2, 3d^1$

2.77 a. $1s^2, 2s^2, 2p^1$

$\boxed{\uparrow\downarrow}$ $\boxed{\uparrow\downarrow}$ $\boxed{\uparrow\,|\,\,|\,\,}$
$1s^2$ $2s^2$ $2p_x^1$

b. $1s^2, 2s^2, 2p^6, 3s^2, 3p^4$

$\boxed{\uparrow\downarrow}$ $\boxed{\uparrow\downarrow}$ $\boxed{\uparrow\downarrow|\uparrow\downarrow|\uparrow\downarrow}$ $\boxed{\uparrow\downarrow}$ $\boxed{\uparrow\downarrow|\uparrow\,|\uparrow}$
$1s^2$ $2s^2$ $2p_x^2\,2p_y^2\,2p_z^2$ $3s^2$ $3p_x^2\,3p_y^1\,3p_z^1$

c. $1s^2, 2s^2, 2p^6, 3s^2, 3p^6$

$\boxed{\uparrow\downarrow}$ $\boxed{\uparrow\downarrow}$ $\boxed{\uparrow\downarrow|\uparrow\downarrow|\uparrow\downarrow}$ $\boxed{\uparrow\downarrow}$ $\boxed{\uparrow\downarrow|\uparrow\downarrow|\uparrow\downarrow}$
$1s^2$ $2s^2$ $2p_x^2\,2p_y^2\,2p_z^2$ $3s^2$ $3p_x^2\,3p_y^2\,3p_z^2$

2.79
a. Not possible
b. Possible
c. Not possible
d. Not possible

2.81

	Atomic Symbol	# Protons	# Neutrons	# Electrons	Charge
a.	$^{23}_{11}\text{Na}$	11	12	11	0
b.	$^{32}_{16}\text{S}^{2-}$	16	16	18	2−
c.	$^{16}_{8}\text{O}$	8	8	8	0
d.	$^{24}_{12}\text{Mg}^{2+}$	12	12	10	2+
e.	$^{39}_{19}\text{K}^{+}$	19	20	18	1+

2.83

Atom	Total electrons	Valence electrons	Principal energy level number
a. H	1	1	1
b. Na	11	1	3
c. B	5	3	2
d. F	9	7	2
e. Ne	10	0 (or 8)	2
f. He	2	0 (or 2)	1

2.85 A loss of electrons by a neutral species results in a cation.

2.87
a. Two
b. One
c. One
d. Two

2.89
a. Li^+
b. O^{2-}
c. Ca^{2+}
d. Br^-
e. S^{2-}
f. Al^{3+}

2.91
a. Isoelectronic
b. Isoelectronic

2.93
a. $1s^2, 2s^2, 2p^6, 3s^2, 3p^6$
b. $1s^2, 2s^2, 2p^6$

2.95
a. (Smallest) F, O, N (Largest)
b. (Smallest) Li, K, Cs (Largest)
c. (Smallest) Cl, Br, I (Largest)

2.97
a. (Smallest) N, O, F (Largest)
b. (Smallest) Cs, K, Li (Largest)
c. (Smallest) I, Br, Cl (Largest)

2.99
a. A positive ion is always smaller than its parent atom because the positive charge of the nucleus is shared among fewer electrons in the ion. As a result, each electron is pulled closer to the nucleus and the volume of the ion decreases.
b. A negative ion is always larger than its parent atom because the positive charge in the nucleus is shared among a larger number of electrons in the ion. Each electron moves farther from the nucleus and the volume of the ion increases.

2.101 Cl^- is larger because it has a smaller nuclear (positive) charge.

Chapter 3

3.1 **a.** Potassium cyanide
b. Magnesium sulfide
c. Magnesium acetate

3.3 **a.** The bonded nuclei are closer together when a double bond exists, in comparison to a single bond.
b. The bond strength increases as the bond order increases. Therefore, a double bond is stronger than a single bond.
The distance of separation and bond strength are inversely related.

3.5 **a.** H—$\ddot{\text{P}}$—H $\overset{\cdot\cdot}{\text{P}}$
          | H$\overset{|}{\underset{\text{H}}{\wedge}}$H
          H

b.   H   H
          | |
    H—Si—H $\ddot{\text{Si}}$
          | H$\overset{|}{\underset{\text{H}}{\wedge}}$H
          H

3.7 **a.** Oxygen is more electronegative than sulfur; the bond is polar. The electrons are pulled toward the oxygen atom.
b. Nitrogen is more electronegative than carbon; the bond is polar. The electrons are pulled toward the nitrogen atom.
c. There is no electronegativity difference between two identical atoms; the bond is nonpolar.
d. Chlorine is more electronegative than iodine; the bond is polar. The electrons are pulled toward the chlorine atom.

3.9 **a.** Nonpolar
b. Polar
c. Polar
d. Nonpolar

3.11 **a.** H_2O
b. CO
c. NH_3
d. ICl

3.13 **a.** Ionic
b. Covalent
c. Covalent
d. Covalent

3.15 **a.** Covalent
b. Covalent
c. Covalent
d. Ionic

3.17 **a.** Li· + :$\ddot{\text{Br}}$· $\longrightarrow$ Li$^+$ + :$\ddot{\text{Br}}$:$^-$

b. ·Mg· + 2:$\ddot{\text{Cl}}$· $\longrightarrow$ Mg^{2+} + 2:$\ddot{\text{Cl}}$:$^-$

3.19 **a.** :$\ddot{\text{S}}$· + 2H· $\longrightarrow$:$\ddot{\text{S}}$—H
                                              |
                                              H

b. ·$\dot{\text{P}}$· + 3H· $\longrightarrow$ H—$\ddot{\text{P}}$—H
                                              |
                                              H

3.21 He has two valence electrons (electron configuration $1s^2$) and a complete N = 1 level. It has a stable electron configuration, with no tendency to gain or lose electrons, and satisfies the octet rule (2 e$^-$ for period 1). Hence, it is nonreactive.
He:

3.23 **a.** Sodium ion
b. Copper(I) ion (or cuprous ion)
c. Magnesium ion

3.25 **a.** Sulfide ion
b. Chloride ion
c. Carbonate ion

3.27 **a.** Magnesium chloride
b. Aluminum chloride

3.29 **a.** Nitrogen dioxide
b. Selenium trioxide

3.31 **a.** Sulfur dioxide
b. Sulfur trioxide

3.33 **a.** K$^+$
b. Br$^-$

3.35 **a.** SO_4^{2-}
b. NO_3^-

3.37 **a.** NaCl
b. $MgBr_2$

3.39 **a.** AgCN
b. NH_4Cl

3.41 **a.** CuO
b. Fe_2O_3

3.43 **a.** Al_2O_3
b. Li_2S

3.45 **a.** SiO_2
b. SO_2

3.47 **a.** $NaNO_3$
b. $Mg(NO_3)_2$

3.49 **a.** NH_4I
b. $(NH_4)_2SO_4$

3.51 Ionic solid state compounds exist in regular, repeating, three-dimensional structures; the crystal lattice. The crystal lattice is made up of positive and negative ions. Solid state covalent compounds are made up of molecules which may be arranged in a regular crystalline pattern or in an irregular (amorphous) structure.

3.53 The boiling points of ionic solids are generally much higher than those of covalent solids.

3.55 KCl would be expected to exist as a solid at room temperature; it is an ionic compound, and ionic compounds are characterized by high melting points.

3.57 Water will have a higher boiling point. Water is a polar molecule with strong intermolecular attractive forces, whereas carbon tetrachloride is a nonpolar molecule with weak intermolecular attractive forces. More energy, hence, a higher temperature is required to overcome the attractive forces among the water molecules.

3.59 **a.** H·
b. He:
c. ·$\dot{\text{C}}$·
d. ·$\dot{\text{N}}$·

3.61 **a.** Li$^+$
b. Mg^{2+}
c. :$\ddot{\text{Cl}}$:$^-$
d. :$\dot{\text{P}}$:$^{3-}$

3.63 **a.** :$\ddot{\text{Cl}}$—$\ddot{\text{N}}$—$\ddot{\text{Cl}}$:
                     |
                  :$\ddot{\text{Cl}}$:

b.   H
           |
    H—C—$\ddot{\text{O}}$—H
           |
           H

c. :S=C=$\ddot{\text{S}}$:

3.65 a. :Cl—N—Cl:
      |
    :Cl:

Pyramidal
polar
water soluble

b.
H
|
H—C—O—H
|
H

Tetrahedral around C
angular around O
polar
water soluble

c. :S=C=S:

Linear
nonpolar
not water soluble

3.67 $[:N\equiv O:]^+$

3.69 $[:O—H]^-$

3.71 Resonance can occur when more than one valid Lewis structure can be written for a molecule. Each individual structure which can be drawn is a resonance form. The true nature of the structure for the molecule is the resonance hybrid, which consists of the "average" of the resonance forms.

3.73
$$\left[\begin{matrix} H & :O: \\ | & || \\ H—C—C—O: \\ | \\ H \end{matrix} \right]^- \longleftrightarrow \left[\begin{matrix} H & :O: \\ | & | \\ H—C—C=O \\ | \\ H \end{matrix} \right]^-$$

3.75
H H
| |
H—C—C—O—H
| |
H H

3.77
H O H
| || |
H—C—C—C—H
| |
H H

3.79 a. Polar covalent
b. Polar covalent
c. Ionic
d. Ionic
e. Ionic

3.81 a. $[:C\equiv N:]^-$
b. $[:Si\equiv P:]^-$

c), d), and e) are ionic compounds.

3.83 a. Angular

:O—S=O:

b. Trigonal planar

O
||
S
/ \
:O: :O:

3.85 a. Polar
b. Nonpolar

3.87 a. $:C\equiv O:$

b.
O
/ \
H H

c. :O=C=O:

3.89 a. CO_2
c. CF_4

3.91 :Cl—Be—Cl:

3.93 A molecule containing no polar bonds *must* be nonpolar. A molecule containing polar bonds may or may not itself be polar. It depends upon the number and arrangement of the bonds.

3.95 Polar compounds have strong intermolecular attractive forces. Higher temperatures are needed to overcome these forces and convert the solid to a liquid; hence, we predict higher melting points for polar compounds when compared to nonpolar compounds.

3.97 Yes

3.99 N_2, O_2, CO, NaCl

Chapter 4

4.1 3.33×10^{-10} g Hg
4.3 Formula mass = 194.20 amu
Molar mass = 194.20 g/mol
4.5 a. DR
b. SR
c. DR
d. D
4.7 $Cu^{2+}(aq) + S^{2-}(aq) \longrightarrow CuS(s)$
4.9 a. 47.9 g NO_2
b. 52.2%
4.11 Examples of other packaging units include a *ream* of paper (500 sheets of paper), a six-pack of soft drinks, a case of canned goods (24 cans), to name a few.
4.13 a. 28.09 g
b. 107.9 g
4.15 39.95 g
4.17 6.0×10^{19} carbon atoms
4.19 1.7×10^{-22} mol AS
4.21 40.36 g Ne
4.23 4.00 g He/mol He
4.25 a. 5.00 mol He
b. 1.7 mol Na
c. 4.2×10^{-2} mol Cl_2
4.27 1.62×10^3 g Ag
4.29 8.37×10^{22} Ag atoms
4.31 A molecule is a single unit comprised of atoms joined by covalent bonds. An ion-pair is composed of positive and negatively charged ions joined by electrostatic attraction, the ionic bond. The ion pairs, unlike the molecule, do not form single units; the electrostatic charge is directed to other ions in a crystal lattice, as well.
4.33 a. 58.44 g/mol
b. 142.04 g/mol
c. 357.49 g/mol
4.35 32.00 g/mol O_2
4.37 249.70 grams

4.39   **a.** 0.257 mol NaCl
      b. 0.106 mol Na_2SO_4

4.41   **a.** 18.02 g H_2O
      b. 116.9 g NaCl

4.43   **a.** 40.0 g He
      b. 2.02×10^2 g H

4.45   **a.** 2.43 g Mg
      b. 10.0 g $CaCO_3$

4.47   **a.** 4.00 g NaOH
      b. 9.81 g H_2SO_4

4.49   **a.** 0.420 mol KBr
      b. 0.415 mol $MgSO_4$

4.51   **a.** 6.57×10^{-1} mol CS_2
      b. 2.14×10^{-1} mol $Al_2(CO_3)_3$

4.53   The ultimate basis for a correct chemical equation is the law of conservation of mass. No mass may be gained or lost in a chemical reaction, and the chemical equation must reflect this fact.

4.55   The subscript tells us the number of atoms or ions contained in one unit of the compound.

4.57   Heat is necessary for the reaction to occur.

4.59   Yes, PbI_2

4.61   If we change the subscript we change the identity of the compound.

4.63   A reactant is the starting material for a chemical reaction.

4.65   A product is the chemical species that results from a chemical reaction.

4.67   **a.** $2C_2H_6(g) + 7O_2(g) \rightarrow 4CO_2(g) + 6H_2O(g)$
      b. $6K_2O(s) + P_4O_{10}(s) \rightarrow 4K_3PO_4(s)$
      c. $MgBr_2(aq) + H_2SO_4(aq) \rightarrow 2HBr(g) + MgSO_4(aq)$

4.69   **a.** $Ca(s) + F_2(g) \rightarrow CaF_2(s)$
      b. $2Mg(s) + O_2(g) \rightarrow 2MgO(s)$
      c. $3H_2(g) + N_2(g) \rightarrow 2NH_3(g)$

4.71   **a.** $2C_4H_{10}(g) + 13O_2(g) \rightarrow 10H_2O(g) + 8CO_2(g)$
      b. $Au_2S_3(s) + 3H_2(g) \rightarrow 2Au(s) + 3H_2S(g)$
      c. $Al(OH)_3(s) + 3HCl(aq) \rightarrow AlCl_3(aq) + 3H_2O(l)$
      d. $(NH_4)_2Cr_2O_7(s) \rightarrow Cr_2O_3(s) + N_2(g) + 4H_2O(g)$
      e. $C_2H_5OH(l) + 3O_2(g) \rightarrow 2CO_2(g) + 3H_2O(g)$

4.73   **a.** $N_2(g) + 3H_2(g) \rightarrow 2NH_3(g)$
      b. $HCl(aq) + NaOH(aq) \rightarrow NaCl(aq) + H_2O(l)$

4.75   **a.** $C_6H_{12}O_6(s) + 6O_2(g) \rightarrow 6H_2O(l) + 6CO_2(g)$
      b. $Na_2CO_3(s) \xrightarrow{\Delta} Na_2O(s) + CO_2(g)$

4.77   Yes. $CaCO_3$

4.79 $Ag^+(aq) + Br^-(aq) \rightarrow AgBr(s)$

4.81   Conservation of mass

4.83   Changing subscripts changes the identity of the compound. Changing coefficients changes the relative number of moles of compound.

4.85   27.7 g B_2H_6

4.87   104 g $CrCl_3$

4.89   **a.** $N_2(g) + 3H_2(g) \rightarrow 2NH_3(g)$
      b. Three moles of H_2 will react with one mole of N_2
      c. One mole of N_2 will produce two moles of the product NH_3
      d. 1.50 mol H_2
      e. 17.0 g NH_3

4.91   **a.** 149.21 g/mol
      b. 1.20×10^{24} O atoms
      c. 32.00 g O
      d. 10.7 g O

4.93   7.39 g O_2

4.95 6.77×10^4 g CO_2

4.97   70.6 g $C_{10}H_{22}$

4.99 9.13×10^2 g N_2

4.101   92.6%

4.103 6.85×10^2 g N_2

Chapter 5

5.1   **a.** 0.954 atm
      b. 0.382 atm
      c. 0.730 atm

5.3   2.91 atm

5.5   Molecules with complex structures, which do not "slide" smoothly past each other, and polar molecules tend to have higher viscosities.

5.7   Evaporation is the conversion of a liquid to a gas at a temperature lower than the boiling point of the liquid. Condensation is the conversion of a gas to a liquid at a temperature lower than the boiling point of the liquid.

5.9 $CO_2 < CH_3Cl < CH_3OH$; Only CH_3OH exhibits London Dispersion Forces, dipole-dipole interactions, and hydrogen bonding. Hence, CH_3OH has the strongest intermolecular forces and therefore, the highest boiling point.

5.11   **a.** Ionic solids generally have high melting points and a tendency to be hard and brittle.
      b. Table salt (NaCl) and calcium chloride ($CaCl_2$)

5.13   In all cases, gas particles are much farther apart than similar particles in the liquid or solid state. In most cases, particles in the liquid state are, on average, farther apart than those in the solid state. Water is the exception; liquid water's molecules are closer together than they are in the solid state.

5.15   Pressure is a force/unit area. Gas particles are in continuous, random motion. Collisions with the walls of the container result in a force (mass $\times$ acceleration) on the walls of the container. The sum of these collisional forces constitutes the pressure exerted by the gas.

5.17   Gases are easily compressed simply because there is a great deal of space between particles; they can be pushed closer together (compressed) because the space is available.

5.19   Gas particles are in continuous, random motion. They are free (minimal attractive forces between particles) to roam, up to the boundary of their container.

5.21   Gases exhibit more ideal behavior at low pressures. At low pressures, gas particles are more widely separated and therefore the attractive forces between particles are less. The ideal gas model assumes negligible attractive forces between gas particles.

5.23   The kinetic molecular theory states that the average kinetic energy of the gas particles increases as the temperature increases. Kinetic energy is proportional to $(velocity)^2$. Therefore, as the temperature increases the gas particle velocity increases and the rate of mixing increases as well.

5.25   The volume of the balloon is directly proportional to the pressure the gas exerts on the inside surface of the balloon. As the balloon cools, its pressure drops, and the balloon contracts. (Recall that the speed, hence the force exerted by the molecules, decreases as the temperature decreases.)

5.27   Boyle's law states that the volume of a gas varies inversely with the gas pressure if the temperature and the number of moles of gas are held constant.

5.29   Volume will decrease according to Boyle's law. Volume is inversely proportional to the pressure exerted on the gas.

5.31   1 atm

5.33   5 L-atm

5.35   5.23 atm

5.37   Charles's law states that the volume of a gas varies directly with the absolute temperature if pressure and number of moles of gas are constant.

5.39   The Kelvin scale is the only scale that is directly proportional to molecular motion, and it is this motion that determines the physical properties of gases.

5.41 No. The volume is proportional to the temperature in K, not Celsius.

5.43 0.96 L

5.45 1.51 L

5.47 • Volume and temperature are *directly* proportional; increasing T *increases* V.
• Volume and pressure are *inversely* proportional; decreasing P *increases* V.
Therefore, both variables work together to *increase* the volume.

5.49 $V_f = \dfrac{P_i V_i T_f}{P_f T_i}$

5.51 1.82×10^{-2} L

5.53 Avogadro's law states that equal volumes of any ideal gas contain the same number of moles if measured at constant temperature and pressure.

5.55 6.00 L

5.57 No. One mole of an ideal gas will occupy exactly 22.4 L; however, there is no completely ideal gas and careful measurement will show a different volume.

5.59 Standard temperature is 273 K.

5.61 0.80 mol

5.63 22.4 L

5.65 1.25 g/L

5.67 0.276 mol

5.69 5.94×10^{-2} L

5.71 22.4 L

5.73 9.08×10^3 L

5.75 172°C

5.77 Dalton's law states that the total pressure of a mixture of gases is the sum of the partial pressures of the component gases.

5.79 0.74 atm

5.81 Intermolecular forces in liquids are considerably stronger than intermolecular forces in gases. Particles are, on average, much closer together in liquids and the strength of attraction decreases as the distance of separation increases.

5.83 The vapor pressure of a liquid increases as the temperature of the liquid increases.

5.85 Viscosity is the resistance to flow caused by intermolecular attractive forces. Complex molecules may become entangled and not slide smoothly across one another.

5.87 All molecules exhibit London forces.

5.89 Only methanol exhibits hydrogen bonding. Methanol has an oxygen atom bonded to a hydrogen atom, a necessary condition for hydrogen bonding.

5.91 Propylene glycol

5.93 Solids are essentially incompressible because the average distance of separation among particles in the solid state is small. There is literally no space for the particles to crowd closer together.

5.95 a. High melting temperature, brittle
b. High melting temperature, hard

5.97 Beryllium

5.99 Mercury

Chapter 6

6.1 A chemical analysis must be performed in order to determine the identity of all components, a qualitative analysis. If only one component is found, it is a pure substance; two or more components indicates a true solution.

6.3 After the container of soft drink is opened, CO_2 diffuses into the surrounding atmosphere; consequently the partial pressure of CO_2 over the soft drink decreases and the equilibrium

$$CO_2(g) \rightleftharpoons CO_2(aq)$$

shifts to the left, lowering the concentration of CO_2 in the soft drink.

6.5 0.125 mol HCl

6.7 Pure water

6.9 4.0×10^{-2} osmol KCl, 2.8×10^{-1} osmol glucose

6.11 a. Electrolyte
b. Nonelectrolyte
c. Electrolyte

6.13 A true solution contains more than one substance with the particles having a diameter less than 1×10^{-9} m. Particles with diameters of 1×10^{-9} m to 2×10^{-7} m are colloids. A suspension contains particles much larger than 2×10^{-7} m.

6.15 Stream temperature is much lower in early spring than mid-August. Henry's law predicts that the concentration of dissolved oxygen in the stream is greater at lower water temperatures. Trout require oxygen and thrive in early spring.

6.17 A solution is described as clear if it efficiently transmits light, showing no evidence of suspended particles. The solution does not have to be colorless to meet these conditions.

6.19 a. 2.00% NaCl
b. 6.60% $C_6H_{12}O_6$

6.21 a. 5.00% ethanol
b. 10.0% ethanol

6.23 a. 21.0% NaCl
b. 3.75% NaCl

6.25 a. 2.25 g NaCl
b. 3.13 g $NaC_2H_3O_2$

6.27 19.5% KNO_3

6.29 1.00 g sugar

6.31 0.04% (m/m) solution is more concentrated.

6.33 2.0×10^{-3} ppt

6.35 Laboratories' managers often purchase concentrated solutions for practical reasons, such as economy and conservation of storage space.

6.37 0.50 M

6.39 a. 1.46 g NaCl
b. 9.00 g $C_6H_{12}O_6$

6.41 0.266 L

6.43 5.00×10^{-2} L

6.45 20.0 M

6.47 0.900 M

6.49 158 g glucose

6.51 0.0500 M

6.53 A colligative property is a solution property that depends on the concentration of solute particles rather than the identity of the particles.

6.55 Salt is an ionic substance that dissociates in water to produce positive and negative ions. These ions (or particles) lower the freezing point of water. If the concentration of salt particles is large, the freezing point may be depressed below the surrounding temperature, and the ice would melt.

6.57 Chemical properties depend on the identity of the substance, whereas colligative properties depend on concentration, not identity.

6.59 Raoult's law states that when a solute is added to a solvent, the vapor pressure of the solvent decreases in proportion to the concentration of the solute.

6.61 One mole of $CaCl_2$ produces three moles of particles in solution whereas one mole of NaCl produces two moles of particles in solution. Therefore, a one molar $CaCl_2$ solution contains a greater number of particles than a one molar NaCl solution and will produce a greater freezing-point depression.

6.63 Freezing Temperature for NaCl Solution = −1.86°C
Freezing Temperature for Sucrose Solution = −0.93°C

6.65 Sucrose

6.67 24 atm

6.69 $A \rightarrow B$

6.71 No net flow

6.73 Hypertonic

6.75 Hypotonic

6.77 1.0×10^{-3} osmol

6.79 Water is often termed the "universal solvent" because it is a polar molecule and will dissolve, at least to some extent, most ionic and polar covalent compounds. The majority of our body mass is water and this water is an important part of the nutrient transport system due to its solvent properties. This is true in other animals and plants as well. Because of its ability to hydrogen bond, water has a high boiling point and a low vapor pressure. Also, water is abundant and easily purified.

6.81

$$H\!-\!\overset{\displaystyle H}{\underset{\displaystyle H}{N}} : \delta^- \; \delta^+ \, H$$
$$\overset{}{\underset{\displaystyle H}{\overset{\cdot\cdot}{O}} : \delta^-}$$

6.83 The number of particles in solution is dependent on the degree of dissociation.

6.85 In dialysis, sodium ions move from a region of high concentration to a region of low concentration. If we wish to remove (transport) sodium ions from the blood, they can move to a region of lower concentration, the dialysis solution.

6.87 The shelf life is a function of the stability of the ammonia-water solution. The ammonia can react with the water to convert to the extremely soluble and stable ammonium ion. Also, ammonia and water are polar molecules. Polar interactions, particularly hydrogen bonding, are strong and contribute to the long-term solution stability.

6.89

$$\overset{\displaystyle H}{\underset{\displaystyle H}{\diagdown}} \overset{\cdot\cdot}{O}: \quad \overset{Na^+}{} \quad :\overset{\cdot\cdot}{O} \overset{\displaystyle H}{\underset{\displaystyle H}{\diagup}}$$

6.91 Polar; like dissolves like (H_2O is polar)

6.93 Elevated concentrations of sodium ion in the blood may cause confusion, stupor, or coma.

6.95 Elevated concentrations of sodium ion in the blood may occur whenever large amounts of water are lost. Diarrhea, diabetes, and certain high-protein diets are particularly problematic.

6.97 0.10 eq/L

6.99 4.0×10^{-2} M

Chapter 7

7.1 **a.** Exothermic
b. Exothermic

7.3 $He(g)$

7.5 $\Delta G = (+) - T(-)$
ΔG must always be positive.

7.7 2.7×10^3 J

7.9 Heat energy produced by the friction of striking the match provides the activation energy necessary for this combustion process.

7.11 If the enzyme catalyzed a process needed to sustain life, the substance interfering with that enzyme would be classified as a poison.

7.13 At rush hour, approximately the same number of passengers enter and exit the train at any given stop. Throughout the trip, the number of passengers on the train may be essentially unchanged, but the identity of the individual passengers is continually changing.

At a busy restaurant during lunchtime, approximately the same number of people will enter and exit the restaurant at any given moment. Throughout lunchtime, the number of people in the restaurant may be essentially unchanged, but the identity of the individuals in the restaurant is continually changing.

7.15 Measure the concentrations of products and reactants at a series of times until no further concentration change is observed.

7.17 Product formation

7.19 joule

7.21 An exothermic reaction is one in which energy is released during chemical change.

7.23 A fuel must release heat in the combustion (oxidation) process.

7.25 The temperature of the water (or solution) is measured in a calorimeter. If the reaction being studied is exothermic, released energy heats the water and the temperature increases. In an endothermic reaction, heat flows from the water to the reaction and the water temperature decreases.

7.27 Double-walled containers, used in calorimeters, provide a small airspace between the part of the calorimeter (inside wall) containing the sample solution and the outside wall, contacting the surroundings. This gap makes heat transfer more difficult.

7.29 Free energy is the combined contribution of entropy and enthalpy for a chemical reaction.

7.31 The first law of thermodynamics, the law of conservation of energy, states that the energy of the universe is constant.

7.33 Enthalpy is a measure of heat energy.

7.35 1.20×10^3 cal

7.37 5.02×10^3 J

7.39 **a.** Entropy increases.
b. Entropy increases.

7.41 $\Delta G = (-) - T(+)$
ΔG must always be negative and the process is always spontaneous.

7.43 Isopropyl alcohol quickly evaporates (liquid $\rightarrow$ gas) after being applied to the skin. Conversion of a liquid to a gas requires heat energy. The heat energy is supplied by the skin. When this heat is lost, the skin temperature drops.

7.45 Decomposition of leaves and twigs to produce soil.

7.47 The activated complex is the arrangement of reactants in an unstable transition state as a chemical reaction proceeds. The activated complex must form in order to convert reactants to products.

7.49 The rate of a reaction is the change in concentration of a reactant or product per unit time. The rate constant is the proportionality constant that relates rate and concentration. The order is the exponent of each concentration term in the rate equation.

7.51 Increase

7.53 A catalyst increases the rate of a reaction without itself undergoing change.

7.55

Non-catalyzed reaction
High activation energy

**Catalyzed reaction
Lower activation energy**

7.57 The rate of the reaction increases four-fold.

7.59 An increase in concentration of reactants means that there are more molecules in a certain volume. The probability of collision is enhanced because they travel a shorter distance before meeting another molecule. The rate is proportional to the number of collisions per unit time.

7.61 Rate = $k[N_2O_4]$

7.63 A catalyst speeds up a chemical reaction by facilitating the formation of the activated complex, thus lowering the activation energy, the energy barrier for the reaction.

7.65 Products

7.67 (A)

7.69 LeChatelier's principle states that when a system at equilibrium is disturbed, the equilibrium shifts in the direction that minimizes the disturbance.

7.71 A dynamic equilibrium has fixed concentrations of all reactants and products—these concentrations do not change with time. However, the process is dynamic because products and reactants are continuously being formed and consumed. The concentrations do not change because the rates of production and consumption are equal.

7.73 The position of the equilibrium addresses the question of whether products or reactants are favored. In a hypothetical equilibrium, if the equilibrium position shifts to the left, that means more reactants are formed. If the equilibrium position shifts to the right, that means more products are formed.

7.75 1. Concentration
2. Heat
3. Pressure

7.77 $K_{eq} = \dfrac{[NO_2]^2}{[N_2O_4]}$

7.79 A physical equilibrium describes physical change; examples include the equilibrium between ice and water, or the equilibrium vapor pressure of a liquid. A chemical equilibrium describes chemical change; examples include the reactions shown in questions 7.81 and 7.83.

7.81 $K_{eq} = \dfrac{[NH_3]^2}{[N_2][H_2]^3}$

7.83 $K_{eq} = \dfrac{[H_2S]^2}{[H_2]^2[S_2]}$

7.85 7.7×10^{-5} M

7.87 **a.** Equilibrium shifts to the left.
b. No change
c. No change

7.89 **a.** False
b. False

7.91 **a.** PCl_3 increases
b. PCl_3 decreases

c. PCl_3 decreases
d. PCl_3 decreases
e. PCl_3 remains the same

7.93 Decrease

7.95 $K_{eq} = \dfrac{[CO][H_2]}{[H_2O]}$

7.97 False

7.99 Removing the cap allows CO_2 to escape into the atmosphere. This corresponds to the removal of product (CO_2):

$$CO_2(l) \rightleftarrows CO_2(g)$$

The equilibrium shifts to the right, dissolved CO_2 is lost, and the beverage goes "flat."

Chapter 8

8.1 **a.** $HF(aq) + H_2O(l) \rightleftarrows H_3O^+(aq) + F^-(aq)$
b. $NH_3(aq) + H_2O(l) \rightleftarrows NH_4^+(aq) + OH^-(aq)$

8.3 **a.** HF and F^-; H_2O and H_3O^+
b. NH_3 and NH_4^+; H_2O and OH^-

8.5 1.0×10^{-11} M

8.7 $CO_2 + H_2O \rightleftarrows H_2CO_3 \rightleftarrows H_3O^+ + HCO_3^-$

An increase in the partial pressure of CO_2 is a stress on the left side of the equilibrium. The equilibrium will shift to the right in an effort to decrease the concentration of CO_2. This will cause the molar concentration of H_2CO_3 to increase.

8.9 In Question 8.7, the equilibrium shifts to the right. Therefore the molar concentration of H_3O^+ should increase.
    In Question 8.8, the equilibrium shifts to the left. Therefore the molar concentration of H_3O^+ should decrease.

8.11 4.74

8.13 4.87

8.15 $Ca \rightarrow Ca^{2+} + 2\,e^-$ (oxidation ½ reaction)
$S + 2\,e^- \rightarrow S^{2-}$ (reduction ½ reaction)
$Ca + S \rightarrow CaS$ (complete reaction)

8.17 **a.** An Arrhenius acid is a substance that dissociates, producing hydrogen ions.
b. A Brønsted-Lowry acid is a substance that behaves as a proton donor.

8.19 The Brønsted-Lowry theory provides a broader view of acid-base theory than does the Arrhenius theory. Brønsted-Lowry emphasizes the role of the solvent in the dissociation process.

8.21 **a.** $HNO_2(aq) + H_2O(l) \rightleftarrows H_3O^+(aq) + NO_2^-(aq)$
b. $HCN(aq) + H_2O(l) \rightleftarrows H_3O^+(aq) + CN^-(aq)$

8.23 **a.** HNO_3
b. CN^-
c. HNO_3

8.25 **a.** Weak
b. Weak
c. Weak

8.27 **a.** CN^- and HCN; NH_3 and NH_4^+
b. CO_3^{2-} and HCO_3^-; Cl^- and HCl

8.29 Concentration refers to the quantity of acid or base contained in a specified volume of solvent. Strength refers to the degree of dissociation of the acid or base.

8.31 **a.** Brønsted acid
b. Brønsted base
c. Both

8.33 **a.** Brønsted acid
b. Both
c. Brønsted base

8.35 HCN

8.37 I^-

8.39 **a.** 1.0×10^{-7} M
b. 1.0×10^{-11} M

8.41 The beaker containing 0.10 M CH_3COOH. CH_3COOH is a weaker acid than HCl, thus, a higher pH than HCl.

8.43 **a.** 2.00
b. 4.00

8.45 **a.** $[H_3O^+] = 1.0 \times 10^{-1}$ M
b. $[H_3O^+] = 1.0 \times 10^{-5}$ M

8.47 11.00

8.49 **a.** $[H_3O^+] = 5.0 \times 10^{-2}$ M
$[OH^-] = 2.0 \times 10^{-13}$ M
b. $[H_3O^+] = 2.0 \times 10^{-10}$ M
$[OH^-] = 5.0 \times 10^{-5}$ M

8.51 A neutralization reaction is one in which an acid and a base react to produce water and a salt (a "neutral" solution).

8.53 **a.** $[H_3O^+] = 1.0 \times 10^{-6}$ M
$[OH^-] = 1.0 \times 10^{-8}$ M
b. $[H_3O^+] = 6.3 \times 10^{-6}$ M
$[OH^-] = 1.6 \times 10^{-9}$ M
c. $[H_3O^+] = 1.6 \times 10^{-8}$ M
$[OH^-] = 6.3 \times 10^{-7}$ M

8.55 The statement is incorrect. The pH = 3 solution is 1000 times as acidic as the pH = 6 solution because pH is a logarithmic function.

8.57 **a.** $[H_3O^+] = 1.0 \times 10^{-5}$
b. $[H_3O^+] = 1.0 \times 10^{-12}$
c. $[H_3O^+] = 3.2 \times 10^{-6}$

8.59 **a.** pH = 6.00
b. pH = 8.00
c. pH = 3.25

8.61 pH = 3.12

8.63 pH = 10.74

8.65 $HNO_3(aq) + NaOH(aq) \rightarrow H_2O(l) + NaNO_3(aq)$

8.67 $H^+(aq) + OH^-(aq) \longrightarrow H_2O(l)$ or
$H_3O^+(aq) + OH^-(aq) \longrightarrow 2H_2O(l)$

8.69 Color change tells us that the proper volume of titrant has been added.

8.71 0.1800 M

8.73 13.33 mL

8.75 **a.** NH_3 and NH_4Cl can form a buffer solution.
b. HNO_3 and KNO_3 cannot form a buffer solution.

8.77 HCl/NaCl is not a buffer solution. It is a strong acid and a salt. The NaOH would produce a significant pH change. On the other hand, CH_3COOH/CH_3COONa is a buffer solution because it is a weak acid and its salt. Therefore, it would resist significant pH change upon addition of a strong base.

8.79 **a.** Addition of strong acid is equivalent to adding H_3O^+. This is a stress on the right side of the equilibrium and the equilibrium will shift to the left. Consequently the $[CH_3COOH]$ increases.
b. Water, in this case, is a solvent and does not appear in the equilibrium expression. Hence, it does not alter the position of the equilibrium.

8.81 $[H_3O^+] = 2.32 \times 10^{-7}$ M

8.83 CH_3COO^-, a conjugate base, reacts with added H_3O^+ to maintain pH.

8.85 pH = 4.74

8.87 $11.2 = \dfrac{[HCO_3^-]}{[H_2CO_3]}$

8.89 The species oxidized *loses* electrons.

8.91 During an oxidation-reduction reaction the species *oxidized* is the reducing agent.

8.93

$$Cl_2 \quad + \quad 2KI \quad \rightarrow 2KCl + I_2$$
substance reduced   substance oxidized
oxidizing agent   reducing agent

8.95 $2I^- \rightarrow I_2 + 2e^-$ (oxidation ½ reaction)
$Cl_2 + 2e^- \rightarrow 2Cl^-$ (reduction ½ reaction)

8.97 An oxidation-reduction reaction must take place to produce electron flow in a voltaic cell.

8.99 Storage battery.

Chapter 9

9.1 X-ray, ultraviolet, visible, infrared, microwave, and radiowave.

9.3 $^{131}_{53}I \rightarrow ^{131}_{54}Xe + ^{0}_{-1}e$

9.5 201 hours

9.7 1/4 of the radioisotope remains after two half-lives.

9.9 Isotopes with short half-lives release their radiation rapidly. There is much more radiation per unit time observed with short half-life substances; hence, the signal is stronger and the sensitivity of the procedure is enhanced.

9.11 The rem takes into account the relative biological effect of the radiation in addition to the quantity of radiation. This provides a more meaningful estimate of potential radiation damage to human tissue.

9.13 Natural radioactivity is the spontaneous decay of a nucleus to produce high-energy particles or rays.

9.15 Two protons and two neutrons

9.17 An electron with a −1 charge.

9.19 A positron has a positive charge and a beta particle has a negative charge.

9.21 • charge, $\alpha = +2$, $\beta = -1$
• mass, $\alpha = 4$ amu, $\beta = 0.000549$ amu
• velocity, $\alpha = 10\%$ of the speed of light, $\beta = 90\%$ of the speed of light

9.23 Chemical reactions involve joining, separating and rearranging atoms; valence electrons are critically involved. Nuclear reactions involve only changes in nuclear composition.

9.25 $^{4}_{2}He$

9.27 $^{235}_{92}U$

9.29 Each isotope contains one proton, and
$^{1}_{1}H$ $1 - 1 = 0$ neutrons
$^{2}_{1}H$ $2 - 1 = 1$ neutron
$^{3}_{1}H$ $3 - 1 = 2$ neutrons

9.31 $^{15}_{7}N$

9.33 Alpha and beta particles are matter; gamma radiation is pure energy. Alpha particles are large and relatively slow moving. They are the least energetic and least penetrating. Gamma radiation moves at the speed of light, is highly energetic, and is most penetrating.

9.35 A helium atom has two electrons; an alpha particle has no electrons.

9.37 $^{60}_{27}Co \rightarrow ^{60}_{28}Ni + ^{0}_{-1}\beta + \gamma$

9.39 $^{23}_{11}Na + ^{2}_{1}H \rightarrow ^{24}_{11}Na + ^{1}_{1}H$

9.41 $^{24}_{10}Ne \rightarrow \beta + ^{24}_{11}Na$

9.43 $^{140}_{55}Cs \rightarrow ^{140}_{56}Ba + ^{0}_{-1}e$

9.45 $^{209}_{83}Bi + ^{54}_{24}Cr \rightarrow ^{262}_{107}Bh + ^{1}_{0}n$

9.47 $^{27}_{12}Mg \rightarrow ^{0}_{-1}e + ^{27}_{13}Al$

9.49 $^{12}_{7}N \rightarrow ^{12}_{6}C + ^{0}_{1}e$

9.51 $^{241}_{95}Am \rightarrow ^{4}_{2}\alpha + ^{237}_{93}Np$

9.53 Natural radioactivity is a spontaneous process; artificial radioactivity is nonspontaneous and results from a nuclear reaction that produces an unstable nucleus.

9.55
- Nuclei for light atoms tend to be most stable if their neutron/proton ratio is close to 1.
- Nuclei with more than 84 protons tend to be unstable.
- Isotopes with a "magic number" of protons or neutrons (2, 8, 20, 50, 82, or 126 protons or neutrons) tend to be stable.
- Isotopes with even numbers of protons or neutrons tend to be more stable.

9.57 $^{20}_{8}O$; Oxygen-20 has $20 - 8 = 12$ neutrons, an n/p of 12/8, or 1.5. The n/p is probably too high for stability even though it does have a "magic number" of protons and an even number of protons and neutrons.

9.59 $^{48}_{24}Cr$; Chromium-48 has $48 - 24 = 24$ neutrons, an n/p of 24/24, or 1.0. It also has an even number of protons and neutrons. It would probably be stable.

9.61 0.40 mg of iodine-131 remains

9.63 13 mg of iron-59 remains

9.65 Radiocarbon dating is a process used to determine the age of objects. The ratio of the masses of the stable isotope, carbon-12, and unstable isotope, carbon-14, is measured. Using this value and the half-life of carbon-14, the age of the coffin may be calculated.

9.67 Fission

9.69
a. The fission process involves the breaking down of large, unstable nuclei into smaller, more stable nuclei. This process releases some of the binding energy in the form of heat and/or light.
b. The heat generated during the fission process could be used to generate steam, which is then used to drive a turbine to create electricity.

9.71 $^{3}_{1}H + ^{1}_{1}H \rightarrow ^{4}_{2}He + energy$

9.73 A "breeder" reactor creates the fuel which can be used by a conventional fission reactor during its fission process.

9.75 The reaction in a fission reactor that involves neutron production and causes subsequent reactions accompanied by the production of more neutrons in a continuing process.

9.77 High operating temperatures

9.79 Radiation therapy provides sufficient energy to destroy molecules critical to the reproduction of cancer cells.

9.81 Background radiation, radiation from natural sources, is emitted by the sun as cosmic radiation, and from naturally radioactive isotopes found throughout our environment.

9.83 $^{108}_{47}Ag + ^{4}_{2}He \rightarrow ^{112}_{49}In$

9.85
a. Technetium-99 m is used to study the heart (cardiac output, size, and shape), kidney (follow-up procedure for kidney transplant), and liver and spleen (size, shape, presence of tumors).

b. Xenon-133 is used to locate regions of reduced ventilation and presence of tumors in the lung.

9.87 Level decreases

9.89 Positive effect

9.91 Positive effect

9.93 Yes

9.95 Relative biological effect is a measure of the damage to biological tissue caused by different forms of radiation.

9.97
a. The curie is the amount of radioactive material needed to produce 3.7×10^{10} atomic disintegrations per second.
b. The roentgen is the amount of radioactive material needed to produce 2×10^9 ion-pairs when passing through 1 cc of air at 0°C.

9.99 A film badge detects gamma radiation by darkening photographic film in proportion to the amount of radiation exposure over time. Badges are periodically collected and evaluated for their level of exposure. This mirrors the level of exposure of the personnel wearing the badges.

Chapter 10

10.1 The student could test the solubility of the substance in water and in an organic solvent, such as hexane. Solubility in hexane would suggest an organic substance; whereas solubility in water would indicate an inorganic compound. The student could also determine the melting and boiling points of the substance. If the melting and boiling points are very high, an inorganic substance would be suspected.

10.3

10.5 Three of the six axial hydrogen atoms of cyclohexane lie above the ring. The remaining three hydrogen atoms lie below the ring.

10.7
a. The monobromination of propane will produce two products, as shown in the following two equations:

$CH_3CH_2CH_3 + Br_2 \xrightarrow{\text{Light or heat}} CH_3CH_2CH_2Br + HBr$

$CH_3CH_2CH_3 + Br_2 \xrightarrow{\text{Light or heat}} CH_3CHBrCH_3 + HBr$

b. The monochlorination of butane will produce two products, as shown in the following two equations:

$CH_3CH_2CH_2CH_3 + Cl_2 \xrightarrow{\text{Light or heat}} CH_3CH_2CH_2CH_2Cl + HCl$

$CH_3CH_2CH_2CH_3 + Cl_2 \xrightarrow{\text{Light or heat}} CH_3CH_2CHClCH_3 + HCl$

c. The monochlorination of cyclobutane:

d. The monobromination of pentane will produce three products as shown in the following equations:

$$CH_3CH_2CH_2CH_2CH_3 + Br_2 \xrightarrow{\text{Light or heat}} CH_3CH_2CH_2CH_2CH_2Br + HBr$$

$$CH_3CH_2CH_2CH_2CH_3 + Br_2 \xrightarrow{\text{Light or heat}} CH_3CH_2CH_2CHBrCH_3 + HBr$$

$$CH_3CH_2CH_2CH_2CH_3 + Br_2 \xrightarrow{\text{Light or heat}} CH_3CH_2CHBrCH_2CH_3 + HBr$$

10.9 The number of organic compounds is nearly limitless because carbon forms stable covalent bonds with other carbon atoms in a variety of different patterns. In addition, carbon can form stable bonds with other elements and functional groups, producing many families of organic compounds, including alcohols, aldehydes, ketones, esters, ethers, amines, and amides. Finally, carbon can form double or triple bonds with other carbon atoms to produce organic molecules with different properties.

10.11 The allotropes of carbon include graphite, diamond, and buckminsterfullerene.

10.13 Because ionic substances often form three-dimensional crystals made up of many positive and negative ions, they generally have much higher melting and boiling points than covalent compounds.

10.15 a. $LiCl > H_2O > CH_4$
    b. $NaCl > C_3H_8 > C_2H_6$

10.17 a. $LiCl$ would be a solid; H_2O would be a liquid; and CH_4 would be a gas.
    b. $NaCl$ would be a solid; both C_3H_8 and C_2H_6 would be gases.

10.19 a. Water-soluble inorganic compounds
    b. Inorganic compounds
    c. Organic compounds
    d. Inorganic compounds
    e. Organic compounds

10.21 a. $C_{19}H_{40}$
    b.

$CH(CH_3)_2(CH_2)_3CH(CH_3)(CH_2)_3CH(CH_3)(CH_2)_3CH(CH_3)_2$

    c. 268.59 g/mol

10.23 a. $CH_3CH_2CH(CH_3)_2$
    b. $CH_3CH_2CH(CH_3)_2CH_2CH_2CH(CH_3)CH_3$

10.25 a.   **b.**   **c.**

10.27 a.   **b.**

    c.   **d.**

10.29 a.   Tricosane.

Pentacosane.

Heptacosane.

b. Tricosane: 324.61 g/mol
     Pentacosane: 352.67 g/mol
     Heptacosane: 380.72 g/mol

10.31 a.   **b.**

10.33
    a.   **b.**

10.35 An alcohol

An aldehyde

A ketone

A carboxylic acid

An amine

10.37 a. C_nH_{2n+2}
    b. C_nH_{2n-2}
    c. C_nH_{2n}

d. C_nH_{2n}

e. C_nH_{2n-2}

10.39 Alkanes have only carbon-to-carbon and carbon-to-hydrogen single bonds, as in the molecule ethane:

$$H-\overset{\overset{\displaystyle H}{|}}{\underset{\underset{\displaystyle H}{|}}{C}}-\overset{\overset{\displaystyle H}{|}}{\underset{\underset{\displaystyle H}{|}}{C}}-H$$

Alkenes have at least one carbon-to-carbon double bond, as in the molecule ethene:

$$\overset{\displaystyle H}{\underset{\displaystyle H}{}}C=C\overset{\displaystyle H}{\underset{\displaystyle H}{}}$$

Alkynes have at least one carbon-to-carbon triple bond, as in the molecule ethyne:

$$H-C\equiv C-H$$

10.41 a. A carboxylic acid:

$$CH_3CH_2-\overset{\overset{\displaystyle O}{\|}}{C}-OH$$

b. An amine: $CH_3CH_2CH_2-NH_2$

c. An alcohol: $CH_3CH_2CH_2-OH$

d. An ether: $CH_3CH_2-O-CH_2CH_3$

10.43

Carbonyl Group

Carboxyl Group

Aromatic Ring

HO

O   NH₂   O

Ester Group

10.45 Hydrocarbons are nonpolar molecules, and hence are not soluble in water.

10.47 a. heptane > hexane > butane > ethane

b. $CH_3CH_2CH_2CH_2CH_2CH_2CH_2CH_2CH_3 >$
$CH_3CH_2CH_2CH_2CH_3 > CH_3CH_2CH_3$

10.49 a. Heptane and hexane would be liquid at room temperature; butane and ethane would be gases.

b. $CH_3CH_2CH_2CH_2CH_2CH_2CH_2CH_2CH_3$ and $CH_3CH_2CH_2CH_2CH_3$ would be liquids at room temperature; $CH_3CH_2CH_3$ would be a gas.

10.51 Nonane: $CH_3CH_2CH_2CH_2CH_2CH_2CH_2CH_2CH_3$
Pentane: $CH_3CH_2CH_2CH_2CH_3$
Propane: $CH_3CH_2CH_3$

10.53 a.
$$\underset{\underset{\displaystyle CH_3CHCH_2CH_3}{|}}{\overset{\displaystyle Br}{}}$$

b.
$$CH_3-\overset{\overset{\displaystyle Cl}{|}}{\underset{\underset{\displaystyle CH_3}{|}}{C}}-CH_3$$

c.
$$CH_3-\overset{\overset{\displaystyle CH_3}{|}}{\underset{\underset{\displaystyle CH_3}{|}}{C}}-CH_2CH_2CH_2CH_3$$

10.55 a. 2,2-Dibromobutane:

$$H-\overset{\overset{\displaystyle H}{|}}{\underset{\underset{\displaystyle H}{|}}{C}}-\overset{\overset{\displaystyle Br}{|}}{\underset{\underset{\displaystyle Br}{|}}{C}}-\overset{\overset{\displaystyle H}{|}}{\underset{\underset{\displaystyle H}{|}}{C}}-\overset{\overset{\displaystyle H}{|}}{\underset{\underset{\displaystyle H}{|}}{C}}-H$$

b. 2-Iododecane:

$$H-\overset{\overset{\displaystyle H}{|}}{\underset{\underset{\displaystyle H}{|}}{C}}-\overset{\overset{\displaystyle I}{|}}{\underset{\underset{\displaystyle H}{|}}{C}}-\overset{\overset{\displaystyle H}{|}}{\underset{\underset{\displaystyle H}{|}}{C}}-\overset{\overset{\displaystyle H}{|}}{\underset{\underset{\displaystyle H}{|}}{C}}-\overset{\overset{\displaystyle H}{|}}{\underset{\underset{\displaystyle H}{|}}{C}}-\overset{\overset{\displaystyle H}{|}}{\underset{\underset{\displaystyle H}{|}}{C}}-\overset{\overset{\displaystyle H}{|}}{\underset{\underset{\displaystyle H}{|}}{C}}-\overset{\overset{\displaystyle H}{|}}{\underset{\underset{\displaystyle H}{|}}{C}}-\overset{\overset{\displaystyle H}{|}}{\underset{\underset{\displaystyle H}{|}}{C}}-\overset{\overset{\displaystyle H}{|}}{\underset{\underset{\displaystyle H}{|}}{C}}-H$$

c. 1,2-Dichloropentane:

$$Cl-\overset{\overset{\displaystyle H}{|}}{\underset{\underset{\displaystyle H}{|}}{C}}-\overset{\overset{\displaystyle Cl}{|}}{\underset{\underset{\displaystyle H}{|}}{C}}-\overset{\overset{\displaystyle H}{|}}{\underset{\underset{\displaystyle H}{|}}{C}}-\overset{\overset{\displaystyle H}{|}}{\underset{\underset{\displaystyle H}{|}}{C}}-\overset{\overset{\displaystyle H}{|}}{\underset{\underset{\displaystyle H}{|}}{C}}-H$$

d. 1-Bromo-2-methylpentane:

$$H-\overset{\displaystyle H}{\underset{\displaystyle H}{|}}{C}-H$$

$$H-\overset{\overset{\displaystyle H}{|}}{\underset{\underset{\displaystyle Br}{|}}{C}}-\overset{\overset{\displaystyle H}{|}}{\underset{\underset{\displaystyle H}{|}}{C}}-\overset{\overset{\displaystyle H}{|}}{\underset{\underset{\displaystyle H}{|}}{C}}-\overset{\overset{\displaystyle H}{|}}{\underset{\underset{\displaystyle H}{|}}{C}}-\overset{\overset{\displaystyle H}{|}}{\underset{\underset{\displaystyle H}{|}}{C}}-H$$

10.57 a. 3-Methylpentane   **c.** 1-Bromoheptane
b. 2,5-Dimethylhexane   **d.** 1-Chloro-3-methylbutane

10.59 a. 2-Chloropropane   **d.** 1-Chloro-2-methylpropane
b. 2-Iodobutane   **e.** 2-Iodo-2-methylpropane
c. 2,2-Dibromopropane

10.61 a. The straight chain isomers of molecular formula C_4H_9Br:

$$H-\overset{\overset{\displaystyle H}{|}}{\underset{\underset{\displaystyle H}{|}}{C}}-\overset{\overset{\displaystyle H}{|}}{\underset{\underset{\displaystyle H}{|}}{C}}-\overset{\overset{\displaystyle H}{|}}{\underset{\underset{\displaystyle H}{|}}{C}}-\overset{\overset{\displaystyle H}{|}}{\underset{\underset{\displaystyle H}{|}}{C}}-Br \qquad H-\overset{\overset{\displaystyle H}{|}}{\underset{\underset{\displaystyle H}{|}}{C}}-\overset{\overset{\displaystyle H}{|}}{\underset{\underset{\displaystyle H}{|}}{C}}-\overset{\overset{\displaystyle Br}{|}}{\underset{\underset{\displaystyle H}{|}}{C}}-\overset{\overset{\displaystyle H}{|}}{\underset{\underset{\displaystyle H}{|}}{C}}-H$$

b. The straight chain isomers of molecular formula $C_4H_8Br_2$:

$$H-\overset{\overset{\displaystyle H}{|}}{\underset{\underset{\displaystyle H}{|}}{C}}-\overset{\overset{\displaystyle H}{|}}{\underset{\underset{\displaystyle H}{|}}{C}}-\overset{\overset{\displaystyle H}{|}}{\underset{\underset{\displaystyle H}{|}}{C}}-\overset{\overset{\displaystyle Br}{|}}{\underset{\underset{\displaystyle H}{|}}{C}}-Br \qquad H-\overset{\overset{\displaystyle H}{|}}{\underset{\underset{\displaystyle H}{|}}{C}}-\overset{\overset{\displaystyle H}{|}}{\underset{\underset{\displaystyle H}{|}}{C}}-\overset{\overset{\displaystyle Br}{|}}{\underset{\underset{\displaystyle H}{|}}{C}}-\overset{\overset{\displaystyle H}{|}}{\underset{\underset{\displaystyle H}{|}}{C}}-Br$$

$$H-\overset{\overset{\displaystyle H}{|}}{\underset{\underset{\displaystyle H}{|}}{C}}-\overset{\overset{\displaystyle Br}{|}}{\underset{\underset{\displaystyle H}{|}}{C}}-\overset{\overset{\displaystyle H}{|}}{\underset{\underset{\displaystyle H}{|}}{C}}-\overset{\overset{\displaystyle H}{|}}{\underset{\underset{\displaystyle H}{|}}{C}}-Br \qquad Br-\overset{\overset{\displaystyle H}{|}}{\underset{\underset{\displaystyle H}{|}}{C}}-\overset{\overset{\displaystyle H}{|}}{\underset{\underset{\displaystyle H}{|}}{C}}-\overset{\overset{\displaystyle H}{|}}{\underset{\underset{\displaystyle H}{|}}{C}}-\overset{\overset{\displaystyle H}{|}}{\underset{\underset{\displaystyle H}{|}}{C}}-Br$$

$$H-\overset{\overset{\displaystyle H}{|}}{\underset{\underset{\displaystyle H}{|}}{C}}-\overset{\overset{\displaystyle H}{|}}{\underset{\underset{\displaystyle H}{|}}{C}}-\overset{\overset{\displaystyle Br}{|}}{\underset{\underset{\displaystyle Br}{|}}{C}}-\overset{\overset{\displaystyle H}{|}}{\underset{\underset{\displaystyle H}{|}}{C}}-H \qquad H-\overset{\overset{\displaystyle H}{|}}{\underset{\underset{\displaystyle H}{|}}{C}}-\overset{\overset{\displaystyle Br}{|}}{\underset{\underset{\displaystyle H}{|}}{C}}-\overset{\overset{\displaystyle Br}{|}}{\underset{\underset{\displaystyle H}{|}}{C}}-\overset{\overset{\displaystyle H}{|}}{\underset{\underset{\displaystyle H}{|}}{C}}-H$$

10.63 a. 2-Chlorohexane   **c.** 3-Chloropentane
b. 1,4-Dibromobutane   **d.** 2-Methylheptane

10.65 a. The first pair of molecules are constitutional isomers: hexane and 2-methylpentane.
b. The second pair of molecules are identical. Both are heptane.

10.67 a. Incorrect: 3-Methylhexane
b. Incorrect: 2-Methylbutane
c. Incorrect: 3-Methylheptane
d. Correct

10.69 a.
$$\underset{\underset{\displaystyle CH_3}{|}}{CH_3CHCH_2\overset{\overset{\displaystyle CH_3}{|}}{C}HCH_3}$$
    The name given in the problem is correct.

b.

CH₃
|
CH₃CH₂CH₂CHCH₂CH₃

The correct name is 3-methylhexane.

c. I—CH₂CH₂CH₂CH₂CH₂—I   The name given in the problem is correct.

d. CH₃CH₂CH₂CH₂CH₂CHCH₂CH₂CH₃   The correct name is 4-ethylnonane.

CH₂CH₃

e. Br   Br
| |
CH₂CH₂CH₂CH₂CH₂CCH₂CH₃   The name given in the problem is correct.

CH₃

10.71 Cycloalkanes are a family of molecules having carbon-to-carbon bonds in a ring structure.

10.73 The general formula for a cycloalkane is C_nH_{2n}.

10.75 **a.** Chlorocyclopropane
b. *cis*-1,2-Dichlorocyclopropane
c. *trans*-1,2-Dichlorocyclopropane
d. Bromocyclobutane

10.77 **a.** 1-Bromo-2-methylcyclobutane: **b.** Iodocyclopropane:

10.79 **a.** 2,5-Dibromo-1,3-dichlorocycloheptane

b. *trans*-1,4-Dimethylcyclooctane

c. 1,3-Dibromo-5-methylcyclohexane

d. 1,2,4-Trimethylcyclopentane

e. 1,1,2,5-Tetramethylcyclohexane

10.81   Cl   Cl

10.83 **a.** Incorrect—1,2-Dibromocyclobutane
b. Incorrect—1,2-Diethylcyclobutane
c. Correct
d. Incorrect—1,2,3-Trichlorocyclohexane

10.85 **a.** Br   Br   **b.**   CH₃

CH₃

c. Cl   **d.** CH₂CH₃

Cl

CH₂CH₃

10.87 **a.** *cis*-1,2-Dibromocyclopentane
b. *trans*-1,3-Dibromocyclopentane
c. *cis*-1,2-Dimethylcyclohexane
d. *cis*-1,2-Dimethylcyclopropane

10.89 Conformational isomers are distinct isomeric structures that may be converted into one another by rotation about the bonds in the molecule.

10.91 In the chair conformation the hydrogen atoms, and thus the electron pairs of the C—H bonds, are farther from one another. As a result, there is less electron repulsion and the structure is more stable (more energetically favored). In the boat conformation, the electron pairs are more crowded. This causes greater electron repulsion, producing a less stable, less energetically favored conformation.

10.93 Because conformations are freely and rapidly interconverted, they cannot be separated from one another.

10.95 One conformation is more stable than the other because the electron pairs of the carbon-hydrogen bonds are farther from one another.

10.97 Combustion is the oxidation of hydrocarbons by burning in the presence of air to produce carbon dioxide and water.

10.99 **a.** $C_3H_8 + 5O_2 \rightarrow 4H_2O + 3CO_2$
b. $C_7H_{16} + 11O_2 \rightarrow 8H_2O + 7CO_2$
c. $C_9H_{20} + 14O_2 \rightarrow 10H_2O + 9CO_2$
d. $2C_{10}H_{22} + 31O_2 \rightarrow 22H_2O + 20CO_2$

10.101 $2C_{16}H_{34} + 49O_2 \rightarrow 32CO_2 + 32H_2O$

10.103 **a.** $8CO_2 + 10H_2O$

b.   CH₃   CH₃
| |
Br—C—CH₃ + CH₃CHCH₂Br + 2HBr
|
CH₃

c. Cl_2 + light

10.105 The following molecules are all isomers of C_6H_{14}.

$CH_3CH_2CH_2CH_2CH_2CH_3$

Hexane

$$CH_3\overset{\underset{\displaystyle CH_3}{|}}{CH}CH_2CH_2CH_3$$

2-Methylpentane

$$CH_3CH_2\overset{\underset{\displaystyle CH_3}{|}}{CH}CH_2CH_3$$

3-Methylpentane

$$CH_3\overset{\underset{\displaystyle CH_3}{|}}{CH}\overset{\underset{\displaystyle CH_3}{|}}{CH}CH_3$$

2,3-Dimethylbutane

$$CH_3\overset{\overset{\displaystyle CH_3}{|}}{\underset{\underset{\displaystyle CH_3}{|}}{C}}CH_2CH_3$$

2,2-Dimethylbutane

a. 2,3-Dimethylbutane produces only two monobrominated derivatives: 1-bromo-2,3-dimethylbutane and 2-bromo-2, 3-dimethylbutane.
b. Hexane produces three monobrominated products: 1-bromohexane, 2-bromohexane, and 3-bromohexane. 2,2-Dimethylbutane also produces three monobrominated products: 1-bromo-2,2-dimethylbutane, 2-bromo-3, 3-dimethylbutane, and 1-bromo-3,3-dimethylbutane.
c. 3-Methylpentane produces four monobrominated products: 1-bromo-3-methylpentane, 2-bromo-3-methylpentane, 3-bromo-3-methylpentane, and 1-bromo-2-ethylbutane.

10.107 The hydrocarbon is cyclooctane, having a molecular formula of C_8H_{16}.

$+ 12O_2 \longrightarrow 8CO_2 + 8H_2O$

Chapter 11

11.1 a.

b.

c. $Cl-C\equiv C-Cl$

d.

11.3 a.

cis-3-Hexene   trans-3-Hexene

b.

trans-2,3-Dibromo-2-butene   cis-2,3-Dibromo-2-butene

11.5 Molecule c can exist as cis- and trans-isomers because there are two different groups on each of the carbon atoms attached by the double bond.

11.7 a.

b.

c.

11.9 The hydrogenation of the cis and trans isomers of 2-pentene would produce the same product, pentane.

11.11 a.

$$H_3C-C\equiv C-CH_3 + 2\,H_2 \xrightarrow{Ni} \text{Butane}$$

2-Butyne   Butane

b.

$$H_3C-C\equiv C-CH_2CH_3 + 2\,H_2 \xrightarrow{Ni} \text{Pentane}$$

2-Pentyne   Pentane

11.13 a. $CH_3CH{=}CH_2 + Br_2 \longrightarrow$

b. $CH_3CH{=}CHCH_3 + Br_2 \longrightarrow$

11.15 a. $CH_3C{\equiv}CCH_3 + 2Cl_2 \longrightarrow$

b. $CH_3C{\equiv}CCH_2CH_3 + 2Cl_2 \longrightarrow$

11.17 a. $CH_3CH{=}CHCH_3 + H_2O \xrightarrow{H^+}$

$$CH_3\overset{\underset{\displaystyle OH}{|}}{CH}CH_2CH_3 \text{ (only product)}$$

b. $CH_2{=}CHCH_2CH_2\overset{\underset{\displaystyle CH_3}{|}}{CH}CH_3 + H_2O \xrightarrow{H^+}$

$$CH_3\overset{\underset{\displaystyle OH}{|}}{CH}CH_2CH_2\overset{\underset{\displaystyle CH_3}{|}}{CH}CH_3 \text{ (major product)}$$

$$CH_2=CHCH_2CH_2CHCH_3 + H_2O \xrightarrow{H^+}$$
$$\underset{\displaystyle CH_3}{|}$$

$$CH_2CH_2CH_2CH_2CHCH_3 \text{ (minor product)}$$
$$\underset{\displaystyle OH}{|} \qquad \underset{\displaystyle CH_3}{|}$$

c. $CH_3CH_2CH_2CH=CHCH_2CH_3 + H_2O \xrightarrow{H^+}$

$$CH_3CH_2CH_2CHCH_2CH_2CH_3$$
$$\underset{\displaystyle OH}{|}$$

$$CH_3CH_2CH_2CH=CHCH_2CH_3 + H_2O \xrightarrow{H^+}$$

$$CH_3CH_2CH_2CH_2CHCH_2CH_3$$
$$\underset{\displaystyle OH}{|}$$

These products will be formed in approximately equal amounts.

d. $CH_3CHClCH=CHCHClCH_3 + H_2O \xrightarrow{H^+}$

$$CH_3CHClCHCH_2CHClCH_3 \text{ (only product)}$$
$$\underset{\displaystyle OH}{|}$$

11.19 a. $H_3CC\equiv CH + H_2O \xrightarrow{H^+}$

$$\begin{array}{cc} H & H \\ | & | \\ H-C-C=C-H \\ | & | \\ H & OH \end{array}$$

$$\longrightarrow \begin{array}{cc} H & H \\ | & | \\ H-C-C-C-H \\ | & || \\ H & H \ O \end{array}$$

Or

$$H_3CC\equiv CH + H_2O \xrightarrow{H^+} \begin{array}{cc} H & OH \\ | & | \\ H-C-C=C-H \\ | & | \\ H & H \end{array}$$

$$\longrightarrow \begin{array}{ccc} H & O & H \\ | & || & | \\ H-C-C-C-H \\ | & & | \\ H & & H \end{array}$$

b.
$$H_3CC\equiv CCH_2CH_3 + H_2O \xrightarrow{H^+} \begin{array}{cccc} H & H & & H & H \\ | & | & & | & | \\ H-C-C=C-C-C-H \\ | & & | & | & | \\ H & & OH & H & H \end{array}$$

$$\longrightarrow \begin{array}{cccc} H & H & & H & H \\ | & | & & | & | \\ H-C-C-C-C-C-H \\ | & | & || & | & | \\ H & H & O & H & H \end{array}$$

Or

$$H_3CC\equiv CCH_2CH_3 + H_2O \xrightarrow{H^+} \begin{array}{cccc} H & OH & H & H \\ | & | & | & | \\ H-C-C=C-C-C-H \\ | & & | & | & | \\ H & & H & H & H \end{array}$$

$$\longrightarrow \begin{array}{ccccc} H & O & H & H & H \\ | & || & | & | & | \\ H-C-C-C-C-C-H \\ | & & | & | & | \\ H & & H & H & H \end{array}$$

11.21 a.

b.

c.

d.

e.

f.

11.23 As the length of the hydrocarbon chain increases, the intermolecular forces between the molecules increase. The stronger the intermolecular forces are, the higher the boiling point will be.

11.25 The general formula for an alkane is C_nH_{2n+2}.
The general formula for an alkene is C_nH_{2n}.
The general formula for an alkyne is C_nH_{2n-2}.

11.27 Ethene is a planar molecule. All of the bond angles are 120°.

11.29 In alkanes, such as ethane, the four bonds around each carbon atom have tetrahedral geometry. The bond angles are 109.5°. In alkenes, such as ethene, each carbon is bonded by two single bonds and one double bond. The molecule is planar and each bond angle is approximately 120°.

11.31 Ethyne is a linear molecule. All of the bond angles are 180°.

11.33 In alkanes, such as ethane, the four bonds around each carbon atom have tetrahedral geometry. The bond angles are 109.5°. In alkenes, such as ethene, each carbon is bonded by two single bonds and one double bond. The molecule is planar and each bond angle is approximately 120°. In alkynes, such as ethyne, each carbon is bonded by one single bond and one triple bond. The molecule is linear and the bond angles are 180°.

11.35 a. 2-Pentyne > Propyne > Ethyne
b. 3-Decene > 2-Butene > Ethene

11.37 Identify the longest carbon chain containing the carbon-to-carbon double or triple bond. Replace the *–ane* suffix of the alkane name with *–ene* for an alkene or *-yne* for an alkyne. Number the chain to give the lowest number to the first of the two carbons involved in the double or triple bond. Determine the name and carbon number of each substituent group and place that information as a prefix in front of the name of the parent compound.

11.39 Geometric isomers of alkenes differ from one another in the placement of substituents attached to each of the carbon atoms of the double bond. Of the pair of geometric isomers, the *cis-* isomer, is the one in which identical groups are on the same side of the double bond.

11.41 a.

b.

c.

d.

e.

11.43 a. 3-Methyl-1-pentene
b. 7-Bromo-1-heptene
c. 5-Bromo-3-heptene
d. 1-*t*-Butyl-4-methylcyclohexene

11.45 a. 1,3,5-Trifluoropentane: $CH_2FCH_2CHFCH_2CH_2F$

b. *cis*-2-Octene:

c. Dipropylacetylene: $CH_3CH_2CH_2—C\equiv C—CH_2CH_2CH_3$

11.47 a. 1-Heptene can only be drawn one way. Therefore, a *cis-trans* isomer does not exist.
b. 2-Heptene can be drawn two ways. Therefore, *cis-trans* isomers do exist.
c. 3-Heptene can be drawn two ways. Therefore, *cis-trans* isomers do exist.
d. 2-Methyl-2-hexene can only be drawn one way. Therefore, a *cis-trans* isomer does not exist.
e. 3-Methyl-2-hexene can be drawn two ways. Therefore, *cis-trans* isomers do exist.

11.49 Alkenes b and c would not exhibit *cis-trans* isomerism.
11.51 Alkenes b and d can exist as both *cis*- and *trans*- isomers.
11.53 a. 1,5-Nonadiene
b. 1,4,7-Nonatriene
c. 2,5-Octadiene
d. 4-Methyl-2,5-heptadiene

11.55

11.57

11.59

11.61 The primary difference between complete hydrogenation of an alkene and an alkyne is that 2 moles of H_2 are required for the complete hydrogenation of an alkyne.

11.63 a.

$$CH_2{=}CH(CH_2)_4CH_3 + H_2O \xrightarrow{H^+}$$

$CH_3CHOH(CH_2)_4CH_3$
Major Product
+
$CH_2OH(CH_2)_5CH_3$
Minor Product

b. $CH_3CH{=}CH(CH_2)_3CH_3 + HBr \longrightarrow$

$CH_3CH_2CHBr(CH_2)_3CH_3$
+
$CH_3CHBr(CH_2)_4CH_3$

c. $CH_3CH_2CH{=}CH(CH_2)_2CH_3 + H_2 \xrightarrow[\text{heat or pressure}]{\text{Pt, Pd, or Ni}} CH_3(CH_2)_5CH_3$

d. $CH_3C{=}CHCH_2CH_2CH_3 + HCl \longrightarrow$ (with CH_3 substituent)

Cl
$CH_3C(CH_2)_3CH_3$
CH_3
Major Product
+
CH_3
$CH_3CHCH(CH_2)_2CH_3$
Cl
Minor Product

11.65 a. H_2 **d.** $19O_2 \rightarrow 12CO_2 + 14H_2O$
b. H_2O **e.** Cl_2
c. HBr **f.**

11.67 a.

$$H_3C—C\equiv C—CH_3 + 2H_2 \xrightarrow[\text{heat or pressure}]{\text{Pt, Pd, or Ni}}$$

2-Butyne

b.

$$CH_3CH_2—C\equiv C—CH_3 + 2X_2 \longrightarrow$$

2-Pentyne

11.69 a. Reactant—*cis*-2-butene; Only product—butane
b. Reactant—1-butene; Major product—2-butanol
c. Reactant—2-butene; Only product—2,3-dichlorobutane
d. Reactant—1-pentene; Major product—2-bromopentane

11.71 $CH_2{=}CHCH_2CH_2CH_3$, $CH_3CH{=}CHCH_2CH_3$,

$CH_3C{=}CHCH_3$, $CH_2{=}CCH_2CH_3$, $CH_2{=}CHCHCH_3$
      CH_3 CH_3 CH_3

11.73 a.

Br
$CH_3CHCH_2CH_3$

b.

I
$CH_3CH_2—C—CH_2CH_2CH_3 + CH_3CHCHCH_2CH_2CH_3$
       CH_3 I CH_3

(major product)   (minor product)

c.

11.75 A polymer is a macromolecule composed of repeating structural units called *monomers*.

11.77 Polyvinyl chloride (PVC) is used in pipes, detergent bottles, and cleanser bottles.

11.79 a.

$$CH_3C{=}CCH_2CH_3 + H_2O \xrightarrow{H^+} CH_3CHCH_2CH_2CH_3$$

(with H on top and bottom of the double-bond carbons; OH on product)

2-Pentene

$$CH_3C{=}CCH_2CH_3 + H_2O \xrightarrow{H^+} CH_3CH_2CHCH_2CH_3$$

(OH on product)

These products will be formed in approximately equal amounts.

b.

$$CH_2C{=}C{-}H + H_2O \xrightarrow{H^+} CH_2CHCH_3 \text{ (major product)}$$

Br (on left); Br OH (on product)

3-Bromo-1-propene

$$CH_2C{=}C{-}H + H_2O \xrightarrow{H^+} CH_2CH_2CHOH \text{ (minor product)}$$

Br (on left); Br (on product)

c.

+ H₂O $\xrightarrow{H^+}$

3,4-Dimethylcyclohexene

+ H₂O $\xrightarrow{H^+}$

These products will be formed in approximately equal amounts.

11.81

a. $CH_2{=}CHCH_2CHCH_3 + H_2O \xrightarrow{H^+} CH_2CH_2CH_2CHCH_3$

(with CH₃ branch; OH on product)

(This is the minor product of this reaction.)

b. $CH_3C{=}CCH_2CH_2CH_3 + HBr \longrightarrow CH_3CH_2CHCH_2CH_2CH_3$

(H on top; Br on product)

OR

$CH_3CH_2C{=}CCH_2CH_3 + HBr \longrightarrow CH_3CH_2CHCH_2CH_2CH_3$

(H on top; Br on product)

c.

+ HBr $\longrightarrow$

d.

$-CH_2CH_3 + H_2O \xrightarrow{H^+}$ $-CH_2CH_3$ (with OH)

11.83 a.

$$CH_2{=}CHCH_2CH{=}CHCH_3 + 2H_2 \xrightarrow[\text{heat}]{Pt} CH_3(CH_2)_4CH_3$$

1,4-Hexadiene   Hexane

b.

$$CH_3CH{=}CHCH{=}CHCH{=}CHCH_3 + 3H_2$$

2,4,6-Octatriene $\xrightarrow[\text{heat}]{Ni} CH_3(CH_2)_6CH_3$

Octane

c.

+ 2H₂ $\xrightarrow[\text{Pressure}]{Pd}$

1,3-Cyclohexadiene   Cyclohexane

d.

+ 3H₂ $\xrightarrow[\text{heat}]{Ni}$

1,3,5-Cyclooctatriene   Cyclooctane

11.85 The term aromatic hydrocarbon was first used as a term to describe the pleasant-smelling resins of tropical trees.

11.87 Resonance hybrids are molecules for which more than one valid Lewis structure can be written.

11.89 a.

b.

c. CH_3CHCH_3

d.

11.91 a.

b.

c.

d.

11.93 Kekulé proposed that single and double carbon-carbon bonds alternate around the benzene ring. To explain why benzene does not react like other unsaturated compounds, he proposed that the double and single bonds shift positions rapidly.

11.95 An addition reaction involves addition of a molecule to a double or triple bond in an unsaturated molecule. In a substitution reaction, one chemical group replaces another.

11.97 a.

+ Br₂ $\xrightarrow{FeBr_3}$ + HBr

b.

$$\text{(benzene)} + Cl_2 \xrightarrow{FeCl_3} \text{(chlorobenzene)} + HCl$$

c.

$$\text{(benzene)} + HNO_3 \xrightarrow[50–55°C]{\text{Concentrated } H_2SO_4} \text{(nitrobenzene, } NO_2) + H_2O$$

11.99

Pyrimidine

11.101

Purine

Chapter 12

12.1 a. 2-Methyl-1-propanol

$$CH_3CHCH_2OH$$
$$\quad | $$
$$\quad CH_3$$

b. 2-Chlorocyclopentanol

Cl

HO—(cyclopentane)

c. 2,4-Dimethylcyclohexanol

OH

H_3C CH_3

d. 2,3-Dichloro-3-hexanol

$$\quad\quad OH$$
$$CH_3CHCCH_2CH_2CH_3$$
$$\quad | \;\; |$$
$$\quad Cl \; Cl$$

12.3 a. The reactant is propene. The major product is 2-propanol and the minor product is 1-propanol. The major product is a secondary alcohol (2-propanol) and the minor product is a primary alcohol (1-propanol). Propene cannot exist as both *cis*- and *trans*- isomers.
    b. The reactant is ethene. The product is ethanol. Ethanol is a primary alcohol. Ethene cannot exist as both *cis*- and *trans*- isomers.
    c. The reactant is 3-hexene. The product is 3-hexanol, which is a secondary alcohol. The reactant 3-hexene can be found as both *cis*- and *trans*- isomers.

12.5 a. Ethanol is a primary alcohol.
    b. 2-Propanol is a secondary alcohol.
    c. 4-Methyl-3-hexanol is a secondary alcohol.
    d. 2-Methyl-2-propanol is a tertiary alcohol.

12.7 a. The reactant is 2-butanol and the product is butanone.
    b. The reactant is 2-pentanol and the product is 2-pentanone.

12.9 Simple phenols are somewhat soluble in water because they have the polar hydroxyl group.

12.11 Ethers have much lower boiling points than alcohols because ether molecules cannot hydrogen bond to one another.

12.13 The longer the hydrocarbon tail of an alcohol becomes, the less water soluble it will be.

12.15 a < d < c < b

12.17 a. CH_3CH_2OH
    b. $CH_3CH_2CH_2CH_2OH$
    c. CH_3CHCH_3
        $\quad | $
        $\quad OH$

12.19 The I.U.P.A.C. rules for the nomenclature of alcohols require you to name the parent compound, that is the longest continuous carbon chain bonded to the —OH group. Replace the –*e* ending of the parent alkane with –*ol* of the alcohol. Number the parent chain so that the carbon bearing the hydroxyl group has the lowest possible number. Name and number all other substituents. If there is more than one hydroxyl group, the –*ol* ending will be modified to reflect the number. If there are two —OH groups, the suffix –*diol* is used; if it has three —OH groups, the suffix –*triol* is used, etc.

12.21 a. 1,4-Hexadiol
    b. 2,3-Pentadiol
    c. 2-Methyl-3-pentanol

12.23 a.

OH

b.

OH   OH

OH

c.

OH

12.25 a. Cyclopentanol
    b. Cycloheptanol
    c. 3-Methylcyclohexanol

12.27 a. Methyl alcohol
    b. Ethyl alcohol
    c. Ethylene glycol
    d. Propyl alcohol

12.29 a. 4-Methyl-2-hexanol

$$CH_3CHCH_2CHCH_2CH_3$$
with CH_3 on the fourth carbon and OH on the second carbon

b. Isobutyl alcohol

$$CH_3CHCH_2OH$$
with CH_3 branch

c. 1,5-Pentanediol $CH_2CH_2CH_2CH_2CH_2$ with OH at each end

d. 2-Nonanol $CH_3CHCH_2CH_2CH_2CH_2CH_2CH_2CH_3$ with OH on second carbon

e. 1,3,5-Cyclohexanetriol

12.31 Denatured alcohol is 100% ethanol to which benzene or methanol is added. The additive makes the ethanol unfit to drink and prevents illegal use of pure ethanol.

12.33 Fermentation is the anaerobic degradation of sugar that involves no net oxidation. The alcohol fermentation, carried out by yeast, produces ethanol and carbon dioxide.

12.35 When the ethanol concentration in a fermentation reaches 12–13%, the yeast producing the ethanol are killed by it. To produce a liquor of higher alcohol concentration, the product of the original fermentation must be distilled.

12.37 The carbinol carbon is the one to which the hydroxyl group is bonded.

12.39 a. Primary
b. Secondary
c. Tertiary
d. Tertiary
e. Tertiary

12.41 a. Primary alcohol
b. Secondary alcohol
c. Primary alcohol
d. Primary alcohol
e. Secondary alcohol

12.43 a. 2-Nonanol is a secondary alcohol:
$$CH_3CHOHCH_2CH_2CH_2CH_2CH_2CH_2CH_3$$
b. 2-Heptanol is a secondary alcohol:
$$CH_3CHOHCH_2CH_2CH_2CH_2CH_3$$
c. 2-Undecanol is a secondary alcohol:
$$CH_3CHOHCH_2CH_2CH_2CH_2CH_2CH_2CH_2CH_2CH_3$$

12.45

Alkene   Alcohol

12.47

Alcohol   Alkene

12.49

Secondary alcohol   Ketone

12.51 a. The predicted products are 1-hexanol (minor) and 2-hexanol (major).
b. The predicted products are 2-hexanol and 3-hexanol. These products will be formed in approximately equal amounts.
c. The predicted products are 5-methyl-3-hexanol and 2-methyl-3-hexanol. These products will be formed in approximately equal amounts.
d. The predicted products are 2,2-dimethyl-4-heptanol and 2,2-dimethyl-3-heptanol. These products will be formed in approximately equal amounts.

12.53 a.

$$CH_3C=CCH_2CH_2CH_3 + H_2O \xrightarrow{H^+}$$
(with H substituents, 2-Hexene)

2-Hexene $CH_3CHCH_2CH_2CH_2CH_3$ with OH on second carbon

2-Hexanol

or

$$CH_3CH_2CHCH_2CH_2CH_3$$ with OH

3-Hexanol

These products will be formed in approximately equal amounts.

b.

Cyclopentene   Cyclopentanol

c. $CH_2=CHCH_2CH_2CH_2CH_2CH_2CH_3 + H_2O \xrightarrow{H^+}$

1-Octene

$$CH_3CHCH_2CH_2CH_2CH_2CH_2CH_3$$ with OH

2-Octanol
(major product)

or

$$CH_2CH_2CH_2CH_2CH_2CH_2CH_2CH_3$$ with OH

1-Octanol
(minor product)

d.

1-Methylcyclohexene

1-Methylcyclohexanol   2-Methylcyclohexanol
(major product)   (minor product)

12.55 a. Butanone
b. N.R.
c. Cyclohexanone
d. N.R.

12.57 a. 3-Pentanone
   b. Propanal (Upon further oxidation, propanoic acid would be formed.)
   c. 4-Methyl-2-pentanone
   d. N.R.
   e. 3-Phenylpropanal (Upon further oxidation, 3-phenylpropanoic acid will be formed.)

12.59 $CH_3CH_2OH \xrightarrow{\text{liver enzymes}} CH_3-\overset{\overset{\displaystyle O}{\|}}{C}-H$

   Ethanol   Ethanal

   The product, ethanal, is responsible for the symptoms of a hangover.

12.61 The reaction in which a water molecule is added to 1-butene is a hydration reaction.

$CH_3CH_2CH{=}CH_2 + H_2O \xrightarrow{H^+} CH_3CH_2\overset{\overset{\displaystyle OH}{|}}{C}HCH_3$

   1-Butene   2-Butanol

12.63

$CH_3CH{=}CH_2 \xrightarrow{H_2O, H^+} CH_3\overset{\overset{\displaystyle OH}{|}}{C}HCH_3 \xrightarrow{[O]} CH_3\overset{\overset{\displaystyle O}{\|}}{C}CH_3$

   Propene   2-Propanol   Propanone
   (propylene)   (isopropanol)   (acetone)

12.65 a.

   b.

   c.

   d.

12.67 Oxidation is a loss of electrons, whereas reduction is a gain of electrons.

12.69

$CH_3CH_2CH_3 < CH_3CH_2CH_2OH < CH_3CH_2\overset{\overset{\displaystyle O}{\|}}{C}-H < CH_3CH_2\overset{\overset{\displaystyle O}{\|}}{C}-OH$

12.71 Phenols are compounds with an —OH attached to a benzene ring.

12.73   Picric acid: 2,4,6,-Trinitrotoluene:

   Picric acid is water-soluble because of the polar hydroxyl group that can form hydrogen bonds with water.

12.75 Hexachlorophene, hexylresorcinol, and o-phenylphenol are phenol compounds used as antiseptics or disinfectants.

12.77 Ethers have much lower boiling points than alcohols of similar molecular mass, but higher boiling points than alkanes of similar molecular mass. The boiling points are higher than alkanes because the R—O—R bond is polar. However, there is no —OH group, so ether molecules cannot hydrogen bond to one another. This is the reason that the boiling points are lower than alcohols of similar molecular mass.

12.79 Alcohols of molecular formula $C_4H_{10}O$

$CH_3CH_2CH_2CH_2OH,$ $CH_3\overset{\overset{\displaystyle OH}{|}}{C}HCH_2CH_3,$

$CH_3\overset{\overset{\displaystyle OH}{|}}{C}HCH_2OH,$ $CH_3-\overset{\overset{\displaystyle OH}{|}}{\underset{\underset{\displaystyle CH_3}{|}}{C}}-CH_3$
   $\underset{CH_3}{|}$

   Ethers of molecular formula $C_4H_{10}O$
   $CH_3-O-CH_2CH_2CH_3$ $CH_3CH_2-O-CH_2CH_3$
   $CH_3-O-\overset{}{\underset{\underset{\displaystyle CH_3}{|}}{C}}HCH_3$

12.81 Penthrane: 2,2-Dichloro-1,1-difluoro-1-methoxyethane
   Enthrane: 2-Chloro-1-(difluoromethoxy)-1,1,2-trifluoroethane

12.83 a. $CH_3CH_2-O-CH_2CH_3 + H_2O$
   b. $CH_3CH_2-O-CH_2CH_3 + CH_3-O-CH_3 +$
      $CH_3-O-CH_2CH_3 + H_2O$
   c. $CH_3-O-CH_3 + CH_3-O-\overset{}{\underset{\underset{\displaystyle CH_3}{|}}{C}}HCH_3 +$

   $CH_3\overset{}{\underset{\underset{\displaystyle CH_3}{|}}{C}}H-O-\overset{}{\underset{\underset{\displaystyle CH_3}{|}}{C}}HCH_3 + H_2O$

   d.

12.85 a. 2-Ethoxypentane
   b. 2-Methoxybutane
   c. 1-Ethoxybutane
   d. Methoxycyclopentane

12.87 a.

   b.

c.

d.

12.89 Thiols contain the sulfhydryl group (—SH). The sulfhydryl group is similar to the hydroxyl group (—OH) of alcohols, except that a sulfur atom replaces the oxygen atom.

12.91 Cystine:

12.93 a. 1-Propanethiol
    b. 2-Butanethiol
    c. 2-Methyl-2-butanethiol
    d. 1,4-Cyclohexanedithiol

Chapter 13

13.1 a.

b.

13.3 a.

b.

13.5 a. 2,3-Dichloropentanal

b. 2-Bromobutanal

c. 4-Methylhexanal

d. Butanal

e. 2,4-Dimethylpentanal

13.7 a. 3-Iodobutanone
    b. 4-Methyl-2-octanone
    c. 3-Methylbutanone
    d. 2-Methyl-3-pentanone
    e. 2-Fluoro-3-pentanone

13.9

13.11 a. Reduction
    b. Reduction
    c. Reduction
    d. Oxidation
    e. Reduction

13.13 a. Hemiacetal
    b. Ketal
    c. Acetal
    d. Hemiketal

13.15

Propanal   3-Hydroxy-2-methylpentanal

13.17 As the carbon chain length increases, the compounds become less polar and more hydrocarbon-like. As a result, their solubility in water decreases.

13.19 A good solvent should dissolve a wide range of compounds. Simple ketones are considered to be universal solvents because they have both a polar carbonyl group and nonpolar side chains. As a result, they dissolve organic compounds and are also miscible in water.

13.21

13.23 Alcohols have higher boiling points than aldehydes or ketones of comparable molecular mass because alcohol molecules can form intermolecular hydrogen bonds with one another. Aldehydes and ketones cannot form intermolecular hydrogen bonds.

13.25 To name an aldehyde using the I.U.P.A.C. Nomenclature System, identify and name the longest carbon chain containing the carbonyl group. Replace the final -e of the alkane name with -al. Number and name all substituents as usual. Remember that the carbonyl carbon is always carbon-1 and does not need to be numbered in the name of the compound.

13.27 The common names of aldehydes are derived from the same Latin roots as the corresponding carboxylic acids. For instance, methanal is formaldehyde; ethanal is acetaldehyde; propanal is propionaldehyde, *etc.*

Substituted aldehydes are named as derivatives of the straight-chain parent compound. Greek letters are used to indicate the position of substituents. The carbon nearest the carbonyl group is the α-carbon, the next is the β-carbon, and so on.

13.29 a.

b.

c.

d.

13.31 a. $CH_3CH(CH_3)CCH_2CH_3$

b. $CH_3(CH_2)_2CCH_2CH_3$

c. $CH_3(CH_2)_3C(CH_2)_3CH_3$

d. $CH_3(CH_2)_5C(CH_2)_6CH_3$

13.33 a. Butanone
b. 2-Ethylhexanal
13.35 a. 3-Nitrobenzaldehyde
b. 3,4-Dihydroxycyclopentanone
13.37 7-Hydroxy-3,7-dimethyloctanal
13.39 a. 4,6-Dimethyl-3-heptanone
b. 3,3-Dimethylcyclopentanone
13.41 a. Acetone
b. Ethyl methyl ketone
c. Acetaldehyde
d. Propionaldehyde
e. Methyl isopropyl ketone

13.43 a.

$$CH_3CHCH_2C\!-\!H$$
with OH below

b.

$$CH_3CH_2CH_2CHC\!-\!H$$
with CH_3 below

c.

$$CH_3CH_2CHCH_2CH_2C\!-\!H$$
with Br below

d.

$$CH_3CH_2CHCH_2C\!-\!H$$
with I below

e.

13.45 Acetone is a good solvent because it can dissolve a wide range of compounds. It has both a polar carbonyl group and nonpolar side chains. As a result, it dissolves organic compounds and is also miscible in water.

13.47 The liver

13.49 In organic molecules, oxidation may be recognized as a gain of oxygen or a loss of hydrogen. An aldehyde may be oxidized to form a carboxylic acid as in the following example in which ethanal is oxidized to produce ethanoic acid.

13.51 Addition reactions of aldehydes or ketones are those in which a second molecule is added to the double bond of the carbonyl group. An example is the addition of the alcohol ethanol to the aldehyde ethanal.

13.53 The following equation represents the oxidation of an aldehyde. The product is a carboxylic acid.

13.55 Ketones cannot be oxidized further.

13.57 The following general equation represents the addition of two alcohol molecules to an aldehyde:

13.59 The following general equation represents the addition of two alcohol molecules to a ketone:

13.61 a.

4-Methyl-2-heptanol → 4-Methyl-2-heptanone

b.

3,4-Dimethyl-1-pentanol $\xrightarrow{[O]}$ 3,4-Dimethylpentanal

c. 4-Ethyl-2-heptanol $\xrightarrow{[O]}$ 4-Ethyl-2-heptanone

d. 5,7-Dichloro-3-heptanol $\xrightarrow{[O]}$ 5,7-Dichloro-3-heptanone

13.63 $R{-}CH_2OH \xrightarrow{[O]} R{-}\overset{\overset{\displaystyle O}{\|}}{C}{-}H \xrightarrow{[O]} R{-}\overset{\overset{\displaystyle O}{\|}}{C}{-}OH$

Primary alcohol   Aldehyde   Carboxylic acid

13.65 **a.** Reduction reaction

$CH_3{-}\overset{\overset{\displaystyle O}{\|}}{C}{-}H + H_2 \xrightarrow{Pt} CH_3CH_2OH$

Ethanal   Ethanol

b. Reduction reaction

Cyclohexanone ${=}O + H_2 \xrightarrow{Pt}$ Cyclohexanol ${-}OH

c. Oxidation reaction

$\overset{\overset{\displaystyle OH}{|}}{CH_3CHCH_3} \xrightarrow{[O]} CH_3{-}\overset{\overset{\displaystyle O}{\|}}{C}{-}CH_3$

2-Propanol   Propanone

13.67 **a.** $+ H_2 \xrightarrow{Pt}$

b. $+ H_2 \xrightarrow{Pt}$

c. $+ H_2 \xrightarrow{Pt}$

d. $+ H_2 \xrightarrow{Pt}$

13.69 **a.** The following equation represents the hydrogenation of butanal. The product is 1-butanol.

$CH_3CH_2CH_2\overset{\overset{\displaystyle O}{\|}}{C}H + H_2 \xrightarrow{Pt} CH_3CH_2CH_2CH_2OH$

Butanal   1-Butanol

b. The following equation represents the hydrogenation of 3-methylpentanal. The product is 3-methyl-1-pentanol.

$CH_3CH_2\overset{\overset{\displaystyle }{}}{\underset{\underset{\displaystyle CH_3}{|}}{CH}}CH_2\overset{\overset{\displaystyle O}{\|}}{C}H + H_2 \xrightarrow{Pt} CH_3CH_2\underset{\underset{\displaystyle CH_3}{|}}{CH}CH_2CH_2OH$

3-Methylpentanal   3-Methyl-1-pentanol

c. The following equation represents the hydrogenation of 2-methylpropanal. The product is 2-methyl-1-propanol.

$CH_3\overset{\overset{\displaystyle O}{\|}}{\underset{\underset{\displaystyle CH_3}{|}}{CH}}\overset{\overset{\displaystyle }{}}{C}H + H_2 \xrightarrow{Pt} CH_3\underset{\underset{\displaystyle CH_3}{|}}{CH}CH_2OH$

13.71 Only (c) 3-methylbutanal and (f) acetaldehyde would give a positive Tollens' test.

13.73 **a.** Hemiacetal

$CH_3CH_2\overset{\overset{\displaystyle O}{\|}}{C}H + CH_3CH_2OH \xrightarrow{H^+} CH_3CH_2{-}\overset{\overset{\displaystyle OH}{|}}{\underset{\underset{\displaystyle OCH_2CH_3}{|}}{C}}{-}H$

b.

$CH_3\overset{\overset{\displaystyle O}{\|}}{C}H + CH_3CH_2OH \xrightarrow{H^+} CH_3{-}\overset{\overset{\displaystyle OH}{|}}{\underset{\underset{\displaystyle OCH_2CH_3}{|}}{C}}{-}H$

13.75 Acetal

a.

$CH_3CH_2\overset{\overset{\displaystyle O}{\|}}{C}H + 2\,CH_3OH \xrightarrow{H^+} CH_3CH_2{-}\overset{\overset{\displaystyle OCH_3}{|}}{\underset{\underset{\displaystyle OCH_3}{|}}{C}}{-}H$

b.

$CH_3\overset{\overset{\displaystyle O}{\|}}{C}H + 2\,CH_3OH \xrightarrow{H^+} CH_3{-}\overset{\overset{\displaystyle OCH_3}{|}}{\underset{\underset{\displaystyle OCH_3}{|}}{C}}{-}H + H_2O$

13.77 **a.**

b.

c.

d.

13.79 a. Methanal
b. Propanal
13.81 a. False
b. True
c. False
d. False

13.83 2 CH$_3$CH (=O) $\xrightarrow{\text{OH}^-}$ CH$_3$CHCH$_2$C—H (=O), with OH

Ethanal   3-Hydroxybutanal

13.85

−OH or enzyme

13.87 CH$_3$CCH$_3$ (=O)

Keto form of
Propanone

Enol form of
Propanone

13.89 a.

CH$_3$CH$_2$CH$_2$—C—CH$_3$, with OH and OCH$_2$CH$_3$

b.

with OH, C—CH$_3$, OCH$_2$CH$_3$ (benzene ring)

c.

cyclopentane with OH and OCH$_2$CH$_3$

13.91 (1) 2CH$_3$CH$_2$OH
(2) KMnO$_4$/OH$^-$
(3) CH$_3$CH=CH$_2$

Chapter 14

14.1 a. Ketone
b. Ketone
c. Alkane
14.3 The carboxyl group consists of two very polar groups, the carbonyl group and the hydroxyl group. Thus, carboxylic acids are very polar, in addition to which, they can hydrogen bond to one another. Aldehydes are polar, as a result of the carbonyl group, but cannot hydrogen bond to one another. As a result, carboxylic acids have higher boiling points than aldehydes of the same carbon chain length.
14.5 a. 3-Methylcyclohexanecarboxylic acid
b. 2-Ethylcyclopentanecarboxylic acid
14.7 a. CH$_3$COOH + CH$_3$CH$_2$CH$_2$OH
Ethanoic acid   1-Propanol
b. CH$_3$CH$_2$CH$_2$CH$_2$CH$_2$COO$^-$K$^+$ + CH$_3$CH$_2$CH$_2$OH
Potassium hexanoate   1-Propanol
c. CH$_3$CH$_2$CH$_2$CH$_2$COO$^-$Na$^+$ + CH$_3$OH
Sodium pentanoate   Methanol
d. CH$_3$CH$_2$CH$_2$CH$_2$CH$_2$COOH + CH$_3$CHCH$_2$CH$_2$CH$_3$, with OH
Hexanoic acid   2-Pentanol

14.9 a.

CH$_3$CHC—OH (=O), with CH$_3$ $\xrightarrow{\text{SOCl}_2}$ CH$_3$CHC—Cl (=O), with CH$_3$ + inorganic products

2-Methylpropanoic
acid

2-Methylpropanoyl
chloride

b.

CH$_3$CH$_2$CH$_2$CH$_2$CH$_2$C—OH (=O) $\xrightarrow{\text{SOCl}_2}$

Hexanoic acid

CH$_3$CH$_2$CH$_2$CH$_2$CH$_2$C—Cl (=O) + inorganic products

Hexanoyl chloride

14.11 a.

H—C—OH (=O) $\xrightarrow{\text{PCl}_3}$ H—C—Cl (=O) + inorganic products

Formic acid   Formyl chloride

b.

CH$_3$CH$_2$—C—OH (=O) $\xrightarrow{\text{PCl}_3}$ CH$_3$CH$_2$—C—Cl (=O) + inorganic products

Propionic acid   Propionyl chloride

14.13 a.

CH$_3$CHCH$_2$C—Cl (=O), with CH$_3$

$\xrightarrow{\text{CH}_3\text{CHCH}_2\text{C—O}^-\text{, with CH}_3}$
3-Methylbutanoate
ion

3-Methylbutanoyl
chloride

CH$_3$CHCH$_2$C—O—CCH$_2$CHCH$_3$ (=O, =O), with CH$_3$ and CH$_3$ + Cl$^-$

3-Methylbutanoic
anhydride

b.

H—C—Cl (=O) $\xrightarrow{\text{CH}_3\text{C—O}^- \text{ (=O)}}_{\text{Ethanoate ion}}$ H—C—O—C—CH$_3$ (=O, =O) + Cl$^-$

Methanoyl
chloride

Ethanoic methanoic
anhydride

14.15 Aldehydes are polar, as a result of the carbonyl group, but cannot hydrogen bond to one another. Alcohols are polar and can hydrogen bond as a result of the polar hydroxyl group. The carboxyl group of the carboxylic acids consists of both of these groups: the carbonyl group and the hydroxyl group. Thus, carboxylic acids are more polar than either aldehydes or alcohols, in addition to which, they can hydrogen bond to one another. As a result, carboxylic acids have higher boiling points than aldehydes or alcohols of comparable molar mass.
14.17 a. Pentanoic acid
b. 2-Pentanol
c. 2-Pentanol

14.19

Propanoic acid   2-Butanol

Butanal   2-Methylbutane

14.21 **a.** Heptanoic acid
     b. 1-Propanol
     c. Pentanoic acid
     d. Butanoic acid

14.23 The smaller carboxylic acids are water-soluble. They have sharp, sour tastes and unpleasant aromas.

14.25 Citric acid is found naturally in citrus fruits. It is added to foods to give them a tart flavor or to act as a food preservative and antioxidant. Adipic acid imparts a tart flavor to soft drinks and is a preservative.

14.27 Determine the name of the parent compound, that is the longest carbon chain containing the carboxyl group. Change the *-e* ending of the alkane name to *-oic* acid. Number the chain so that the carboxyl carbon is carbon-1. Name and number substituents in the usual way.

14.29 The I.U.P.A.C. name for adipic acid is hexanedioic acid.

14.31 **a.** $CH_3(CH_2)_2CH(CH_3)CH_2COOH$

     b. $CH_3(CH_2)_2C(CH_3)(CH_2CH_3)COOH$

     c.

14.33 **a.** I.U.P.A.C. name: Methanoic acid
        Common name: Formic acid
     b. I.U.P.A.C. name: 3-Methylbutanoic acid
        Common name: β-Methylbutyric acid
     c. I.U.P.A.C. name: Cyclopentanecarboxylic acid
        Common name: Cyclovalericcarboxylic acid

14.35

Butanoic acid   Methylpropanoic acid

14.37 **a.** $CH_3CH_2CCH_2CH_2COOH$ (with CH_3 substituents)

     b. $CH_3CHCHCH_2COOH$ (with CH_3 and Br)

     c.   benzene ring with COOH, O_2N, NO_2

     d.   cyclohexane ring with COOH and H_3C

14.39 **a.** I.U.P.A.C. name: 2-Hydroxypropanoic acid
        Common name: α-Hydroxypropionic acid
     b. I.U.P.A.C. name: 3-Hydroxybutanoic acid
        Common name: β-Hydroxybutyric acid
     c. I.U.P.A.C. name: 4,4-Dimethylpentanoic acid
        Common name: γ,γ-Dimethylvaleric acid
     d. I.U.P.A.C. name: 3, 3-Dichloropentanoic acid
        Common name: β,β-Dichlorovaleric acid

14.41 **a.** 3-Bromobenzoic acid (or *meta*-bromobenzoic acid or *m*-bromobenzoic acid)
     b. 2-Ethylbenzoic acid (or *ortho*-ethylbenzoic acid or *o*-bromobenzoic acid)
     c. 4-Hydroxybenzoic acid (or *para*-hydroxybenzoic acid or *p*-hydroxybenzoic acid)

14.43 In organic molecules, oxidation may be recognized as a gain of oxygen or a loss of hydrogen. An aldehyde may be oxidized to form a carboxylic acid as in the following example in which ethanal is oxidized to produce ethanoic acid.

$$H_3C-\overset{O}{\overset{\|}{C}}-H \xrightarrow{[O]} H_3C-\overset{O}{\overset{\|}{C}}-OH$$

     Ethanal   Ethanoic acid

14.45 The following general equation represents the dissociation of a carboxylic acid.

$$R-\overset{O}{\overset{\|}{C}}-OH \rightleftharpoons R-\overset{O}{\overset{\|}{C}}-O^- + H^+$$

14.47 When a strong base is added to a carboxylic acid, neutralization occurs.

14.49 Soaps are made from water, a strong base, and natural fats or oils.

14.51 **a.** (oxidation series)

     b. (oxidation)

     c. $\xrightarrow{[O]}$ No Reaction

14.53 **a.** CH_3COOH

     b.
$$CH_3CH_2CH_2-\overset{O}{\overset{\|}{C}}-O-CH_3 + H_2O$$

     c. CH_3OH

14.55 **a.** The oxidation of 1-pentanol yields pentanal.
     b. Continued oxidation of pentanal yields pentanoic acid.

14.57

 a. (acid) + $NaOH \longrightarrow$ (sodium salt, O^-Na^+) + H_2O

 b. (acid) + $KOH \longrightarrow$ (potassium salt, O^-K^+) + H_2O

 c. 2 (acid) + $Ca(OH)_2 \longrightarrow$ (calcium salt, Ca^{2+}) + $2H_2O$

14.59 The structure of the calcium salt of propionic acid is $[CH_3CH_2COO^-]_2Ca^{+2}$. The common name of this salt is calcium propionate and the I.U.P.A.C. name is calcium propanoate.

14.61 Esters are mildly polar as a result of the polar carbonyl group within the structure.

14.63 Esters are formed in the reaction of a carboxylic acid with an alcohol. The name is derived by using the alkyl or aryl portion of the alcohol I.U.P.A.C. name as the first name. The *-ic* acid ending of the I.U.P.A.C. name of the carboxylic acid is replaced with *-ate* and follows the name of the aryl or alkyl group.

14.65 a.

b.
$CH_3CH_2CH_2CH_2CH_2CH_2CH_2CH_2CH_2-C(=O)-O-CH_2CH_2CH_2CH_3$

c.
$CH_3CH_2-C(=O)-O-CH_3$

d.
$CH_3CH_2-C(=O)-O-CH_2CH_3$

14.67 a. Ethyl ethanoate
b. Methyl propanoate
c. Methyl-3-methylbutanoate
d. Cyclopentyl benzoate

14.69 The following equation shows the general reaction for the preparation of an ester:

$$R-C(=O)-OH + R-OH \underset{}{\overset{H^+, heat}{\rightleftharpoons}} R-C(=O)-OR + H_2O$$

Carboxylic acid + Alcohol ⇌ Ester + Water

14.71 The following equation shows the general reaction for the acid-catalyzed hydrolysis of an ester:

$$R-C(=O)-OR + H_2O \underset{}{\overset{H^+, heat}{\rightleftharpoons}} R-C(=O)-OH + R-OH$$

Ester + Water ⇌ Carboxylic acid + Alcohol

14.73 A hydrolysis reaction is the cleavage of any bond by the addition of a water molecule.

14.75 a.
$CH_3CH_2CH_2-C(=O)-O-CH_2CH_3$
b.
$CH_3CH_2-C(=O)-OH + CH_3CH_2OH$
c. $CH_3CH_2CH_2OH$
d.
$CH_3CH_2CHCH_2(Br)-C(=O)-O^- + CH_3CH_2OH$

14.77 a. Isobutyl methanoate is made from isobutyl alcohol (I.U.P.A.C. name 2-methyl-1-propanol) and methanoic acid.

$CH_3CHCH_2OH + HCOOH \rightarrow HCOCH_2CHCH_3$ (with CH_3 branches)
Isobutyl alcohol Methanoic acid Isobutyl methanoate

Isobutyl alcohol is an allowed starting material, but methanoic acid is not. However, it can easily be produced by the oxidation of its corresponding alcohol, methanol:

$$CH_3OH \overset{[O]}{\rightarrow} HCHO \overset{[O]}{\rightarrow} HCOOH$$
Methanol Methanal Methanoic acid

b. Pentyl butanoate is made from pentanol and butanoic acid.

$CH_3(CH_2)_3CH_2OH + CH_3CH_2CH_2COOH$
Pentanol Butanoic acid
$\rightarrow CH_3CH_2CH_2COCH_2(CH_2)_3CH_3$
Pentyl butanoate

Pentanol is an allowed starting material but butanoic acid is not. However, it can easily be produced by the oxidation of its corresponding alcohol, 1-butanol:

$$CH_3CH_2CH_2CH_2OH \overset{[O]}{\rightarrow} CH_3CH_2CH_2CHO$$
Butanol Butanal
$\overset{[O]}{\rightarrow} CH_3CH_2CH_2COOH$
Butanoic acid

14.79 Saponification is a reaction in which a soap is produced. More generally, it is the hydrolysis of an ester in the presence of a base. The following reaction shows the base-catalyzed hydrolysis of an ester:

$$CH_3(CH_2)_{14}-C(=O)-O-CH_3 + NaOH \rightarrow$$
$$CH_3(CH_2)_{14}-C(=O)-O^- Na^+ + CH_3OH$$

14.81

Salicylic acid Methyl salicylate

14.83 Compound A is
$CH_3CH_2CH_2CH_2-C(=O)-O-CH_3$

Compound B is
$CH_3CH_2CH_2CH_2-C(=O)-OH$

Compound C is CH_3OH

14.85 a.

$$CH_3CH_2-\overset{O}{\overset{||}{C}}-OCH_2CH_2CH_3 \underset{\longleftarrow}{\overset{H^+,\ heat}{\rightleftharpoons}} CH_3CH_2-\overset{O}{\overset{||}{C}}-OH$$

Propyl propanoate   Propanoic acid

$$+\ CH_3CH_2CH_2OH$$

1-Propanol

b.

$$H-\overset{O}{\overset{||}{C}}-OCH_2CH_2CH_2CH_3 \overset{H^+,\ heat}{\rightleftharpoons} H-\overset{O}{\overset{||}{C}}-OH$$

Butyl methanoate   Methanoic acid

$$+\ CH_3CH_2CH_2CH_2OH$$

1-Butanol

c.

$$H-\overset{O}{\overset{||}{C}}-OCH_2CH_3 \overset{H^+,\ heat}{\rightleftharpoons} H-\overset{O}{\overset{||}{C}}-OH$$

Ethyl methanoate   Methanoic acid

$$+\ CH_3CH_2OH$$

Ethanol

d.

$$CH_3CH_2CH_2CH_2-\overset{O}{\overset{||}{C}}-OCH_3 \overset{H^+,\ heat}{\rightleftharpoons}$$

Methyl pentanoate

$$CH_3CH_2CH_2CH_2-\overset{O}{\overset{||}{C}}-OH\ +\ CH_3OH$$

14.87 Acid chlorides are noxious, irritating chemicals. They are slightly polar and have boiling points similar to comparable aldehydes or ketones. They cannot be dissolved in water because they react violently with it.

14.89 Acid anhydrides have much lower boiling points than carboxylic acids of comparable molecular mass. They are also less soluble in water, and often react with it.

14.91 a. PCl_3, PCl_5, or $SOCl_2$

b.

$$CH_3-\overset{O}{\overset{||}{C}}-O^-$$

c.

a cyclohexane ring with $-\overset{O}{\overset{||}{C}}-O^-$

14.93 a.

benzene ring with $-\overset{O}{\overset{||}{C}}-OH\ +\ HCl$

b.

$$2\ CH_3-\overset{O}{\overset{||}{C}}-OH$$

14.95 a.

$$CH_3(CH_2)_8-\overset{O}{\overset{||}{C}}-O-\overset{O}{\overset{||}{C}}-(CH_2)_8CH_3$$

b.

$$CH_3-\overset{O}{\overset{||}{C}}-O-\overset{O}{\overset{||}{C}}-CH_3$$

14.97 a. $CH_3(CH_2)_6\overset{O}{\overset{||}{C}}Cl$ chain with $\overset{O}{\overset{||}{C}}Cl$

b. $CH_3(CH_2)_2\overset{O}{\overset{||}{C}}Cl$ chain with $\overset{O}{\overset{||}{C}}Cl$

c. $CH_3(CH_2)_7\overset{O}{\overset{||}{C}}Cl$ chain with $\overset{O}{\overset{||}{C}}Cl$

14.99 The following equation represents the synthesis of methanoic anhydride:

$$HCO^-\ +\ H\overset{O}{\overset{||}{C}}-Cl \rightarrow H\overset{O}{\overset{||}{C}}-O-\overset{O}{\overset{||}{C}}H$$

Methanoate anion   Methanoic chloride   Methanoic anhydride

14.101 a.

$$CH_3CH_2OH + CH_3CH_2-\overset{O}{\overset{||}{C}}-O-\overset{O}{\overset{||}{C}}-CH_2CH_3 \longrightarrow$$

$$CH_3CH_2-\overset{O}{\overset{||}{C}}-OCH_2CH_3$$

$$+$$

$$CH_3CH_2-\overset{O}{\overset{||}{C}}-OH$$

b.

$$CH_3CH_2OH + CH_3-\overset{O}{\overset{||}{C}}-O-\overset{O}{\overset{||}{C}}-CH_3 \longrightarrow$$

$$CH_3-\overset{O}{\overset{||}{C}}-OCH_2CH_3 + CH_3-\overset{O}{\overset{||}{C}}-OH$$

c.

$$CH_3CH_2OH + H-\overset{O}{\overset{||}{C}}-O-\overset{O}{\overset{||}{C}}-H \longrightarrow$$

$$H-\overset{O}{\overset{||}{C}}-OCH_2CH_3 + H-\overset{O}{\overset{||}{C}}-OH$$

14.103 a. Monoester:

$$HO-\overset{O}{\overset{||}{\underset{OH}{P}}}-OCH_2CH_3$$

b. Diester:

$$HO-\overset{O}{\overset{||}{\underset{OCH_2CH_3}{P}}}-OCH_2CH_3$$

c. Triester:

$$CH_3CH_2-O-\overset{O}{\overset{||}{\underset{OCH_2CH_3}{P}}}-OCH_2CH_3$$

14.105 ATP is the molecule used to store the energy released in metabolic reactions. The energy is stored in the phosphoanhydride bonds between two phosphoryl groups. The energy is released when the bond is hydrolyzed. A portion of the energy can be transferred to another molecule if the phosphoryl group is transferred from ATP to the other molecule.

14.107

$$CH_3-\overset{O}{\overset{||}{C}}\sim S-COENZYME\ A$$

The squiggle denotes a high energy bond.

14.109

$$\begin{array}{c} H \\ | \\ H-C-O-NO_2 \\ | \\ H-C-O-NO_2 \\ | \\ H-C-O-NO_2 \\ | \\ H \end{array}$$

bonding between the N—H bond of one amide and the C=O group of a second amide results in very high boiling points.

15.49 The I.U.P.A.C. names of amides are derived from the I.U.P.A.C. names of the carboxylic acids from which they are derived. The *-oic acid* ending of the carboxylic acid is replaced with the *-amide* ending.

15.51 Barbiturates are often called "downers" because they act as sedatives. They are sometimes used as anticonvulsants for epileptics and people suffering from other disorders that manifest as neurosis, anxiety, or tension.

15.53 **a.** I.U.P.A.C. name: Propanamide
  Common name: Propionamide
  b. I.U.P.A.C. name: Pentanamide
  Common name: Valeramide
  c. I.U.P.A.C. name: N,N-Dimethylethanamide
  Common name: N,N-Dimethylacetamide

15.55 **a.** $CH_3CH_2\overset{O}{\overset{\|}{C}}NH_2$

  c. $CH_3CH_2\overset{CH_2CH_3}{\underset{\;}{CH}}-\overset{O}{\overset{\|}{CH}}\overset{}{\underset{CH_2CH_3}{C}}NH_2$

  b. $CH_3(CH_2)_2\overset{O}{\overset{\|}{C}}\overset{}{\underset{CH_2CH_3}{N}}CH_2CH_3$

  d. $CH_3(CH_2)_4\overset{O}{\overset{\|}{C}}NHCH_3$

15.57 **a.**

  b.

  c.

  d.

  e.

15.59 N,N-Diethyl-*m*-toluamide:

Hydrolysis of this compound would release the carboxylic acid *m*-toluic acid and the amine *N*-ethylethanamine (diethylamine).

15.61 Amides are not proton acceptors (bases) because the highly electronegative carbonyl oxygen has a strong attraction for the nitrogen lone pair of electrons. As a result they cannot "hold" a proton.

15.63

Lidocaine hydrochloride

15.65

Penicillin BT

15.67 **a.**

$CH_3-\overset{O}{\overset{\|}{C}}-NHCH_3 + H_3O^+ \longrightarrow$

N-Methylethanamide

$CH_3COOH + CH_3N^+H_3$

Ethanoic acid   Methylammonium ion

  b.

$CH_3CH_2CH_2-\overset{O}{\overset{\|}{C}}-NH-CH_3 + H_3O^+ \longrightarrow$

N-Methylbutanamide

$CH_3CH_2CH_2COOH + CH_3N^+H_3$

Butanoic acid   Methylammonium ion

  c.

$CH_3\overset{CH_3}{\underset{\;}{CH}}CH_2-\overset{O}{\overset{\|}{C}}-NH-CH_2CH_3 + H_3O^+ \longrightarrow$

N-Ethyl-3-methylbutanamide

$CH_3\overset{}{\underset{CH_3}{CH}}CH_2COOH + CH_3CH_2N^+H_3$

3-Methylbutanoic acid   Ethylammonium ion

15.69 **a.**

$CH_3CH_2-\overset{O}{\overset{\|}{C}}-O-\overset{O}{\overset{\|}{C}}-CH_2CH_3$

  b.

$CH_3CH_2-\overset{O}{\overset{\|}{C}}-NH_2 + NH_4^+Cl^-$

  c.

$CH_3CH_2CH_2-\overset{O}{\overset{\|}{C}}-Cl + 2CH_3CH_2NH_2$

15.71

15.73 Glycine:

Alanine:

15.75

15.77 In an acyl group transfer reaction, the acyl group of an acid chloride is transferred from the Cl of the acid chloride to the N of an amine or ammonia. The product is an amide.

15.79 A chemical that carries messages or signals from a nerve to a target cell

15.81 **a.** Tremors, monotonous speech, loss of memory and problem-solving ability, and loss of motor function
b. Parkinson's disease
c. Schizophrenia, intense satiety sensations

15.83 In proper amounts, dopamine causes a pleasant, satisfied feeling. This feeling becomes intense as the amount of dopamine increases. Several drugs, including cocaine, heroin, amphetamines, alcohol, and nicotine increase the levels of dopamine. It is thought that the intense satiety response this brings about may contribute to addiction to these substances.

15.85 Epinephrine is a component of the flight or fight response. It stimulates glycogen breakdown to provide the body with glucose to supply the needed energy for this stress response.

15.87 The amino acid tryptophan

15.89 Perception of pain, thermoregulation, and sleep

15.91 Promotes the itchy skin rash associated with poison ivy and insect bites; the respiratory symptoms characteristic of hay fever; secretion of stomach acid

15.93 Inhibitory neurotransmitters

15.95 When acetylcholine is released from a nerve cell, it binds to receptors on the surface of muscle cells. This binding stimulates the muscle cell to contract. To stop the contraction, the acetylcholine is then broken down to choline and acetate ion. This is catalyzed by the enzyme acetylcholinesterase.

15.97 Organophosphates inactivate acetylcholinesterase by binding covalently to it. Since acetylcholine is not broken down, nerve transmission continues, resulting in muscle spasm. Pyridine aldoxime methiodide (PAM) is an antidote to organophosphate poisoning because it displaces the organophosphate, thereby allowing acetycholinesterase to function.

Chapter 16

16.1 It is currently recommended that 45–55% of the calories in the diet should be carbohydrates. Of that amount, no more than 10% should be simple sugars.

16.3 An aldose is a sugar with an aldehyde functional group. A ketose is a sugar with a ketone functional group.

16.5 **a.**

b.

c.

16.7 **a.** D-
b. L-
c. D-

16.9

D-Galactose

16.11 α-Amylase and β-amylase are digestive enzymes that break down the starch amylose. α-Amylase cleaves glycosidic bonds of the amylose chain at random, producing shorter polysaccharide chains. β-Amylase sequentially cleaves maltose (a disaccharide of glucose) from the reducing end of the polysaccharide chain.

16.13 A monosaccharide is the simplest sugar and consists of a single saccharide unit. A disaccharide is made up of two monosaccharides joined covalently by a glycosidic bond.

16.15 The molecular formula for a simple sugar is $(CH_2O)_n$. Typically n is an integer from 3 to 7.

16.17 Mashed potato flakes, rice, and corn starch contain amylose and amylopectin, both of which are polysaccharides. A candy bar contains sucrose, a disaccharide. Orange juice contains fructose, a monosaccharide. It may also contain sucrose if the label indicates that sugar has been added.

16.19 Four

16.21

D-Galactose   D-Fructose
(An aldohexose)   (A ketohexose)

16.23 An *aldose* is a sugar that contains an aldehyde (carbonyl) group.

16.25 A tetrose is a sugar with a four-carbon backbone.

16.27 A ketopentose is a sugar with a five-carbon backbone and containing a ketone (carbonyl) group.

16.29 **a.** β-D-Glucose is a hemiacetal.
b. β-D-Fructose is a hemiketal.
c. α-D-Galactose is a hemiacetal.

16.31

D-Glyceraldehyde   L-Glyceraldehyde

16.33 Stereoisomers are a pair of molecules that have the same structural formula and bonding pattern but that differ in the arrangement of the atoms in space.

16.35 A chiral carbon is one that is bonded to four different chemical groups.

16.37 A polarimeter converts monochromatic light into monochromatic plane-polarized light. This plane-polarized light is passed through a sample and into an analyzer. If the sample is optically active, it will rotate the plane of the light. The degree and angle of rotation are measured by the analyzer.

16.39 A Fischer Projection is a two-dimensional drawing of a molecule that shows a chiral carbon at the intersection of two lines. Horizontal lines at the intersection represent bonds projecting out of the page and vertical lines represent bonds that project into the page.

16.41 Diastereomers are a pair of stereoisomers that are not enantiomers.

16.43 Dextrose is a common name used for D-glucose.

16.45 D- and L-Glyceraldehyde are a pair of enantiomers, that is, they are nonsuperimposable mirror images of one another.

16.47

a.
```
        O
        ||
        C—H
HO——*——H
H ——*——OH
HO——*——H
HO——*——H
      CH2OH
```

b.
```
        O
        ||
        C—H
H ——*——OH
H ——*——OH
      CH2OH
```

c.
```
        O
        ||
        C—H
HO——*——H
H ——*——OH
HO——*——H
H ——*——OH
HO——*——H
      CH2OH
```

16.49

a.
```
  HC=O        HC=O        HC=O        HC=O
H—C—OH     HO—C—H     HO—C—H     H—C—OH
H—C—OH     HO—C—H     H—C—OH     HO—C—H
  HC=O        HC=O        CH=O        HC=O
   A           B           C           D
```
The stereoisomers are A, C, and D. Compounds A and B are identical and they are meso compounds because they have an internal plane of symmetry. Compounds C and D are enantiomers. Compound A is a diastereomer to both compounds C and D.

b.
```
  CH2OH       CH2OH       CH2OH       CH2OH
H—C—Br      Br—C—H      Br—C—H      H—C—Br
H—C—CH3     H3C—C—H     H—C—CH3     H3C—C—H
  CH2OH       CH2OH       CH2OH       CH2OH
   A            B           C           D
```
Therefore, there are four possible stereoisomers. The two pairs of enantiomers are A with B and C with D. Compounds A and B are both diastereomers to compounds C and D.

16.51

a.
```
  CH2CH3      CH2CH3      CH2CH3      CH2CH3
H—C—OH      HO—C—H      HO—C—H      H—C—OH
H—C—OH      HO—C—H      H—C—OH      HO—C—H
  CH2CH3      CH2CH3      CH2CH3      CH2CH3
   A            B           C           D
```

The stereoisomers are A, C, and D. Compounds A and B are identical and they are meso compounds because they have an internal plane of symmetry. Compounds C and D are enantiomers. Compound A is a diastereomer to both compounds C and D.

b.
```
    O            O            O            O
    ||           ||           ||           ||
    C—CH2OH      C—CH2OH      C—CH2OH      C—CH2OH
H—C—F        F—C—H        F—C—H        H—C—F
H—C—Cl       Cl—C—H       H—C—Cl       Cl—C—H
    C—CH2OH      C—CH2OH      C—CH2OH      C—CH2OH
    ||           ||           ||           ||
    O            O            O            O
    A            B            C            D
```
There are four possible stereoisomers. Compounds A and B are enantiomers, and compounds C and D are enantiomers. Compounds A and B are diastereomers to both compounds C and D.

16.53 Anomers are isomers that differ in the arrangement of bonds around the hemiacetal carbon.

16.55 A hemiacetal is a member of the family of organic compounds formed in the reaction of one molecule of alcohol with an aldehyde. They have the following general structure:
```
        OH
        |
   R ———OR
        |
        H
```

16.57 The reaction between an aldehyde and an alcohol yields a hemiacetal. Thus, when the aldehyde portion of a glucose molecule reacts with the C-5 hydroxyl group, the product is an intramolecular hemiacetal.

16.59 When the carbonyl group at C-1 of D-glucose reacts with the C-5 hydroxyl group, a new chiral carbon is created (C-1). In the α-isomer of the cyclic sugar, the C-1 hydroxyl group is below the ring; and in the β-isomer, the C-1 hydroxyl group is above the ring.

16.61 β-Maltose and α-lactose would give positive Benedict's tests. Glycogen would give only a weak reaction because there are fewer reducing ends for a given mass of the carbohydrate.

16.63 Enantiomers are stereoisomers that are nonsuperimposable mirror images of one another. For instance:
```
     O                   O
     ||                  ||
     C—H                 C—H
H—C—OH              HO—C—H
   CH2OH                CH2OH
 D-Glyceraldehyde    L-Glyceraldehyde
```

16.65 An aldehyde sugar forms an intramolecular hemiacetal when the carbonyl group of the monosaccharide reacts with a hydroxyl group on one of the other carbon atoms.

16.67 A ketal is the product formed in the reaction of two molecules of alcohol with a ketone. They have the following general structure:
```
        OR
        |
   R ———OR
        |
        R
```

16.69 A glycosidic bond is the bond formed between the hydroxyl group of the C-1 carbon of one sugar and a hydroxyl group of another sugar.

16.71

β-Maltose

16.73 Milk

16.75 Eliminating milk and milk products from the diet

16.77 Lactose intolerance is the inability to produce the enzyme lactase that hydrolyzes the milk sugar lactose into its component monosaccharides, glucose and galactose.

16.79 A polymer is a very large molecule formed by the combination of many small molecules, called monomers.

16.81 Starch

16.83 Homopolysaccharides are a class of polysaccharides that are composed of a single monosaccharide.

16.85 Starch, glycogen and cellulose are examples of homopolysaccharides. These homopolysaccharides are all made up of glucose.

16.87 The glucose units of amylose are joined by α (1 → 4) glycosidic bonds and those of cellulose are bonded together by β (1 → 4) glycosidic bonds.

16.89 Glycogen serves as a storage molecule for glucose.

16.91 The salivary glands and the pancreas

Chapter 17

17.1 a. $CH_3(CH_2)_7CH=CH(CH_2)_7COOH$
   b. $CH_3(CH_2)_{10}COOH$
   c. $CH_3(CH_2)_4CH=CH—CH_2—CH=CH(CH_2)_7COOH$
   d. $CH_3(CH_2)_{16}COOH$

17.3

$$CH_3(CH_2)_{12}\overset{\overset{\displaystyle O}{\|}}{C}—OH + CH_3CH_2OH \underset{heat}{\overset{H^+}{\rightarrow}} CH_3(CH_2)_{12}\overset{\overset{\displaystyle O}{\|}}{C}\text{-O-}CH_2CH_3$$

Tetradecanoic acid   Ethanol   Ethyl tetradecanoate

17.5

$$CH_3CH_2CH_2\overset{\overset{\displaystyle O}{\|}}{C}—O—CH_2(CH_2)_3CH_3 \underset{heat}{\overset{H^+}{\rightarrow}}$$

Pentyl butanoate

$$CH_3CH_2CH_2\overset{\overset{\displaystyle O}{\|}}{C}—OH + CH_3(CH_2)_3CH_2OH$$

Butanoic acid   Pentanol

17.7

$$CH_3\overset{\overset{\displaystyle O}{\|}}{C}—O—CH_2(CH_2)_2CH_3 + KOH \rightarrow$$

Butyl acetate

$$CH_3\overset{\overset{\displaystyle O}{\|}}{C}—O^-K^+ + CH_3(CH_2)_2CH_2OH$$

Potassium acetate   Butanol

17.9

$$CH_3CH_2CH=CHCH_2CH=CHCH_2CH=CH(CH_2)_7COOH + 3H_2$$

All cis-9,12,15-Octadecatrienoic acid

$$\downarrow Ni$$

$$CH_3(CH_2)_{16}COOH$$

Octadecanoic acid

17.11 a.

b.

17.13

Steroid nucleus

17.15 Receptor-mediated endocytosis

17.17 Fatty acids, glycerides, nonglyceride lipids, and complex lipids

17.19 Lipid-soluble vitamins are transported into cells of the small intestine in association with dietary fat molecules. Thus, a diet low in fat reduces the amount of vitamins A, D, E, and K that enters the body.

17.43 The essential fatty acid linoleic acid is required for the synthesis of arachidonic acid, a precursor for the synthesis of the prostaglandins, a group of hormonelike molecules.

17.45 Aspirin effectively decreases the inflammatory response by inhibiting the synthesis of all prostaglandins. Aspirin works by inhibiting cyclooxygenase, the first enzyme in prostaglandin biosynthesis. This inhibition results from the transfer of an acetyl group from aspirin to the enzyme. Because cyclooxygenase is found in all cells, synthesis of all prostaglandins is inhibited.

17.47 Smooth muscle contraction, enhancement of fever and swelling associated with the inflammatory response, bronchial dilation, inhibition of secretion of acid into the stomach.

17.49 The name of these fatty acids arises from the position of the double bond nearest the terminal *methyl group* of the molecule. The terminal methyl group is designated omega (ω). In ω-3 fatty acids the double bond nearest the ω methyl group is three carbons along the chain. In ω-6 fatty acids, the nearest double bond is six carbons from the end.

17.51 Omega-3 fatty acids reduce the risk of cardiovascular disease by decreasing blood clot formation, blood triglyceride levels, and growth of atherosclerotic plaque.

17.53 The decrease in blood clot formation, along with the reduced blood triglyceride levels and decreased atherosclerotic plaque result in improved arterial health. This, in turn, results in lower blood pressure and a decreased risk of sudden death and heart arrhythmias.

17.55 Omega-3 fatty acids are precursors of prostaglandins that exhibit anti-inflammatory effects. On the other hand, omega-6 fatty acids are precursors to prostaglandins that have inflammatory effects. To reduce the inflammatory response contribution to cardiovascular disease, it is logical to increase the amount of omega-3 fatty acids in the diet and to decrease the amount of omega-6 fatty acids.

17.57 A glyceride is a lipid ester that contains the glycerol molecule and from 1 to 3 fatty acids.

17.59 An emulsifying agent is a molecule that aids in the suspension of triglycerides in water. They are amphipathic molecules, such as lecithin, that serve as bridges holding together the highly polar water molecules and the nonpolar triglycerides.

17.61 A triglyceride with three saturated fatty acid tails would be a solid at room temperature. The long, straight fatty acid tails would stack with one another because of strong intermolecular and intramolecular attractions.

17.63

17.65

17.67 Triglycerides consist of three fatty acids esterified to the three hydroxyl groups of glycerol. In phospholipids there are only two fatty acids esterified to glycerol. A phosphoryl group is esterified (phosphoester linkage) to the third hydroxyl group.

17.69 A sphingolipid is a lipid that is not derived from glycerol, but rather from sphingosine, a long-chain, nitrogen-containing (amino) alcohol. Like phospholipids, sphingolipids are amphipathic.

17.71 A glycosphingolipid or glycolipid is a lipid that is built on a ceramide backbone structure. Ceramide is a fatty acid derivative of sphingosine.

17.73 Sphingomyelins are important structural lipid components of nerve cell membranes. They are found in the myelin sheath that surrounds and insulates cells of the central nervous system.

17.75 Cholesterol is readily soluble in the hydrophobic region of biological membranes. It is involved in regulating the fluidity of the membrane.

17.77 Progesterone is the most important hormone associated with pregnancy. Testosterone is needed for development of male secondary sexual characteristics. Estrone is required for proper development of female secondary sexual characteristics.

17.79 Cortisone is used to treat rheumatoid arthritis, asthma, gastrointestinal disorders, and many skin conditions.

17.81 Myricyl palmitate (beeswax) is made up of the fatty acid palmitic acid and the alcohol myricyl alcohol—$CH_3(CH_2)_{28}CH_2OH$.

17.83 Isoprenoids are a large, diverse collection of lipids that are synthesized from the isoprene unit:

17.85 Steroids and bile salts, lipid-soluble vitamins, certain plant hormones, and chlorophyll

17.87 Chylomicrons, high-density lipoproteins, low-density lipoproteins, and very low density lipoproteins

17.89 The terms "good" and "bad" cholesterol refer to two classes of lipoprotein complexes. The high-density lipoproteins, or HDL, are considered to be "good" cholesterol because a correlation has been made between elevated levels of HDL and a reduced incidence of atherosclerosis. Low-density lipoproteins, or LDL, are considered to be "bad" cholesterol because evidence suggests that a high level of LDL is associated with increased risk of atherosclerosis.

17.91 Atherosclerosis results when cholesterol and other substances coat the arteries causing a narrowing of the passageways. As the passageways become narrower, greater pressure is required to provide adequate blood flow. This results in higher blood pressure (hypertension).

17.93 If the LDL receptor is defective, it cannot function to remove cholesterol-bearing LDL particles from the blood.

The excess cholesterol, along with other substances, will accumulate along the walls of the arteries, causing atherosclerosis.

17.95 The basic structure of a biological membrane is a bilayer of phospholipid molecules arranged so that the hydrophobic hydrocarbon tails are packed in the center and the hydrophilic head groups are exposed on the inner and outer surfaces.

17.97 A peripheral membrane protein is bound to only one surface of the membrane, either inside or outside the cell.

17.99 Cholesterol is freely soluble in the hydrophobic layer of a biological membrane. It moderates the fluidity of the membrane by disrupting the stacking of the fatty acid tails of membrane phospholipids.

17.101 L. Frye and M. Edidin carried out studies in which specific membrane proteins on human and mouse cells were labeled with red and green fluorescent dyes, respectively. The human and mouse cells were fused into single-celled hybrids and were observed using a microscope with an ultraviolet light source. The ultraviolet light caused the dyes to fluoresce. Initially the dyes were localized in regions of the membrane representing the original human or mouse cell. Within an hour, the proteins were evenly distributed throughout the membrane of the fused cell.

17.103 If the fatty acyl tails of membrane phospholipids are converted from saturated to unsaturated, the fluidity of the membrane will increase.

Chapter 18

18.1 a. Glycine (gly):

b. Proline (pro):

c. Threonine (thr):

d. Aspartate (asp):

e. Lysine (lys):

18.3 a. Alanyl-phenylalanine:

b. Lysyl-alanine:

c. Phenylalanyl-tyrosyl-leucine:

18.5 The primary structure of a protein is the amino acid sequence of the protein chain. Regular, repeating folding of the peptide chain caused by hydrogen bonding between the amide nitrogens and carbonyl oxygens of the peptide bond is the secondary structure of a protein. The two most common types of secondary structure are the α-helix and the β-pleated sheet. Tertiary structure is the further folding of the regions of α-helix and β-pleated sheet into a compact, spherical structure. Formation and maintenance of the tertiary structure results from weak attractions between amino acid R groups. The binding of two or more peptides to produce a functional protein defines the quaternary structure.

18.7 Oxygen is efficiently transferred from hemoglobin to myoglobin in the muscle because myoglobin has a greater affinity for oxygen.

18.9 High temperature disrupts the hydrogen bonds and other weak interactions that maintain protein structure.

18.11 Vegetables vary in amino acid composition. No single vegetable can provide all of the amino acid requirements of the body. By eating a variety of different vegetables, all the amino acid requirements of the human body can be met.

18.13 An enzyme is a protein that serves as a biological catalyst, speeding up biological reactions.

18.15 A transport protein is a protein that transports materials across the cell membrane or throughout the body.

18.17 Enzymes speed up reactions that might take days or weeks to occur on their own. They also catalyze reactions that might require very high temperatures or harsh conditions if carried out in the laboratory. In the body, these reactions occur quickly under physiological conditions.

18.19 Transferrin is a transport protein that carries iron from the liver to the bone marrow, where it is used to produce the heme group for hemoglobin and myoglobin. Hemoglobin transports oxygen in the blood.

18.21 Egg albumin is a nutrient protein that serves as a source of protein for the developing chick. Casein is the nutrient storage protein in milk, providing protein, a source of amino acids, for mammals.

18.23 The general structure of an L-α-amino acid has a carbon in the center that is referred to as the alpha carbon. Off the alpha carbon, there is an amino group on the left, a carboxyl group to the top, and a hydrogen to the right. In addition, there is a side chain, R, attached to the bottom of the alpha carbon.

$$H_3^+N-\overset{\displaystyle COO^-}{\underset{\displaystyle R}{\overset{|}{\underset{|}{C}}}}-H$$

18.25 A zwitterion is a neutral molecule with equal numbers of positive and negative charges. Under physiological conditions, amino acids are zwitterions.

18.27 A chiral carbon is one that has four different atoms or groups of atoms attached to it.

18.29 Interactions between the R groups of the amino acids in a polypeptide chain are important for the formation and maintenance of the tertiary and quaternary structures of proteins.

18.31

L-Serine   L-Threonine   L-Cysteine

L-Tyrosine   L-Asparagine   L-Glutamine

18.33 A peptide bond is an amide bond between two amino acids in a peptide chain.

18.35 Linus Pauling and his colleagues carried out X-ray diffraction studies of protein. Interpretation of the the pattern formed when X-rays were diffracted by a crystal of pure protein led Pauling to conclude that peptide bonds are both planar (flat) and rigid and that the N—C bonds are shorter than expected. In other words, they deduced that the peptide bond has a partially double bond character because it exhibits resonance. There is no free rotation about the amide bond because the carbonyl group of the amide bond has a strong attraction for the amide nitrogen lone pair of electrons. This can best be described using a resonance model:

The partially double bonded character of the resonance structure restricts free rotation.

18.37 **a.**

b.

c.

18.39 The primary structure of a protein is the sequence of amino acids bonded to one another by peptide bonds.

18.41 The primary structure of a protein determines its three-dimensional shape and biological function because the location of R groups along the protein chain is determined by the primary structure. The interactions among the R groups, based on their location in the chain, will govern how the protein folds. This, in turn, dictates its three-dimensional structure and biological function.

18.43

18.45 The secondary structure of a protein is the folding of the primary structure into an α-helix or β-pleated sheet.

18.47 **a.** α-Helix
b. β-Pleated sheet

18.49 A fibrous protein is one that is composed of peptides arranged in long sheets or fibers.

18.51 A parallel β-pleated sheet is one in which the hydrogen bonded peptide chains have their amino-termini aligned head-to-head.

18.53 The tertiary structure of a protein is the globular, three-dimensional structure of a protein that results from folding the regions of secondary structure.

18.55

$$COO^-$$
$$H_3^+N—C—H$$
$$CH_2$$
$$S$$
$$S$$
$$CH_2$$
$$H_3^+N—C—H$$
$$COO^-$$

18.57 The tertiary structure is a level of folding of a protein chain that has already undergone secondary folding. The regions of α-helix and β-pleated sheet are folded into a globular structure.

18.59 Quaternary protein structure is the aggregation of two or more folded peptide chains to produce a functional protein.

18.61 A glycoprotein is a protein with covalently attached sugars.

18.63 Hydrogen bonding maintains the secondary structure of a protein and contributes to the stability of the tertiary and quaternary levels of structure.

18.65 The peptide bond exhibits resonance, which results in a partially double bonded character. This causes the rigidity of the peptide bond.

18.67 The code for the primary structure of a protein is carried in the genetic information (DNA).

18.69 The function of hemoglobin is to carry oxygen from the lungs to oxygen-demanding tissues throughout the body. Hemoglobin is found in red blood cells.

18.71 Hemoglobin is a protein composed of four subunits—two α-globin and two β-globin subunits. Each subunit holds a heme group, which in turn carries an Fe^{2+} ion.

18.73 The function of the heme group in hemoglobin and myoglobin is to bind to molecular oxygen.

18.75 Because carbon monoxide binds tightly to the heme groups of hemoglobin, it is not easily removed or replaced by oxygen. As a result, the effects of oxygen deprivation (suffocation) occur.

18.77 When sickle cell hemoglobin (HbS) is deoxygenated, the amino acid valine fits into a hydrophobic pocket on the surface of another HbS molecule. Many such sickle cell hemoglobin molecules polymerize into long rods that cause

the red blood cell to sickle. In normal hemoglobin, glutamic acid is found in the place of the valine. This negatively charged amino acid will not "fit" into the hydrophobic pocket.

18.79 When individuals have one copy of the sickle cell gene and one copy of the normal gene, they are said to carry the *sickle cell trait*. These individuals will not suffer serious side effects, but may pass the trait to their offspring. Individuals with two copies of the sickle cell globin gene exhibit all the symptoms of the disease and are said to have *sickle cell anemia*.

18.81 *Denaturation* is the process by which the organized structure of a protein is disrupted, resulting in a completely disorganized, nonfunctional form of the protein.

18.83 Heat is an effective means of sterilization because it destroys the proteins of microbial life-forms, including fungi, bacteria, and viruses.

18.85 Even relatively small fluctuations in blood pH can be life threatening. It is likely that these small changes would alter the normal charges on the proteins and modify their interactions. These changes can render a protein incapable of carrying out its functions.

18.87 Proteins become polycations at low pH because the additional protons will protonate the carboxylate groups. As these negative charges are neutralized, the charge on the proteins will be contributed only by the protonated amino groups ($—N^+H_3$).

18.89 The low pH of the yogurt denatures the proteins of microbial contaminants, inhibiting their growth.

18.91 An essential amino acid is one that must be provided in the diet because it cannot be synthesized in the body.

18.93 A complete protein is one that contains all of the essential and nonessential amino acids.

18.95 Chymotrypsin catalyzes the hydrolysis of peptide bonds on the carbonyl side of aromatic amino acids.

18.97 In a vegetarian diet, vegetables are the only source of dietary protein. Because individual vegetable sources do not provide all the needed amino acids, vegetables must be mixed to provide all the essential and nonessential amino acids in the amounts required for biosynthesis.

18.99 Synthesis of digestive enzymes must be carefully controlled because the active enzyme would digest, and thus destroy, the cell that produces it.

Chapter 19

19.1 a. Pyruvate kinase catalyzes the transfer of a phosphoryl group from phosphoenolpyruvate to adenosine diphosphate.

b. Alanine transaminase catalyzes the transfer of an amino group from alanine to α-ketoglutarate, producing pyruvate and glutamate.

c. Triose phosphate isomerase catalyzes the isomerization of the ketone dihydroxyacetone phosphate to the aldehyde glyceraldehyde-3-phosphate.

d. Pyruvate dehydrogenase catalyzes the oxidation and decarboxylation of pyruvate, producing acetyl coenzyme A and CO_2.

19.3 a. Sucrose
   b. Pyruvate
   c. Succinate

19.5 The induced fit model assumes that the enzyme is flexible. Both the enzyme and the substrate are able to change shape to form the enzyme-substrate complex. The lock-and-key model assumes that the enzyme is inflexible (the lock) and the substrate (the key) fits into a specific rigid site (the active site) on the enzyme to form the enzyme-substrate complex.

19.7 An enzyme might distort a bond, thereby catalyzing bond breakage. An enzyme could bring two reactants into close proximity and in the proper orientation for the reaction to occur. Finally, an enzyme could alter the pH of the microenvironment of the active site, thereby serving as a transient donor or acceptor of H^+.

19.9 Water-soluble vitamins are required by the body for the synthesis of coenzymes that are required for the function of a variety of enzymes.

19.11 A decrease in pH will change the degree of ionization of the R groups within a peptide chain. This disturbs the weak interactions that maintain the structure of an enzyme, which may denature the enzyme. Less drastic alterations in the charge of R groups in the active site of the enzyme can inhibit enzyme-substrate binding or destroy the catalytic ability of the active site.

19.13 Irreversible inhibitors bind very tightly, sometimes even covalently, to an R group in enzyme active sites. They generally inhibit many different enzymes. The loss of enzyme activity impairs normal cellular metabolism, resulting in death of the cell or the individual.

19.15 A structural analog is a molecule that has a structure and charge distribution very similar to that of the natural substrate of an enzyme. Generally they are able to bind to the enzyme active site. This inhibits enzyme activity because the normal substrate must compete with the structural analog to form an enzyme-substrate complex.

19.17 a.

ala-phe-ala

b.

tyr-ala-tyr

19.19

19.21 The common name of an enzyme is often derived from the name of the substrate and/or the type of reaction that it catalyzes.

19.23 1. Urease
   2. Peroxidase
   3. Lipase
   4. Aspartase

5. Glucose-6-phosphatase
6. Sucrase

19.25 **a.** Citrate decarboxylase catalyzes the cleavage of a carboxyl group from citrate.
  b. Adenosine diphosphate phosphorylase catalyzes the addition of a phosphate group to ADP.
  c. Oxalate reductase catalyzes the reduction of oxalate.
  d. Nitrite oxidase catalyzes the oxidation of nitrite.
  e. *cis-trans* Isomerase catalyzes interconversion of *cis* and *trans* isomers.

19.27 A substrate is the reactant in an enzyme-catalyzed reaction that binds to the active site of the enzyme and is converted into product.

19.29 The activation energy of a reaction is the energy required for the reaction to occur.

19.31 The equilibrium constant for a chemical reaction is a reflection of the difference in energy of the reactants and products.
Consider the following reaction:

$$aA + bB \rightarrow cC + dD$$

The equilibrium constant for this reaction is:

$$K_{eq} = [D]^d[C]^c/[A]^a[B]^b = [\text{products}]/[\text{reactants}]$$

Because the difference in energy between reactants and products is the same regardless of what path the reaction takes, an enzyme does not alter the equilibrium constant of a reaction.

19.33 The rate of an uncatalyzed chemical reaction typically doubles every time the substrate concentration is doubled.

19.35 The rate-limiting step is that step in an enzyme-catalyzed reaction that is the slowest, and hence limits the speed with which the substrate can be converted into product.

19.37

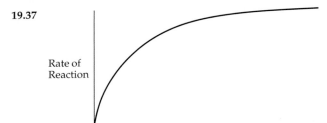

Concentration of Substrate

19.39 The enzyme-substrate complex is the molecular aggregate formed when the substrate binds to the active site of an enzyme.

19.41 The catalytic groups of an enzyme active site are those functional groups that are involved in carrying out catalysis.

19.43 Enzyme active sites are pockets in the surface of an enzyme that include R groups involved in binding and R groups involved in catalysis. The shape of the active site is complementary to the shape of the substrate. Thus, the conformation of the active site determines the specificity of the enzyme. Enzyme-substrate binding involves weak, noncovalent interactions.

19.45 The lock-and-key model of enzyme-substrate binding was proposed by Emil Fischer in 1894. He thought that the active site was a rigid region of the enzyme into which the substrate fit perfectly. Thus, the model purports that the substrate simply snaps into place within the active site, like two pieces of a jigsaw puzzle fitting together.

19.47 Enzyme specificity is the ability of an enzyme to bind to only one, or a very few, substrates and thus catalyze only a single reaction.

19.49 Group specificity means that an enzyme catalyzes reactions involving similar molecules having the same functional group.

19.51 Absolute specificity means that an enzyme catalyzes the reaction of only one substrate.

19.53 Hexokinase has group specificity. The advantage is that the cell does not need to encode many enzymes to carry out the phosphorylation of six-carbon sugars. Hexokinase can carry out many of these reactions.

19.55 Methionyl tRNA synthetase has absolute specificity. This is the enzyme that attaches the amino acid methionine to the transfer RNA (tRNA) that will carry the amino acid to the site of protein synthesis. If the wrong amino acid were attached to the tRNA, it could be incorporated into the protein, destroying its correct three-dimensional structure and biological function.

19.57 The first step of an enzyme-catalyzed reaction is the formation of the enzyme-substrate complex. In the second step, the transition state is formed. This is the state in which the substrate assumes a form intermediate between the original substrate and the product. In step 3 the substrate is converted to product and the enzyme-product complex is formed. Step 4 involves the release of the product and regeneration of the enzyme in its original form.

19.59 In a reaction involving bond breaking, the enzyme might distort a bond, producing a transition state in which the bond is stressed. An enzyme could bring two reactants into close proximity and in the proper orientation for the reaction to occur, producing a transition state in which the proximity of the reactants facilitates bond formation. Finally, an enzyme could alter the pH of the microenvironment of the active site, thereby serving as a transient donor or acceptor of H^+.

19.61 A cofactor helps maintain the shape of the active site of an enzyme.

19.63 Thiamine (B_1) is found in the coenzyme thiamine pyrophosphate. Riboflavin (B_2) is found in both flavin mononucleotide and flavin adenine dinucleotide. Niacin (B_3) is found in both nicotinamide adenine dinucleotide and nicotinamide adenine dinucleotide phosphate. Pyridoxine (B_6) is found in both pyridoxal phosphate and pyridoxamine phosphate. Cyanocobalamin (B_{12}) is found in coenzyme deoxyadenosyl cobalamin. Folic acid is found in tetrahydrofolic acid. Pantothenic acid is found in coenzyme A. Biotin is found in biocytin.

19.65 At the temperature optimum, the enzyme is functioning optimally and the rate of the reaction is maximal. Above the temperature optimum, increasing temperature begins to denature the enzyme and stop the reaction.

19.67 Each of the following answers assumes that the enzyme was purified from an organism with optimal conditions for life near 37°C, pH 7.
  a. Decreasing the temperature from 37°C to 10°C will cause the rate of an enzyme-catalyzed reaction to decrease because the frequency of collisions between enzyme and substrate will decrease as the rate of molecular movement decreases.
  b. Increasing the pH from 7 to 11 will generally cause a decrease in the rate of an enzyme-catalyzed reaction. In

fact, most enzymes would be denatured by a pH of 11 and enzyme activity would cease.

c. Heating an enzyme from 37°C to 100°C will destroy enzyme activity because the enzyme would be denatured by the extreme heat.

19.69 High temperature denatures bacterial enzymes and structural proteins. Because the life of the cell is dependent on the function of these proteins, the cell dies.

19.71 A lysosome is a membrane-bound vesicle in the cytoplasm of cells that contains approximately fifty hydrolytic enzymes. Some of the enzymes in the lysosomes can degrade proteins to amino acids, others hydrolyze polysaccharides into monosaccharides, and some degrade lipids and nucleic acids. The lysosome contains these enzymes to prevent degradation of large biological molecules that are important to maintain cell integrity.

19.73 Enzymes used for clinical assays in hospitals are typically stored at refrigerator temperatures to ensure that they are not denatured by heat. In this way they retain their activity for long periods.

19.75 a. Cells regulate the level of enzyme activity to conserve energy. It is a waste of cellular energy to produce an enzyme if its substrate is not present or if its product is in excess.

b. Production of proteolytic digestive enzymes must be carefully controlled because the active enzyme could destroy the cell that produces it. Thus, they are produced in an inactive form in the cell and are only activated at the site where they carry out digestion.

19.77 In positive allosterism, binding of the effector molecule turns the enzyme on. In negative allosterism, binding of the effector molecule turns the enzyme off.

19.79 A proenzyme is the inactive form of an enzyme that is converted to the active form at the site of its activity.

19.81 Blood clotting is a critical protective mechanism in the body, preventing excessive loss of blood following an injury. However, it can be a dangerous mechanism if it is triggered inappropriately. The resulting clot could cause a heart attack or stroke. By having a cascade of proteolytic reactions leading to the final formation of the clot, there are many steps at which the process can be regulated. This ensures that it will only be activated under the appropriate conditions.

19.83 *Competitive enzyme inhibition* occurs when a structural analog of the normal substrate occupies the enzyme active site so that the reaction cannot occur. The structural analog and the normal substrate compete for the active site. Thus, the rate of the reaction will depend on the relative concentrations of the two molecules.

19.85 A structural analog has a shape and charge distribution that are very similar to those of the normal substrate for an enzyme.

19.87 Irreversible inhibitors bind tightly to and block the active site of an enzyme and eliminate catalysis at the site.

19.89 The compound would be a competitive inhibitor of the enzyme.

19.91 A proteolytic enzyme catalyzes the cleavage of the peptide bond that maintains the primary protein structure.

19.93 The structural similarities among chymotrypsin, trypsin, and elastase suggest that these enzymes evolved from a single ancestral gene that was duplicated. Each copy then evolved independently.

19.95

tyr-lys-ala-phe

19.97 Elastase will cleave the peptide bonds on the carbonyl side of alanine and glycine. Trypsin will cleave the peptide bonds on the carbonyl side of lysine and arginine. Chymotrypsin will cleave the peptide bonds on the carbonyl side of tryptophan and phenylalanine.

19.99 Analysis of blood serum for levels of certain enzymes can confirm a preliminary diagnosis that was made based on disease symptoms or a clinical picture. When cells die, they release their enzymes into the bloodstream. Enzyme assays can measure amounts of certain enzymes in the blood.

19.101 Creatine kinase-MB, and aspartate aminotransferase (AST/SGOT)

19.103 Urease is used in the clinical analysis of urea in blood. In a test called the blood urea nitrogen test (BUN), urea is converted to ammonia using the enzyme urease, the ammonia becomes an indicator of urea. This allows for the levels of urea to be measured. This measurement is useful in the diagnosis of kidney malfunction.

Chapter 20

20.1 a. Adenosine diphosphate:

b. Deoxyguanosine triphosphate:

20.3 The RNA polymerase recognizes the promoter site for a gene, separates the strands of DNA, and catalyzes the polymerization of an RNA strand complementary to the DNA strand that carries the genetic code for a protein. It recognizes a termination site at the end of the gene and releases the RNA molecule.

20.5 The genetic code is said to be degenerate because several different triplet codons may serve as code words for a single amino acid.

20.7 The nitrogenous bases of the codons are complementary to those of the anticodons. As a result they are able to hydrogen bond to one another according to the base pairing rules.

20.9 The ribosomal P-site holds the peptidyl tRNA during protein synthesis. The peptidyl tRNA is the tRNA carrying the growing peptide chain. The only exception to this is during initiation of translation when the P-site holds the initiator tRNA.

20.11 The normal mRNA sequence, AUG-CCC-GAC-UUU, would encode the peptide sequence methionine-proline-aspartate-phenylalanine. The mutant mRNA sequence, AUG-CGC-GAC-UUU, would encode the mutant peptide sequence methionine-arginine-aspartate-phenylalanine. This would not be a silent mutation because a hydrophobic amino acid (proline) has been replaced by a positively charged amino acid (arginine).

20.13 A heterocyclic amine is a compound that contains nitrogen in at least one position of the ring skeleton.

20.15 It is the N-9 of the purine that forms the *N*-glycosidic bond with C-1 of the five-carbon sugar. The general structure of the purine ring is shown below:

20.17 The ATP nucleotide is composed of the five-carbon sugar ribose, the purine adenine, and a triphosphate group.

20.19 The two strands of DNA in the double helix are said to be *antiparallel* because they run in opposite directions. One strand progresses in the $5' \rightarrow 3'$ direction, and the opposite strand progresses in the $3' \rightarrow 5'$ direction.

20.21 The DNA double helix is 2 nm in width. The nitrogenous bases are stacked at a distance of 0.34 nm from one another. One complete turn of the helix is 3.4 nm, or 10 base pairs.

20.23

20.25

20.27 The prokaryotic chromosome is a circular DNA molecule that is supercoiled, that is, the helix is coiled on itself.

20.29 The term *semiconservative DNA replication* refers to the fact that each parental DNA strand serves as the template for the synthesis of a daughter strand. As a result, each of the daughter DNA molecules is made up of one strand of the original parental DNA and one strand of newly synthesized DNA.

20.31 The two primary functions of DNA polymerase III are to read a template DNA strand and catalyze the polymerization of a new daughter strand, and to proofread the newly synthesized strand and correct any errors by removing the incorrectly inserted nucleotide and adding the proper one.

20.33 3'-TACGGGCTCGACTAACTAGTCT-5'

20.35 The *replication origin* of a DNA molecule is the unique sequence on the DNA molecule where DNA replication begins.

20.37 The enzyme helicase separates the strands of DNA at the origin of DNA replication so that the proteins involved in replication can interact with the nitrogenous base pairs.

20.39 The RNA primer "primes" DNA replication by providing a $3'-OH$ which can be used by DNA polymerase III for the addition of the next nucleotide in the growing DNA chain.

20.41 DNA $\rightarrow$ RNA $\rightarrow$ Protein

20.43 Anticodons are found on transfer RNA molecules.

20.45 3'-AUGCCCGUAUCCGGAAUUUCGAUCGAA-5'

20.47 *RNA splicing* is the process by which the noncoding sequences (introns) of the primary transcript of a eukaryotic mRNA are removed and the protein coding sequences (exons) are spliced together.

20.49 Messenger RNA, transfer RNA, and ribosomal RNA

20.51 Spliceosomes are small ribonucleoprotein complexes that carry out RNA splicing.

20.53 The *poly(A) tail* is a stretch of 100–200 adenosine nucleotides polymerized onto the 3' end of a mRNA by the enzyme poly(A) polymerase.

20.55 The *cap structure* is made up of the nucleotide 7-methylguanosine attached to the 5' end of a mRNA by a 5'-5' triphosphate bridge. Generally the first two nucleotides of the mRNA are also methylated.

20.57 Sixty-four

20.59 The reading frame of a gene is the sequential set of triplet codons that carries the genetic code for the primary structure of a protein.

20.61 Methionine and tryptophan

20.63 The codon 5'-UUU-3' encodes the amino acid phenylalanine. The mutant codon 5'-UUA-3' encodes the amino acid leucine. Both leucine and phenylalanine are hydrophobic amino acids, however, leucine has a smaller R group. It is possible that the smaller R group would disrupt the structure of the protein.

20.65 The ribosomes serve as a platform on which protein synthesis can occur. They also carry the enzymatic activity that forms peptide bonds.

20.67 AUG GCU GGG CUU UGU AUG UGG UAU UCU AUU GGG UAA

20.69 The sequence of DNA nucleotides in a gene is transcribed to produce a complementary sequence of RNA nucleotides in a messenger RNA (mRNA). In the process of translation the sequence of the mRNA is read sequentially in words of three nucleotides (codons) to produce a protein. Each codon calls for the addition of a particular amino acid to the growing peptide chain. If one of those codons has been altered by mutation, it may now call for the addition of the wrong amino acid to the growing peptide chain. This could result in improper folding of the protein and in loss of biological function.

20.71 An ester bond

20.73 A point mutation is the substitution of one nucleotide pair for another in a gene.

20.75 Some mutations are silent because the change in the nucleotide sequence does not alter the amino acid sequence of the protein. This can happen because there are many amino acids encoded by multiple codons.

20.77 UV light causes the formation of pyrimidine dimers, the covalent bonding of two adjacent pyrimidine bases. Mutations occur when the UV damage repair system makes an error during the repair process. This causes a change in the nucleotide sequence of the DNA.

20.79 **a.** A *carcinogen* is a compound that causes cancer. Cancers are caused by mutations in the genes responsible for controlling cell division.
  b. Carcinogens cause DNA damage that results in changes in the nucleotide sequence of the gene. Thus, carcinogens are also mutagens.

20.81 A *restriction enzyme* is a bacterial enzyme that "cuts" the sugar–phosphate backbone of DNA molecules at a specific nucleotide sequence.

20.83 A selectable marker is a genetic trait that can be used to detect the presence of a plasmid in a bacterium. Many plasmids have antibiotic resistance genes as selectable markers. Bacteria containing the plasmid will be able to grow in the presence of the antibiotic; those without the plasmid will be killed.

20.85 Human insulin, interferon, human growth hormone, and human blood clotting factor VIII

20.87 4096 copies

20.89 The goals of the Human Genome Project were to identify and map all of the genes of the human genome and to determine the DNA sequences of the complete three billion nucleotide pairs.

20.91 A genome library is a set of clones that represents all of the DNA sequences in the genome of an organism.

20.93 A dideoxynucleotide is one that has hydrogen atoms rather than hydroxyl groups bonded to both the 2' and 3' carbons of the five-carbon sugar.

20.95 Sequences that these DNA sequences have in common are highlighted in bold.
  a. 5' **AGCTCCT**GATTTCATACAGTTTCTACT**ACCTACTA** 3'
  b. 5' AGACATTCTATCTACCTAGACTATG**TTCAGAA** 3'

  c. 5' **TTCAGAA**CTCATTCAGACCTACTACTATACCTTGG GAGCTCCT 3'
  d. 5' **ACCTACTA**GACTATACTACTACTAAGGGGACTATT CCAGACTT 3'
  The 5' end of sequence (a) is identical to the 3' end of sequence (c). The 3' end of sequence (a) is identical to the 5' end of sequence (d). The 3' end of sequence (b) is identical to the 5' end of sequence (c). From 5' to 3', the sequences would form the following map:

```
   ___b___
          ____c____
                   ___a___
                          ___d___
```

Chapter 21

21.1 ATP is called the universal energy currency because it is the major molecule used by all organisms to store energy.

21.3 The first stage of catabolism is the digestion (hydrolysis) of dietary macromolecules in the stomach and intestine.
  In the second stage of catabolism, monosaccharides, amino acids, fatty acids, and glycerol are converted by metabolic reactions into molecules that can be completely oxidized.
  In the third stage of catabolism, the two-carbon acetyl group of acetyl CoA is completely oxidized by the reactions of the citric acid cycle. The energy of the electrons harvested in these oxidation reactions is used to make ATP.

21.5 Substrate level phosphorylation is one way the cell can make ATP. In this reaction, a high-energy phosphoryl group of a substrate in the reaction is transferred to ADP to produce ATP.

21.7 Glycolysis is a pathway involving ten reactions. In reactions 1–3, energy is invested in the beginning substrate, glucose. This is done by transferring high-energy phosphoryl groups from ATP to the intermediates in the pathway. The product is fructose-1,6-bisphosphate. In the energy-harvesting reactions of glycolysis, fructose-1,6-bisphosphate is split into two three-carbon molecules that begin a series of rearrangement, oxidation-reduction, and substrate-level phosphorylation reactions that produce four ATP, two NADH, and two pyruvate molecules. Because of the investment of two ATP in the early steps of glycolysis, the net yield of ATP is two.

21.9 Both the alcohol and lactate fermentations are anaerobic reactions that use the pyruvate and re-oxidize the NADH produced in glycolysis.

21.11 Gluconeogenesis (synthesis of glucose from noncarbohydrate sources) appears to be the reverse of glycolysis (the first stage of carbohydrate degradation) because the intermediates in the two pathways are the same. However, reactions 1, 3, and 10 of glycolysis are not reversible reactions. Thus, the reverse reactions must be carried out by different enzymes.

21.13 The enzyme glycogen phosphorylase catalyzes the phosphorolysis of a glucose unit at one end of a glycogen molecule. The reaction involves the displacement of the glucose by a phosphate group. The products are glucose-1-phosphate and a glycogen molecule that is one glucose unit shorter.

21.15 Glucokinase traps glucose within the liver cell by phosphorylating it. Because the product, glucose-6-phosphate, is charged, it cannot be exported from the cell.

21.17 Glucagon indirectly stimulates glycogen phosphorylase, the first enzyme of glycogenolysis. This speeds up glycogen degradation. Glucagon also inhibits glycogen synthase, the first enzyme in glycogenesis. This inhibits glycogen synthesis.

21.19 ATP

21.21

Adenosine triphosphate

Adenosine diphosphate   Inorganic phosphate group

21.23 A coupled reaction is one that can be thought of as a two-step process. In a coupled reaction, two reactions occur simultaneously. Frequently one of the reactions releases the energy that drives the second, energy-requiring, reaction.

21.25 Carbohydrates

21.27 The following equation represents the hydrolysis of maltose:

β-Maltose

β-D-Glucose

21.29

21.31 The hydrolysis of a triglyceride containing oleic acid, stearic acid, and linoleic acid is represented in the following equations:

Glycerol

$HO-\overset{O}{\overset{\|}{C}}-(CH_2)_7CH=CH(CH_2)_7CH_3$
Oleic acid
+
$HO-\overset{O}{\overset{\|}{C}}-(CH_2)_{16}CH_3$
Stearic acid
+
$HO-\overset{O}{\overset{\|}{C}}-(CH_2)_7CH=CHCH_2CH=CH(CH_2)_4CH_3$
Linoleic acid

21.33 The hydrolysis of the dipeptide alanyl leucine is represented in the following equation:

Alanyl leucine

$$H_3{}^+N-CH-\underset{\underset{CH_3}{|}}{\overset{\overset{O}{\|}}{C}}-O^-$$

Alanine

$+$

$$H_3{}^+N-CH-\underset{\underset{CH_2}{|}}{\overset{\overset{O}{\|}}{C}}-O^-$$
$$\underset{\underset{CH_3}{|}}{CH}-CH_3$$

Leucine

21.35 Glycolysis is the enzymatic pathway that converts a glucose molecule into two molecules of pyruvate. The pathway generates a net energy yield of two ATP and two NADH. Glycolysis is the first stage of carbohydrate catabolism.

21.37 Glycolysis requires NAD^+ for reaction 6 in which glyceraldehyde-3-phosphate dehydrogenase catalyzes the oxidation of glyceraldehyde-3-phosphate. NAD^+ is reduced.

21.39 Two ATP per glucose

21.41 Although muscle cells have enough ATP stored for only a few seconds of activity, glycolysis speeds up dramatically when there is a demand for more energy. If the cells have a sufficient supply of oxygen, aerobic respiration (the citric acid cycle and oxidative phosphorylation) will contribute large amounts of ATP. If oxygen is limited, the lactate fermentation will speed up. This will use up the pyruvate and re-oxidize the NADH produced by glycolysis and allow continued synthesis of ATP for muscle contraction.

21.43 $C_6H_{12}O_6 + 2ADP + 2P_i + 2NAD^+ \rightarrow$
Glucose $2C_3H_3O_3 + 2ATP + 2NADH + 2H_2O$
                              Pyruvate

21.45 a. 7
    b. 2
    c. 6
    d. 4
    e. 1
    f. 9
    g. 5
    h. 10
    i. 3
    j. 8

21.47 Isomerase

21.49 Enediol

21.51 A kinase transfers a phosphoryl group from one molecule to another.

21.53 NAD^+ is reduced, accepting a hydride anion.

21.55 Enolase catalyzes a reaction that produces an enol; in this particular reaction, it is phosphoenolpyruvate.

21.57 To optimize efficiency and minimize waste, it is important that energy-harvesting pathways, such as glycolysis, respond to the energy demands of the cell. If energy in the form of ATP is abundant, there is no need for the pathway to continue at a rapid rate. When this is the case, allosteric enzymes that catalyze the reactions of the pathway are inhibited by binding to their negative effectors. Similarly, when there is a great demand for ATP, the pathway speeds up as a result of the action of allosteric enzymes binding to positive effectors.

21.59 ATP and citrate are allosteric inhibitors of phosphofructokinase, whereas AMP and ADP are allosteric activators.

21.61 Citrate, which is the first intermediate in the citric acid cycle, is an allosteric inhibitor of phosphofructokinase. The citric acid cycle is a pathway that results in the complete oxidation of the pyruvate produced by glycolysis. A high concentration of citrate signals that sufficient substrate is entering the citric acid cycle. The inhibition of phosphofructokinase by citrate is an example of *feedback inhibition*: the product, citrate, allosterically inhibits the activity of an enzyme early in the pathway.

21.63

$$CH_3-\overset{\overset{O}{\|}}{C}-H \xrightarrow[\quad NADH \quad\quad NAD^+ \quad]{} CH_3CH_2OH$$

Acetaldehyde   Ethanol

21.65 The lactate fermentation

21.67 Yogurt and some cheeses

21.69 Lactate dehydrogenase

21.71 This child must have the enzymes to carry out the alcohol fermentation. When the child exercised hard, there was not enough oxygen in the cells to maintain aerobic respiration. As a result, glycolysis and the alcohol fermentation were responsible for the majority of the ATP production by the child. The accumulation of alcohol (ethanol) in the child caused the symptoms of drunkenness.

21.73 The first stage of the pentose phosphate pathway is an oxidative stage in which glucose-6-phosphate is converted to ribulose-5-phosphate. Two NADPH molecules and one CO_2 molecule are also produced in these reactions. The second stage of the pentose phosphate pathway involves isomerization reactions that convert ribulose-5-phosphate into other five-carbon sugars, ribose-5-phosphate and xylulose-5-phosphate. The third stage of the pathway involves a complex series of rearrangement reactions that results in the production of two fructose-6-phosphate and one glyceraldehyde-3-phosphate molecules from three molecules of pentose phosphate.

21.75 The ribose-5-phosphate is used for the biosynthesis of nucleotides. The erythrose-4-phosphate is used for the biosynthesis of aromatic amino acids.

21.77 Gluconeogenesis is production of glucose from noncarbohydrate starting materials. This pathway can provide glucose when starvation or strenuous exercise leads to a depletion of glucose from the body.

21.79 The liver

21.81 Lactate is first converted to pyruvate.

21.83 Because steps 1, 3, and 10 of glycolysis are irreversible, gluconeogenesis is not simply the reverse of glycolysis. The reverse reactions must be carried out by different enzymes.

21.85 Steps 1, 3, and 10 of glycolysis are irreversible. Step 1 is the transfer of a phosphoryl group from ATP to carbon-6 of glucose and is catalyzed by hexokinase. Step 3 is the transfer of a phosphoryl group from ATP to carbon-1 of fructose-6-phosphate and is catalyzed by phosphofructokinase. Step 10 is the substrate-level phosphorylation in which a phosphoryl group is transferred from phosphoenolpyruvate to ADP and is catalyzed by pyruvate kinase.

21.87 The liver and pancreas

21.89 *Hypoglycemia* is the condition in which blood glucose levels are too low.

21.91 a. Insulin stimulates glycogen synthase, the first enzyme in glycogen synthesis. It also stimulates uptake of glucose from the bloodstream into cells and phosphorylation of glucose by the enzyme glucokinase.
    b. This traps glucose within liver cells and increases the storage of glucose in the form of glycogen.
    c. These processes decrease blood glucose levels.

21.93 Any defect in the enzymes required to degrade glycogen or export glucose from liver cells will result in a reduced ability of the liver to provide glucose at times when blood glucose levels are low. This will cause hypoglycemia.

21.95 Glycogen phosphorylase catalyzes phosphorylysis of a glucose at one end of a glycogen polymer. The reaction involves the displacement of a glucose unit of glycogen by a phosphate group. As a result, glucose-1-phosphate is produced.

$$\text{Glycogen(glucose)}_x + n\text{HPO}_4^{2-} \longrightarrow \text{Glycogen(glucose)}_{n-x} + n\text{glucose-1-phosphate}$$

21.97 In glycogen degradation, phosphoglucomutase converts glucose-1-phosphate to glucose-6-phosphate. In glycogen synthesis, phosphoglucomutase converts glucose-6-phosphate to glucose-1-phosphate.

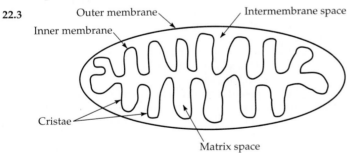

21.99 Glucokinase converts glucose to glucose-6-phosphate as the first reaction of glycogen synthesis.

Chapter 22

22.1 Mitochondria are the organelles responsible for aerobic respiration.

22.3

Outer membrane

Intermembrane space

Inner membrane

Cristae

Matrix space

22.5 Pyruvate is converted to acetyl CoA by the pyruvate dehydrogenase complex. This huge enzyme complex requires four coenzymes, each of which is made from a different vitamin. The four coenzymes are thiamine pyrophosphate (made from thiamine), FAD (made from riboflavin), NAD^+ (made from niacin), and coenzyme A (made from the vitamin pantothenic acid). The coenzyme lipoamide is also involved in this reaction.

22.7 *Oxidative phosphorylation* is the process by which the energy of electrons harvested from oxidation of a fuel molecule is used to phosphorylate ADP to produce ATP.

22.9 $NAD^+ + H:^- \rightarrow NADH$

22.11 During transamination reactions, the α-amino group is transferred to the coenzyme pyridoxal phosphate. In the last part of the reaction, the α-amino group is transferred from pyridoxal phosphate to an α-keto acid.

22.13 The purpose of the urea cycle is to convert toxic ammonium ions to urea, which is excreted in the urine of land animals.

22.15 An amphibolic pathway is a metabolic pathway that functions both in anabolism and catabolism. The citric acid cycle is amphibolic because it has a catabolic function—it completely oxidizes the acetyl group carried by acetyl CoA to provide electrons for ATP synthesis. Because citric acid cycle intermediates are precursors for the biosynthesis of many other molecules, it also serves a function in anabolism.

22.17 The mitochondrion is an organelle that serves as the cellular power plant. The reactions of the citric acid cycle, the electron transport system, and ATP synthase function together within the mitochondrion to harvest ATP energy for the cell.

22.19 The intermembrane compartment is the location of the high-energy proton (H^+) reservoir produced by the electron transport system. The energy of this H^+ reservoir is used to make ATP.

22.21 The outer mitochondrial membrane is freely permeable to substances of molar mass less than 10,000 g/mol. The inner mitochondrial membrane is highly impermeable. Embedded within the inner mitochondrial membrane are the electron carriers of the electron transport system, and ATP synthase, the multisubunit enzyme that makes ATP.

22.23 Coenzyme A is a molecule derived from ATP and the vitamin pantothenic acid. It functions in the transfer of acetyl groups in lipid and carbohydrate metabolism.

22.25 Decarboxylation is a chemical reaction in which a carboxyl group is removed from a molecule.

22.27 Under aerobic conditions pyruvate is converted to acetyl CoA.

22.29 The coenzymes NAD^+, FAD, thiamine pyrophosphate, and coenzyme A are required by the pyruvate dehydrogenase complex for the conversion of pyruvate to acetyl CoA. These coenzymes are synthesized from the vitamins niacin, riboflavin, thiamine, and pantothenic acid, respectively. If the vitamins are not available, the coenzymes will not be available and pyruvate cannot be converted to acetyl CoA. Because the complete oxidation of the acetyl group of acetyl CoA produces the vast majority of the ATP for the body, ATP production would be severely inhibited by a deficiency of any of these vitamins.

22.31 An aldol condensation is a reaction in which aldehydes or ketones react to form larger molecules.

22.33 Oxidation reduction

22.35 A dehydrogenation reaction is an oxidation reaction in which protons and electrons are removed from a molecule.

22.37 **a.** 1
     b. 6
     c. 2
     d. 2
     e. 4
     f. 2
     g. 1
     h. 2

22.39 True

22.41 Three

22.43 Two ATP per glucose

22.45 The function of acetyl CoA in the citric acid cycle is to bring the two-carbon remnant (acetyl group) of pyruvate from glycolysis and transfer it to oxaloacetate. In this way the acetyl group enters the citric acid cycle for the final stages of oxidation.

22.47 The high-energy phosphoryl group of the GTP is transferred to ADP to produce ATP. This reaction is catalyzed by the enzyme dinucleotide diphosphokinase.

22.49

$$\begin{array}{c} COO^- \\ | \\ C{=}O \\ | \\ CH_2 \\ | \\ COO^- \end{array} \quad + \quad H_3C{-}\overset{\displaystyle O}{\overset{\displaystyle \|}{C}}{-}S{-}CoA + H_2O \quad \longrightarrow$$

Oxaloacetate   Acetyl CoA

$$\begin{array}{c} COO^- \\ | \\ CH_2 \\ | \\ HO{-}C{-}COO^- \\ | \\ CH_2 \\ | \\ COO^- \end{array} \quad + \quad HS{-}CoA + H^+$$

Citrate   Coenzyme A

The importance of this reaction is that it brings the acetyl group, the two-carbon remnants of the glucose molecule, into the citric acid cycle to be completely oxidized. Through these reactions, and subsequent oxidative phosphorylation, the majority of the cellular ATP energy is provided.

22.51 The conversion of citrate to *cis*-aconitate is an example of the dehydration of an alcohol to produce an alkene (double bond). The conversion of *cis*-aconitate to isocitrate is an example of the hydration of an alkene, that is, the addition of water to the double bond, to produce an alcohol.

22.53 This reaction is an example of the oxidation of a secondary alcohol to a ketone. The two functional groups are the hydroxyl group of the alcohol and the carbonyl group of the ketone.

22.55 It is a kinase because it transfers a phosphoryl group from one molecule to another. Kinases are a specific type of transferase.

22.57 An allosteric enzyme is one that has an effector binding site and an active site. Effector binding can change the shape of the active site, causing it to be active or inactive.

22.59 Allosteric enzymes are an efficient means to regulate a biochemical pathway because they bind to effectors, such as ATP or ADP, that alter the shape of the enzyme active site, either stimulating the rate of the reaction or inhibiting the reaction.

22.61 The citric acid cycle is regulated by the following four enzymes or enzyme complexes: pyruvate dehydrogenase complex, citrate synthase, isocitrate dehydrogenase, and the α-ketoglutarate dehydrogenase complex.

22.63 Energy-harvesting pathways, such as the citric acid cycle, must be responsive to the energy needs of the cell. If the energy requirements are high, as during exercise, the reactions must speed up. If energy demands are low and ATP is in excess, the reactions of the pathway slow down.

22.65 ADP

22.67 The electron transport system is a series of electron transport proteins embedded in the inner mitochondrial membrane that accept high-energy electrons from NADH and FADH$_2$

and transfer them in stepwise fashion to molecular oxygen (O_2).

22.69 Three ATP

22.71 The oxidation of a variety of fuel molecules, including carbohydrates, the carbon skeletons of amino acids, and fatty acids provides the electrons. The energy of these electrons is used to produce an H$^+$ reservoir. The energy of this proton reservoir is used for ATP synthesis.

22.73 The electron transport system passes electrons harvested during oxidation of fuel molecules to molecular oxygen. At three sites protons are pumped from the mitochondrial matrix into the intermembrane compartment. Thus, the electron transport system builds the high-energy H$^+$ reservoir that provides energy for ATP synthesis.

22.75 a. Two ATP per glucose (net yield) are produced in glycolysis, whereas the complete oxidation of glucose in aerobic respiration (glycolysis, the citric acid cycle, and oxidative phosphorylation) results in the production of 36 ATP per glucose.
  b. Thus, aerobic respiration harvests nearly 40% of the potential energy of glucose, and anaerobic glycolysis harvests only about 2% of the potential energy of glucose.

22.77 Transaminases transfer amino groups from amino acids to ketoacids.

22.79 The glutamate family of transaminases is very important because the ketoacid corresponding to glutamate is α-ketoglutarate, one of the citric acid cycle intermediates. This provides a link between the citric acid cycle and amino acid metabolism. These transaminases provide amino groups for amino acid synthesis and collect amino groups during catabolism of amino acids.

22.81 a. Pyruvate
  b. α-Ketoglutarate
  c. Oxaloacetate
  d. Acetyl CoA
  e. Succinate
  f. α-Ketoglutarate

22.83 Transaminase binds to the amino acid in its active site. Then, the α-amino group is transferred to pyridoxal phosphate, producing pyridoxamine phosphate. The amino group is then transferred to an α-keto acid.

22.85 Hyperammonemia

22.87 a. The source of one amino group of urea is the ammonium ion and the source of the other is the α-amino group of the amino acid aspartate.
  b. The carbonyl group of urea is derived from CO_2.

22.89 Anabolism is a term used to describe all of the cellular energy-requiring biosynthetic pathways.

22.91 α-Ketoglutarate

22.93 Citric acid cycle intermediates are the starting materials for the biosynthesis of many biological molecules.

22.95 An essential amino acid is one that cannot be synthesized by the body and must be provided in the diet.

22.97

$$\begin{array}{c} \overset{\displaystyle O}{\overset{\displaystyle \|}{C}}{-}COO^- \\ | \\ CH_3 \end{array} + CO_2 + ATP \quad \longrightarrow \quad \begin{array}{c} \overset{\displaystyle O}{\overset{\displaystyle \|}{C}}{-}COO^- \\ | \\ CH_2 \\ | \\ COO^- \end{array} + ADP + P_i$$

Pyruvate   Oxaloacetate

Chapter 23

23.1 Because dietary lipids are hydrophobic, they arrive in the small intestine as large fat globules. The bile salts emulsify these fat globules into tiny fat droplets. This greatly increases the surface area of the lipids, allowing them to be more accessible to pancreatic lipases and thus more easily digested.

23.3 Starvation, a diet low in carbohydrates, and diabetes mellitus are conditions that lead to the production of ketone bodies.

23.5 (1) Fatty acid biosynthesis occurs in the cytoplasm whereas β-oxidation occurs in the mitochondria.

(2) The acyl group carrier in fatty acid biosynthesis is acyl carrier protein while the acyl group carrier in β-oxidation is coenzyme A.

(3) The seven enzymes of fatty acid biosynthesis are associated as a multienzyme complex called *fatty acid synthase*. The enzymes involved in β-oxidation are not physically associated with one another.

(4) NADPH is the reducing agent used in fatty acid biosynthesis. NADH and $FADH_2$ are produced by β-oxidation.

23.7 The liver regulates blood glucose levels under the control of the hormones insulin and glucagon. When blood glucose levels are too high, insulin stimulates the uptake of glucose by liver cells and the storage of the glucose in glycogen polymers. When blood glucose levels are too low, the hormone glucagon stimulates the breakdown of glycogen and release of glucose into the bloodstream. Glucagon also stimulates the liver to produce glucose for export into the bloodstream by the process of gluconeogenesis.

23.9 Insulin stimulates uptake of glucose and amino acids by cells, glycogen and protein synthesis, and storage of lipids. It inhibits glycogenolysis, gluconeogenesis, breakdown of stored triglycerides, and ketogenesis.

23.11

Cholate

Chenodeoxycholate

23.13 A micelle is an aggregation of molecules having nonpolar and polar regions; the nonpolar regions of the molecules aggregate, leaving the polar regions facing the surrounding water.

23.15 A triglyceride is a molecule composed of glycerol esterified to three fatty acids.

23.17 Triglycerides, cholesterol, and phospholipids are packaged into a protein-coated shell to produce the class of plasma lipoproteins called chylomicrons. Chylomicrons carry dietary triglycerides from the intestine to all tissues via the bloodstream.

23.19 Triglycerides

23.21 The large fat globule that takes up nearly the entire cytoplasm

23.23 Lipases catalyze the hydrolysis of the ester bonds of triglycerides.

23.25 Acetyl CoA is the precursor for fatty acids, several amino acids, cholesterol, and other steroids.

23.27 Chylomicrons are plasma lipoproteins (aggregates of protein and triglycerides) that carry dietary triglycerides from the intestine to all tissues via the bloodstream.

23.29 Bile salts serve as detergents. Fat globules stimulate their release from the gallbladder. The bile salts then emulsify the lipids, increasing their surface area and making them more accessible to digestive enzymes (pancreatic lipases).

23.31 When dietary lipids in the form of fat globules reach the duodenum, they are emulsified by bile salts. The triglycerides in the resulting tiny fat droplets are hydrolyzed into monoglycerides and fatty acids by the action of pancreatic lipases, assisted by colipase. The monoglycerides and fatty acids are absorbed by cells lining the intestine.

23.33 The energy source for the activation of a fatty acid entering β-oxidation is the hydrolysis of ATP into AMP and PP_i (pyrophosphate group), an energy expense of two high-energy phosphoester bonds.

23.35 Carnitine is a carrier molecule that brings fatty acyl groups into the mitochondrial matrix.

23.37 The following equation represents the reaction catalyzed by acyl-CoA dehydrogenase. Notice that the reaction involves the loss of two hydrogen atoms. Thus, this is an oxidation reaction.

23.39 An alcohol is the product of the hydration of an alkene.

23.41 Six acetyl CoA, one phenyl acetate, six NADH, and six $FADH_2$

23.43 112 ATP

23.45 95 ATP

23.47 The acetyl CoA produced by β-oxidation will enter the citric acid cycle.

23.49 Ketone bodies include the compounds acetone, acetoacetone, and β-hydroxybutyrate, which are produced from fatty acids in the liver via acetyl CoA.

23.51 Ketosis is an abnormal rise in the level of ketone bodies in the blood.

23.53 Matrix of the mitochondrion.

23.55

Acetoacetate   β-Hydroxybutyrate

23.57 In those suffering from uncontrolled diabetes, the glucose in the blood cannot get into the cells of the body. The excess glucose is excreted in the urine. Body cells degrade fatty acids because glucose is not available. β-oxidation of fatty acids yields enormous quantities of acetyl CoA, so much acetyl CoA, in fact, that it cannot all enter the citric acid cycle because there is not enough oxaloacetate available. Excess acetyl CoA is used for ketogenesis.

23.59 Ketone bodies are the preferred energy source of the heart.

23.61 Cytoplasm

23.63

23.65 The phosphopantetheine group allows formation of a high-energy thioester bond with a fatty acid. It is derived from the vitamin pantothenic acid.

23.67 Fatty acid synthase is a huge multienzyme complex consisting of the seven enzymes involved in fatty acid synthesis. It is found in the cell cytoplasm. The enzymes involved in β-oxidation are not physically associated with one another. They are free in the mitochondrial matrix space.

23.69 Glycogenesis is the synthesis of the polymer glycogen from glucose monomers.

23.71 Gluconeogenesis is the synthesis of glucose from noncarbohydrate precursors.

23.73 β-oxidation of fatty acids

23.75 The major metabolic function of the liver is to regulate blood glucose levels.

23.77 Ketone bodies are the major fuel for the heart. Glucose is the major energy source of the brain, and the liver obtains most of its energy from the oxidation of amino acid carbon skeletons.

23.79 Fatty acids are absorbed from the bloodstream by adipocytes. Using glycerol-3-phosphate, produced as a by-product of glycolysis, triglycerides are synthesized. Triglycerides are constantly being hydrolyzed and resynthesized in adipocytes. The rates of hydrolysis and synthesis are determined by lipases that are under hormonal control.

23.81 In general, insulin stimulates anabolic processes, including glycogen synthesis, uptake of amino acids and protein synthesis, and triglyceride synthesis. At the same time, catabolic processes such as glycogenolysis are inhibited.

23.83 A target cell is one that has a receptor for a particular hormone.

23.85 Decreased blood glucose levels trigger the secretion of glucagon into the bloodstream.

23.87 Insulin is produced in the β-cells of the islets of Langerhans in the pancreas.

23.89 Insulin stimulates the uptake of glucose from the blood into cells. It enhances glucose storage by stimulating glycogenesis and inhibiting glycogen degradation and gluconeogenesis.

23.91 Insulin stimulates synthesis and storage of triglycerides.

23.93 Insulin is secreted when blood glucose levels are high. It facilitates the uptake and storage of glucose by target cells to restore normal blood glucose levels. Glucagon is secreted when blood glucose levels are too low. It stimulates release of glucose into the blood to restore normal levels.

Credits

Chapter 1

Opener, p. 2: © Karl Weatherly/PhotoDisc/Getty RF; Medical Perspective p. 3(top): © Creatas/PunchStock RF; p. 3(bottom): © Digital Vision/PunchStock RF; Human Perspective p. 5: © Corbis RF; 1.2a: © Geoff Tompkinson/SPL/Photo Researchers, Inc.; 1.2b: © Dr. Parvinder Sethi; 1.2c: © David Parker/Segate Microelectronics/SPL/Photo Researchers, Inc.; 1.2d: Courtesy APHIS,PPG, Otis Methods Development Center, USDA; 1.3a: © The McGraw-Hill Companies, Inc./Louis Rosenstock, photographer; 1.3b: © The McGraw-Hill Companies, Inc./Jeff Topping, photographer; 1.3c: © The McGraw-Hill Companies, Inc./Louis Rosenstock, photographer; 1.4(both): © The McGraw-Hill Companies, Inc./Ken Karp, photographer; 1.6c: © The McGraw-Hill Companies, Inc./Ken Cavanagh, photographer; p. 20: © DV545/Getty RF; 1.8a-c, 1.10a-d: © The McGraw-Hill Companies, Inc./Louis Rosenstock, photographer; Human Perspective p. 28: © Corbis RF; 1.12: © The McGraw-Hill Companies, Inc./Louis Rosenstock, photographer; Human Perspective p. 33: © Vol. 12/Getty RF.

Chapter 2

Opener, p. 31: © Comstock Images/Jupiter RF; 2.1: © IBM Corporation, Almaden Research Center; 2.6: © Yoav Levy/Phototake; Chemistry Perspective p. 49(left): © Earth Satellite Corp./SPL/Photo Researchers, Inc.; Chemistry Perspective p. 49(right): © Dan McCoy/Rainbow; Human Perspective p. 51: © Vol. 2/PhotoDisc/Getty RF; p. 55: © The McGraw-Hill Companies, Inc./Stephen Frisch, photographer; 2.14: © The McGraw-Hill Companies, Inc./Jacques Cornell, photographer.

Chapter 3

Opener, p. 80: © Getty RF; 3.2c: © The McGraw-Hill Companies, Inc./Trent Stephens, photographer; Medical Perspective p. 83: © Comstock Images/Picture Quest RF; p. 94: © Pixtal/age fotostock RF; 3.14: © Charles D. Winters/Photo Researchers, Inc.

Chapter 4

Opener, p. 122: © Science Source/Photo Researchers, Inc.; 4.1, 4.3: © The McGraw-Hill Companies, Inc./Louis Rosenstock, photographer; p. 140(top): © The McGraw-Hill Companies, Inc./Charles D. Winters, photographer; p. 140(bottom): © The McGraw-Hill Companies, Inc./Louis Rosenstock, photographer; p. 141: © The McGraw-Hill Companies, Inc./Stephen Frisch, photographer.

Chapter 5

Opener, p. 160: © Corbis RF; A Human Perspective p. 162: © The Image Bank/Getty Images; 5.2a,b: © The McGraw-Hill Companies, Inc./Louis Rosenstock, photographer; 5.5: © Peter Stef Lambert/Stone/Getty Images; p. 174: © BrandX/Picture Quest RF.

Chapter 6

Opener, p. 186: © Brand X Pictures/Punchstock RF; 6.1: © Kip Peticolas/Fundamental Photographs; Human Perspective p. 190: © J.W. Mowbray/Photo Researchers, Inc.; 6.4: © The McGraw-Hill Companies, Inc./Louis Rosenstock, photographer; 6.6a-c © David M. Phillips/Visuals Unlimited; Medical Perspective p. 205(top): Courtesy of Rita Colwell, National Science Foundation; 6.7: © C. Paxton & J. Farrow/Photo Researchers, Inc.; 6.8a,b, Human Perspective p. 207: © The McGraw-Hill Companies, Inc./Louis Rosenstock, photographer; Medical Perspective p. 211: © AJPhoto/Photo Researchers, Inc.

Chapter 7

Opener, p. 218: © The McGraw-Hill Companies, Inc./Connie Mueller, photographer; Medical Perspective p. 225(both): © The McGraw-Hill Companies, Inc./Louis Rosenstock, photographer; 7.9: © The McGraw-Hill Companies, Inc./Ken Karp, photographer; p. 232: © Design Pics/Punchstock RF; 7.15, 7.16: © The McGraw-Hill Companies, Inc./Ken Karp, photographer.

Chapter 8

Opener, p. 252: © Comstock/Jupiter Images RF; 8.1: © The McGraw-Hill Companies, Inc./Mark Dierker, photographer; p. 258: © Digital Vision/Getty RF; 8.4a: © The McGraw-Hill Companies, Inc./Louis Rosenstock, photographer; 8.4b, 8.6a,b: © The McGraw-Hill Companies, Inc./Stephen Frisch, photographer; p. 267, 268a,b, 269: © The McGraw-Hill Companies, Inc./Louis Rosenstock, photographer; Medical Perspective p. 273: © The McGraw-Hill Companies, Inc./Auburn University Photographic Services; Medical Perspective p. 275: © PhotoDisc/Getty RF; p. 276a: © The McGraw-Hill Companies, Inc./Louis Rosenstock, photographer; p. 276b: © The McGraw-Hill Companies, Inc./Connie Mueller, photographer; p. 276c: © Brand X Pictures/Punchstock RF; 8.7(both): © The McGraw-Hill Companies, Inc./Stephen Frisch, photographer; Medical Perspective p. 280: © AAA/Photo Phototake.

Chapter 9

Opener, p. 286: © Corbis RF; 9.3: © Gianni Tortoli/Photo Researchers, Inc.; Green Chemistry p. 298(top): NASA; 9.6: © U.S. DOE/Science Source/Photo Researchers, Inc.; p. 299: © Stockbyte/Punchstock RF; 9.7: © Blair Seitz/Photo Researchers, Inc.; Medical Perspective p. 302(top): © The McGraw-Hill Companies, Inc./Louis Rosenstock, photographer; Medical Perspective p. 302(bottom): © Javier Larrea/age fotostock RF; 9.8b: Courtesy Bristol-Myers Squibb Medical Imaging; 9.9: © U.S. DOE/Mark Marten/Photo Researchers, Inc.; 9.10: © The McGraw-Hill Companies, Inc./Louis Rosenstock, photographer; 9.11: © Scott Camazine/Photo Researchers, Inc.

Chapter 10

Opener, p. 312: © Digital Vision/Punchstock RF; p. 313: © Vol. OS22/PhotoDisc/Getty RF; Green Chemistry p. 315: Courtesy Ocean Drilling Program/NOAA; Chemistry at the Crime Scene p. 323: © Vol. 43/PhotoDisc/Getty RF; Green Chemistry p. 325: © Digital Vision/Punchstock RF; Green Chemistry p. 335: © Corbis RF; Green Chemistry p. 335(bottom): © OS23/Getty RF; p. 336: © Corbis RF; p. 337: © Fotosearch RF; Medical Perspective p. 339: © Corbis Royalty Free.

Chapter 11

Opener, p. 348(top): © Digital Vision/Getty RF; p. 348(bottom): © Vol. 12/PhotoDisc/Getty RF; p. 349(top): © Vol. 19/PhotoDisc/Getty RF; p. 349(bottom): © Banana Stock/Punchstock RF; Medical Perspective p. 354: © Vol. 77/PhotoDisc/Getty RF; Medical Perspective p. 355: © Steven P. Lynch; 11.3(top): © Ingram Publishing/Superstock RF; 11.3(center top): © Photodisc/Getty RF; 11.3(center bottom): © Steven P. Lynch; 11.3(bottom): © Digital Vision/Getty RF; p. 364: © PhotoDisc/Getty RF; 11.5: © The McGraw-Hill Companies, Inc./Ken Karp, photographer; p. 370: © Superstock/Alamy; Green Chemistry p. 374: © Moodboard/Corbis RF.

Chapter 12

Opener, p. 390(top): © C Squared Studios/Getty Images RF; p. 390(bottom): © Corbis RF; p. 392: © Digital Vision RF; 12.3: © Vol. 12/PhotoDisc/Getty RF; Medical Perspective p. 395(top): © Vol. 18/PhotoDisc/Getty RF; 12.4: © Corbis RF; p. 396: © Comstock/Punchstock RF; Chemistry at the Crime Scene p. 407: © Vol. 88/PhotoDisc/Getty RF; 12.8: © Corbis RF; 12.9: © Vol. OS22/PhotoDisc/Getty RF; Kitchen Chemistry p. 413: © PhotoDisc/Getty RF.

Index

METRIC PREFIXES

Multiple	Prefix	Symbol	Submultiple	Prefix	Symbol
10^{12}	tera	T	10^{-1}	deci	d
10^{9}	giga	G	10^{-2}	centi	c
10^{6}	mega	M	10^{-3}	milli	m
10^{3}	kilo	k	10^{-6}	micro	μ
10^{2}	hecto	h	10^{-9}	nano	n
10^{1}	deka	da	10^{-12}	pico	p

CONVERSION FACTORS

Length:
1 meter (m) = 39.37 inches (in)
1 inch (in) = 2.54 centimeters (cm)
1 Ångstrom (Å) = 10^{-10} m

Mass:
1 kilogram (kg) = 2.205 pounds (lb)
1 pound (lb) = 453.5 grams (g)
1 atomic mass unit (amu)
   = 1.661×10^{-24} grams (g)

Volume:
1 liter (L) = 1000 milliliters (mL)
   = 1000 cm^3
1 liter = 1.057 quarts (qt)

Energy:
1 calorie (cal) = 4.18 joules (J)

Temperature:
°F = 1.8°C + 32
$$°C = \frac{(°F - 32)}{1.8}$$
K = °C + 273.15

Pressure:
1 atmosphere (atm) = 14.7 lbs in^{-2} (psi)
1 atm = 760 millimeters of mercury
   (760 mm Hg = 760 torr)

PHYSICAL CONSTANTS

Avogadro's number	6.022×10^{23} units mole^{-1}
Speed of light	3.0×10^{8} m sec^{-1}
Gas constant (R)	0.08205 L-atm K^{-1}-mol^{-1}
Mass of an electron	9.11×10^{-28} g
	or
	5.40×10^{-4} amu
Mass of a proton	1.67×10^{-24} g
	or
	1.007 amu
Mass of a neutron	1.68×10^{-24} g
	or
	1.009 amu
Volume of one mole	
of ideal gas	22.4 L (@ 273 K)